Sir
EDWARD GREY

A BIOGRAPHY OF
LORD GREY OF FALLODON

KEITH ROBBINS

CASSELL·LONDON

CASSELL & COMPANY LTD
35 Red Lion Square, London WC1
Sydney, Auckland
Toronto, Johannesburg

First published 1971

I.S.B.N. 0 304 93746 0

Printed by the Camelot Press Ltd,
London and Southampton
F.371

To Janet

Preface

The foreign policy of Sir Edward Grey will be debated for many years to come. Doubtless, many detailed studies will appear which may amplify the emphasis of this volume. The author is indebted to those which have already appeared. It is, however, the natural tendency of writers on specific aspects of foreign policy to assume that their particular topic was the subject chiefly engaging the Foreign Secretary's attention. In this respect, a new biography provides an opportunity to link together the different strands of policy, both domestic and foreign. While the reader will often find a summary and assessment of recent scholarly work, he will be reminded that no policy can be fully understood apart from the character of the Foreign Secretary himself.

That Sir Edward's private papers seem completely to have disappeared is the sort of misfortune a student of his life comes to expect. Both his wives predeceased him; two brothers were killed in Africa (by a lion and a buffalo respectively); both his family home and his fishing cottage were destroyed by fire; he had no children, and he suffered severely in his last twenty years from increasing blindness. I am most grateful to the large number of people who have helped in the search, though unsuccessful, for the papers. If any readers have any knowledge of them, I should be pleased if they would write to me.

The biography has therefore been written largely on the basis of letters from Grey to be found in many collections, both private and public. I am indebted to the owners for their kindness in making them available, for their permission to make quotations from copyright material or to use photographs, and, in some cases, for their generous hospitality. To appear in a list is scant reward, but space forbids more personal acknowledgment. I am also grateful to many other helpers, too numerous to name, who have provided information, or shared their memories of Sir Edward Grey with me. Without all this co-operation, the book could not have been written.

I am most grateful to Her Majesty the Queen for her gracious permission to quote from papers in the Royal Archives at Windsor; papers in the Public Record Office have been used by permission of H.M. Stationery Office.

I must also thank the following individuals and institutions: Beatrix,

Sir Edward Grey

Lady Aldenham; The Beaverbrook Foundations and Mr A. J. P. Taylor; The University of Birmingham Library; The Bodleian Library, Oxford; Colonel the Hon. and Mrs H. Bridgeman; The British Library of Economics and Political Science; The Trustees of the British Museum; The Brotherton Library, The University of Leeds; Mr Hubert Butler; Cambridge University Library; Mr Mark Bonham Carter; Churchill College Library, Cambridge; Mrs O. S. Clarke and Lieutenant-Colonel R. L. Clarke; Mrs Elizabeth Clay; The Library of Congress; Mr Gerald Curtis; Sir Peter Curtis; Katharine, Lady Darwin; Mrs Pauline Dower; The Department of Palaeography and Diplomatic, The University of Durham; Mr H. Seton Gordon; Lady Graves; Sir Robin Grey, Bt; Mr Peter Gwyn; Dr A. R. B. Haldane; Viscount Harcourt; The Earl of Harrowby; Harvard College Library; Dr Cameron Hazlehurst; The Dowager Countess of Iddesleigh; Professor A. K. S. Lambton; Mr S. McKenna; Mr Edward Marsden; Mrs Lucy Masterman; Mr H. G. Matthew; Mrs Mary Moorman; Lord Mottistone; Mr A. B. L. Munro Ferguson; The National Library of Australia; The National Library of Scotland; The National Library of Wales; The National Portrait Gallery; The Warden and Fellows of New College, Oxford; Mr Peter Newbolt; The University of Newcastle upon Tyne; A. H. Noble, W. S. on behalf of Lord Elibank; Sir Malcolm Perks; Lord Ponsonby; Mary, Duchess of Roxburghe; The Hon. Sir Steven Runciman and Viscount Runciman; The Hon. Godfrey Samuel; Mr L. P. Scott; The Hon. Margaret Sinclair; Earl Spencer; *The Times* Archives; Susan, Lady Tweedsmuir; The Earl and Countess Waldegrave; A. P. Watt & Son; Westfield College, The University of London; Captain Francis Widdrington; The Warden and Fellows of Winchester College; Yale University Library; Mrs Janet Young.

For permission to quote from published works I must also thank the Longmans Group Ltd for G. M. Trevelyan, *Grey of Fallodon*; A. P. Watt & Son and the Estate of Viscount Grey of Fallodon for Grey of Fallodon, *Twenty-Five Years*; A. P. Watt & Son, the Kraus Reprint Corporation and the Hon. M. Sinclair for J. A. Spender, *The Life of Sir Henry Campbell-Bannerman*.

In those cases where it has not been possible to trace the holder of copyright, or where it may have been overlooked, the author offers his apologies.

Finally, I must thank Professor G. E. Aylmer for commenting on my typescript.

K. R.

Contents

List of Illustrations

Introduction

The eminence of Sir Edward Grey is only precariously established. Historians cluster round Lloyd George, Churchill, Asquith or Curzon sniffing eagerly for scandal and devoted to their brilliance. The last years of Liberal England have been meticulously chronicled by those anxious to capture the spirit of delight before the onset of tragedy. For their part, to dampen romantic enthusiasm, social historians stress the extent of mass poverty and the harshness of industrial life. One thing all are agreed upon: in the summer of 1914 an era ended. Sir Edward Grey, looking out of the Foreign Office window on the morning of war, saw the gas lights being extinguished. Sadly he observed that the lights were going out all over Europe and they would not be lit again in his lifetime. It was his one memorable phrase.

Despite the enthusiasm for this period of English history, the neglect of Grey surprisingly persists. Yet, judged on current form, no Foreign Secretary is ever likely to emulate his record of eleven years' continuous service at the Foreign Office. It might be argued that long service is no guarantee of distinction, but even so, the fact that Grey was seemingly indispensable in itself requires explanation. Some further reason for the reluctance of historians must therefore be found. The chief answer must be that Grey is an enigma. It is easy to write about men with transparent ambition who deliberately choose to make politics their career. They can then be studied within an agreed framework. The gentleman politicians are much more difficult to handle, and perhaps Sir Edward Grey supremely so. Neither his admirers nor his critics know quite what they should say about him. For everyone who ponders his record as Foreign Secretary, there is someone who instinctively thinks of him as an author or bird-lover. Few individuals and even fewer historians combine his interests in equal measure, and judgments for and against him share the common quality of intolerance.

The verdict on the one side insists that Grey would have done better to stick to fishing and his ducks. If he was so engrossed in nature, he should never have strayed into politics. And, in particular, it was disastrous for him to be associated with foreign affairs, where his want of experience combined fatally with his insularity. In office he was the quintessence of incompetence—the amateur statesman. More scurrilous versions of this attack insinuate that the countryside remained his chief preoccupation at the Foreign Office—that he only condescended to make occasional appearances in London. All the while, his thoughts were concentrated on the breeding habits of his ducks at the expense of the great affairs of state which were supposedly his concern. Supporters of 'nature' Grey have unwittingly pandered to this portrait. They know little of his political activities and care less. His greatness for them had nothing to do with foreign affairs. On his death, an enthusiastic bird-lover urged that a fitting national memorial to the statesman would be a statue in a public park of Grey with a fishing-rod in one hand and feeding his ducks nestled at his feet out of the other. The idea was not adopted. Nevertheless, part of the memorial subscription was allotted for the establishment of the Edward Grey Ornithological Institute at Oxford. Equally, his only previous biographer, G. M. Trevelyan, has perhaps contributed to this impression. For all its fine qualities, his book is suffused with a rather oppressive sentimentality. It is a requiem for a Northumbrian way of life shared both by subject and biographer. Not surprisingly, therefore, it neglects some of the puzzles about Grey's career and makes some of the rough places smoother than they should be.

There is, however, a third view which neither mocks nor praises the country gentleman lost in the great world but rather considers such an approach superficial. Grey's love of nature was not insincere, but it did not absorb the whole man. His hatred of politics was not false, but it is not the whole story. Like others of his class before and since, duty may have driven him into politics, but once in, he fought with the best for what he wanted. As for his pleas for release, he protested too much, and when in his prime showed little disposition to give up his office. In particular, a generation of German historians after the First World War refused to rise to the bait offered by the simple fisherman. Grey could not really be so straightforward, and if he was not, then he must be Machiavellian to an unsuspected degree. It is curious that contemporary German historians, busily discovering that their political leaders had feet of iron, have resurrected Grey as the model of simpleminded rectitude in politics.

The fascination of Sir Edward Grey is that all of these interpretations could be true. The aim of this biography is to look at his career as a whole. The enigma of his personality may still remain, but that character will be seen in the context of his family, his friends, his county, his class, his office and his nation. Few men mould their own structure, few men are completely moulded by it; in the interaction lies the excitement.

THE GREYS OF
HOWICK AND FALLODON

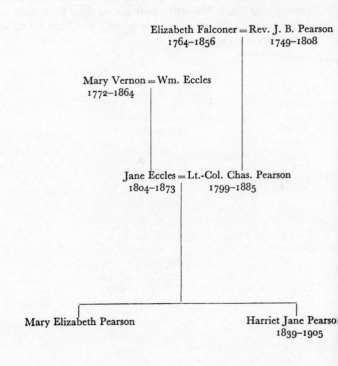

Elizabeth Falconer = Rev. J. B. Pearson
1764–1856   1749–1808

Mary Vernon = Wm. Eccles
1772–1864

Jane Eccles = Lt.-Col. Chas. Pearson
1804–1873   1799–1885

Mary Elizabeth Pearson   Harriet Jane Pearson
1839–1905

1) Dorothy Widdrington = EDWARD GREY   Alice
    d. 1906   1862–1933
2) Pamela Glenconner   Viscount Grey of Fallodon
    d. 1928

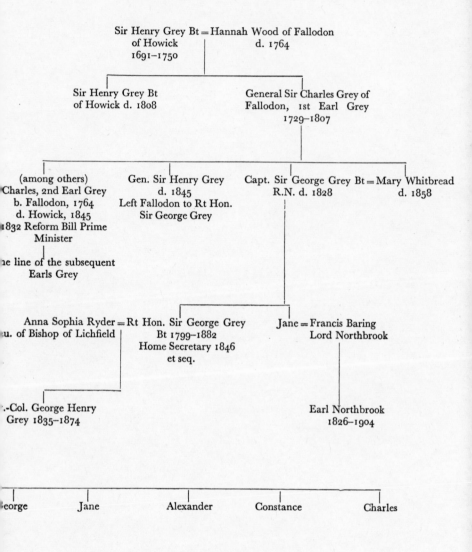

Sir Henry Grey Bt = Hannah Wood of Fallodon
of Howick   d. 1764
1691–1750

Sir Henry Grey Bt   General Sir Charles Grey of
of Howick d. 1808   Fallodon, 1st Earl Grey
                                      1729–1807

(among others)   Gen. Sir Henry Grey   Capt. Sir George Grey Bt = Mary Whitbread
Charles, 2nd Earl Grey   d. 1845   R.N. d. 1828   d. 1858
b. Fallodon, 1764   Left Fallodon to Rt Hon.
d. Howick, 1845   Sir George Grey
1832 Reform Bill Prime
     Minister

the line of the subsequent
      Earls Grey

Anna Sophia Ryder = Rt Hon. Sir George Grey   Jane = Francis Baring
u. of Bishop of Lichfield   Bt 1799–1882   Lord Northbrook
                          Home Secretary 1846
                               et seq.

.-Col. George Henry   Earl Northbrook
Grey 1835–1874   1826–1904

George   Jane   Alexander   Constance   Charles

B

1

A House and a Name

It would have been very difficult for Edward Grey to have escaped some connexion with political life. Numerous chairmen at political meetings found a ready introduction by referring to the great Lord Grey of the Reform Bill. They welcomed Sir Edward for his conspicuous abilities and unflinching adherence to the principles that had ever added lustre to the name of Grey. But Edward was not in fact a direct descendant of the second Earl Grey. His great-grandfather was a younger brother of the famous politician. Their father, the first Earl, had formerly been General Sir Charles Grey of Fallodon, a tough, blunt soldier who had fought at Minden in 1759 and then with distinction in the American War of Independence. He ended his career in the West Indies in the 1790s, happily capturing a number of the wealthy French sugar colonies for the British Crown.

At this juncture, the award of the earldom notwithstanding, the Grey family was of provincial rather than national eminence. Sir Charles lived and died at Fallodon in Northumberland, where the majority of his children, including his eldest son, were born. He took a firm line with his younger children at least and they could not expect tender treatment from him. Edward's great-grandfather, George, was left to make his own way of life. After a short time at Winchester, he went to sea and his ship, the *Roebuck*, was sent to the North American station, then the scene of war. He was only eleven years and three months. He was moved to the *Resolution* in 1780 and, at the tender age of thirteen, was made a Lieutenant in that ship. His vessel was involved in Rodney's engagements in April 1782 and, the Captain and senior Lieutenants being killed or badly wounded, he commanded the ship after the battle. He subsequently had the satisfaction of receiving as his new Captain an officer who had objected to passing him as a Lieutenant on account of his youth.

In 1783 he returned home and begged his parents to let him receive a formal education. The request was refused and, bitterly disappointed, he went back to sea.[1] In 1795 he married Mary, daughter of old Samuel Whitbread. The Whitbreads and the Greys were already connected. Mary's half-brother, Samuel Whitbread, M.P., had already married George's sister Elizabeth, whom he had of course met through his friendship with 'Reform Bill' Charles.[2]

George's tough naval life was in marked contrast to the leisured, not to say frivolous, life of his elder brother.[3] No one ever accused Captain George Grey, R.N., of indolence. After the award of a baronetcy in 1814 he became Commissioner in Residence at Portsmouth dockyard. With his wife, he took a keen interest in the welfare of sailors and attempted to soften some of the hardships of naval life. Both had come under the influence of the Evangelical party, and numbered amongst their friends William Wilberforce and the Rev. Charles Simeon. Under this inspiration they started missions to seamen. They had two children, George and Jane. Such was the reputation of public schools in the early years of the century that they refused to expose their son to the temptations of such institutions.[4] George was sent to an Evangelical clergyman for private instruction and then, since his father was determined that he should receive a full education, he went up to Oriel College Oxford in 1817 when he was eighteen. His friends at university were drawn from the same religious background and he seems to have contemplated taking orders. But after classics at Oxford, he moved to London to take up law, being called to the Bar in 1826. In the following year he married Anna Sophia, the daughter of the Rt Rev. and Hon. Henry Ryder, Bishop of Lichfield and Coventry and a leading member of the Evangelical party. The match was approved, although mother felt compelled to write to daughter admonishing her 'not to be persuaded by your dear companion into the belief that so much exercise is good for your health. . . .'[5]

The first Baronet died in 1828 'with a remarkable *cheerful* and thankful spirit' despite being in great pain. 'He continually contrasted his own state with that of the poor—often exclaiming when receiving any attention or assistance—"What shall I render to the Lord for all his Mercies". . . .'[6] With his uncle gaining such national fame, it is hardly surprising that the second Sir George's thoughts turned to politics. After the passing of the Reform Bill he became a candidate for Devonport and was elected in December 1832. Although a strong Evangelical, he had rejected the pressures of a society for the returning of religious men to parliament. Vital religion was of very great importance, but 'everybody looks for the best lawyer tho' his religious principles may be very different from what we might wish. It is the same with a General & to a certain extent must be so I think with a Politician or a Statesman. . . .'[7] Within three years, Sir George was Under-Secretary for the Colonies and a few months before Melbourne's Government fell in 1841 came into the Cabinet as Chancellor of the Duchy of Lancaster. He was a moderate Whig with a general interest in social questions. He paid a generous tribute to his fellow Evangelical, Lord Ashley, when the latter brought before the House the report of the commission on the mines (1843) with its revelations of the treatment of women and children in particular.[8] Outside the Commons, although not specially wealthy, he immersed himself in a wide variety of charitable activities. He was a member of the committee of the Church Missionary Society and the British and Foreign Bible Society. More practically, he was a member of the Metropolitan District Visiting Society and devoted his Sunday afternoons when in London to making the acquaintance of the poor of St Giles. As a private member, he introduced a Bill for the erection of public baths and wash-houses in towns. He approved of concessions to Dissenters in respect of University Entrance and supported the Maynooth Grant in 1845. Clearly, in view both of his connexions and application, a solid political career lay in front of him.

Despite his north-eastern heritage, Sir George had been born in Gibraltar and until 1845 lived and worked in the south of England. In that year, however, he inherited Fallodon on the death of an unmarried uncle, General Sir Henry Grey. Fallodon had come into the Grey family through the marriage of Sir George's great-grand-father, Sir Henry Grey of Howick, with a certain Hannah Wood. Her father had erected a red-brick house with stone facings early in the eighteenth century when he bought the small estate. Because of the disturbed state of the Border, country houses were late appearing in North Northumberland. There had been a smaller house on the site built in the mid-seventeenth century by a Puritan merchant from Berwick. He had built the high brick walls enclosing the fine garden and sheltering it from the winds off the sea. The first Earl Grey, as the younger son, had inherited the Fallodon house and estate, but his elder brother had caused a house to be built only four miles or so away at Howick. Later, Howick was to be the home of the Earls Grey, and it was there that Grey of the Reform Bill died, in the

3

year Sir George inherited Fallodon. Lady Grey's relatives ventured north to this outpost and found both place and people so different from the south, being 'quite on the old half feudal system'. However, the poor seemed well and much attached to the family. Their good health had to be put down to their consumption of barley and oat cakes 'and such like'.[9] All in all, the move to Northumberland was deemed a success. The Bishop's widow was only concerned that Sir George might hurt himself indulging in that favourite pastime of Victorian politicians—tree felling. 'Don't let Grey *lend his hands* to the work of cutting down his trees,' she wrote, 'he will do himself a bad mischief—I know he will. . . .'[10]

Sir George was determined to put down roots in the county of his ancestors. He gave up his safe seat at Devonport and in the General Election of 1847 he fought and won North Northumberland—long regarded as virtually a possession of the Percy family with their seat at Alnwick. He became Home Secretary in the Russell Government. In office he showed himself efficient and discreet, although he brought down upon himself the wrath of Lord Ashley for his enforcement of the 1847 Factory Act in such a way that some of its provisions were evaded. Ashley called him 'fearful, vacillating and showing no principle'. Grey would seem to be enmeshed in a typical mid-Victorian clash between undoubted good feeling and what were believed to be the immutable laws of economics.[11] However, his greatest claim to fame lies in his handling of the Chartist demonstrations in London in 1848. His cool reaction to the situation was much admired and he was lauded as 'the man who saved England'. 'Well, my dear Annie,' his mother-in-law wrote, 'London is not in flames thanks to your dear Husband & our merciful God, who sent a seasonable rain. . . .'[12]

When the 1852 General Election came, it was doubtful whether Sir George would be able to save his seat in North Northumberland. He owed his success in 1847 very largely to the fact that the local Tories were in some disarray following the 'treachery' of Peel in repealing the Corn Laws. In 1852, however, party feeling had recovered and, led by Sir Matthew White Ridley of Blagdon, the Tories were determined to oust Grey. They did have problems. The Conservative who sat with Grey, Lord Ossulston, was reluctant to face a contested election for financial reasons, but these were overcome. Eventually, after Sir George had been electioneering for months, two Tories were put up. The landowners had clearly led the way, with the Duke of Northumberland at their head, but their own tenant farmers had stiffened their resolution rather than been coerced into compliance. Grey was denounced as a demagogue, an associate of the notorious troublemakers, Cobden and Bright. Despite the lateness of their entry, the Tory pair triumphed. Of the seven polling districts into which the constituency was divided, only in Berwick did Sir George do well, his vote exceeding the combined Tory poll. In an overwhelmingly rural constituency the Whig landowners were no match for the Tory.[13] No Whig ever again succeeded in sitting for North Northumberland while the constituency survived. Grey had the consolation of knowing that though they had no votes to help him, he had aroused support amongst the great body of non-electors. A total of £400 was raised by a subscription among working men as a token of their esteem. He was presented with a silver salver and candelabrum with the inscription: '. . . from more than thirteen thousand of the working men of Northumberland, in testimony of their gratitude for his support of the just, wise, and beneficial measure of Free Trade, their respect for his private worth, and for the eminent integrity and ability which have distinguished his public career'.[14]

In 1852 and succeeding years the leading families easily exercised political control over the north of the county. Any notion of democracy as the word would be understood today, either in local or parliamentary government, seemed very far away. Fortunately for Sir George, patronage could also work on his side. A member of the Howard family, being a sound Whig, obligingly resigned his seat at Morpeth and at a by-election in early 1853 Sir George was returned unopposed. The Morpeth electorate had been increased to 300 by the Reform Act and had been reduced to returning a single Member, but since 1832 it had not had to bother with a contested election. The Earl of Carlisle had simply nominated a member of his family who had been returned unopposed. Sir George was similarly untroubled for twenty years and only if he had persisted in his candidature for the election of 1874 would Morpeth have had the privilege of a contest. Instead, after the Reform Act of 1867 the miners constituted a clear majority of the electorate and felt that they had a national duty to their class to elect one of their own men. Morpeth became the pocket borough of the Northumberland Miners' Union, and Thomas Burt sat from 1874 until after the First World War. Burt, while naturally self-conscious, professed his admiration for the great Whig families of the area.[15]

However, while Sir George increased his reputation in the county, his national career did not advance much further in his Morpeth period. He became Colonial Secretary in 1854 under Aberdeen and in the following year reverted to the Home Office under Palmerston. In Palmerston's Cabinet of 1859 he became again Chancellor of the Duchy of Lancaster and two years later became Home Secretary for the third time. He never took office under Gladstone. He was obviously moderately successful as a Home Secretary but not deemed worthy of higher office. Until the end of his career he remained a widely respected moderate Whig. Attempts were made by 'advanced Liberals' to draw him into active political work in North Northumberland, but his replies were distinctly chilling. He wrote to old Earl Grey in late 1874 that 'I do not see at present on what common basis the different sections of the so called Liberal party can unite. But the case might be different if the "advanced Liberals" were willing to support a candidate of liberal but not extreme views. . . .' Earl Grey replied in complete agreement. He could understand forming a party to promote some important public object on which the members agreed and for the sake of which they were willing to waive their views on minor matters: 'This was the principle on which the old Whig party was formed & acted.' But, he continued, 'to try & form a party first & then to look out for some public questn. on which they can agree is contrary to every notion of public duty on which I was brought up. A party so formed is a mere faction.' In any case he felt that 'contested elections & the preparations made for them beforehand are in themselves very bad things—they excite angry passions & animosities & interfere greatly with social comfort. . . .'[16] A decade later it was to be Edward Grey who would be doing just these disagreeable things.

Sir George and Lady Grey had but one child, a son born in 1835. His grandmother was replete with wholesome advice for her daughter on his upbringing. The vital matter was *unity in the Parents' management*—'not that this can be the same always in little points but *dear baby* should never hear this proclaimed. I have felt myself compelled to make such an admonition because I set you such, my poor dear child, such a bad example in a contrary system. . . .'[17] But as Georgy grew up, his parents were disappointed to find that his ambition was to join the Army, and Sir George demurred. Soldiering was an idle profession and a man was easily corrupted by drinking and gambling. Only the advent of the Crimean War made him change his mind and allow his son to see service in the Crimea with the Rifle Brigade. After that he went with his battalion to India during the Mutiny. It was clear that he would not go into politics. He seemed, however, an admirable young man to have as a companion for the Prince of Wales, six years his junior. Having been approached, Sir George wrote to his cousin General Charles Grey, Comptroller of the Household, that his son was very sensible of the honour for which he was being considered. He would accept the appointment with a most grateful feeling and endeavour to show himself worthy of the favourable opinion held of him.[18] In November 1858 he came to stay with the Royal Family, and Queen Victoria noted: 'He is very nice and gentlemanly and I hope will make a good companion for Bertie.' A week later his appointment as equerry was announced.[19] In approaching Sir George, the Prince Consort had expressed the view that 'It would give us great pleasure if this connection of service which during many years has existed between the parents, should be continued between our son and yours.'[20] Almost immediately, young George went with the Prince on a continental tour, and General Bruce, who was in charge of the party, reported in his favour: 'The Prince evidently takes to him. It is not easy for any one at once to seize the peculiarities of H.R.H.'s character, but I have very strongly warned Grey that the mere amusement of the Prince, although when kept within due bounds a laudable object, should be entirely subordinate to other and more important considerations.'[21] A little later, Bruce concluded: 'It is really most fortunate to have a person of his age uniting so many qualifications for the post.'[22]

In 1860, young George married Harriet Jane Pearson, a twenty-one-year-old girl of charm but no great distinction; it was rumoured that he might have looked higher in his choice. It is strange that Edward Grey's mother and her family were totally ignored by his previous biographer, especially since she survived her husband by thirty years. Not that the Pearsons were a family to court publicity. Her father, Lieutenant-Colonel Charles Pearson, was living near Worcester when his two daughters were born. In 1852 the family moved to Cheltenham where Harriet was brought up and her parents continued to live after her marriage. Colonel Pearson's father, the Rev. John Betteridge Pearson, was descended from a long line of Shropshire clergymen who had intermarried with minor gentry of the county and tradesmen from Shrewsbury. Early in his career, he had been curate of a church in Lichfield. Dr Johnson's stepdaughter, Miss Porter, so much admired his ministrations that she left him £10,000, her house and a collection of Johnsoniana.

Unfortunately, a manuscript of the doctor's dictionary was sub-sequently put away in a loft and consumed by rats. However, the good Johnsonian walking-stick survived and was appropriately inherited by Edward Grey. This change in the curate's fortunes enabled him to marry Elizabeth, daughter of the Rev. James Falconer, at one time Archdeacon of Derby. Falconer had estab-lished himself in a comfortable but ugly house in the Cathedral Close at Lichfield. His comfort was increased by profitable specula-tion in the Trent and Mersey Canal. He had married Mary, daughter of Thomas Hall of Hermitage, Cheshire, and she retained the Jacobite traditions inherited from her mother's family. As a child, Harriet, in her grandmother's presence, was never allowed to call the Pretender anything but Prince Charles Edward. Stories of the toast to the King over the water were recalled such as would have scandalized the Whig citadels of Northumberland. The father of Harriet's mother, Jane Eccles, had been a young solicitor in Manchester. He was a clever man of modest background and his appointment as solicitor to the Duchy of Lancaster had placed valuable business in his hands. His advance helped overcome family objections to his marrying Mary Vernon. Her father, that is to say Harriet's great-grandfather, was a man of some refinement in Cheshire county society. He had travelled widely in France and shared in the current horticultural enthusiasms. To him belongs the satisfaction of being the first man to grow pines in Cheshire.[23]

Harriet Pearson therefore came from a comfortable provincial background. Her family had no national pretensions and no political ambitions. She was herself a modest woman, without intellectual distinction or particular artistic accomplishment.[24] It is not altogether clear how she came to meet and marry George Grey, but it seems likely that an introduction was made through a relative of hers, Captain William Eccles, who had served with Grey in India. On her engagement she wrote that she hardly deserved such happiness and added: 'It appears that *he* mentioned it to Sir George & Lady Grey three years ago, but that being so young they advised him to *wait* two or three years, & so it was not till fairly settled in his present position that he came forward. . . .'[25] On their marriage, the couple took a small house in London. There, in 1862, Edward Grey, their first child, was born.

Since old Sir George was anxious to have them near him, the young Greys then moved back to Fallodon. George had resigned from the army and only retained his royal duties. His father made over to him the Home Farm of some two hundred acres. Lady Elizabeth Waldegrave visited Fallodon in September 1866 and was taken on a tour of the estate. She learnt how Sir George had added to its size by buying up property as it came on the market. One of these properties was subsequently the subject of negotiation with George Hudson, the 'Railway King'. He wished to drive the main line to Scotland through it. Sir George agreed and asked such a moderate sum that Hudson had put into the railway deeds the clause empowering the possessor of Fallodon to stop any train to take up or set down a guest visiting the house. So was the convenience obtained whereby a future Foreign Secretary could join the fast train from King's Cross and be set down within a few hundred yards of his house. In consolidating the estate, Sir George's expectation was that he would be able to build up a valuable property for his son. Lady Grey was less enthusiastic. Property investment was no doubt sound for the future, but she would have preferred a little more ready capital available.[26]

When not required by his royal master, young George spent most of his time on the farm at Fallodon. He was easy-going and liked country life and pursuits. Edward remembered him as handsome and full-bearded—never happier than when out hunting, shooting or fishing. However, he was in courteous but open rebellion against the Evangelical discipline and intellectual seriousness of his parents. For so many of the second generation, the Evangelical outlook lost its appeal, and they drifted, it seemed, into hedonism or papistry. Lady Grey had even herself to suffer the sorrow of a younger brother, George, succumbing to the temptations of Rome and the even greater humiliation of a younger sister who was not simply content with conversion but became a nun. Old Mrs Ryder could hardly be consoled.[27] George Grey did not follow this path. Instead, in the words of Lady Elizabeth Waldegrave, herself an Evangelical, she found 'young George very much given up to his own comforts' and this extended to his wife and children. For example, they made little attempt to make themselves as inconspicuous as possible in what was their father's house. She found him 'rather a John Bull fine gentleman', but the only apparent blemish on his moral life was his vice of smoking. Fortunately he had the decency to retire at 10.30 in the evening for this purpose. It was the only time in the day, his mother lamented, when he read anything other than the newspapers. There was no disguising that this was a disappointment to both parents with their serious interests. But there were consolations. His

9

influence with the Prince of Wales was all on the right side—he discouraged Sunday travelling and wished that His Highness would not smoke *so* much. He had been 'over educated', and Grey was making him more manly by encouraging hunting. The visitor was also concerned about the 'education' of young Edward. Regrettably, the duty of teaching him hymns devolved upon Grandmama. Lady Grey, who organized the village Sunday School, was a vigorous teacher. Someone had once mentioned the possibility of setting aside a schoolroom in the house, but young George declared that he would never allow his children in such a place. Nevertheless, he was deemed a good father. The child Edward knew that if he cried, 'away he goes'. Despite these tensions between the generations and the somewhat wayward disposition of young George, the household at Fallodon seems to have been contented enough.[28] Harriet, who sang prettily, got on *very well indeed* with her parents-in-law.[29] In turn, their concern for her grew with their fears that George, far from convincing the Prince of Wales of the iniquities of travel on the Lord's day, might himself be corrupted. However, young George was never away from Fallodon for too lengthy a period. Children arrived at Fallodon at regular intervals. After thirteen years of married life, Edward had been followed by Alice, George, Jane, Alexander, Constance and Charles.

In 1871, at the age of nine, Edward was sent to a small preparatory school of rather uncertain standards at Northallerton in the North Riding. It seems to have been a somewhat primitive institution. The boys were made to stand up while going through a prepared lesson, but no regular marks were kept. Nor were there organized games. A field was set aside for rough and tumble. Two years later Edward left to attend a more distinguished academy with more distinguished pupils. Temple Grove, at East Sheen, was a great mansion surrounded by large and beautiful grounds. One hundred and twenty boys and a dozen masters carried on a great classical tradition in spartan conditions. French and German were taught by little-regarded foreigners. However, it was efficient, with a regular system of marks and 'placings' designed to encourage the competitive instincts. It was the first time that Grey had measured himself against others. He seems to have thrived on it, reaching the top class and showing skill at cricket and football. He crowned his career by becoming head of the school. In retrospect, however, Grey came to feel that even at this stage he made use of his brain 'simply to excel in competition, without having interest in the subject or any natural aptitude for it'. There were others at the school, like Montague James, who were considered to be real scholars, but while they chuckled appreciatively over their Aristophanes, Grey was more likely to be found applauding or executing a cover drive. Although he loved Fallodon, he was happy at this school, it was 'a going concern'.[30]

George Grey died unexpectedly in the middle of December 1874. He was at Sandringham, apparently perfectly well, when illness struck. Princess Alexandra was there and sent a description of the sad affair to her husband. When the symptoms became serious Harriet was sent for from Northumberland. Not well herself, she arrived to find her husband in violent pain and hardly able to breathe. Hearing that Princess Alexandra was in the house Grey asked to see her: 'I shall never forget the sad and solemn impression it made upon me, feeling that this was the leavetaking of a dying man and one whom we all were so fond of.' His wife asked if she should send for little Edward from school but he had dissented; 'I shall be gone before he comes.' It was all 'too sad'.[31] Queen Victoria noted in her journal: 'How very dreadful ... Col. Grey had been the picture of health and strength and was only 39. ...'[32] Bertie came to see her and the Queen noted: 'He looks very ill and was greatly distressed and grieved about poor Col. Grey's death. He intends to go to the funeral which is to be in the North, and will be very trying for him. ...'[33] It was reported that at Sandringham Mrs Grey had been wonderfully calm, unlike Edward, who had been finally summoned; 'the poor boy ... is greatly distressed'.[34] For a moment, it seemed likely that there would be a double loss. Old Sir George was extremely ill himself and had not been informed that his son was dying. When he was informed of the death he had a severe fainting fit. His son's funeral took place a few days later. The Prince of Wales, despite the intense cold and his mother's concern, was there. Behind the coffin walked the widow, old Sir George (to everybody's alarm) and little Edward. The Prince sorrowed for the death of 'one of the truest and most devoted of friends'.[35] Sir George, looking forward to a quiet retirement and in ill health, suddenly found himself saddled with fresh responsibilities. Harriet was left alone to face life with seven young children. Edward, at twelve, found himself the head of the family: smitten for the first time, but not the last, with sudden unpredictable loss and grief.

The boy was then sent to Winchester. His grandfather must have felt that the conduct of public schools had sufficiently improved for him to risk allowing his grandson to attend. Private tutorship was in any case falling out of fashion. The domestic circumstances at Fallodon also made it seem desirable for Edward to go away to school. Old Sir George delighted in his grandchildren, reading books aloud to them, but this was no substitute for a formal education. Nor would it have been conceivable that the boy should have received his secondary education locally. The nearest local grammar school was a dozen miles away at Alnwick, though in any case Edward's community was with his social peers in the country as a whole, not with the local lads in his isolated part of Northumberland. At public school, the traditions and standards of his class would receive fresh stimulus and reinforcement. In this regard, Winchester was an admirable choice. It continued to maintain a close link with the Church, probably closer than any other leading public school. Between 1820 and 1870, more Wykehamists entered the Church than any other single profession with the exception of law, and at mid-century the father of nearly every other Wykehamist was a parson. The parents of boys at Winchester born, like Grey, in the decade 1860–9 were drawn 30% from the Church, 22% from the professions, 11% from business, 16% from the forces, 4% from Government service; 14% were gentlemen of leisure and a mere 0·3% were farmers. It is noteworthy, however, that with a few exceptions, the sons of the leading political families did not go to Winchester. Nor, in turn, did Winchester produce many politicians.[36]

Winchester had recently received the attentions of the Clarendon Commissioners anxious about the standards of education.[37] Only a few years before their visit a competitive examination for scholarship students, 'College' men, had been introduced. Previously, the Scholars had been selected more according to the strength of their Wykehamist connexions. In 1867, George Ridding, himself a Wykehamist and a clergyman, became Headmaster. The changes he introduced were chiefly concerned with the improvement of the teaching system rather than with what was taught. Ridding, like the Commissioners, was convinced that the study of the classics was the basis of a sound education. Like other Victorian headmasters, he tried to develop the facilities for organized games as a means of curbing violence and lawlessness. Out of his own pocket he reclaimed land for playing-fields, and this did improve the discipline of the school. Life at Winchester was, however, still quite rough and tough. Ridding was a keen philologist and 'compiled grammar sheets of Gothic and comparative accidence in Italian, Spanish, Walla-

chian, French, Dutch, German, English, Danish', but his notion that
this would create wide linguistic competence in his boys seems to
have failed in respect of at least one of his pupils.[38]

In September 1876, Grey went into Du Boulay's house. At
Winchester, the prefectorial system was established before the
influence of Arnold's Rugby led to its general adoption in schools.
The prefects at Winchester had already a long tradition of power
and not all Housemasters were able to control them successfully.
The head of the house was W. W. Palmer, who had been at Temple
Grove. Later in life, he and Grey were to have official relations when
Palmer, as Lord Selborne, was High Commissioner in South Africa.
Grey was Palmer's study fag and admired the high tone which he
set in the house. Edward was admitted to the school in the highest
class of scholars. To some of his contemporaries he seemed somewhat
lonely and introspective, while at the same time being perfectly at
ease socially if the occasion required. In due course he became head
of house, winning general respect. His academic progress was more
ambiguous. He did not achieve a reputation as a scholar, though he
performed quite adequately for the Headmaster in the upper part of
the school and never disgraced himself. But the Grey legend was
already being formed. His juniors were convinced that he was a
'jig' (clever) but did no work.[39] However, if he should turn his mind
to the subject he was quite capable of tossing off Greek or Latin
verses of alpha standard. He could equally have carried off prizes if
the idea had appealed to him. Putting aside the hero worship, it is
difficult to decide just how able Grey was. He himself subsequently
explained his indifferent performance as being due to the blunting
of his competitive zeal. Initially he moved rapidly up the school
until he reached a division from which promotion in under a year
was impossible. Grey claims not to have known of this convention,
and when a don, fully aware of it, manipulated his position in class,
Grey was furious. It seemed that no matter how well he did he was
not to be allowed to succeed. Confronted with this injustice, Grey's
ambition wilted and he never regained his zeal.[40] While this
recollection may be correct, it hardly explains everything, for he did
not excel in other conventional aspects of school life either. He
neither debated nor wrote and, despite his reputation for brilliance
at ball games, did not demonstrate this publicly by appearing for
school elevens. Such diffidence might seem conceited, and indeed
there is a streak of arrogance in Grey, but his preference for more
solitary activities is better explained by his circumstances. He had

13

no father to consult, and while he loved and respected his grandfather, writing regularly to him, the generation gap was too wide for close communication. It was in fishing, therefore, rather than in school games, that he delighted, taking every opportunity to fish the Itchen. Here he developed his particular skill with a dry fly. Fishing, Grey himself recalled, was not a pastime, it was a passion. On one occasion, a crowd of boys was late for 'Name Calling', absorbed in watching Grey land a large trout. When the boys explained themselves to the Headmaster, he summarily dismissed them: 'Yes, yes, Grey caught a fish.'

In his vacations Grey usually went back to Fallodon, though the grandparental regime was somewhat rigorous. Lady Grey had been brought up to believe that it was indelicate to eat a whole hen's egg, so bantams were kept for her and grandchildren were only allowed half an egg.[41] Edward, however, enjoyed his grandfather's company and they often went on walks together. Sometimes he also stayed in Cheltenham when his mother was visiting her parents. The grandparents visited the family there on one occasion in 1876. Besides its other attractions, Cheltenham was the sort of town which appealed to Sir George. It was, he wrote to his cousin, 'unusually free from Ritualism. There is I am told only one among the many churches in which it is to be found.'[42]

About half the boys in Grey's age group at Winchester went on to university and of these nearly 70% went to Oxford. The closest connexion existed, of course, between Winchester and New College, but Grey did not follow this path. He went to Jowett's Balliol. Wykehamist influence was by no means confined to New College. In 1880, the year Grey went up, Winchester, despite its small size, was the source of nearly one-eighth of Balliol freshmen and the Wykehamist contingent exceeded the representation of any other school. Five years earlier, Eton, Harrow, Rugby and Winchester between them accounted for nearly half the freshmen. In 1880, it took a dozen public schools to provide this proportion.[43] The other Balliol freshmen came from minor public schools, grammar schools or overseas. In this sense Balliol was an extension of Winchester. Although Grey does not seem to have carried over close friendships from school, there were many familiar faces, perhaps too many, when he came to dine in Balliol Hall.[44]

It was supposed amongst Grey's acolytes at Winchester that the only question at Oxford was not whether he could succeed but whether he had a mind to. His grandfather was anxious to help him and suggested that he might go to the Vicar of Embleton, the local parish, for coaching in the vacations. The Vicar was Mandell Creighton, subsequently Dixie Professor of Ecclesiastical History at Cambridge, and Bishop in succession of Peterborough and London. The living was in the hands of Merton College, Oxford, where Creighton had previously been a Fellow. Although born and educated in the far north of England, Creighton's translation from Merton Common Room to the Northumberland coastal belt was a shock for him. His friendship with old Sir George meant a lot to both men. Creighton habitually had pupils during the long vacation and was quite prepared to have Edward, suggesting that he should stay for some weeks at the vicarage. The best thing he could do was 'to show him how to work, and I have been pleased with the testimony of pupils, not only that they did work here, but that they actually began to enjoy the process'.[45] Creighton was at this time writing his *History of the Papacy* and his own concentration was meant to be an example to the young. Edward was installed in the drawing-room of the fine peel-towered vicarage. Certain hours were set aside for work and during these Edward had no alternative but to read the set books for Classical Moderations. The sole distraction was to gaze out of the window at the gardener and envy him his work in the open air. However, he managed to do sufficient reading to obtain a Second in the autumn of 1881. The following year his grandfather died. He became Sir Edward Grey, the owner of an estate of 2,000 acres and enough income for a life of pleasure and leisure. But he also inherited a tradition, and there were six younger siblings to think of.

The Second in Classical Mods. satisfied Grey. Greats was a long way off and could wait a while. The idleness which had threatened at Winchester now triumphed. He got out of Oxford as much as he could, walking and fishing. He became a polished 'real' tennis player, being the Oxford champion in 1883 and thrashing his Cambridge opponent in the inter-varsity competition. At night he would on occasion gamble, though never to a degree which caused financial embarrassment. Nor was he above the activities of the more adventurous bloods. Alfred Spender, who was sharing rooms in a somewhat unlikely way with Lord Weymouth, heir to the Marquess of Bath, recorded one such assault in his diary in February 1882. Their oak (outer door) was firmly barred against the assailants, who were after Weymouth, but red-hot pokers were to hand and the attackers bored their way through. A seventeen-stone Balliol gentleman completed the good work and the party carried Weymouth off. Sir Edward Grey, as Spender later discovered, directed the operation.[46] It was not even as though his failure to work was accompanied by shining performances at the Union. Jowett could have pardoned, indeed welcomed, such activities as essential training for a public man. The Master, as part of his policy of introducing chosen undergraduates to men of the world, invited Grey to meet Robert Lowe, Lord Sherbrooke, who was his guest in college. Cosmo Lang, subsequently Archbishop of Canterbury, was present and heard the Master say crisply: 'Lord Sherbrooke, let me introduce a young man, the bearer of an honoured name to which at present he is doing very little credit—Sir Edward Grey.' The implication was clear. Edward was neglecting his opportunities. On that occasion, Grey laughingly acknowledged the justice of the remark, but did little about it.[47] He came back to Balliol in October 1883 with Greats before him in the following May. It was apparent that time had caught up with him and that his performance would be a fiasco. So he explained his feelings to a disappointed Jowett. The Law School, he thought, would offer an easier option and, although the Law tutor did not warm to this explanation for the change, the Master agreed to the plan. There was little improvement. When the 1884 Balliol soccer team came to be photographed, one of the players was described as 'absent'. The entry in the Balliol minute-book for January 1884 provides the explanation: 'Sir Edward Grey, having been repeatedly admonished for idleness, and having shown himself entirely ignorant of the work set him in vacation as a condition of residence, was sent down, but allowed to come up to pass his examination in June.'[48]

Edward spent February and March 1884 at Fallodon all alone. There was no question of being bored or depressed. He loved his house and the burns and beaches of Northumberland. He did a certain amount of work, but enjoyed life in the open air more. He bought his first pairs of waterfowl and by the late spring had a wide variety on his ponds. The temptation must have been to forget Oxford altogether, especially since Creighton was moving to Cambridge and could no longer prod him. The Master, however, had not forgotten him. Unusually for a man in disgrace, he was summoned down for a week-end. Grey was apprehensive, but there was a large company and Jowett said nothing to him. At last, Grey had to explain that he needed to depart early from the breakfast table to catch his train north. The Master bade him good-bye and then followed him into the passage adding pleadingly: 'You will read, won't you?' Grey did come back to Balliol in the summer and achieved a Third in Jurisprudence.[49]

His Oxford career was now ignominiously over. The life he had led had been one of pure pleasure and, as he recalled, it was of a kind which could not be enjoyed at any other time of life. True, it had led to nothing, but he had not been scarred and, having been successfully idle, the way was now cleared for serious things. Of course, as at Winchester, some of his Balliol contemporaries later recorded the belief that although he did little in their time, 'we all knew' that he might do anything. It is difficult to see on what this confidence was based and how far it was really a contemporary feeling. Grey did indeed have a 'name', but then, so did others. George Nathaniel Curzon did not rest idly on his, and in comparison Edward Grey seemed a most inferior person. Although they overlapped, they rarely met or shared friends. Then there were men like Asquith, who had come up to Balliol exactly ten years before Grey, without a 'name' but who had carved one for themselves by their academic achievement. Asquith and Grey did not, however, meet at Oxford, since the former had moved to London in 1875. Balliol meant much to these three, but it did not mean the same thing. It must be doubtful, for example, whether Grey carried away theories and views, absorbed from Jowett and Green, which were to modify existing political doctrine and lay the intellectual foundations of the 'new Liberalism'.[50] It is, indeed, difficult to know who would have been more surprised, Jowett or Grey, if either had known that within eighteen months of leaving Oxford he would be a Member of Parliament.

2

Political Initiation

When Sir Edward returned to Fallodon in the summer of 1884 he was twenty-two and seemingly in no mood to commit himself to anything demanding. The life of a country gentleman could have stretched before him and he could have enjoyed himself in country pursuits. The Wykehamists at Balliol in his year became lawyers or civil servants, ending their days in such excellent positions as Deputy Chairman of H.M. Customs or member of the Board of Revenue. Grey did not follow in their footsteps. If he was to enter public life it would be as a politician. Suddenly, it seems, he made up his mind. He would try. Since he had done so little at Oxford, the obvious answer was to find a position which would enable him to observe politicians and civil servants at work. Having so decided, he did not have to start on the outer fringes of politics. While he was at school, Lord Northbrook, who lived nearby, befriended him and made available a stretch of the Itchen for fishing. Northbrook was a nephew of old Sir George, his father having married George's only sister, Jane. Observers detected a considerable similarity in manner and attitude between uncle and nephew. Northbrook had returned from India, where he had been a competent if not outstanding Viceroy. In 1884, as First Lord of the Admiralty, he was a somewhat uneasy member of Gladstone's Cabinet. Edward wrote to him requesting 'serious and unpaid employment'. Northbrook (who was a Baring) knew that his kinsman, Sir Evelyn Baring, would be in London for an Egyptian conference in the summer, and an arrangement was made for Edward to serve Baring as a secretary for the duration. A Ryder cousin reported great family pleasure at his decision to go into politics. 'All the Whigs are warmly welcoming the young man,' she wrote. 'I hope he will walk in his grandfather's ways though of course like all the Greys he must be a Liberal. Still a man like Uncle George is a blessing whichever side he is on.'[1]

In July 1884 the House of Lords rejected a Government Bill to extend the county franchise on the grounds that it should have been accompanied by a Redistribution Bill. Edward Grey received an invitation to chair a meeting to be held in Alnwick in protest. He accepted from a common sense of fairness 'and a feeling that the people among whom I had been brought up, and my own neighbours in the country, ought to have what had been given in the towns in 1867'.[2] Lord Northbrook now found Grey 'very keen on politics' and when the Egyptian conference ended wrote to the Chancellor of the Exchequer asking if he would take Grey on as an unpaid assistant private secretary. Baring had reported very favourably on his ability and application.[3] So, in October, Edward started work at the Treasury, living in London with his mother and family. The experience was rewarding. Looking back over these months, in January 1885, he noted that official life had given him business habits. Whereas six months previously he had hardly formed one political idea, now he had many. Then he knew no Political Economy, now he even had glimmerings of original ideas. Politics, social problems, moral philosophy and culture had become his consuming interests.[4] There is a touching naïveté about these remarks, but the prospect of action had clearly stimulated his intellectual curiosity.

Meanwhile, in Northumberland, the political scene was stirring. Edward, coached by Creighton, made a second political speech and addressed a number of other meetings. He now had firm political intentions. In the 1880 election, the Tories had retained both seats in Northumberland North. Earl Percy, son of the Duke of Northumberland, headed the poll, followed by Sir Matthew White Ridley. The sole Liberal candidate had come 500 votes behind Ridley. The constituency contained approximately 67,000 inhabitants, but there were only 4,376 voters. Berwick-upon-Tweed also returned two Members, as befitted its historic importance. Its population stood at over 13,500, with a registered electorate in 1880 of 1,443. At the General Election, the Liberals had gained both seats, but lost one subsequently in a by-election.[5] When the constituency boundaries were altered and the electorate extended, the Liberal chances in North Northumberland would improve. Meanwhile, Creighton exhorted him not to waste time. He should study questions and divide his opinions into three categories: matters of firm conviction, matters where more information was required and subjects where he would be prepared to do whatever was wanted. 'It will be a great thing', Creighton concluded, 'to fight Percy, and will cover you with glory.'[6] If he should win, he would be a marked man. Grey followed his advice and read Mill's *Political Economy*, Seeley's *Expansion of England* and the more radical suggestions in George's *Progress and Poverty*, leavening his diet with the poetry of Virgil, Tennyson, Milton and Wordsworth.[7]

The Liberal Party nationally was in a state of some turmoil, and no less so in Northumberland. While Grey wanted the candidature, other powerful county figures were not so convinced of his suitability. Opposition probably came from two sources. There were those constituents for whom the toppling of Percy had little significance if he were merely to be replaced by Grey. It would be simply another round in an ancient contest. While this new young Grey might repeat the lofty sentiments of Liberalism, was he prepared to give some solid pledges on particular issues? For example, would he say something about the Disestablishment of the Church of England, an issue which, under the previous franchise, candidates could ignore? North Northumberland had the highest proportion of Non-conformists of any county constituency in the country.[8] Admittedly, the great majority of these were Presbyterians, who felt less strongly than other Nonconformists, nevertheless the question now mattered. To Grey it was a great bore. After he had gained the candidacy, he drove to Belford to thank the local Liberal Association. The occasion was not a success. Edward was not in his best form. Nothing excused his languid behaviour, except perhaps a wasp sting, but he moaned that 'the people drivelled badly about Disestablishment and the opening of Museums on Sundays etc'.[9] Such was his haste to return to Fallodon after the experience that the wheels of his cart seemed hardly to touch the ground, and it took him only an hour to travel the ten miles home.

The real danger to Edward's candidature came, however, not from disgruntlement at the grass roots among those about to be enfranchised. In the event, they would still vote for him. The chief threat came from within his own social class, indeed even within his own family. The traditions of the Greys were those of political freedom, not those of social radicalism. There was some danger that Edward, with his new enthusiasm for politics, might be captured by wild and woolly notions. Radicalism, in this rural context, meant the land question.[10] In the spring of 1885 he made a number of speeches on which critics seized: 'I never read a more weak schoolboy production in my life,' old Earl Grey was informed; 'not one sound argument in it – I feel humiliated that such could have proceeded from a Northumberland man, and a Grey.'[11] Edward claimed that he had been misreported, though Creighton warned him that this was no defence: 'The more you say, the more chances you give them of setting you in a false light ... success in life is to the thick of skin.'[12] In this situation Edward turned to his cousin Albert, nephew and heir of old Earl Grey and Liberal Member for South Northumberland since 1880. 'I have never advocated', he wrote, 'that the State was to establish men as owners who had not money to buy land ... but what I do feel strongly is the mischief of places like Alnwick and Wooler being cramped and kept back, because with many people willing and able to buy, the large estates will not allow them to do either. At the same time, I have explicitly refused to pledge myself to a scheme of compulsory sale.'[13] In March, Albert came to see him at the Treasury and warned him that his unsound Radical views as to fixity of tenure and fair rents were ruining his chances of adoption.[14] Hinting at his uncle's displeasure, he refused to accept the presidency of the Liberal Association. Edward understood the position but would not retract: 'As to Lord Grey, I fancy that the thunderbolt will be discharged at me sooner or later if I stand for the division, and politically and publicly I don't funk it.' He did not disguise, however, that it went sorely against the grain 'to see the head of the family ally himself with the bigoted Toryism of the Percies'.[15] Rumours of Edward's radicalism had also spread among the Ryders and an uncle was firmly of the opinion that he was 'communistic'.[16]

For a time, the situation depressed Edward, and he contemplated giving up. However, he continued making public speeches, although compromising by eliminating fixity of tenure from his programme on the grounds that he had not yet discovered a practical bill to embody the principle. He declined an offer to stand for a Manchester constituency and wrote privately: 'If they run me here well and good; but I don't think the labours of a seat in Parliament are peculiarly to be longed for and I shan't be half sorry to have a few years longer to educate and open my mind before stepping into publicity.'[17] By this stage he had almost come to hope that he would not be selected, thinking that he did not have enough 'thought at my back'. The selection troubles rather disgusted him and he wrote revealingly to Albert, who was having similar difficulties: 'I wouldn't complain so much if they were going to run a genuine labour candidate ... but they will disgrace themselves if they put up some middle class clap trap politician against you.'[18] However, in mid-summer 1885, he heard that he was going to be chosen as the Liberal candidate.[19]

Edward was to contest the new division of Northumberland (Berwick-upon-Tweed). The town had lost its separate representation and was merged with part of the old North Northumberland county constituency. His opponent was the sitting Member, Earl Percy. According to the 1881 census, Berwick division had a population of over 55,000 and there were nearly 10,000 registered electors in 1885. Grey conducted an energetic campaign, speaking throughout the summer in village after village. He enjoyed these meetings, but finding new material for speeches was 'a most wearisome matter'. As the election came near, local excitement mounted. Shortly before the poll, he went to speak at the small village of Crookham and 'when we were about half a mile from it we were met by a thousand people, all roaring and screaming, and part of them with torches, and they took out the horses and pulled us up to the chapel where Edward was to speak. The row was fearful when we got out, and still worse when we got inside. . . . They were very pleased with the speech . . . and when it was over we were again dragged to a man's house where we had tea . . . and those wretched people dragged us *two whole miles* on our way to Belford.'[20] The only issue in the campaign was the toppling of the Percy. Edward wrote to Lord Northbrook hoping that he could persuade Lord Rosebery to speak for him in Alnwick: 'it might be thought not unworthy of even such a great man to give one push to help topple over the Percy influence. . . .'[21] The Duke of Northumberland possessed an estate of over 150,000 acres and landlord influence was still a potent factor in elections.[22] A great landlord, in a poor year, could legally refuse to remit a percentage of the rent and only charge a figure which the farm seemed reasonably capable of bearing. If he did remit, he expected in return a certain amount of compliance and this would normally include political support. Pollock's *Land Laws* stated that 'in the case of holdings from year to year it may not be unfairly said that being of the landlord's political party is often a tacit condition of tenancy'.[23] However, influence notwithstanding, Grey achieved his great symbolic victory with a majority of 1,413 votes. Afterwards, to recover from their exertions, Percy and Grey went fishing together.[24]

Edward had halted his campaign for a fortnight in the middle of October 1885 in order to get married. His bride was Dorothy

Widdrington, the eldest child of S. F. Widdrington of Newton Hall. Their friendship had not been a long slowly maturing affair. Newton-on-the-Moor, about sixteen miles south of Alnwick, was beyond the reach of horses for a day visit from Fallodon. It was Creighton, with his keen eye for young men of promise, and even keener one for young ladies, who formed the link between them. She had first got to know the vicar in 1873 when she was thirteen. The Creightons had gone to stay at Newton and visits were subsequently exchanged over a period of years. Dorothy was not an easy girl and welcomed his advice. She described herself as being in a perpetual state of self-defence, and the hostility and superiority, which some sensed in her attitude, was basically because she was afraid of other people. The Widdringtons were another old Northumbrian family and, not being a boy, she had stayed at home for her education. She had grown up loving the wide open countryside which surrounded her home. A succession of governesses had tried to teach her, but she had not been co-operative. In 1881, her mother took her to London for classes but the visit was not a success. According to Ella Pease, an intimate friend, writing after Dorothy's death, it was her relations with her mother which were at the root of many of Dorothy's problems. Mrs Widdrington tried to make Dorothy a social figure and her daughter would not respond.[25] The summer and winter of 1882 were spent in Switzerland and it was not until 1883 that Dorothy was presented at Court. Predictably, she hated what she called the artificiality of society and wrote: 'I do wish the time was come to leave this horrid London. I *do* long to go back to Newton so.'[26]

She first met Edward in the winter of 1884–5, the first time for several years that she had been at home. She was persuaded to hunt and go to a few balls but made no secret of her dislike for social life. The admiration of men was firmly rejected, since she would become a nurse and never marry. At this stage, Grey was no exception. However, the Widdringtons came to London at Easter 1885 for the season and Dorothy and Edward met frequently at balls. He succeeded in breaking her fierce reserve and within months their engagement was announced. Dorothy wrote to Ella Pease that there must have been some who felt that he was too young and ought to have 'done better' but the Grey family had been very kind.[27] Old Lady Grey was 'quite gratified & believes that she will have a very happy influence over Edward who is very radical in politics at present'.[28] The excitement of the election had jolted Dorothy out of

23

her customary introspection. When they settled into a little house in Hereford Square in February 1886 she was full of enthusiasm for her husband's career. The family was pleased that she seemed such a sensible wife, for they were, 'for their position', very poor and had to watch expenditure carefully.[29] Dorothy read the newspapers and, although from a Conservative family, learnt to identify herself with the Liberal cause. But would this interest last? She was just twenty-one, without friends in London and without inclination for social life. While she could look attractive, she always did so with a certain disgust that anyone should think this important. She liked reading in an eclectic manner, but her chief devotion remained to the countryside, where she liked to believe that she could 'be herself'.

At twenty-three, Grey was the youngest member of the new House of Commons, but it was a matter for speculation how long he would remain in Parliament. He had identified himself with Liberalism at a time when the party seemed on the verge of disintegration. His own campaign had made him aware of the divisions on the land question, but in addition there was Ireland and the party leadership. Grey had already assessed both Gladstone and Chamberlain. When working at the Treasury, he attended meetings of the Eighty Club, which had been formed by his cousin Albert from among members who had fought the election of 1880.[30] The committee, composed largely of promising young members and candidates, organized dinners at which the great men of the party spoke on political topics. The general tendency was 'Radical'. In April 1885, when Chamberlain addressed the club, Grey seconded the vote of thanks, making his first speech in the circle of 'coming men'.[31] While he congratulated Chamberlain in public, in private he was less impressed by the speech, which had been powerful and immensely clever, but rather unfair to Goschen. Chamberlain seemed not to understand the disposition and motives of men less advanced than himself and 'a man of really large sympathy could hardly be so unfair, so harsh and so one sided as he is'.[32] On the other hand, Edward was no Gladstonian either. The old man's handling of Gordon and the Sudan was disastrous, and his great eloquence had generated a certain egotism. Gladstone could not now bear any cause or principle, which he espoused, to fail. In June 1885 Grey had half an hour with Gladstone after dinner and explained his position, in particular his diffidence in expressing his own individual opinions against those of older, wiser candidates. Gladstone replied that he understood but encouraged him to persist with his candidature, on the grounds that one was never too young to begin learning. Grey was fascinated by his conversation and 'his personal character', though his criticisms did not disappear.[33]

Preoccupied as he had been by his campaign and wedding, the young member had much to learn about the situation at the top of his party. Gladstone, with his dislike of men with 'fads' and 'crotchets', was looking for an issue which would galvanize all Liberals. Was Ireland the answer? Chamberlain, after a visit to Gladstone in mid-October 1885, reported that the leader was talking of a policy 'which would necessarily throw into the background those minor points of difference about the schools and small holdings which threaten to drive the Whigs into the arms of the Tories or into retirement'.[34] Chamberlain was taken aback. He wanted programme politics, in which definite and practical schemes were suggested to solve particular problems. Both men shared a desire for party unity but also talked of a willingness to split rather than sacrifice principle and conviction. Chamberlain did not accept that the Irish question took precedence over the social questions which involved the whole of the United Kingdom. In any case, with an expanded electorate, it was ridiculous to embark on Ireland as a way of shelving disagreement about land reform, for the Whigs were expendable. For his part, Gladstone, finally convinced of the merits of Home Rule, regarded the 'sectionalists' as expendable.

This was the crisis which immediately confronted Grey in the early months of 1886. It tested the loyalties and taxed the wisdom of older men. Dorothy wrote that politics was both very interesting and rather disappointing: 'The Irish bother is so fearfully unsatisfactory, people taking up Home Rule not because they think it will do any good, but because they can't see anything much better to do. Everyone prodding his neighbour to speak out, and then dropping on him when he does so. It is really a most unpropitious time to have gone into Parliament.' A split was inevitable but 'an immense deal depends on how, when, and where the split with one's party is made. . . .'[35] Grey was careful not to make a maiden speech and was under some pressure not to accept Gladstone's policy. In his case, the appeals were even more difficult to resist, since Albert Grey and Sir George Otto Trevelyan were among the principal organizers. His cousin knew very well that he did not idolize Gladstone, and was in a position to warn that the Northumberland Whigs might withdraw their support, if he backed the Government. Edward also liked Trevelyan and had approved of his campaigns for rural

suffrage. Moreover, Sir George Otto's father had played an important part in securing him the constituency nomination. Yet, though
there were these personal complications, Grey resisted their
appeals. There was also pressure of a more fundamental kind from
Creighton, who wrote from Cambridge to express his dismay at the
trend of politics: 'If the coming democracy is going to turn Parliament into a large vestry, if reforms of the House of Lords, and
Disestablishment of the Church, are to be the objects of legislative
energy, the future can only be disastrous. England is in difficulties
in every part of her Empire: she is isolated in Europe, she is neither
liked nor trusted. The democracy must be told these things till it
has grasped them. It will not save its Indian Empire by reforming
the House of Lords.' He urged Grey to read Maine's recently
published book, *Popular Government*. Creighton thought the anxieties
it expressed had to be carefully considered.[36] Lord Northbrook too
finally lost confidence in Gladstone, whom he now described as
decadent: '. . . his hasty adoption of Home Rule, his hasty and ill-
considered and impracticable Bills, his ambiguous utterances in the
House of Commons and his deplorable endeavour to set class against
class in the country, is most melancholy.'[37] Personal and ideological
pressures all seemed to be pointing one way, but Grey resisted them.
It seems that he read John Morley's articles in the *Pall Mall
Gazette* and was convinced by them that 'coercion was not, under
modern conditions, possible as a permanent system of governing
Ireland'.[38] Home Rule was therefore the only alternative.

Grey had therefore to fight his second election in a period of six
months in unpropitious circumstances. The Hon. F. W. Lambton
opposed him as a Liberal Unionist and there was no Conservative
candidate. Many of the Whig families were profoundly disturbed by
the new political and social climate. Sir Charles Trevelyan had a few
years earlier protested at the tone of the *Newcastle Daily Chronicle*,
which was made up of '*communism*, *Jingoism* and *Low Sport* and . . .
positively conducive to political and personal demoralisation'.[39]
Earl Grey, at eighty-four 'tall, dry, spare, gaunt and lame' led the
house of Howick against Edward.[40] Having spent £941 on his
previous campaign, he only spent £625 on his 1886 contest,
whereas his opponent spent £750. Nevertheless, he managed to hold on
to the seat. His total vote was down by 600, although Lambton only
topped Percy's 1885 total by 400. In the neighbouring constituency
of Hexham, the sitting Liberal candidate lost 1,000 votes but his new
Liberal Unionist opponent was down 400 on the previous Con-

servative poll. In the Wansbeck division, the sitting Liberal lost 600 votes but his Liberal Unionist opponent lost 1,000 of the previous Conservative total. Judged by these local comparisons, Lambton's good performance demonstrated the strength of the Whig swing to Liberal Unionism. Nationally, approximately a third of the Liberal M.P.s elected in 1885 repudiated Gladstone's leadership. In the Northumberland county constituencies only Albert Grey did so, standing for Tyneside this time as a Liberal Unionist. Although he added 500 votes to the previous Tory total and his opponent lost 1,600 of his own old Liberal poll, Albert lost by the narrow margin of 120 votes.[41] Edward now had the difficult task of writing to him. He made it clear to his cousin that he would not support coercive measures 'unless they are coupled with large concessions in the nature of Home Rule: i.e. I shall oppose coercion as a policy; no Govt. of course intends it as a policy, but in default of any other it has lately become such. . . .'[42]

Throughout the next two years of the Tory Government, Ireland remained Grey's chief concern. He criticized those who pressed for the rigid enforcement of law in Ireland 'as if forsooth government and social order depended through thick and thin on one particular system of law in every age and under every condition. Why can't they realise that the far greater danger to Government and social order in Ireland at this moment arises from the condition and origin of the law itself.'[43] Writing again to his friend Alfred Pease, M.P. for York, he declined to join in a bottomless condemnation of agitation in Ireland: 'Of course the Irish agitators are violent and the Plan of Campaign is illegal, but one can't deplore the violence and illegality without deploring the necessity. There is no parallel between agreements made in England under perfect freedom of contract, and the rents of a starving peasantry in Ireland.'[44] And when he finally made his maiden speech in February 1887 he chose to speak on the bankruptcy of the Government's Irish policy.[45] It looked, he wrote to Albert Grey, as though the Government was going to throw over the landlords pretty completely and strengthen Parnell's hands at the same time by infuriating the people. Parnell might well be succeeded by secret societies and he doubted whether the Government had the machinery to cope with them.[46] Although Grey had followed Gladstone, he also recognized the force of Chamberlain's argument, in the abortive moves for Liberal reunion in 1887, that all other Liberal reforms could not be postponed until Home Rule had been

27

realized.[47] The 1886 General Election might seem to imply perpetual opposition for the Liberals with a Home Rule platform, but power if it was left in abeyance. Grey was not one of those Gladstonians who talked of fighting and fighting again until Home Rule was secured. He found himself associating with a group of young members with a similar unease, and together they tried to work out an alternative.

Asquith and Haldane already formed a pair. Throughout the early eighties both men were seeking to make their name and fortune at the Bar. For Asquith, despite his Oxford reputation, success was by no means easy. He had no private income and when without work at the Bar had to seek money from lecturing, writing text-books and journalism. Married, with three sons, and living relatively quietly in Hampstead, he was a barrister of ten years' standing when he entered the House in 1886. Asquith's friendship with Haldane was very close and for half a dozen years they had dined together several times a week.[48] Haldane was a Scot whose parents had insisted that he resist the snare of Balliol. Instead, at sixteen, he was a student at Edinburgh University, which he followed later by study in Göttingen and Dresden. He was attracted to metaphysics as much as to law, and while his power of retaining information was unrivalled, his power of expression was weak. He was unmarried and acted out a family role as honorary uncle to the Asquith boys. While making a considerable sum at the Bar he also had the advantage of a private income and a small estate at Cloan in Perthshire. In 1886, Asquith was thirty-three, Haldane thirty and Grey a mere twenty-four. In the presence of the barristers, Grey's third in Jurisprudence hardly counted for much. He had no outside reputation to sustain him in the Commons and lived on his private income. Nevertheless, he had beaten Asquith to the House and with his age and name could afford to wait patiently for some years.

Grey recognized Asquith's qualities from the beginning. He found his maiden speech in March 1887 'about the best 35 minutes I've ever heard, well delivered and fresh and strong to a degree'.[49] Yet, though closely associated with Asquith, he was never intimate with him, Balliol notwithstanding. Their relationship, even at this early stage, was a working one. Edward never accompanied Asquith on his fairly frequent journeys to the continent, nor did they dine together regularly. Although they were both married men, their domestic situations were only superficially similar. Mrs Asquith liked life at home with her children, while her husband was increasingly drawn into higher social circles. Dorothy Grey had no children and, after a few country house parties in her first year of marriage, she made it clear that they interfered with her desire to make herself perfect. 'If you don't go and say nothing about it,' she claimed, 'nobody ever finds out.'[50] Like Edward, she had fallen in love with the Itchen valley, and Lord Northbrook had put a cottage at their disposal for week-ends. By 1888 she could write: 'I believe we have arrived at the state when we have got all the good out of people that we shall ever get.'[51] Some might find these comments a trifle premature in a young woman of twenty-three. There was no prospect of children. When they returned from their honeymoon, Dorothy told her husband that she had discovered in herself a strong aversion to the physical side of marriage. He then suggested that they should live together as brother and sister.[52] Dorothy felt that she ought to undertake social work with a Charity Organization Committee. She took flowers to factory girls in the East End during their dinner hours, but she became acutely embarrassed and gave it up. It was not an encouraging atmosphere for a young politician, and hardly surprising that no social friendship with Asquith developed.

Haldane was different. Despite many obvious differences, they had much to offer each other at this stage in their careers. Haldane was always thinking about policy and strategy and Grey was eager to learn. But where Haldane mumbled, Grey was acquiring the reputation of a clear, straightforward and persuasive speaker, who kept the ear of the House. While Haldane had a porky presence calculated to reduce some circles to mirth, Grey was a lithe, handsome young man with clear features. Love of Northumberland also drew them together. Moreover, Haldane got on surprisingly well with Dorothy.[53] He was not a fisherman nor an athlete (at a swimming party at Mells, the impact of Haldane striking the surface of the water had shattered his costume), but neither was Grey interested in German metaphysics. All in all, the combination of their attributes could make them a formidable pair.

It was Haldane, who fancied his organizing powers, who tried to work up something of a coherent group. It would include Sydney Buxton, Tom Ellis and Arthur Acland. Of these, Grey immediately found Buxton congenial and often went fishing with him or sent reports of his solitary achievements. Ellis came from a Welsh background totally alien to Grey but within a few years they were on Christian-name terms—something never achieved with Asquith.

29

Acland was in something of a different category. He was fifteen years Grey's senior and full of ideas, particularly about education, but a somewhat unstable personality to whom, despite Creighton's recommendation, Grey does not seem to have been particularly drawn. Some combination of these men, with others, met informally as the 'Articles Club' and enjoyed a number of private dinners as they discussed the renewal of the Liberal Party. They also used meetings of the Eighty Club in their drive to find a progressive policy to counter the efforts of the 'extreme Socialist party'. Writing to Munro Ferguson, an associated Scottish Liberal M.P., Haldane outlined their aim of capturing the public confidence by constructive propositions, 'which should by means of these not only attain a position from which to criticise with the utmost firmness and frankness the people with whose names we were at present being labelled, i.e. Labouchere and company, but at the same time, while perfectly loyal to our front bench, stimulate it to really lead the party'.[54] This is an example of the prose which led people to doze in Haldane's speeches. In fact, neither Haldane nor Grey were 'perfectly loyal' to the front bench in the division lobbies. Asquith was already more conforming in his voting behaviour. Grey in 1888 had spoken and voted for Balfour's Irish land purchase scheme, despite his party's opposition to it unless accompanied by a Home Rule bill. He also struck out independently in favour of payment for M.P.s.[55]

John Morley was the rather odd choice as Senior Friend of the group. Nothing pleased him more than to have achieved a circle of acolytes.[56] Haldane publicly described himself as a 'Morleyite', having been assured by the master that he was a man with a future. Everybody diligently read *On Compromise* and was suitably impressed. Even Haldane was prepared to thin his Teutonic gruel with maxims culled from Condorcet. Morley was willing to guide them because he was alarmed by the dangerous radicalism which was always linked with the unmentionable Labouchere. The great London dock strike had begun in August 1889 and to Morley it was symptomatic of the restless politics of the capital. It was certainly necessary to deal with social problems, but in such a way that 'the unhealthy elements in London Radicalism should be extinguished or at least countered and prevented from becoming contagious. The "healthy" Liberalism of the provinces, of Scotland, and of Wales must be enabled to predominate.'[57] As Asquith put it in a letter to Buxton, the only member of the group to have a London seat, the 'better kind' of Radicalism was unduly backward in putting out constructive proposals, but now was their chance to remedy the situation, while keeping in touch with the 'worthiest elements' on the front bench.[58] Asquith, Haldane, Grey and others dined at Morley's on 13 November to try to work out a programme. Six days later, Grey chaired a meeting of the Eighty Club at which Morley gave an address on 'Liberalism and Social Reform'. The member for Newcastle surprisingly believed that the safe progress of the country depended on the 'solid, serious, reflective Liberalism of the North-East of England'. He then outlined a social programme such as might keep the Tyne quiet but would hardly dampen the flames on the Thames.[59] The group continued to operate to some extent in the following year, 1890, convinced that what they were doing was more important than the official party rituals.

The party leadership was aware of the dangers of the Irish obsession, but it was difficult to find alternative issues on which agreement was possible. Irish Home Rule was thus still necessary to stall the vociferous demands of competing groups within the party. For his part, Sir William Harcourt complained of lack of co-operation from the young men 'like E. Grey who *can* speak, [but] won't. Asquith [who] will never do a day's work for us in the House . . .'[60] They in turn found Harcourt conceited and impossible to deal with. Sir William could not help noticing that it was Rosebery and not himself who chiefly received invitations to a further series of dinners organized by Haldane and Asquith. Grey attended these dinners on several occasions and it was because of this association that the general label of 'Imperialist' came to be loosely attached, although for all three their primary concern was with the cohesion of the white colonies rather than fresh colonial annexation in Africa. Unless this is understood, the links of the group with both Morley and Rosebery at the same time cannot be understood.[61] In November 1890, Haldane and Grey exchanged views on the progress of their campaign of mild dissidence. Edward remained determined to vote for Balfour's impending Irish Land Purchase Act, arguing: 'Up to the present moment our course has been intelligible to the public and it must remain so. In our comparatively private position we must sketch roughly in outline only and on a large scale; otherwise nobody will take the trouble to understand us; very few of the public read our speeches, hardly any remember them, but nearly everybody knows when we vote for Land Purchase and remembers the votes.' Grey wrote from Ireland, where he recorded his impression that 'about 90 per cent of the present Irish party have done their work in politics and that if new blood doesn't flow in pretty quickly the Unionists will yet be given a great opportunity. Balfour is doing good work in Ireland. . . .'[62] When the Parnell divorce scandal broke shortly afterwards, it seemed to Grey even more unlikely that absolute insistence on Home Rule would be possible.[63]

Although Haldane and Grey seemed to be having some success with their attempt to make names for themselves, the former was badly depressed and talked about giving up politics. He had been disappointed in love and the Greys were privy to the whole affair. Edward tried to cheer him up. He argued that it was a mistake to look for direct results in public life. Haldane's influence would always be indirect 'and it will be your privilege never to be able to measure it. If it were not for you I do not think I should have even the hold on public life which I have now. . . . I should say for instance that Asquith owes some of the very best of himself to you; in knowing you both I feel as if it was so.' By such coaxing he restored his friend's self-confidence. Edward himself was in remarkably buoyant form. He knew moods of black depression, but his fundamental conviction that life was glorious never left him. He admitted that this was both his strength and weakness, for 'a life of pleasure seems possible to me; it promises satisfaction; I know with my intellect that this is not true, but I dare neither look nor listen for fear I should not be able to resist'. Then again, when he looked at himself frankly, 'there comes with more justification than to you a doubt of my powers to be effective in public life. On the other hand I have felt lately a little consciousness of power which I never had before. I am tending and encouraging it carefully. . . .'[64]

This growing confidence—he was still only twenty-eight—was matched by Dorothy's happiness. She seemed, albeit temporarily, reconciled to her circumstances. To her joy, they had just purchased a cottage of their own at Itchen Abbas which they frequently visited. Dorothy also felt more relaxed in Northumberland, although her relations with her parents were strained and she scarcely went near them. Her mother made a point of telling any acquaintances they had in common that they had to choose between friendship with herself or with her daughter.[65] But things were better for Dorothy at Fallodon. For three years after their marriage Lady Grey, Mrs Grey and Edward's sisters remained in the house and she felt inhibited by their presence. In 1888 they made homes elsewhere and Dorothy was able to feel that Fallodon was her own home.

Grey's maturing judgment was strengthened by his immersion in literature, especially in Wordsworth, whose appeal was deeply significant. His resonance for a man like Grey scarcely needs elaborating. Wordsworth had no easy optimism about the inevitable benefits of progress. He *felt* strongly and intensely and gave to his readers 'the assurance that moral choices were significant events in the universe' and that 'human life was always surrounded by immense forces, in comparison with which railways, committees and parliaments were trivial'.[66] Edward felt this too, and the difficulty of his life was to keep a balance. His sense of the triviality of business gave him a detachment which some of his colleagues could neither understand nor tolerate. It was not merely the difficult disposition of his wife which seemed at times to threaten his whole political career. He felt the yearning for the simple life as strongly as she did. It could yield him a pleasure which more sophisticated men found incomprehensible.[67] He was not 'clever' in the sense that he revelled in intellectual activity or was tempted by abstract reasoning. Rooted in the land, he thought of his politics in rural metaphors. There were no universal laws in horticulture or politics. Just as plants and birds could only flourish under certain conditions, and these conditions fluctuated unpredictably, so with political principles and institutions. He was the only politician who, talking of the 'ever-broadening stream of Liberalism', would be thinking of the damage to the land. Big cities oppressed him immeasurably. His 'love of nature' was not a soppy escapism from the 'real world', except in the conceptions of some of his admirers. The escapists were his colleagues and critics who lived in the country because gentlemen did, or who thought bird-watching or fishing mere pastimes and not to be taken seriously.

Grey's increasing self-confidence led him to seek more speaking engagements on the party's behalf, although in 1891 he was not confident of its future success.[68] Despite talk of a recovery, the crisis of identity was very far from being resolved. He contrived to steer a clever course, careful not to carry his dissent on Ireland too far and at the same time vaguely being known for his sympathy with 'progressive' causes.[69] In the latter area, Haldane continued to buzz busily, fixing up meetings between devotees irrespective of party label. Grey was not sure what this intellectual activity amounted to, writing in September 1891 that 'the Liberal party has to learn lessons which only a long minority can teach it. Liberals, Socialists and Labour men are all far too cocksure; and not till each element is well purged of its cocksureness will a decent party be formed out of the whole.'[70] The meeting of the National Liberal Federation at Newcastle in the following month was perhaps an example of this over-confidence. Superficially, it was a great display of party unity, but it masked fundamental differences. The Federation represented grass-roots Liberalism, and its incoming President, Dr Spence Watson, a latterday John Bright, was determined to make its views more plainly apparent to the party leadership. Gladstone paid his first visit to Newcastle for thirty years to take part, though he still considered himself aloof from the pressures of party organizations. While he endorsed the 'Newcastle programme' in general terms, he was fortunately able to believe that he was not committed to it. At this meeting, Grey, as a rising local figure, moved the motion on Ireland. After praising the Irish people for their moderation through-out their ordeal, he successfully urged the council to look 'with unshaken confidence to Mr Gladstone, upon his return to power, to frame and—in spite of idle menaces from the House of Lords—to pass a measure which shall fully satisfy the just demands of Ireland and leave the Imperial Parliament free to attend to the pressing claims of Great Britain for its own reforms'.[71] After Newcastle, the party now had a variety of goodies on offer—Home Rule, Disestab-lishment in Wales and Scotland, local veto, abolition of plural franchise, triennial parliaments, taxation of land values, abolition of entail and extension of small-holdings being among the most important. But it was just this 'programme' that the old-style party leadership dreaded. Where was the strong compelling theme? The impression had been created that the Liberal Party was little more than an accidental alliance of diverse pressure groups. Moreover, once there was an element of precision, the path was open to endless squabbles such as would break out between various factions in the temperance movement. Equally Nonconformists would want to know why Disestablishment was only promised for Wales and Scotland.

Whatever the qualms of the leadership about 'dictatorship from below' and the 'programme' itself, Grey swung himself into the new style of campaigning. His speeches in the ensuing months were simply rhetorical embellishments of the programme. The Irish Question still dutifully came first, for 'so long as Ireland returned eighty members in favour of Home Rule, Unionist policy was proclaimed a failure'. Liberals believed that a union of hearts was possible with the Irish people after Home Rule. After that, however, 'the wage-earners were entitled to first attention because they were the class the country most needed'. He denied that Liberals were setting class against class, for that could only be done 'if the classes who monopolised power refused to other classes their fair share'.[72] In an article in the *Co-operative Wholesale Annual* he repeated that Members of Parliament should be paid. As he wrote to Buxton, 'It all keeps on coming round to giving electors a perfectly free choice of candidates—to do so is safe, not to do so is dangerous—that's the essence of it all. . . .'[73] His difference over Ireland with his cousin Albert did not prevent a continuing exchange of views. What about Proportional Representation, Albert asked, should it not become Liberal policy? Edward read Sedgwick's *Elements of Politics* on the subject and found difficulties to match the attractions. He was not going to be caught by 'faddism'. It was 'out of the range of practical politics at present'. Profit-sharing? It was 'well worth while for any landowner with a high sense of duty and a touch of enthusiasm to try it', but it would not catch on generally, since 'to reconcile the farmers to it will need a much larger interest on capital and to make the hands *keen* a bigger bonus would have to fall to their share'. A general rise in farm prices might make this possible, but this in turn would have its complications.[74]

The political questions Grey took up were, therefore, generally matters connected with the land. The Tories had passed the Local Government Act of 1888, which substituted elected county councils for administration by the justices of the peace at quarter sessions. Grey criticized the Tories for failing to introduce what he called 'real' local government. They had been like 'mutes at a funeral' during the passage of the Bill. The county councils should have been supplemented by local authorities elected by manhood suffrage. Until parish councils were established, real land reform would be impossible. They should be able to acquire land compulsorily for public purposes such as providing cottages, stores, reading-rooms, schools, libraries, public halls and recreation grounds. Moreover, allotments should be available as an antidote to the restlessness and depression characteristic of much village life. The dull and spiritless (often the majority) would, he believed, be encouraged by being able to grow vegetables for their own families on land made available at reasonable rents. The paramount importance of all reform was the interest of the community. 'It is solely the acquisition of a permanent interest for the community which will justify arbitrary interference and will make it possible.'[75]

35

In midsummer 1892, Lord Salisbury advised the Queen to dissolve Parliament. The Tories had been in office for six years and had a majority of just over sixty. Gladstone, a spry eighty-three, led his party to the polls for the sake of his duty to Ireland. If the Liberals were victorious, he would make his last effort. In his constituency, however, Edward Grey found that the 'House of Lords & Irish questions and other general topics are of course listened to by all audiences with more or less interest if they were brightly put, but village people are not excited about them.' He was writing to Sir George Otto Trevelyan, now back in the Liberal fold after a temporary absence with Mr Chamberlain. In 1885 and 1886, he continued, the people had been keen on getting the vote and had used it to his advantage, but now 'they are much less clear what they want done with the vote. To a great extent one has to put ideas into their heads, instead of reasoning on a basis of ideas which are already there.' They wanted manhood suffrage but were not clear what they wanted to do with it. In his campaign, Grey was stressing the need for parish councils, through which villagers would gain some real share of power. This sometimes caught on. Sir Edward had no hesitation in pointing out that Religion, Justice and Education were all on a 'thoroughly undemocratic footing'. The monopoly price of land in some districts was a scandal and, while he did not advocate elected magistrates, it would be helpful to have qualified ones. Disestablishment and Disendowment were not yet practical in England but he would have no objection if Trevelyan (who was going to speak for him) stressed the unpopular basis of the Church.[76]

This campaign of rural reform notwithstanding, Grey had a difficult election. Morley reported to Harcourt at the end of June that after a bad start he was rapidly making up ground though at a very late stage. Dorothy reported that the spirits of supporters had been going down and there seemed a very good chance of Edward's opponent winning.[77] Grey had little permanent organization and had to drum up support at election time. However, he retained his seat, just topping 4,000 votes, his lowest poll, with his opponent only 442 votes behind. Nationally, the Liberals had been hoping to regain much ground lost in 1886, but they were not entirely successful. There was a majority of forty for Home Rule, but the Liberals were dependent for their majority on the Irish. The Ministers did not resign at once but waited for their defeat in August on a motion of no confidence. Gladstone became Prime

Minister for the fourth time. Dorothy Grey, while reflecting on the delights which defeat would have brought, nevertheless confessed to her friend Mrs Herbert Paul that 'Edward quite wants to be in the House . . .'[78] It would be interesting to see whether Mr Gladstone 'quite wanted' him in the Government.

3

Junior Office

It never occurred to Grey that he would be sent to the Foreign Office as parliamentary Under-Secretary. When the appointment was announced, he wished he was 'bringing a little more knowledge into the Foreign Office with me, but I hope to be able to learn & apply quickly'.[1] Dorothy would have preferred the Local Government Board, where it would have been 'most interesting to try and instil a really fine public spirit into small local governments newly created on the right lines'. Indeed, such a position seemed more in accordance with his expressed interests than was the Foreign Office. 'I am trying', Dorothy wrote to Bishop Creighton, 'to remember which of Dizzy's novels contains a man who prided himself on possessing a gallery of the portraits of Under-Secretaries whose chiefs were in the Lords. They are splendid beings it seems.'[2] Grey's friends had done well—only Haldane had been completely ignored —and Asquith as Home Secretary and Acland as, in effect, Minister of Education were in posts of importance. In this respect, Edward was a little perturbed, writing to Buxton: 'We shall lose our freedom and may be turned into clerks, instead of people who are doing something to develope and expand Liberal principles.'[3] Nevertheless, he did not refuse the invitation, writing to Gladstone that he could not but feel 'that you have paid me a very great compliment in asking me to undertake the work. . . . The position will probably be more important and difficult than any which I had expected to occupy so early in public life.' He expressed his gratitude for the confidence shown in him and would do his duty to the best of his ability.[4] Old Lady Grey, living on in Torquay, was delighted: 'He is only 30 years of age—younger than his beloved grandfather was when he first began his political life. . . .'[5]

No clear explanation of Gladstone's choice has ever been forthcoming. He liked young men of good Whig stock, though he knew

Grey was not an uncritical admirer. He had in fact first offered the post to his son Herbert, who had declined.[6] Rosebery may have suggested Grey, though he had still to accept office himself when the offer was made. In any event, it was important that the two men should get on well together. At forty-five, Rosebery seemed on the verge of a brilliant career, yet he hesitated before again accepting the Foreign Office. Gladstone, Morley and Harcourt had all to write begging letters. His wife had died in 1890 and he replied: 'The eighteen months that I have spent in seclusion have convinced me that I was not intended or fitted for a political life. . . .'[7] No one doubted Rosebery's intelligence, even brilliance, but he was moody and mysterious. Moreover, having been persuaded into accepting office, he tended to feel that he had accepted it on his own terms. Grey had not been to stay with Rosebery, although they had both been guests at dinners given by other members of the informal group. Being only five years older than Asquith, Rosebery was nearer to them in age than to other senior members of the party like Harcourt or Morley. Rosebery's biographer remarks of Grey that, like his subject, he was 'idealistic, imaginative and rich' and addicted to solitude. Sir Edward's wealth was not in fact comparable, but they certainly had in common a wildly oscillating attitude to politics.[8] Dorothy still looked upon political life as an 'experiment'. In his new post Edward would have 'opportunities for speaking, fighting and understanding, and if we find we cannot keep our hearts in towns, nor live rightly, crowded up with horrible people, we shall still be young, and other things will be possible to us'.[9] In keeping with his new position, before Parliament reassembled, Edward took her to Cloan for what she described as a 'very funny' visit. She felt 'unworthy of brilliant society and I believe this is partly because I try to play up to it and fail'. Haldane was host and the company included Asquith and Miss Margot Tennant. Margot had now reached the half-way stage in the two and a half years it took her to decide to marry the Home Secretary. Asquith looked 'worried and sad, whether about Margot or the Home Office I don't know'. Dorothy was embarrassed by the frank way in which Margot talked. From Cloan, the party then paid an experimental visit to the Trades Union Congress and lunched with the Webbs. The delegates looked 'such very splendid capable men' but Dorothy felt 'it was no good our being interested in it all because we have only got to do with foreign parts'.[10]

The task of a parliamentary Under-Secretary was, superficially, straightforward. He had to represent the views of his master in the Commons and, although having direct access to the Foreign Secretary, he had little part in policy-making. Decisions were reached in Cabinet and it was then his responsibility, properly briefed, to explain them to the Commons. 'It was not for him to take upon himself the responsibility of indiscretions; he had to be discreet without being unnecessarily reserved.'[11] Put more concisely, being Under-Secretary meant that one drank less, but talked more, than the Foreign Secretary.[12] Edward felt no sense of inferiority about his lack of expertise. Some previous Under-Secretaries had schooled themselves for their responsibilities by travel and reading. Dilke, for example, regarded his tenure as the first step up the ladder to the Secretaryship of State. Curzon, who was to succeed Grey in 1895, had spent the bulk of his time, since becoming an M.P. in 1886, making a name for himself as an authority on the East. Edward was not overawed by Curzon's *majestas*, writing to his cousin: 'He's quite a success: perfect delivery, wonderful command of language, and never dull, added to which the "appearance" so well known to all his friends attracts favourable attention. . . .' Yet, 'he never makes his opponents feel uncomfortable'.[13] The Greys had mustered one visit abroad, in the winter of 1887–8, when they spent several months in India. They had not greatly enjoyed the trip and Edward could not be persuaded to repeat the experiment. Why go to the Pamirs when the Highlands were available with much less inconvenience? Success in office did not depend on acquiring intimate knowledge about inaccessible parts of the world, but rather on gaining the 'feel' for ministerial responsibility. Aided by his distinctive clean-shaven, moustacheless appearance, Grey had to establish his personality on the House in a direct and convincing way, without giving rise to the suspicion that he was trying to usurp his master.

Grey enlarged his experience by being fortunate enough to come into office with a Cabinet divided on foreign policy. Somewhat surprisingly, Gladstone had previously announced his intention of maintaining continuity and Rosebery held him to this promise. After dining with the Foreign Secretary on 7 September 1892, Lord Esher noted: 'He is absolute at the F.O. He informs his colleagues of very little, and does as he pleases. If it offends them, he retires . . .'[14] The friction created by this attitude was not long suppressed. The issue was the future of Uganda. The British East Africa Company had run into difficulties and threatened to withdraw from the area.

Should it be allowed to do so? Most of the leading members of the Cabinet felt that it should. No Government should give official support to every trading company which ran into difficulties. Yet, in 1890, Lord Salisbury had tried to use government money in support of the company's plan for a railway from the coast to Uganda—though there was some doubt about his precise intentions. Both Gladstone and Rosebery claimed to be expounding Salisbury's views. The Foreign Secretary wanted to confirm British influence in Uganda and at the same time show his colleagues that he meant to control policy. Pressure groups agitating about the alleged consequences of withdrawal—a revived slave trade and fighting between 'Protestants' and 'Catholics'—helped Rosebery.[15] Gladstone and Harcourt discounted these rumours and did not appear in a mood for compromise. Rosebery in turn became broody and meditated resignation. If he did, the Government might collapse, and on 29 September a compromise was reached. The Prime Minister agreed to support the Company into the early part of 1893 while further inquiries were undertaken. Gladstone wrote to Rosebery that he had never known a Prime Minister and a Foreign Secretary go before the Cabinet with diverging views: 'It is the union of these two authorities by which foreign policy is ordinarily worked in a Cabinet; not that I have the smallest fear that this incidental miscarriage of ours will occur again.'[16] Rosebery acknowledged the special responsibility of the Prime Minister, but insisted that no departmental head could disengage himself from policy. In November, the Cabinet agreed to the dispatch of Portal's mission of inquiry but did not know that Rosebery had instructed Portal to conclude treaties with native chiefs of such a nature as to make withdrawal impossible.

In this situation, the task of a Government spokesman in the Commons was not easy. Sooner or later, in making a statement on Uganda, Grey was bound to say something which would offend one or other section of the Cabinet. His own sympathies were necessarily with his chief. The crisis had blown up so suddenly that he had no time to consider the question dispassionately. When Rosebery was being violently assailed by radical critics, the Foreign Secretary dropped a hint to the Prime Minister: 'Do not ignore Edward Grey, who is able and ready to speak if the discussion on foreign affairs goes on.'[17] On this occasion, Grey managed to please all concerned. His intervention was deft but not definite, informative but not illuminating.

It was another matter with Grey's speech on 21 March in which he stoutly defended Rosebery's Uganda policy. Labouchere alleged that he was taking sides against the Prime Minister and Edward was forced to write a hasty disclaimer. Nothing was further from his mind than that his statement should have been considered wanting in respect and he deeply regretted any offence he might inadvertently have caused.[18] He also had some explaining to do to the Foreign Secretary for, to judge from Harcourt's comment, 'You have put the fat in the fire', he had clearly boobed. 'It has been the misfortune of most of the Greys', he alleged, 'to become unpopular with their colleagues and for the present I am afraid I have leapt into the most unpopular position on the Government Bench.' It was a disarming opening, and Rosebery repeated it to his friends with obvious delight. Grey felt that he was bound to say something when a comment had been made about the ambiguous position of the Government over Uganda. He had not advocated the direct annexation of Uganda but had insisted that it would have been disgraceful not to send Portal's mission. Looking back, he thought the incident 'could not have been helped if I spoke at all. Mr G's speeches have laboured to imply that Portal's mission would lead to evacuation: mine implied (it did not assert) that the mission might lead to reoccupation.' He acknowledged that but for one or two personal friends, the Government Bench would rather he had been 'confused and drunk than clear and sober. You cannot overestimate the disgust that is felt. . . .'[19] Rosebery had no intention of pressing for his resignation. Talking to Sir Edward Hamilton, he said that Grey would have done better to keep silent as he intended doing himself, but evidently 'the speech which was ready would come out'.[20] The row blew over, but from it Grey learnt the value of silence. Events took their course and a year later, shortly after Rosebery had himself become Prime Minister, the protectorate over Uganda was announced.

The Ugandan question had been fought over so strongly because it was a symbol of the Government's attitude to 'Imperialism'. Terms like 'Imperialist' and 'Anti-Imperialist' are not very revealing. Despite his biographer's assertion that Asquith was 'in close agreement' with Rosebery on foreign affairs, and was classified as an 'Imperialist', he disagreed sharply with the Foreign Secretary on Uganda. He had no interest in the head waters of the Nile or in the protection of Uganda from slave-raids. Grey also found that Haldane was also against occupation in principle, while reluctantly conceding that it might have to be done. So much for the enthusiasm of the 'Liberal Imperialists'! Nor were the older generation of 'Anti-Imperialists' anxious to end the British Empire. The differences can be more exactly stated by the terms 'expansionist' and 'consolidationist'. The latter term, which could embrace Morley, Harcourt and Gladstone himself, defines those who essentially believed that to add further to the Empire would stretch Britain's resources. The naval and military expenditure needed to protect it would be too great. The Liberals were already, rather unwillingly, having to give careful consideration to the problem of Imperial Defence.[21]

Rosebery took issue with this view. The Empire was large, but what had to be considered was not 'what we want, but what we shall want in the future'. British restraint would not lead to a general colonial moratorium and would only mean that existing colonies might acquire unfriendly neighbours. It might therefore be necessary to advance in order to hold and it was too late to decide that European intervention in Africa was a mistake.[22] Grey shared this general position but recognized that 'Liberalism' might be a casualty. Imperial sentiment did not blind him to the irony of the situation. In November 1892, he dined with Rosebery, to meet Cecil Rhodes, subsequently describing him as 'not exactly what you call a Liberal: he has a new version of "one man, one vote" for South Africa, viz. that he, Rhodes, should have a vote, but nobody else should'.[23] Grey also possessed a young man's distrust of the virtues of compromise, believing that at bottom all Gladstone's troubles in Egypt and the Sudan, and in Africa generally, were due to a fatal want of firmness. He was therefore able to support Rosebery with growing conviction, especially in the matter of Egypt. Working for Baring, as he had done some eight years previously, had given him a personal insight into its problems. Once again, on this issue, Rosebery was in a minority in the Cabinet. The 'big three' pressed for eventual evacuation and opposed any increase in British commitments. Rosebery told the Queen that the only firm support he gained for the contrary position came from Bryce—another reputed 'Anti-Imperialist'. In January 1893, Lord Cromer (as Baring had just become) was involved in a crisis which suddenly revealed how flimsy the basis of British occupation was. He requested further troops, but the Prime Minister declared that he would rather set fire to Westminster Abbey—probably the most potent threat in his armoury—rather than agree to such a proposal. Predictably Rosebery took the opposite view. Eventually a compromise was

43

reached, and the Abbey was spared the attentions of an unexpected pyromaniac.[24]

These excitements were beyond the sphere of an Under-Secretary, nevertheless, in his station, observers reported favourably on Grey's progress. Arthur Balfour found him the most striking figure among the younger men on the ministerial side. Hamilton noted in his diary in July 1893 that 'so well has Edward Grey done at the F.O. that but for his being a commoner R. said that he (E. Grey) apparently possessed qualifications that might fit him for promotion some day from the Under-Secretaryship to the Secretaryship of State'.[25] In the late autumn of 1893 there was some talk of Grey being invited to become Viceroy of India—a post which it was proving difficult to fill. Rosebery refused to put Grey forward on the grounds that '. . . it would be a thousand pities if his Parliamentary career were interfered with. Edwd. Grey would come back from India shelved politically—probably with a peerage and with at any rate a position lost: while he was one of the very few men who might be regarded as making for a leader in the House of Commons.'[26] What were these 'qualifications'? Above all, the fact that he impressed the House, not by brilliance of speech or sharpness of retort but by soundness of grasp and sincerity of tone. The ear of the House mattered supremely when the opinion of the political élite, not the anonymous mass, assessed promotion prospects. Despite Gladstone's reputed remark that the difficulty with Grey was his fondness for the phrase 'I go a-fishing', Edward does in fact seem to have studied Foreign Office questions seriously. He felt better equipped to pass a Foreign Office test than he had ever done a school or university examination—a comparison which still left scope for improvement. Like a new boy at school, he had started off doing the right things. He dutifully stayed in London over Christmas while his colleagues of senior rank fled to the country. The Greys had taken a modest house in Grosvenor Road costing them £200 a year and invited the Herbert Pauls to share their small Christmas dinner. There was 'a sort of protest in having a very small dinner, when everybody else is having parties in large country houses and violating the natural repose of the country in the depth of winter'.[27]

The Grosvenor Road house had been taken as much for its nearness to trains from Waterloo as for its closeness to the House of Commons. Practically every week-end during the spring and summer of that long parliamentary session of 1893, Edward and Dorothy walked to the station before there was any traffic about,

and breakfasted in their Hampshire cottage at eight. It was only
reluctantly that they returned to London on the following Monday
morning. Dorothy remained devoted to her books and solitude.
'Where there is so much that is unworthy how can we remain pure?'
she wrote to Edward from Fallodon in September 1893. 'If our life
outside politics was to be muddy and doubtful, the contrast would
not be so great, but every little bit of purity in us, every little bit of
heaven shared, is one more shadow cast on the blackness of town
life, with its unworthy aims, mistakes, and general devilishness.'[28]
Dorothy's mood became blacker and she wrote to her brother-in-law
George: 'The strongest hatred we feel now is of people, any people;
they are all horrid and there is no health in them; they are mean and
selfish. If they see that one is happy, they are jealous and hate one;
if they see one is miserable, they feel triumph. If one does any good,
gratitude is a weight. If one makes mistakes, they are never
forgotten. . . . All human relations are a mockery it seems to me. . . .'[29]
If Edward was to preserve his wife's balance, or even sanity, it began
to look as if he would have to abandon his promising career.

Normally, Grey worked in the Foreign Office during the morning
and adjourned to the cellar-room of the Commons after lunch. The
noise which often penetrated the ceiling on those summer days was
the House discussing Ireland. Foreign affairs took up most of Grey's
time, but the centrepiece of politics was still the Home Rule
question. The Prime Minister was tooling up for a final futile assault.
Ostensibly a Cabinet Committee was drafting the Bill, but neither
Rosebery nor Harcourt sat on it. Gladstone agreed to consider items
in the Newcastle 'programme' when the Home Rule Bill passed
through the Commons. The Prime Minister introduced his measure
in February, and after a summer of argument it passed its third
reading early in September. Three days later it was crushingly
rejected in the Lords. Rosebery gave the Bill but a tepid blessing
before marching his little flock into the lobbies in one final gesture.
There was no outcry in the country. The Prime Minister either had
no plans for a dissolution or could not persuade his colleagues to
agree to them. Neither did he announce his resignation. There was
pronounced irritation at the wasted year, but no one had the courage
to ask Gladstone to go. The situation might have been easier if a
successor were apparent, but neither Rosebery nor Harcourt
commanded complete support. Finally, on 27 February 1894, the
Prime Minister announced his resignation and on 4 March,
Rosebery kissed hands as his successor. Harcourt was bitterly

45

disappointed. He had more experience than Rosebery and sat in the Commons, but even if his colleagues agreed with his views, they seldom agreed with him. His querulousness was notorious and it was probably a temporary personal feud with his erstwhile lieutenant, Morley, which cost him the position. For a fleeting moment, it had seemed that Rosebery was a model of balance and composure.

Grey was pleased with the outcome, but while he admired his chief, he was also aware of his weaknesses. 'He will have a very rough time,' he wrote to Dorothy, 'and he seems to be facing it, but I wish he was a little more buoyant and would ride over all but the biggest waves instead of plunging through them and getting the brine in his eyes.'[30] Rosebery's style of sea-bathing, coupled with some rather nautical pranks played by his colleagues, was to lead to the drowning of his Government in fifteen months. Grey himself contributed an unexpectedly big splash. However, for the moment, Lord Kimberley moved across from the Colonial Office to become Grey's new master. Asquith seems to have made a discreet little fuss about Grey not replacing some of the deadwood in the Cabinet, but Edward himself seems neither to have desired nor expected promotion. Kimberley was a congenial elder statesman with a wide knowledge of books and man, although even Grey found his partiality for discussing the effect of gales on the Norfolk landscape not altogether to the point. Still, the Foreign Secretary was clear enough on paper and behind him stood Rosebery, who did not disguise his continuing interest in foreign affairs. Unfortunately for the harmony of the Government, Harcourt, as Leader of the Commons, decided that he had to be fully informed on all aspects of foreign policy.

The first and last Rosebery Government was a sorry spectacle. Rarely can a collection of able and intelligent men have quarrelled so splendidly. A formula for co-operation between Rosebery and Harcourt was supposed to exist. The Prime Minister pledged himself to Welsh and Scottish Disestablishment as a gesture to the remote and vocal, while he kept Morley in office as Chief Secretary for Ireland for the same reason. With Harcourt promising a further dip into the Newcastle bag, a miracle might after all happen. Rosebery moved quickly to dispel this possibility. Speaking in the Lords in reply to a challenge from Salisbury to go to the country over Home Rule, the Prime Minister went so far as to agree that 'before Irish Home Rule is conceded by the Imperial Parliament, England, as the predominant member of the partnership of the Three Kingdoms, will have to be convinced of its justice and equity'.[31] To faithful Gladstonians this seemed tantamount to accepting the postponement of Home Rule until an English majority supported it. Rosebery's attempts to gloss over the speech did not appease the rank and file. The Cabinet, which had felt the weight of Mr Gladstone's burden, was more disturbed by the subsequent party confusion than by the speech itself. Struggling to find an issue to unite the party, Rosebery alighted on the House of Lords. All sections of the party could be persuaded that its reform was necessary to clear the way to their desired Elysium. But there were difficulties. The Queen had chosen Rosebery as her servant in part because she trusted him not to do anything wild, like destroying the only really independent House, as she liked to term it. Besides it was doubtful whether feeling in the party was strong enough to mount an attack simply on the Upper House. The Lords ought to be trapped into rejecting many more Liberal bills and thus be seen to be holding back the tide of social progress. If this was so, someone would have to decide which measures to bring forward. Yet it was because of his inability to make this choice that Rosebery first thought of an attack on the Lords. The cause of the Government was not advanced. Meanwhile the Prime Minister was at loggerheads with Harcourt over the latter's proposal to include Death Duties in his Budget.

Despite his official concern with foreign affairs, Grey did make some public speeches on these matters and from this time onwards they were increasingly reported in the national press. In July 1894 he proclaimed that the people would have to declare their will on the future of the Lords. Some of its privileges would have to be removed as they were indefensible, but he made it clear that he did not favour single-chamber government.[32] In a speech at Oldham in October he revealed that despite the obstacles placed before it, the Government was a success. While he agreed that the Liberal Party was bound in honour not to allow the Home Rule question to drop until a satisfactory settlement had been reached, 'social and labour questions were being neglected' and they would have to be solved 'because there were now millions of men in the country living from hand to mouth'.[33] He warned Liberals that with the formation of an Independent Labour Party there would have to be great and sweeping changes if their party was to keep abreast. His sympathies, in a general way, were with broad measures of social reform rather than with sectarian pressure for Welsh Disestablishment.[34]

As regards his own office, he had now measured his responsi-

E

bilities and had a little more scope, since Rosebery was not his immediate superior. In these years, France and Britain seemed to be constantly clashing throughout the world. In 1893, the two countries had come near to conflict over Siam, whose independence Britain wished to see preserved as a buffer between India and French Indo-China. The French seemed bent on destroying that independence and claimed certain territory. In August, French gunboats subjected Bangkok to several days of blockade before the Siamese accepted all the major French demands. British ships had been sent to Siamese waters for the protection of British subjects but there was always the danger that an 'incident' might develop. Rosebery was restrained by Gladstone, who informed him that he had cherished the old idea of a French alliance from his youth. The Foreign Secretary duly desisted from sending stronger Notes to the French. To his surprise, when he became Prime Minister, Rosebery found he was restrained by other factors. It did seem that short of a declaration of war there was no way of persuading the French to renounce their gains, and he could not persuade his colleagues that French designs on Burma were as serious a danger as the Russian threat. It was against the wishes of the 'Imperialist' Secretary of State for India, Sir Henry Fowler, that troops were sent to the Burmese/Siamese frontier. Harcourt made it clear that the whole business was quite absurd. Rosebery found this typical. Whenever Britain was in dispute with another country, Harcourt seemed invariably to believe that Britain was in the wrong. Kimberley tried to smoothe matters by arguing that the old buffer-state concept was inapplicable and that negotiations should be sought with France on a fresh basis. Happily, the Government was able to leave this task to its successors. Because of his previous Indian experience, Kimberley was obviously most helpful to the Prime Minister on this question and Grey's involvement seems to have been minimal.[35]

Sir Edward was much more interested in the problem of Britain and France in Africa. When the Government formally made Uganda a British protectorate, old Earl Grey, now ninety-two, applauded his speech on the subject. The Government had made a considerable advance with the policy 'of not seeking to found a great British Empire in Africa but to help the African population to reach a condition in which they will be able to govern and protect themselves in alliance with England'.[36] Edward replied that it would have been a disgrace to leave Uganda to its fate, but he disclaimed any personal responsibility, or rather stressed collective responsibility. In office he had been learning the necessity of compromise, with the result that it was 'very difficult to decide how much is due to one's own personal opinion and how much to that of friends or colleagues, but as regards Uganda I am sure that the main question has now been decided rightly. . . .' He could not feel the same confidence about Africa as a whole, because of the great jealousy of the various European Powers. Each was forcing the other on in a most disagreeable way. Large as Africa was, it had limits, and the European Powers would, hopefully, accept boundaries within which each could work undisturbed. He feared, however, that 'the oldest and best known part of Africa, viz. Egypt, will remain a vexed question longer than any. . . .'[37] His fears for the Nile valley were quite justified.

The revolt of the Mahdi in 1881 meant that the Sudanese were most unwilling to accept a reimposition of purely Egyptian suzerainty. It was also true that Egypt could not reimpose it without British support. In this situation, the task of defining Egypt's boundaries was necessarily delicate. In the summer of 1894 Grey reported to Kimberley that Chamberlain had raised with him the question of these boundaries. He had replied that the time was not ripe for definition. While it was necessary to assert that Egypt's frontiers marched with what were now Britain's in Uganda, the problem was one of procedure. The consent of Egypt and possibly of Turkey would have to be obtained. The best answer was that 'the Anglo-German Agreement makes it clear that everything from Wadelai to Alexandria belongs either to us or to Egypt, or if you prefer, is in the sphere of influence either of us or of Egypt, but that the exact boundaries where one leaves off and the other begins, must be settled between Egypt and ourselves and that no third Power can intervene'. Kimberley wanted to discuss the problem, and warned that 'we must be *very* careful what we say'.[38] Later in the year, Anglo-French rivalry switched to West Africa and relations between London and Paris remained cool. In January 1895 Grey found Europe 'a disheartening spectacle'. Apparently no nation was moved by any aspiration 'except the sort of malevolent and bastard enthusiasm, which exists in France and Germany, for large slices of Africa, from which they will eventually derive no other satisfaction than that of having kept other people out & for that they will have to pay heavily'. He did not deny an element of selfishness in British policy. Sir Henry Fowler had achieved something of a debating success for the Government in his defence of the Indian Cotton

Duties, but Grey frankly admitted their basically selfish character. Yet there was something peculiar about the British. Grey instanced the way in which, following reports of fresh massacres, British public opinion had shown 'a genuine disinterested indignation about Armenia'. European apathy made action impossible, but no other nation, except perhaps the United States, was capable of such concern.[39]

This disinterested indignation was followed a few months later by indignation of a less rarified kind. In February 1895, statements were made in the French Chamber suggesting that a French advance on the Upper Nile from the East would put France in a good position to re-open the whole Egyptian question. There were rumours in the press that secret expeditions were already in preparation. In the Commons on 11 March, Grey was asked to state that the whole Nile waterway was within the British sphere and that no foreign occupation would be permitted. Sir Edward allowed himself to be pressed into replying that 'the Egyptian and British spheres together do cover the whole Nile waterway'. This had been his position in his letter to Kimberley in 1894. Later in the month, however, news of French successes on the Niger prompted fresh fears that they would be repeated on the Nile. On the morning of 28 March, Grey was confronted with two questions, one concerning French activities on the Niger and the other asking for news of a French expedition which was believed to be heading for the Upper Nile. To the former query Grey replied that inquiries were being made in Paris and to the latter he replied that he had no knowledge of any such expedition. He did not add that the Prime Minister at least suspected that one might have started. However, later that evening, the questioner returned to the subject of the Nile when, in view of recent events in West Africa, it might have been expected that he would again refer to the Niger. The questioner warned the Government that if the French occupied some portion of the Nile, the British position in Egypt would become untenable. It was in answer to this point that Grey made his famous 'declaration'.[40]

Sir Edward claimed that Germany, Italy and the Congo Independent State recognized the British position and that no other Power disputed it. Then he was subsequently reported as saying that 'in consequence of the claim of Egypt in the Nile valley, the British sphere of influence covered the whole of the Nile waterway'. In a letter to *The Times* Grey stated that he had been misreported and that he had repeated his earlier phrase that 'the British and Egyptian spheres of influence together cover the whole of the Nile water-way'.[41] This misreporting, if such it was, formed only a minor element in the subsequent row. Grey continued, stressing that he could not believe the rumours, 'because the advance of a French expedition under secret instructions, right from the other side of Africa, into a territory over which our claims have been known for so long, would not be merely an inconsistent and unexpected act, but it must be perfectly well known to the French Government that it would be an unfriendly act, and would be so viewed by England'. He hoped it would be possible to rely on the sense of justice and fairness of the French Government and people.[42]

This 'declaration' bristles with interpretative problems. Firstly, it has been widely supposed that Grey was merely the mouthpiece of Rosebery. The Prime Minister had seen Kimberley the day before and presumably discussed the situation. Certainly, the French Ambassador, Courcel, believed that the declaration was stage-managed by Rosebery. Yet, if this were the case, it was hardly necessary for Grey to write to the Prime Minister privately explaining what he had said. Grey's statement was, of course, very convenient for Rosebery. His private secretary wrote that if it had been premeditated this could not have been done without the sanction of the Cabinet. As it was, Lord Rosebery had been able 'to commit the Cabinet to a policy of which, I should think, none of them cordially approve, and to which not a few are violently opposed. . . .'[43] Grey denied the story which subsequently appeared in the press that he came to the debate with a prepared statement referring to the Nile. In his memoirs he explains that 'whatever language I had thought of using about West Africa, where there were conflicting claims and action, and where both British and French officials were active, was not suitable to the question of the Nile valley. I therefore transferred to the subject of the Nile the firmness I had been authorized to show about competing claims in West Africa. . . .'[44] In the past, this explanation had convinced nobody except his previous biographer. It has, however, recently been observed that this account is in fact quite plausible. The objection that Grey had already used his prepared Niger answers falls to the ground when it is realized that the declaration was given in answer to a debate later on that same day. In the morning Kimberley had told the French Ambassador that he thought the Nile would be referred to in the House of Commons but he did so in such a casual way that he clearly did not expect it to assume its subsequent significance. In the emergency of the moment, Grey used a phrase which he had used in his correspondence with Kimberley in 1894.

Whatever its origins, the statement caused a furore. Writing to the Prime Minister, Grey was unrepentant: 'It seemed to me at the time that it was necessary to speak clearly and that if I did not things with France must go from bad to worse: at any rate to speak clearly was the only chance of improving matters.'[45] Rosebery had no intention of letting him resign, writing to Kimberley that 'nothing shd be done to diminish, impair, or reflect upon the present position of E. Grey. He is one of the most important members of the Govt. for his being outside the Cabinet is the direct cause not of his failure, but of his great success as reptve. of the F.O. Moreover he is persona gratissima to the H. of C., popular, admired, and respected.'[46] Grey himself was unperturbed. Sir Edward Hamilton met him at dinner on the evening after his speech and commented that it 'improved his already good position in the House of Commons. If he sticks to political life, he is certain to make his mark. . . .'[47] The Cabinet did not repudiate the declaration, though there was strong opposition from Harcourt and Morley. Harcourt had not been present at the debate, but opposed what he termed the 'menacing tone' towards France. It would inevitably lead to the situation which it was designed to avoid—a French demonstration. Nor could the French Foreign Minister, Hanotaux, be expected to come to a friendly settlement. Even after Kimberley assured Harcourt that he had not given Grey particular instructions, he insisted that he should in future see all answers which it was proposed that the Under-Secretary should deliver. Only by this means could the Leader of the House be reconciled to Rosebery and Kimberley discharging their offices from the Lords. After some argument, a patched-up accommodation on this point was temporarily reached.[48]

In his correspondence with Harcourt, the Foreign Secretary denied that the declaration constituted a threat; war was never contemplated. Yet the French Ambassador reacted very strongly, and the crisis did seem very serious. Just how serious, must in part depend upon whether the phrase 'unfriendly act' used by Grey did, at that time, have the precise significance of a warning which could only be followed by an ultimatum. The evidence seems to suggest that Grey had no such formal diplomatic usage in mind—a view which is perhaps substantiated by his subsequent use of 'unfriendly' in a purely descriptive sense.[49] Certainly, careful attention to the text of Grey's remarks, which were firm but courteous, seems to discredit the suggestion that the declaration was 'the first note of the hysteria which was to overwhelm foreign policy toward the end of the century'. In any case, it is a curious charge to bring against a man normally criticized for his addiction to traditional diplomatic method.[50] Grey's statement received additional publicity because Chamberlain seized upon it and repeated on three occasions in his speech that French activities constituted 'an unfriendly act'. Sir Edward was aware that Chamberlain was 'lying in wait' and that if he had not spoken the Government could have been accused of dodging a request for a clear statement—'which would I think have been really dangerous in its effect upon the attitude of the French. . . .'[51]

After all the fuss, the rumours of a Nile expedition were found to be baseless. Harcourt regarded this discovery as a vindication of his criticism. The French were no more likely to march upon the Nile than they were upon the Volga. But Grey's case did not depend upon there actually being a French expedition under way; indeed, he only dared make such a firm statement because there was no imminent danger of a clash. It was a public warning to the French, its substance having already been put in private, that such a mission should not be attempted in the future. As such, the warning was apposite. The French had become aware of Far Eastern intrigues between Germany and Russia and did not want to risk a major crisis. Naturally, Hanotaux rejected Grey's claim, but his tone was moderate and his wording left the way open for future talks. For his part, Kimberley had no wish to exacerbate the affair and, without going back on the principle, stressed his willingness to talk. Grey himself was quite determined that the principle which he had established should not be lost. On 24 April he informed Rosebery that the British flag had been taken down the river to Dufile and a treaty made there. The men on the spot had done the utmost possible 'to anticipate other people and make our right down the Nile good by treaty'. They had been acting contrary to instructions and would no doubt have to be reprimanded, but they had placed a trump card in British hands.[52] At that point, the Liberal Government had only two months to run, and it was to be left to others to resolve the question of the Upper Nile.

It is difficult to evaluate the foreign policy of the Rosebery Government. Like the administration as a whole, it lurched from side to side with no certain goal. When the Prime Minister was able to give his complete attention to problems he showed a penetrating grasp, but this only happened infrequently. The general problems of his Government oppressed him and with his loss of sleep went his sense of balance and proportion. But as a period of apprenticeship for Grey it could hardly have been bettered. The Grey 'declaration' is one of the few acts of the Government to be remembered. There had, of course, been other important decisions—the refusal to join with other Powers in coercing Japan after her defeat of China in 1894 is one example—but they attracted less attention. In retrospect Grey was quite critical of the way in which Rosebery's hostility towards France allowed Germany a great deal of scope. In particular, he instanced the growth of German influence in Turkey, which was also aided by the British concern for the Armenians. In 1910 he recalled that 'we were expected to give way whenever British interests conflicted with German interests'.[53] It is likely, however, that he exaggerated the extent to which he was critical of Rosebery's attitude towards France. His own actions, in any case, hardly contributed to an improved atmosphere. No special fear of Germany survives in what letters are available from this early period, although in a letter to Buxton, the Colonial Under-Secretary, at the end of 1894, he remarked concerning Samoa that 'the secessionists in Australia ought to understand that if they were not a British Colony, Germany would take Samoa tomorrow and do just as she pleased there. . . . If the secessionists ever get their way, Germany and France will teach them a few smart lessons.'[54]

The Government was defeated by a Tory stratagem on 21 June. The issue was the allegedly insufficient supply of cordite for the Army. There was not enough powder in this charge to bring down a Government in a healthy condition, but the Cabinet had no stomach for a struggle and the only issue was whether to resign at once, dissolve or prepare for a future dissolution. Grey was not among the small minority who wanted to continue. 'The situation', he wrote to Rosebery on the following day, 'had already become distressing over the Welsh Bill and would soon have become impossible.'[55] Rosebery and Harcourt managed to reach agreement on the final decision of the Government, that resignation was preferable to dissolution. Amazed at this latter-day harmony, the Cabinet agreed.

Grey's position was now paradoxical. He was a young man of thirty-three with a growing reputation and encouraging prospects. Yet these prospects were bound up with the fortunes of a party which had just closed a period of government in ignominious fashion. No one cared to prophesy when the Liberals would be back. In the meantime Grey had an important task ahead of him. He had won the national real tennis amateur championship at the Queen's Club in 1889 and 1891. During his period of office, from 1892 to 1894, he had suffered the ignominy of being runner-up. It was time to redeem his mis-spent years—as he did successfully in 1895, 1896 and 1898. That apart, however, Grey had been closely connected with Rosebery, but who could tell what leadership to expect from that strange figure? Then there were personal considerations. He had written to Rosebery in March 1895 that he felt an obligation to do all he could to serve him and the Government in his existing position. If he ever put forward a personal claim it would be 'to cut myself loose, but that will not be yet. . . .'[56] Dorothy, however, still loathed London life. Lady Monkswell was at dinner with her on 10 May and noted that 'for a very pretty & admired woman [she] looks as displeased as anyone I know. . . .'[57] She would much rather have been down at the cottage, where Edward would be able to spend ten days with her over Whitsuntide. It was with this situation in mind that Grey declined the Privy Councillorship which Rosebery offered on the resignation of the Government: 'It would certainly be quoted and regarded as an undoubted pledge and earnest of future public work', he wrote, 'and that is why I shrink from it. My wish is to let my work and my public position be emphasized and noticed now as little as possible that I may leave it, when an honourable opportunity comes . . . .'[58] Nevertheless, at the dissolution, he agreed to stand again for Berwick-on-Tweed.

4

Lack of Direction

As was only to be expected, the Liberals fared badly in the General Election of 1895. On balance, they lost nearly a hundred seats and the great bulk of these were in England. In all parts of the country the swing against them was noticeable—in agricultural districts their dismal performance can partly be explained by their failure to solve the crisis in farm prices. In Wales alone did Liberalism remain solid, though even here there was an adverse swing of 7%. The party had sustained its worst defeat of the century, and the Tories could anticipate power for a generation. The Liberal members of 1895 were not very different from their immediate predecessors, with a large contingent drawn from trade, industry and the professions, and only a small number of working men and landowners. The great majority of Liberal M.P.s now sat for industrial constituencies.

Grey's achievement in adding over 300 votes to his majority in an agricultural area was therefore a success against the tide. He was not enthusiastic about his campaign. After the defeat of the Government he had written in his *Cottage Book*, 'I shall never be in office again and the days of my stay in the House of Commons are probably numbered. We are both very glad and relieved. . . .'1 However, they dragged themselves away from the Itchen valley to fight the battle. Edward's opponent was Lord Warkworth, another member of the Percy family. Dorothy found the general propriety of the campaign 'really distressing'. The meetings were so respectable and a lot of serious people asked serious questions. Dorothy admitted that their eventual victory was due to the people who had improvised an election organization, for 'they had no attention and no advice for the last three years and at a moment's notice it is found that in every village there are devoted souls who from real love of Liberalism have kept the threads of everything'. The squires, parsons and publicans had supported Warkworth as never before, but to no avail. Yet the victory was embarrassing since it made it 'more difficult to get free from politics, but we are just as decided as ever that it must be done'.[2]

This little local triumph could not alter the fact that nationally the party was in a precarious state. Rosebery was still the leader and, typically, thought the defeat a great blessing to the Liberal Party. 'Do you not remember', he wrote to Ripon, 'my prophesying to you that the fall of the late government must be followed by an inevitable smash up. We have offended every interest by the Newcastle programme (to which I have never adhered): three leaders proclaimed three different policies . . . but there was a more general & deeply rooted cause—Mr. G's general policy since 1880.'[3] These convictions were seemingly supported by the election defeats of Harcourt and Morley—Morley, most symbolically, in Newcastle itself. Harcourt was re-elected in July, but Morley had to wait until February 1896 when, like many others, he had to flee to Scotland for a seat. Rosebery had failed to capture the imagination of the electorate and it was not clear how far he was going to exert himself. Naturally he at once resumed his quarrel with Harcourt and for a time it seemed he might force him to resign the leadership in the Commons, but this plan failed. A clumsy arrangement was reached whereby Rosebery was the leader of the party, but Kimberley led it in the Lords and Harcourt in the Commons. Other ex-Cabinet members began to feel that the party's fortunes would never revive while there was this unfortunate personal tangle at the top, and they unsuccessfully sought a permanent reconciliation. On the face of it, Rosebery had only to wait, for Harcourt was nearing seventy, and, with every year that passed, it was more unlikely that the party would wish to be saddled with another Grand Old Man. Yet Rosebery was so listless and indecisive that his friends could not decide whether he really wanted to keep the leadership. Grey continued to support Rosebery and attended the pre-session meeting which the party leader held at Mentmore in February 1896. He also chaired a meeting of the Eighty Club in March 1896 in which Rosebery recommended the mysterious policy of 'concentration' as a remedy for the ills which afflicted the party. Surprisingly, despite the slights and splits, the party put up a better performance in the first half of 1896 than could reasonably have been expected. Perhaps the Liberals could yet recover.

Grey's personal vacillations paralleled the behaviour of the party leadership. On the one hand, he continued to express in private his detestation of public life and on the other, he clearly remained strongly interested in foreign affairs, where a number of developments attracted his attention. Firstly, there was the Venezuelan crisis. The boundary dispute between British Guiana and Venezuela was already more than half a century old and Britain and Venezuela had severed diplomatic relations on the subject in 1887. The new factor in the situation was the increased interest taken by the United States. There were protests about British imperialism and allegations that the heavy British investment in South America was a prelude to the extension of British control. Senator Lodge's claim in March 1895, 'We are a great people; we control this continent; we are dominant in this hemisphere', was widely believed.[4] Richard Olney, who became American Secretary of State in June, was determined to take a firm line. In his note of 20 July he asserted that union between a European and an American state was 'unnatural and inexpedient', that the United States was 'practically sovereign' on the continent. Britain should therefore agree to submit the boundary question to arbitration. Olney subsequently justified his strong language by claiming that 'in English eyes the United States was then so completely a negligible quantity that it was believed only words the equivalent of blows would be really effective'.[5]

Salisbury and Chamberlain, his Colonial Secretary, were studiously unmoved. When the Prime Minister finally replied he rejected the American claim firmly but courteously. It was not the case that American questions were for American decision alone—the Monroe doctrine had never entailed this proposition. 'The Government of the United States is not entitled to affirm as a universal proposition, with reference to a number of independent States for whose conduct it assumes no responsibility, that its interests are necessarily concerned in whatever may befall those States, simply because they are situated in the Western Hemisphere.'[6] President Cleveland was not pleased and in his presidential message of 17 December he reaffirmed that the Monroe doctrine did apply to the Anglo-Venezuelan dispute and asked Congress to make money available for a commission of investigation. If this commission should decide in favour of Venezuela, it would be his duty 'to resist by every means in its power as a willful aggression upon its rights and interests the appropriation by Great Britain of any lands or the exercise of governmental jurisdiction over any territory' which belongs to Venezuela.[7] Although there were qualifications in the statement,

American opinion had been roused, and Salisbury was confronted with a message which was tantamount to an ultimatum.

The Opposition was fully aware of the gravity of the situation. Harcourt and Rosebery were not on speaking terms and had to exchange opinions through an intermediary, usually Asquith. They both agreed, however, that war would be a disaster. Harcourt, whose second wife was American, curiously wrote to Chamberlain (who enjoyed a similar marital state) that 'we semi-Americans' ought to accept arbitration without reservation.[8] Grey's initial reaction was less well-disposed towards the United States. If Cleveland did not appoint a decent commission, it meant that the Americans were deliberately seeking war. 'There is perhaps some danger', he wrote to Buxton, 'that they may think we are so hampered by difficulties with Russia, France and Germany that they can make a little score off us with perfect safety. This would delight them no doubt so much that they would be loath to forego an opportunity.'[9] He hoped this would not happen. Writing to Munro Ferguson, who was acting as Rosebery's private secretary, Grey recognized that the strength of American feeling on the Monroe doctrine 'and the extension of it lately to limits which Monroe never dreamt of' was 'only the natural growth of ideas and aspirations'. Britain did not in the least want to stand in the way of them, but it should be pointed out to the United States that 'if they are to champion these South American Republics, they must exercise some control over them'.[10] On 11 January 1896, the day the Cabinet met to consider the matter, he wrote that he hoped Salisbury would put an end to the 'squabble' with America.[11] Salisbury was in fact reluctant to go back on his previous stand, but his colleagues forced his hand and he agreed to open negotiations with the United States. Eventually, after months of haggling, agreement was reached. An important concession had been made to the United States, and it was one with which Grey was in full agreement.

Salisbury's colleagues might have given him more support if the Venezuelan crisis had not coincided with the excitement caused by the Jameson Raid. The Transvaal mining boom of the 1880s had brought into the country a great many people, called Uitlanders by the Boers, whose presence constituted a threat to Boer supremacy. For their part, the immigrants (of British and European stock) protested about their lack of rights. A scheme was evolved by Rhodes, to which Chamberlain was privy, whereby an uprising in Johannesburg would be followed by an invasion from Bechuanaland.

This force was to consist of police, put at the disposal of the British South Africa Company. However, the Johannesburg conspiracy collapsed, though the plotters did not make sufficient allowance for the zeal of the Company's Administrator, Dr Jameson. On the evening of 29 December he led a force of some five hundred men into the Transvaal, hoping to take Johannesburg, 180 miles away, before the Boers noticed. On the morning of 2 January they were trapped, and they surrendered to avoid further casualties. The British High Commissioner and Chamberlain had already disavowed them.

The South African affair made Grey 'quite miserable'. He admired Jameson and liked him personally, but could not understand why he had acted so recklessly. It was perhaps possible that 'the Boers put a very lying spirit out to draw him into a trap, and that Jameson and his people really believed their friends in Johannesburg were on the point of being shot down. . . .' The Raiders were handed over for trial in London, which Grey felt was better than 'a long spell of a Boer prison'. Grey was shocked by the arrest of the Johannesburg conspirators and the death sentence passed on them: 'A couple of hundred years ago one would have been used to having one's friends sent to the Tower and beheaded, but it makes me sit up to have this sort of thing going on now.' President Kruger was now in a position to make strong terms and Rhodes's wings would be clipped —'no 180 miles an hour for him . . .'[12]

Sir Edward's reactions were in part determined by his family connexions with Southern Africa. Two of his cousins were wounded taking part in the Jameson Raid.[13] His younger brother George was in Africa and had taken part in the overthrow of the Matabele in 1893. The Greys had obviously closely followed this fighting.[14] The work of the pioneers as they opened up Southern Rhodesia was watched with interest. Financial weakness handicapped the enterprise and even the resources of the British South Africa Company were inadequate. The Company was forced to allow unofficial white settlers and prospectors to recruit their own labour and collect taxes on its behalf. This open-air life of prospecting and hunting was just the kind of precarious, dangerous life which appealed to George Grey. The European grasp was still shaky, as the Matabele rebellion of 1896 demonstrated. With the departure of Europeans to fight with Jameson, the Matabele saw their chance. After the earlier war, tribal authority had been ignored, cattle confiscated and land seized. In effect, the administration had acted as though the Africans no longer existed as a factor in the local balance of power. Since the Matabele had little to lose, their rebellion was a desperate affair and only suppressed at a cost of more than £7 million in circumstances which endangered the Company's charter. British troops had to be called in, and some extension of British political authority seemed inevitable. The Administrator of Rhodesia from 1896–8 was none other than Albert Grey, who had succeeded his uncle two years earlier and was now the fourth Earl Grey. Rhodes was forced to negotiate and come to terms with the Matabele, who obtained a promise of more land, a proper system of native administration, and machinery for redress of grievances. Rebel leaders as well as loyalists were appointed as salaried spokesmen of the people.[15] George Grey had raised a troop known as 'Grey's Scouts', who had distinguished themselves in the fighting. Edward had again closely followed his brother's activities and admired his bravery. Naturally, he saw the problem through his brother's eyes. The work of colonization had to go forward. For the moment, the white man could not stand in any other relation to the black than that of ruler and ruled. But within that basic framework, George Grey 'never lent any countenance to the view that to trust natives as people who had rights would weaken the authority of the Whites over them'.[16] Edward never went to Africa in his life, but through George and to a lesser extent through Albert, he came to feel that he had a certain personal grasp of the realities of the situation.

The abortive Jameson Raid was followed in swift succession by a friendly telegram from the Kaiser to President Kruger congratulating him on maintaining his country's independence. The telegram aroused a storm of protest in Britain. The Kaiser had hopefully believed that his message would remind the British that they could no longer do what they liked and draw their attention to the advantages of friendly association with the Triple Alliance. Germany's allies, Austria and Italy, argued in vain that it might have the opposite result. Salisbury did not lose his temper, but equally felt no increased affection for Berlin. The immediate result of the telegram was to increase the popularity of the Raiders, and German intervention goes some way towards explaining the curious behaviour of the Liberals during the official inquiry into the events.[17] After a few months, the Kaiser made conciliatory gestures and relations improved. Nevertheless, Grey feared that if Britain did have to intervene in South Africa, 'Germany will no doubt put on the screw in Egypt and be as nasty as she can every-where'. His prognosis for the future was gloomy: 'The fact is that the success of the British race has upset the temper of the world, and now that they have ceased quarrelling about provinces in Europe and have turned their eyes to distant places, they found us in the way everywhere. Hence a general tendency to vote us a nuisance and combine against us.'[18]

Because of this tendency, Grey strongly opposed any unilateral commitments by Britain. The Liberals as a party were pressing the Government on the further Turkish massacres in Armenia during 1895-6. Salisbury defended his inaction on the grounds that from Archangel to Cadiz there was not a soul who cared whether the Armenians were exterminated or not. Since the Great Powers were unwilling to take collective action, because of their separate interests in Constantinople, there was nothing Britain could do. The seizure of the Ottoman Bank in Constantinople, by armed Armenians, led to a further bout of slaughter in Turkey and fresh protests in Britain. Earlier in the year Rosebery had attacked the failure of the European Powers to protect the Armenians, though he had specifically refrained from advocating unilateral action. Grey agreed with him and awaited the outcome of the Cabinet delibera-tions with interest. In November 1895 Chamberlain had argued in the Cabinet that Britain would occupy a stronger position in Europe as the friend of Russia than as the friend of the Triple Alliance. The Prime Minister objected to 'cutting Austria adrift', but when the Austrian Foreign Minister pressed for a British promise to defend Constantinople against Russia, as the price for the renewal of the existing Mediterranean Agreements between the two countries, Salisbury was not prepared to pay.[19] Grey, too, thought that 'a bold and skilful Foreign Secretary' might detach Russia from Britain's list of active enemies without any great sacrifice of interests. 'I have never been very devoted', he wrote, 'to the blue eyes of the Mediterranean and if Old Sarum has the pluck to do a bold stroke of policy and play the dog in the manger there less, I for one should be glad.' Unless Russia was bent on annexing Persia, 'room could easily be found for her wants and ours both in Asia and Europe: and if Russia stands aside we ought to be able to deal easily with any combination of European navies which is possible at present'.[20]

Careful consideration of policy along these lines was far removed from the mood of the party as a whole. The Armenian question led

to Rosebery's resignation on 8 October 1896. After some initial
reluctance, Gladstone had been persuaded out of retirement and had
addressed a public meeting in Liverpool on 24 September. He
urged Salisbury to free Britain from the fetters of the concert of
Europe, though he did not specifically advocate war. Rosebery felt
called upon to make his own position clear, and the return of Mr
Gladstone, seemingly as difficult to destroy as the Ottoman Empire,
oppressed him. Misleading press reports of Harcourt's speech to his
constituents on 5 October led him to believe that Sir William had
lined up with the Gladstonians. Rosebery was now a mass of
contradictory impulses. On the one hand, he wanted to strike out in
a bold new direction; on the other, he wanted to have done with the
whole wearisome business. He brooded in isolation for a fortnight
without consulting his disciples, and on the morning of 8 October
readers of *The Times* were the first to discover that he had resigned
the party leadership. The next day he delivered a moving valedic-
tory speech in Edinburgh. He paid tribute to Gladstone but made it
clear that their views differed: 'It is . . . against a solitary and
feverish interest in the East that I enter my protest.' He also
praised Asquith, implying that the party should look to him for
leadership in the future.[21]

Edward Grey was not with Haldane, Asquith and others in
Edinburgh for this moving, if baffling, occasion. At the height of
the Armenian crisis he had retreated to the Shetland isles for a
month's fishing.[22] From Lerwick he had written to Rosebery early
in September with exemplary detachment that 'Foreign affairs and
men are the two interesting things in politics at present: other
subjects have no life in them.'[23] 'You are stronger now both in the
party and in the country', he wrote on reading the resignation
speech: 'the first consideration is not under present circumstances
worth much, what the second may be worth events alone can prove.
Party politics are in an abnormal state: the play of forces in the
country will not let them continue so and you will now, if you wish
it, play a powerful part when new questions arise and new developments in politics show themselves.' Time would have to do its work,
for 'there is at present no Liberal party worth leading: the party in
Parliament is numerically small. . . . These men in the House of
Commons won't follow Asquith or Morley or Harcourt any better
than anyone else. Leadership is for the present impossible. . . .'[24]
Predictably, other party reactions were not of a piece. While
Asquith appreciated the praise bestowed on him, he felt that Rose-

F

bery had acted selfishly. The older men, like Ripon and Spencer, felt that he had abandoned them to the mercies of Harcourt without much of a fight. Arthur Acland still clung to the notion that Rosebery would be the man to lead a crusade for social reform. Haldane, who some years before had obligingly accepted the mission of making Rosebery 'great', had to think again. Morley and Harcourt said nothing.

The effect of Rosebery's resignation on Grey was to reopen the whole question of his political career. The leadership of Kimberley in the Lords and Harcourt in the Commons was not an exciting prospect. Even before the resignation he had confessed from his fishing retreat that 'up here politics seem less of a necessity than ever and I have lost instead of gaining any material for such discourses as I am booked for in the autumn'.[25] To complicate matters, Dorothy was miserable and unwell with heart disease. She wanted Edward to give up politics and devote himself to his Northumberland estate. After meeting her in November 1896, Lady Monkswell wrote: 'Lady Grey also has a contempt for children and does not desire any. She is a very handsome, delightful & clever woman, something over 30, but could anybody be more "madly with her blessedness at strife"? If Sir Edward Grey goes on he is bound to be Foreign Minister when the Liberals come in; there is no one else in the running.'[26] But would he go on, and would the Liberals ever return?

At this point, Chamberlain invited him to join a Royal Commission to inquire into the economic and social problems of the British West Indies, in particular those connected with the sugar industry. The investigations might last for some months and during that time he would necessarily be away from the House of Commons. Asquith, Haldane and Rosebery all advised him not to accept.[27] Absence from the House was serious enough, but the greater danger to his prospects arose from the fact that other commissioners might want to tamper with Free Trade principles. It would be decidedly embarrassing for a leading Liberal to be involved in such a situation —the Tories might make capital out of it. It was on these grounds that Morley advised him not to go, writing to Harcourt: 'It would be a great pity if a youngster with Grey's prospects were to entangle himself in the smallest degree with any such abominations.'[28] Harcourt replied in typical fashion: 'On the whole I think he had better Jingoise in England than Zollvereinise in the Indies—besides if he went it might look like secession.'[29] Yet despite this sage advice, he decided to go, writing to Rosebery: 'I think you are quite right that an ambitious man had better refuse, but I side with the unambitious. . . .'[30]

The commissioners, who were paid two guineas a day on land and half a guinea a day at sea for their pains—hardly enough to cover the expenses of wine and gratuities to the steward, as Grey complained—left England in January 1897.[31] Dorothy accompanied them since the climate was thought to be good for her health. Besides the chairman, Sir Henry Norman, a former Governor of Jamaica, the other members were the Fabian Sydney Olivier, a civil servant in the Colonial Office, and Sir David Barbour, a former Finance Member in the Government of India. The sugar islands were now sad relics of the prosperous prizes which they had been when Edward's great-great-grandfather had captured some of them for the Crown. The major European Powers had begun to subsidize their own sugar-beet industries by means of export bounties. European sugar swamped the British market so that by the end of the century West Indian sugar constituted less than a tenth of total sugar imports. The situation was catastrophic in the islands. Investment fell, unemployment rose, wages dropped and the island Governments faced bankruptcy. Chamberlain gave Grey an assurance that he kept an open mind on the problem, but it was obvious that a system of countervailing bounties was in his mind. The commissioners worked hard, travelling from island to island and across to British Guiana. Edward revelled in the sights and sounds of the islands. Off duty, he made comparisons between the indigenous birds and more familiar English species. He also found Richardson's *Pamela* an ideal distraction from the problems of sugar. Dorothy stayed in Dominica, recuperating and looking at the wild life. She did her best to understand the situation, writing: 'If something very large isn't done to help the planters quite soon, there won't be a white man left in the islands: and it seems a pity, because the islands are so very beautiful, and the niggers are so very ugly.'[32]

The commissioners returned in May and their report was published in August.[33] They recommended that the Government advance nearly £600,000 in grants and loans to improve methods of cultivation, organization and communication. The fruit trade was to be encouraged as an alternative. The commission fudged the central issue of the bounties. All agreed that abolition of the continental bounty system would be the biggest single encouragement to an increase of prosperity and that the Government should try to persuade the states concerned, but Grey and Barbour were not prepared to strengthen its negotiating hand by approving retaliatory duties. The Colonial Secretary then tried to persuade his colleagues that the bounty system was indefensible and that it was absolutely wrong that the United Kingdom should profit by the ruin of its oldest colonies. They were not convinced, though they did authorize fresh negotiations on the bounty question, but these proved abortive. In March 1898, Chamberlain, with Grey's support, successfully moved the allocation of £120,000 as a first instalment—a high figure for the time. In return the Colonial Secretary asked for control over taxation and expenditure so that he could really begin to develop the imperial estate. His colleagues were still unhappy. Balfour, for example, did not like the proposed plan to subsidize the fruit industry against the competition of its American rival.[34] Grey found his West Indian experience profoundly depressing: 'The small islands will be poor affairs without sugar—as is the natural state under normal conditions of small islands which are not near large markets. I have seen no criticism which in the least shakes my opinion that the case against countervailing duties is conclusive on their merits: putting free trade and fair trade theories and phrases altogether out of the question and looking at things solely with regard to what is practical and expedient.'[35] The Government should prepare for the worst, although there was always the chance that the expanding United States market might keep the trade going for some time. Indeed, while Chamberlain no doubt had some very clever plans, he feared that 'even without bounties the British market will live normally upon German beet and the West Indies remain dependent upon the U.S. market'.[36]

While in the West Indies, Grey naturally lost close touch with political developments at home. He wrote to the Chief Whip, Tom Ellis, that he had not seen English newspapers for weeks and would be anxious to receive instruction from him on his return.[37] The fears of the party leaders that his trip would cause him to wobble on Free Trade had not proved justified. Nevertheless, the situation at the top of the party was still delicate. Before leaving the country Sir Edward had publicly declared that 'although Lord Rosebery had resigned, he believed that they felt no less confidence in his leadership than they did before'. The party needed time for 'freedom of thought and discussion' before trying to regain power.[38] Such remarks could not have endeared him to Harcourt, since speeches of this kind, made by Rosebery's disciples, were deliberately designed to make it clear that the throne was still vacant. This uncertainty made it impossible for Harcourt to consolidate his position. As a result, many leading Liberals were afraid to say anything in public lest they be 'labelled'. For this reason, Grey could not have chosen a better time to take some months in the sun. There was one subject in particular on which Harcourt would have liked Grey to have maintained a permanent silence—the question of the Nile valley.

Since his famous 'declaration' of March 1895, Sir Edward had not allowed his interest in Egypt and the Sudan to languish. Morley had already reported to Harcourt that Grey was likely to vote with the Government on the Sudan. Not that he was impatient for a settlement. While the Khalifa was strong he in effect held the Nile valley against all comers, stopping development and progress, but he was 'an enemy of all the world and the mischief to us and Egypt was negative and stationary'.[39] For his part, Salisbury wanted to be sure that when that power was challenged there would not be any repetition of the Gordon fiasco. Meanwhile, he was anxious to humour France and he cultivated good relations with the French Ambassador, Courcel. He would probably have been content to let this situation drift on had it not been for the Italian reverses in East Africa. These prompted him to authorize an Egyptian expedition from Egyptian territory to strike against Dongola. This decision was not connected with the French approval on 30 November 1895 of secret preparations to send a Major Marchand on a peaceful mission to the Nile with the intention of provoking an international conference on its future. It was to take Marchand some time to arrive at his destination.

Meanwhile, the success of the Dongola expedition—the whole province was under Kitchener's control by September 1896—led Grey to believe that the Khalifa was 'rotten' and that the time had come for a move against him. It was necessary to press on, he told Munro Ferguson, in order to 'prevent new developments, which were not on the cards as long as the Khalifa's power was not known to invite attack'. By the summer of 1897 the Anglo-Egyptian forces were poised to attack the heart of the Mahdist state.[40] As the military advance continued, Grey was fully aware that his name was likely to be very frequently mentioned. In November 1897 he warned Rosebery that 'my speech about the Nile Valley is likely to come up again and there may be more rows and rumours about it. . . .' If it did come up, 'I shall stand up for what I have said. . . . I suspect that Salisbury has let the question of French expeditions both to the

Nile and West Africa go to sleep. He has been woken up about West Africa and may be woken up about the Nile by things going too far.'[41] What else would be said from the Opposition front bench was a matter for speculation! Harcourt, the chief critic of his declaration, would find it difficult to attack a Government policy which could quote it in support.

The Nile valley question interested Grey for obvious reasons, but while it developed Grey kept something of a watching brief on other aspects of foreign affairs. While he was in no sense 'shadow' Foreign Secretary—though nor was anyone else—there were few important foreign questions which altogether escaped his attention. The question of Crete provides one example. In January 1897 there had been a serious rebellion against Ottoman rule with the objective of union with Greece. Salisbury neither wanted Greece to set the Balkans alight nor to see the Cretans handed over to Turkish vengeance. Again, it was up to the Concert of Powers to act and not Britain alone. The Powers did in fact agree on a settlement whereby Crete was given autonomy under nominal Turkish suzerainty conditional on the withdrawal of both Greek and Turkish troops. The Sultan was prepared to accept, but the optimistic Greeks insisted on declaring war on him in April 1897 and were forced to sue for an armistice by the end of the month. In the ensuing negotiations, Britain was able to preserve for Greece far better terms than she dared expect, including the Cretan autonomy statute. By this yardstick, Grey was well satisfied, having written in May that if Salisbury made this an essential condition of all he did there was no cause to strike attitudes about whether or not Crete should be annexed to Greece.[42] He thoroughly applauded the Prime Minister's use of the Concert, for 'if Greece had annexed Crete he believed Turkey would have annexed Athens'. His criticism fastened on the fact that 'there was something in Lord Salisbury which induced him too early to reconcile himself to a pessimistic view of the situation and to give it up as hopeless'. He concluded on a fine party note that the British position in the area had been fatally compromised by Disraeli's policy and the Conservative decision to uphold the Ottoman Empire at the expense of the Christian peoples.

In the same speech he was also able to score points off the Government for their handling of the North Indian frontier. Curzon, he claimed, had persuaded his colleagues to retain the fort of Chitral in an exposed position among notably turbulent clans. In the summer of 1897 these clans erupted into revolt and for a time it seemed that the Indian Army might be threatened with its most serious situation since the Mutiny. By a combination of good luck and severity, order had been restored, but Grey alleged that the Government had gravely miscalculated. Had the Liberals remained in power after 1895 they would have withdrawn from Chitral.[43] Curzon, who had been to Chitral, took the opportunity to deride Opposition speakers who, until the outbreak, could not have named a single tribe on the frontier.[44] Perhaps, after all, there were advantages to be gained from travel in the Pamirs.

The lesson which the Greco-Turkish war had confirmed for Salisbury was that the Eastern question in its traditional nineteenth-century sense had little serious interest for Britain. 'On the other hand our interest in Egypt is growing stronger . . . the idea that the Turkish Empire is on the verge of dissolution has been dissipated . . . the only policy which it seems to me is left to us by the Cabinet's decision . . . [is] to strengthen our position on the Nile (to its source) and to withdraw as much as possible from all responsibilities at Constantinople.'[45] The consolidation of Egypt was making steady progress. Berber had been evacuated by the Mahdist garrison and fell without resistance in August 1897. In April 1898 Kitchener achieved a decisive victory and in September, after the battle of Omdurman, the Mahdist state in the Sudan had ended.[46] The politicians were, however, aware that Kitchener's work might not be over. On 19 September he met Major Marchand at Fashoda and from then until 4 November, when Marchand was ordered to withdraw, war seemed very near. Popular excitement over events in the Sudan was high throughout the summer and Grey shared this state of emotion. He wrote to his friend Katharine Lyttelton, whose soldier husband was about to fight in the Sudan: 'Don't you feel already how all the trivial things are losing their hold? All the horrible little worries and busy-nesses and plannings, which creep upon one in numbers and cling and cluster upon the spirit and drain its energy and make it anaemic and weak—all these cannot stand the throbbing of a pulse which is stirred, and fall from one and shrink and perish on the ground, and you feel that you are standing erect and strong and clean. . . .'[47]

Since the Government had cited his declaration in Kitchener's instructions, Grey's name figured prominently both in diplomatic circles and in the public mind. Harcourt wrote to his son on 12 September that it was 'strange to see how the old affair of the Anglo-Belgian Treaty and Grey's foolish speech is coming to the front à propos of Fashoda. It may lead to some awkward revelations.'[48] His primary concern now had to be for the unity of the party and he did his best to avoid speaking about Fashoda at all. As usual, since it was September, the author of the declaration was to be found in Scotland fishing. But his pulse began to throb sufficiently for him to leave the delights of the island of Mull and make his way south. He was at Fallodon by 27 September and wrote from there a letter of encouragement to Tom Ellis, who was in fact mortally ill. Edward reported that his fishing had been very successful and he had seen 'nobody connected with politics since the Session ended'. The Government seemed to be getting a little better 'after having had several nasty shakes. Kitchener has done something to rescue its prestige, but I don't think Salisbury will polish off the difficulty at Fashoda quite as quickly as his supporters would like.'[49] Rosebery reappeared in Gladstonian fashion to approve any steps which the Government might feel necessary to support Kitchener. He also took the opportunity to claim credit for the Grey declaration, though the burden of his message was an appeal for national unity. As soon as he spoke, there was a fluttering among the acolytes who believed that a decisive reassertion of leadership was near. His followers chimed in with messages of support for the Government—Asquith, Fowler and then Grey himself on 27 October stated unequivocally: 'Egypt is the Nile and the Nile is Egypt.'[50] Even Bryce supported the Government, though in milder, donnish tones. Harcourt and Morley did seem isolated, and they exchanged letters lamenting that 'as to official Liberalism its mouth is closed by the estoppal of Grey's speech. . . .'[51] Finally, Harcourt was compelled to speak in support of the Government but at the same time he warned: 'We should all abstain from language of vulgar swagger, or of provocation, or of menace, which might embarrass their conduct or precipitate their action.'[52] Colleagues, like Grey himself, were making strong speeches without any kind of consultation and Harcourt could go on no longer. He presented his colleagues with the decision in the middle of December and, in a message reminiscent of his predecessor's, he ventured to state that he felt that he had received less than full support for his efforts.

Harcourt conceived his resignation as a blow against the spirit of the Grey declaration, yet at the same time he warmed to Grey personally. The letter Grey wrote after the resignation was announced gave him more pleasure than any other. In a speech at North Shields on 14 December, Sir Edward went out of his way to praise Harcourt and stress the difficulties under which his leadership had laboured.[53] Despite their differences, they had a way of handling them which did not interfere with their personal relations. To the end of his days Sir George Otto Trevelyan remembered how in some connexion Grey, as a very young member, 'quietly rebuffed and silenced Harcourt amidst the amazed delight of all Harcourt's colleagues'. He believed that the history of the future was contained in that incident.[54] When Grey read of Harcourt's resignation in the newspaper he had a speaking engagement that same evening and, having overcome his shock, had composed the tribute which Harcourt had so liked.[55] When Grey had become Foreign Under-Secretary, Sir William told him to break up his fishing rod since the ball was now at his feet. Edward replied that he wasn't sure that he wanted the ball.[56] Now, as he retired, Harcourt wrote: 'For you, my dear Edward, I have always felt the strongest attraction derived not only from hereditary attachment, but from esteem of your character and admiration of your ability. I have had my full share of the nineteenth century, and the twentieth belongs to you. You have already established for yourself a first place in the regard and respect of the House of Commons—the only solid foundation for a public career.'[57] He was glad to know that the party had in store a man so well fitted to accomplish its work. 'Grey', he told Buxton, 'is made of the right stuff and after all there is *some* advantage in being a gentleman.'[58] To Fowler he was even more explicit: 'I think E. Grey's speech excellent and very handsome towards me. I have certainly done all I could to bring him forward, feeling that he is the young hope of the party.'[59] Grey replied gratefully acknowledging Harcourt's forbearance, admitting that they had different points of view on some questions. As for the future, 'My wife and I are still not sure that we quite welcome the prospect of the twentieth century, if our share in it is to be so full as you most generously anticipate. But the future of the Liberal Party and of anyone who belongs to it, is a secret which time still guards jealously, and all our meetings and speeches are not throwing any light upon it yet.'[60]

'Far and away the best thing', Grey wrote to Haldane on 16 December, 'would be for Asquith to give up the Bar and throw himself into this position, and in the work of it, his qualities and powers would develope, and by the next Election he would have gained an influence far greater than he has ever yet had.'[61] To Buxton he wrote of Campbell-Bannerman that 'he would carry the thing on very cleverly & in pretty good style, but he would not make the running as Asquith might, & he is delicate in health. There remain but Fowler or Bryce. . . .'[62] There were even faint murmurings in favour of Grey himself, since it was becoming clear that Asquith would not push himself, largely, it was felt, because with his five children he could not afford to give up his career.[63] But there were not enough advantages in being a gentleman for Grey to challenge Campbell-Bannerman effectively—even if he had wanted to. In addition, there was always Rosebery to add his customary quota of confusion, so Grey believed that the party could look forward to a session of quarrelling—Harcourt 'really did a lot in keeping the peace for the last session or two'. But perhaps the merrier the better, since 'Parties must gravitate towards a more normal condition, and if the tendency is that way, the more they are shaken, the quicker will the tendency work'.[64] He also believed that a good shaking would tend towards the ascendancy of Rosebery and the only question was whether he would be prepared 'to take a more regular and less detached part in politics'.[65] Waiting for Rosebery was to prove a wearisome business.

Edward helped to pass the time by writing a book on fly-fishing. Fishing remained his passion when Parliament was in recess. The cottage in late spring and early summer was where Grey was most at home. London was where great decisions were made, but 'there is an aspect of London which is inevitable and becomes most oppressive in hot June days. There is the aggressive stiffness of the buildings, the brutal hardness of the pavement, the smell of the streets festering in the sun, the glare of the light all day striking upon hard substances, and the stuffiness of the heat from which there is no relief at night—for no coolness comes with the evening air, and bedroom windows seem to open into ovens. . . .'[66] The quality of this writing is testimony to the intensity of his feeling. The book is full of skilful description of the angler's craft and praises the solace to be derived from the pursuit of fish. Not every young Liberal politician would have chosen this subject for his book, but then Edward still liked to believe that he did not come into this category. There was some amusement to be derived from the reviews. Predictably it was found 'too fishing for the bookish and too bookish for the fishing'.[67] To Herbert Paul, who said that the book was too good for a sporting library, Edward replied that he was 'possessed with the feeling that we live in a world, which in spite of much that is distressing, is beautiful beyond expression, & to put some of that feeling . . . was what I most cared to do'.[68] That year there had indeed been much that was distressing. In the spring of 1898 Dorothy seemed near to death and when they left the cottage in July Edward wrote: 'We are very grateful and perhaps all that happened before we came this year has made us more than usually fearful and sad at leaving it.' By September, however, he could write: 'Dorothy has continued to improve and my anxiety has gradually faded away and even changed into good spirits. She is much better: we are going to live quietly all this autumn & winter, but we are enjoying life.'[69] A month later this quiet life was disturbed by a war which broke out in South Africa.

5

Fishing in Troubled Waters, 1899-1902

In January 1899 Haldane reported that Grey was 'very keen indeed about Politics'.[1] After a quiet start, the 'merry scenes' which Sir Edward forecast began to materialize. Campbell-Bannerman began his leadership in a deliberately relaxed style and had written to Rosebery urging him to think of the future rather than the past. The appeal seemed to have succeeded until Rosebery broke his silence in May 1899 and, claiming to speak in a 'disembodied' way, urged a combination of the old Liberal spirit with the new Imperial mood.[2] Harcourt and others rushed in with predictable contradictions. More interesting was the reaction of his erstwhile followers. Asquith was upset by the speech, drafting a letter (which he did not send) doubting the plausibility of reconstructing the Liberal Party on the basis of an amalgam of Unionism and Jingoism. This seemed to offer doubting middle voters the maximum of inducement to become or remain Tory.[3] It was not without significance that since Campbell-Bannerman was sixteen years his senior, Asquith might reasonably expect to be his successor. The return of Rosebery might complicate matters for him. Grey and Haldane both remained respectful but were becoming restless. They hoped that the advent of the South African war might create circumstances in which he would throw off his mask of indifference and disenchantment—if mask it was.

In February 1897 Sir Alfred Milner was appointed High Commissioner of South Africa and Governor of Cape Colony. His appointment marked a new phase in the complicated history of the country. Asquith chaired a remarkable farewell dinner for him at the end of March. The Colonial Secretary and other Government ministers were present, as were Haldane and Morley for the Liberals. Unable to attend, both Rosebery and Harcourt sent fulsome letters of good wishes. The impression given, and no doubt intended, was that the entire nation was behind Milner in his mission—which included responsibility for the transaction of business with the two Boer states, the Orange Free State and the South African Republic (the Transvaal). Grey was in the West Indies but wrote privately to express his delight at the appointment. He went on to say that there was 'no one in whom I should feel more confidence than in you in such a place'. Grey feared that it looked as if 'the use of force could not be avoided: this will not be pleasant for, though the direct consequences of the use of force in such a case seem so certain, the indirect consequences may be so far reaching and incalculable. . . .'[4] Despite the recent assertion that Asquith, Grey and Haldane were 'among his closest and oldest friends', it is not clear how intimately Grey knew Milner or under what circumstances they met. The 'Balliol set' has been exaggerated, since Milner had gone down from Oxford and was working as a journalist in London for several years before Grey went up. Asquith was an old Oxford friend and it was probably through him that the two men met.[5]

The situation in South Africa had been dramatically changed by the discovery of gold in the Transvaal. Hitherto, the British had been able to believe that in due course the Boer republics would be driven to accept subordinate status by the logic of British power. But the great potential wealth of the Boers now meant that Afrikaner nationalists thought time was on their side. After the fiasco of the Jameson Raid, the dispatch of Milner, with his formidable administrative reputation, was another attempt to maintain British interests. Sir Alfred spent his first months getting to grips with the complicated situation. While contemporaries often saw the problem as a contest between Briton and Boer, it was in fact three-sided for there was also the relationship of both white groups to London, not to mention the question of the black majority. The standard Liberal recipe, that good relations between Briton and Boer would pave the way to a fair settlement of the native question, was deceptively simple. Milner quickly appreciated this and wrote to Asquith that he was 'quite confident of being able to get over the Dutch-English difficulty if it were not so horribly complicated by the Native question. . . .' The paradox was that 'you might indeed unite Dutch and English by protecting the black man, but you would unite them against yourself and your policy of protection'.[6] Asquith, Grey and Haldane saw Milner when he came back to England on leave at the end of 1898 and, on his return to South Africa, he spared no pains to keep them informed of his views.

75

Milner had now become convinced that it was essential to stir events to crisis point.[7] Chamberlain shared his view that political control over the Transvaal was necessary in order to consolidate the imperial position both in South Africa and as a whole, but he had to consider public opinion at home and the attitude of the continental Powers. Milner's public case against the Transvaal rested largely on the condition of the 'Uitlanders', those who had entered the country in the wake of the gold strikes and were largely of British nationality. President Kruger, who had been freshly confirmed in office, took the view that these miners were a transient population who did not merit the franchise. Not unnaturally, he also wished to preserve the Afrikaner character of his state and saw these new-comers as a threat to its traditions. Milner needed the support of the Uitlanders and managed to gain enough signatories to warrant sending to Chamberlain a petition claiming that British intervention was necessary to gain their political rights. After all, it was observed, there was an Afrikaner Government in the Cape. In May 1899 Milner sent his famous 'Helot' dispatch with its passionate charges against the South African Republic. At the Bloemfontein conference which followed and limited itself to the franchise question, Milner insisted that the Uitlanders should have the franchise after five years' residence. Kruger was prepared to reduce the period from fourteen to seven years, but no compromise could be reached and tension mounted.

Throughout this period, Milner was very anxious to be on good terms with his Liberal friends. He noted with alarm Campbell-Bannerman's public speech on 17 June in which he warned the Government that Liberals could see no justification for war in South Africa. In a letter of 13 July, Grey too warned Milner that public opinion was so strongly against war that the franchise question would be a totally insufficient justification. He defended public opinion against the charge that it had become slothful from peace and prosperity. He was confident that it would have '*insisted* upon war about Fashoda last year, if the French had not given way. . . .' Nor was Grey himself convinced that war would be 'either right or wise', though he agreed that the matter had to be treated not as a Transvaal or Uitlander question simply, but as a South African question. Was it not wise, he concluded, to make use of the 'enlightened' Afrikaners of the Cape? After all, Kruger's concessions at Bloemfontein were a great advance on previous offers and it seemed to him that the plan 'should be accepted on the understanding that it is carried out to the letter and applied fairly and effectively. If he reverses it afterwards or obstructs its working the whole thing must be reopened at once.' Grey was careful to add that he had discussed his suggestions with Asquith, but with no one else.[8]

In his reply of 7 August, Milner was adamant. Some of the things he had done were, he admitted, real mistakes, but others only appeared so because of ignorance of local conditions. The notion that the Cape Dutch, the 'enlightened' Afrikaners, were the party of the future who would win over their brethren in the Transvaal to the merits of the Empire was, he feared, one such illusion. Only a minority of the Cape Dutch were actively 'disloyal', but in his view 'too high a price is paid for conciliating that half of the population which is at heart averse from us, when the process involves the alienation of the other half which is still thoroughly loyal. And especially when the latter section, if only given a fair chance, command the future.' Of course the Afrikaners wanted peace in South Africa since they were not the 'under-dogs'. 'In the Colony, where they have a majority in Parliament, the rule of the majority prevails. In the Transvaal, where they are a minority, that minority keeps political power exclusively in its own hands.' The Afrikaners of the Cape wanted 'a reformed and enlarged but still distinctly Afrikander—i.e. non-British, not to say anti-British, Republic'. Milner claimed that he wanted 'a Republic in which both elements will have fair play, as in the Cape, as in Canada. And leave the rest to the future.' Milner took Grey up on local details, but his basic concern was with South Africa as it affected the Empire as a whole. Such a republic as he described might not be pro-British, but it would not be anti-British and therefore would not be '*that* danger to British South Africa which a pure Afrikander State, armed to the teeth, and incessantly intriguing against us both in South Africa and in Europe, is'. He admitted that the Transvaal was not an immediate threat, but its potential was very great. The British in other parts of South Africa wanted to see the Transvaal become British, but if the Imperial Government could not even secure equality of treatment for Britons in that state, then its prestige was gravely weakened. Therefore, he concluded, 'We must do something substantial to improve the position of our clients, or lose all reputation and political influence, even in what will remain nominally British South Africa. Such a result must, in my opinion, be avoided at any cost, even the cost of war. . . .'[9]

The negotiations on the franchise question continued throughout the summer with little success. Finally, on 8 September, Milner made his last offer, couched in conciliatory language. Grey was following these negotiations carefully, sending on letters from Milner to Rosebery, though he commented: 'I don't think the Franchise is a good issue to fight about and should have preferred taking strong action based upon misgovernment of the British Uitlanders, demanding Home Rule for the Rand as the only possible guarantee that our fellow subjects there would be decently treated. But we are committed to the Franchise now and must make the best of it.'[10] He remained against war and thought 'the tangle into which the negotiations have got is past understanding'.[11] When Kruger rejected the offer, Grey reported to Rosebery that this action had 'put him in the wrong even with John Morley'. Nevertheless, 'the issue between a five and seven years franchise is a ridiculous one to go to war upon, and the Government must put the real issue before the country before they go any further'.[12] Kruger's action 'made things very difficult for the friends of peace'. Writing again to Rosebery at the end of September he now considered the last British demands 'very moderate' and 'if Kruger will go on refusing them I don't see how we can refuse to vote for the means of enforcing them. The demands can't be dropped.' Writing to Munro Ferguson on 1 October he thought war seemed inevitable: 'the younger Boers think they can beat us, and if so they won't give way'.[13]

A few days later, Grey reported his estimate of the situation in Britain to Milner. He believed that the latest diplomatic efforts had convinced a large section of the population that Kruger was shifting his ground in order to evade a settlement. Therefore, while there would be 'vehement and persistent opposition to war from a minority in Parliament and in the country' a majority would now agree that war was inevitable. However, Grey was far from being 'mesmerized' by Milner to the extent of being totally uncritical of his diplomacy. He criticized the publication of the 'Helot' dispatch: 'it should have been published only when negotiations had failed and Parliament was being summoned as we now expect'. His second main criticism was of the Colonial Office for its 'foolish and mischievous' insistence upon the claim to 'Suzerainty' over the Transvaal. This contention should have been dropped and a paragraph to this effect inserted in Chamberlain's dispatch of 8 September. Nevertheless, he agreed with Milner's main objective, which he took to be 'a substantial representation for Uitlanders in the Transvaal and to leave the future to the play of natural forces'.

He concluded that 'Kruger may never have meant the negotiations to lead to any real redress or reform: that he and others may have been playing for an independent Afrikander South Africa; and I do understand and sympathize with your statement of the grievances and resentments of the British part of South Africa. It may be that war had to come: the time seems near, when those of us who are not sure that diplomacy could have succeeded, may have to say that war was inevitable. I wish this had been made more clear first. . . .'[14] On 9 October, Kruger sent his ultimatum to Britain. She was to remove her troops from the republican border in Natal and submit outstanding questions to arbitration. The British Government did not reply and two days later war broke out.

Now that the war had actually come, Grey wanted to get the best of both worlds. 'I admit the necessity of it', he wrote, 'and that it must be carried through but it has no business to be popular, and the cry of Revenge for Majuba dishonours us and destroys our reputation for good faith. I should like to break the heads of all the Music Halls first and then go out and teach the Boers gravely and sternly the things which they do not know.'[15] Yet while he disliked popular emotion, he had to admit: 'The war gives me a sort of stirring all down the backbone: I hope that means that I should do well under fire, but I don't know. It seems as if one had no right to be staying at home and talking: it is a different thing altogether to Indian Frontier and Nile wars, in which I didn't feel the least ashamed of not being.'[16] For her part, Dorothy felt that the Transvaal had been working to take the Cape and Rhodesia for a number of years. She also thought about the native population: 'Bad as we are in some ways there is much more hope of kindness for them under us than under the frankly brutal government of the Dutch. . . .' If there was enough fighting 'all our ugly national faults would be blotted out'.[17] On the other hand, she wrote to Creighton, now Bishop of London, to lament: 'The Primrose League clergy are particularly bloody-minded just now.'[18] She turned to a life of St Francis of Assisi since the present clergy were all 'scratching each other's eyes out and singing "Britons Never" before their services'. While she was unhappy about the war, 'what is to be done while people will go on making this devastating torrent of children & expecting them to be fed?' The Empire seemed to her faintly absurd. Edward's brother George had just returned to Bulawayo after an eight-month journey into the heart of the Zambesi country: 'He seems to have been annexing territory or making spheres of influence of some sort.

I am glad he should enjoy himself but I daresay there will be a horrid little war about it someday.'[19]

Grey stuck to his strong line from the outset. Due to the difficulties Campbell-Bannerman encountered in bringing his wife and himself back from the continent, the meeting of the 'ex-Cabs' did not take place until two days after the war had broken out. The party leader had written privately to Herbert Gladstone that 'the national dignity is not so much involved as to justify our closing ranks with the Government and putting out of sight the feeble grounds of the war. . . .'[20] Nevertheless, in his first speech after the recall of Parliament, on 17 October, he accused the Boers of having 'committed an aggression which it was the plain duty of us all to resist'. But he tempered this approval with strong criticism of Government diplomacy and asked for a statement from a Minister that no attempt was being made 'to avenge the military disaster of another year'.[21] It was clearly the speech of a man who was aware that his colleagues were seriously split. John Dillon, the Irish Nationalist, at once proposed an amendment, seconded by the ever-ready Labouchere, calling for an end to the war by arbitration. The amendment attracted only 54 votes, only 21 of these being Liberal or Radical. Fowler, Grey, Haldane and 35 other Liberals voted with the Government. A further amendment, deploring the conduct of the negotiations, was moved on the following day by Philip Stanhope. Harcourt intervened, dismissing the idea that the Opposition had nothing to do but approve the policy of the Government whose provocative diplomacy had led to disaster. When this amendment came to be voted on, Campbell-Bannerman gave up the attempt to control the party. There were 186 Liberal votes to be distributed and of these, 94, almost exactly half, voted for the amendment, which was lost by 135–362. Of the other 92, 15, including Grey, voted with the Government, the rest followed Campbell-Bannerman's 'leadership' and abstained. Of those who voted for Stanhope's amendment, 21 had also voted for Dillon's motion. The two extremes of the party were therefore small though the '15' contained greater talent than the '21'. Mr Jenkins's treatment of this vital initial vote is confusing. Contrary to his suggestion, Campbell-Bannerman did not leave himself 'united with Asquith, Fowler, Grey and Haldane' since (Asquith apart!) they voted *with* with the Government. Nor did his abstention separate him from the 135 members who went into the lobby with Stanhope, since of that total, only 94 were Liberals. Contrary to the suggestion that he was isolating himself dangerously by appearing to ally with the Liberals who did not vote for Stanhope, his action in abstaining, together with 77 others of his party, was perfectly compatible with a resolve to lead from the centre.[22]

'Feeling ran pretty high last night', Grey wrote to Rosebery on the morning after the debate; 'the front bench difficulties were great and resulted in a deadlock as regards that particular debate. It seems to me impossible that there should not be a direct conflict of tone in subsequent speeches. Either the war is a necessary one, or it is not: if the former, it should be justified: if the latter, it should be denounced in every speech for some time to come. I intend to justify it.'[23] Firmness of tone was matched by action. Grey now became the leader of those Liberals who felt that the Government was right to resort to force. Over the week-end after the debate, he brooded on his course of action while staying at Fallodon. When he got back to London he wrote again to Rosebery that in his opinion 'the difference in the party is cut deeper than ever'. It was not simply the Government's mistakes which had caused the war, and it was dishonest to pretend so. The Government deserved to be turned out, but for other reasons. He was convinced that the votes did not represent the true state of feeling in the party—'people did not realise how much the division that evening must govern the line & tone of subsequent speeches; and there was of course no guidance, except Harcourt's and Morley's, from the front bench'. He concluded: 'You cannot feel more independent than I do at this moment.'[24] This spirit contrasted strongly with the depression of his like-minded colleagues. Fowler, unusually, said that he felt his age, while Asquith, anxious not to commit himself too soon, was all for keeping quiet. Grey felt that it was 'impossible to make any attempt to conceal the differences', and, aided and abetted by Haldane, was going to 'let himself go' at a speech on 25 October in Glasgow in favour of the independent candidate for the office of Rector of Glasgow University.[25] Although they intended to 'shew a little sport' in Glasgow, the candidate, who happened to be Lord Rosebery, was assured that there would be no attempt to commit him, even by implication, to anything he said. For the first time in his career, Grey began to take the lead.

Sir Edward's speech in Glasgow dispelled, as it was meant to, any impression that the Liberal Party was united against the war.[26] While not omitting all criticism, he firmly stated that the war must go forward. On the following day, in a speech in Bath accepting the freedom of the city, the future Lord Rector claimed that 'the party of Liberal Imperialism is destined to control the destinies of this country'. He also took the occasion to reveal that Chatham was 'the first Liberal Imperialist'. On hearing this news, Harcourt snorted at such nonsense. Edward Grey should blush for shame on hearing his ancestors maligned by such tosh. Campbell-Bannerman and his associates had grown somewhat resigned to the splendid inevitability of Rosebery's gestures and it was Grey who most aroused their anger. He was alleged to have broken an informal front-bench understanding to refrain from making divisive public speeches and they suspected a plot. Rosebery was indeed in private urging his friends to 'unfurl their flags' although they were left in doubt as to whether Rosebery would fly his own standard. Grey, in fact, no longer needed a nod from Dalmeny. He spent three hours in conversation with Rosebery early in November and the master had then pointed out that the Glasgow speech represented a more advanced line than his own. Perhaps Rosebery still harboured against Milner the fact that he had been the brain behind Harcourt's infamous proposal of Death Duties. Sir Edward did not disagree, but added, rather pointedly, that while Rosebery's remarks about Liberal Imperialism were perfectly splendid, it was not possible for him, and others, 'who have several speeches to make and to wrestle with constituents, to keep within the same limits: we had to argue and to say whether we were in the right or the wrong in this war with the Boers: it was impossible . . . to avoid discussing the merits of the war'.[27]

Meanwhile, Campbell-Bannerman did not leave all the speaking to the Roseberyites. He was adept at appearing the plain man surrounded by literary and intellectual meteors, who flashed brightly, but then suddenly went out. Writing to Buxton, he suggested that 'all these philosophic and historical students with whom we have to deal are beyond my modest range. I do not see where the lofty principles of Imperialism come into this sordid quarrel.' Unlike most plain men, however, he could also be witty. In a speech in Birmingham on 24 November he noted that 'every one nowadays appears to cultivate some peculiar species of his own of what is called Imperialism, and to try to get some qualifying adjective of his own before the word'. He did not want to differ from other people, so he had his own species called 'Common-sense Imperialism'.[28] The technique was deliberately deflationary. His point was that the happy British family scattered throughout the world had ample room for its activity without acquiring new dominions. He qualified this remark by saying that acquisition was sometimes inevitable, but

even so the direction in which he was moving was now clear.
'C.-B. has cut the painter of the dinghy in which Rosebery, Grey and
Fowler may drift off by themselves', wrote Harcourt with relief.[29]
For his part, Grey made three more widely reported public speeches
on the war in November.[30] He wrote to Buxton in December that he
had only one more political speech planned—'which is a relief as I
have said all I want to about the war, and the audiences look so
weary when I talk of anything else'.[31] He made no attempt to be
conciliatory and had the satisfaction of knowing that the bulk of the
Liberal press was on his side. In November, the pro-Boer editor of
the *Daily Chronicle*, H. W. Massingham, was dismissed and the paper
swung into the centre. Noting the change, Grey was satisfied that the
'*Westminster* is alone of any daily paper in opposing the war. The
Westminster doesn't seem to me to have been very clear always & I
thought it rather rot of it to say that I was more extreme than the
Government. . . .'[32]

Like the other leading Liberals, Grey does not seem to have had
any difficulty with his constituency party. He reported to Haldane
that he had discussed the war but 'those who differ with me are in a
hopeless minority'. The weak link in his campaign was Asquith.
Grey's fear was that Campbell-Bannerman and others would
attempt to mark off Asquith from them. If that were the case, 'I
shall show my teeth', Grey wrote to Haldane.[33] The party leader was
much to blame for the confusion for his ridiculous idea 'that we
could go through the whole of this war without taking a line'.[34] Sir
Edward was also on the watch for Chamberlain, who was trying to
exploit the situation by distinguishing between the loyal support
shown by Asquith, Grey and Fowler, and the conduct of the rest of
the Opposition. Grey had to be able to attack the Government as
well, in order to preserve his Liberal base. He made much of the
Government's failure to clear the nation's honour after the Jameson
Raid. This piece of bungling had meant that the Transvaal armed
with impunity. More importantly, however, the military disasters of
mid-December allowed all Liberals to attack the Government, that is
when the situation had been held in check. Grey was furious with the
tone of Balfour's speeches in Manchester defending the Government.
He seemed to be implying that the entanglement at Ladysmith
was an Act of God for which there was no human responsibility.
'All this is monstrous', he wrote to Buxton in mid-January 1900.
'I am prepared to give any vote which will express this feeling.
But I suppose Bryce will get up and say that the Boers are an injured

people, who are not responsible for the war and that will damn our case and make me damn him.' The Government deserved to be turned out for slackness and incompetence, though he feared that the Opposition was hardly ready to replace it. 'You see,' he concluded, 'I am no better than *The Times*, *Morning Post*, etc., but I am clear of having urged the Government into war, though I defended it afterwards.'[35]

Grey relished his new position. He admitted to an inclination to 'splash about & not make the sacrifice of being careful' since caution seemed hardly to matter in the prevailing conditions. His impression was that Rosebery's position in the country was improving, though local Liberal Party workers were depressed by the divisions.[36] Formally, therefore, attempts were made to emphasize the good relations prevailing among the leadership. When Campbell-Bannerman was too ill to address the annual meetings of the National Liberal Federation, Grey, and not someone of his own views, replaced him. According to Spence Watson, Grey discharged his task with 'ability and tact' praising Sir Henry for unselfishly accepting a position 'which was not favourably reported upon by his predecessor'.[37] Had anyone else been the leader, there might well have been a split which would have been irreparable. The large audience cheered him enthusiastically. Privately, however, Grey reported to Rosebery that the warm welcome accorded him had largely been due to the fact that there had been a great row at the Federation on the previous day and 'having blown off their steam, they were the more easily reconciled to a comparatively peaceful meeting'.[38] The tide of war seemed to be turning in the British favour with the occupation of Ladysmith, Bloemfontein, Mafeking and Johannesburg by May 1900.

The prospect of peace seemed, momentarily, to improve relations within the party, but at the end of July the Liberals achieved their most spectacular split of the war. Against the wishes of the leader, Sir Wilfrid Lawson, a 'pro-Boer' Liberal, whose choice of awkward causes was only mitigated by his wit in presenting them, moved a token reduction in the Colonial Office vote.[39] Out of the blue, Grey found himself in the middle of a crisis. Asquith passed on a message from Campbell-Bannerman that if the party should split on this amendment, he would resign. The anti-war members were determined to support Sir Wilfred and Haldane pressed Grey to speak against it. Asquith dithered in the middle, pointing to the consequences. In the event, Grey decided to speak and carried nearly 40

Liberals into the lobby with the Government. A slightly smaller figure including Bryce, Morley, Reid and Lloyd George voted with Lawson.[40] The position was so humiliating that Sir Henry's resignation was confidently predicted. It seemed the moment for Grey and Haldane to address themselves to Lord Rosebery.

Haldane wrote immediately after the division was known. Although Campbell-Bannerman might change his mind in the morning, it was likely that he would resign and depart for Marienbad. Even if he did reconsider on this occasion, he would not go on much longer. In that event, 'if you choose to emerge and lead the Liberals who may be called "Lord R's friends" with Asquith & Grey as lieutenants in the House, I think things will work out. . . .'[41] Grey was equally explicit. Only if Rosebery was leader of the party, with Asquith as deputy in the Commons, could a strong and successful Opposition be built up. Meanwhile, he did his best to quash any moves to find a formula on South Africa which would reunite the party.[42] Once again, the plot failed to thicken. Sir Henry did not resign and Grey lacked any clear signal from Rosebery.

The manifest Liberal disarray and apparent victory in the war seemed to provide a good reason for the Government to call a General Election. Grey took a more prominent part in the Liberal campaign nationally than he had ever done before, helped by the fact that he was unopposed in his own constituency. Unusually for him, he was travelling all day, speaking in the evenings and, at the end, 'nearly used up'. He was determined to speak for as many Liberal candidates of his persuasion as possible. He was campaigning against Chamberlain, who made no distinction between different sections of the Opposition—a vote for a Liberal is a vote for the Boers—and one of whose objectives seems to have been to destroy the Liberal Imperialists. Rosebery held aloof from the campaign until the last moment, when he issued an open letter attacking the Government but declaring that a peace settlement should not endanger the sacrifices made by the nation. Although Grey reported that things were going badly, that 'the Liberal Party is disintegrated everywhere', the result was not total disaster. They actually gained a few seats on their 1895 total, though they lost a few if their total at the dissolution is the yardstick of their performance. Too much should not be made of the closeness of the popular vote, since more than 150 Tories and Liberal Unionists were returned unopposed.[43] Chamberlain complained privately to his wife that the baser sort on the other side had fought the election with the 'greatest malignity', and only one man, Sir Edward Grey, had repudiated their disgraceful proceedings.[44]

The General Election did not affect the fundamental position of the Liberal Party. Haldane, Fowler and others continued to address private pleas to Rosebery to draw his sword and lead them. Grey shared their desire but wrote that the former leader had but two years to come into the open and in the meantime he might 'at any time get an ultimatum from some of us that we are not going on any more without him'.[45] Grey and Haldane increasingly adopted an air of open contempt for the party leader and the 'old gang' of Bryce, Harcourt and Morley. They allowed themselves to be associated with the activities of the Liberal Imperial Council formed earlier in the year by Sir Robert Perks, the member for Louth, a wealthy Wesleyan and legal associate of Sir Henry Fowler. A believer in 'sound' Imperialism, it was the mission of the Council to make sure that 'our sober-minded, hard-working industrial leaders who have the sound idea that Peace is our first interest, should not take fright at the term "Imperialism" & think that we are following in the wake of Beaconsfield'. In fact, he did not altogether like the title of the Council but claimed that 'the Liberal revolt against the Little England policy is too strong just now for our men to drop the word "Imperial"'.[46] Perks constantly plied Rosebery with information designed to convince him that the country was seeking his return. The 'old men' regarded the Council with extreme distaste. Harcourt wrote to Earl Spencer that he was 'sorry to know that E. Grey has gone in thick and thin with the Perks and Fowler gang. . . .'[47] Following the election Perks optimistically told Rosebery that in the parliamentary party there were 142 supporters, 33 opponents and 7 doubtfuls. He therefore doubted the wisdom of pushing the Council. Should they not concentrate on gaining control of the existing Liberal organizations? Rosebery was noncommittal.[48] The pushing Perks was disliked by the more thoroughbred members of the party—his surname caused them endless delight. Even the fact that he shared a rooted dislike for the Pope and all his works could not save him in the eyes of Harcourt. Haldane, on the other hand, urged his merits: 'Don't underrate Perks. He is a man of really powerful intelligence, immense wealth and influence and a great deal of character. He cannot be overlooked and his name does not matter. . . .'[49]

Campbell-Bannerman was not in fact inclined to dismiss him. He wrote to Ripon at the end of October that he had felt compelled 'to fire a shot across the bows of Mr Perks and his crew mainly because they were bragging and puffing themselves and seeking to attract the neophytes'. The warning had little effect, for in the middle of November the Council formally dissociated itself from Campbell-Bannerman's leadership. At Dundee on 15 November Sir Henry attacked the Council in scorching terms. Privately he wrote to Sydney Buxton, who was rather in the confidence of both sides, that he was not going to sit by and let those pretentious fellows take command of the ship and order out half the crew. He claimed to have no objections to their opinions—'being I hope a Liberal and also an Imperialist enough for any decent man'—but the effect of putting the two words together was too explosive for him. Campbell-Bannerman had also taken the opportunity in his speech to deliver a less than warm invitation to Rosebery to return—'the door has always been open'. Privately he wrote that it was time for the ex-leader to be in or out: 'as long as he is merely looking over the wall, there will be no peace for us'. Sir Henry stressed again and again that the Liberal Party was a combination and had to rub along as best it could on South Africa. 'Grey and his very superior set', he wrote, 'must be content not to be asserting their superiority at every turn. Honest fellows have swallowed annexation much against the grain. . . . The sacrifices and reticences ought not to be all on one side.'[50]

The 'very superior set' was in no mood for such compromise. The day after the Dundee speech, Grey, Asquith and Haldane dined together. Grey was furious at its tone and sent an ultimatum to Campbell-Bannerman ('no suggestion of ours made him & no power could have stopped him', wrote Haldane to Rosebery[51]). In his letter, Grey made it clear that he regarded Milner as 'the best man for the place of administrator' and stressed that he would resist moves being made elsewhere in the party to censure him and attack his appointment as administrator of the newly occupied territories. He regretted the tone of the Dundee speech and declared that if he had to speak he would feel bound to put the case for the Liberal Imperialists. As regards the general situation, he felt the party could not go on as it had been doing since the resignation of Mr Gladstone. It was becoming necessary to make it clear whether the differences were really small or whether they were great. Sir Henry replied in conciliatory terms, making it clear that not Liberal Imperialism, but the Liberal Imperial Council was the target of his criticism. Grey accepted the invitation to have a chat on problems and softened his assault by paying tribute to the way in which Campbell-Bannerman had coped with the difficulties. Yet he reiterated that the attempt to reach a compromise in the middle had resulted, in his judgment, in increased vitality at both extremes: 'each is contending for the ascendancy, one in the hope of getting you entirely on their side & pushing Rosebery further off; the other in the hope of bringing Rosebery back as leader. Anything would be better than the continuance of this exhausting uncertainty. . . .' The only way this could be achieved would be by a lead being given in strong terms which, though it might temporarily divide, would provide a rallying call in the long run.[52] After their meeting, the two men papered over the cracks for the time being. Sir Henry refused to give any assurance about Milner, though in fact he did squash the Radical campaign for a while. He also declined a handsome offer from Harcourt in December to rejoin the shadow Cabinet. For their part, Grey and Haldane spoke with the party in the censure motion moved on Chamberlain, by Lloyd George. This reduced the rumours that they were about to go over to the Tories. The death of Queen Victoria at the end of January 1901 helped to dampen down controversy at a dangerous time. So, somehow or other, Campbell-Bannerman managed to hang on in the hope of better days. It is possible that he would not have survived if Rosebery had given Grey and Haldane the least real encouragement. Sir Edward did his best to inspire his return, writing to him after his Rectoral Address on the subject of the Empire that it made him feel 'that a rift was made in the clouds'. But nothing happened. He informed Rosebery of his brisk exchange with Campbell-Bannerman in which he had urged that it was 'necessary to deal with facts'. He had felt Sir Henry's invitation to return had not been sufficiently fulsome but added 'that is your affair'.[53] Rosebery did not dissent from this latter judgment and reacted by spending most of the spring of 1901 travelling in Europe. Indeed, he was out of the country for three months in that decisive year. Even when he was in the United Kingdom he flitted between his various houses in an enigmatic manner. If Rosebery was to return, the unofficial time-limit which Grey had given was beginning to run out.

All these political calculations were based on the assumption that the war in South Africa was virtually won. Lord Roberts had returned home at the end of 1900 in triumph, leaving Kitchener to conduct the mopping-up operations—or so it was thought. Although Roberts had formally annexed both republics as British colonies, the brilliant guerilla tactics of the Boers meant in fact that early in 1901 the British forces simply controlled the towns and the railways. British lines of communication were constantly endangered with the risk of serious disaster. After the elation of the previous year, the news that the war was very far from being won had a depressing effect at home. 'There is no doubt', Haldane wrote to Milner at the beginning of March, 'that the country here is getting tired of fighting; but I have no fear of any such mistake being made as an insistance on any change of policy. The anti-annexationists are becoming fewer every day. On the other hand I think Chamberlain's popularity is on the wane. . . .' The demands for his correspondent's recall had been squashed, 'even Lloyd George taking a leading part in doing so'.[54] Soon, however, the military situation led to further party disagreements. Kitchener decided that the Boers could never be defeated in the open veldt, but they could be forced into submission if they were deprived of food. Their farms were burnt, their cattle captured, their crops destroyed and their families concentrated into camps. According to an Afrikaner historian: 'Malnutrition and contagious diseases caused a high rate of mortality, particularly amongst children. In July 1901 the death rate stood at 116 per thousand per annum; by October it had risen to the appalling figure of 346 per thousand.'[55] As information about the camps began to filter through, Campbell-Bannerman decided to raise the whole question publicly. His general position in the party was stronger than it had been for some time. Lloyd George had engineered the capture of the *Daily News* with Cadbury money and, as Harcourt put it, the paper was restored to the 'ancient faith'. Its editor, E. T. Cook, a notable scourge of the pro-Boers, was 'shunted'.[56] The *Daily Chronicle* did a summersault in the opposite direction at about the same time, but the capture of the *News* was regarded as the greater triumph.

Sir Henry was therefore in a confident frame of mind when, flanked by Morley and Harcourt, he made a speech at a London dinner on 14 June. 'A phrase often used is that "war is war",' he remarked, 'but when one comes to ask about it one is told that no war is going on, that it is not war. When is a war not a war? When it is carried on by methods of barbarism in South Africa.'[57] Campbell-Bannerman subsequently protested that he had intended no slur on the army, but he would not withdraw the offending word 'barbarism'. Four days later, Lloyd George raised the issue in the House of Commons. Quite apart from their genuine sentiments, the

Radicals were determined to cause a stir in reaction to the fuss which had been made of Milner on his leave at the end of May. Milner had been met at the station by the Prime Minister and whisked away to the King, from whose presence he emerged Lord Milner of St James's and Cape Town, a Privy Councillor and a Freeman of the City of London. These honours were too much for Morley, who denounced the hero as an 'imitation Bismarck'. This phrase touched the Liberal Imperialists on the raw. Grey had prefaced his impending return with the words: 'You will be able to decide what most wants saying to us in England and to say it with more effect than any member of the Government. . . .' Sir Edward had warned Milner that attacks on him were to be expected but that the four main points about South Africa—successful prosecution of the war, annexation of the Boer territories, temporary direct Imperial Government followed by eventual representative Colonial Government and Milner's own position as Administrator—were in no real danger. The prospect of a crisis did not disturb Grey, 'our pro-Boers must either subside or some of us must have it out with them. . . .'[58] He jauntily went down to Southampton to greet Milner when he docked, finding him 'a little worn and rather older, but very sound and fit and unstrained. In other words like a man in hard condition.'[59] Not finding Morley's 'admirable Sermons' to the point, Haldane told Milner that 'Grey is not in a mood to sit still, no more am I.'[60] Grey did reply to Morley in a public speech at Berwick, but it was Campbell-Bannerman's speech which gave him an exceptional opportunity, for it had offended many in the party who had been prepared to jog along under his leadership. It really seemed as if the showdown, so long forecast, was about to occur.

Lloyd George's censure motion on the camps, moved on 18 June, saw the Liberal leadership completely split. Asquith, Grey, Haldane and some fifty other Liberal M.P.s abstained, and some seventy voted for Lloyd George with their leader. Asquith's public association with his friends was also significant. On the morrow of the 'methods of barbarism' speech he wrote to Sir Henry: 'Through no fault of yours, the proceedings were turned into an aggressive demonstration by one section of the party. . . . I am very glad I was not there, and shall do all I can to discourage reprisals, but I do not know with what success. . . .'[61] Four days later, however, he was writing privately to Perks in different terms: 'The banquet of last Friday, with its incidents and consequences, seems to me to suggest that it is time for those of us who are not willing that the official and propagandist machinery should be captured by Lloyd George and his friends, to bestir themselves. . . .' He followed this by a speech in strong terms to a London Liberal gathering in which he declared that the views he shared with his friends on the war might be right or wrong, but they had not sought to make them a test of Liberal orthodoxy. He now stressed 'in the plainest and most unequivocal terms' that they did not repent, neither would they recant.[62] It seemed that Asquith had come off the fence and was pushing himself to the fore.

In January 1899, Arthur Acland reported to Asquith that Grey was hopeful that 'you & he may do a good bit if you have time to spare from law and society, and he from his country pursuits'.[63] In the intervening couple of years, Grey had been more active than Asquith and taken a bolder stand. He was now pleased that Asquith had moved, for hitherto he had been thought 'rather lacking in personality: but this is his doing'. Grey expressed his views in conversation with a new friend, Henry Newbolt the poet, on 27 June. Campbell-Bannerman was 'a good old fellow' and he did not want a revolt against his leadership unless it became necessary, 'but we do want a leader, and a change of party tactics'. He did not deny that the question of the camps was 'a nasty one' but conditions were improving and gave Sir Henry no right to make charges of 'barbarism'. 'The object of effort should not be to turn out the Government—that will come in time. It should be to create a real party with real tactics and methods of its own. Anti-Chamberlainism won't do—it is not a policy. There must be something started that will last for another two or three generations.'[64] It was with this end in view that some of Asquith's supporters arranged for a dinner to be held on 19 July in honour of his recent speech. Other friends declined to come on the grounds that the dinner was openly divisive. On the same grounds, on 10 July, Sir Henry himself wrote to Asquith asking that the dinner be postponed until the entire party could attend and the affair had lost 'all that tinge of sectional feeling'. Asquith replied in conciliatory terms, but gave the impression that the arrangements were too far advanced for cancellation. In fact, the Liberal Imperialists were determined to go ahead, Grey most of all. He wrote on 7 July: 'Politics have suddenly become very interesting to me, because I think I may be in the beginning of new things—even fishing has gone to the wall.'[65] Grey had asked Rosebery to preside over the dinner, but the invitation was declined. Apparently, he told Asquith, Rosebery 'did not want to embarrass you by saying anything which might put the fat in the fire before the dinner was held'. Grey himself felt that 'making the fat frizzle couldn't hurt us, but . . . I thought it would be better that you should not be privy to any letter he wrote'. Grey had also told Rosebery of their annoyance at Campbell-Bannerman's suggestion of a dinner of union at which he should preside.[66] The original dinner would go ahead.

At this stage Rosebery decided that it was time to complicate matters. Without warning, his letter appeared in *The Times* on 17 July declaring that the Liberal Party had to make up its mind on the war. 'Neutrality and an open mind make up an impossible attitude. The war is either just or unjust, the methods either uncivilised or legitimate. But this is not a transient difference of opinion. It is based on a sincere fundamental and incurable antagonism of principle with regard to the Empire at large. . . .'[67] He prefaced his remarks with a declaration that he would not return to party politics. The organizers of the dinner were furious and for the first time Grey ventured to criticize his former leader in public. While hoping that his detachment would not last, he reminded both Rosebery and his own audience that 'lookers-on see most of the game. Yes, but they do not influence the result.'[68] Then, even more irritatingly, Rosebery went to speak at a City Liberal Club lunch on 19 July (the dinner to Asquith was to follow in the evening) and there declared: 'I must plough my furrow alone. That is my fate, agreeable or the reverse; but before I get to the end of that furrow it is possible that I may find myself not alone.'[69] In his own speech, Asquith was careful not to be offensive to the radical wing of the party and linked his espousal of Imperialism abroad to a conscious policy of social reform at home. There was no open challenge to the leadership of the party and its impact in the press was somewhat blunted by Rosebery's carefully timed proclamation of detachment.

Since Grey had presided at the dinner to Asquith, Rosebery's intervention placed him in a most awkward situation. Who was he to support? Campbell-Bannerman, with some justice, regarded Grey, prompted by Haldane, as the foremost conspirator. When Sir Henry had asked for a vote of confidence at a party meeting on 9 July, Grey had been the most outspoken critic, saying that Campbell-Bannerman himself had created difficulties as well as suffered from them. Sir Henry believed that Grey and Haldane had foisted the dinner upon Asquith, for 'those gentry have made A.

their tool in a great plot against me'.[70] The leader underestimated Asquith's own willingness to emerge, but otherwise he was substantially correct. Ironically, at this point Asquith was being advised by Arthur Acland: 'Your difficulty in the future might be to keep Grey in the paths of Liberalism. I don't feel that he is essentially & necessarily a Liberal as I think you are. On the other hand he is not a bit of a Tory. He is intensely self critical and liable to throw over the party some day on some point where he thinks honour or consistency to himself demands it.'[71] Knowing as he did the part Grey was playing, Asquith replied that he saw no reason for anxiety.

Meanwhile, Sir Edward had to think of an answer to Rosebery. He decided to distinguish between the City Liberal speech and the letter to *The Times*, asking Rosebery to ignore his criticisms of the latter. 'The letter', he wrote, 'gave me the impression of a spectator in a great coat about to enjoy, but not to exercise freedom: the speech is that of a man stripped for combat. . . .' Rosebery's plough was a source of great fascination. Grey claimed that his own furrow was in the same direction: 'We ought not therefore to come into conflict, but the situation needs delicate handling and for the present there is some soreness.' Pointedly Grey remarked that but for Asquith's stand 'there would have been a secession of myself and a few, but *very few*, others from the Liberal party before you had come back. Now, if there is a split, it will be a much less one sided affair.' He and Haldane were now 'very chivalrously' disposed towards Asquith.[72] It was doubtful whether Asquith would regard himself for ever as a nightwatchman keeping his end up before the appearance of the star batsman, especially in view of that gentleman's expressed reluctance to play his best shots in public. Seemingly without embarrassment, however, Rosebery wrote to Asquith congratulating him on his speech and expressing the hope that politics would not impair their personal relations. Broker Haldane saw Rosebery on 21 July and tried to explain that Asquith was hurt 'from the *appearance* of the great sacrifice & effort of his life being jumped upon'. Although, of course, it was appearance only, Haldane insisted that Rosebery should see that Asquith's furrow was being ploughed 'at great pain to himself'.[73] Asquith replied on 22 July, expressing friendly sentiments and wishing Rosebery well with his ploughing. He hoped that the furrow would not be divergent but that sooner or later, and the sooner the better, it would be one 'in which E. Grey & I & all your real friends & associates can lend a hand'.[74] As the summer passed, Grey became disconsolate. What was the point in conducting a conspiracy if Rosebery declined to play and at the same time frustrated the efforts of Asquith to establish himself? As he wrote to Dorothy in August 1901: 'To be an ally of a man of genius, you have either to pay the price which he asks (sometimes an impossible one) or serve him for nothing.'[75]

The autumn did not bring any fresh hopes. Dorothy wrote at the end of October: 'We have not seen Rosebery lately, so can't give you any news of the secret furrow. Asquith and E. are in very good heart, but don't expect things to straighten out very quickly.'[76] Asquith and Grey were closer together politically than ever before, although social intimacy did not develop and Asquith did not visit Fallodon. Haldane remained Grey's closest associate and it was at Cloan that the three men usually came together. Rosebery received the report of one such gathering held in October; 'We shall go ahead', Sir Edward wrote, 'for what we are worth & the Liberal party will either get better or be smashed to pieces; in other words the party system will either be re-established for the working of our politics, or it will disappear. The immediate situation is not very hopeful, but it is interesting & that is a change for the better since a year ago.'[77]

Meanwhile, the guerilla war in South Africa continued. Kitchener had recently threatened the Boer leaders with banishment, and their men with loss of their land if they did not surrender. The ultimatum was rejected, but in fact the overwhelming numerical superiority of the imperial forces was beginning to tell. Criticism of British methods still flourished in the Liberal Party. The supersession of Milner remained a favourite radical objective, but Grey remained adamant in his defence. Yet one forms the impression, as 1901 drew to a close, that all factions were wearying of the struggle and seeking a means of reconciliation.

It was in this context that Rosebery arrived at Chesterfield in mid-December to make a speech. This intention had been disclosed some six weeks earlier and the Derbyshire town was thronged with people who would not normally think of visiting it in December —indeed, of visiting it at all. The ranks of the Liberal Imperialists would have been trimmed if the special train ordered by Perks for the faithful had met with an accident. Although the press was full of rumour about the speech, Rosebery kept its contents a surprise to the end. When he rose to speak, flanked by Grey, Asquith and Fowler, they must have been as apprehensive as they were expectant.

The speech was indeed surprising. He began by defending the military methods which had been employed in South Africa, but at the same time he accused the Government of incompetence in its dealings with the Boers. There would have to be a negotiated settlement and he put the blame for failure to make progress largely on Milner's rigidity. Rosebery did not confine himself to South Africa. The Liberal Party had not held effective power for sixteen years, and it would not do so again while there were 'men who sit still with the fly-blown phylacteries of obsolete policies bound round their foreheads, who do not remember that while they have been mumbling their incantations to themselves, the world has been marching and revolving. . . .' On its clean slate the party had to write policies adapted not to 1885 or 1892 but to 1901 or 1902. Liberals should not dissociate themselves from the new sentiment of Empire which had captured the nation. The party should be free from commitments to the Irish and to the tatty remnants of the Newcastle programme. Rosebery concluded that he did not appeal merely to party, but to the people as a whole who yearned for a system which would satisfy the criterion of 'Efficiency'.[78]

With his friends, Edward Grey now felt confident that at long last Rosebery had decided to abandon his detachment and in due course resume the leadership. He sent Rosebery his 'unqualified congratulations'. Some people had suggested that they differed over South Africa, but there was not 'a single conclusion in your speech to which I don't give a whole hearted assent. . . .' All in all, Rosebery had succeeded in making dry bones live: 'there was a new light upon the whole & when you went upon new ground, as in the possible development of bringing the Boers to ask for peace, I felt that I would follow. . . .' He now intended to take action. He was going to write to Campbell-Bannerman saying that he would no longer abide by the party agreement made at the Reform Club meeting on 9 July and that 'the conflict between your views & his renders it necessary for me to make my choice and that he ought to be told that I go with you'. An extraordinary euphoria enveloped the Liberal Imperialists. Haldane felt that everything now could be left to him to organize, writing to Rosebery: 'There is no more that you need do for the moment. Asquith & Grey & others will work out details in the next few days & the rest may be left to grow.'[79]

Although Grey made no reference in his letter, the euphoria could not altogether disguise the fact that, particularly in regard to

Milner, his views did not altogether coincide with Rosebery's. Grey therefore had some explaining to do. In letters he stressed the points on which Rosebery diverged from Campbell-Bannerman, and ignored those on which he had hitherto diverged from Rosebery. He argued that when Parliament reassembled Sir Henry would insist that the party concentrate on three points—that the war was being carried on by methods of barbarism, that overtures of peace should be made to the Boers, that Milner was to be recalled. Rosebery had contradicted these three points and therefore Grey declared that he had 'made his last speech upon the Reform Club compact platform, & shall speak next time entirely on Rosebery lines & disown all others. The consequences will be what they will be. I hadn't an idea what Rosebery was going to say & was delighted as I heard it all unfolded.'[80] Other friends were less easily persuaded. Alfred Spender, the editor of the *Westminster Gazette*, wrote expressing surprise that he should have agreed with the Chesterfield speech. Sir Edward was stung and replied that such an interpretation was 'the most damnable misconstruction either of Rosebery's speech or of my speeches'. In high dudgeon he listed points of agreement and provided quotations from his own speeches to prove that 'allowing even some small differences there is really not a word of mine to be unsaid in accepting it'. He now felt that the party ought to have split back in July, 'those of us who wanted to attack the Government on Rosebery lines could then have ignored C-B.'. Now the onus was on Sir Henry to drop anything in his line inconsistent with what Rosebery had proclaimed, for 'the moral of it all is that if there is to be union behind Rosebery, the nonsense must be dropped'. He added that he had not had a political conversation with Rosebery since July. Then, in what developed into a lengthy letter (itself an illustration of his enthusiasm), Grey returned to what he saw as the real problem in South Africa. It was all very well to be conciliatory towards the Boers at the end of hostilities, but he believed that the worst difficulties from a British point of view would come from the 'British' element in South Africa. Those in the fighting forces were bound to have their pride 'and yet we have got to carry them with us in what we do for the Boers. Then there is the cursed little gang of financiers whose mines are to be taxed: can't you foresee their machinations, the articles in their press about Taxation and Representation. . . . And with the Boers think of the large & patient mind, & the infinite tact wanted & the courage to deal liberally with them.' That was where the Liberal Party was needed, but it had no influence—'discredited, dissipated & ruined because, except for Asquith, everyone of our leaders let the "kissing factionists with ardent eyes" run the whole party unreproved in a time of national crisis'. Those who, like himself, had tried to keep a sane balance, had only succeeded in sacrificing themselves: 'To the other side we are trimmers, to our own we are hateful; and there remains for us now nothing but to cling to the faint hope that the genius of Rosebery may succeed in redeeming a party which seems past redemption.'[81]

These strong words, even though they were for Spender the man, not Spender the editor, were echoed in a letter three days later to the Liberal Chief Whip, Herbert Gladstone. He reiterated his support for all references in the Chesterfield speech to South Africa. However, he thought the speech could only have an impact if the points where it differed from Campbell-Bannerman's line were stressed. Therefore, he would take his side explicitly with Rosebery and withdraw his recognition of Sir Henry's leadership unless he in turn totally accepted Rosebery's line. He concluded that it was tragic 'to think of where and what the Liberal party might be, if it had developed the Rosebery point of view from the beginning. . . .' Gladstone refused to be stampeded. He replied that it came as a surprise to learn that a Rosebery line had been available 'from the beginning'. He tried a touch of humour by saying that in his position he was a kind of telephone exchange (the metaphor still had a certain freshness at this juncture) and that if the situation were not so serious, it would have been amusing to listen to all the messages from the Liberal leaders about each other. The Chief Whip then bluntly stated that Rosebery had severely criticized Milner, although he had stopped short of demanding his recall. If Rosebery were to become Prime Minister tomorrow could Milner really with dignity remain? As for 'methods of barbarism', had not enough been said on the subject already? As he saw the situation, "C-B. offers to co-operate with R. on his lines for settlement. C-B. *and others* think that R's line is very different to that of Asquith's and yours. You *& others* think R's line incompatible with C-B.'s. In the main I think R. is with you on the war, & that C-B. is with him on the settlement.'[82] It was, of course, a Chief Whip's solution, too pat to be satisfying, but in urging Grey to maintain party unity, he had both observed a difference between Rosebery and Grey which Sir Edward would have preferred to gloss over, and also reminded him that Campbell-Bannerman too had his convictions. To expect him to drop his views when they conflicted with Rosebery's was asking too much.

Grey was undeterred. From Fallodon on 2 January he wrote to Sir Henry in order to make his position clear: 'If you & Rosebery work together, I have no more to say, & no new departure to make; if on the other hand you & he decide that you cannot co-operate I must say this—that I go with him.'[83] Sir Henry was astonished at his temerity and thought the letter a piece of 'D——d egotism and impertinence'. The points on which they were alleged to differ were 'nonsense'.[84] It was apparent that the Chesterfield magic had not rubbed off on the party leader. He agreed that Rosebery's views on peace and war went far and were not unreasonable, 'though it is unfortunate that they run counter to the very two things our people in the country care most about—Milner and the Camps. . . . Aaron, K.C. [Asquith], and Sir E. Hur [Grey], who were there to hold up the prophet's hands, must have held up their own at some of the things they were expected to swallow with avowed gratitude. So far good.' The rest of the speech about clean slates and efficiency was an affront to Liberalism and 'pure claptrap'.[85] Campbell-Bannerman went to 'beard the Douglas in his halls'—a phrase befitting an encounter between two Scotsmen. There was no progress. Rosebery said he was definitely out of the party. Quite apart from other matters, Ireland would bar the way. While Sir Henry believed their views on the war were in substantial agreement, Rosebery's private record of the conversation was rather different. He formed the impression that Campbell-Bannerman had definitely thrown himself into the arms of the pro-Boers, where his sympathies had really always been. The two men fell out over the recording and communication of this conversation and never had anything else to say to each other on politics. In his complacent, rather cocky way, Campbell-Bannerman had written Rosebery off, and although his eccentricities would no doubt continue to annoy, he need no longer worry. His acolytes, however, were more dangerous. The leader was out of touch with Asquith and aware that Haldane 'in his heavy way' was asking Liberals to choose their man. And Grey had sent that letter. His first instinct was to let him go, but he was persuaded that Grey's standing in the party had reached considerable proportions and that secession was infectious. So, on 4 January, he gave Grey a frank reply, pointing out that Sir Edward did not seem to be as well informed about Rosebery's views and intentions as he was. Rosebery would not come back. In these circumstances, he hoped that Grey would not feel it necessary to break with the party.[86]

Three weeks after the Chesterfield speech, the euphoria of the Liberal Imperialists was already dying down. Rosebery was manifesting his usual withdrawal symptoms. Manager Haldane anxiously wrote to him: 'I think you should make a sign to Grey & Asquith. We are all anxious to help, but we all feel we have been a little sat on. They have made their signals. . . .'[87] On 13 January, Sir Henry made a speech emphasizing the points of agreement within the party on the questions of war and the settlement. But on the following day, Asquith made it clear that no compromise was possible and that the Boers had to be convinced of the finality of the result and the hopelessness of ever renewing the struggle. When Parliament met a few days later, it was obvious that the Liberal Party was again in chaos. Edward Grey sat ostentatiously below the gallery in isolation from his nominal leaders. Yet while these defiant gestures were all very well in their way, they led nowhere if Rosebery failed to rise. By the end of January Edward was writing gloomily to Dorothy: 'I hear nothing from R., and what I hear of him is rather tiresome and petty. He has a habit of hiding his light, and making it seem as if the light that was in him was darkness. I am all for letting him go his own way, but I don't think I can help him much to play his game at present. It is an *underground* game, which is all right for him; but for us, who are in the House here, it is difficult to take part in it without playing the *underhand* game. We are in contact with much from which he is free.'[88] Then, late in February, came the open rupture between Rosebery and Campbell-Bannerman. As well as on domestic matters, Rosebery wrote to *The Times*, it was obvious 'that our views on the war and its methods are not less discordant. I remain, therefore, outside his tabernacle, but not, I think, in solitude.'[89] Grey welcomed this moment of 'definite separation' since it was a relief to see the *status quo* broken up—'The last seven years have been a nightmare of futility.'[90]

This rupture seemed to make it necessary for the different sections of the party to institutionalize their opinions. At the end of February, the Liberal League, successor to the Liberal Imperial Council, was announced.[91] Perks had been meditating this change for several months. Despite pressure from Herbert Gladstone, Perks had succeeded in persuading William Allard, the Liberal organizer for the Home Counties, to become its chief agent. Rosebery became

President, with Asquith, Grey and Fowler as Vice-Presidents. The purpose of the League was obvious—to boost Rosebery and to provide a haven for those Liberals who rejected the official leadership and its 'obsolete' policies. Asquith's position in the League was ambivalent. In an open letter to his constituents on 1 March he clearly aligned himself with Rosebery, both on foreign and domestic issues. Yet on 14 March he publicly opposed 'any aggressive movement against his fellow-Liberals' and would not support moves 'to destroy or weaken the general organisation of the party'.[92] Fowler too, although a firm Roseberyite, was not pressing for a complete break. At the end of December 1901 he had still considered it the wisest policy 'to try to draw C-B. to the side of Rosebery and *not* to drive him into the ranks of Labby and Lloyd George & Co. . . . Our policy is not to break up the party—we aim at its unity on a solid & country inspiring policy & we can do that best by remaining inside the party and adopting what we call "a policy of permeation".'[93] By the middle of March, although the situation was still uncertain, Grey recognized that Rosebery was not likely to capture the party. He told Milner that 'Rosebery has broken definitely with C-B; the bulk of the Liberal party in the House huddle round the latter, and the existing organizations or a majority of them, are with him; R. has a large following outside. Whether he will capture the party; or whether R's section will be driven out & C-B left with a surviving rump, it is too soon to say; or perhaps a corresponding split may come amongst the Conservatives and a large middle party come into being & hold the field for a while. . . .'[94] For the first few months of its existence it seemed that the League might emerge as a powerful force with the backing of the Harmsworth press, though its objectives were uncertain. However, at long last, in the middle of May 1902, the South African war ended. While it would be absurd to suppose that differences within the party would disappear overnight, the ostensible cause of them had at least been removed. After all, it was supposed to be the duty of the Opposition to oppose the Government, and it did Liberals no harm to turn their minds once again in this direction.

6

Prelude to Power

When the South African war ended, Grey was forty, a man in his prime, with nearly seventeen years of parliamentary experience behind him. His physical presence was impressive with his sharp, well-defined features, and his movements were lithe and athletic. It came as no surprise to learn that he excelled at such games as tennis and racquets. He also liked good food and wine. Although a disciple of Haldane in such matters, he had so far not matched his friend's rotundity. The pattern of life which he and Dorothy had established since their marriage remained fixed. They tried to open the cottage in March or April and then spend as much time there as possible. When the Liberal Party seemed to be dining itself to destruction in the summer of 1901, Edward ruefully confessed that his time had been 'sadly broken by politics' and he had been unable to savour the roses and honeysuckle to the full. At the cottage Dorothy and Edward usually kept themselves to themselves. In any case, few of his colleagues could have tolerated the rule that politics was never to be discussed on this holy ground. Together they fished, watched birds, admired flowers and walked. Then, early in June, the cottage was usually closed, and they departed northwards to Fallodon and Scotland. Dorothy would sometimes stay there for at least part of the winter. Edward stayed in London during the parliamentary session, travelling north whenever he could. As far as his constituency was concerned, he could largely rely on his name and reputation. Yet the need for formal party organization even penetrated North Northumberland. Dorothy helped organize the middle-class ladies of Berwick and Alnwick into Women's Liberal Associations. She wrote to a friend in October 1901: 'We have just begun to pay attention to this constituency. We had never done it at all before, but it would be so flat to lose the seat before Rosebery comes out of his furrow.' She helped organize an evening party in

Berwick for five hundred people and reflected: 'I wonder if that sort of thing does any good.'[1]

Fallodon and Northumberland remained Grey's first love, but the amount of time he was able to spend there was limited. Indeed, for several years at the beginning of the century the house was let for the summer months and they stayed in the cottage. 'Fallodon is let again this year,' he wrote gloomily in April 1903, 'that is another of the delights of politics; it confers on you the double privilege of being some hundreds a year out of pocket & of being unable to live at home.'[2] Was it worth going on? If Liberal fortunes improved and he kept in the race, then a seat in the Cabinet seemed likely, but if not, then he had now reached the age when he had to think seriously of an alternative. In July 1898 he had been elected a director of the North Eastern Railway Company. The salary of some £400 a year had helped him to recoup some of his political expenses. The North Eastern was a fine company to join, and although Grey never flattered himself that he was a real railway man, he came to find the work unexpectedly engrossing. It brought him into close contact with industrial and commercial questions, thus complementing his political specialization in foreign affairs.

The North Eastern took its name in 1854 after the merger of the Leeds Northern, the York and Midland, and the York, Newcastle and Berwick companies. After amalgamation with the famous Stockton and Darlington Company in 1863, the North Eastern gained a virtual monopoly of the running in Northumberland and Durham, the North and East Ridings of Yorkshire and a large stake in the West Riding. Its lines penetrated into Westmorland and Cumberland and by virtue of its running powers over the North British line north of Berwick, the N.E.R. was able to play its part in pulling trains from York to Edinburgh. To do this, it had a fine stock of locomotives replete with shining brass. With its headquarters in York, the company was very much a northern institution. Grey came to know a good deal about the region's commercial life, though he never paraded this knowledge. On average about twenty times a year he assembled in the boardroom in York, for only occasionally did the directors meet in Newcastle or London. By the turn of the century, the strong Quaker tradition on the board had become somewhat attenuated. Fellow directors now included industrialists like Sir Hugh Bell the ironmaster, and landowners like Sir Matthew Ridley. Besides the fact that they were gentlemen, they all had in common a strong attachment to their region. They

invariably stayed in the comfort of the Station Hotel before trans-
acting their business. Grey found this situation very congenial.[3]

In matters of industrial relations, the N.E.R. led the field among
the railway companies in that it recognized the railway unions. All
the others resisted this move on the grounds that it jeopardized the
strict standards of discipline necessary in a public service. In fact,
it has been suggested that most railway directors were convinced
that they needed to retain as much control as possible over wages
and hours without the hindrance of collective bargaining. Financi-
ally, the golden days of the railways were over. Costs, in the form
of taxation, materials and labour were steadily rising through the
nineties. Charges, however, were controlled and largely held steady
by a Railway and Canal Commission after an act of 1894. The
Commission tended to listen to the demands of traders and others
to keep transport costs down. Profit margins were therefore being
squeezed and the railway industry was heading for the strikes which
were to occur in the first decade of the century.[4] The N.E.R. was not
immune from these pressures, but astute management, combined
with the profitability of the main east-coast route to Scotland,
helped to make it much more prosperous than many of its contemporaries. The decision to recognize the unions, which had been
taken back in 1889, was also believed to contribute to better
relations within the company. To a sceptical director of another
railway company, Grey wrote that it was right to have discussions
with union officials. Of course, they put forward demands with
strong backing, but face-to-face encounters helped to overcome
many difficulties. 'I suppose', he added, 'the other lines think they
can smash the Union or prevent its being formed in their systems,
but I believe that Unions will form anyhow and that in the long
run you can deal better with organised than with unorganised
labour.'[5]

Several more years convinced Grey that there was something
solid and definite about railway work—'One can sit with one's feet
on the ground instead of standing on one's head hurraying with
one's heels, which is about all one can do in opposition, though
one goes on mouthing about public affairs.'[6] In December 1904,
when he was offered the chairmanship of the board, he accepted:
'. . . it is a big job, but interesting. It will make a hole in my time:
I can't help that. I have done nearly 20 years of political work,
mostly opposition. I am not prepared to spend the next twenty
years doing the same sort of thing to the exclusion of definite and

useful work like the railway.' The arrangement was that if the Liberals should win the next election (which his Tory co-directors felt unlikely) and Grey were invited to join the Cabinet, he would be free to resign—'but barring that one contingency, I am now, I hope, settled for life. After 20 years' work I shall retire & fish a little before I die (D.V.).'[7] His letter to Rosebery was on similar lines. He was weary of the 'sterile work of opposition'. Dorothy too was delighted, writing to Munro Ferguson that she supposed there would be 'a lot of grindstone about the work, and most of the salary will have to be saved to replace past election expenses, but I have ordered a new tea-table and some extra bulbs. It's rather a fine salary you know, £2000 a year! . . . It may even be that we shall want one of the better sort of Grosvenor Road houses. . . .'[8] Sir Edward enjoyed his new responsibilities—'I live in a whirl of trains & speeches & weekends in the North: sometimes I imagine I am a Chairman of a Railway, sometimes that I am an M.P., sometimes that I am married, sometimes that I am not: I am all of these by turns, but not one of them for long enough to make it seem real.'[9] Clearly, he had found an acceptable alternative career for himself, yet, despite his own rather gloomy estimate, the Liberal Party was undoubtedly recovering and he was deeply involved in its future.

Arthur Balfour succeeded his uncle, Lord Salisbury, as Prime Minister in July 1902. Earlier in the spring, Balfour had introduced his controversial Education Bill. He proposed to abolish the old school boards throughout the country and make county and county borough councils responsible for all secondary and technical education. Local authorities were to maintain standards not only in the board schools but also in the voluntary (Church) schools. The managers of these latter were to provide the buildings and appoint the teachers but their running expenses were to be paid for out of the local rates. The proposals led to a storm of protest. Balfour had particular difficulty with Chamberlain, who feared that Liberal Unionists of Nonconformist stock might be tempted by this measure to return to their old allegiance. For Nonconformists complained that Church teaching was being subsidized from the rates, even though the 'undenominational' religious instruction was being provided in other schools. Here was one war-cry for the Liberal Party, and Lloyd George in particular took it up eagerly. Even Asquith waded in with denunciations of the Government's reactionary measure. Probably influenced by Haldane, Grey felt it would be a mistake to try to wreck the Bill on the old religious cry.[10] Therefore, although he stressed Nonconformist grievances for party reasons, he gave his approval to the basic notion that local authorities should assume responsibility for education.

The unity which this agitation gave to the Liberals, coupled with the obvious lack of enthusiasm of Chamberlain, gave rise to the feeling that Balfour was 'riding for a fall'. Some Tories, Grey wrote to Rosebery, took it as a matter of course that a Liberal Government would take over if Balfour promised to support it for a year or two. Even if this were true, Grey was firmly against the idea: 'Such a Govt. would be a pure Ministry of Affairs in a position neither of power nor of dignity. I for one wouldn't give up my railway director-ship to be in it.' If the idea were mooted, Liberals should gain specific promises of support for some British and Irish measures, one of which should amend the Education Bill. If Balfour refused this support, then no Liberal Government could be formed without discarding essential Liberal measures—'If Balfour agreed you would have a real justification for taking office & be able after two years to appeal to the country with the credit both of Liberalism & Efficiency in Affairs, the latter helped I hope by having Kitchener in the Cabinet & perhaps Milner.'[11] At least one significant difficulty about the proposal that Rosebery should approach Balfour on these lines was that Rosebery was not the leader of the party. Grey and Haldane still refused to acknowledge that he was a lost cause. The South African war had seen Grey as a fighting politician—Dorothy wrote: 'Edward has lately taken to politics and things have been raspingly difficult to manage'—but for all his somewhat reckless activity, Campbell-Bannerman was still the leader.[12] In so far as Rosebery had failed to rise to the bait, Grey could hardly be blamed, but for a group supposedly devoted to 'Efficiency', they were sur-prisingly inefficient themselves. There is indeed something pathetic about the gyrations of this group of Liberals. They had sensed for years that something was wrong with the party, but they lacked a clear-cut alternative. Although their attempts to cajole or coerce Rosebery came to nothing, their activities are not to be dismissed as the intrigues of a fastidious few. The loss of Asquith, Grey and Haldane, if they stuck together, was something the old-guard leadership could not afford if the Liberals were to provide a strong Opposition. While Campbell-Bannerman might consider them 'the superior set', it seemed that an important section of the party in the country believed they were 'the coming men'.

In this situation, Grey and his friends drifted, hoping vaguely for the disintegration of the two existing parties and loosely (for it was difficult to see what the notion meant) attached to the doctrine of 'Efficiency'. It seemed possible to him 'that in this century Parliamentary Government will break down & be discarded as outworn, but what the new system will be and in what country it will be evolved I cannot foresee'.[13] For a while the group became very thick with Sidney Webb as he and Haldane vied with each other in the production of elaborate reforms. At the end of February 1902, Beatrice noted in her diary: 'Asquith, Haldane, Grey, Munro Ferguson and the [Jack] Tennants, form a little family group into which they have temporarily attracted Sidney by asking him to their little dinners and informal meetings.' The Webbs lived just a little further down the Grosvenor Road from the Greys, but intimacy was hardly to be expected. Mrs Webb was not impressed by Sir Edward, he was 'a slight person: he has charm of appearance, of manner and even of character; but he is I fear essentially a "stick" to be used by someone else!' She found something pathetic in a remark he made at dinner that politicians were now expected to make their own causes. The trouble with Grey was not only that he had no original ideas, but that he apparently had no notion of work as the main occupation of life. Politics, she lamented, was 'merely with him an episode in his daily life, like his enjoyment of nature, books, society, sport (mostly nature and sport be it said)'. Nor did the wives help. Both Margot Asquith and Dorothy Grey found themselves in the unusual position of being lashed from the same source. Lady Grey was deemed to be 'a fastidious aristocrat, intensely critical of anyone to whom work is the principal part of life. She is clever enough to see that work alone counts, and yet knows, in her heart of hearts, that neither she nor her husband are capable of it.' Yet the more she saw of Sir Edward the more, against her will, she liked him. After entertaining him and other 'Limps' in November 1902 she wrote: 'Like Balfour he is a man of exquisite flavour; he is high-minded, simple, kindly and wise, without being able or clever—an ideal element in a Cabinet containing some strong master-mind.' He would never be that mind himself and, still obsessed by the gospel of work, she doubted whether he could sustain an eight-hour day for ten months of the year. But undoubtedly his temperament had 'an exquisite poise—far above human passions and human prejudices—in an atmosphere rarefied by public spirit, fastidious honour and widely diffused human fellowship. . . .'[14] While undoubtedly there was some truth in these observations, Beatrice Webb was never very good at understanding how men of Grey's stamp operated. She had her image of the fisherman-king, and she would stand by it. There were, of course, extraordinary deficiencies in her own outlook. In February, discussing Grey's lack of original ideas, she actually wrote in her diary that he had none 'beyond foreign and colonial policy (whatever that may mean) . . .'

Haldane and Sidney Webb mercifully felt that foreign policy had a meaning. They invited Grey, as an 'expert' in the subject, to join the rather pretentious political dining club which they launched at the end of 1902 under the title of the 'Co-Efficients'. 'Haldane told me of the dining Club', Grey wrote to Webb, '& I see much advantage in it & should like to attend. . . .'[15] Each diner was supposed to make a contribution to the efficiency of the whole—economics, finance, the armed services, journalism and the colonies were all represented in this Cabinet, and H. G. Wells represented himself. Wells did not like Grey, who apparently had a brain 'almost incredibly fixed and unaware of the violent mutability of things. His air of grave and responsible leadership was an immense delusion. . . .'[16] The Hon. B. Russell, an as yet unregenerate member, claimed subsequently to recall war with Germany being spoken of 'without too much apprehension' and to have heard Grey advocating an arrangement with France and Russia.[17] But, as Leo Amery wrote, as a brains trust with a definite political object, the Co-Efficients petered out almost as soon as they began. Individuals continued to dine together for a number of years, but all hope of devising a programme which broke decisively with Gladstonianism and appealed to elements in both existing parties was shattered by the speech made by Joseph Chamberlain at the Town Hall in Birmingham on 15 May.

Chamberlain had spent the winter of 1902–3 in South Africa on a tour. While away, he brooded on the future of the Empire, and as he explained in his speech, he had come to feel that the Empire would disintegrate unless it could be held together economically by preferential duties. At the same time he advocated retaliatory duties against foreign countries. In September 1903, Balfour accepted Chamberlain's resignation and balanced this by accepting those of three Free Trade Ministers, including the Chancellor of the Exchequer, Ritchie. Shortly afterwards, the Duke of Devonshire also resigned and, with Chamberlain a free-lance, the disarray of the Government seemed complete. The Liberals were presented with a great opportunity.

Before Chamberlain's Birmingham speech, Grey had been decidedly pessimistic, writing: 'I hate politics as much as ever & can't write about them: I think this Govt. will flicker out in a year or two & a ministry will be reformed under Chamberlain. I see no prospect of Liberals coming in before 1910 & have no more thoughts of office than for the last several years. . . .'[18] Three days after the speech, the Co-Efficients met for dinner at Grey's house and Leo Amery remembered making 'an impassioned appeal to him not to let a small theoretical issue prevent his joining in a great Imperial movement which might revivify the whole of our political and social life'.[19] He believed that he had moved Grey, but not sufficiently. Hewins, a Liberal who did become a Chamberlainite, met Grey a few weeks later and also thought he was wavering. In a letter, which does not survive in Hewins's papers, Grey reputedly said that he would not regret a victory for Chamberlain.[20] But while much has been made of this alleged wavering—on rather flimsy evidence from partisan sources—the significant fact is that Grey did not fall. Indeed, were it not for these testimonies, other evidence would suggest that he remained as keen a Free Trader as any Liberal.[21] The difficulty for Grey at this time was that every political issue was linked to the leadership question. The new issue raised by Chamberlain gave Rosebery an occasion 'to speak strongly not only as an individual but as a party man . . . a speech on these lines would strengthen both the Liberal League & your own position.'[22] A month later he wrote again, regretting Rosebery's refusal to allow his name to be associated with the Free Trade Union—an *ad hoc* body set up to counter the Tariff Reform League. In vain he pleaded that the Free Trade Union was not being run against the Liberal League. 'We are in for a big fight', Grey implored him, 'in which no half measures will do and in which no in-and-out part is possible for anybody.'[23]

In August and September 1903, when the government crisis came to a head, the Greys retreated to the North of England and Scotland. Edward was writing an article on the fiscal question and found this task more congenial within easy reach of salmon rivers. On their way south, they were to spend a few days with Rosebery at Dalmeny and then Grey had 'a horrid lot of meetings' planned for October. At Dalmeny, Haldane joined them and the two men then launched a further assault on Rosebery. The suggestion was being aired that

Earl Spencer, who had been Gladstone's personal choice to succeed him, should lead the party. It was argued that, under the strain of his wife's ill-health, Campbell-Bannerman was losing interest in the leadership and would hand over to Spencer, whose views on the Boer War had largely agreed with his own, whereas he would not make way for one of the younger men. In Haldane's words, Grey 'went splendidly' at Rosebery, but to little effect.[24] In turn, Grey refused to look at a self-pitying memorandum drawn up by Rosebery to explain why he could not form a Government, declaring that a national crisis would compel reconsideration of any reason. Rosebery then expressed the utmost contempt for Spencer and declared that he was going to work for an Asquith ministry. 'This is what passed,' Haldane concluded his report to Asquith, 'and it was very definite. I left it to Grey and he was like a rock. You must lead us accordingly.' In his letter Grey endorsed the idea that Asquith should become leader at some stage: 'you could I think carry the point that you must be leader in the House of Commons; but having carried this (which would mean the deposition of C-B), it would be urged upon you & your friends that it would be un-generous and unnecessary to insist upon jumping over Spencer too. . . .' Grey added that 'under no circumstances would I take office with C.B. as Prime Minister in any Govt. in which C-B was leader in the House of Commons. . . .'[25] The idea of a Spencer ministry continued to have some attractions—Lord Tweedmouth, for example, sketched one in the spring of 1904 with Campbell-Bannerman at the Foreign, Rosebery at the Colonial and Grey at the War Office. But these were little more than after-dinner exercises and the unfortunate Spencer had a serious illness in 1905 which put him out of the running. In any case, Free Trade still had to be saved.

Asquith conducted a countrywide campaign rebutting Chamberlain's claims in a series of splendid speeches. Reading one such in *The Times*, Grey wrote to say that it was 'quite first rate in every way—powerful in attack & fertile in suggestion & you send your figures like arrows straight to the mark'.[26] Dorothy went to hear Chamberlain when he came to speak in Newcastle in October 1903 and found the orchid rather faded. He only warmed up in his speech when he was getting his knife into Rosebery. She didn't think people were convinced that everybody would be better off under his system. There was little cheering on this occasion, though she admitted that this was 'probably because the people were all upper class in two-guinea seats'.[27] Grey made a number of spirited speeches himself and his article on 'Mr Chamberlain's Fiscal Policy' appeared in the *Monthly Review*, edited by Newbolt. Since Grey's figures were less certain of their target than Asquith's, his arguments were mainly political. He could not believe in the reality of this 'alleged Imperial crisis' nor accept that only by introducing Preferential Tariffs could disruption be avoided. He claimed that the issue was not one between those who desired the closer union of the Empire and those who were indifferent to it. He was as strongly in favour of the Empire as anyone, but attempting to bind it together economically was not feasible. In the case of Canada, for example, 'the protection of the Canadian manufacturer against the British manufacturer is still an essential condition of any offer of the Canadian Government'. And there were more serious considerations than merely economic. Many, like him, believed that the British Imperial ideal could be compatible with 'the growing sympathy and union of sentiment throughout the English-speaking race'. An attempt to penalize United States grain, in favour of Canadian, would destroy this sympathy. In general, protection would mean for Britain 'an artificial increase in the cost of production for which we shall receive no compensating benefit; we shall certainly incur some tariff wars with other countries, and when they are over we shall be lucky if we find ourselves with tariffs against us not more unfavourable on the whole than they are now'.[28] It was in 1859 that the British Government had recognized the right of the self-governing colonies to levy protective duties on British produce. 'I do not believe it is possible to get our self-governing colonies to become Free Trade', Edward wrote to his cousin Albert, '& I fear that Chamberlain will simply drag us into Protection. Old Lord Grey was right in his attempt to prevent them from taxing our Imports. . . .'[29] The article had been written before Chamberlain's resignation was announced, but he told Herbert Gladstone that he thought the argument still stood. Balfour, he believed, was trying to keep the party together while Chamberlain educated the country. Balfour intended to hang on as long as possible but he might be forced into a dissolution. In which case, the party should press for the reform of higher education, the taxation of land values, housing for the working classes and the amendment, but not repeal, of the Education Act. He doubted whether these claims would get much of a hearing in the general defence of Free Trade from the immediate peril.[30]

Activity of this kind gives the lie to the criticism of Grey written by Lloyd George in brilliant paragraphs in his memoirs. There it is claimed that Sir Edward's position was due to the care with which he kept almost entirely out of the clash of party conflicts. 'Even when he was busily negotiating faction inside his Party he preferred to remain behind the lines, leaving the actual fighting to Lord Rosebery, Mr. Asquith, and Mr. Haldane.' In a paragraph which he subsequently decided not to print, he was even more scorching. Grey 'never took any part in the toil and unpleasantness of Opposition during the long years when the Liberals were in Opposition after 1886. He never took part in debates in the House of Commons, except occasionally in the knightly tournaments which were arranged about once a year; he rarely appeared on the platform at Liberal gatherings up and down the country.' The real work of opposition was left to the 'bowmen and billmen' of the party, amongst whom, it seems, Lloyd George was to be found. When the party was battling in the 1886, 1895 and 1901 Parliaments, Lloyd George 'hardly ever saw Sir Edward Grey in the House'. Finally, the indictment concluded, Grey's real interest in politics began 'with the victory and the sharing of its spoils. The choicest of these must be reserved for him and his friends. Then he became active and threatened serious trouble in the Party if his wishes were not respected.' It was when power was reached that Sir Edward Grey came in. 'You would not expect Sir Willoughby Patterne to plough and sow. He only turned up at Harvest Home, when the sheaves were distributed.'[31] To continue the metaphor, while there is a grain of truth in the charge, most is chaff. Grey was certainly never anxious to take on speaking engagements for their own sake—however galling it was to Lloyd George, he never needed to speak to make his name. He was not above telling the Whips that with three or four major speeches planned for November he was heavily booked until Christmas. Given his background, Grey could not become the silver-tongued, grass-roots politician held up, for some reason, as the ideal. Lloyd George did not like those qualities of reticence and restraint which made many of his generation, brought up on Carlyle, see in Grey the ideal of the 'strong silent man'. He added: 'In the War and post-War days of Clemenceau, Foch, Lenin, Mussolini, Roosevelt and Hitler—all talkers—that legend has become a little mildewed. The strongest men of history have never been silent.' In the years after 1933—when Lloyd George wrote these words—some of the talkers fared less well.

As has been seen, from the period of the Boer War onwards, Grey by no means left Rosebery, Asquith and Haldane to do the real work. The irony is that in 1904, one of the years when Grey was supposed to be surveying the harvest, he was one of the few Liberal leaders to agree to speak for Lloyd George in Caernarvon itself. He told Herbert Gladstone that he would not be able to attend an ex-Cabinet meeting because of this engagement: 'I am sorry this isn't compatible with being in London the same afternoon. Caernarvon appears to be on the fringe of the Celtic fringe & very remote.'[32] Not only was it very remote, it was very curious. Having delivered what the *North Wales Observer* described as 'an eulogy of Mr. Lloyd George', Grey sat down, awaiting a reply from the local Member. To his amazement, however, a bard, conveniently stationed near the platform, mounted it, and delivered an extensive ode in Welsh on the same subject. In response, Lloyd George quipped that if Chamberlain ever came to Caernarvon, he would place a prohibitive tariff on poetry.[33] Relations between Grey and Lloyd George seemed very friendly. Moreover, in the previous month, December 1903, Perks reported a conversation with Lloyd George to Rosebery. The Welshman had little to say in favour of Haldane or Asquith as 'the former, & also in some measure the latter, is under the influence of people with whom they "spend week-ends"—that neither of them is a "real democrat"—that personally he has much more confidence in Grey than in Asquith'.[34]

It is also misleading to suppose that in these years Grey maintained a bland indifference to internal problems. 'Naturally enough', wrote Wells, 'he could see very little to complain of in the condition of the country.'[35] In fact, he possessed a shrewd awareness of what was going on in the relations between Liberalism and Labour. His attitude to labour questions was modestly 'progressive'. In the engineering dispute of 1897, for example, he had condemned the employers for trying to break the unions, while at the same time believing that the union leaders had provoked trouble. As for the eight-hour day, no one could really tell how much it would cost until the experiment was tried. Both as a railway director and as a north-eastern M.P., he knew that dissatisfaction and unrest were just below the surface. In 1900, the Labour Representation Committee, combining both trade unions and socialist societies, was formed. The following year, the success of the Taff Vale Railway Company in suing the Amalgamated Society of Railway Servants made it clear that trade-union funds were not, as had been supposed, afforded absolute protection. The repercussions ran through the trade-union world and led to increased support for the L.R.C. In 1903, at Barnard Castle in County Durham, Arthur Henderson, a former Liberal agent, triumphed over Liberal and Conservative opponents. The implications were ominous. Gladstone turned to Grey for advice since the constituencies were in some disarray. Grey said that there was little he could do to put things right in Durham. His sphere in Northumberland was over fifty miles away, with a very different social and economic climate. But he was prepared to repeat publicly what he had said already for a decade, that 'Labour should have more direct representation in the House of Commons & every Liberal should not only admit this but wish it'. Constituencies should be apportioned so that a Labour candidate should not spoil Liberal chances and vice versa. Henderson had now clearly vindicated the Labour claim to Barnard Castle '& should now not only be left in peace but supported'.[36] Gladstone did in fact succeed in concluding a secret agreement of this kind with Ramsay MacDonald, the secretary of the L.R.C. After the election of Will Crooks as member for Woolwich in 1903, Grey told students at Edinburgh University, where he had been an unsuccessful candidate for the office of Lord Rector: 'I look upon the result of Woolwich with the greatest satisfaction, because it seems to me to prove that the wage-earning classes, who are numerically far the greatest of the population, are gaining in power and strength and concentration and organisation and political purpose. That is what should happen. . . .'[37] But it was one thing to advocate the adoption of working-class candidates and another for local parties to give them preference over professional or business men. It was also extremely difficult to tell how distinct this 'Labour Party' considered itself to be. Yet there seemed little cause for alarm about the social fabric when Sir Edward could exchange over breakfast quotations from Wordsworth with Thomas Burt, the miner and his grandfather's successor as M.P. for Morpeth.[38] But then, perhaps in different ways, both men were becoming anachronistic?

While the party was drawing together on the issues of protection and education, it would be wrong to suppose that its troubles were over. In particular, the party was not united on the Irish question. Both in his Chesterfield speech and subsequently, Rosebery made it clear that he would have nothing further to do with Gladstonian policy for Ireland. Grey found Rosebery's reference to the Irish 'harshly put' but was afraid that 'the statement he made is true, as to the present position'.[39] A few months earlier, Grey had written to Herbert Gladstone to explain his position in some detail and, if possible, without emotion. He contended that 'the Irish intend to make the Liberal Party dependent upon their support—the British electors will never trust us as long as we are. The only way out is to be independent, by which I mean that I would not support the taking of office dependent upon the Irish vote.' But, as his record in the past showed, he felt a deep sense of obligation towards Ireland 'and in that spirit I shall always be moved in speaking of Irish affairs. Things must advance towards Home Rule, but I think it must be step by step.' If they were sensible, the Irish would recognize that they would benefit if the Liberal Party regained the confidence of the British electorate. He hoped he would be able to co-operate on Irish matters, but there was 'a difference between co-operation & dependence, & Redmond's attitude & tone have been so overbearing that it is necessary to repudiate dependence'.[40] Speaking to the Oxford University Liberal League in May 1903 he urged members 'not to lose sight of the Irish question, but to equip themselves by knowledge of Irish history. . . .' He had always felt, he continued, that 'since they failed to settle the Irish question by controversy, that at last, in time, if they were patient, they might see it settled by consent. . . .'[41] Whatever Gladstonians like Morley might think, Grey considered his attitude to be plain common sense. Writing to the secretary of the Liberal League in May 1904 he stated clearly: 'What the League is opposed to is an *independent* Irish Parliament. Mr Gladstone's Home Rule was a *subordinate* Irish Parliament. Ireland will get much more local self-government, but in my opinion it will be realized by degrees & not by one big step as Mr Gladstone proposed.'[42]

Grey was right in assuming that Balfour would try to hang on as long as possible in the hope that the latent tensions among the Liberals might again rival those in his own party. Certainly, as well as Ireland, whenever the South African question cropped up, the fragility of the new-found Liberal unity was apparent. The introduction of Chinese indentured labour into the Transvaal mines, sanctioned by the Balfour Government and Milner, caused great fury on the Liberal benches. When the ordinance was put to the Commons in February 1904, Asquith and Grey voted against, but Haldane abstained. The Radicals now hunted Haldane. Grey wrote to Dorothy that journalists like Massingham thought they could exclude Haldane from the next Government, 'and they are so elated by things generally that they think they can exclude us all, including Asquith, and have a real Radical government of their own. What a futile thing it would be—all froth!' He found Haldane unpredictable. So often he had higher ideals than the bulk of the party, but now he differed on the narrow point that without Chinese labour there would be a deficit in the Transvaal revenue.[43] Haldane stayed, and the Liberals hung precariously together. In April 1905, Grey wrote to his cousin Albert, the newly appointed Governor-General of Canada, that Balfour was unlikely to last beyond June. He would not forecast the result of an election—'the anticipation of dissolution has quite upset all political work and it is urgent that an election should take place & put an end to the rot'.[44] In order to clear the political air, the country had to pronounce on Free Trade. But in August, Balfour was still there and Grey's language was stronger. The parliamentary session had been the most barren that he had ever experienced: '. . . I think worse of Balfour's public conduct than I can tell you in a letter or than you would care to hear. He has been so spoilt by the exercise of his own powers of casuistry, which are enormous, & by living in an atmosphere of adulation and Christian names, that he has lost the ordinary sense of right and wrong.'[45]

The Liberals therefore had to depart for the recess still in a state of uncertainty. Fortune seemed to be favouring them in the country, as Dorothy wrote; '. . . we are in the thick of winning by-elections, and the Liberal party is now thought sure of a majority independent of the Irish. . . .'[46] Inevitably, the Greys departed for the north of Scotland; equally inevitably, Campbell-Bannerman departed for Marienbad. In the first few days of September, Haldane and Asquith came to visit Edward at his fishing lodge, Relugas, in Sutherland (the Asquiths were staying some fifteen miles away). Haldane had decided that the time had come to put into practice the understanding he had with Grey that they would not serve under Campbell-Bannerman if he remained in the Commons. On his own account, the initiative came from Haldane since Grey 'hated to have to make any move'. The three men then resolved, in the so-called 'Relugas Compact', not to join a Campbell-Bannerman Cabinet unless he went to the Lords. Asquith suggested that Haldane should inform the King of this decision (Haldane had lately come into contact with the King on educational questions), since it might affect his choice of Ministers. Grey did not dissent from this move, but felt that Asquith should see Campbell-

Bannerman himself as soon as possible and inform him of the situation.[47] Although the three men were clearly out for their own ends, their doubts about Sir Henry in the Commons were genuine and shared by others not of their opinions. In October 1903, Gladstone had reported to Asquith a conversation with Campbell-Bannerman in which the leader had himself expressed serious doubts about his physical ability to take on such a heavy load. In February 1905, Grey claimed that even Morley had been persuaded to agree that Asquith should become leader of the Commons if the Liberals came in.[48] Although the Relugas pact was a secret, rumours that something like it existed had been current for a number of years. For example, in September 1903, Ripon wrote to Spencer, 'I hear that the intrigues against C.B. have not ceased & that Asquith, Fowler & E. Grey are supposed to be likely to refuse to join a Liberal government if he remains Leader in the House of Commons. Can this be true?'[49]

Haldane brought the decision of his friends to the attention of the King in a constitutionally dubious way, and in a manner of which they doubtfully approved. He wrote to Knollys, the King's private secretary, informing him of the decision but stressing that they would serve cheerfully if they could have sufficient safeguards—Asquith to be leader of the Commons and Chancellor of the Exchequer, Grey to have the Foreign or Colonial Office, and the Woolsack for himself. Knollys, writing on his own account, urged in reply that even if Sir Henry stayed in the Commons, the trio might serve their country and party better by joining his Government. Haldane was perturbed, and on 27 September wrote to Asquith urging him to see Campbell-Bannerman as soon as possible on the latter's return from the continent. In his conduct, Haldane was certainly outrunning Grey's intentions. Departing at last from his fishing for railway business in London, Sir Edward wrote to Asquith on 2 October to stress that it was 'too soon to put a pistol to C.B.'s head. If he shows himself willing to discuss the formation of the next Govt. he should be told what we think & feel. But we want it to come to him in a friendly way & not as if we were trying to force him in a way which he might think premature & unfriendly.' He would have liked Rosebery to have been Government spokesman in the Lords, but that seemed out of the question (they had kept their intentions secret from Rosebery) and Asquith should therefore lead the Commons. But, not knowing what Haldane had already told Knollys, Grey added: 'it is too soon in any case to stipulate for definite offices; your leadership in the H. of C. is the most important point & should be made alone first'.[50] Three days later, Haldane was dining with the King at Balmoral and believed that he had persuaded him. His Majesty would tell Sir Henry that he had doubts whether anyone but a young man could be both Prime Minister and leader of the Commons. He would suggest a peerage. Very pleased with himself, Haldane now felt that it only remained for Asquith to see Campbell-Bannerman.

The party leader was delayed on the continent and it was not until 13 November that Asquith was able to see him. Sir Henry made it clear that it would be with great reluctance that he would leave the House of Commons, despite suggestions that he ought to, made by 'that ingenious person, Richard Burdon Haldane'. They provisionally discussed other posts in a new Government. Asquith could have the Exchequer but it became clear that Master Haldane was by no means a certain Lord Chancellor. As for the Foreign Office, Campbell-Bannerman said that he was considering Lord Elgin, a former Viceroy of India, for the position. Asquith was very firm, according to his wife, that Grey was 'the *only* man, and that it was clear in his mind that Grey's appointment as Foreign Minister would be popular all over Europe'. Asquith believed he had made an impression, though he could see that 'C.B. had never before realised how urgently Grey is needed at the Foreign Office'. Sir Henry had apparently been thinking of Grey for the War Office. Asquith had certainly taken Grey's advice and not taken his pistol; indeed, if his wife's account is correct, he had not even mentioned that his mission was to inform Sir Henry that he and two colleagues had contracted not to serve in the Government whose composition they discussed.[51] It is not clear what Asquith said to Grey when they met shortly afterwards.

A few days later, Asquith again saw Campbell-Bannerman, and Grey may well have accompanied him. This time their talk concerned Ireland. In a speech at the end of October, Rosebery had demanded that Home Rule should either be announced as a major measure for immediate consideration or abandoned for the time being. But if the party was to keep together, any such clear-cut statement was impossible. Grey, Asquith and Campbell-Bannerman hammered out a compromise and the leader spoke in his constituency on 23 November with their agreement. He reiterated that the Liberal Party was still committed to 'full self-government' for Ireland (a highly ambiguous term) but it could not have the priority previously given to it by Gladstone. The Irish would have to accept devolution 'step by step', with the proviso that it would lead to the larger policy in the end. This declaration, vague in some respects though it was, represented a move in the direction of the Asquith–Grey approach, though it appears to have been acceptable to Morley. Seemingly the party had closed ranks for the election—if election there was to be. Grey was afraid that Balfour would resign, in which case he was strongly against the Liberals accepting office. Balfour ought to be made to go on till January 1906 when there could be a dissolution. 'If he refuses & C.B. refuses it is possible that the King may ask Chamberlain to form a Govt. & he may do so & dissolve on Protection, but that will split the Conservative party. For us to take office now will enable Balfour & Chamberlain to unite.'[52] Two days after the speech, Morley sounded out Grey and reported back to Campbell-Bannerman. He wanted Asquith to lead the Commons but beyond that would accommodate himself to any distribution of offices. He did not 'press for F.O.; would not at all object to C.O. which will be in the firing line with Chamberlain always attacking . . . would not care who went to F.O. if he were safe & sensible; does not know much about Elgin for the office. . . .' Of course, throughout, Grey's tone was 'altogether pleasant and like a gentleman'.[53]

Speculation on the problem of offices was replaced by an unexpected and dangerous crisis for the Liberals. Rosebery was roaming the West Country speaking for the Liberal League and, while Grey and Morley were having their discussion, made a speech in Bodmin denouncing Home Rule and what he took to be the implications of Campbell-Bannerman's Stirling speech. Home Rule impaired the unity of the Free Trade party and indefinitely postponed social and educational reform. He declared once and for all that he would not serve under such a banner. It was at once widely assumed that Rosebery spoke for Asquith, Grey and Haldane. All three were in fact furious, though they had only themselves to blame in so far as they had not told Rosebery of their agreement with Campbell-Bannerman.[54] Asquith hastily sent a telegram to Grey urging him to repudiate Rosebery's interpretation of the Stirling speech, which was 'perfectly innocuous sense'. Grey did so in a speech at Newcastle-under-Lyme and wrote sadly and sharply to Rosebery: 'C.B.'s Stirling speech wasn't intended to be as you take it. Asquith discussed Ireland with him in London; got an assurance that C-B agreed with his (A's) Irish declaration; and Asquith now telegraphs to me that he regards the sense of C-B's speech which you have denounced, as quite innocuous. I can't desert Asquith & I want to defend you. I feel dead beat at last.'[55] Rosebery was unrepentant. Without the knowledge of Asquith's conference with Campbell-Bannerman, he had taken the speech at what he believed was its face value—and he had not been alone in his interpretation. Campbell-Bannerman should now clarify the position publicly. Grey admitted that he should have been informed, but would not support him further. Sir Henry spoke again, but refused to make any further concession to Rosebery's position. Now that full publicity was concentrated on the issue, to downgrade Home Rule deliberately would only provoke a crisis with the strong Home Rulers in the party. Rosebery too was adamant and stressed that Campbell-Bannerman could close the whole affair simply by saying that his interpretation was wrong and that Asquith and Grey were right. Why then didn't he? Wearily Grey replied that Sir Henry must be responsible for the consequences of his own silence, but that with the possible exception of Robert Reid, everyone had deciphered the Stirling speech as he himself had done. Everybody knew what the limit of Irish policy had to be in the next Parliament and 'this being so I think it is a pity to make more of the Irish question than need be; it is not really the test issue for the next election'. If Rosebery wanted any consolation, he would not join any Government unless assured that his interpretation was correct.[56]

The Tories rejoiced to see the Liberals once more in disarray. It was known by Saturday, 2 December, that Balfour was going to resign on the following Monday or Tuesday. Asquith also knew that Campbell-Bannerman was prepared to form a Government. Balfour's decision had probably been taken before the Bodmin speech, but he could have been encouraged by it to feel that the Liberals would not be able to agree on a Cabinet. On the Saturday evening, Grey received a telegram from Asquith urging him to travel down to London on the following day. Edward was irritated. He had only just returned to Fallodon after an absence of eight months and felt 'very independent'. Like Lord Grey of the Reform Bill, once in Northumberland, he liked to stay there. On his way south to Parliament in 1808 his distinguished ancestor wrote home from an inn at Grantham that he dreamed of his family, house and horse and became 'very confident that my stay in the place I hate most will be short. . . .'[57] Edward never dreamed of horses, but otherwise shared the feelings completely. The next few days would determine whether his stay in the place he hated most would last a very long time. It is almost impossible to say what he really felt about office. He held himself bound by the 'Relugas Compact' without realizing how frayed it had already become. On 25 November he reported to Asquith his version of his discussion with Morley. He had insisted that Campbell-Bannerman's translation to the Lords was a *sine qua non*, while Haldane's elevation to the Woolsack was the only office on which there should be no compromise. He had not made a point of the Foreign Office for himself 'provided it was in safe hands (e.g. not Bryce) to which J.M. cordially assented. . . .' Morley anticipated that there would be no difficulty in forming a Government.[58]

Campbell-Bannerman arrived in London from Scotland at midday on Monday, 4 December, and saw Asquith and Grey later in the day. The fact that he apparently found no difference of thinking between him and them must mean that they did not discuss the formation of the Government. Grey had informed Asquith by letter that Rosebery was still asking for a public statement from the party leader on the Irish question and that he had told Rosebery that unless he received an assurance from Campbell-Bannerman, he would not join the Government. But he was apprehensive, writing: 'I fear this portends something fresh. If Rosebery makes a statement publicly to this effect I shall follow it by again challenging C.B. to say that R's interpretation is right; but this won't tend to edification & I shan't say it very pleasantly to C-B.'[59] To Rosebery he wrote: 'Asquith, R.B.H. & I have gone too far to refuse office immediately & I go to hear whether the conditions, which I consider the essential minimum, are conceded; but I go very sadly . . . now the time has come I wish I was staying out more than ever. It isn't certain that I shall not, but I guess & fear.'[60] By Monday night, it seems that Grey could give his assurance to Rosebery and his first condition had been met.

There still remained the question of Campbell-Bannerman and the Lords. At some stage Asquith must have told Grey that he had decided to accept office even if the Prime Minister remained in the Commons. While Grey could hardly have been pleased by this defection, he seems neither to have been surprised nor especially angry. On the same day, after their initial joint interview with Campbell-Bannerman, he wrote to Asquith that he did not want him 'to risk your personal position more than you think absolutely necessary. C.B. gave me the impression that he was quite prepared to form a government without any of us; he never once suggested that my abstaining would make the formation of a Govt. difficult, though I had suggested that it might raise difficulties as regards yourself.' He added: 'If you go in without me eventually I shall be quite happy outside & I shan't think it in the least wrong of you to go in. My own personal position makes it exceptionally easy for me to stay out. I want therefore to go in to make the best of a bad or hopeless job as I think it. But if it comes to the worst I hold you quite free to do otherwise.'[61] At ten that Monday night, Grey did go in to see Campbell-Bannerman. The interview was short and sharp. Sir Henry described Grey as coming to him 'all buttoned up and never undoing one button' to demand that he go to the House of Lords. It is not known what Grey said about Asquith and Haldane, for on this occasion he was acting simply for himself. Campbell-Bannerman was not very alarmed since he knew he already had Asquith and the loss of Haldane would not occasion any pain. The services of Grey he did value, though the interview with Asquith on 13 November reveals that he had not thought of him automatically for the Foreign Office—or was at least intent on creating that impression. Somewhat piqued, Campbell-Bannerman told Grey that he would consider his suggestion and the interview terminated abruptly. When Sir Edward got back to the Athenaeum he wrote to Campbell-Bannerman thanking him for his patience in listening to a disagreeable suggestion, 'I should not have said it unless it was really vital to me that under present conditions Asquith should lead in the House of Commons at the beginning of the new Parliament.'[62]

Grey then went back to Haldane's flat in Whitehall Court where he was staying. One or two things rankled, he wrote to Asquith on the following morning, in particular 'the discourtesy of forming a Govt. without giving Rosebery the chance even of expressing regret that he can't join it' and the slighting of Haldane.[63] Asquith had sent Sir Henry a long letter, which Grey had seen, imploring him to consider Haldane for the Lord Chancellorship, but it had apparently made no difference. In aligning himself with Haldane, Grey seemed to be making his own exclusion certain. Presumably before receiving this letter, Asquith had another discussion with Campbell-Bannerman on the morning of Tuesday, 5 December. Sir Henry gave his account of Grey's visit. He had found him 'a regular Grey' with 'all the defects of his qualities'—by which he presumably meant his awkward, honest obstinacy once he had believed he had fastened on to an issue of principle. Asquith defended him and again returned to the theme of the burden which Sir Henry would have to shoulder. On the general issue, Asquith said that he was being placed 'in a cruel and impossible position if under the circumstances Edward Grey refused to take Office; he was his dearest friend as well as supporter, and to join a Government without such a friend would be personal pain to him, as they had never worked apart from one another'.[64] Thereupon, Campbell-Bannerman went off to Buckingham Palace to be made Prime Minister. Despite the King's concern for his health, he had decided to fight on in the Commons. Asquith wrote to Grey that he formed the impression that Sir Henry 'was rather smarting from the way in which you had presented the case to him, and that he would therefore regard it as a "humiliation" now to recede'. But if Grey could conveniently construct 'something in the nature of a golden bridge' he might still yield.[65]

At Whitehall Court, late into the night, Grey and Haldane accordingly experimented with various models before coming up with a new plan. Grey wrote to Dorothy that he was surprised that Campbell-Bannerman had taken his 'really outrageous (from me to him) proposal in perfect temper'. So, on the morning of 6 December, Edward put forward his new proposal. He suggested that Campbell-Bannerman should indeed stay in the Commons as Prime Minister, but that Haldane should take the Woolsack and lead the Government in the Lords. Asquith discussed this proposition with Morley amongst others. Morley was now proclaiming that Campbell-Bannerman was not 'a big man'. He should either have ordered Grey from his room or accepted his proposal. Following this enlightening thought, Asquith went to see Grey and found him in 'an uncompromising three-cornered humour'; the trouble with him was that he was 'not only perfectly fearless but prides himself upon his own characteristics'. Pessimistic, and not liking to be open to the charge of abandoning his friends, Asquith made a personal appeal to the Prime Minister to go to the Lords and 'solve the difficulty'. Sir Henry said he would have to consult his wife—an ominous sign. Disconsolate, Asquith motored back to Hatfield House, his base during these curious proceedings.[66]

Meanwhile, Sir Henry went his own way. Lord Elgin, whom he had considered for the Foreign Office, was now offered the Colonial Office, which he accepted. Even more bizarrely, he telegraphed to Cairo to offer the Foreign Office to Lord Cromer, who was hardly a Liberal and had played no part in British domestic politics.

Cromer at once declined. There was a certain amount of amusement to be derived from offering the post to the man for whom Grey had worked as an unpaid private secretary twenty years previously. On the afternoon of 7 December, Edward wrote to Dorothy that the Prime Minister had definitely decided to stay in the Commons and not to put Haldane on the Woolsack. Asquith was joining the Cabinet on the grounds that failure to do so would split the party. Grey did not blame him for taking this course. He himself wrote another letter to Campbell-Bannerman stating his feelings in detail: 'I have always regarded the prospect of political office with great personal reluctance; it would be intolerable to be in office without giving complete & absolute support to all that was said by the head of the Government in both Houses; and as things are it is better for me to stay outside retaining my freedom, but with every intention of giving public support to Liberal policy so long as I retain my public position. . . .' He sent this puzzling letter 'to be sure that there has been no misunderstanding'.[67]

Haldane now took a hand. In his autobiography, he wrote that on 7 December he had 'definitely decided that under no circumstances would I enter without him [Grey]'—an empty declaration since no one had yet offered him anything. Since Grey had just decided to reject the offer of the Foreign Office which Asquith had been authorized to make, the outlook for Haldane looked bleak. Then, presiding over a meeting of the Committee on Technical Education, two messengers brought relief of a somewhat confusing kind. The Prime Minister offered him the post of Attorney-General, or 'something else'. That something else turned out to be the War Office. Then began the difficult process of persuading himself that he ought to accept. He went back to see Grey who, symbolically, was lying on a sofa in the massive Haldane library. A vigorous bout of 'mental wrestling' then ensued. Haldane took leave to doubt whether the desire 'to keep a second line of defence for Free Trade' (a curious political judgment advanced as 'the only tenable ground from an ethical point of view') was sufficiently substantial to justify refusal. After an hour of such stuff, it may have occurred to them that they were being ridiculous. The compact was already broken, the offices were theirs and an election could be won. They walked together to endure forty-five minutes of moral exhortation from Arthur Acland, specially brought to London for the purpose by the editorial kingmaker, J. A. Spender. On Haldane's insistance, the two men ended the evening with excellent fish in a private dining-room at the Café Royal.[68] Haldane then dashed over to see the Prime Minister to say that he would take the War Office if Grey went to the Foreign Office. Sir Henry allowed him to make the offer, and Grey's acceptance was communicated the following morning. Gleefully, Haldane wrote to Asquith that he had induced Grey to reconsider his position. Asquith was delighted, for Grey at the F.O. was 'a great thing'. Soberly, Grey himself wrote to Rosebery: 'The decision is taken at last & I have today agreed to go into the Cabinet & take all the consequences, which that entails. I go to the F.O.'[69] Rosebery replied handsomely, but both men were aware that personally, the chief consequence it entailed was the end of their old political relationship. Edward Grey was no longer an apprentice; he had arrived.

7

The Foreign Office under
Campbell-Bannerman, 1905-8

Grey's extraordinary behaviour in the first week of December 1905
very nearly excluded him from the office which he was to hold
continuously for the next eleven years. The muddle into which he
had got himself was compounded of loyalty and obstinacy, ambition
and disinterest. It was a perfect example of the kind of behaviour
which both friends and enemies described as 'Greyish'. While there
is little evidence to support the view that Campbell-Bannerman
would have preferred anyone rather than Grey, he was clearly
prepared to leave him out. Nor is there any justification for the
view that Grey's membership of the Commons told in his favour.
The Prime Minister toyed with Elgin, approached Cromer and, in
default of Grey, might well have accepted Asquith's suggestion of
Lord Crewe. Indeed, discussing the subject in October 1904,
Haldane had been at pains to argue that Grey's membership of the
Commons should not disqualify him, 'the impossibility of combining
the work of that office with the obligation of the House of Commons
being in his opinion exaggerated'.[1] As things turned out, it was
fortunate for Grey that he was in the Commons, but it was fortuitous.
Nor is there much in the view that the Prime Minister was reluctant
to have Grey because he was an 'Imperialist'. If so, it is curious that
he should telegraph to the pro-consul in Cairo as an alternative.
Sir Henry's personal feelings, such as they were, sprang rather from
the fact that Grey had spent a large part of the previous six years
trying to unseat him. At the point when he was at last gaining his
reward, it would have been surprising if he had not derived a certain
satisfaction from Grey's discomfiture. And for his part, Grey did
not resent this—once in, he declared that he had shot his bolt:
'As to the Government, the only declarations of policy which count

are those of the Prime Minister; having entered his Government my statements will be in line with his as long as I am in it.'[2]

If Grey had not gone to the Foreign Office, it would have been because of a clash of personality and generation, not because he was considered 'unfit' for the post. Yet there were fundamental doubts, some of which were publicly expressed. It was observed that in comparison with Grey, Sir Charles Dilke bristled with information about foreign affairs and boasted innumerable political contacts on the continent. But his past misdemeanours still ruled him out. Interestingly, at least in the middle nineties, Dilke had a high opinion of Grey and bracketed him with Lloyd George as the coming man in the Liberal Party. On Dilke's advice, the journalist and military writer, Spenser Wilkinson, went to interview Sir Edward and came away most impressed by the balanced, unruffled way in which his deliberately nasty questions were answered.[3] Of the other Liberal former Foreign Under-Secretaries, James Bryce could hardly be accused of neglecting to travel. There was hardly a region of the globe which he had not strenuously visited. In addition to his great book on the American Commonwealth, he had scaled Mount Ararat. The trouble with Bryce, however, was that he knew too much and his colleagues were apt to use him as a reference book rather than a guide to action. What could be better, in the circumstances, than to make the learned Home Ruler of Ulster stock the Chief Secretary for Ireland? Other lesser figures had also been grooming themselves for office by travel and could only lament that their diligence had not been rewarded. Even a complete outsider, Ramsay MacDonald, had peregrinated in anticipation of a future call. The 'cosmopolitan' Lloyd George lamented that Northumberland was good enough for Grey.

That Grey did not travel has remained the stock criticism of him ever since. No one, however, can define an ideal Foreign Secretary. Theoretically he should be the politician best equipped to understand, represent, define and express his own country's needs and objectives, together with a keen perception of foreign attitudes and the reasons for them. In practice, to some extent, these two requirements cancel out. A Foreign Secretary who has studied, worked or travelled abroad can suffer from a pull of loyalties similar to that sometimes experienced by diplomats. When a Foreign Secretary considers himself an expert in his own right on a particular subject or area, his own recollections and emotions may cloud the issue and he is a poor judge of his own partiality. It is in this sense that a little personal experience is a dangerous thing, tending to superficiality and misplaced confidence. Edward Grey was totally uncontaminated by any experience of 'abroad', apart from his visits within the Empire to India and the West Indies. For his class and background, Grey's insularity was amazingly complete. Sharing neither the Teutonic proclivities of Haldane nor the Gallic delights of Campbell-Bannerman, he could judge the policies of continental powers unclouded by personal ties. To an uncanny degree, both at home and abroad, he was the typical Englishman. Much more so than Palmerston, 'the most English minister', with his Irish peerage, childhood spent abroad, university education in Edinburgh and fluency in languages. Of his successors, Grey stands closest to Halifax and Douglas-Home, Bevin and Brown, and four-square Englishness, whether of the rural or urban variety, undoubtedly has its advantages. It brings a politician closer to the concerns of the majority of the population, yet it obviously has its dangers. While Grey admirably fitted an image of England, he lacked that historical conception of European development which might perhaps have sharpened his perceptions and aided his diplomacy. Such a suggestion is, however, extremely general, and it is more difficult to demonstrate in what particular respect he was handicapped.

Even recent works of unimpeachable historical scholarship continue to repeat tired myths that 'the new minister was a north-country gentleman thrust into a great office by a sense of duty to his country and obligation to his party'. He is credited with force of character, elegance of expression, devotion to principle and a certain liberal moral view of the world. Offsetting these, 'at least initially', were 'his lack of experience and his scanty acquaintance with European history and statesmen'.[4] His lack of personal acquaintance may be freely conceded, though the extent to which his predecessors had cultivated personal friendship must not be exaggerated. As for his 'lack of experience', he had of course never been Foreign Secretary before, nor indeed served in the Cabinet, but that apart he was as experienced as any member of his party and generation could be. Any serious study of his career before 1905 should dispel the notion that he was summoned from his estates to the Foreign Office, at the call of duty, with nothing to aid him but his Roman nose. His previous biographer, feeling it necessary to excuse his lack of travel, stressed that he never saw himself as the destined successor of Salisbury and Lansdowne, but this too is an

K

oversimplification. Asquith and Haldane certainly thought of him as a future Liberal Foreign Secretary. As for Grey himself, while he frequently expressed doubts about politics as a whole, he assumed that if he were to come into a Government it would be at the Foreign Office, or possibly the Colonial Office. After 1895, during the years of Opposition, he expressed his views on most major domestic issues, but he was regarded as a foreign-affairs 'expert' and consulted as such, though not systematically, by Harcourt, Morley and Campbell-Bannerman. It was in this capacity that he was invited to join the Co-Efficients. The divisions which rent the party during the Boer War quite naturally meant that sections of the party which rejected his 'Imperialism' were loath to credit him with any standing as a foreign-affairs spokesman. His private comments and public statements in these years only gain authority in retrospect. Even here, however, the position is ambiguous. It does not necessarily follow that because Liberals were quarrelling among themselves on imperial or colonial questions, they were also doing so, or were doing so in the same groups, when it came to foreign policy. Preoccupied by the imperial war and its aftermath, it is indeed difficult to detect the existence of a Liberal foreign policy at all from 1899 to 1905. As late as the spring of 1903, Asquith was still rejecting the notion of 'conferences between colleagues', on the grounds that it was wrong to 'cut the knots with a knife'.[5] These were hardly circumstances for the formulation of a Liberal foreign policy. Thus, despite his lack of official position, it is tempting to believe that Grey's scattered private and public thoughts on foreign policy, unsystematic though they were, could not be exceeded in their scope by any other leading Liberal with the possible exception of James Bryce.

These years, 1899 to 1905, were of great importance for Britain's international position. Whether or not 'splendid isolation' ever existed in its full sense, there was a feeling that it would have to cease, for Britain's position seemed overexposed. While, on one level, it was possible to regard the victory in the Boer War as a great feat by a United Empire, it was also possible to see the degree to which the war had left Britain vulnerable. Although there still remained a strong traditional opposition to the conclusion of treaties of alliance, the break was near. It became increasingly clear that some support was needed in the Far East against the advance of Russia. Soundings took place initially with Germany, but the Germans were not willing to antagonize Russia in Europe for the sake of their relatively small interests in China.[6] Despite initial inhibitions, in the absence of the United States, Japan was the obvious power to deal with. An alliance with Japan was finally concluded at the end of January 1902. It provided for British neutrality in the event of a war between Japan and one power (i.e. Russia) or British belligerency if Japan went to war with two hostile powers (i.e. Russia and France). A secret article provided for the maintenance of some British naval presence in Far Eastern waters. In terms of the commitment undertaken, this treaty was a major development in British foreign policy, although at the time many looked upon it as a local Far Eastern agreement without wider significance. In the Commons the debate on the treaty was surprisingly limited. Harcourt and Campbell-Bannerman both doubted whether the step was necessary and regretted the restriction on British freedom, but took their opposition no further. In his speech in the Commons Grey welcomed the agreement in stronger terms than either of his colleagues and spoke of Japan becoming Britain's partner.[7]

The Anglo-Japanese agreement was a much more limited and convenient response to the danger of Russian expansion than an Anglo-German agreement would have been. The idea of an Anglo-German alliance had been mooted both in 1898 and in 1901, but nothing was achieved. In his speech at Leicester on 30 November 1899, Chamberlain talked of the 'natural alliance' between 'the Teutonic race and the two branches of the Anglo-Saxon race', but felt that a formal alliance might not be necessary so long as there was an alliance in the minds of statesmen. The speech caused a sensation—even more so when Bülow declared that Germany did not depend on British goodwill and that she would not stand aside 'while others pick the plums out of the cake'. The idea lapsed, at least for the time being. Grey thought the speech clumsy and inept —Chamberlain 'really must be kept out of foreign politics or he will make everything impossible, even friendship with America'. Secondly, he strongly opposed a German alliance both because, like Salisbury, he did not believe an alliance was necessary and also because he disliked the methods of German diplomacy. In any case, he believed that German public opinion was strongly anti-British.[8]

Grey certainly held that a triple alliance between the United States, Britain and Germany was an absurdity, but close relations between the United States and Britain were vital. Britain would have to accommodate herself to the world role the United States was beginning to assume. Grey therefore allowed himself to comment on the Spanish-American war of 1898 that the struggle on which the

United States was engaged was one 'to stir up our blood, and makes us conscious of the ties of language, origin, and race'.[9] Despite the rhetoric, he was conscious that the Anglo-American relationship 'was consummated largely by a succession of British surrenders'.[10] Writing to Andrew Carnegie, the peaceful millionaire, in October 1901, Grey stated: 'I have always felt that it was folly for us to argue about the Monroe Doctrine. The Monroe Doctrine is, whatever the United States says it is, and what we have to consider is how far we can meet it.' The Isthmian canal question was a case in point. Under the old Clayton–Bulwer treaty of 1850 Britain had a large stake in the prospective Isthmian canal. Fifty years later Grey had to admit that the interests of the two countries 'are really nothing like equal. It is true that with our great mass of shipping and far ranging trade we are interested in the question, but the United States have a political and strategic interest in it which is far greater.' He therefore concluded that both British sentiments and British interests were involved 'in growing attachment politically to the United States. We should look now upon a quarrel between them and us with the same horror that we should upon civil war.' Canadian questions were the only ones likely to present real difficulties, for Canada had her own sentiments and feelings.[11] There were indeed a number of contentious Canadian-American questions. Opinion in Ottawa still rankled at the British part in the arbitration of certain disputed territory to the United States. Grey admitted in 1903 that 'if the U.S. Govt. had met the Alaska question with a simple defiance [it] is a very awkward one [question] and a real one. If the U.S. Govt. choose, they can make a great difficulty between us & Canada by picking quarrels with Canada, which we should be reluctant to fight for.' All he could suggest was 'it should be our care not to predispose the U.S. Govt. to do this'.[12]

Grey therefore anticipated no danger from across the Atlantic, though he masked British decline in rather flabby sentiment. The dangers he did apprehend came chiefly from Europe and European rivalry elsewhere in the world. He had welcomed the Anglo-Japanese alliance as a safeguard against Russia, but was not Russophobe. It was the Triple Alliance that gave him most concern. When, in 1902, he heard the news that Italy, despite her continuing membership of the Triple Alliance, had come to an arrangement with France, he was delighted, 'because it makes it possible for us to get on good terms with France too, which is much better than clutching at the skirts of the Triple Alliance, considering the feeling of the Germans about us'. He told Herbert Gladstone that he had no wish to attack the Government on this matter and was going off to York on railway business, commenting: 'The front bench has so many ex-F.O. under secs that I am sure I can be spared'—an indication of his ambiguous position in relation to foreign affairs.[13] He expressed himself more fully about Germany in a private letter to Henry Newbolt in January 1903. They had been talking about Kipling, and Grey confessed that he 'always sets my teeth on edge, but Kipling apart I have come to think that Germany is our worst enemy & our greatest danger. I do not doubt that there are many Germans well disposed to us, but they are a minority; and the majority dislike us so intensely that the friendship of their Emperor or their Government cannot be really useful to us. As a matter of fact the German Government has behaved very badly to us in China.' He admitted that it might be argued that bygones should be bygones. Even so, he continued, 'I believe the policy of Germany to be that of using us without helping us: keeping us isolated, that she may have us to fall back on. Close relations with Germany mean for us worse relations with the rest of the world especially with the U.S., France & Russia.' He wanted Britain 'to have closer relations, if possible, with France & Russia and I believe they are possible'. He admitted that things were being said in the press and elsewhere against Germany by Kipling and men of lesser talent, 'but in public affairs it seems that everything has to be overstated & put almost brutally, if it is to have any effect. This is one of the things that makes public life so distasteful. . . .' The repudiation of Kipling, he thought, 'must be left to those, who wish us to lean towards Germany & this I do not. . . .'[14]

Despite his tough attitude towards France at the time of the Fashoda crisis, it therefore comes as no surprise that he warmly endorsed Lansdowne's attempts to achieve a reconciliation. When the entente with France was concluded in 1904, Grey welcomed it in the Commons on the grounds that whereas Europe had seemed to be divided into two camps, the Triple and the Dual Alliances, there was now a tendency to obliterate the hard and fast lines between them. 'Italy has made her arrangements with France directly. Austria has made her own arrangements with Russia directly. And we in our turn have now taken part in making a sort of arrangement with a view to creating greater frankness and friendliness between ourselves and France.'[15] Although there were some Liberal critics of the agreement, Grey's views were generally supported—even in circles which later turned against him.[16] On this question he broke directly with Rosebery, the most distinguished critic of the agreement. Writing in August 1905, Grey felt 'more and more that Rosebery is wrong about Germany, and I feel it so strongly that if any government drags us back into the German net I will oppose it openly at all costs'.[17] But at the same time he deplored the tone of the anti-German campaign in some sections of the British press. It is therefore clear that for years before taking office, Grey feared that if French independence were destroyed, British chances of opposing German hegemony in Europe were slight.

The Russo-Japanese war broke out in February 1904 and continued until the Treaty of Portsmouth in September 1905. Grey seems not to have shared the anxieties of those Liberals who feared that Britain would be drawn into the conflict.[18] Nevertheless, the war led to a fresh negotiation of the alliance, and speaking at the end of May 1905, Grey pronounced in favour of renewing it. When the treaty was published as a parliamentary paper on 26 September, there was a lively correspondence between Campbell-Bannerman, Morley, Ripon, Spencer and Asquith on the Liberal attitude. They were all uneasy and it is clear that the main worry was the impact on India: 'I think it objectionable', Spencer wrote, 'that we should allow the idea to exist that we cannot defend India ourselves, & also it may lead to difficulties with our native population there. . . .'[19] Grey sent his views to Asquith: 'I don't object to the Anglo-Japanese agreement, unless the Indian part will have a bad effect on native opinion in India. . . . If we are to run the risk of having to go to war on behalf of Japan in the Far East, there should be some corresponding risk undertaken by her on behalf of us. To make it quite clear that the alliance is defensive we must renounce any forward designs beyond the Indian frontier & our pre-existing obligations to Afghanistan. I have never liked the latter, but it is an old story & we can't back out of it now.'[20] A year earlier he had been perturbed by the progress of the British mission to Tibet, writing that it was 'the old story—we magnify the reasons for interfering & belittle the consequences of interference'.[21] On these terms he welcomed the renewed and extended agreement with less reservation than some of his colleagues.[22]

Late in October 1905, when the break-up of the Government seemed imminent, Grey made a major speech on foreign affairs, collecting his ideas together. Hoping for wide publicity, he wrote in advance to Spender, of the *Westminster Gazette*. He feared that 'the impression has been spread abroad with some success by those interested in spreading it, that a Liberal Government would unsettle the understanding with France in order to make it up to Germany'. He was going to fight this, for 'I think we are running a real risk of losing France & not gaining Germany, who won't want us, if she can detach France from us'.[23] In his speech he stressed three cardinal aspects of British foreign policy which the Liberal Party would not change. The first was friendship with the United States, the second was the Anglo-Japanese agreement and the third the Anglo-French entente. As regards the latter, although there had been some difficulties since signature, there would have been more serious ones if no agreement had existed. A Liberal Government would make new friendships but 'you can never make a new friendship which is worth having by backing out of an old one'. The estrangement between Britain and Russia, he believed, was not rooted in the present, but solely in the past, and patient work by both Governments could improve matters. As regards Germany, he did not believe that the Governments could do much, since the antagonism went deep into the press and public opinion of both countries. He suggested that matters could improve on condition that 'the relations of Germany with France on all matters which come under the French Agreement should be fair and good also'. Finally, he stressed the need for continuity in foreign policy in a democracy: 'I wish at the present moment to emphasise the fact that the friendship of the people of this country is as sure and as well worth having as that of any monarch or autocratic government in the world.'[24]

Whether or not Grey consulted other Liberal leaders before making this speech, most of them would have agreed with its contents. Grey's anxieties about Germany were more pronounced than most of his colleagues, but even Bryce, who started with the hope that 'if ever we come in we may succeed in improving relations with Germany', admitted that 'between the vicious nagging and misrepresentation we may expect from our own Jingo press and the frequently rude aggressiveness of the German Government this may prove to be a difficult task'.[25] Campbell-Bannerman had something of a shock from a conversation with the King at Marienbad in August, reporting to Spencer: 'He has great apprehensions of war between France & Germany, & in that event what should we do? He discussed the personal relations of the Royal families & also the sentiments of the peoples: the growth of the G. navy etc. War between ourselves & G. deplorable but might be inevitable.'[26] Sir Henry deprecated the possibility—'the two nations, apart from military & ruling class & press have no desire to quarrel'. Nevertheless, Campbell-Bannerman needed some advice and was relieved to hear from Spencer that he saw 'no cause for immediate alarm as to German relations'. He suspected that the King's use of the word 'probability' was under the inspiration of 'our friend "Jack" [Fisher] who is very bellicose and who is the worst possible counsellor on anything, at least beyond his métier'.[27] From these remarks in September 1905 one might conclude that he would not readily countenance any immediate steps on the premise of likely war, though he remained firmly attached to the French agreement. At a different level, Liberal commentators, like Grey's friend Herbert Paul, were anxious to stress the importance of this entente: 'England and France standing together', he wrote in the *Nineteenth Century* for November, 'are at this moment the best security for the peace of Europe, and French sympathies can only be retained if both parties in England show themselves equally anxious to retain it'.[28] Spender of the *Westminster Gazette*, digesting Grey's letter of 19 October, wrote two days later to Strachey of the *Spectator*, that the situation was more complicated than simply 'standing together'. He did not want to see a change of policy towards Germany, or any weakening of the agreement, but felt that 'a change of *feeling* is necessary even to the permanence of the understanding with France'. The French were very puzzling. They had implored him to attempt to tone down the anti-German remarks in the British press since the French public did not want to get involved in an Anglo-German quarrel. Then, when he had done something very modest in this direction, he had been warned to stop because the French public felt Britain was deserting them. French diplomacy with regard to Morocco had been inept and it was clear that Germany was going to pick a quarrel with France as a means of getting at Britain, and 'if the quarrel goes on the French will bye and bye ask whether the understanding with us is worth the practical inconvenience of this friction'. In this triangular relationship, Spender concluded, 'we can't live on this razor's edge between doing too much and doing too little but shall infallibly topple over on one side or the other, unless feeling grows more stable'.[29] It was on this razor's edge that Grey was going to have to live for many years, and a few months before taking office he had a very fine apprehension of its sharpness.

The only general element in Grey's October speech at which some

Liberal opinion jibbed was the doctrine of continuity. There were always those Liberals, especially in the country, who wanted to see a distinctively Liberal foreign policy. But even if he could conceive what the enterprise meant, Grey had no wish, except incidentally, to advance the cause of 'world Liberalism'. He believed that 'the national interest' existed and it was the duty of both Tory and Liberal Governments to clarify and defend it. Together with his colleagues at the Indian and Colonial Offices, he controlled the external relations of the greatest Empire in the world. Opinions differed as to whether this giant was now a 'weary Titan'. Certainly Grey was against further expansion. 'I hope', he wrote to Herbert Samuel in 1902, 'that Africa is now so divided up that neither philanthropic nor political reasons will lead to our taking more of it. If that Continent has a commercial future we have secured that our share of it shall be a large one. Our business now is to develope what we have got, wisely and with discrimination.'[30] But did Britain have the energy, will and skill needed to accomplish this task? Already the relations between Britain and the self-governing colonies caused some difficulties, particularly—as in the case of Britain, Australia and the Anglo-Japanese alliance—when there appeared to be a conflict of interest. Paradoxically, for a reputed 'Imperialist' Grey by no means made the preservation of the British Empire his chief priority. He took little pains to conciliate growing colonial nationalism and adopted rather a 'take it or leave it' attitude. For example, when the Colonial Premiers came to London for their conference in 1903 he wrote: '. . . The object of bringing Colonial Premiers here is to keep in touch with Colonial opinion. Hitherto from our anxiety to conciliate them it has led rather to their ascendancy over us than to ours over them.'[31] The implication was that he would favour a more determined assertion of United Kingdom interests. This feeling was no doubt prompted by an apprehension of European dangers, but it also seems to coincide with a certain flagging of sentiment on his part after the Boer War.

To think of Britain as a European power involved not only a psychological adjustment but also a reassessment of her strategic posture. Deep changes of this kind are, however, given a certain bogus clarity by historians in retrospect. While Grey seemed to be moving in a 'European' direction, in 1903 he was still a big-navy supporter. He felt Britain was spending too much on the armed services 'because we are spending too much on the Army'. Even if it were necessary to spend as much, 'we should be in an infinitely stronger position if we were spending two-thirds of that on the Navy and one-third on the Army, instead of spending on each of them equally'. This was because 'if your Navy is strong, your position is secure, and if you unfortunately become involved in a war, you have time to develop your striking force, and meanwhile you are safe from the attacks of your enemy. . . .'[32] In Opposition, he gave strong support to Fisher's naval reforms—even chairing a committee of inquiry into the best method of manning the new navy —and approved the plans for concentrating the fleets.[33] Changes in the structure of the army, central government, higher education, especially technical education, were all included in the general programme of 'Efficiency' which the Liberal Imperialists advocated. The claim of the Liberal League, Grey wrote, 'to a share in Patriotism & Efficiency is a reply to the Tory claim of a monopoly of these'.[34] He took part in the debates on army reform and even gained the praise of L. S. Amery for his efforts. While it would be pretentious to claim that Grey was in any sense a military authority, he took a greater interest in such matters than he has been sometimes credited with.[35] Sir Edward also took a more favourable attitude than did leading Liberals of the old generation to Balfour's proposals for a Committee of Defence. While Campbell-Bannerman was anxiously writing to Spencer in March 1903: 'I shall be in the House tomorrow as A. J. B. is to explain the new Cabinet Council of Defence . . . I confess I do not like making soldiers & sailors actually *members* of the Council', Grey's fears were that nothing would come of the project. 'Far be it from me to say I have no hopes that this new Council of Defence may do better,' he said publicly in the same month, 'but at present it is only in the chrysalis stage, and we cannot be expected to raise shouts of exultation till we see the results of it. . . .'[36] When Balfour established the Committee of Imperial Defence in 1904 with service chiefs and political heads meeting together to formulate plans for imperial and home defence, Grey gave general approval.[37] All of these moves were made in response to something of a panic about Britain's economic and military capacity. In matters of trade, Grey believed 'foreign competition is becoming more real: it used to be a bogey, but other nations have been creeping up to us and we shall not be able to maintain the lead, if we waste our power'.[38]

Most clever people tend to assume that cleverness is the one thing needful, but the Foreign Secretary had to operate within a bureaucratic and a political system where other personal attributes—such as ability to listen to an argument or to take a decision—have equal if not greater significance. He had to sit in a Cabinet which might be preoccupied by domestic problems remote from his chief concern, but he could not ignore them, for his foreign policy depended on the success of the Government as a whole. Only in a very limited sense, therefore, is it possible to argue that Grey was solely concerned with 'foreign affairs'. Looked at from Grey's vantage point, the Cabinet did not seem likely to pose too many problems. His relationship with Campbell-Bannerman, once the awkwardness of the immediate past rubbed off, was not likely to prove too contentious. Although the Prime Minister would naturally be concerned in the major issues of policy, he was not in fact especially interested in foreign affairs and unlikely to interfere extensively. Grey would have some dealings with Lord Ripon, the Lord Privy Seal, who at seventy-nine seasoned the Cabinet with experience and Roman Catholicism. Ripon had sided with Campbell-Bannerman during the South African war, but was personally well-disposed to Sir Edward, having served in government with his grandfather. The Foreign Secretary would also come into contact with Morley on matters where the defence of India was closely related to other questions of general foreign policy. Relations with Morley, he must have supposed, would be unpredictable. Morley, at sixty-eight, was something of an old nanny, though periodically inclined to regard Grey as one of the children who had come on well under his care. However, he could be difficult and there was no telling what might happen when a notionally 'anti-Imperialist' was made Secretary for India. Grey would also have to collaborate on some issues with the Colonial Secretary, Lord Elgin, a man in his late fifties, but he was not likely to regard him as a very formidable figure. He might well receive more pertinent communications, certainly lengthier ones, from Elgin's under-secretary in the Commons, the thirty-two-year-old Winston Churchill. Initially, Grey delighted in Churchill's company, writing to Dorothy after the latter's election victory, 'Happy and brilliant Winston'. Besides Haldane at the War Office, he was also on friendly terms with the First Lord of the Admiralty, Lord Tweedmouth. The Greys had spent a number of enjoyable holidays at his wife's highland lodge, Guisachan, where they fished while Haldane wrote his Gifford lectures. As Chief Whip, Herbert Gladstone had known as much about the internal situation of the party as anyone, but he was to find it quite difficult enough to master the Home Office without worrying about other matters. Grey could rely on his solid political relations with Asquith to negotiate any difficulties with the Treasury. Bryce was likely to find Ireland absorbing enough but Lloyd George, at the Board of Trade, might develop the unfortunate idea that 'trade' gave him an entrée wherever he chose. The other domestic ministers were not likely to stir far beyond their patches. He found John Burns's love of London quite extraordinary, while the Postmaster-General, Sydney Buxton, was his oldest fishing friend. He was also on good terms with junior ministers like Walter Runciman and Herbert Samuel. As his own under-secretary in the Commons he had Lord Edmond Fitzmaurice, the younger brother of the previous Unionist Foreign Secretary, Lord Lansdowne. Since, however, for the first time since 1868 the Foreign Secretary was himself in the Commons, the office was less significant than when Grey himself held it a decade earlier. Apart from Bryce's appointment to the Washington Embassy in 1907, with Birrell substituting for him in Ireland, the only Cabinet changes throughout the Campbell-Bannerman ministry were the promotion of McKenna to replace Birrell and the elevation of the First Commissioner for Works, L. Harcourt.

As regards the bureaucracy, the Foreign Office was of course the only department of state with which Grey was familiar, but in the decade since he had left, it too was changing. Sir Thomas Sanderson, who had become Permanent Under-Secretary in 1894, was on the point of retiring and with him went many traditions. He has been called the 'last great super-clerk' and when Salisbury was in his prime had not considered it his place to advise his minister, except on the rare occasions when he was specifically asked. But, with age, Salisbury's general scorn for bureaucracies had to be tempered and a change in their relationship began. At the same time, there was also some demand for a change in the system whereby intelligent men spent the greater part of their day performing clerical functions which others, less gifted, could have managed. Perhaps the most able of Sanderson's assistants was Francis Bertie, who became ambassador to France in 1905 and did everything he was instructed, and more, to strengthen the entente with France. Bertie's suspicions of Germany were shared in general by some of the younger able men, like Louis Mallet and William Tyrrell of the Foreign Office, and Charles Hardinge and Reginald Lister of the Diplomatic Service—the two at this stage being distinct institutions. These men all regarded the Liberal Party with some suspicion and feared that it might neglect what they considered the 'German threat'. From their point of view, Grey was probably as good an appointment as they could have hoped for. In the summer of 1905, Lansdowne appointed Hardinge to succeed Sanderson. Hardinge had last-minute doubts on the score of expense. Mallet urged Bertie to overcome his friend's hesitation, writing: 'Everyone hopes he will come here. There is much to be done in the way of reorganization and the importance of having someone who will keep the Liberals straight . . . is overwhelming.'[39]

Grey's arrival at the Foreign Office therefore coincided with the advent of a pushing, vigorous new Permanent Under-Secretary with different ideas about his function from those of his predecessor. He was going to establish a policy-making bureaucracy rather than preside over a sophisticated aristocratic clerical agency. Hardinge was but four years older than Grey and had served in a wide variety of embassies as well as at the Foreign Office itself. He was very familiar with the European diplomatic scene and was also highly thought of at Court. He also thought highly of himself. The relationship, therefore, was much more likely to be one between equals than of master and servant. Within a few months, Hardinge had secured the appointment of Mallet, since described as the most violent of the anti-Germans, as Grey's private secretary.[40] In addition, there was Eyre Crowe, the brilliant son of a German mother who played a leading role in the reform of the Foreign Office and from 1906 to 1912 served as senior clerk in the Western Department, becoming thereby 'the key anti-German figure in the Grey stable'.

In the excitement of the discovery that these men of the new model Foreign Office both had views of their own and expressed them to each other, there has been an increasing tendency to see Grey as a cypher for their purposes. The relationship between Grey and his officials is not easy to pin down. The seeker after 'influence' is apt to find the ground submerging under him. Hosts of 'key decision makers' can be observed in their strategic positions, but on close examination their 'decisions' often seem to vanish. Grey was efficient in his office. Writing to Churchill in December 1905, Lord Hugh Cecil warned him that 'gaseous' success—shining as a firework on platform and in the House—was all very well 'but the further steps require a reputation as a good administrator, a skilled & industrious official—the sort of reputation Edward Grey eminently has. . . .'[41] The problem is further complicated by Grey's manner and method. He did not often pronounce in isolation, but liked to hear and have a full expression of views, however contentious they were. This style gave many men the feeling that when Grey took action on lines which they had urged, they caused it. But it is dubious to infer that Grey only had a mind of his own when in some instances, it can be shown that he disagreed with advice from leading officials. Even before coming into office, he was well aware that certain officials were known to have 'anti-German' reputations and was quite capable of making allowances. Besides, whether they were right or wrong, he did not need them to tell him to keep a wary eye on Germany.

The immediate situation in December 1905 and January 1906 was one of hectic confusion. Although Sir Matthew Ridley had remained a director of the N.E.R. while Home Secretary in a Conservative Government, Grey resigned his chairmanship in accordance with his previous agreement. As he wrote to his cousin Albert, things were in a whirl and there was no chance of a Christmas holiday with 'an active opponent in my constituency & I have got to get hold of the biggest office in the Empire & fight a contested election simultaneously between now and the end of January. It's never been done before under modern conditions & I may not survive it.'[42] The only consolation was that Dorothy was feeling fitter than she had done for nine years—although that was not saying very much. She had gone through a phase of dreading the Foreign Office, writing to a friend, 'This last fortnight has been quite the most horrid that we have ever had, and it is a great grief to both of us that E. is in a Govt. without Rosebery. We shan't be able to judge for a long time whether he was right to go in or not, but as he has, I am very glad he has work which interests him so much. There is a lot of flummery about the Foreign Office, and I try not to think about how badly I shall do my small part of the work, but I shall try very hard. . . .'[43]

The contest in Berwick seemed hard going. Grey told the Prime Minister that he was arranging to be in London for the first three working days of every week and to spend the other three in the constituency. Although Foreign Secretary, foreign affairs played no part in his campaign. Along with most Liberals, the defence of Free Trade was his main platform but he also stressed the need for expanded Higher Education and further land reform. In this election, as usual, different constituencies polled on different days

The boroughs declared first and showed substantial swings to the Liberals—amongst those defeated were Balfour and his brother. On 19 January, Grey wrote to Campbell-Bannerman in a curiously detached way: 'The elections are wonderful & give much cause for reflection: the future will be interesting.'[44] When his own poll was declared on 25 January, Grey achieved his greatest electoral success as Member for Berwick. For the first time he topped 5,000 votes and had a majority of 2,240. For the first time, a Tory candidate, on this occasion the subsequent Tory Minister, Thomas Inskip, failed to achieve 3,000 votes. When the final results were declared, the full extent of the Unionist defeat could be seen. There were 377 Liberals, 83 Irish Nationalist and 53 Labour and on the other side 132 Conservatives and 25 Liberal Unionists. The Government thus had an absolute majority of 84 and all seemed set for an outstanding term of office.

8

Crises and Consolidation, 1905-8

Each day the Foreign Secretary has to adjust his policy. All over the world, events of importance occur which require analysis and decision. A man may stare in vain at the evidence and search for the vital link between disparate pieces of information. Images jostle in the mind at various levels of explanation. In the world of 1905, men with different values and social systems coexisted uneasily together. Yet, knowing the disaster of 1914, it is impossible to view the years in between with complete detachment. In writing about international relations, the historian must press the ongoing flow of contact and communication into assimilable, and no doubt inadequate, compartments. He talks of abstractions like 'Anglo-American relations' or 'naval races', isolating and particularizing, yet trying to preserve an awareness of the underlying interconnexions. While we parcel problems into convenient categories, it is important to remember that this pattern emerges only with the passage of time.

Grey came into office at a time of crisis. He had no time to ponder deeply on his principles or play himself in gently. On 31 March 1905, the German Kaiser had chosen to visit Tangier. It was widely supposed that his purpose was to warn France that her peaceful penetration into Morocco had not gone unnoticed. He revealed that Germany had great and growing interests in the area and these could only be preserved if its independence was respected. France and Britain had, however, found it very difficult to respect the independence of Islamic states on the Mediterranean littoral, partly because it was difficult to see what the phrase could mean. It seemed inevitable that such states could not survive the impact of Europe. The conventional Liberal hope was instead that Germany should get a fair share. Even here there were exceptions, for the

Radical journal, *The Speaker*, deplored German attempts to 'foment resistance to one of the most justifiable of all cases of moral pressure on a backward state'.[1] It was another matter, however, if the real objective of German policy was to disrupt the Anglo-French entente. The German demand for an international conference caused a crisis in France and the resignation of the Foreign Minister, Delcassé, in June 1905. Initially, British observers were inclined to believe that the Germans, having achieved this triumph, would be inclined to let the matter drop, since the French Prime Minister, Rouvier, would be amenable. There were, however, those in Germany who felt that there was an opportunity for repairing relations with Russia and disrupting her alliance with France. After all, what help had France been to the Russians in their war with Japan? In July 1905, in an unguarded moment on a yacht in the Baltic, the Kaiser was able to persuade the Tsar to sign a treaty, which would nullify the Dual Alliance. His ministers subsequently persuaded the Tsar to change his mind. Nevertheless, the Germans were not dispirited and seemed to sense that a major transformation of the European alliance system was within their grasp. Since Russia was pre-occupied by internal dissension, France was isolated and, when the Germans pressed, agreed to the conference. The difficulty was to see what Germany really wanted. It would have helped if the Germans themselves knew. On the one hand, the Chancellor, Bülow, seemed at times to want to settle the affair if he could obtain compensations from France elsewhere in Africa. Yet the French offers never seemed to be taken up. A great deal of speculation (both at the time and subsequently) centred on the intentions of Holstein, the so-called *éminence grise* of the German Foreign Office. Historians now seem to feel certain that Holstein would never have gone to war, but at the time it seemed plausible to contend that he wished to push France very far. It was known in Germany that the Anglo-French entente did not contain a provision for military co-operation. The notion of striking while France was demoralized and Russia prostrate was at least a matter for speculation. Policy, therefore, was fluid and waited on events.[2]

The crisis could not have come at a worse moment for Grey. The Government was in office, but had not been confirmed in power. There were some who believed that Grey, as a follower of Rosebery, might therefore accept a consolidation of German influence over France. Grey had no such intentions and recognized that the forthcoming conference would be 'difficult if not critical'. The

L

French were very anxious to know whether they might hope for any British assistance, other than diplomatic and verbal. In this respect, the Prime Minister's statement on 21 December that the entente would be maintained did not clarify the position. Grey's first steps were therefore precautionary. He listened to ideas for concessions to Germany and at the same time counselled close contact with France. This was all the more necessary because the French oscillated between far-reaching concession and stern intransigence. The Greys then left town to spend a sentimental Christmas with Rosebery where there was a good squash court, an expert to play with, Madeira to restore one, and not too much holly.

Christmas goodwill did not extend to the international scene. Grey received a letter from Repington, the military correspondent of *The Times*, telling of his conversations with the French military attaché, Huguet, who expressed concern about British intentions. Cambon, the French Ambassador, had been expressing similar anxieties to the King, and the C.I.D. was considering possible British action in the event of the conference failing. Grey replied to Repington on 30 December that he stood by anything which Lord Lansdowne had said to the French. But had Lansdowne said anything to encourage military and naval conversations with France? Grey himself professed later to believe that talks had started, but this opinion has been vigorously challenged. A recent author suggests that on this question 'Grey . . . had a curious talent for convincing himself that what he wanted to believe really was the truth'.[3] Lansdowne himself recollected that in his final months 'military and naval experts got together and talked about possible schemes of co-operation as was their business, and talked indiscreetly as they always do'. General Grierson, the Director of Military Intelligence, made a tour of the Franco-Belgian frontier in March 1905 and, to judge from his later capacity for indiscretion, his accompanying French colleagues must have formed a shrewd impression of his purpose. Equally, although Fisher, the First Sea Lord, always opposed consultations with France for fear that this might commit him to military co-operation on French soil, in preference to his own plan for a raid on Schleswig-Holstein, it is likely that he dropped large hints about his willingness to 'have a go'—Delcassé at least seems to have known of them. It therefore seems plausible that 'while there was no *joint* Anglo-French attempt to concert strategy against Germany before Delcassé's resignation, there was nonetheless a series of unilateral declarations of support made to the French by English service chiefs'.[4] While Lansdowne naturally played down their significance, the French emphasized them. In any case, in his first fortnight of office, amidst all his other concerns, Grey was poorly placed to conduct an elaborate inquiry into the subtle differences between 'talks about talks', official conversations, unofficial but authorized talks, indiscretion officially connived at and sheer indiscretion. Probably correctly, he believed that 'something' had been said to encourage the French. His duty now was to state the position clearly.

It must already have become clear to officials and soldiers with whom Grey talked that he attached more importance to the entente as an end in itself than Lansdowne had done. On 3 January, he warned the German Ambassador that in the event of war between Germany and France, public feeling might be such that Britain could not remain neutral. He emphasized that if the conference went well, the entente would not be used to prejudice German interests. Meanwhile, the secretary of the C.I.D., Sir George Clarke, continued his investigations into the military situation and concluded that any military co-operation, if undertaken at the outset, should take the form of direct participation in the defence of the French frontier.[5] On 8 January, Grey wrote to Haldane, expressing his concern and asking him to have an answer ready if the Government were compelled by popular feeling, as he put it, to go to the aid of France. The following day Grey himself saw Clarke, who revealed his contacts with the French military attaché. Both men agreed that these 'unofficial' soundings should continue and that it was best not to inform the Prime Minister at this stage. He did not report this conversation when, on the same day, he sent his summary of the situation to Campbell-Bannerman in Scotland. He regretted their lack of personal contact at such a delicate time, but stated that he had confined himself to diplomatic support for the French. The War Office, he added, ought to be ready to answer the question, 'What could they do if we had to take part against Germany, if for instance the neutrality of Belgium was violated?'[6] The following day, he had his first famous interview with Cambon, who spoke of the possibility of German aggression. Grey could only promise neutrality—'a benevolent neutrality if such a thing existed'. Cambon was not satisfied and urged that unofficial naval and military conversations should take place—'some communications had he believed already passed, and might he thought be continued'. Neither Government would be committed. In his own record, Grey wrote that he 'did not dissent from this view', although three days later he minuted, somewhat lamely, that 'I did not dissent but I reserved my opinion, because I did not know what they were.' He instructed that his dispatch to Bertie in Paris, recounting the conversation with Cambon, should not be sent to the Prime Minister, but retained for the time being in the department. Instead, he wrote a personal letter to Sir Henry, enclosing an abbreviated version of the conversation and omitting any reference to military discussions.[7] Meanwhile, Mallet urged Bertie to write a strong dispatch to Grey pointing out that if Britain could promise nothing more than simple neutrality in a war provoked by Germany, France might submit. This Bertie did.

Grey, however, had gone up to Northumberland to campaign. He met Haldane there and asked him for his views about the conversations. Haldane replied that there had been some 'general conversations' before his time, but none at the scientific General Staff level where they might be really useful. Such talks could, however, be arranged and, on his own account, Haldane undertook to go to London and consult with the Prime Minister. 'This I did', he wrote, 'and had a full talk with him a few days later.'[8] Although in his memoirs Haldane claims that both Grey and himself were agreed that Campbell-Bannerman should first be consulted, in fact he was not. Sir Henry was not in London to have the conversation with Haldane approving the military talks. On 15 January, Grey wrote to Bertie that the Prime Minister had said that he could not be in London before 25 January. The letter continued that it was Haldane who 'had authorized me to say that these communications might proceed between the French Military Attaché and General Grierson direct'. There is no mention of any higher approval.[9] The day before the Algeciras conference opened on 16 January, the military conversations were put on an 'official' footing and on the 17th, Haldane reported that they were under way.[10] The British seemed prepared to send an army of eighty to a hundred thousand men to the continent to fight alongside France. Grey and Haldane had moved adroitly to gain their point before the Prime Minister knew of the position. Grey was convinced by his inquiries that British troops 'won't save France unless she can save herself. We can protect ourselves for we are more supreme at sea than we have ever been.' He still disliked promising support in advance for that would transform the entente into an alliance 'and alliances, especially continental alliances are not in accordance with our traditions'.

While detesting 'the idea of another war now' he wrote unequivocally to Bertie that 'if France is let in for a war with Germany arising out of our agreement with her about Morocco, we cannot stand aside, but must take part with France'.[11] However, he assumed that in the last resort Germany would back down—an assumption that the Germans made about Britain. In all the controversy over the military conversations, it is important to remember that, a few years earlier, Grey had been a 'blue water' man and not an advocate of military expansion or an expeditionary force.

The details of the crisis in Anglo-French relations were, at this stage, quite unknown to the majority of the Cabinet. On 19 January, Grey wrote requesting an interview with the Prime Minister when both men were back in London. The matter was 'difficult and delicate' and the French wanted a reply by the end of the month. He reported that the prospects for the conference looked better, though 'evasion of difficulties' rather than a settlement seemed the best that could be expected. Asquith, he said, had been shown 'what had passed' and he would discuss matters with Lord Ripon.[12] The Prime Minister was in no hurry to return from Scotland but inquired whether Grey wanted the answer to the French confirmed by the Cabinet before it was sent. Sir Edward replied that he would rather not commit himself before they had discussed the matter.[13] Grey talked with Ripon on 22 January, and they must have mentioned the question of a closer alliance with France, although not, it seems, the status of Belgium.[14] Ripon was clearly against a military commitment, having written to the under-secretary, Fitzmaurice, that if the conference broke down and serious trouble with Germany arose 'and we decline, as I think we ought to decline, to go farther than diplomacy will reach, I cannot but fear a cry of "perfide Albion" and a destruction of the present friendship between the two nations'. The situation required great wariness 'but we may trust Grey for that'.[15]

Whatever criticism is levelled against Grey for his failure to bring the matter to the Cabinet, the chief responsibility must rest with the Prime Minister. On 27 January, Clarke gave Campbell-Bannerman a report and found him 'not at all inclined to be alarmed at what I told him we had done'.[16] Grey then joined the Prime Minister at Windsor for the week-end, when the subject must have been discussed. Cambon, writing on 1 February, believed that the two men, together with the King, agreed to keep silent and not inform the Cabinet.[17] Grey himself never made any such admission. He subsequently agreed that he ought to have brought the matter to the attention of his colleagues at their meeting on 31 January and it is reasonable to suppose, despite later denials on his part, that he expected some opposition.[18] Not unnaturally, he never advanced this reason himself. In his memoirs, he explained that Ministers were hurrying about the country and difficult to contact—which was true enough earlier in January, but not of the first Cabinet meeting at the end of the month. He also contended that the conversations were technical and non-binding, and therefore not the concern of the Cabinet as a whole. This contention has been severely dealt with: '. . . if Grey thought they were not important enough to go to the Cabinet, then he was not fit to be Foreign Secretary'.[19] If this be true, so is it *a fortiori* of the Prime Minister. After all, Sir Henry had previous departmental experience at the War Office and he of all people should have been suspicious of such an argument. But accept it he did (or at least he appeared to) even if he sensed a danger of creating an 'honourable undertaking' to France. If Cambon's purported 'revelation' is indeed correct—and it would be interesting to discover his source of information—Sir Henry's attitude still remains to be explained. Painted as the victim of a Grey–Haldane conspiracy, he has indeed been let off too lightly. He had only himself to blame for staying in Scotland, remote from discussion, at a time of serious international crisis. Some believe that his acquiescence in the talks was against his own better judgment and dictated by a concern for the precariously established unity of the party. This explanation is not convincing. Of course he wanted to keep the party together, but he was in a position to state on what terms. Far from Grey being in the Cabinet as a representative of a party 'too strong for the Prime Minister to defy', he had just trounced this section in no uncertain fashion.[20] Haldane was in the Cabinet by special favour, while Grey knew that he had not been considered indispensable. The election results, now available, had strengthened the 'Centre' of the party against the 'Imperialist' wing. Nor was the French issue one on which Grey and Haldane could raise the rather battered banner of Rosebery in revolt. With all these factors in his favour, there was absolutely no cause for the Prime Minister to give in to Grey if he seriously disagreed with him. If the Prime Minister and Ripon actually opposed the military conversations, and were not merely understandably anxious about them, they should have raised the subject in Cabinet where, according at least to historians, they would have received much support.

Certainly, the episode shows Grey in a determined mood, keen to establish his authority in his domain from the outset and, aided by a somewhat lazy Prime Minister, not beyond some sharp practice for the purpose. However, the notion that this conception of the relations between Foreign Secretary and the Cabinet was 'new' is somewhat forced. And the view that 'more than ever before', foreign policy fell into the control of one man, is hyperbole. In this particular instance, at a time of serious crisis, in peculiar circumstances, leading members of the Government with departments involved took decisions which they did not communicate to their colleagues. No doubt the information should have been revealed as soon as the immediate crisis was past—though it is possible to suggest that they would have been amazed if they could have realized what great weight some historians have placed upon the episode. Nevertheless, there is something acutely docile about the attitude of those who did not know, but who later, as will be seen, complained loud and long of being kept in ignorance. Might it not have occurred to them to ask questions? If they had done so, it is unlikely that they would have been given a direct lie. Indeed, their complaint was that they had not been informed, not that they had been misinformed. Fitzmaurice later claimed that if no one else told the Lord Chancellor, Loreburn—one of the most vehement subsequent protesters—of the conversations with Cambon, then he did.[21] Haldane stated that the German Secret Service was aware of the talks within a matter of months, and he discussed the subject with the Kaiser in September 1906. Even journalists like Spender knew at an early stage, though Grey had not informed them.[22] The suspicion cannot be avoided that those at the time who did not know, did not especially wish to know.

Grey's crucial meeting with Cambon on 31 January followed the Cabinet meeting in the morning. The Foreign Secretary again stressed that conversations were now taking place officially and Germany had been warned that if she attacked France because of Morocco, British public feeling might be so aroused as to compel the Government to go to war. If Cambon wanted a more formal agreement, Grey was sure his colleagues would want to have more say in French Moroccan policy. The inference was clear. Nevertheless, the French Ambassador pressed for an assurance, which Grey declined to give. If any change was made, it would turn the entente into an alliance, and Grey could not authorize this himself—thereby hinting that there might be difficulties in the Cabinet if a formal proposal were brought before it. It was best to leave matters where they stood. Sir Edward reiterated his personal opinion that Britain would not fight to give France Morocco, but she would go to war to save the entente. Sanderson, performing his last official act, added that if the Cabinet gave a pledge to assist, without mentioning the matter to Parliament, it was liable to impeachment if it tried to implement that pledge. The lesson was again clear. Cambon should be satisfied with what he had obtained and to press for more might endanger what had been achieved.[23] And, quite apart from Cabinet feeling, there is no evidence that Grey himself wanted a formal commitment.

Tension at the Algeciras conference did not abate.[24] Disagreement now centred on the control of the Moroccan police. France pressed for a control shared between herself and Spain, while Germany proposed various schemes to prevent this. The British delegate, Nicolson, resisted attempts early in February to persuade him to urge concessions on the French. Grey then wired to express his full support for a stand favourable to France. The breakdown of the conference now seemed likely and Grey cautiously tried to find a way out of the impasse. By 15 February he wrote to Nicolson suggesting that the French might make a concession on the State Bank, another vexed question, in return for German acquiescence in the police proposal—though he would not press the point. Criticized by the German Ambassador for his stand, Grey replied that Germany should be less obsessed about her political influence in Morocco and seek sound economic guarantees instead. He pointed out that Britain, with a much larger share of Moroccan trade than Germany, also wished to see the 'open door' preserved. These attempts to achieve a breakthrough failed. German proposals that a neutral Power should assume control were unacceptable to France and Hardinge urged Grey to continue giving her support. His chief contention was that 'if France is left in the lurch an agreement or alliance between France, Germany and Russia in the near future is certain'. The spectre of the Björko treaty lingered on. These comments were made on a memorandum drawn up by Grey himself on 20 February in which he argued that if war did break out between France and Germany, it would be very difficult for Britain to keep out. An expectation had arisen in France and if this were disappointed, 'the French will never forgive us'. On the other hand, the prospect of being involved in a European war was 'horrible', while to fight Germany at a moment of her own choosing would court disaster. 'An entente between Russia, France and ourselves would be absolutely secure', he wrote. 'If it is necessary to check Germany it could then be done.' On the assumption that the conference failed, he would urge France to make a great effort 'and if need be some sacrifice' to avoid war.[25] He had in mind the concession of a port or coaling station to Germany on the North African coast, and took steps to discover the naval view. This willingness did not please Mallet. Although Tweedmouth stated that the Navy would acquiesce if the general situation required it, Mallet believed that it would be interpreted in Germany as a sign of weakness. In making the entente, he believed, Britain was on the right road and Germany would not risk a war with the two Powers for some years to come, but to weaken French feeling might prove fatal. Grey then withdrew his suggestion on these grounds.[26]

It seemed, therefore, that the conference was doomed to collapse. All parties were considering how best they could pin responsibility for failure on their opponents. But at the end of February the first indications of German willingness to give way became apparent. On 3 March, France forced the issue by calling for the police question to be discussed in full conference and when only Austria and Morocco voted with Germany against the proposal, her weakness became apparent. Holstein's view that Germany would be able to gain territorial concessions from France, after the conference, in return for co-operation over Morocco, was discredited and he resigned several weeks later. The Austrians then advanced a compromise proposal whereby France or Spain, in proportion, would have exclusive control over every Moroccan port except Casablanca. This seemed the ideal formula, but the French remained unyielding. On 10 March, Grey wrote to Campbell-Bannerman that the French were showing a disposition 'not to accept the last German concession, which really gives them the substance. It will be most unfortunate if they do not come to an agreement now. . . . The Germans in effect climbed down & declared for peace.'[27] The French saw no reason for magnanimity and kept up the pressure on Grey as well as on Germany. They floated rumours that British willingness to accept the Austrian proposal showed that Britain and Germany had come to a private arrangement, and France was being left in the lurch. Grey now felt that France was being unreasonable, risking the substance for the shadow, but he was constantly cornered into making fresh declarations of support. Hardinge, and probably even Nicolson, demurred at fresh support in this instance, fearing that if the conference broke down because of the status of Casablanca, Britain would have to support whatever violent action France might take in consequence. Then President Roosevelt's mediation surprised the European Powers by appearing to believe that declarations in favour of Moroccan territorial integrity were meant literally. He seemed to want joint Franco-Spanish control in all ports as an obstacle to partition. Grey supported French objections to this proposal, describing a mixed force as 'unworkable'. In the end, by the terms of the General Act of Algeciras signed on 7 April, a mixed police force was to be stationed in Tangier and Algeciras under the command of a Swiss; France and Spain divided the policing of the other ports between them. The only consolation for Germany was the quasi-international presence in the two major ports which would give her a negotiating stake should Morocco be directly partitioned. It was a poor reward for so much effort. A diplomatic success, however, is often more embarrassing than a defeat, and so it was with Algeciras. Since the crisis followed so soon upon his coming into office, the Foreign Secretary had little alternative but to respond much as Lansdowne would probably have done. As the events developed, however, Grey found himself upholding the entente as the first principle of his foreign policy, but in so doing his freedom of manœuvre seemed severely restricted.

The conclusion of the first Moroccan crisis found Grey a sadder and more melancholy figure than when it began. On 1 February, after his interview with Cambon, Grey lunched in his room at the Foreign Office with John Morley. Later he went to a defence committee meeting. It was there that his private secretary brought a telegram to say that Dorothy had been thrown out of a carriage and was unconscious. She had gone for a drive along the lanes north of Fallodon and her horse shied. The head groom had warned her that the horse was in a highly nervous state and likely to bolt, but she had insisted. She was carried into the schoolhouse at Ellingham, still unconscious. Edward caught the evening train north and arrived in the small hours of 2 February. He knew at once that the situation was grave. In the morning he wrote to Haldane in deep distress that there was a chance, but only a chance, that Dorothy would recover. She had a fracture at the base of her skull. On his arrival, her left leg and arm were paralysed, but they were so no longer. The prolonged unconsciousness and suspense were dreadful. He asked that his man-servant should send up his tall hat, black overcoat and trousers. In the early hours of 4 February, she died, without regaining consciousness.[28] It was the second death to strike Edward within a year. In June 1905, his mother had died, when she was confidently expected to recover. Then he had written: 'The death of Mother brings mortality home to one more than anything I have known; it is like a landslide in my past. My life would not have been without hers and hers is gone.'[29] The death of his wife struck him even more sharply. A few days later, according to her wish, Dorothy was cremated at Darlington. After the short service, Mrs Creighton came to stay at Fallodon: 'My feeling is that I want just one friend by me to whom I can talk about Dorothy. I can do that to you & you more than anyone may give me help as to how to face going on alone.' To Haldane he wrote: 'We are companions in sorrow until life ends. I shall feel the need of friends, a thing I have never felt while I had her love every day. . . .' For a while, he shared a flat with Haldane in Whitehall Court and subsequently they both took houses in Queen Anne's Gate.[30]

There can be no doubt about the loss Grey suffered. Society had never been able to comprehend Dorothy since she had deliberately given it little chance. The great world meant nothing to her. Her books, few close friends and the quietness of the country were her pleasures. In public she seemed nervous and brittle. The way in which she secreted herself 'in the funny little hole where they lived in Grosvenor Road' was thought quite astonishing.[31] Even her close friends felt there was something sad in her neglect of her own family, in particular her blind old father.[32] In her last few years she became more relaxed and even attempted to overcome her dislike of the sight of children. Edward had never wished not to have an heir, but had not wavered in his devotion to her. Mrs Creighton, herself a widow, but also a mother, embarked on a memoir of Dorothy and to her Edward wrote: '. . . now you have the love between you & the children & can cherish it gratefully. I have none but even so feel no want of them; I have known enough & had enough to fill my life.'[33]

In the immediate aftermath, work was the great solace. He wrote to the Prime Minister offering his resignation, having no wish to attempt what he was not fit for, but adding 'for myself the best chance is to work & to begin at once; I shall try and if I find I haven't the strength I will give it up'.[34] A week later he was able to write to Herbert Paul: '. . . I am slowly feeling my way now; what there is I cannot tell yet, but it is not all pain, and death is not an end, and the memory of our great happiness, unimpaired to the end of her life, will not be denied a happiness of its own even now.'[35] On 17 February he was back at Fallodon for the week-end and feeling terribly lonely and depressed. A few days later he wrote: 'This week is being the worst I have had: & the struggle is very hard; the persistent absence of any wish to live on tells on one's strength so. This week is worse than last week; the cold & weight of the separation are more felt; it is three weeks since we last spoke to each other; a longer time than there has ever been for more than 20 years. . . . I have got well into my work here & used to the people I have got to see about it, but I dread the House of Commons.'[36] He experienced fits of longing which could not be satisfied, then 'I feel like a prisoner in a cell who beats his head against the walls; but these fits pass or cease at any rate while I do my work. . . .'[37] In letters such as these, chiefly to his women friends, like Katharine Lyttelton, Eleanor Paul and, probably, to Pamela Tennant, he was able to drop the mask of stern resolution which he wore in the Office. In the male world of the House of Commons, the Foreign Office and the Clubs, he seemed to demonstrate an admirable English fortitude. His Cabinet colleagues admired his resolution, but apart from Haldane and Buxton they had little share in his personal life. Grey had what he described as 'an unusual gift of solitude, the power to enjoy being alone' whereas Asquith seemed constantly to need company.[38] Perhaps the most important consequence of his wife's death was to turn Grey spiritually into an old man. To all external appearance he was, at forty-three, physically fit and at the beginning of a long political career. For Edward, on the other hand, the future seemed only likely to record the ebbing of a past happiness, a future in which life and work degenerated into a routine without expectation.

German diplomacy at Algeciras had done nothing to shake Grey's determination to stand by the French entente. If the scope of German interests had been more precisely stated, he might have been less willing to support France when, as he himself admitted, her attitude was somewhat unreasonable. Although in his memoirs he denied making use of the term 'Balance of Power', he nevertheless saw the European situation in these traditional terms. Reiterating what were alleged to be the lessons of history, he minuted on 9 June

1906: 'The Germans do not realise that England has always drifted or deliberately gone into opposition to any power which establishes a hegemony in Europe.'[39] In deference to French anxieties, he certainly discouraged plans for a meeting between the King and Kaiser. He told Cambon on 20 June that if a choice had to be made between France and Germany, 'public opinion here would be as decided on the French side as ever'. But it is an exaggeration to suggest that henceforth, 'his anxiety was always, not that relations with Germany were bad, but that they might become too good'.[40] If Germany abandoned what Grey conceived to be her pursuit of hegemony (which he did not define), then relations could indeed become good. But he remained suspicious of what he regarded as premature attempts to blur differences with Germany in the summer and autumn of 1906—whether these came from King Edward, visiting mayors and journalists, or even Richard Burdon Haldane. He did not need to be instructed in this caution by the 'anti-Germans' in the Foreign Office; indeed, on the question of exchanges with Germany, Hardinge welcomed them and this was one reason for a disagreement with the British Ambassador in Paris. The flimsiness of 'Liberal Imperialism' as a guide to foreign policy is nowhere more clearly seen than in Grey's relations with Haldane. The Secretary for War had been honoured by an invitation to attend military manœuvres in Germany, and the French started to flap. Grey felt their touchiness was extreme, but nevertheless urged Haldane not to find himself involved in celebrating the anniversary of the victory over France at Sedan. On 3 September he wrote quite seriously to his friend: 'I think you enjoy a whirlwind and I suspect you of having enjoyed being in the centre of this. In hurricanes I believe there is always a calm spot at the centre. I can't say that I enjoy whirlwinds; being here alone I have however been able to see the ludicrous aspect of this one. It may alas! have serious consequences; we must wait and see. I want to preserve the entente with France, but it isn't easy, and if it is broken up I must go.'[41] Despite the humour, Haldane had clearly been warned. Journalistic 'experts' like the Radical H. N. Brailsford, who was confidently giving his opinion that Grey knew 'absolutely nothing of foreign affairs . . . Haldane manages all that for him', would have had a surprise if they had read private correspondence.[42] Basking in the euphoria of his German visit, Haldane even told the Kaiser, no doubt with Grey in mind, 'Many of my countrymen had lived all their days in an island and were more apt to misunderstand

Germany than those who had lived much there.'[43] Such patronizing comment did not get him very far when he returned to his island. Grey was very firmly in control of his Foreign Office, deciding which of his colleagues would be bothered with the important dispatches to read.

In December 1906, Grey wrote to President Roosevelt to explain the obvious merits of his European policy. Britain was not anti-German, but she wished to be independent of Germany. Hence the entente with France would be strengthened and there might be an arrangement with Russia. These arrangements were defensive in character, for if the entente were broken up, France would have to make her own terms with Germany. What the British people resented, he believed, was what he called 'mischief-making' by Germany. Economic rivalry 'and all that' did not give much offence. Here, once again, the Boer War seemed to represent a significant stage, for Britain had now had enough of war for one generation. His contemporaries had had enough excitement, they had lost a little blood and now were sane and normal.[44] These feelings about Germany were given a much more coherent form in the famous memorandum which Eyre Crowe produced to greet the New Year. Crowe described the entente as hardening, following the German attempt to break it up over Morocco. It was taking on an importance not present in its original conception. As for Germany, either she was bent on a conscious policy of gaining European hegemony or she was drifting awkwardly in a vague and unpractical way. In any event, in the past her aggressiveness had apparently been met by concession after concession. The lesson of Algeciras, however, was that while Germany's legitimate colonial and naval ambitions should be conceded, in other matters firmness paid. Grey ordered that the memorandum should go to the Prime Minister, Ripon, Asquith, Morley and Haldane, together with his own comment. He described it as 'most valuable. The review of the present situation is both interesting and suggestive, and the connected account of the diplomatic incidents of past years is most helpful as a guide to policy. The whole Memorandum contains information and reflections, which should be carefully studied. The part of our foreign policy with which it is concerned involves the greatest issues, and requires constant attention.' How deeply Grey was influenced by this document is another matter. He would certainly never have expressed himself with such length or with such thoroughness. It is perhaps sufficient to say that in its main lines of argument it confirmed his own less intellectual view that the Kaiser was 'very restless and cannot help scheming'.[45]

Time and again throughout 1907, Grey reaffirmed his adherence to the entente. For example, there was a clash in April after a meeting in Paris between the new French Prime Minister, Clemenceau, and Campbell-Bannerman. Clemenceau had been rash enough to ask directly whether France could rely on Britain's support in the event of war with Germany. Sir Henry replied that public opinion would not allow British troops to be used on the continent. The French Prime Minister exploded, questioning the value of military conversations and saying that the effect of this refusal on his colleagues would be disastrous. It was left to Grey to pick up the pieces. After consulting the Prime Minister, he wrote to Paris that the British public was indeed reluctant to undertake obligations which would commit them to a continental war, but he then stressed that Sir Henry had not said that British troops would never be employed on the continent. To say the least, there was a difference of emphasis between Grey and the Prime Minister, although there does not seem to have been a clash between them on the matter.[46]

Next it was the turn of the Crown, aided by the faithful retainer, Haldane, to cause a disturbance. In April, the King requested that the Kaiser be invited to England. Despite the fact that a return visit was due, Grey was not enthusiastic. Hardinge, however, persuaded him that a visit would not do any harm. A few months later, the Permanent Under-Secretary had second thoughts. Shortly before accompanying the King on a continental tour which would include encounters with the German and Austrian Emperors, Hardinge admitted that 'great efforts are being made by Germany to break up the Franco-Russian alliance and the Anglo-French "entente"'.[47] Grey was very alarmed at what he termed 'a tendency in our Press to whittle away our obligations to France about Morocco' and to emphasize the troubles France was having. Specifically, he told Haldane that he did not want Bülow to accompany his sovereign to London: 'the Emperor has a habit of turning visits into demonstrations which is tiresome. All the other sovereigns are so much quieter. . . .' Although Grey did succeed in preventing Bülow from coming, he was still on guard lest his friend dilate publicly on the intriguing theme that the Kaiser was both an Englishman and a German. The French did not appreciate such sentiments. This concern for French susceptibilities reached its ludicrous height in October, when Grey vetoed a proposal that the band of the Coldstream Guards should play in Germany. There was too much embracing going on, and the Germans could not expect both the band and a royal invitation to London.[48] He demanded that the War Office should never entertain such projects without first clearing them with the Foreign Office. King Edward was furious over the incident and wondered what his cousin would say if he learnt that the Foreign Secretary had denied him the right to send abroad one of his own military bands. The constant theme of Grey's correspondence remained, as he wrote to Campbell-Bannerman in September 1907: 'If the Germans succeed in detaching France from us we shall soon get the rough side of German diplomacy again.'[49] He felt similarly about Spain: 'It would be a great calamity if Spain from lack of other support fell under German influence & let Germany get a footing in Spanish affairs.' Britain should help Spain 'by offering her an undertaking to help her protect her islands & Morocco coast against aggression in return for guarantees to us on her part, which would increase the security of Gibraltar'.[50] After months of negotiation, Britain and France did exchange Notes in the middle of May expressing their willingness to preserve the *status quo* in the Mediterranean and that part of the Atlantic which washed the shores of Europe and Africa. Grey privately assured Cambon that if Germany threatened this agreement he would regard Britain's obligations under it as comparable with those of the 1904 agreement concerning Morocco.

It is, therefore, true to say that in the years of the Campbell-Bannerman Government, Grey had come to see what he called German bullying as the main threat to British security. It would be tempting to regard Grey's initial inflexibility on this question as his greatest error. Certainly, he found himself being driven to give France more support than he had thought would be necessary. But flexibility for its own sake is not always a virtue. To be equally open and sympathetic to both France and Germany presupposed that both states were equally powerful—which they manifestly were not. If, because of her own strength, Britain could have afforded to be indifferent to the fate of France, then Grey's support for her was gratuitous and provocative. The Foreign Secretary, however, could only operate within the area of the given, and, as will be seen, the Government's priorities left him little alternative. The power necessary to be totally indifferent and independent either did not exist, or imposed unacceptable constraints. Sir Edward's determination in his first years of office was to make the strength of his attachment to France clear to Germany. When this fact had been absorbed, he would be prepared to talk with Berlin.

Grey had inherited the French entente from Lansdowne, though he gave it a fresh importance. The Anglo-Russian agreement was his own achievement and it was much more controversial than the reconciliation with France. In contrast to other members of his party, Grey had never been a Russophobe. From the outset he was anxious to come to terms with Russia when the moment was right. Not surprisingly relations between the two countries were poor when Russia was at war with Britain's ally, Japan. It even seemed possible that war might result when the Russian Baltic Fleet opened fire on British fishing boats in the North Sea. Public opinion refused to believe that even the Russian Navy was so incompetent as to believe that these vessels were really Japanese submarines. But the crisis passed, and the defeated, demoralized Russia of early 1906 seemed a more likely candidate for an agreement than a victorious Power. It was recognized that various factions in St Petersburg preferred the idea of a reconciliation with Germany. Count Witte, for example, who had negotiated the peace treaty with Japan, still favoured a continental coalition. It was also alleged that, as in the case of Delcassé, German pressure had led to the resignation of the Russian Foreign Minister, Lamsdorff, in May 1906. Grey had also been informed that if Britain did not reach agreement with Russia on the future of Persia, then Germany might well interfere there and pose as much of a problem as she did for France over Morocco. Confronted by a report that the Persians were going to turn to Germany for a loan, Grey suggested to the Russian Ambassador that their two countries should provide it instead. On 28 May 1906, Nicolson arrived in Russia as the new British Ambassador, and on the following day proposed to the new Russian Foreign Minister, Isvolsky, that official talks should begin. These negotiations, however, were to drag on for another year, facing breakdown on a number of occasions, before they met with success.

In his conduct of the negotiations, Grey had general support within the Foreign Office. Hardinge, who had served in St Petersburg, had returned an advocate of agreement. He gave the negotiations his full support, since earlier experience in Tehran had convinced him that complete British influence over Persia could not be regained. Nicolson, his successor in Russia, had also served in

M

Persia, and quite simply held no high opinion of the Persians. Spring-Rice, however, who had acted as chargé in the interim, was appointed Minister in Persia and quickly showed a sympathy with the Persian reform movement. Within the Cabinet, Grey had little to worry about. The Prime Minister, Ripon, and Asquith all favoured the agreement and were kept informed on the progress of the negotiations, though the Foreign Secretary kept a fairly tight personal supervision. The key relationship was obviously with Morley, the Secretary for India. The views of the Government of India could be expected to be hostile, and Morley would need to be strong. Fortunately for Grey, he was in favour of an agreement, writing that 'for the same reasons that make Germany seek coldness or a quarrel between us and Russia, we ought to do what we can to baulk her'.[51] The objections were more likely to come from backbench Liberal opinion.

The Liberals had enthusiastically welcomed the creation of the parliamentary Douma in Russia after the 'revolution' of 1905. In April 1906, concerning a possible private loan, Grey wrote to Campbell-Bannerman that he did not want to interfere, but warned: 'We may some day be accused of having sided with reaction against reform in Russia.'[52] That day was not far off. The Tsar chose to dissolve the Douma shortly before Campbell-Bannerman had to address a visiting Russian parliamentary delegation. Somewhat embarrassed, Sir Henry improvised with his famous phrase, 'La Douma est morte: vive la Douma.' In response to Grey's congratulations, the Prime Minister replied that 'mere platitudes would not do. I think what I did say was free from offence yet was, I think, effective for good.'[53] Nevertheless, Sir Edward had some explaining to do to the Russian Ambassador, while if Campbell-Bannerman had not made some such comment, his backbenchers would have required an answer. As it was, with news of fresh pogroms against the Jews, the image of Russia was hardly favourable, and many Liberals felt it intolerable that a Liberal Government should contemplate an agreement with such a country. The Foreign Secretary was therefore apprehensive before the opening of the new session of Parliament in the autumn of 1906. The new members had now acquired the art of asking questions and 'there is so much in foreign affairs which attracts attention and had much better be left alone'.[54] Grey believed that the defence of British interests was his duty, and not the encouragement of the Russian constitutional movement. If an agreement was necessary to safeguard these interests, it should take precedence over the 'independence' of states like Persia. Those possessed of responsibility without power, like journalists and academic critics, found his toughness increasingly unpalatable.

In March 1906, Robertson, then serving in the Intelligence Division, produced a memorandum on the military considerations involved in an entente with Russia. He declared that Persia was 'the crux of the whole question. *We should oppose anything tending to impair its territorial integrity. . . .*' If Russia were allowed a better foothold in the north or to establish her influence on the Gulf, then Britain should have similar rights as regards Seistan and the exit of the Gulf. If Russia did forego her great interests, Britain could support her against Germany in Asiatic Turkey. Germany would not like this arrangement, but then, she would not like any British agreement with Russia. However, 'Germany's avowed aims and ambitions are such that they seem bound, if persisted in, to bring her into collision with us sooner or later, and therefore a little more or less enmity on her part is not a matter of great importance'.[55] On the Russian side, however, especially in diplomatic and military circles, it was felt that in course of time, Persia would naturally gravitate into the Russian sphere. In these circumstances, Grey's September proposals, suggesting a division of spheres, with Britain installed in Seistan and Persian Baluchistan, were sceptically received. Isvolsky replied that he would claim the northern sphere, leaving the middle open to all parties, but admitted that many of his colleagues still felt that Persia should fall entirely under Russian influence. In response, Grey and Morley were even prepared to contemplate a Russian presence on the Gulf, but the King and the Viceroy would not hear of it.

The only way by which Isvolsky could gain an agreement with Britain was to convince his colleagues that Germany would not fundamentally object to it. He therefore visited Berlin at the end of October 1906 to explain the position. A little later he was amazed to learn that no objection was raised. From the British side, however, it looked suspiciously as though he was double-dealing with Germany, and Nicolson was therefore anxious to speed up negotiations. Relations were also complicated by the vexed question of the Baghdad Railway. Grey was not averse to reaching agreement with Germany on participation in the building of the line, but he did not want to act without France and Russia. The French were amenable, though Grey feared that their financiers might be kept too long for an answer and lose interest, but Russian fears were more fundamental and difficult to remove. To reach agreement with Germany on the railway might jeopardize the prospect of an entente with Russia. Indeed, it was probably fear of German penetration into the Middle East which made an agreement with Britain attractive to Russia. So, on 20 February, Isvolsky presented proposals to Nicolson which were substantially satisfactory and met the British insistence that the Russian zone of Persia should not touch the Afghan frontier. The only subsequent snag concerned the status of the Gulf. The Government of India did not like the small size of the British sphere and gained royal support for the notion that the Russians should be made to recognize British special interests in the Gulf. While Nicolson believed that Isvolsky could not go so far for fear of offending Germany and his own pro-Germans, Hardinge said such a statement was needed to carry the agreement in Britain. In the event, Grey supplemented the convention by a note reaffirming the British position and Isvolsky assented to it.[56] At last, the Foreign Secretary got his agreement, though, as he wrote to Campbell-Bannerman, without Morley 'we should have made no progress at all for the Govt. of India would have blocked every point: Morley has removed mountains in the path of the negotiations'.[57] Sir Henry congratulated him on his achievement.

In view of later history, it has been rare for these congratulations to be echoed. At the time, Grey was under strong pressure from opposite quarters. To Curzon, who led the attack in the Lords, the agreement represented an imperial abdication: 'It gives up all that we have been fighting for for years. . . . The efforts of a century sacrificed and nothing or next to nothing in return.'[58] Grey, however, maintained that Russia's hold on Northern Persia was unshakeable, whereas the British position in the south was weak. It was for this reason that he subsequently maintained: 'What we gained by it was real—what Russia gained was apparent.' There is nothing strange in the fact that Grey maintained this view despite Russia's troubles in 1905–6. He both needed and yet was afraid of her. He could not afford to risk a war against her for fear of how Germany would exploit it, so he took advantage of a possibly temporary moment of weakness to gain a division-of-spheres agreement which he believed in the last resort was non-enforceable. His claim that 'we were freed from an anxiety that had often preoccupied British Governments; a frequent source of friction and a possible cause of war was removed . . .' was quite clearly not the case.[59] Yet, granted his determination not to go to war, the only conceivable strategy was to make a public agreement in the hope that, by constant reference to it, the Russians might not stray too far from the path. The question was not whether Britain was stronger than Russia, but whether in the international situation Britain could afford to antagonize her. Those critics who dismissed his reliance on a scrap of paper or jeered at his apparent belief that the Russians were men of honour who could be trusted were telling him nothing that he did not already know. Of course, Grey was 'not a world statesman. His horizon was limited to Europe', but it was in Europe that he believed the dangers to the British Empire existed.[60]

Sir Edward was also criticized by Radicals and Socialists for buttressing the Russian Government and failing to respect Persian independence. In his memoirs, Grey admitted that the independence and integrity of Persia did not in fact exist at the time of the agreement. The complaint against him was that his own actions did nothing to challenge this situation. Late in 1905, Persia was stirred by a movement of Tehran merchants, inspired by leading mullas, demanding the dismissal of an oppressive Grand Vizier. The Government reacted with strong measures against the mobs. In the summer of the following year, some ten thousand or more people took sanctuary in the grounds of the British Legation. From there they successfully demanded a new constitution for Persia. The chargé d'affaires, Grant Duff, seemed to the new Russian Minister in Persia, Hartwig, to be aiming to overthrow the Shah in the pursuit of British interests. The sympathies of the Legation for the constitutional movement were well known and were used in St Petersburg by the opponents of the Anglo-Russian agreement. The Russian Ambassador in London denied that Grey was secretly bent on unseating the Russians in the north by supporting the reform movement. Sir Edward was a constitutionalist as regards Russia but not for Persia; '*il trouve cela folie*'.[61] But the new British Minister did not find the idea ludicrous. He could not resist the irony of a situation where 'the Russians are engaged in spoiling their own Duma at home and teaching the Shah how to spoil his Mejlis [Parliament] here. The dear Liberals at home are trying to get social recognition from the Russian Emperor, and to obtain this are encouraging him in his policy of extinguishing the liberties of Persia.'[62] Spring-Rice constantly wrote to Grey urging support for the reform movement and casting doubt on Russian intentions. When the Anglo-Russian agreement was signed he wrote critically, boldly stating that 'there is at least a prima facie case for those who are ready to criticise you for all you do either in co-operation with an autocratic power or in opposition to the liberties of smaller nations'.[63] When, in the following summer, the Shah staged a counter-coup with the assistance of his Russian-officered Cossack corps, the first Parliament was dissolved. The wrath of the Persian constitutionalists was directed more against Britain than against Russia. The Russians had done what was expected of them, 'what was unexpected, incomprehensible, and painful was Britain's participation in the rape of Persia'. They were shocked by 'the atmosphere of uncertainty and hypocrisy that Sir Edward Grey managed to create, and the sudden realization that Britain was not the moral force they had believed her to be'.[64] It is little wonder that from this angle a contemporary historian of Iranian descent describes Grey as 'the ruthless politician with the deceptively mild exterior'.

In the conflict between what Grey believed to be the strategic needs of the British Empire and his mild belief in the progress of constitutionalism, there was little doubt which would triumph. Grey perceived the politics of Persia through a haze of mullas and he did not believe their ideas could conform so nearly to the tenets of English Liberalism as some of his friends urged. The Empire, even annexes like Persia, was no doubt in some sense 'Liberal' although the progress towards constitutionalism seemed to bristle with difficulties. The threat to Britain itself seemed to Grey the most important problem with which he had to deal. Paradoxically, during the very years of his personal preoccupation with Europe, different forms of nationalism in the Middle and Far East were stirring and endangering the imperial structure.

The paradox of the Liberal Empire was nowhere more apparent than in Egypt. Cromer was confronted by an awkward situation in April 1906. The Sultan of Turkey had occupied some disputed areas at the base of the Sinai Peninsula. The British regarded this intrusion as the violation of a long-standing convention concerning the area and a threat to the status of Egypt. Cromer therefore requested an increase in the British garrison. In a letter to the Prime Minister, Grey supported the request, adding: 'The armament may induce the Turks to settle the Sinai Peninsula question, if so that will be something gained: but in any case things have become so disturbed (and I fear that intrigues of German agents are keeping them so disturbed) that they will get worse, if something is not done.'[65] The view that Germany was meddling in the affair was also shared by Hardinge and Crowe, Fitzmaurice and Ripon. The Mediterranean Fleet was prepared and an ultimatum sent to the Sultan on 3 May, to expire ten days later. Abdul Hamid drew back—which was very fortunate, for it was far from clear what precise punitive action was going to be taken if he remained obdurate. Campbell-Bannerman again congratulated Grey: 'I fully concur in all you have done about the Turkish squabble . . . the most important thing is to shew that we will not yield to the wishes of the Turk.'[66] Even though Grey contradicted his private remarks by writing to Lascelles in Berlin that he did not suppose the German Embassy was involved, his main reflection was that the Akaba incident did fall into a pattern of German penetration through Ottoman Turkey to the south and east.[67] This fact helps to explain his reluctance to rush into reconciliation with Germany following Algeciras, and gave further impetus to an Anglo-Russian rapprochement.

The situation in Egypt was not, however, quite what it seemed. Cromer had been surprised by the Egyptian reaction to the crisis. He had professed, quite sincerely in his own way, to be acting in defence of Egypt's rights, but found himself under attack in the local press for seeking to undermine Islam. This feeling certainly did exist, but the majority of Egyptians were probably not anxious to establish a new Islamic Empire. The agitation was 'primarily a movement of protest against the British and a feeling of affinity for Ottoman resistance to a common enemy. It was one of the great mistakes of Lord Cromer to view the nationalist movement in Egypt almost entirely as a recrudescence of traditional values, rather than a movement drawing inspiration from the West and led by men produced by Egypt's modern institutions.'[68] The unpleasant, indeed baffling, fact seemed to be emerging that what to Grey had been a timely defence of a constitutionally complex, but British-ruled, state against a decaying Turkey was seen by many of its inhabitants in a very different light. Even more curiously, forces were stirring which would challenge even the supposition that European control over Turkey itself was inevitable sooner or later.

Something of this tension was disclosed by the Dinshawai incident of June 1906. Some British army officers out pigeon-shooting near the village of Dinshawai shot and wounded the wife of the local Imam. They were surrounded by the villagers and two British officers were wounded; in their alarm, they fired on the villagers.

One of the officers died, and, on their arrival, relieving troops killed a bystander. Over fifty Egyptians were arrested and brought before a special Tribunal presided over by the Coptic Christian Minister of Justice, accompanied by three British officials and one other Egyptian. Severe verdicts were passed on 27 June, including the sentencing of four men to death and many to terms of hard labour and public flogging. They were carried out on the following day.[69] Grey had a hurried conversation with the Prime Minister and Asquith, but decided to take no action, although he found the verdicts startlingly severe. Cromer had left for London before the verdicts were announced and came to see Grey on his arrival. The more the Foreign Secretary studied the affair, the more uncertain he became. Nevertheless, he considered that he had been right not to interfere, since the authority of the man on the spot had to be upheld. In the Commons, Grey declared that severe action of this kind was justified, because acts of violence in Egypt were increasing. The real object of the sentences, therefore, was to uphold the prestige of the British agency by showing that only a limited amount of political resistance would be tolerated. If necessary, Britain would retain her position in Egypt by force.[70]

Whatever the rights and wrongs of Dinshawai, it was a decisive stage in the evolution of modern Egyptian nationalism. It provided just the kind of issue to unite discontented urban journalists and intellectuals with the peasant masses. Cromer was nearing the end of his administration in Egypt, and was conscious that after the incident the Liberal Government would not bestow their complete confidence in him. In March 1907 he resigned, though for months afterwards Grey had dutifully to defend his record. In August, Hardinge wrote to Bryce describing what a wonderful effect 'his calm and fearless moderation has upon the House'. Redmond's description of the Dinshawai incident 'succeeded in raising a feeling of hostility which taxed all Grey's skill to allay—as it was . . . 40 Liberals . . . joined the Irish and Labour parties against the Govt.'[71] The political consequences were therefore not confined to Egypt. George Bernard Shaw took up his pen on behalf of the fellahin. More knowledgeably, Wilfrid Scawen Blunt, an Arab sympathizer of long standing, fed Irish and Radical members of parliament with information from Egyptian sources. He was disgusted by the ease with which Grey calmed these critics with promises of reform in Egypt. Sir Edward had indeed warmly supported the appointment of Eldon Gorst as successor to Cromer, and hoped quite genuinely that he would be able to adopt a more conciliatory attitude towards Egyptian opinion. In fact, even to blame Grey too severely for his attitude towards the shooting is to overestimate the power of the London Government. Confronted by what amounted to a *fait accompli* by a jittery local administration which claimed that neither the Egyptian Government nor the British Agency had the legal right to interfere, Grey had little alternative but to take a stronger line than, left to himself, he would have advised. Speaking privately, he considered that: 'The Denshawai sentences erred grossly on the side of severity and the harm done by them here and in Egypt was many fold greater than any leniency. And I have had for two years to defend them in public!'[72] In October 1907, after correspondence with the Lord Chancellor, he told Gorst that the prisoners should be released after serving eighteen months, as an act of justice, and he would take the responsibility.[73]

The future of South Africa seemed to provide the British Empire with a test of another kind. Although Grey drifted away from Milner, he still had strong views on South African questions. He had a personal link with Milner's successor as High Commissioner, Lord Selborne, his fag-master at Winchester. The Liberals kept him in office until 1910, and in December 1905 Sir Edward wrote to make his own position clear. He now felt that Chinese labour should cease to come to South Africa for, whatever the immediate economic benefits, it was 'a bad foundation on which to build up an industry'. It was better for mining to develop slowly without the Chinese than rapidly with them. He also declared himself in favour of suspending the existing Lyttelton constitution and introducing immediate self-government in the Transvaal. It was better to grant this magnanimously than to wait for the Representative Assembly to extort it from an apparently reluctant Imperial Government.[74] After long discussions, the Cabinet took a line on South Africa in keeping with Grey's private thoughts. Before writing to Selborne, Grey had been in touch with the Colonial Secretary urging that further importation of Chinese should stop. Elgin agreed.[75] The considerations which chiefly influenced Grey in the direction of magnanimity towards the Boers were, as one would expect, closely connected with general foreign policy. Significantly, before the beginning of the Algeciras Conference he wrote to Elgin that although he did not believe war likely, it was possible, and 'in view of this it would be well for contingencies in S. Africa to be provided for'.[76] In February 1906, the Colonial Secretary wanted to discuss the alleged German intrigues with the Boers, and these anxieties led Grey to approve a settlement which might prevent Boer treason in the event of general war.[77] These considerations took precedence over the position of non-whites. In this respect the Liberals held themselves to be bound by the terms of the Treaty of Vereeniging which ended the war. Besides, it was clear that English and Afrikaans-speaking South Africans could and would unite under the banner of colonial self-government against any strong imposition by the Imperial Government. Grey knew that the situation was still fragile and was kept informed by Elgin of the difficulties he was experiencing with the Natal Government in the aftermath of the native rebellion of 1906–7.[78] The Liberals knew that their South African policy was a gamble but, amidst all their other difficulties, they had no power to coerce both white communities.

The Colonial Conference of 1907 was of course not primarily a concern of Grey's, nevertheless he necessarily had views on the pressing questions concerning the status of the self-governing parts of the Empire. At the conference, no real agreement on administrative and constitutional matters was possible—the decision to set up a continuing Secretariat within the Colonial Office was an unsatisfactory compromise. Administrative arrangements necessarily had repercussions on the framing of a common foreign policy. Writing to his cousin, the Governor-General of Canada, Grey raised no objection to the notion of a Canadian, paid for by the Canadian Government, being attached to the British Embassy in Washington, though it should be understood that the Ambassador would be free to accept or reject his advice as he saw fit.[79] But how much further should this process go? Elgin thought the proposal for a sort of Canadian Foreign Office a dangerous one—'if Canada had a F.O. our friend Deakin would certainly claim one—& so on, and where would it stop?'[80] Grey was obviously not quite so alarmed, partly because he was already aware of the delays and inefficiencies which resulted from the lack of any such department in Ottawa. Elgin was not reassured, fearing that the request for a separate F.O. 'might lead the self-governing colonies on to claims which ought to be inconvenient to the Imperial F.O. Perhaps I exaggerate the risk.'[81]

As far as the 'Imperial F.O.' was concerned, the problem of Canada was intimately connected with Anglo-American relations. On coming into office, Grey wrote to the British Ambassador in Washington, Sir Mortimer Durand: 'All we want is that the U.S.

Govt. should realize that the present British Govt. is just as well disposed to the U.S. as their predecessor was.'[82] In fact, Grey probably made a more determined effort to establish intimate relations with the United States than any of his predecessors. But it was by no means easy to keep the quartet of Britain, the United States, Canada and Newfoundland in harmony. The Canadians were still smarting from their setback in the Alaskan boundary dispute, feeling that the London Government had put its desire to stand well with the United States before Canadian interests. For his part, Earl Grey, the Governor-General, was anxious to see all matters of contention between the United States and Canada settled and thus remove sources of embarrassment for Britain. In May 1906, after certain preliminary exchanges, the American Secretary of State, Elihu Root, proposed the settlement of all out-standing questions in a letter to the British Ambassador. The most complicated disputes concerned fishing rights in the North Atlantic and sealing in the Baring Sea. The Canadian Government, however, was far from anxious to enter into negotiations. Laurier, the Prime Minister, did not believe that the United States would permit the entry of Canadian fish, duty-free, in return for Canadian agreement to abandon pelagic sealing. By the end of 1906, it seemed unlikely that the negotiators would get down to serious business.[83]

The subject caused Grey some concern, since the increasing international role being played by the United States under Roosevelt seemed to make good relations essential. As Grey confessed in a letter to Roosevelt after the Algeciras conference, 'We *had* feared you might be an ally of the Emperor there, but in the event I felt it was not so. . . .' He was anxious to convince the President of the merits of his European policy, while at the same time, there was a real friendly feeling towards the United States. Since he recognized that the American was a distinctive type, a 'new man', he now shied away from 'Anglo-Saxon race feeling', but stressed the fact that language and religion brought the two countries together in a special way.[84] Grey had been described to Roosevelt by St Loe Strachey as a 'Radical Whig'—the sort of man he could expect to find congenial. In his reply, the President stated that good relations between Britain and France were 'an excellent thing from every standpoint'. But Germany's future course seemed to interest the President less than Japan's. Grey had found himself quite unable to forecast what would happen in the Far East and, after extensive speculation, Roosevelt agreed. The President concluded that

Japanese immigration on the West Coast of Canada and the United States meant that the two countries had a common problem and he looked forward to an exchange of views.[85] This troublesome question placed Grey in some difficulty because of the Anglo-Japanese alliance. Commenting on a letter from Roosevelt which Strachey had forwarded, Grey replied in October 1907: 'I sympathise with the desire of great countries not to be swamped by alien races, where that desire arises from patriotic and national feeling. But I am alarmed when this desire takes the form of keeping out every thing, both goods and men, coming from outside, and refusing to face any kind of competition. Without some competition, no community will progress, and no country can be developed. My remarks do not apply much, if at all, in the case of Canada, where the population is increasing rapidly and the country is being developed. But they do apply in the case of Australia.' The whole problem would have to be handled with great delicacy and tact.[86] Sir Edward wanted to maintain good relations with Tokyo which he believed were for the benefit of the Empire as a whole. In an interview with the Canadian Minister, Mackenzie King, in March 1908, Grey deprecated the suggestion that the Japanese were likely to break agreements they had made on the question of immigration. Nevertheless, he had to admit that 'if the Japanese did fail to observe their agreement with Canada, we should certainly not plead the Anglo-Japanese Alliance as hampering Canada in preventing Japanese immigration'.[87] As his remarks indicate, Grey also experienced a similar difficulty with regard to Australian fears of Japanese expansion.

Sir Mortimer Durand had not been a success as British Ambassador in Washington and it was necessary to think of someone who would get on well with Roosevelt—whom Grey described as 'so very brisk and keen'. The King favoured sending Hardinge, but Grey told the Prime Minister that he could not afford to lose his services: 'I now consider him invaluable where he is, & he really cannot be spared from his present place.'[88] Somewhat forlornly, Grey tried to press Rosebery into service, but he declined. Spring-Rice, the Minister in Persia and personal friend both of Grey and Roosevelt, was canvassed, but in the end the choice fell upon James Bryce. Grey explained that the Americans 'wanted someone whose appointment they could take as a compliment to themselves'. Bryce satisfied this requirement and, into the bargain, was reputed to understand how the American Senate worked.[89] Bryce's arrival in Washington in March 1907 was the signal for another attempt to deal with the points of friction. He warned Grey that progress would be difficult: 'Canada, tho less vexatious and irresponsible than Newfoundland, is in no humour for "deals" or compromises, or at least not such as the U.S. are likely to agree to....'[90] Arbitration was probably inevitable, though the Canadians were shy of this since the Alaskan award. Bryce felt that there was no chance of Canadian fish entering the United States market duty-free. He planned instead to try to settle lesser matters, in the hope that a better atmosphere for tackling the more controversial topics might thereby be created. When the two colonial Prime Ministers, Laurier and Bond, were in London for the Colonial Conference, Grey and Elgin tackled them but found it 'impossible to make real progress'. While the Newfoundland Premier would agree to arbitration on the whole fishing problem, Laurier was not keen and Grey felt 'reluctant to make a proposal to the United States which would give offence to Canada....'[91] However, in August 1907 the Canadians did consent to arbitration, and there seemed to be some progress on the boundary question. This optimism was to some extent illusory, for Newfoundland turned awkward and Grey wrote angrily: 'Bond's position really amounts to this, that we ought at his bidding to use the British Navy to impose upon Americans by force whatever he asks.'[92] Bryce was also exasperated, writing to Grey in March 1908: 'The Canadians are quite heart-breaking in their habits of procrastination and delay....'[93] The Foreign Secretary fully sympathized but was 'quite unable to help, for in substance it is more Canada's affair than ours, and the Colonial Office has been pegging away at the Canadian Government'.[94] Bryce's tenacity was rewarded a couple of months later when agreement was finally reached on the fishing question. The boundary problem, however, was still unresolved. Bryce was convinced that the delays had shown that, whatever the Colonial Secretary might think, there was a need for a Canadian External Affairs Department. Hardinge agreed, but also feared that Australia might stake a similar claim and that would not be desirable, 'however, we must risk that'.[95] After a year as Ambassador, Bryce seemed to be effectively consolidating Anglo-American relations without undue 'hustling' of the Canadians.

Grey was fond of referring to the Foreign Office as 'the biggest job in the Empire', and his responsibilities were indeed global. The pressure of events in Europe seemed to be driving him to an increased concern with the defence of the United Kingdom, but excessive concentration on the major crises of European history has led commentators to neglect the fact that Sir Edward presided over 'the Imperial F.O.'. In the first two years of office, he had shown a shrewd awareness of the connexions between fishing off the North American coast, building a railway to Baghdad, authorizing military conversations with France and securing Seistan. It was not a bad achievement for someone widely esteemed for his knowledge of the migratory patterns of birds.

9

Domestic Constraints, 1905-8

Success in foreign policy depends, in the last resort, upon power; without military and naval strength, the Foreign Secretary would have been gravely handicapped in his diplomacy. Grey was therefore closely interested in Cabinet decisions on defence spending. In turn, of course, the military and naval estimates seriously limited the amount of money available for other projects. Many Liberals, however, had strong objections to such an ordering of priorities. Domestic needs should be met first, and only then should 'defence' be considered.

The Liberals had the misfortune to come into office at a critical stage in naval building. The Balfour Government had authorized the construction of the Dreadnought—the battleship whose superior speed, engines and guns made all earlier types obsolete. Fisher, the First Sea Lord since October 1904, had co-operated with his political chief to produce a construction programme aimed at maintaining the two-Power standard, that is to say, keeping the Royal Navy supreme over the two next largest navies in the world. The potential expansion of the German navy was very much in Fisher's mind. The incoming Government inherited a commitment to build four large ships a year—a provision which could be expanded if necessary. The extent to which Dreadnought building sapped Britain's numerical superiority in conventional battleships had not been fully appreciated. Initially, the Government accepted its predecessor's programme, but then backbench pressure made itself felt. At the Cabinet on 10 July 1906, Asquith, the Chancellor of the Exchequer, urged the reduction of the programme from four to two. This, he argued, would be perfectly compatible with supremacy, since the Russian navy was out of the reckoning and the French were not likely to combine with Germany. Tweedmouth, the First Lord, argued that such a reduction did mean the abandonment of the two-Power standard. The Prime Minister then invited Grey to sit on a committee with himself, Asquith, Tweedmouth and Fisher in order to resolve the matter. They compromised by suggesting three ships for the 1906–7 estimates. The construction of the third ship was delayed until it was known whether any international agreement could be reached at the second Hague Conference due in 1907. Grey supported this compromise, for it now meant that there were solid naval reasons for making sure that the possibility of a Franco-German combination was indeed a myth. As has been well said, 'Old Age Pensions were financed by the entente cordiale.'[1] The very people most anxious for Britain to be detached from both France and Germany were those whose social concerns made them unwilling to pay the military and naval price which could make such detachment feasible. Even Asquith wrote to the Prime Minister in December 1906, regretting the fact that the savings on the navy were very small. They represented a 'very poor and inadequate fulfilment of our pledges in regard to reduction of expenditure on fighting services'. He opposed the proposal to build a large new dockyard at Rosyth, and expressed his lack of confidence in the Sea Lords. Having regard to the sketchy programmes and inferior shipbuilding resources of others, British naval supremacy was so completely assured that there was no cause to be rushed into 'these nebulous and ambitious developments'.[2]

The question of naval construction is a perfect example of the difficulties confronting Grey. As a result of the July 1906 decision, he had to maintain both that the navy was not weakened and that Britain was not forcing the pace. Balfour was not alone in observing that the two arguments did not cling together. The Germans wanted to know why they should be called upon to accept the *status quo* in perpetuity because of the exigencies of Liberal Party politics. The Kaiser made it clear that he would not discuss disarmament, since 'each State must decide for itself the amount of military force which is considered necessary for the protection of its interests. . . .'[3] Grey refused to accept that his plan for a limitation of armaments was a plot to keep Germany inferior: 'I want people here and in Germany, who will have to vote the money, to realize that it is he [the Kaiser], who has forced our hand in spite of our wish to limit expenditure.'[4] He explained to Roosevelt that if Britain and Germany were to agree to limit or even stop new construction for a few years, then the rest of Europe would do the same. Russia, however, would be allowed to rebuild her battered fleet.[5] It was this provision which aroused German suspicions. Roosevelt replied that the limitation of armaments was certainly desirable, though he did not think it would have very great effect in diminishing the likelihood of war. The strengthening of the Hague Court was of more consequence than disarmament: 'Even here, however, we can accomplish anything at all only by not trying to accomplish too much. . . .'[6] It was, in fact, obvious that no large-scale disarmament agreement was likely. In the instructions to the British delegation, Grey did not even want the subject raised if it were likely to lead to friction. He was now inclined to favour the idea that the Great Powers should disclose their plans for naval construction in advance, before disclosing them to their Parliaments for approval. Such exchanges might lead to useful negotiations and reductions before the Governments were publicly committed to their programmes. Grey did not feel very sanguine about the chances of success, speaking in the House of Commons in August 1907 of the 'pathetic helplessness of mankind under the burden of armaments'. If only there were sufficient good will, it ought to be possible for the nations to reduce the burden, but 'the difficulty in regard to one nation stepping out in advance of the others is this, that while there is a chance that their courageous action may lead to reform, there is also a chance that it may lead to martyrdom'.[7]

The British delegation for the talks at the Hague was almost equally divided between advocates of courageous action and opponents of martyrdom. The leading plenipotentiary was the venerable old Quaker lawyer, Sir Edward Fry. Eyre Crowe came from the Foreign Office to deter prospective martyrs. Grey showed his customary concern for French susceptibilities, declaring that a German proposal for an appeal court was aimed at dividing Britain and France. He therefore told Fry that it would be 'very necessary to avoid being drawn into an appearance of co-operation with Germany against France: the French are very sensitive at this moment. . . .'[8] Fry assured him that care would be taken, though Crowe felt that the old man was quite guileless and there was something pathetic about his attempts to gain German support for his proposed resolution on armaments. Crowe tried to convince Fry that conventions of the kind he proposed were useless apart from making 'that silly person, the world, believe that the cause of humanity is thereby advanced'. The old man admitted that 'it is all really empty make believe' though he clung to the idea that it all served some good purpose.[9] On 17 August, he brought forward

Grey's idea of an exchange of information about prospective naval plans. But while the proposal was accepted, there was no discussion on how it should be implemented. Marschall, the German delegate, professed to regard the whole business as a masterly example of British deception. Suddenly, the British had discovered that a situation had been reached where freedom, humanity and civilization demanded limitation of armaments, 'that is to say the perpetuation of a state of things which is to the present advantage of England'. Germany and Austria-Hungary consequently ensured that the British plan was taken no further. Marschall claimed that France really agreed with Germany, but could not stand out against Britain, while no one quite knew where the Russians stood. Crowe, on the other hand, took a very different view. Germany, Austria, Italy and their satellites had wrecked everything in the most open manner. The most sinister development, in his opinion, was that the Russians sided with Germany rather than with France. He believed that the dominating influence in the conference was fear of Germany. She had followed her traditional course, 'cajoling and bullying in turn, always actively intriguing'. The Scandinavian countries had intimated that they wanted to go with Britain, but were deterred by fear of German ill-will. Crowe professed to be puzzled that the whole conference had practically united against Britain on every question involving naval warfare. Even the Americans acted in a way which seemed to him quite contrary to their interests. It does not seem to have occurred to him that other nations might have found something bullying in the British attitude to freedom of capture at sea.[10]

The failure of the Hague conference notwithstanding, the Cabinet decided in November 1907 that the naval estimates ought not to exceed the sum agreed for the previous year. In mid-December, however, Tweedmouth reported that the Admiralty could not agree to this suggestion. The Cabinet went over the matter on 21 January 1908, and Harcourt, Lloyd George, Burns, McKenna and Morley opposed any increase. They claimed to carry a third of the parliamentary party with them and could therefore bring the Government down if they chose. On 4 February, the Cabinet bowed before this pressure and agreed on a programme which Fisher was to be persuaded to accept. Fisher, however, threatened resignation and eventually persuaded the Prime Minister to accept an increase. Sir Henry explained to the King that the increase was not caused by further shipbuilding beyond the accepted figure, but by expenditure on works which were formally paid for out of loans. In this first real battle in the Cabinet on estimates, Grey had been firmly on the Admiralty side.

A week later came a sensation. The First Lord's private secretary, opening the morning mail on 18 February, found a blue registered envelope which contained a letter from the German Kaiser. Amongst other things, His Majesty stressed in this unusual communication that it was 'absolutely *nonsensical* & *untrue* that the German Naval Bill is to provide a navy meant as a "Challenge to British Naval Supremacy". The German Fleet is built *against* nobody at all. It is solely built *for* Germany's needs in relation with that country's growing trade. . . .' He concluded: 'This perpetual quoting of the "German Danger" is utterly unworthy of the great British nation with its world wide Empire & its mighty Navy which is about 5 times the size of the German Navy; there is something very ludicrous about it.' Tweedmouth sent the letter to Grey and the Foreign Secretary approved the proposed reply. He also agreed that the First Lord should send a copy of the forthcoming estimates, which had not yet been presented to Parliament. The King was also informed. Tweedmouth claimed in reply that there was nothing in the estimates which should offend Germany. He then went to stay with Lord Rothschild at Tring, taking the original letter with him. Grey had stressed that in his reply Tweedmouth should not take up any of the points in the letter.[11] Hardinge got to hear of the Kaiser's epistle and tackled the Foreign Secretary about his decision to allow the estimates to be forwarded to Berlin. Sir Charles reported that he had rubbed into Grey 'what a foolish thing he & Tweedmouth had done . . . and how indefensible such an action would prove if it were ever known to the public, which I am glad to say is not likely'. Grey did not take kindly to this advice and became 'very Greyish', although Hardinge thought he had convinced him of his mistake. How was the Foreign Secretary's behaviour to be explained? Hardinge believed that certain people, both in the Cabinet and outside, told Grey that the Foreign Office was anti-German and hinted that he was being run by the Office. So, there were occasions when Grey acted entirely on his own, just to remind his servants that however much he agreed with them, and was 'quite sound on the whole', he did not depend upon them.[12] Unfortunately for the Government, the matter did come into the open, when Colonel Repington, the military correspondent of *The Times*, published a letter in the paper on 6 March, entitled 'Under which

King?' The clear implication was that the Kaiser had been putting private pressure on a Minister of the Crown. An awkward situation seemed likely to arise, but the Opposition accepted Government assurances that the estimates had been settled before the Kaiser's letter was received. Grey's role in the matter is a reminder that while he could be touchy about the band of the Coldstream Guards going to Germany, he could also forward unpublished estimates to the Kaiser.

At the War Office, Haldane had to operate under the same constraints as applied in the case of naval expenditure. He had to be able to promise drastic army reform on a tight budget. Haldane regarded the whole question as a great challenge to his administrative and organizational ability. He also knew that there would be only too many anxious to see him fail. Grey, of course, was not among that number, for the crisis of the early months of 1906 had made him fully aware of Britain's precarious military position. The question, as Lord Esher remarked, was whether steps could be taken in good time. He paid Grey the unexpected compliment of being 'the only man who possesses the power of anticipation'.[13] From the outset, Haldane made it clear that the army had to be ready to serve overseas and could not be conscripted. The emphasis therefore had to be on mobility and efficiency. It would make up in quality what it lacked in quantity. By July 1906 he was ready with his plans for an Expeditionary Force of some 150,000 men with specialist groups. Battalions were brought back from South Africa and the Mediterranean, and certain battalions of Guards were abolished. Haldane had been careful to stress the cost-effectiveness of his policy. Critics seized on this to argue that the Liberals were putting cheapness before everything, but in general there was remarkably little criticism and the proposals came into effect from the beginning of 1907.[14] Conservative critics still insisted that the Expeditionary Force was no match in size for the conscript armies of continental states. All the while, Haldane continued to develop his army council into a General Staff which would assist in planning and executing his designs. The question still seemed to be one of time, as Esher wrote: 'The foreign policy of E. Grey, or any other Secretary of State, might land us any day in a similar plight. We have an Army in excess of our requirements for "small wars"—and wholly inadequate to the demands of a great war.'[15]

The next problem was the creation of an efficient home defence force and reserve for possible overseas service. Here Haldane encountered the vested interests of the Militia, Yeomanry and Volunteers. They wished basically to remain as they were, men who could be called up in an emergency for home defence, rather than amalgamate and become mere supports for the Expeditionary Force. Haldane decided to ride boldly over the opposition and create a new Territorial Army out of the Yeomanry and Volunteers, and a Special Reserve from the Militia. The Territorial Army would be administered by local county associations. His scheme was referred to a Cabinet committee on which Grey sat, in company with Asquith, Morley, Burns, Sinclair and Haldane himself. According to Sinclair, Asquith, Burns and Morley asked the questions, while Grey was rather silent.[16] Following a session early in January 1907, Haldane was convinced that all would go well if people were convinced that 'the Liberal Government is the one government that can produce a business-like and economical army'.[17] When the committee reported to the full Cabinet, Asquith and Grey were warm in support, and even Burns and Morley most appreciative. The initial Opposition reaction to the bill when it was introduced in the spring was to claim that no such reorganization was feasible. There was no guarantee that men would re-engage for units which might be regarded as mere store-houses for the front line. However, the measure triumphed with unexpected ease in the Commons in June and an unenthusiastic Lords let it through. Haldane seemed to be coming into his own. Grey wrote to his family that there was 'such a gratifying recognition on all sides of the fine work he has done and of what a great man he is'.[18] The creation of the Territorial Army in April 1908, together with Haldane's other reforms, was an indication that foreign policy was coming into closer alignment. The achievement was Haldane's, yet the support of Grey, even if not frequently expressed, was invaluable. Discussing such questions with the two men in August 1907, Almeric Fitzroy remarked of Grey: 'there is such prudent suavity in his handling of delicate themes, such breadth of judgment in his outlook, such patience in his attitude towards troublesome problems. . . .'[19]

The impression must not be given, however, that the Campbell-Bannerman Government produced a precise and integrated defence policy. The drive for reform had come from within the departments and was not co-ordinated. If one asked, as the Campbell-Bannerman Government came to an end, what its strategic thinking had been, it would be difficult to produce a coherent answer. Despite his foreign policy of support for France and his authorization of the military conversations, Grey himself was by no means converted to sending major military assistance to the continent. Fisher was still arguing vigorously for a raiding force of some 70,000 British troops to give effect to the activity of the Fleet and quoted Grey's view, that it would be 'a projectile to be fired by the Navy' in his support. Even more explicitly, in May 1908 Grey backed up a statement of Hardinge's that the British army could never have more than a moral effect since it could never be more than 150,000 men, by stating that 'the real counterforce to the German army must be the French and Russian armies, while we maintain naval supremacy'.[20] The military talks with France continued in secret, and although Grey approved the revised British plan sent to him by the War Office in July 1907, he apparently 'had no further reports of the Anglo-French staff talks'.[21] The Prime Minister had been persuaded to let the Committee of Imperial Defence continue in existence, but he did not want it to advise on strategy or supervise the departmental reforms. Only fifteen meetings were held during this Government and during this period, Grey was assiduous in attendance. At its meeting on 28 February 1907, for example, the Committee received a paper which convincingly argued that in the event of a rupture with Turkey, it would be wrong to attempt a landing in the Gallipoli Peninsula. Grey stated that this report would be duly noted in the Foreign Office so that the department could 'recognize the limitations of our power of offence against that country'.[22] Campbell-Bannerman's reserve in the use of the C.I.D. was partly because of a fear that it constituted a dangerous weapon with which the Services might bully the Cabinet. But since the Cabinet devoted little time to strategy, there was a curious uncertainty, not least on the part of the Foreign Secretary, about what actually would happen in the event of war.

Except in times of serious international crisis, the concerns of the Foreign Secretary bring him least into contact with public opinion. Grey's interventions in home politics during the Campbell-Bannerman ministry were limited. Throughout 1906, the Prime Minister worked his colleagues very hard, and the Liberals had a group of minor Acts to their credit—including an Agricultural Holdings Act which especially delighted Grey.[23] But its major Bills, on Education and Plural Voting, were both rejected by the Lords. Grey strongly favoured the Education Bill and, with Lloyd George, in a significant partnership, seems to have been prepared to accept the challenge offered by the upper House. The Cabinet overruled them.[24] In the summer of 1907, the Prime Minister warned the Commons that his Government would not tolerate a situation in which its legislation was constantly wrecked. He then outlined a scheme for a conference between duly selected members of both Houses if a Bill sent up from the Commons failed to become law. If this conference failed to reach agreement, the Bill could be re-introduced in the Commons and again sent to the Lords. If the Lords still rejected it, on passing through the Commons once again, it would have the force of law, whether or not the Lords rejected it once more. As later events were to show, Grey was by no means happy with this scheme. In any case, Sir Henry merely dangled the threat before the Commons and by no means all Tories were convinced of its reality. By the autumn of 1907, the Cabinet was becoming restless, for although the speech from the throne in February had promised a Licensing Bill, an Irish Education Bill and an Eight Hours Bill for miners, amongst other measures, nothing more had been heard of them. The Prime Minister had given strong personal backing to a Bill increasing the number of smallholdings in Scotland, but the Lords had rejected it. The upper House also severely emasculated an Irish Bill on evicted tenants. In a speech at the end of October, Lloyd George warned that if 'when the Liberal Statute Book is produced it is simply a bundle of sapless legislative faggots fit only for the fire, then a real cry will arise for a new party'. He added, significantly, 'Many of us here in this room will join in the cry.'[25] The President of the Board of Trade further advanced his position by settling what threatened to be a crippling railway strike. Lloyd George received royal congratulations in person and, in adding his own, Grey also reported that Ballin, the German shipowner and companion of the Kaiser, had a tremendous opinion of him. Yet this success could not remove Grey's fear that the country was in for a bad winter. Shipbuilding was almost at a standstill, and other trades were bound to be affected in time. The high Bank Rate was bound to restrict trade everywhere.[26] The Prime Minister, who had lost his wife, was increasingly unwell and unable to concentrate. The great Liberal Government did not seem to be achieving anything, and by-election losses brought home to the leadership that this situation could not last indefinitely. Writing to Bryce in March 1908, Grey did not attempt to hide the fact that the party had lost ground in the country, though he hoped that with a compromise on Education and a modified Licensing Bill, this could be recovered. The Liberal problem, he added, was always 'that a strong and earnest minority demands legislation, which when it is introduced offends the rest of the country'. People supported an Eight Hours Bill, but jibed at a rise in the price of coal. They supported a Licensing Bill, but then discovered that investors did not like losing their money and drinkers objected to the price going up. He concluded, somewhat half-heartedly, that 'after all, one use of a Liberal majority is that it should spend itself in doing things which are right, and which could not be done without it'.[27]

During these two years, Grey had also to accustom himself to life without Dorothy. Dates, anniversaries and recollections came to play an increasing part in his life. He contrived as much as possible to keep up his old habits, with visits to the cottage and to Fallodon, but of course the work never really left him. He described Foreign Office work as 'like the Greek Furies, it pursues one incessantly & one may not rest & read. I fly from it every Saturday evening but it catches me up on Sunday morning.'[28] When at Fallodon he did his official work directly after breakfast and then went out walking on his own. He was resolved not to give politics up 'because that would be trying to anticipate another world in this one, and I know that can't be done, certainly not now'.[29] In July 1906, he wrote from his cottage that he felt 'very worn out; there is more sense now of not having strength for my work than there was. . . .' A few days at Fallodon made him feel much better. He reflected that it might be when 'one is quiet and at rest one *can* feel the past & its influence better; just as a reflection is clear & distinct when the pool is smooth & still'.[30] The pressure of work was such that there was a danger that he might 'lose all my friends, if office lasts much longer for simple want of time to see them. . . .'[31] Late autumn on the Itchen brought little comfort, 'there was no song of birds, nothing bright, no life stirring to take me out of myself, and there was the end of many things to be seen . . . waiting for winter'.[32] His first Christmas as a widower he spent on his own at Fallodon; 'it was very bad for the first day or two at Fallodon; I don't quite know why—perhaps it was because of the vivid memory of this time last year, when the election was beginning. . . .'[33] The question of death constantly interested him. He found that he had 'settled unconsciously into a great wish that I may die easily without the disturbance and devastation of long pain. When one ceases to be anxious about death one becomes more anxious about the manner of it. . . .' While other forms of suffering might purify and ennoble, he found it hard to believe that this was true of physical pain. He found grey hairs coming fast in fresh places on his head, and was glad, for he tried to be old.[34]

As the first anniversary of Dorothy's death approached, he felt that he had been through the full cycle of moods. Writing from Fallodon he admitted the temptation 'to stay here, & walk about amongst the things we planted together, & to think of past days, as if I had no more to do with life & just to wait'.[35] Strength, he told Mrs Creighton, was what he now needed: 'I cannot feel interest in politics at all, nor in my work as I should; it continues to die away and that makes things very hard for there is so much work and it is so incessant. However, the struggle goes on. . . .'[36] Whatever these private feelings, he kept his full round of official engagements and dinners, although not without lamenting that he had to dress up— 'the better the season of the year the more functions & flummery are piled upon one & office is not a human life at all'.[37] The moments spent fishing, dining with friends like the Lytteltons or Tennants, listening to singing, or talking of poetry and books with Sir Henry Newbolt were infinitely preferable to the great occasions of state. Christmas 1907 he did not spend on his own, but with Eddie and Pamela Tennant at the Glen. It was 'just a happy children's Christmas which left the grown ups free to walk about the hills & read & talk quietly'.[38] With Newbolt he usually talked of birds through dinner—Sir Henry wondered 'what he manages to talk to other people about while the servants are in the room— birds are a perfect passe-temps from the diplomatic point of view'. After dinner, they would exchange quotations from Wordsworth, or Newbolt would expound Hegel or Bergson. Sir Edward admitted that he was not a great reader of German philosophy. Plato really contained all that was lasting in philosophies, since 'philosophy never affects mankind unless it is put into the form of poetry, as Plato used it'.[39] Sir Edward would never hear anything said against Wordsworth or Plato. He scorned Francis Galton's attempts to establish Wordsworth's insanity; it showed 'insufficient development' in Galton. For Grey, what could only be partly understood was more interesting than the rest; it was evidence that the limitations within which men existed were not absolute. 'Galton sitting in Plato's cave would have explained to his comrades that the shadows thrown into the cave from outside were unreal and sheer illusion, because he could not touch or handle them, or felt nothing when he did. But for all that, the passing shadows would have remained the most interesting thing to the people in the cave.'[40] In March 1908, they postponed discussion of a Cabinet or party split on the future navy estimates, to dream of the future of civilization. There would be a reaction against the city and people would live in Sussex cottages with gardens and woods. People would come to get used to motors and telephones, and would smile at the idea of being 'rushed' by them. The population of England would fall as the country gradually lost the supremacy of wealth based on steam-power. Switzerland, Norway and New Zealand would be the states of the future, based on water and electricity.[41]

Away from Grey's smoking-room, full of the scent of lilies-of-the-valley, azaleas and hyacinths from Fallodon, the political reality was that old Sir Henry Campbell-Bannerman could not go on much longer. On 1 April he wrote to the King to say that his doctors now advised immediate resignation, which he submitted formally two days later. King Edward requested Asquith to form a Government, summoning him to Biarritz for the purpose. Grey wrote to Sir Henry thanking him for his consideration and the kindness 'which have made it so easy and pleasant for me to serve under you'. He was frank enough to admit that 'the difficulties I made when the Government was formed were short-sighted and ill-judged and we all feel now that troubles, which your presence at the head of the Government kept in abeyance, will have to be faced. . . .'[42] It was a matter of opinion whether the new Prime Minister would be able to face them successfully.

10

The Asquith Government, April 1908–December 1909

The Liberal Party received Asquith as its leader with a sense of inevitability unaccompanied by marked enthusiasm. There had been various murmurings in favour of Grey, but they had not come to anything. Lord Knollys, the King's private secretary, wondered whether Asquith was 'quite the right stamp of man for Prime Minister' and thought that the King might send for Grey.[1] Lady Randolph Churchill told her son that Sir Edward would be Prime Minister and he would be in the Cabinet. J. A. Spender, however, noted that Grey was steadily refusing to emerge from the Foreign Office. Runciman thought that Grey would be foolish to compete with Asquith.[2] There is no evidence that Sir Edward considered himself a serious contender. For his part, the new Prime Minister symbolized Grey's importance to him by telegraphing from Biarritz that the Foreign Secretary should be invited to dinner immediately as soon as he returned.

As Foreign Secretary in the Campbell-Bannerman Government, Grey's position had never seriously been challenged. Radicals like the journalist, A. G. Gardiner, in a sketch first published in 1908, predictably criticized his foreign policy: 'he has committed this country to the support of the most reactionary government in Europe and has given a tendency to events which is rapidly hardening Anglo-German relations into a condition of permanent antagonism. The entente under him has taken a sinister colour. . . .' Nevertheless, crediting Grey with high aims and stainless honour, he speculated on his political future. It depended, in his estimation, on whether the centre of gravity in Liberalism shifted to right or left. 'If to the right, then the highest place in the State is within his scope, for though he is superficially little in sympathy with the eager

185

spirit of the new Liberalism, he is not essentially at variance with it. The Whig temperament is in him a restraint upon the tongue rather than a restraint of thought.'[3] His standing in the Asquith Government was therefore high from the outset. Nevertheless, the effect of the changes made by the new Prime Minister was to make Grey's position somewhat uncomfortable. In particular, Lloyd George and Churchill held a very wide interpretation of their duties at the Treasury and Board of Trade respectively. Not that the pattern of alignment within the Cabinet was straightforward; once again, domestic and foreign issues criss-crossed in an unpredictable manner. And in the disputes of the next few years, Grey played a larger general role in the affairs of the Government than he had done previously. Foreign affairs, of course, remained his overriding concern.

The second major crisis to confront Sir Edward as Foreign Secretary concerned the situation in the Balkans. The conflict in this area had long engaged the attention of influential Liberals who expected their Government to play an active role. The Anglo-Russian rapprochement seemed to give Britain a firmer base for intervention than had been the case for some years. The deterioration in Austro-Russian relations early in 1908 seemed to make co-operation with Russia even easier. At the end of March, Grey wrote to Bryce in Washington that he believed at long last that the time was ripe for the Powers to present proposals for reform in Macedonia to the Sultan. Though the jealousies between the Powers were not to be underestimated, there was now a chance that they could reach agreement.[4] The Macedonian problem was but one aspect of the general situation in the Balkans, where resistance movements operated in the areas still under Turkish control. Sporadic violent uprisings were suppressed with equal violence. The Macedonian question was peculiarly intractable because the 'Macedonians' were variously believed to be Serbs, Greeks, Bulgars or just plain Macedonians. Grey was anxious to be able to demonstrate some improvement in the Balkans as the fruit of Anglo-Russian co-operation, since his agreement was coming under fresh criticism. When the Foreign Secretary informed the House of Commons that the King and the Tsar were to meet at Tallinn in the summer, Keir Hardie brought a motion of censure which attracted 59 votes. In his speech, Grey told the members that if reconciliation with Russia was made impossible he would resign. The two monarchs, accompanied by Hardinge (though Asquith felt that a minister would be a better choice in future) and Isvolsky, discussed the situation in Macedonia, the Near East and the general European scene. Hardinge argued that 'it was absolutely necessary that England and Russia should maintain towards each other the same cordial and friendly relations as now exist between England and France, which in the case of England and Russia are, moreover, inspired by an identity of interests of which the solution of the Macedonian problem was not the least'.[5]

The Macedonian problem was not, however, to be solved. A fresh complication ensued with the success of the Young Turk revolution in the summer of 1908 and the overthrow, though not the deposition, of the Sultan, Abdul Hamid. While the events were welcomed by English Liberals, the leaders had not come to power to preside over the liquidation of European Turkey. Indeed, the Committee of Union and Progress, which was the secret society behind the revolution, grew and spread in Macedonia itself. In the words of its historian, the Young Turk revolution was a nationalist uprising 'which aimed at the overthrowing of the regime of Abdul Hamid and its replacement by a stronger government which would put an end to foreign interference and the intolerable conditions under which the Turks had been living. . . .' The movement was liberal to a point, but the nationalistic elements far outweighed the liberal. 'Very little thought was given to the non-Turkish elements in the Ottoman Empire . . . other than that they must perforce all become Ottomans in a revived and powerful empire. . . .'[6] The movement came as a surprise to Grey, and immediately confronted him with a dilemma.[7] He decided that it was more important to regain the British position in Constantinople by showing goodwill towards the new regime rather than offend it by pressing for further reform in Macedonia. There were, nevertheless, complications for Britain in such an attitude. For example, the demand for a constitution in Egypt would gain great force and the British power of resisting it would be very much diminished. In the meantime, Grey wrote, 'Our course is clear; we must be ready to help the better elements, to wait upon events, and give sympathy and encouragement when required to the reform movement.' Shortly afterwards, however, he was writing: 'We must be careful not to give Russia the impression that we are reverting to the old policy of supporting Turkey as a barrier against her and should continue to show willingness to work with Russia when possible. . . .'[8] The situation was clearly one of considerable delicacy, for to an extent Grey was in fact reverting to such a policy. He used the improvement of the British position to frustrate the construction of the Baghdad Railway under German-Turkish auspices. British capitalists were surprisingly reluctant to open up the new opportunities before them and in matters of trade, contracts and concessions, Grey, following precedent, 'was prepared to protect but not to lead'.[9]

The attempt to reassert the British political and economic position could not but strain the attempted Anglo-Russian venture in the Balkans. Isvolsky was anxious to raise the vexed question of the Straits.[10] On 2 July he wrote to the Austrian Foreign Minister, Aehrenthal, suggesting that if Austria-Hungary supported Russia in her attempts to open the Dardanelles, Russia would in turn support the annexation by the Habsburgs of Bosnia and Herzegovina, and the Sanjak of Novi-Bazar. In these latter territories, Austria legally administered and stationed troops respectively, but there were those in Vienna who now wanted to see both areas transferred from Ottoman to Habsburg suzerainty. It seemed, therefore, that the Russian Foreign Minister was seeking a personal triumph. These suspicions hardened when Isvolsky and Aehrenthal, seemingly taking advantage of events in Constantinople, met in Moravia in September and came to a verbal agreement regarding Bosnia, Herzegovina and the Straits. In addition, there was a further source of potential Anglo-Russian discord. Prince Ferdinand of Bulgaria was also anxious to take advantage of the situation and was looking for a pretext to declare himself completely independent. If he should take this step, the Russians might feel obliged to support him or risk the growth of Austrian influence in Sofia. If this happened, the British might have to choose between Russia and Turkey.

Early in October came the news Grey feared. Bulgaria declared herself a sovereign state, and the Austrians annexed Bosnia and Herzegovina unilaterally, although they waived their rights in the Sanjak by way of compensation to Turkey. Grey wrote at once to Asquith that the Austrian action in supporting Bulgaria—that action in turn being a calculated flouting of the Young Turk regime —was 'monstrous'. 'I propose', he added, 'that we should be the Turk's friend in the contest: inclination and policy both point that way, for the Young Turk regime is the injured and deserving party. . . .' He intended to state publicly that Britain could not 'recognize the right of any Power to alter an international Treaty without the consent of the other Powers parties to it. . . .' The Prime

Minister telegraphed that he entirely agreed.[11] It was obvious, however, that short of an unlikely war, the events were *faits accomplis*. Grey therefore concentrated on using the device of non-recognition to help the Turks gain some counter-concession by diplomacy.

The crisis was at its height when Isvolsky, complaining that he had been deceived by Aehrenthal, arrived in London to see the Foreign Secretary. He stated that he had not in fact agreed to Austrian annexation of Bosnia and Herzegovina, though Grey was sceptical. Isvolsky then painted a dire picture of the situation in St Petersburg. If he were dismissed, the Anglo-Russian agreement would be doomed. He had to be able to take the Tsar a 'peace offering' and agreement to the passage of Russian warships through the Straits would be ideal for this purpose. Grey was not in principle averse to a change in the provisions relating to the use of the Straits, but felt that the moment was quite inopportune to press for a further concession from the Turks. The Cabinet met on 12 October to consider the matter, and endorsed the opinion that the time was not ripe. Isvolsky's suggestion that the Straits should be closed to all but the Black Sea states was equally unacceptable. Public opinion 'would not support any Government which, for no consideration to us, abandoned what has always been regarded as a valuable Treaty right. . . .'[12] Isvolsky expressed his grave disappointment at this decision, but Grey did not budge. Hardinge thought the Cabinet was being silly—a not uncommon feeling on his part. However, later on 12 October, Isvolsky returned, with the suggested solution that in the event of war, Turkey should observe her neutrality by giving equal facilities for passage through the Straits to all the belligerents. When Grey put this idea to his colleagues, the element of reciprocity it involved carried the day. Isvolsky managed to find the encouragement to Russian ambition sufficient for his purposes. The King was persuaded to send the Tsar a letter in praise of the Foreign Minister's skill. As Hardinge wrote to Bryce, 'The danger seems, for the moment, to have been averted, and if we can only maintain the present situation for the next month, snow will fall in the Balkans. . . .' He considered that the Turks had behaved with great forbearance. However, he feared that even if the Bosnian and Bulgarian questions could be patched up, there still remained 'that wretched little Servia who, I fear, is bent on mischief unless she can get some territorial compensation for the loss of her national aspirations'. Hardinge also felt sure that Aehrenthal's action had been largely at the instigation of

Berlin—an indication that Anglo-German relations were little better.[13]

It was on relations with Berlin that Grey had his first serious brush with some of his colleagues. A hardening hostility had serious implications for the bright new visions of social reform. Lloyd George had already started on his scheme for old age pensions, and tried to enlist the Prime Minister in favour of financing them by reducing military or naval expenditure rather than by resorting to fresh taxation. Asquith appointed a Cabinet committee to go into the question. Churchill sniffed around eagerly for possible economies and the scent took him in the direction of Haldane. The Secretary of State for War was disinclined to cut military expenditure. Lord Esher was called in by Asquith to help resolve the crisis. He had been most helpful in resolving a recent little difficulty caused by the King, exuberantly and independently creating the Tsar an Admiral of the Fleet. Esher found Churchill wild and unpractical, though he appreciated the difficulty of forcing Haldane's hand. He commented that if Churchill thought himself Napoleon, he would not get very far: 'Men of the Grey, Crewe and Asquith type (notably the former) are so unlike the adventurers that Napoleon swept out of his path. Our rulers have roots which go deep down into the political soil.'[14] At any rate, they went deep enough to fend off the call for extensive cuts in defence expenditure.

Substantially defeated in this approach, Lloyd George and Churchill realized that an alternative was to settle Anglo-German difficulties themselves. In August 1908, both Lloyd George and Churchill in public talked about the need to improve relations with Germany. Grey was displeased, as was the King. The Prime Minister agreed with Grey that the substance of Lloyd George's remarks (made in Germany while on a visit with the ostensible object of examining the German welfare system) had not been objectionable, but he should never have consented to be interviewed at all on naval matters while abroad. He would make this clear, without 'scolding' the Chancellor. As regards Churchill, Grey was rather more inclined to regard him as simply impetuous, writing at the end of the Campbell-Bannerman ministry that Winston 'knows nothing about the F.O. work, and thinks that because a Parliamentary Under-Secretary can travel and pick and choose and gallop about the field and toss his head and sniff what breeze he pleases, therefore a Foreign Secretary can do the same'.[15] It was, of course, far from being the case that Grey himself wished to see a continuing spiral of defence expenditure. He authorized Hardinge to raise the matter with the German Emperor when he accompanied the King on a visit to Cronberg in August 1908. The Kaiser there maintained that no cause for apprehension in England as to the German naval programme could exist. The German programme was not a new one 'and it had become a point of national honour that it should be completed. No discussion with a foreign Government could be tolerated. . . .'[16] In face of such intransigent comments, there was little even Lloyd George and Churchill could do. Already, however, Grey was quietly beginning to wonder whether it might be possible to show goodwill to Germany, on matters removed from direct naval rivalry, in the hope that this might prove a more acceptable path to agreement. The question of giving the Germans facilities at Walfisch Bay (the imperial enclave within German South-West Africa), or even its outright cession was being considered in the summer of 1908. He was in correspondence with Lord Crewe, the Colonial Secretary, on the subject in June and both men were aware that objections were likely to come from South Africa. This indeed proved to be the case and Grey wrote that it was a factor which could not be got over. Grey was rather disappointed: 'German intrigues in S. Africa are now futile. Neither Boers nor British would entertain them and railway or no railway the Germans can do nothing by force against a united South Africa as long as we keep command of the sea. . . .' He wanted 'to make it clear to the Germans that it is not we who have forbidden the colony to make any arrangements, though we uphold the colonial view. . . .' He told Crewe that his comments were not official—'this question is so entirely a South African one that it is hardly for the F.O. to argue with the C.O. about it'.[17] Presiding over the 'Imperial F.O.' was becoming a difficult job.

The German attitude on the naval question seemed so negative that Grey had little hesitation in ignoring the claims of some colleagues, like Loreburn, that a fresh approach should be made. To have undertaken worthless negotiations would only have provoked the French to fever pitch. They were already bad enough in their worries. Through various channels, Clemenceau contrived to cast doubt on British usefulness as a possible support. It was a great misfortune 'that at a moment so pregnant with disagreeable possibilities you are tinkering at your army and have, relatively speaking, neither men, arms nor ammunition'.[18] Grey passed on these friendly comments to the Prime Minister, who was not very sympathetic. Clemenceau was very ignorant, he replied in September 1908, 'if he imagines that we are going to keep here a standing army of half or three quarters of a million of men, ready to meet the Germans in Belgium, if and when they are minded to adopt that route for the invasion of France'.[19] Sir Edward quietened Loreburn's fears by writing that: 'For the present the Near Eastern complications overshadow all other Foreign Affairs, and as regards these France stands more in the good books of Germany and Austria than anyone else does, and there is no prospect just now of a quarrel arising on her account with anyone. . . .'[20] Loreburn's hopes of greater understanding between Britain and Germany were also somewhat dimmed by unfortunate incidents, like the *Daily Telegraph* affair. At the height of the Bosnian crisis the newspaper published what purported to be an interview given by the Kaiser to a certain Colonel Stuart Wortley. He claimed a desire to improve Anglo-German relations, instancing as evidence of his goodwill, his refusal to join France and Russia in a continental alliance at the time of the Boer War. This exercise, a personal whim of the Emperor's, back-fired badly. It was received with astonishment and then amusement in Britain, and caused him considerable trouble with his Ministers. Grey was not very amused: 'I am very tired of the Emperor—he is like a great battleship with steam up and the screws going but no rudder & you cannot tell what he will run into or what catastrophe he will cause. Anyhow the country with the biggest army in the world has been made a fool of in public by its own Emperor & that is an uncomfortable thing for the country fooled & laughed at will seek some object on which to vent its ill-temper. I am glad we are an island. . . .'[21]

In the aftermath of the annexation of Bosnia, Anglo-Austrian relations deteriorated sharply. Grey considered the attacks on Britain in the Austrian press to be grossly unfair. He told the Austrian Ambassador, Count Mensdorff, that 'if the consequences of the annexation of Bosnia had been within my control, I should not have taken the serious view which I had of the Austrian action. It was precisely because the feeling which had been aroused in Turkey, Russia, Italy, Servia and Montenegro was so strong and spontaneous that I thought the situation serious. . . .'[22] On Christmas Day, 1908, he wrote gloomily to Bryce that the Near East was not getting settled—'D'Aehrenthal with his short sighted trickery has uncorked several bottles'.[23] Hardinge optimistically hoped for 'the federation of the small Slav states of the Balkans with Turkey to support them' and looked for a Turkish victory if Bulgaria should be rash enough to attack.[24] Fortunately, however, Grey's patient support of Turkey was rewarded in the middle of January, when the Austrians agreed to pay a substantial sum in compensation to Constantinople. The Austrians may have felt that British naval movements in the Mediterranean (which were designed to prevent Greece annexing Crete) were an indication of willingness to support Turkey if war broke out. Grey had no such design. As he told the Prime Minister, he had simply let it be known to the Italian Foreign Minister that war between Austria and Turkey could doubtfully be limited, and Britain might intervene.[25] To the Austrian Ambassador, he denied that the British position had been determined by hostility to Germany. 'The balance of power in Europe was preserved by the present grouping, and I should not think of wishing to disturb it', he added.[26] What did alarm him was Aehrenthal's seemingly reckless disregard for the fragility of the situation; 'a breach of the peace will provoke a conflagration greater than anyone can foresee: he is living in a fool's paradise. It is dangerous to light a fire out of doors when there is a lot of combustible material about. . . .'[27]

Grey and Hardinge both hoped that with the Austrian payment to the Turks, 'Bulgaria will now be much more moderate and conciliatory in her attitude'.[28] But by the end of January, Hardinge was gloomy. There was a distinctly warlike feeling in the Bulgarian capital, Sofia. Diplomatically, the situation was now very complicated. Russia was unwilling to see undue pressure put on the Bulgarians because this would only contribute further to the loss of her traditional influence with them. The British Minister in Sofia was equally reluctant to drive them into the arms of Vienna. The British Ambassador in Constantinople, however, insisted that some payment should be made to placate Turkish feelings. Once again, the delicate balance of British policy was exposed. Fortunately, a solution was found whereby the Russians helped Bulgaria to pay a substantial sum to Turkey. Grey was quite explicit in his reason for accepting this proposal: 'If I had refused to support . . . the result would have been a diplomatic separation between Russia and us that would have reacted unfavourably on the whole of our relations.'[29]

The final legacy of the Bosnian crisis was the problem of Serbian compensation from Austria. In February 1909, as Hardinge put it,

'We are having a very strenuous time with Balkan affairs.' There was no question of Vienna making any concessions, indeed a strong party advocated a punitive expedition against Serbia and the exaction of a promise of 'good neighbourliness'. Britain would not countenance any suggestion that it should be for Turkey to ease the situation by herself making compensation in lieu. Equally, Grey made it clear to Isvolsky that Britain would not give military support if war broke out between Serbia and Austria, with Russia aiding the former. It was 'almost incredible' to Hardinge that Austria should contemplate such a venture, but unless Isvolsky could be worked up 'to the pitch of telling the Servians that they are not to expect any territorial compensation', war seemed inevitable.[30] If there was to be peace, the Serbs would have to accept what they would no doubt regard as 'humiliating' terms. This was, indeed, what happened. Berlin intervened by putting pressure on the Russians to accept the Austrian annexation of Bosnia, and, since they were not really prepared to go to war, they did so. Grey continued to hold out, and put on a show of disapproval at the Russian action, but a little later followed suit.

Although Grey could claim substantial success for his policy of supporting Turkey, the final Austro-German success in denying Serbia any compensation exposed the ineffective nature of the Anglo-Russian entente in the Balkans. Granted the prevailing feelings among them, the notion of a federation of Balkan states in alliance with Turkey—which was canvassed as an alternative strategy—was little more than a pious hope. It was difficult to feel much confidence in the success of British policy in the area, though, as Hardinge admitted, the situation could change with 'kaleidoscopic rapidity'. For the moment, in the summer of 1909, Anglo-Russian relations were cool. St Petersburg knew that British support had stopped short of military intervention and that France, her ally, had been lukewarm throughout. Once again, humiliation at the hands of Austria had been her fate. Rather than be exposed in this way again, pressures to seek an accommodation with Germany could be expected to increase. They could perhaps be countered if the Russian agreement were turned into a formal alliance, but since the Cabinet would not accept the idea, neither Hardinge nor Grey pursued it very far. The great obstacle was Russian behaviour in Persia, which continued to antagonize many Liberals. The friction between British and Russian diplomatic representatives in Tehran had been serious enough to be brought before the Cabinet.

Amidst all his other concerns, Grey tried to keep out of Persian affairs in 1908. He professed to hope that, with Russian co-operation, a reform programme could be imposed on the Shah, though, as has been observed, this ignored the fact that 'the shah and the court party, whatever their protestations, had no intention of implementing such a programme'.[31] When the question of an Anglo-Russian loan to the Shah was mooted, Grey also experienced difficulty with his colleagues. Morley tried, though in the end unsuccessfully, to argue that he had supported the Anglo-Russian agreement as a way of divesting India of concern with Persian affairs. He therefore saw no reason why a contribution from sorely pressed India should be expected—though in the end he agreed to contribute a quarter of the promised international loan.[32] In May 1909, again under British and Russian pressure, the Shah swore allegiance to the constitution for the fourth time, but on this occasion was too late. The various factions which made up the Constitutionalist movement were determined to advance on Tehran and oust him. Reputedly, a British official, having joined his Russian colleague in a warning not to proceed, slipped back to see the leaders, ostensibly in search of his cigarette case, and whispered: 'Go to Tehran and be assured.'[33] By July, the Shah had fled to the Russian Legation and was deposed in favour of his boy son. In the following months, the National Assembly resumed its work. The British Minister reported that, putting aside *amour propre*, he was 'disposed to rejoice at the failure of our programme'. Under the lately deposed Shah there was never a real chance of a constitutional regime working satisfactorily. Now the field was 'open for a second and more promising experiment in parliamentary government'.[34] While this was no doubt splendid for the Persians and their British Liberal sympathizers, it did not help Grey's attempts to work with the Russians. He was sceptical about the possibilities of a revitalized Persia being able to withstand Russian pressure. In this respect, the dilemma confronting British policy, as Grey saw it, was very similar throughout the Near East. He was not ideologically opposed to the progress of constitutional movements. About events in Turkey, for example, he wrote in August 1908, 'I am more interested in that than in anything that has happened while I have been in office. The change in Turkey is pregnant with consequences. . . .'[35] Nevertheless, he retained a cool detachment and doubted whether, on their own, these could survive against pressure from the north. Nor was it clear to him that if Britain were to support the revitalized Near Eastern states against Russia, they had a sufficient identity of interest with the British Empire to be reliable partners. This was the great danger with his Turkish policy—there was a strong risk that the new regime would consider acting as long-stop for British policy in the Balkans an unrewarding occupation and seek her own relations with the Central Powers. In so far as the new regimes were basically nationalist in outlook, Grey was further handicapped by the fact that, in contrast to Germany, Britain was already an imperial Power in the area and herself experiencing pressures, both in Egypt and India, of a similar kind. No policy in the Near East could clear a way through all these problems, but the course pursued by Grey took them all into account, though leaving them largely unresolved.

Although the Balkan and Near Eastern crises had some impact on Anglo-German relations, the naval question was at the centre of discussions between London and Berlin. It also, of course, had important domestic repercussions. The pressures for a reduction in naval expenditure had been defeated early in 1908, but at the end of the year they were clearly building up once again. Just before Christmas, Grey wrote to Asquith outlining a proposed interview with the German Ambassador. In view of the supposed capacity of Germany to build twenty-one, or at least seventeen, Dreadnoughts by April 1912, he would say that he was ready to discuss future building plans with Germany, but if the offer was not taken up, Parliament would be asked to take the necessary steps. This letter was written after some preliminary exchanges in the Cabinet. The First Lord of the Admiralty, McKenna, who had been appointed by Asquith to cool the shipbuilding ardours of the Sea Lords, now took their view. He submitted estimates which would provide for at least six Dreadnoughts and an increased expenditure of £3 million. Churchill and Lloyd George, who fought these proposals, with Grey and McKenna as their chief opponents, believed that they had succeeded in cutting back these extravagant demands. Hence Grey's proposal that he approach Metternich to try to discover the truth. On 30 December, McKenna wrote to Grey reiterating his belief that Germany meant to build to the full extent of her capacity. He argued that: 'If by any spurt Germany can once catch us up we have no longer any such superior building capacity as would ensure our supremacy.'[36] The Foreign Secretary was very impressed by this argument.

After receiving the Prime Minister's approval, Grey duly had his interview with Metternich on 4 January. The Ambassador, in reply, cast doubt on the accuracy of the figures suggested by the Admiralty for German naval construction, and repeated that this programme was now fixed by law. He did not take up Grey's offer to have discussions on the situation and simply reiterated that German building was not in competition with Britain. The Foreign Secretary then reported to Asquith, and a serious crisis seemed to be brewing. Since, on a number of occasions, Grey had made it clear publicly that he regarded naval supremacy as vital for the maintenance of a successful foreign policy, it looked as though he might become very obstinate. The differences in the Cabinet were genuinely political rather than personal. Asquith and Grey remained on good terms. The Prime Minister had himself but a few weeks before endorsed the two-Power standard, and Grey wrote to Margot Asquith that her husband was in great form—he 'only shines out bigger in contrast to the curs that yap at his heels'.[37] Grey continued to have a high regard for Churchill's bounding energy. The fact that he did not attend Churchill's wedding in September had no personal significance. The ceremony had such associations for him that he now declined all invitations.[38] Since personal relations still remained good, it seemed that a way out of the crisis might be found. Asquith began by telling Churchill that he quite shared his sense of urgency about social proposals, in particular, unemployment. His chief hope, however, remained that the naval excitement would melt away by itself. Others shared the view that this might happen. For example, Hardinge was writing to Bryce that the Germans showed 'some signs of slackening' in their naval programme. He attributed this to Asquith's firm adherence to the two-Power standard. He had always maintained that 'our best way of stopping or of obtaining a modification of, the German naval programme, would be a complete declaration of our intentions'.[39]

However, the naval issue did not vanish in the night. Primed by the Sea Lords, McKenna stuck to his position in the Cabinet. In answer, Churchill circulated a paper casting doubt on the reality of the German danger. Lloyd George wrote a long letter to the Prime Minister lamenting that the party seemed likely to embark on a sterile controversy which would depress its supports in the country and undermine its parliamentary effectiveness. His alignment with Churchill was clear, though he left himself room for compromise. These two were supported in argument, though not in intimacy, by Morley, Burns and Harcourt. On 3 February, Grey again saw Metternich, who repeated his denial of the notion that German shipbuilding competed in any sense with British. In return, Grey tried to explain the enormous emotional significance of the navy for the average Englishman. If supremacy at sea were challenged, the security of the Empire was at stake. It was as if one of Germany's land neighbours were to collect an army more powerful than her own. After this conversation, Grey wrote to Asquith that the House of Commons would demand to know how many ships would be needed to maintain the superiority which was the objective of the building programme. Like others, he had advocated retrenchment at the last election, 'but I always excepted the Navy from my promises, and in any case promises must be subordinate to National Safety'.[40]

A series of Cabinet meetings in the middle of February failed to produce agreement. The point at issue, Asquith reported to the King, was whether to lay down six Dreadnoughts at once, or four with an option to lay down a further two—if German construction seemed to warrant it. There was still 'great difference of opinion', with Churchill, Harcourt, Burns and Morley for the smaller, and Grey, Runciman, Crewe and Buxton for the larger. Lloyd George proposed a compromise programme to be spread over a certain number of years so as to equalize the burden of expenditure. Asquith himself, Grey and Crewe would have accepted this settlement, but Harcourt and Runciman felt that it would impair parliamentary control. McKenna stuck throughout to his original proposal.[41] In an attempt to resolve the deadlock, a small Cabinet committee, consisting of Asquith, Grey, Morley and Lloyd George, explored the question further. Without success, Grey attempted to persuade Morley that the critical time would prove to be in 1912: 'If we err at all we must err on the side of safety; we must be in advance rather than in arrears; for the former error is reparable, the latter is not.' In typical fashion, he continued that his own ambitions were so dead that he thought the United Kingdom would be happier without an Empire and with a population of ten millions. However, he did not think his colleagues would thank him for expressing such views! As things stood, he would resign unless the Navy Estimates provided a sufficient margin of safety against possible German strength in 1912–13.[42] Churchill countered Grey's arguments with two points. First, he suggested that airships rather than Dreadnoughts should be built, since the latter would be impotent against the former. Grey was a little bewildered, though he was beginning to doubt whether there were 'any such things as facts! Providence is so fond of qualifications.' Secondly, Churchill claimed that no difference existed between them on the paramountcy of public safety. 'There is no difference between us which would —if the facts are proved—prevent McKenna laying down every ship exactly as he plans it now.' Grey had also argued that unless six ships were ordered, there would be a dangerous public panic, not to mention naval resignations. Even if all these fears were justified, which Churchill doubted, he thought it would be a weak government to be influenced by such considerations. 'Are you willing', he concluded, 'to see the Government broken irretrievably rather than postpone for a few months during wh. the facts may be proved . . .'[43] Grey's reply, unfortunately, does not seem extant, but clearly, his agreement would be vital in any eventual solution. In the midst of this crisis, Asquith wrote to his wife: 'E. Grey is a great stand-by always, sound, temperate and strong.'[44]

At last, during the Cabinet on 24 February, Asquith was able to find a solution acceptable both to McKenna and Grey, and to Churchill and Lloyd George. Oddly enough, the compromise now involved eight ships, rather than six. Four Dreadnoughts were definitely to be laid down, and the House was to be asked to pass an act to make forward contracts so that, if it saw fit, the Government could place orders for four additional ships to be laid down not later than April 1910. The 'economists' had singularly little to show for their efforts. Curiously, however, Hardinge wrote to the King's private secretary to let him know that he was 'fairly disgusted' with the solution. He felt that the Government would not commission the extra ships, and the compromise was 'meant to throw dust in the eyes of the public by promising more than it is the intention of the Govt. to carry out'. He then permitted himself some very strong words about his political master: 'I always told you that Grey is a weak man. I thought that success had given him confidence & even strength but as regards the latter characteristic I was mistaken. I expect that nothing can ever make a weak man a strong one and that it is a great mistake to think otherwise. The outlook is gloomy. . . . W. Churchill is the one man in the Cabinet who knows what he wants and how to get it.'[45] 'Strong men' and 'weak men' depend on the perspective of the observer. From another angle, it might be argued that Grey showed his strength in accepting a compromise which his Permanent Under-Secretary found inadequate. In any event, Hardinge quite wrongly assessed the significance of the compromise he condemned and in so doing underestimated the object of his scorn.

In view of Hardinge's comments, lamenting his lack of control over Grey, there is a delicate irony in the fact that in this, and succeeding months, the popular journalist, W. T. Stead (born, curiously, in Grey's home parish of Embleton), was campaigning with the slogan: 'Let the country and foreign nations understand that Sir Edward Grey is master in his own office, and not Sir Charles Hardinge.' In particular, Hardinge was alleged to be holding up the progress of disarmament. On an earlier occasion, Grey wrote to the Prime Minister that he did not worry about anything Stead wrote. In his view, there was less chance of doing anything effective with the Germans if there was a public campaign. Nor was he very impressed by the truth of Stead's allegations about himself. 'He has an insane idea that Bertie and C. Hardinge are in a conspiracy to defeat any reduction of expenditure on armaments and that I am their tool. . . .' The Foreign Secretary proposed to say nothing, for to argue publicly would only increase Stead's sense of his own importance.[46] When Hardinge was attacked again, Grey wrote to St Loe Strachey that Hardinge and Bertie had nothing to do with the line taken about armaments at the Hague 'but in any case if attacks are to be made upon Civil Servants, no self-respecting man will stay in the service'.[47]

In the immediate aftermath of the Cabinet crisis of early 1909, relations were somewhat strained. In private conversation early in March, Grey allegedly remarked: 'Winston, very soon, will become incapable from sheer activity of mind of being anything in a cabinet but Prime Minister.'[48] For some reason, talk of Churchill naturally led Grey on to talking of Napoleon. However, the Foreign Secretary was not perturbed; the chief object of his concern was to try to discover the truth about German intentions. On 5 March he suggested to the German Ambassador that facilities should be offered to the Naval Attachés to examine the number of ships under construction in both countries. He also asked for clarification of the German building programme, since speculation only produced suspicion. On 10 March, Metternich stated that Germany would not have the thirteen ships, which were being talked about, ready until the end of 1912, instead of the spring, as he had first suggested. He was less than frank about the collecting together of materials which could be used in accelerating the programme, and he had to admit that the Emperor would not allow any exchanges between experts. Sir Edward was now confused as to what exactly was being built and he was very wary. Nothing he heard led him to suggest any changes in Britain's estimates. Fisher, the First Sea Lord, was delighted by Grey's staunchness, writing to the King: 'Your Majesty has one splendid servant in the Cabinet—the Foreign Secretary. He is as much above all the rest of them as Mr. Balfour is above all his colleagues!' Haldane, on the other hand, was a 'veritable Judas'.[49] Fisher's flattering remarks were no doubt the result of a long conversation he had had with Grey on 4 March. The Foreign Secretary then outlined his understanding of the Cabinet's compromise decision. It meant that the extra four ships would be ordered, but not paid for, when the Admiralty advised it. Fisher interjected: 'We say "now".' On Fisher's account, Grey further said that if there were then any difficulty in the Cabinet, that would be the time for 'reconsideration'.[50]

The conversations with Metternich reinforced the earlier stand taken by Grey and McKenna in the Cabinet. Asquith himself seems to have become, for the moment, more alarmed than he had been earlier. All three, however, were in some political difficulty. The Opposition could naturally accuse the Government of incompetence in not realizing the gravity of the situation if they said the position was very serious. But unless they said it was grave, they would have trouble from their own supporters who were already horrified by the increased expenditure and sceptical of the German 'threat'. Dissension reappeared in the Cabinet itself on 19 March when Lloyd George, angry at the rejection of his proposal for a tax on land values, lost his temper. Grey may well have taken the brunt of his biting tongue, for Asquith took the trouble to write to him after the meeting, saying that, with the doubtful exception of Winston the Chancellor's remarks were resented by the whole Cabinet. He explained that the week's events had been 'a complete debacle for them and their ideas'. No doubt Churchill and Lloyd George could not help reflecting on how they would have looked if they had resigned with, according to Winston, '90 per cent of the Liberal party behind them'.[51]

A few days later, Grey was embarrassed to learn that J. L. Garvin, the editor of the *Observer*, was telling people that he had it on the authority of the First Sea Lord that Grey was insisting in the Cabinet that the four extra ships should be built and was threatening resignation if they were not. Fisher had indeed been supplying Garvin with considerable information which had been used in the newspaper to support the campaign for naval expansion. Suspecting this, Grey wrote to Fisher saying that Garvin 'must be brought to book'. The First Sea Lord was now in an awkward position, and, without permission, sent Grey's letter on to Garvin inviting him to reply. The editor claimed that he had been misrepresented, and that he had spoken only to his proprietor, Lord Northcliffe, and to Chirol of *The Times*. Fisher, he claimed, had not asked him to publish a statement. The First Sea Lord was delighted with this reply—and even more pleased that an article Garvin had written on the naval question had raised the temperature of the agitation. But Grey was only partly mollified. He replied that the alleged private conversations, not the article, were the substance of his complaint. In his view, anything a public man said in public was fair comment. His unexpressed views were a matter for legitimate conjecture, and if he was indiscreet in private he willingly accepted the consequences. What was intolerable, however, was that 'others who are in official & confidential relations should make statements about his individual views, upon which statements can be founded in the press whether correct or incorrect contrasting his position with that of his colleagues'. Grey was angry with Fisher, both on the general issue of communicating information, and on the narrower issue of passing on his letter to Garvin. The following day, 23 March, the two men met at dinner and Fisher wrote to Garvin: 'I fear he & I are estranged but it can't be helped and the best thing is silence.'[52]

In view of his prominent role in the naval controversy, it was fitting that Grey should make the major speech for the Government in reply to the Opposition motion of censure. This speech, at the end of March 1909, was probably his most important thus far. He began by sharing with his own backbenchers a disgust at the amount being spent by the great countries of Europe on their armies and navies. But unilateral disarmament was not the solution. Britain would probably become the conscripted appendage of some stronger Power if that happened. The Navy remained the basis of British defence and, in contrast to the German Navy to Germany, its strength was of vital importance to national security. Because this was so, he felt that Germany should take the first step towards reducing her naval expenditure, whereupon Britain would certainly follow suit. Such an arrangement would necessarily have to be on the basis of British naval superiority. If this could be achieved, he concluded, there would be a feeling of increased security and peace in Europe. A first step in this direction would be the exchange of information between experts. This speech, together with a shorter one from the Prime Minister, seems to have given considerable satisfaction to the House and dampened the new cry, 'We want eight and we won't wait.'[53] The Home Secretary, Gladstone, described Grey's speech as 'a most notable statement'. As a speaker, Sir Edward was 'sui generis', his 'cool impressive delivery kept the House in the closest attention from beginning to end'.[54] It drew an eulogy from Balfour. Hardinge, sitting in the gallery, told the King that the speech had had a good effect from a Foreign Office point of view. He was convinced that the four extra Dreadnoughts were necessary, and if they were not ordered, 'Sir Edward will leave the Cabinet'. In so far as the speech had been designed 'to convince the British public that so long as he remained a member of the Cabinet, the national security would not be endangered . . .', he thought it had succeeded.[55]

Asquith, however, still hedged on the issue of further construction. In view of the denials and disclaimers from Germany which both preceded and followed Grey's speech, he had fresh doubts about the fundamental position. He was also reluctant to sanction the extra expenditure. Grey, however, kept up the pressure. He passed on the news that Italy and Austria-Hungary were believed to be building Dreadnoughts. This news 'ought to decide us to use our own powers as to beginning the extra four ships this year', and he asked that the Cabinet should decide as soon as the Budget was settled.[56] It seems likely that the Austrian building programme led the Prime Minister to believe that the extra four were indeed necessary. With surprisingly little trouble, the Cabinet agreed, and McKenna announced the decision in the Commons on 26 July. A disgruntled group of Liberal M.P.s realized that they had been out-manœuvred. Having obtained his objective, Grey admitted to Asquith in September that there was 'clearly no imminent danger from Austrian Dreadnoughts, although it was difficult to dispose of fears based on statements, known to be exaggerated, but which could not be completely disproved'.[57] For the time being, with this decision, some of the tension went out of the naval crisis.

Edward Grey was largely responsible for the fact that eight ships were finally ordered. McKenna had advocated the Admiralty's case resolutely, but he lacked sufficient political weight to win. Grey's support of the Navy seems to have been on general grounds of strength, rather than because of particular support for Fisher in the battle he was waging, and losing, to prevent the adoption of an extensive continental military strategy. The Foreign Secretary seems to have played very little part in these discussions. It was Hardinge who represented the Foreign Office on the sub-committee of the C.I.D. appointed by Asquith in October 1908 to consider the military needs of the Empire. At a meeting of that sub-committee on 23 March 1909, Hardinge had declared that the only grounds on which the French could base any hopes of military assistance were the 'semi-official' military conversations, and the force contemplated in these talks was 'a comparatively small one'.[58] No one asked any further questions. The sub-committee's report, accepted by the C.I.D. in the summer of 1909, clearly envisaged a possible European role for the Expeditionary Force. The practical importance of such a decision was, however, still limited. The navy was unco-operative and a year later no transport tables had been drawn up for the movement of the Expeditionary Force to the continent. Grey must have been informed of these proceedings, although he did not himself attend a C.I.D. meeting either in 1909 or 1910. If he had strong views, he evidently did not feel called upon to express them in this forum. Even if he did maintain a lingering sympathy for the naval viewpoint, circumstances were bringing his collaboration with Fisher to an end. The struggle between the First Sea Lord and Admiral Lord Charles Beresford had broken out again, and the situation could not be allowed to continue. Grey sat on a committee of inquiry, chaired by Asquith, together with Crewe, Morley and Haldane. When its report was published in August 1909, both men professed to find encouragement in it, but Fisher had in reality been expecting stronger Government backing. It was clear that he would have to go, and in due course his resignation was announced, to take effect from the end of January 1910. It is unlikely that Grey fought very hard on his behalf. Their personalities were not really very sympathetic and the Garvin incident had marred their earlier co-operation. At an earlier stage of the Beresford–Fisher struggle, Grey had been 'on the wobble' in the direction of Beresford, and he probably wobbled again.[59]

The Foreign Secretary's support of a big navy did not mean that he welcomed naval expenditure for its own sake, or saw it as a means of distracting the public from events at home. He was prepared to entertain discussions with Germany, although he adhered to his view that the Germany Navy was an optional extra.

It may be, of course, that it was because he took this line that he was not, as far as one can tell, a fervent advocate of a large B.E.F. for the continent. It made him vulnerable to a German charge that this, too, was an optional extra for Britain. Despite the tense Balkan situation in the early months of 1909, Grey was quite prepared for Hardinge to accompany the King on another visit to Germany in February. The Permanent Under-Secretary had been told by Grey to congratulate the German Chancellor on the conclusion of a Franco-German agreement concerning Morocco. In Germany, the two men talked in general terms with the aim of improving the general atmosphere, avoiding such contentious matters as naval armament and the Baghdad railway. Although Bülow's position as Chancellor was felt to be in danger, the visit was 'a great success on the whole'. Presumably on Grey's orders, only a portion of Hardinge's report was issued to the Cabinet. Hardinge told Bryce, who was sent a full copy, that there was a good deal of leakage from the Cabinet, which had the habit of finding its way into the columns of the *Manchester Guardian*.[60] In the following months, quite apart from the detailed exchanges on the naval question, the notion of a more general settlement was aired. Then came a change of Chancellors in Germany, Bethmann Hollweg replacing Bülow in the middle of July. Already certain private approaches had been made on the Kaiser's behalf by the shipowner, Albert Ballin. His counterpart on the British side was the financier, Sir Ernest Cassel. Bethmann, however, was determined to assert his position from the outset, declaring to the Kaiser that Anglo-German relations were his department. Indeed, on 21 August, the new Chancellor proposed a thorough-going revision of Anglo-German affairs such as would lead to a good understanding; the naval question could be an aspect of this general settlement. A fortnight previously, Grey had written to Hardinge that the possibility of some slackening in German naval expenditure did not seem hopeless, and the initiative seemed promising.[61]

While the Foreign Secretary welcomed the proposals for a naval agreement, the idea of a separate Anglo-German arrangement was disturbing. He preferred that 'it should be one not between two Powers alone but between the two great groups of Powers'.[62] Despite Bethmann's request that this approach should be kept secret from any other Powers, Grey decided to avoid possible complications, if the news leaked out, by informing both Paris and St Petersburg. Mallet, now an assistant Under-Secretary, was frankly suspicious of the proposal, but Grey and Hardinge were prepared to wait and see. Further exchanges took place in October and the proposals were received early in the following month. The situation was such that a subtle German offer might have had some chance of success. As has been seen, Anglo-Russian relations were in a poor state, and the Russian agreement was subject to continuous Liberal criticism. Earlier in the year, Grey had written claiming that conditions inside Russia were improving. What his critics did not understand, was that it was no use expecting too much in a short time. It did not follow that 'because we now have telegraphs and telephones and trains, therefore the progress of a nation from re-actionary to free government ought now to be . . . much more rapid. . . .'[63] In these circumstances, Grey would not entertain the suggestions that came from the St Petersburg Embassy that the agreement should be turned into an alliance. When the Tsar visited Britain in August 1909, it was felt advisable that he should penetrate no further into the heart of the country than a yacht anchored off the Isle of Wight. An agreement with Germany, in addition to its intrinsic merits, would have the effect of restoring Grey's position with some of his restless backbenchers.

The proposals, however, were disappointing. Grey had looked for some indication of naval reduction, but Germany was only prepared to slow down the rate of construction. Politically, the British were to be assured that Germany was not contemplating aggressive designs against Russia, France or any other Power. But, should Germany be forced into a war by provocation 'she must have the certainty of not finding England on the side of her opponents'.[64] Crowe's worst suspicions were aroused by this proposal. Hardinge was more restrained, but held that in the absence of modifications in the existing German naval programme, the suggestions went much further than was compatible with the Government's foreign policy. Grey agreed, but did not want to stir up feelings by an outright rejection. His information on the talks between Cassel and the President of the Baghdad Railway Company, Dr Gwinner, seemed to suggest that progress was being made. Germany offered a 50 per cent share of the southern section, while Turkish customs were to be increased to enable the Turks to make good their kilometric guarantee for the construction of the line. The view in London was that if agreement could be reached so as to give Britain a majority share, then a settlement was quite possible. On the other hand, strong suspicion existed that the German Government was using

The rebuilt Fallodon Hall

Grey at Winchester: Du Boulay's house, 1877.
Grey is sitting on the extreme right in the middle row

The young Foreign Under-Secretary, 1892

Dorothy Grey: portrait by Weigall, 1885

Cartoon by Harry Furniss, drawn not later than 1910

Above right: Grey, Churchill and Crewe in 1910

Right: Ambassador to Washington:
Bryce, Reading, Grey and Curzon in 1919

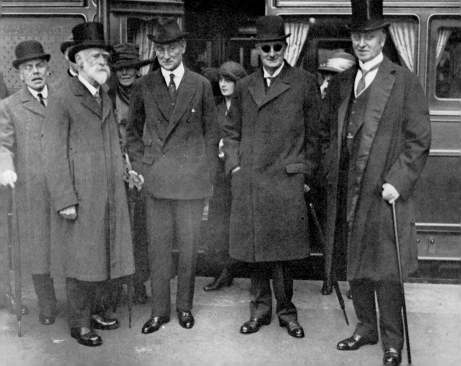

Portrait by Sir James Guthrie, 1928

Grey and robin

Last portrait, 1932

agreement on this question as a lever to assist the general agreement. It was, therefore, convenient that the imminent dissolution of the House of Commons enabled Grey to allow the matter to 'lie dormant' for a while. Churchill had already circulated his colleagues urging that the only real constraint on German building was the difficulty of getting money. The overflowing expenditure threatened 'every dyke by which the social and political unity of Germany is maintained'. He asked: 'Will the tension be relieved by moderation or snapped by calculated violence? Will the policy of the German Government be to soothe the internal situation, or to find an escape from it in external adventure?' It was a question to which the British Cabinet did not know the answer. Churchill later claimed that this was 'the first sinister impression that I was ever led to record'.[65] This development, and others, made the 'triumph of the Lloyd George–Winston set' with its 'very prejudicial effect on our foreign policy' rather unlikely.[66] Writing to Bryce in the middle of December about the German proposal, Grey himself doubted 'whether much will come of it', and in this view he spoke for most of his colleagues.[67] Besides, the first thing in all Liberal minds, at the end of the year, was to win the election.

Politics at home throughout 1909 was dominated by Lloyd George's spring Budget and its repercussions. In late 1908, the Chancellor had been anxious about the possibility of war, because it would upset his Budget plans. In the naval struggle, Grey and Lloyd George had been on opposite sides, but this does not necessarily imply that Grey was hostile to the Chancellor's 'revolutionary' taxation changes. Certainly, to the public, the Cabinet presented a united front. Dutifully, Grey replied to a correspondent who had abused the Chancellor, that Loyd George was a colleague with whom he had always been on the best of terms. The Budget 'raises the money required in a way which presses much less, I believe, upon the poorer classes than any alternative that could be devised'.[68] When Lord Rosebery denounced the Budget, Grey was not afraid to refute him publicly. The Budget was good, he told the National Liberal Club, who were honouring him at dinner, by whatever general principle it was tried; it took taxes from superfluities and taxed people in proportion to their ability to pay. Nevertheless, it is unlikely that he greeted Lloyd George's oratorical assaults without wincing privately. The Foreign Secretary spent the August Bank Holiday in 1909 with the Buxtons at their house in Sussex. Having

P

passed the evening playing 'tip and run' with the children, he turned to discussing the Budget with the house party. Although he calculated that the new Land Tax, together with an insurance against Death Duties, would cost him some £70 per annum, he accepted that the principle was right. The conversation then became more frivolous, and Grey launched an attack on Brighton as a pleasure place. A fellow guest did not dare quote Lloyd George's 'delightfully naïve' assessment that he liked Brighton because 'You have all the healthiness of the sea combined with the amenities of the town.'[69] It was certainly true that many men who, a generation ago, would have been in Cabinets, and would have made quite good ministers 'of a good English type', no longer were there. They had been replaced by 'new men and manners: less solid men & worse manners'.[70] This was mere nostalgia. Whatever the lack of discretion and refinement in some of the new men, Grey had no real wish to return to a political system entirely managed by an aristocratic, though fluid, governing élite. The pace and style of change was all-important, for 'what is wanted in politics is an idealist who can estimate rightly the limits of what is possible in his own generation'.[71] So with Lloyd George and his Budget.

The Finance Bill made its weary way through all its stages in the Commons. The Opposition obstructed at every possible point, with much sleep lost and many tempers frayed. Apart from an Irish Land Bill, there was little else that the Government could concern itself with. Having been introduced on 29 April, it was not until 4 November that the Bill was finally passed. The number of divisions had been exhausting, though Grey did not expose himself to too many of them. A week later, Lord Lansdowne, the Opposition leader in the Lords, announced that he would move that the House would not be justified in assenting to the Bill until it had been carefully submitted to the judgment of the country. This announcement ended several months of mounting speculation. In August, Grey had publicly remarked that Balfour and Lansdowne were keeping two doors open; their wishes were known, but not 'the extent of their nerve'.[72] Their Lordships, not entirely to the dismay of some Liberals, firmly shut the door in their debate at the end of November. As the Cabinet had agreed beforehand, the Government refused to go on. A general election was to take place in late January. In his speech at the beginning of the campaign, Asquith stated that the Liberals would not take office without obtaining the necessary safeguards. In fact, as events were to show, it was difficult to be sure what these safeguards were, and whether Asquith had been promised them. Grey wrote to Bryce that the Government was clearly in for a big fight. He himself had no scruple in attacking the Lords for what they had done about the Budget but he was 'afraid of a breakaway in our party for a Single Chamber & that would mean a split. I want a Second Chamber, but I do not like entrusting real powers to one unless it is mainly elective.'[73]

Sir Edward also confessed to Bryce that 'a county contested election & the F.O. work combined make an ordeal which depresses, but it will be over in six weeks & the older one gets the more one realises that time passes'. He had now been four years in office and come to terms with his own grief. The private themes of his life remained constant; reflection on time and death, on the transience and permanence of love. He now felt that he could give more patience, understanding, unselfish sympathy to a woman than ever before, 'only I couldn't give the love to anyone but Dorothy'. His point of reference remained in the past. He felt a sense of security 'because the worst that could happen has happened to me & cannot happen again'.[74] The pressure of work meant that he had little time for deep reflections, but 'if life is long there will be plenty of time . . . if life is short there will be less need for them. But I do long for them. . . .'[75] Despite the constant strain, he admitted in December 1908 that physically he was 'damnably well. Now & then I get very tired towards the end of a week, but an easier day & two hours extra sleep sets me up again.'[76]

He continued to husband his resources by living quietly, but it was not easy to get much rest. Writing to Newbolt at the end of April 1909 he sadly reported: 'My holiday was wrecked by Constantinople & Persia: I made an attempt to salmon fish & had two days of it at Rosehall and one Sunday on which I walked up a lonely glen amongst many pairs of curlews & heard ravens & lunched by a burn in the sun. Then I had to decide to return to London just as the fishing was at its very best. I do long to be free to enjoy country life again.'[77] Frequent visits to Fallodon were impossible, but he still contrived to stay at the cottage. He enjoyed dining with his small circle of political and literary friends, but made no attempt to become a society figure. As the veteran political journalist, Sir Henry Lucy, remarked: 'Not elsewhere in either hemisphere do the high heavens look down upon the Foreign Secretary of a great Empire in his shirt-sleeves digging up potatoes for his Sunday dinner.'[78] What was more, he had planted them himself. Not that Grey was a recluse. He appeared, not without a certain inner loathing, at such State dinners and occasions as befitted his office. He dutifully did his spell as minister in residence at Balmoral. His relations with his colleagues were agreeable, though, with few exceptions, not intimate. The Prime Minister remained a very old political friend, but that was how the relationship remained. Haldane he saw frequently. His relations with Morley were surprisingly close, and he spent a number of week-ends combing through books in Morley's library and exchanging thoughts on great men. Churchill's perpetually unblinkered vision irritated him, but he still found the man attractive. Congratulating Winston on his part in settling a coal dispute in the summer of 1909, Grey could not resist adding in an avuncular, sentimental way, 'have a free happy & glorious week-end'. Buxton remained a friend of long standing. Walter Runciman had become his neighbour at Doxford and, on the occasions when the two men coincided in Northumberland, they bicycled vigorously about the countryside.

As a relief from Foreign Office papers, he read modern novels like E. M. Forster's *A Room with a View*, or Conrad's *The Mirror of the Sea*, or the latest Meredith. Gibbon was a continual source of delight. As was the Bible. The Evangelical certainties and severities of his grandparental home had deserted Edward with the passage of time. In a typically English fashion, he now blended the Old and New Testaments with Plato and Wordsworth. 'The Jews', he wrote to Buxton early in the nineties, 'were a wonderful people, but they never were a complete epitome of all human nature & the parts which they did not share were & are as real as those which they do.' Yet he did now feel that they had grasped something infinitely better than any other nation, and no longer shared the view that 'God's choice of such an inconceivably stupid & wicked people' was 'an unreasonable, unjustifiable & perverse prejudice'.[79] When at home in Northumberland, he regularly went to Embleton parish church, though he did not often receive the sacrament. The sense of sanctity was not alien to him, and he did not confuse it with solemnity. Worship did not cease as he left the churchyard. A rapture seized him as he strode across the moor and reached his favourite haunt—Rhos Castle Camp—where he could survey the castle-strewn coast of North Northumberland. He would picnic and sleep among the heather and birds, praising the Lord for his goodness. 'The beauty of the world', he reflected, '. . . is for all who have eyes to see and hearts to feel. I shall die grateful for what I have had, whether I die soon or late, and whatever happens to me between now and then.'[80]

Such was the Foreign Secretary. A man who on his forty-seventh birthday wished he were thirty years older; who did not really like work, but had not had a day completely free from it for over three years; whose affections were out of doors, but whose hours were spent immured in the Foreign Office. Rod in hand, Grey once declared to Esher that 'A man's character . . . is formed not by environment, not by action, but by what he thinks when he is alone.'[81] It was an eminently 'Greyish' sentiment. He had come to terms with his own inner loneliness, and the loneliness of high office posed few fresh problems. Though outwardly, he looked and felt younger in body than his contemporaries, 'it seems to be at variance with what I feel in spirit'.[82] At its best this discrepancy meant maturity, and at its worst, fatalistic resignation.

11

A Year of Elections, 1910

The year 1910 was the year the Foreign Secretary almost forgot foreign affairs. He spent the first and last months of the year heavily involved in electioneering, an activity which had lost some of its former charm. 'The election was dreadful', he wrote to Mrs Creighton at the end of January; 'F.O. work all morning & 3 meetings an evening.' The political situation was very uncertain but also very interesting: 'I doubt my being long in office'.[1] Despite the fact that he described himself as being young in body, he always emerged from an election campaign feeling considerably older in spirit. Not that his seat was in any real danger. He had been the sitting Member for twenty-five years, and it would take a formidable candidate to rival his combination of qualities. During the course of the campaign, Sir Edward declared that the ownership of land did not in itself confer any kind of political right. In opposing Lloyd George's land taxes, landed families were trying to assert such rights and he hoped his audience would give them no support. When he sat down, an old farmer rose to move the vote of thanks. 'We are proud of Sir Edward', he declared, 'not because he is Foreign Minister of this country, nor because his word is heard with respect in every foreign country, but, first and foremost, because he belongs to one of our oldest landlord families.' No one, not even Sir Edward himself, seemed to be in the least amused or surprised.[2] Grey polled virtually the same total of votes as he had done in 1906 but his opponent put on nearly five hundred. Nationally, the Liberal position was far worse. The party lost its overall majority and depended on Labour and Irish Nationalist support, the figures being Liberal 275, Conservative 273, Irish Nationalist 82, and Labour 40.

Writing to Grey just before all the results were known, Churchill considered that the situation was 'not unfavourable', but 'we must act with decision and unity at every point. We have had five years of power, & our attitude should be that while willing & able to go on & carry out our large plans, we will only do so on our own terms. The King, the Irish, the Labour Party & the nation at large must understand that. . . .'[3] This was brave talk, and so long as the Government tackled the House of Lords and Home Rule, it was probably justified. But just what did 'tackling' the House of Lords mean? There were those Liberals who assumed that the new Government would proceed along the lines of Campbell-Bannerman's 1907 resolution. They fondly believed that the Prime Minister would have gained the necessary royal approval to create peers before the election. The result simply meant that he now had the authority of the country. This was not the case. Asquith went through the campaign with the knowledge that the King thought the Government policy tantamount to the destruction of the House of Lords, and he would insist on a second general election, so that the country could express its mind on a particular proposal. The Prime Minister's first task was therefore to disillusion many of his own supporters. It is little wonder that he fled to Cannes as soon as possible after the election, and even on his return, was in a curiously listless mood.

Nothing would have persuaded Grey to go to Cannes, and in this odd situation, colleagues turned to him for advice on the course to be adopted. It was going to prove more difficult to agree on a 'particular project' than many people imagined. The so-called C-B veto as outlined in 1907 had in fact been pushed through by the Prime Minister against the advice of a Cabinet committee which had gone into the subject and produced its own proposal—the so-called Ripon plan. The committee proposal embodied the following propositions: firstly, if either House refused to pass, or amended, a Bill from the other House, then that Bill should stand adjourned until the next session; secondly, if that House refused to reconsider, then the other House could claim a joint vote; thirdly, for such a joint vote, the House of Lords should be represented by 100 Peers, consisting of all Peers who were members of the Government, not exceeding 20, and the rest to be chosen by the House itself; fourthly, these Peers and the House of Commons should deliberate and vote together on the points of difference and their decision would be binding on both Houses.[4] Grey had originally found a proposal along these lines more congenial, and the obvious temptation was to resurrect it. In the aftermath of the election, Sir Edward seemed to be taking a strong stand. Hardinge wrote to the King's private secretary on 27 January reporting Grey as saying that the moderate section of the Cabinet would deal firmly with Lloyd George. The Foreign Secretary 'thinks also that there will very soon be a split over the question of the H. of Lords, Navy and Home Rule & that he with others will have to go'. Grey was 'in favour of leaving the H of Lords question till the old and new budgets have been dealt with, especially as he anticipates a split in the Cabinet over the Naval Estimates'. Asquith would then have to decide 'whether to stick to Grey & his lot or to Lloyd George. If Asquith throws in his lot with L.G. about the navy he and others will certainly resign. Moreover he says that he will not agree to any Home Rule project being made into law by this Parliament nor to the adoption of the C.B. resolution which means Single Chamber Govt. . . .'[5] Grey was supposed to be 'full of brave words at present'.

To judge from an unusually long letter he wrote two days later to Runciman, Grey was taking the matter seriously, even canvassing support with which to confront Asquith on his return. Sir Edward ruled out any possibility of compromise with Balfour—'we must fight the Lords battle out, but it must be on big lines'. He thought that the C-B plan would not rouse the country, and that it would lay the party open to the charge of being in effect a Single Chamber party. He wanted 'something much bigger—a clean sweep of the privileges of Peers and a good scheme for an elective Second Chamber. I should like to go to the country on Finance for the Commons & a scheme for an elective Second Chamber & let the Tories fight for the hereditary principle against it.' He went into a little more detail and then concluded: 'We must show ourselves big people if we are to win a big fight & I would spend no time fiddling on with the so-called "C-B" plan or manœuvring for position.'[6] At this point, a problem of terminology arises. Many subsequent commentators, and clearly Hardinge, believed that Grey's expressed opposition to the C-B plan was the result of his 'moderation' or 'conservatism'. The tone of this letter to Runciman, however, makes it clear that he was quite ready for a 'big fight', but the scope of the reform should be really comprehensive and strike at the hereditary principle. It clearly emerges that Grey's concern, whatever the Palace might hope, was simply the preservation of a bi-cameral legislature. It seemed to him that 'some of our unofficial people & most of our press (I except the W.G.) seem to be discussing the problem before us without any attempt to think it out & with a strong desire to run their heads against a brick wall, which is evidence rather of the thickness of their skulls than of their intelligence'.[7] In the next few days, he strongly pressed his views, either personally or by letter, on Crewe, Churchill, Haldane and Runciman, gaining their general support for the proposition that the 'C-B' plan was inadequate.

On his return, Asquith found a letter from Grey talking about 'the great issue' at great length. In Grey's judgment, the Liberals would only carry the country if they showed great strength and unity of purpose. There was 'the certainty of a split amongst ourselves, and defeat, if we drift towards a Single Chamber. If we cannot agree upon a Single Chamber policy, we cannot agree at all.' He therefore proposed a Bill establishing the right of the House of Commons to control finance and a Bill abolishing the political privileges of Peers and substituting an elective Second Chamber. Seemingly as an afterthought, he added: 'Balfour will endeavour to destroy confidence in us and get it for himself on the question of the Navy. This we should defeat by our own Navy Estimates, and I assume that we shall do this.'[8] Sir Edward was rather in the mood to make assumptions of this kind. After two Cabinets on 10 and 11 February, Hardinge wrote: 'Grey is very pleased with himself & considers that he & his group have won all along the line in the Cabinet. He told me this morning that the present is a fine opportunity for boldness, and that the Cabinet would tell the Irish to go & be damned. I cannot imagine to myself Asquith doing this & I think Grey is much too uncompromising. The difference is that Asquith wants to remain in office & Grey does not care whether he remains or not.'[9] For the rest of February, in a long series of lengthy meetings, the Cabinet tried to reach a formula. Its spirits were drooping and on 25 February the Prime Minister had to report in his letter to the King that some Ministers, seeing no possibility of stable government, were in favour of resigning forthwith. Instead, a Cabinet committee was appointed, and the ministers decided to forgo the pleasure of further meetings for some ten days, while it reported. As expected, its suggestion was a variant of the 'C-B' plan, embodied in three resolutions. The first stated that the Lords could not touch a money Bill—and the Speaker should determine what was and what was not a money Bill. The second stated that a Bill should pass through the Commons in three successive sessions (not necessarily in the same parliament) in order to become law against the wishes of the Lords. The third reduced the length of parliaments from seven to five years.

The proposals did not please the Foreign Secretary and on 14 March he reacted publicly, claiming that it would be disastrous for the Liberals to be labelled the Single Chamber party, indeed, that it would be death and damnation as well. On the following day he wrote to Crewe that he saw 'no way out of the veto difficulty, unless it is announced that the limitation of the veto (in C.B. form) is proposed & will be used only to secure the passage of a Bill to establish a new Second Chamber. Unless this is said we steer straight on the single Chamber rock. Another solution would be to revert to the original Cabinet proposal of a joint sitting, but that I suppose the party would not stand.'[10] Grey warned Asquith that he intended to bring the matter up at the Cabinet on the 16 March. The Prime Minister reported Grey's views to the King, but said that there was 'a considerable difference of opinion on this point in the Cabinet, and after an animated but perfectly friendly discussion, the further consideration of the matter was adjourned to the next meeting'.[11] Sir Edward then brooded for nine days before sending his letter of resignation to Asquith. He stated that he would have accepted the 'Ripon' plan, but he could not accept the bare and simple 'C-B' veto: 'I cannot give a silent vote for this and I cannot speak upon it without placing a limitation and expressing opinions upon it, which you will at once be challenged to repudiate or to confirm. If you confirm them you will, as far as I can judge of the present disposition of the Irish, the Labour party and many Liberals, break up the majority; if you repudiate them I must resign.'[12] Asquith was not pleased, writing to Crewe: 'I have had a tiresome letter from E. Grey.'

Although Grey acted on his own in resigning, he had the support of Runciman, who intended to make it clear to the Prime Minister that 'Grey is not speaking or acting alone. Whether Haldane will have the pluck to do his part & take risks, remains to be seen. I have had no talk with Crewe for a week & I cannot tell what he thinks now.'[13] His correspondent, McKenna, replied that 'if Grey goes out I go too'. Many things in the Government's conduct could not be justified, 'notably going through the election on a public misunderstanding of the Albert Hall speech' and failure to legalize the taxes. He did in fact substantially agree with Grey on the question of the Lords, but that apart, Grey had been 'in some sort my political conscience'. He also knew that 'but for him I should have been beaten on the Navy Estimates last year'.[14] Asquith was forced to make concessions. Grey was satisfied by the preamble to the Parliament Bill in which the Government declared its intention 'to substitute for the House of Lords as it at present exists a Second Chamber constituted on a popular instead of a hereditary basis, but such a substitution cannot immediately be brought into operation'. In the meantime, it was 'expedient to make such provision as in this Act appears for restricting the existing powers of the House of Lords'.[15] Successive Governments who have wilted before the task of reforming the Upper House have Grey to thank for their unhappy labours.

After this miserable period, it seemed that the Liberals were recovering their nerve and morale. Lloyd George reintroduced his Budget and it had a successful passage through both Houses by the end of April. The main issue was now the question of the veto. This time, if the Lords failed to accept the resolutions, Asquith had warned that the Government would either resign or recommend a dissolution. In no case would it recommend a dissolution 'except under such conditions as will secure that in the new parliament the judgment of the people as expressed in the election will be carried into law'.[16] The obvious inference from these remarks was that the King would grant a dissolution and, if it should prove necessary, create a large number of peers. Having heard the Prime Minister's triumph, but before parliament adjourned for a ten-day recess at the end of April, Grey had disappeared to the North of Scotland. He admitted that it might seem 'rather scandalous that I should have come here while there is a political crisis but I feel very pleased at having bolted. . . .' He claimed that he was not really being naughty, because it had been settled that the Budget would be sent to the Lords unchanged. If the Lords refused it, then there would be a crisis, although 'we would not commit ourselves as to what we would advise the King to do'.[17]

Little did his ministers realize that they were never going to be able to advise the King. Edward forestalled the possibility by dying on 6 May. By sailing to Portugal, the Prime Minister missed the event. Grey had a genuine sense of loss, though he had never been a courtier and the King's pleasures had not been his own. When staying at Balmoral, the King had taken him for walks along paths familiar to Edward's father. Although the notion that the King substantially intervened in foreign policy now has few supporters, there were a number of brushes between the two men. These chiefly occurred on points where the King felt that he was acting within his rights, and harmlessly, but where Grey insisted that there were political implications. For example, Grey expressed his dislike of the King's action in making the Tsar Admiral of the Fleet, without prior reference, at Tallinn in June 1908. The King was sufficiently annoyed to reject Asquith's suggestion that Grey should fill a vacancy in the Order of the Garter. Instead, he offered Grey the Grand Cross of the Royal Victorian Order, but this time it was Grey's turn to decline. The King, Lord Esher noted, was 'dreadfully hurt'.[18] In the last week of the King's life, Grey was involved in attempts to prevent him from being forced to give guarantees to the Government. Sir Edward had asked to see the King, who was not very willing to grant an audience. Hardinge said it would be in the interests of all concerned if one could be arranged. The King always made 'a great impression' on Grey, though he quite understood the King's feelings about him.[19] Hardinge later heard that an audience had been granted and commented: 'Although Grey is a broken reed to lean on he still professes himself to be opposed to asking for guarantees.' He hoped the King would speak 'pretty straight to him if the constitutional question is touched upon'.[20] The audience either never took place or had no importance because of the King's death. Death was the one factor in the political situation which no one had reckoned with. When, shortly afterwards, Hardinge left the Foreign Office to become Viceroy of India, the death of the sovereign and the transfer of the Permanent Under-Secretary meant a new context in which Grey had to work. Nicolson, Hardinge's successor, never approached with the new King the relationship which Hardinge had enjoyed with his father.

King George V was not ill-informed, but there was a considerable feeling that it would be unwise to press him for such a major constitutional decision so soon after ascending the throne. Given the new situation, the Cabinet was prepared to attend a constitutional conference with the Opposition leaders, in an attempt to resolve the deadlock by this means. The Government was represented by the Prime Minister, Crewe and Birrell; the Opposition by Balfour, Lansdowne, Austen Chamberlain and Cawdor. In a letter to Crewe just before the first meeting in mid-June, Grey lamented that the 'C-B' plan had been adopted, instead of the Cabinet's original proposal, in 1907, of Joint Sessions. 'If only the other side would agree to anything like the Ripon plan & call it a compromise, there would be a way of escape, but I fear this is too much to hope for.'[21] The sessions were adjourned for the summer at the end of July without making very much progress. They did, however, have an unexpected effect on Lloyd George. They opened up for him a vista of a Coalition Government with agreement between the two parties on the major issues of the day. In mid-August, he drafted a memorandum on this theme addressed to Asquith, but which only reached him at the end of October, via a number of Opposition letter-boxes. Grey had been privy to the scheme before that date. On 6 October, Churchill wrote to Lloyd George that the effect of the scheme on democratic political organizations was uncertain, but 'if we stood together we ought to be strong enough either to impart a progressive character to policy, or by withdrawal to terminate an administration which had failed in its purpose'. He proposed that they should dine within a few days 'and talk to Grey all about it'.[22] Their desire to approach Grey is a little surprising, but no doubt they felt that his approval would be an important weapon with the Prime Minister. The three men had dinner together, and then, on 26 October, Grey wrote to Asquith that on reflection, he was favourable to Lloyd George's 'big scheme', though he recognized the difficulties. He was afraid that if the resumed conference broke up without agreement, the Liberal Party would break up 'and a time of political instability, perhaps of chaos, to the great detriment of the country' would ensue. The Opposition was paralysed and useless, 'but behind us there are explosive & violent forces which will split our party and I do not believe we can resume the old fight against the Lords by ourselves without divisions'.[23] Asquith was not very impressed, either by the argument or by Lloyd George's 'missionary operations'.[24] This bizarre episode ended when the constitutional conference broke up in the first week of November.

At its meeting on 10 November, the Cabinet decided in favour of a dissolution, and Asquith had the difficult task of obtaining his guarantees. With some reluctance, the King agreed to use his prerogative to make Peers if requested. Dissolution took place on 28 November and it was clear by Christmas that the Liberals had more or less preserved their position. There was a much lower turnout, not entirely due to the big increase in the number of uncontested seats as compared with January. The Conservatives lost one and the Liberals three; Labour and the Irish Nationalists gained two each. Although its normal majority was slightly increased, so was the Government's dependence on the minority parties. Grey was well satisfied with this result. Although he could not know it, he had fought his last election. On a smaller poll, his majority increased by three votes. Sir Edward had always found elections rather puzzling. After the polls had closed his workers would tell him, usually pretty accurately, by how many votes he would be in. Grey professed bewilderment and would say: 'Gentlemen, I do not know how you do it.'[25] The repetitious nature of political debate oppressed him in this campaign more than usual. Having at one point described the Opposition proposal for a referendum in the event of deadlock between the Houses as 'a Pig in a Poke', he felt inclined to stop in the middle of subsequent speeches and ask his brother, 'Is that the 6th or only the 5th time . . . ?'[26] He thought the only thing which would stand in the way of a reasonable settlement would be a decisive swing to the Tories—or to the Liberals for that matter. Although the *status quo* was confirmed, 'This time the Election was peculiarly horrible, because two sets of men who had spent the autumn in amicable discussion finding out how well they got on personally and what points of agreement they had, spent the election in denouncing each other. I am weary . . .'[27] His Tory opponent wrote: 'I had rather a nice fight in Northumberland, & was rather well pleased with the result, so much so that I mean to have another go at Sir Edward. From his speeches & his election address you would think that the Liberals were Tories compared to the men of Mr Gladstone's days. . . . He doesn't appear ever to have heard of such a man as Lloyd George or such a place as Limehouse. . . .'[28] Another attempt to distinguish Grey from some of his colleagues was made by his friend Henry Newbolt in a letter to *The Times* in the first week of the campaign. It caused Grey considerable embarrassment and he hastened to say that it was very unfair to put him on a separate pinnacle—Asquith, Crewe, Morley, Loreburn, Haldane, to mention only a few, were equally deserving of praise. Newbolt had been disgusted by the language of Lloyd George's Mile End speech, but Grey would not be drawn into condemnation. He only remarked that 'the impression which people gather from platform speeches of the respective parts played by members of the Government in forming the policy of the Party is in fact very wide of the mark'. Even if he would not have made such a speech himself, he would not dream of condemning his colleague publicly.[29]

Quite apart from his own personal feelings and predilections, Grey's preference for discussion rather than demagoguery was also a product of his office. Given what he conceived to be Britain's exposed position, nothing could give greater delight abroad than the spectacle of a nation rent by constitutional and political quarrels. Fortunately, as it happened, the international situation in 1910 was relatively quiet.

The attempt by Bethmann Hollweg to interest Britain in an extensive agreement seemed simply to disappear in the welter of events surrounding the December election. On 22 March, the German Ambassador reminded Sir Edward that the result was now known and asked for a statement. Grey replied that, since there appeared to be no possibility of a reduction in the German naval programme, public opinion would not countenance an agreement.[30] Hardinge wrote to Bryce that the Germans had been told plainly that it was no use talking of agreement while there was no change in this position.[31] However, Grey did not want exchanges to cease, suggesting to the German Chargé at the end of March that 'the key to smooth relations in many respects between the two countries might be found in a settlement of the Bagdad Railway question'.[32] The British Ambassador had an interview with Bethmann Hollweg in the middle of April, but the German stress remained on treating this question in a general political agreement with England. For all the language of goodwill, the Chancellor's proposals were received with scorn by Crowe and Mallet. Neither was the Foreign Secretary impressed.[33] The tension in Anglo-German relations had slackened, but the prospects of agreement seemed as far away as ever. Through the summer, both sides restated their positions formally and deliberately, but there was no breakthrough.[34] Dismally, Grey wrote to the British Ambassador in Berlin: 'I am afraid Tirpitz will fight hard against anything. He uses all that we say or do as a pretext for standing off from us.'[35]

The lack of progress naturally irritated the more impatient members of the Cabinet, who were hoping that an Anglo-German success could lift the Government's domestic fortunes. The itch to try their own hand at negotiation could not be suppressed. Churchill informed Grey in May that he had discussed the subject of the Austrian Dreadnoughts with the German Ambassador. He had told Metternich that as a Radical Member of Parliament 'not at all directly concerned in F.O. or Admiralty policy' but one concerned with financial economy and Anglo-German closer friendship, he deeply regretted that rumours of Austrian Dreadnought construction, which he had steadily disbelieved, were in fact only too true.[36] Grey appreciated Churchill's correctness on this occasion, but in general he disliked such approaches. The effect, he believed, was only to encourage the Germans in their already strong conviction that in due course Britain would have to accept their terms. When the Lord Chancellor, Loreburn, raised the subject of closer collaboration between Britain and Germany at a Cabinet on 20 July, Grey gave a general summary of the conversations, but stressed 'the inexpediency of entering into any engagements with Germany which would be of such a character as to lead to misunderstanding and perhaps loss of friendship with France and Germany'. The whole Cabinet approved the memorandum of 29 July setting out the British interpretation of the negotiations.[37]

It was not until the middle of October that the German reply was received. Since there was little sign of movement in the German position, further exchanges could then easily have developed into a series of unprofitable complaints. In a letter to the British Ambassador on 26 October, Grey rehearsed his experience of dealing with Germany and concluded: 'I desire friendship: but it must not be on terms which would involve the old disadvantages'.[38] The Germans would gain little by cataloguing the occasions on which it was alleged that Britain systematically opposed German interests. Britain was also capable of drawing up such a list. However, at the end of the year a slight easement appeared. On 16 December, Grey was informed by Metternich that, without a prior political agreement, the German Government now agreed to the exchange of information between the two Admiralties. In return, Grey revealed that the whole question of a 'political formula' was being considered by the Cabinet. Now that the Government had just been confirmed in office, the matter would be further explored in the coming year. He wanted 'to see something which would make it clear that the Triple Alliance and what was called the "Triple Entente", though they were regarded by some as different camps, were not really opposite camps'. Since Germany had 'settled' her difficulty with France as to Morocco, he contended that there were no longer antagonistic aims between the different Powers. Metternich interposed that France still had not renounced the idea of a war of revenge for Alsace-Lorraine. Grey replied that France could not be expected to renounce the lost provinces, but he did not believe an attack on Germany, for this purpose, played any part in her relations with other Powers. The tone of this conversation was mildly encouraging.[39]

In all his diplomatic dealings, Grey refused to be hurried or bullied into an agreement for the sake of agreement. While not sharing the complete scepticism of some Foreign Office opinion, he believed that the pace of negotiation had to be slow and deliberate. His concern to keep the control of policy in his own hands was, in part, the result of his analysis of the confusing situation prevailing in Germany. There, the tension between the volatile Kaiser and Bethmann Hollweg, Kiderlen and Tirpitz, led to confusion of counsel and statement, a confusion which was only in part deliberate. The promptings and initiatives of his colleagues were therefore received with a caution which could be interpreted as disdain. Some of the suggestions were indeed a little fatuous. In the autumn of 1910, the Portuguese inconveniently had a revolution. It caused Grey considerable difficulty, because of the good relations between Buckingham Palace and the deposed royal family.[40] Churchill opposed recognizing the new regime until such time as genuinely free elections had been held to test popular support. Here, he thought, was a sphere for joint Anglo-German action, which might lead on to higher things: 'You have so often spoken of your desire that we should find some external question upon which we could frankly co-operate. Is this one?'[41] More brazenly, Lloyd George was still not averse to making his own statements to the press on the subject of Germany, without consultation. Haldane sympathized: 'Ll.G. is irritating in the extreme. Just when you are talking with Bethmann-Hollweg to have these interviews going on.'[42]

Throughout the exchanges with Germany, Grey had stressed that he would not sacrifice his agreements with France and Russia. In fact, after the Franco-German agreement on Morocco in February 1909, the bombardment of anxious requests from France slowed down. Indeed, if anything, there was concern at French activity, which seemed to be working against British interests, particularly in Turkey. A few scattered attempts were made to discuss the condition of the British Army, but the subject was usually avoided. As long as the naval race continued, Paris recognized that France became valuable to Britain and was simply content to let events take their course. There were some moments of anxiety, but not of great substance. Pichon, the French Foreign Minister, came to England for the funeral of King Edward in May and was aghast to discover that Orleanist princes were given precedence over him in the funeral procession. The French Embassy communicated Pichon's distress and Grey wrote a very fierce note to the Lord Chamberlain's Office, protesting about this insult to a Great Power.[43] By the end of the year, however, there was some apprehension in Paris that

Q

an Anglo-German naval agreement might after all be a possibility.

Questions of etiquette apart, relations with France seemed almost serene, but it was otherwise with Russia. As usual, Persia was both the source and setting of Anglo-Russian disagreement. Grey continued to hope, against the evidence, that genuine co-operation in the region was possible. This seemed to mean that Britain deferred to Russia in dealings with the Persian constitutional government. For example, the Persians asked Britain and Russia for a loan to restore order in the country. The Russians proposed a larger loan with stringent conditions and the British concurred. The National Assembly found these conditions humiliating and rejected them. Instead, the Persian Government tried to raise a loan privately and a number of London bankers were interested. When it seemed likely that Seligman brothers, a private firm, might supply the money, the Russians objected. They disliked any move which would increase the independence of Persia. Grey, in turn, did not want to encourage an offer which would offend St Petersburg. Seligman had little alternative but to withdraw, in October 1910, when it became clear that Foreign Office support was being given to a more pliable institution, the Imperial Bank of Persia. Persian frustration at such moves led to a protest meeting in Istanbul against Anglo-Russian tyranny over Persia and led to an appeal to the Kaiser as 'the only European monarch animated by friendly feelings towards Islam'. The Russians did not show great zeal in restraining the ex-Shah from making contacts in Northern Persia, and the country's Foreign Minister suffered the humiliation of being dunned by bailiffs for the ex-Shah's pension payment.[44]

It would have been surprising if such events had not revived criticisms of the Anglo-Russian agreement. The classic study of the Persian Revolution by Professor Edward Browne of Cambridge was published in 1910 and provided ammunition for the critics. Browne had no time for Grey, believing that he was 'so ignorant, that he hardly knows the Persian Gulf from the Red Sea'. An illustration of the anxious feeling can be found in a letter from G. M. Trevelyan, later Grey's admiring biographer, to Walter Runciman. While recognizing that it was *ex parte*, Trevelyan urged Runciman to read the book. Grey and Nicolson ought to read it too. The Persians 'are not perfect, and by European standards are asses . . . but if once we find ourselves engaged with the destroyers of Finland in a squabble with Germany and Turkey to defend a practical partition of Persia, we are ruined'. He expressed his distrust of the Foreign

Office and Nicolson's zeal for Russia. If Britain could not make friends with Germany or meet her half-way, armament expenditure would only increase, 'social reform will stop, and some day war may supervene'. He accepted that Grey did not want to get involved in Persia 'but Gladstone did not want to stop in Egypt'.[45]

Yet, to 'stand up to Russia' was not easy. In the middle of that same October, Grey had received information that the Kaiser and the Tsar were to meet at Potsdam at the beginning of November. Persia would obviously be discussed. This news, together with the recent replacement of Isvolsky as Russian Foreign Minister by Sazonov, seemed to indicate a shift in Russian policy. No one was sure how far the Russians would go with Germany. To stir up a diplomatic quarrel about the Russian presence in Persia at this time seemed madness. However incredible this might seem to English critics of Grey who found him too 'Russian', a strong factor in the downfall of Isvolsky had been the feeling that 'at this time our Minister of Foreign Affairs is not Isvolskii but . . . Grey, that we do everything to please England'.[46] At their meeting in Potsdam on 5 November, the two Emperors came to an agreement, though the details were not finally worked out until August 1911. Russia's special interests in Persia, that is to say in the sphere as defined by the Anglo-Russian agreement, were recognized. Germany promised not to seek concessions in the Russian zone and professed to have only 'commercial ends'. In return, not without reluctance, the Russians agreed to connect Tehran with the Baghdad railway when completion of the relevant section made this feasible. News of the agreement was received in London with some dismay. Grey could have responded by encouraging the Imperial Bank to go ahead with its loan before the Persian Government had satisfied the Russian conditions. Nicolson strongly advised against this course. In the end, early in January 1911, the loan was made, after the Russians had secured a favourable consolidation of the various debts owed them. The weakness of the British position was apparent and, given Sazonov's desire to improve Russo-German relations, more difficulties could be expected.

The situation in the Near East as a whole remained unsettled and uncertain. It remained difficult to judge what direction the new Turkish Government would take. Grey remained under pressure from some of his backbenchers to improve the conditions in the Balkans, particularly Macedonia. But to press for this would only alienate the regime from Britain. German influence was already

growing and it was difficult enough to maintain British commercial influence as matters stood. Although it is certainly true that
the Foreign Office did not accept a responsibility for trade promotion
as a whole, Grey was quite prepared to urge the British Ambassador
to give 'all assistance that you properly can to Armstrong-Vickers
group against foreign competition'. Sir Edward knew that the
British position in Constantinople was in jeopardy. His Ambassador
warned in September 1910 that in the event of war between Turkey
and Greece, 'Young Turkey, once she makes up her mind to fight
will act with great rapidity and will not be deterred as she used to be
by advice'.[47] The following month, Grey warned the Prime Minister:
'I think it is premature to assume that the new regime in Turkey will
definitely adopt and pursue an oppressive and aggressive policy, but
we must be on our guard against possible developments. . . .'[48]

A basic anxiety of British policy-makers throughout the Near East
was that Pan-Islamic solidarity might revive, and if India were
involved, the whole structure of the Empire might be in danger.
Not surprisingly, it was hard for the Foreign Office to disentangle
the puzzling mixture of religious feeling and 'secular' nationalism
which was astir. Nowhere was this more apparent than in Egypt.
There, Cromer's successor, Sir Eldon Gorst, had initiated a policy
of gradual liberalization. He wished to limit direct British control
by expanding the role of the Egyptian council of ministers. He also
promulgated a law in the summer of 1909 giving Egyptians greater
powers of administration through provincial and local councils.
Yet these concessions did little to settle the unrest. Nationalist
groups opposed the Khedive and his ministers. Already, they were
beginning to agitate about the status of the Suez Canal and the
British occupation. To complicate matters further, there was an
economic recession and strife between Moslems and Copts. Grey
had given full backing to Gorst's policy. Early in May 1910
Hardinge wrote to Gorst that he had 'urged Sir Edward two or
three times during the last eighteen months to pull up a bit, as I
saw that the Egyptians were getting out of hand. He, however,
thought otherwise . . .'[49] The assassination of the Prime Minister,
Boutros Pasha, seemed to show that Hardinge's fears were justified.
The Liberal Government had to face strong criticism for allowing
too many concessions and bowing before disorder. The turn of
events seems also to have convinced the Foreign Secretary that a
strong line was again needed. As it happened, ex-President Roosevelt
appeared in England, ready and willing to help.

After shooting his way through East Africa, Roosevelt arrived in London in May 1910. Especially in Egypt and the Sudan, he had been impressed by the work of British officials and soldiers on his trip. He was aware that they felt they were being let down by London, and took it upon himself to say something in their favour. The behaviour of the English in Egypt was making them 'look flabby'. He told the King of his intention, who warmly approved, as did Cromer. Then he saw Grey, whom he had not previously met. The two men at once warmed to each other and Grey was anxious that Roosevelt should deliver his speech. Subsequently, Roosevelt wrote: 'Asquith and Morley would, I knew, and as Grey showed that he knew, disapprove, but this was evidently in Grey's mind merely another reason why I should make it.'[50] Aware that a row was likely, Roosevelt was prepared to disavow meeting Grey, but the Foreign Secretary declared that he would be willing to state publicly that he approved the speech. Therefore, at the Guildhall on 31 May, Roosevelt roundly declared: 'You have given Egypt the best Government it has had for at least two thousand years', but weakness could ruin this work. 'Weakness, timidity and sentimentality may cause even more far-reaching harm than violence and injustice.' Some nation had to govern Egypt or it would sink into a welter of chaos once more. That nation should be the British.[51]

The speech did indeed cause a storm, although the two men were not perturbed by it. Grey had arranged that they should take a short walking-tour through the Itchen Valley and then in the New Forest. In such surroundings, they were able to spend the time profitably, testing each other's knowledge of birds. It was all so much better than an official Foreign Office luncheon, and the occasion lingered long in the memories of both men. In the last year of his life, Grey wrote to Theodore's son: 'Your father has been very much in my mind lately. . . . How stimulating he would have found the difficulties of the times, and how interesting it would have been to see what he would have done.'[52] Of the politicians Roosevelt met—and Churchill he refused to meet—Lloyd George struck him as *the* man of power, although very emotional. But all in all, taking internal and external politics together, Grey was the man to whom he was really drawn. He was not, like Balfour, a brilliant man, or, like Lloyd George, a born leader, but he was 'a kind of high-minded public servant, as straight in all private as in all public relations, whom it is essential for a country to have'.[53]

Roosevelt's private remarks about Grey's 'straightness' might have brought a smile to the face of some of his colleagues, who believed that he had been less than 'straight' with them in the matter of the Guildhall speech. It is a moot point whether the Prime Minister knew of Roosevelt's intentions. Lord Crewe, the Colonial Secretary, certainly did not and was understandably displeased. Grey, who told Bryce that he had come independently to Roosevelt's views on Egypt, was unabashed. The speech, he told Crewe, was a great tribute to the British in Africa generally. Some people would be annoyed by what he had said about Egypt, 'but then I think it is healthy that that particular sort of person should be shocked by someone else as well as by his own Government occasionally. . . .' Crewe still thought the speech 'a pity'. He did not agree that it was 'sentiment' which was in fact doing the mischief; 'the harm comes not from a moral source, but from intellectual indolence, which misapplies political maxims in countries like Egypt by treating them as if they were fundamental truths. . . .'[54]

Sir Edward had not thought up the Guildhall speech, but he had made adroit use of it to establish his viewpoint in the Cabinet. When Roosevelt's comments were referred to on 13 June in the debate on Egyptian administration, the Foreign Secretary stood firmly by them and admitted that he had approved the speech in advance. Taken as a whole, it was 'the greatest compliment to the work of one country in the world ever paid by the citizen of another'. Balfour, and other Opposition spokesmen, welcomed the speech. The critics came from the Liberal backbenches, where the remarks were regarded as insulting and improper. Wilfrid Scawen Blunt was furious. The Irish M.P.s, on whom he relied to raise opposition, had betrayed him, because they had not dared offend Roosevelt. He attributed Grey's willingness to talk with Americans to the fact that, unusually, there was no difficulty with language. Egypt and Islam would only be saved by Kaiser Wilhelm and the Ottoman Army.[55] British policy in Egypt might have been different, if it could have been regarded in isolation, but this was impossible. So, the Gorst experiment faded and in 1911 Kitchener, a soldier, replaced him. The inference was obvious.

Blunt's enthusiasm for Arabs and their disinterested patron, the Kaiser, was eccentric, but another African colonial problem saw the emergence of a much more formidable campaigner, E. D. Morel. For several years before the advent of the Liberal Government,

Morel had been campaigning against the injustices and abuses of King Leopold's personal rule in the Congo. He skilfully directed his Congo Reform Association until it exerted formidable pressure for a change in the status and administration of the Congo.[56] In its early years, it worked quite cordially with the Foreign Office. After pressure, chiefly from Britain, Belgium agreed in 1908 to annex her sovereign's state. This step was recognized by the other Powers, with the exception of Britain and the United States. Grey wanted the Belgians not merely to annex the state, but also to reform the administration. When the abuses had been removed, as he hoped they soon would be, Britain would recognize the change. For its part, the C.R.A. intended to keep up the pressure on Grey, Morel writing in February 1909 that it would be 'both impossible and intolerable to permit an indefinite prolongation of the present situation'.[57] As spring and summer passed, it became apparent that the Belgian assurances were disappointing, and insufficient to justify recognition. Morel's anger could not be contained and he busily organized lecture tours and protest meetings and published pamphlets, all urging some 'definite action'. Morel had 'definitely given up' Grey (Morel was always very definite about everything), 'he will do nothing on his own initiative unless the public compel him'.[58]

In their concentration upon the Congo, Grey's critics took little notice of the delicate European situation. Already, Belgian feeling had been offended by the British refusal to recognize the annexation. Further 'definite action' would only encourage pro-German feeling in Belgium. This did not worry Morel, for he felt that France was at the bottom of all African problems, and he threatened to 'expose' the land of his birth. The British people would be invited to consider 'whether the advantages conceivably derivable from any Continental alliance were worth the abandonment by England of her moral duty and her moral obligations'. A giant campaign, from Land's End to John o' Groats, would be launched against the entente cordiale, if the Government left the Congo natives to their fate.[59] Grey was not indifferent to the Congo atrocities, but he was not the man to be hurried into rupturing Anglo-Belgian relations. Quite apart from the damage it would do, he was not sure what this action would achieve. As he wrote to Churchill, the Congo question would have been simple if Britain had been prepared to say that 'unless things were put right within a certain time we would ourselves take the place in hand'. He was not aware that this course had been

advocated and failing it, the only alternative was patient pressure.[60]
Fortunately, however, the death of King Leopold removed a major
obstacle in the path of improvement, and if progress continued, it
seemed at the end of 1910 that recognition would be granted quite
shortly.

E. D. Morel went off on a tour of West Africa, full of venom
against 'that weak-kneed invertebrate politician whose name is
Grey'.[61] No one seemed to find any incongruity in the fact that it
was Lord Cromer, no less, who presided over the committee which
raised for Morel a sum of four thousand guineas, in public appreciation of his work. When Morel returned in the spring of 1911, his
eager pen was anxious to find a fresh means of attacking the Foreign
Secretary. In this resolve, he was not to find himself alone, nor, in
Europe, America, Africa and Asia, was there any shortage of
subjects.

12

Policy under Attack, 1911

Politicians have found it convenient to begin their War Memoirs in 1911 and historians have often followed their example. Yet the fact of war in the summer of 1914 should not automatically compress the three preceding years into a prelude. Certainly, Europe seemed near war in 1911, yet after the immediate crisis was over, it was widely believed that international relations were healthier than they had been for years. The ascent to disaster was not constant.

Exhausted by archives and intoxicated by political science, some historians have lately stressed the domestic background to international conflict. The cluster of crises afflicting Britain from 1911 onwards—labour unrest, the feminist revolt, the Irish question—has proved irresistible. We gather that all who clamoured for 'preparedness and foreign-policy pugnacity held reactionary, ultra-conservative, or protofascist views on domestic affairs'. It seems that there were 'few if any liberal conservatives or reformers in . . . the pro-Entente wing of the Unionist and Liberal parties in England'. While some urged war as an antidote to revolution, Grey is linked with those 'left of the centre' who tended to be afraid of war as a precipitant of social revolution. His policy, it is implied, was conditioned by this fact.[1] The crudity of this hypothesis, not to mention its inconsistency, hardly needs stressing, and Grey's attitude towards war can be stated more shortly. He hated the prospect of mass-slaughter in a European war. He admired courage and bravery in soldiers, but no one could be less 'militarist' in disposition. A recent work which purports to describe the spirit of Europe in the 'Age of Imperialism' attributes to Sir Edward a memoir in praise of a dead 'bellicose idealist' and endows him with something called a 'militant mentality'.[2] However, the offending memoir was written by his cousin.

Edward Grey consorted with Quakers and genuinely appreciated their spirit, though he could not share their beliefs. He studied Norman Angell's book *Europe's Optical Illusion* before it gained its later fame as *The Great Illusion*. Yet preparedness remained the necessary watchword. As for social revolution, he recognized the realities of social change and did not resist their implications. But pace remained all-important. Without shame or disguise, he watched the social scene from a position of comfort. He recognized that power was passing from the House of Commons to the Trade Unions. Men in the great industries had to have a share in the control of them. If both sides in industry were unyielding, there could be civil war, but he relied on the spirit of compromise, inherent in the English character, to save the country from catastrophe. He had followed Wordsworth too closely through the agonies of the French Revolution to expect great bliss at a second dawn. Life would be more difficult for those, like himself, who had been used to more than £500 a year, but the changes were necessary and he could survive them. Grey went further than most of his contemporaries, to 'Right' or 'Left'. As he looked out on 'hideous cities' and the 'ghastly competition' of his boasted civilization, he felt horror. If God shared his view, 'then the great industrial countries will perish in catastrophe, because they have made the country hideous and life impossible'.[3]

After its victory in the General Election, the obvious first business of the Government was to settle the constitutional issue. The Parliament Bill was passed by a majority of 121 in the Commons on 15 May. After weeks of debate, interrupted by the coronation, the Lords sent down their amendments to the Commons. Asquith refused to accept them and the Lords then had to decide, in the knowledge that if the Bill were rejected, the Government had the King's consent to create the necessary peers. Amidst scenes of great drama, the Lords passed the Bill by a small majority. The triumph on this occasion was clearly Asquith's. Grey still hankered after reform of the Upper House, but he made no difficulty this time. The Foreign Secretary's role in these events was minimal but, at least according to Margot Asquith, memorable. In the debate on 24 July when the Lords' amendments were considered, a concerted uproar kept Asquith on his feet for thirty minutes, trying to speak. Margot 'realised slowly that Henry was being howled down'. She sent a note to Edward Grey: 'They will listen to you—so for God's sake defend him from the cats and the cads!' When Grey rose, the stillness was apparently formidable. White and silent, he stared at the enemy and then spoke: 'If arguments are not to be listened to from the Prime Minister there is not one of us who will attempt to take his place.' Amidst cheers, he sat down. For the first and last time, G. P. Gooch saw the Foreign Secretary 'flushed and angry'.[4]

After the drama of the Parliament Act, the Cabinet returned to the question of relations with Germany. The Foreign Secretary now found himself in a new position. The centrality of the problem had led to a feeling that the Cabinet as a whole should associate itself more closely with policy. The Prime Minister became Chairman of a Cabinet Committee on Foreign Affairs, the other members being Grey, Morley, Crewe, Lloyd George and Runciman. The committee was charged with the task of drawing up a memorandum which the British Ambassador in Berlin was to submit to the Imperial Chancellor. It was not easy to reach agreement, but the document was finally presented to the Cabinet on 8 March and handed over in Berlin sixteen days later. The Cabinet had insisted that the tone of the reply should be one of 'unmistakeable cordiality', but Grey won his point that nothing should be said which could lead to misinterpretation in France and Russia.[5] In return, Grey was prepared to consider the simultaneous conclusion of a political and a naval agreement. He hoped that the Baghdad railway question might prove a useful starting-point for discussion. The Germans were aware that France and Russia had been informed of these proposed exchanges. Grey had thwarted those members of the Cabinet—normally critics of 'secrecy'—who did not wish them to be informed. Fears in the Foreign Office that this new committee was a device to limit the scope of the Foreign Secretary had so far not proved correct.

Many Liberals in Parliament and in the country were becoming restive at the apparent deadlock on the naval question and annoyed at the annual rejection of their demands for defence cuts. The Foreign Secretary was coming under attack for his failure to gain the necessary political easement between the two countries. In a debate on 13 March, Arthur Ponsonby, seconding a motion for the reduction of armaments, declared that it was deplorable that the Liberal Party should have embarked upon 'this profitless and provocative expenditure on armaments'. He believed that were it not for the importance of the constitutional question, the Government would only have been saved from defeat by the votes of the Opposition. In reply, Grey made one of his most important speeches.

He did not deny that armaments expenditure constituted a heavy burden and characterized those states which claimed to be most 'civilized'. If the process went on, either war would occur, or the mass of men would revolt against the taxation it entailed. In the meantime, unilateral disarmament would solve nothing. Patience might eventually produce an agreement with Germany for mutual reduction of expenditure, but he warned that Germany regarded her Naval Law as a necessary and unchallengeable measure. He concluded by sharing with his critics the conviction that in the long term the only real solution was the substitution of law for force, and the acceptance of arbitration. In the short term, he stressed the benefits to be gained by exchanging information.[6] This speech was not merely designed to appease his critics, it represented his real convictions.

A few weeks before, there had been a point when he had felt like resigning. No principle was involved, but he had just suffered a further personal loss. His brother George, after spending Christmas at Fallodon, returned to Africa. There he had the misfortune to be fatally mauled by a lion when out hunting. Edward had been closest to him, and the brothers planned to make Fallodon their joint home when George finally returned from Africa. The blow was a heavy one. Asquith wrote to Knollys that 'Edward Grey is completely knocked down by the death of his brother. . . . He wished to give up altogether & at once, but of course I would not hear of this.' Grey havered for a week and took a rest. By early April, however, Harcourt described him as being 'in a much better frame of mind'.[7]

There was, however, little to encourage him in the German reply of 9 May. The exchanges were now virtually deadlocked. Grey told the Cabinet that the terms 'do not close the door to further negotiations, but, so far at any rate as naval expenditure is concerned, they are of an unsatisfactory and discouraging character'.[8] At the end of May a further draft dispatch on the exchange of information was submitted to the Cabinet for approval, but few now anticipated an early breakthrough.

The deadlock in Anglo-German relations seemed to make it all the more important to secure the British position outside Europe. Walking in the New Forest with Roosevelt was, no doubt, symbolic of Anglo-American intimacy, but a rather empty gesture in so far as Roosevelt was unlikely to regain office. President Taft was more difficult to deal with. Bryce had been plodding on with American-Canadian issues and some progress had been made with the intricate questions of fishing and sealing. The work, however, was exhausting and Bryce took some extended leave in South America. Even there, Grey exhorted him to see 'how much the Germans are doing to push themselves in South America. . . .'[9] The Ambassador returned to Washington in January 1911 and found himself in the middle of a debate on the vexed question of American-Canadian trade reciprocity.[10] Traditionally, Canadian opinion had been concerned to 'compute a balance of how much she gained by any improvement in Anglo-American understanding as against how much she gave up in order to make it possible'.[11] Now, however, it was the turn of the United Kingdom to become anxious. To Canadian businessmen, trade across the border was already more important than trade with the mother country. When, therefore, on 21 January, a Reciprocal Trade Agreement between the United States and Canada was announced, Grey was alarmed and wrote to his cousin, the Governor-General: 'It would be disastrous if Canada went so far as to give the United States preferential rates which were not extended to British goods, and thereby discriminated against British trade.'[12] If this could be avoided, then he had no objections. In the event, however, despite the fact that the Laurier Government had come as near to negotiating with the United States on equal terms as any previous Canadian Government, the Conservatives, helped by some injudicious American remarks, raised the annexation bogey and repudiated the agreement when they came into office.

This rejection was important not only in itself, but also for its repercussions on the pursuit of a full Anglo-American Arbitration Treaty. Bryce had concluded an Arbitration Convention in 1908, but since this excluded questions involving 'vital interests' and 'national honour' it was not felt to be fully comprehensive. Influential groups and individuals, financed by Andrew Carnegie, now gave great prominence to the idea of international arbitration. President Taft took up the idea, and in the early months of 1911 a draft treaty was prepared which the British Cabinet approved. Quite apart from the benefit to Anglo-American relations, Grey saw this agreement in a more general light. 'The effect of such agreements', he wrote to Bryce, 'upon disarmament and the *morale* of international politics should be considerable.'[13] These hopes were dashed when it became clear that despite Presidential approval, or perhaps because of it, the Arbitration Treaty would not be accepted by the Senate, except in an emasculated form. Grey was prepared, he told Bryce in September, to sign a general Arbitration Treaty with the United States, but not with all nations indiscriminately.[14] By the spring of 1912, both Bryce and Grey were disappointed men, and it was clear that nothing could be done until the Presidential election in November 1912.

The discussions with the United States again brought the question of Anglo-Japanese relations into prominence. In February and March, the Cabinet had to consider whether British obligations to Japan clashed with the proposed Arbitration Treaty. Grey reported at the end of March, that, according to the Japanese Ambassador, his Government would not object to the exemption of an Anglo-American agreement from the operation of the Alliance. It was therefore agreed to propose a renewal of the Anglo-Japanese treaty.[15] But, leaving aside American dislike of the Alliance, were there not equally strong feelings in Australia and Canada? Was it not wise to find out? The Prime Minister resisted the notion that the subject could be profitably discussed at the forthcoming Imperial Conference. Nicolson, too, felt that it would be better not to discuss the subject there. These views were shared by Grey.[16] He was prepared to discuss the matter privately, but did not want it to come up at one of the plenary sessions. The Australians, in his view, required 'a good deal of education', for 'the logical conclusion of denouncing the Alliance would be that Australia and New Zealand should undertake the burden of naval supremacy in China seas. This they are neither willing nor able to do.' He did not believe there was the least danger of Japan attempting forcible measures on the American side of the Pacific.[17]

The Foreign Secretary's reluctance had largely been dictated by his concern for secrecy. When it was possible for him to address the delegates in the context of a C.I.D. meeting, he was quite prepared to do so. Thus, on 26 May, the colonial leaders were treated to a lengthy exposition of British foreign policy—a more detailed survey, in fact, than he ever gave his own colleagues. The Foreign Secretary was guardedly hopeful of an improvement in relations with Germany, and praised the benefits which had been gained from the Anglo-Russian agreement. He declared emphatically that 'we are not committed by entanglements which tie our hands'. But, if a single Power, or group of Powers, looked like gaining such a dominating position in Europe, 'the question might arise as to whether we ought to take part by force in European affairs'. Mindful of his audience, however, he stressed that 'if we did it would be solely because Sea Power, and the necessity of keeping the command of the sea, was the underlying cause and motive of our action'. Finally, Grey discussed Japan, announcing the Government's intention to renew the Alliance. He did his best to calm colonial anxieties by making it clear that there would be no provision about immigration which would interfere with colonial control. He also declared that the alternative to the Japanese Alliance—the reinforcement of the British fleet in the Pacific—was out of line with current naval thinking.[18]

Sir Edward described his speech, and the discussion which followed, as a 'consultation'. The creation of colonial navies made it all the more essential that the foreign policy of the Empire should be a common policy. If it was to be common, it must be one 'on which the Dominions must be taken into consultation, which they must know, which they must understand, and which they must approve'. Nevertheless, whatever the rhetoric, in practice Grey did not initiate any meaningful process of consultation.[19] Despite the occasional imparting of information, the foreign policy of the Empire continued to be made in Whitehall, however important Colonial pressure on particular points might be. If Grey was an 'Imperialist', he had little enthusiasm for colonials in conference. On the occasion of the previous conference he had written to his cousin in Canada that a conversation with him gave 'a stronger impression of a United Empire than can be got from any number of Deakin's speeches or from all the Premiers at a Conference'.[20] In 1908, he agreed to address the Victoria League, though confessing that if he really spoke his mind he would say: 'I think there is too much tendency here to slobber over the Colonies, and they are too much given to spit at us; I except Canada from this criticism, but for Australia it might be put even stronger. . . .'[21] It was not without a little relief that His Majesty's servants in London said farewell to their brethren from across the seas and returned to their customary routines.

The Moroccan crisis of the summer was not altogether unexpected. For months past there had been disturbances in the hinterland of the country which might provide the French with the pretext they needed to complete their penetration. Grey had watched these developments with some anxiety. He did not wish to encourage the

French, and even Crowe considered their policy 'vicious', fearing that they were contemplating making a bargain with Germany at British expense.[22] There was, indeed, considerable public and private discussion in France on the precise value of the entente. If war should actually come, France had no guarantee at all. Crowe shared this view, minuting in February 1911 that 'an entente is nothing more than a frame of mind, a view of general policy which is shared by the government of two countries, but which may be or become so vague as to lose all content'.[23] In the early months of 1911, therefore, the French conducted a number of probes to discover whether there was any chance of extending the relationship, but Grey was firmly discouraging. Bent as it was on naval talks with Germany, Grey knew that such a proposal had no chance of success with the Cabinet. Early in April 1911, Grey circulated a report from the British military attaché in Paris to Asquith, Haldane and Morley. It gave an account of a conversation with General Foch, in which he pointed out the need for closer Anglo-French military conversations. Nothing would be better than British military assistance, but France could not be expected to make her planning arrangements—reserving rolling stock for example—unless there was a reasonable certainty that the help would be forthcoming. Otherwise, scarce resources would be better deployed elsewhere.[24] At this point, Grey thought it wise to inform, or remind, the Prime Minister of the origins of the 1906 military conversations. He stressed that no promises had been made—'our hands must be free' —but that the military experts had convened. 'What they settled I never knew', Grey wrote in 1911; 'the position being that the Govt. was quite free, but that the military people knew what to do if the word was given. Unless French war plans have changed; there should be no need for anything further, but it is clear we are going to be asked something.'[25]

It has been observed that in this letter, Grey failed to mention the 1907 staff exchanges, which had taken place with explicit Foreign Office approval, and the resumption of military conversations by Sir Henry Wilson after his appointment as D.M.O. in August 1910. 'The Foreign Secretary's ignorance of these developments', it is contended, 'plus his confession that "what they settled I never knew" suggests that Grey's conduct and control of British foreign policy left something to be desired.'[26] There are some puzzles here. It is dangerous to infer from the fact that Grey did not mention these developments, that he did not know of them. If Grey had kept the origins and nature of the conversations secret for five years from his supposed Liberal Imperialist intimate (and Asquith's ignorance or purported ignorance is astonishing) then he was perfectly capable of revealing to the Prime Minister only as much as he thought good for him. It is, unfortunately, impossible to establish with precision just what Grey did know, and it may be necessary to distinguish between types of 'knowledge', between what he really knew and what he officially knew. Grey did distinguish in his mind between the exchanges of 'experts' and his own political role. It was not the business of the Foreign Secretary to 'know' the details of the military arrangements—any more than it was the business of Sir Henry Wilson to play politics. But just as Wilson did play politics, may not Grey also have known more than he officially claimed to know? Certainly, in the early months of 1911, Wilson, Grey and Haldane were busily tackling the problem of how to move the four divisions destined for the continent from their mobilization areas to their ports of embarkation.[27] The criticism that 'on the one hand, he consistently refused to extend the political nature of the entente; on the other, he consistently refused to appreciate that the staff talks negated much of his prudent approach to Anglo-French relations' and that he committed the 'grave error of failing to control the talks . . .' therefore underestimates the subtlety of the situation.[28] Whatever he really knew, or intelligently surmised, it was convenient, if not vital, to be able to tell the French that he did not 'know' about the military aspect. Far from his failure to control the talks negating his prudent approach to Anglo-French relations, it alone made it possible. It is, of course, arguable that military and political thinking should have been integrated at the highest level, but to have done so would have destroyed the entente as such.

The dispatch of the German gunboat, the *Panther*, to Agadir on 1 July came as a great surprise. The Foreign Office was bewildered. Since Grey himself was out of town, Nicolson, the Permanent Under-Secretary, received Metternich's verbal explanation. Germany had watched with concern French military activity in Fez, which seemed to contravene the Act of Algeciras without sufficient justification. The German Government could not ignore the interests of its subjects in the southern part of the country and had taken steps to protect them. Germany was quite ready to reach a settlement with France and Spain in which British assistance would be welcomed.[29] Nicolson was alarmed, but in another respect

R

pleased. Throughout the spring and early summer, he had been worried by the pressure within the Cabinet for continuing the talks with Germany on the naval question. The friendly impression made by the Kaiser during his visit in May to attend the unveiling of a memorial to his grandmother had all been part of a deliberate 'softening-up' campaign. A sufficiently large number of people had been impressed for Nicolson to feel that the entente policy was in danger. Crowe, too, believed that the 'excellent relations' now claimed to exist between Germany and Britain were designed to give Germany a free hand in dealing with France. Once again, Morocco would be the testing-ground of the entente, and they wanted a firm stand behind France. Shortly before the emergency Cabinet on 4 July, Nicolson wrote to Grey urging him to support the French request that a vessel be sent to a nearby port.[30]

The Foreign Secretary, however, was not to be rushed into precipitate action by his permanent officials—the position in the Cabinet was too delicate for that. Crowe's knowledge of Germany he respected, though he did not slavishly follow his advice. He was less respectful towards Nicolson, who had been Under-Secretary for almost a year. Grey could only blame himself for any disappointment he felt. In general, ambassadorial appointments were made after a process of consultation involving the Foreign Secretary, his private secretary, the Permanent Under-Secretary, the Prime Minister, his private secretary, and finally, the King and his private secretary. In the case of Nicolson, however, it would seem that Grey and Hardinge largely handled the matter without reference either to Downing Street or the Palace. It is possible that Grey wished to avoid comment in the Cabinet.[31] In the event, however, Sir Arthur was not a very efficient administrator, and his dislike of the Liberal Government obtruded too conspicuously for political convenience. His years at St Petersburg had not dimmed his enthusiasm for Russia, nor his desire to turn the entente into an alliance. His cultural pessimism accorded ill with Liberal optimism. Perhaps this rift suited the Foreign Secretary. By the summer of 1911, Grey was an established Minister. No new Permanent Under-Secretary could have established with him the relationship which Hardinge had been able to develop after 1906.[32]

In fact, the Cabinet, at its meeting to discuss the crisis on 4 July, refused to send a ship as a counter-demonstration. His colleagues authorized Grey to tell the German Ambassador that Britain could not allow the future of Morocco to be settled behind her back.

They also insisted that the French should realize that concessions would be expected of them, since their action had made a return to the *status quo* impossible. The British interests to be safeguarded were, Asquith concluded, no German port on the Mediterranean shore, no new fortified port anywhere on the Morocco coast and the 'open door' for British trade. Grey informed Cambon that while Britain preferred that compensation to Germany should be outside Morocco, even this was not ruled out. This attitude startled and angered the French, and while it has been surmised that Grey bowed before Cabinet pressure, no evidence exists that he was himself seriously upset by the decision, at this stage.

In the light of German discussions with France on compensation, the British Cabinet reviewed the position on 11 and 19 July. It agreed that France could not be expected to cede her entire Congo possessions, and a fresh set of proposals should be considered. Grey then urged that a conference be called and Germany told that in the event of her refusing to attend, steps would be taken to protect British interests. At this point, however, he encountered opposition. The Lord Chancellor, Loreburn, claimed that direct British interest in Morocco was insignificant, and such steps might end in war. Morley, Harcourt and Burns were also unhappy and a long animated discussion ensued. In the end, it was agreed to postpone a communication to Germany. In the meantime, the French were to be asked whether they wished to prevent, at all costs, the admission of Germany to Morocco. For its part, the British Government did not consider such admission a *casus belli*. The British note to Germany of 4 July had still not been acknowledged and a jittery feeling was developing.[33]

While himself clear that 'We cannot go to war in order to set aside the Algeciras Act and put France in virtual possession of Morocco . . .', Grey was disturbed by the tone of the Cabinet. He feared 'lest irreparable harm may have been done by continued silence and inaction'.[34] Nicolson and Crowe, convinced that a trial of strength was involved, pressed for a strong commitment to France. Grey was more restrained, knowing the delicate balance in the Cabinet. However, on 21 July, in the continued absence of a reply, Grey was instructed to inform the German Ambassador that Britain would welcome a settlement based on concessions in the French Congo, but if this failed, she would not recognize any other solution to which she had not been a party.[35] Later in the evening, the Chancellor of the Exchequer spoke at the Mansion

House. His purpose, he subsequently declared, was to 'warn Germany of the peril into which her Ministers were rushing her so heedlessly'.

Earlier in the afternoon, he had been to see Grey to gain his approval, and submit a draft of his speech. There had been no objection. Lloyd George declared that Britain was not to be treated 'as if she were of no account in the Cabinet of Nations . . . peace at that price would be a humiliation intolerable for a great country like ours to endure'. There has been much dispute as to whether the speech was a warning to Germany or to France. Certainly, it was interpreted in Berlin as support for France, and welcomed in Paris as such. Nicolson was delighted, as was Grey's private secretary, Tyrrell, who wrote that the speech 'has saved the peace of Europe and our good name'. Lloyd George was now thought entirely 'sound' and his co-operation with Grey 'delightful to watch'.[36] But to see the speech in its traditional light as a warning to Germany does not necessarily mean that it was not also a useful warning to France. Fear that the Foreign Office was only being supplied with an edited version of the Franco-German discussions was present even amongst the firmest supporters of France. For example, on 15 July, Crowe had minuted: 'If we can rely on France telling us frankly and fully what goes on between her and Germany, there is no reason for us to stir. . . . Previous experience should however put us on our guard against too implicit reliance on French openness in matters of this nature. There is a grave risk of British economical interests in Morocco being bartered away surreptitiously by France to Germany before we are told of what is going on.'[37]

While Metternich protested against the public method adopted by the British Government, Kiderlen declared that Germany did not in fact seek Moroccan territory. If progress was not made, however, she might have to demand a return to the *status quo*. He insisted that this explanation be kept private. It would seem that having originally sponsored German 'interests' in southern Morocco to give him a *pied-à-terre* in negotiation with France, it was now extremely difficult for him to shake them off. Tension remained high, and the Franco-German exchanges continued throughout August and September. By the middle of October, the Germans were prepared to reach an agreement which gave them certain territory from the French Congo. Those Germans who could not understand why Germany had settled for such terms, put it down to the British attitude. In fact, it would seem that Kiderlen had never expected territorial compensation in Morocco itself, and if, by a final irony, he had gained southern Morocco, a report which he had himself commissioned during the crisis argued that German acquisition would be an economic disaster.[38] But even if the limited German aims were realized, their methods had aroused fresh suspicions abroad. In Germany also, there were those who supposed that it had been the intention to acquire a portion of Morocco. Thus, as Grey subsequently wrote, 'the consequences of such a foreign crisis do not end with it. They seem to end, but they go underground and reappear later on.'[39]

On the British side, it has been supposed that Grey and Asquith 'sought to reduce radical influence by both the content of the pronouncement and the participation of the pronouncer'. Certainly, they had no wish to encourage 'radical' influence, but if the 'radicals' were exerting a strong influence over the direction of policy, it is a little surprising that Lloyd George should have chosen this moment to break ranks. No evidence survives of any 'deal' involving the three men. If he had stayed on the 'radical' side, Lloyd George would have avoided the wrath of Loreburn and Morley. The Lord Chancellor wrote to Grey on 27 July imploring him to make clear publicly 'that we have no wish to interfere between France & Germany, and to undo the effect of Lloyd George's speech'. Commenting on the protest delivered by the German Ambassador, Morley wrote to Asquith that he felt 'the justice of every word of the language that Metternich was instructed to use about the speech. . . . I utterly dislike and distrust the German methods. They are what they have always been. But that is no reason why we should give them the excuse of this provocation. . . .'[40] Instead, Lloyd George joined the small group of ministers —Asquith, Grey, Churchill and Haldane—who seem to have managed the crisis throughout the summer. August was a very hot month, and much to his disgust, Grey was tied to London. Lady Lyttelton was rash enough to choose these circumstances to ask whether he had read Nietzsche. He had not: 'I imagine it to be strained, unwholesome & unnecessary but I don't know what it is. I believe he put an end to his own life.' Putting such frivolity aside, he reported that the Moroccan situation seemed to be improving: 'The Prussians are a tiresome, cynical people. They think the time has come for them to get something, & they will get something, but not as much as they thought.'[41] One other colleague, Mr Churchill, kept him company in London 'for love of the crisis' as Grey put it.[42]

Churchill had now joined Lloyd George in fevered apprehension of the danger and both men were frantically making amends for their previous blinkered existence. They busily exchanged military plans and were ardent in their determination to keep Grey 'all progged up'. The Home Secretary was assiduous in his attendance on Sir Edward, taking him off regularly for a swim at the Automobile Club. This exercise, as Grey dryly remarked, would cool Churchill's ardour, while it revived his own spirits. The Foreign Secretary was no more going to be swept away by this enthusiasm than he had been in the past by Churchill's passion for economy. Nevertheless, their personal relations were very good. In June, Winston had asked him to be godfather to young Randolph, writing to his wife: 'He likes and wistfully admires our little circle.'[43]

Another little circle assembled for a special meeting of the Committee of Imperial Defence on 23 August. The dispatch of the *Panther* had been the signal for Sir Henry Wilson to attend busily to the Anglo-French staff talks and the preparation of the B.E.F. He also saw Grey and, in the presence of Crowe and Haldane, stressed that Britain had to join in the war on the same day as the French and send all six divisions. He found these suggestions were agreed to, but without much heartiness. Grey did not impress him: 'an ignorant, vain, and weak man, quite unfit to be the Foreign Minister of any country larger than Portugal. A man who knows nothing of policy and strategy going hand in hand.'[44] Whatever the truth of this contention, Wilson was in the fortunate position of being able to conduct his policy without the hindrance of a Cabinet. He did, however, have to reckon with the opposition of the First Sea Lord to the idea of a major continental involvement. To try to resolve this disagreement was the purpose of the meeting on 23 August. Present were Asquith, Grey, McKenna, Haldane, Lloyd George, Churchill and the service chiefs. To their subsequent chagrin, Morley, Harcourt and Crewe were not invited. A long discussion ensued. Admiral Sir Arthur Wilson declared that the Navy was not in a position to convey the B.E.F. to France on the outbreak of war. Sir Henry Wilson, for the Army, could not accept this. In order to support his arguments, he had virtually to admit that the Army had agreed with the French on the importance of immediate transportation. Presumably, this was news to Churchill, Lloyd George and McKenna. Grey took very little part in the discussions. Only two of his contributions were of any significance. He stated rather weakly that British military support would be 'of great moral value' to the French. As to the Belgians, 'he thought that they would avoid committing themselves as long as possible in order to try and make certain of being on the winning side'. On the general issue, he came down without much enthusiasm on the side of the Army. So far as he could judge, 'the combined operations outlined were not essential to naval success, and the struggle on land would be the decisive one. . . .'[45] It seemed that the Admiralty had lost this encounter.

Other members of the Government now began to be alarmed. The day after the C.I.D. meeting (though in ignorance of it), Runciman wrote to Harcourt that he found 'in the most unexpected quarters . . . *a positive desire for conflict*'. He respected the opinions of Grey and Haldane, even if he disagreed with them, but the new 'rampageous strategists' would upset the balance of the Cabinet. The only way to hold them in check was to reach a definite decision at the Cabinet not to land a single British soldier on the continent during the crisis.[46] Two days later, Harcourt replied with news of the C.I.D. meeting: 'It was to decide on where and how British troops could be landed to assist a French Army on the Meuse!!!' Harcourt said that he would resign rather than accept such 'criminal folly'.[47] They would have been even more alarmed if they had known that on the following day Lloyd George observed the thunderclouds gathering and the chances of war multiplying. Everybody seemed to the Chancellor to 'take it all much too carelessly'. He urged Churchill to find out all he could about Russian strength and to press Grey. It was essential to know what 'Russia is capable of before we trust the future of Europe to the hazard. We are even now almost at the point where we cannot recede.'[48] Grey replied to Churchill that the Russians had given an official assurance to France, but agreed that it would be useful for the military authorities to find out from the French what the Russians really could do.[49] The Foreign Secretary passed on this concern about Russia to Asquith and learnt that the Prime Minister had formed the impression that the Russians were either not ready for war, or afraid of the unpopularity of war in such a cause, or both.[50] Grey therefore stressed to Lloyd George that he was urging the French to enlarge their French Congo offers. Unless Germany was really bent on war, it seemed to him unlikely, 'but after the crisis is over the whole question of future developements of Foreign policy will have to be considered very carefully & coolly in the light of recent events'.[51]

The Prime Minister now began to get a little alarmed. He cast his mind back to the report of the conversation between General Foch and the British military attaché back in April. Such talks now seemed 'rather dangerous; especially the part which refers to possible British assistance. The French ought not to be encouraged, in present circumstances, to make their plans on any assumptions of this kind.' In reply, Grey studiously painted a very different picture of the international situation from the Churchill–Lloyd George vision. The Germans were proceeding 'leisurely' with the negotiations, which were entering upon 'exceedingly tedious but not dangerous ground'. Nevertheless, he was alarmed by Asquith's short pronouncement: 'It would create consternation if we forbade our military experts to converse with the French. No doubt these conversations and our speeches have given an expectation of support. I do not see how that can be helped.'[52] The Prime Minister's unease before the prospect of military intervention grew rapidly in the weeks after the C.I.D. meeting. It was undoubtedly a genuine distaste, but was also very convenient, because a major Cabinet crisis was brewing. The news of the C.I.D. meeting having leaked out, Lord Morley, with wounded pride, demanded assurances that vital information would not be withheld from Cabinet Ministers. The Prime Minister was relieved to have Grey's view that the Moroccan crisis looked like resolving itself into 'prolonged haggling'.[53] This meant that he could devote himself to the tiresome task of consoling Morley.

The subject came before the Cabinet on 1 November and it was a stormy session. Haldane had the task of explaining the origin of the military conversations. The Prime Minister attempted to cool tempers by declaring that all questions of policy had been and would be reserved for the Cabinet. Grey concurred. The Cabinet broke up without coming to any conclusion.[54] A fortnight later, the subject was resumed and there was a long, animated discussion. Grey (who must have been the main target of the critics) declared that at no stage had 'our freedom of decision of action in the event of war between France and Germany' been compromised. Loreburn expostulated and threatened to resign. Morley and Harcourt were equally angry. In the end, it was agreed that no communications should take place between the General Staff and other staffs which could 'directly or indirectly, commit this country to military or naval intervention'. Secondly, if such communications related to concerted action by land or sea, they should not be entered into 'without the previous approval of the Cabinet'. On Asquith's draft, Grey wrote: 'I think the last paragraph is a little tight'; for the first time in his career he had been defeated. Morley was eager to report that one very eminent Minister had received the rating he deserved.[55] It remained to be seen whether he survived.

Although the Cabinet crisis centred on the Moroccan question, it also reflected a certain unease in the party as a whole. The Agadir crisis had coincided with industrial unrest and very hot weather. Lloyd George had played a conspicuous part in settling the railway strike and was congratulated both by Prime Minister and Foreign Secretary. Nevertheless, the industrial scene was still unsettled. By November, the issue of votes for women was adding a further strain to relationships inside the Cabinet. Although Grey and Asquith were in substantial agreement on foreign policy, they were at loggerheads on the suffrage question. Sir Edward had been a strong supporter of votes for women, and had been the speaker for Winston Churchill at a famous election meeting at Manchester in October 1905. Both men were invited by Christabel Pankhurst to state their position. Rather curiously, Grey alienated the ladies by refusing to declare his own sympathies. Since this was not to their liking, they caused a disturbance and were removed, shouting at the police and threatening to spit. Grey adhered to his convictions and, in an attempt to forestall further violence, tried to prod Asquith into taking action. In March 1911, Scott of the *Manchester Guardian* saw both Haldane and Grey in an attempt to persuade them to speak in support of a Conciliation Bill at a public meeting. Grey declined, pleading pressure of work, but stating his intention of speaking in the Commons on the subject. Haldane also refused, though, Scott thought, for a less adequate reason. 'Grey', he wrote, 'is far & away the bigger man.'[56] That particular Conciliation Bill died in the Commons in May. Further agitation took place, but there seemed little prospect of Government action. Then, in November, Lloyd George publicly stated his readiness to move an amendment to an adult suffrage bill (which was under discussion) in favour of women. Grey at once aligned himself with the Chancellor of the Exchequer, and a different kind of Cabinet struggle began.

Asquith's personal opposition to female suffrage was well known, and he was delighted to find Churchill anxious to undertake the job of keeping the Government together. Winston wrote to the Master of Elibank, the Chief Whip, that the Government was getting into very great peril on the issue. Female suffrage was unpopular in the country and Lloyd George's attitude was incomprehensible. It would be a tragedy to go down on 'Petticoat politics!' Since Lloyd George and Grey were 'working themselves up, they will have to go, if female suffrage is knocked out'. He urged a referendum on the subject, with men and women polling separately. He urged the same course on Grey. He lamented a situation in which Sir Edward and 'George' might 'persuade yourselves that women's suffrage is not merely the most important but the *only* question in politics'.[57] On the Opposition benches, F. E. Smith was quick to see that the Government could fall on this issue. The Chief Whip flapped, urged the leading contenders to meet, and lamented the bad effect on party morale. This was, indeed, something of a silly season for the leading Liberals, though the strength of convictions on the matter must not be underestimated. Feelings were smoothed over, but the underlying cause of them was not resolved. At the height of the antagonism, Harcourt wrote to Grey: 'Your public appearance on the Suffrage platform has reluctantly brought me out into the open and I am now actively organising against you and your pernicious opinions.' The letter concluded with an invitation to come and shoot partridges, but this did not diminish the sharp political division.[5]

This letter is most instructive. Harcourt was a prominent 'radical' critic of Grey's foreign policy, perhaps with some aspirations to succeed him, yet he was clearly not 'radical' on the suffrage question. On this matter, possibly as a debt to a memory, Grey was much more 'radical' than many of his colleagues who are normally honoured by this description. Nor was it an isolated example. Payment of Members was introduced in 1911, and this was something Grey had been advocating, with more persistence than many, for over twenty years. He was a firm supporter of the National Insurance Bill, writing that though it might be unpopular for a few years, it would be 'a great solid good'.[59] Nor did he neglect to give some consideration to the problems of industrial unrest. In 1911, he gave a lecture in a memorial series for a former colleague on the board of the N.E.R. In it, he stressed that industrial workers now had a power and consciousness of their own existence which was quite new. 'They will not stand being played with, nor allow their problem of existence to be pushed on one side by international questions.' Amidst wild talk of the imminence of war, he declared that he neither expected it nor saw any need for it. He had heard it said that any powerful Government might seek to divert attention from internal troubles by indulging in external adventure. While this might have been the case in some instances, it seemed to him foolishness. If a great war came, these industrial issues might temporarily be suspended, but afterwards interest in them would be quickened. It was quite possible that 'the next country, if any, which had a great and successful war, unless it were purely a war of defence against aggression, would be the first to have a social revolution'.[60] There was no way of dodging the issues involved in social and industrial change.

In view of these comments, it is perhaps not quite so strange as it first appears, to find the Foreign Secretary closely involved with the problems of the coal industry in the first months of 1912. The Miners' Federation had decided on a national strike in favour of a minimum wage. Notices were due to expire on 29 February, and shortly before, the Cabinet appointed Asquith, Grey, Lloyd George and Buxton to try to bring both sides together in a settlement. The move failed, and the strike began, though the Cabinet team remained in being. In the middle of March, they met both sides in three days of talk—again without success. The Cabinet, with some dissension—a surrender to Syndicalism, said Churchill—agreed to an emergency Bill for settling minimum rates on a local basis, but not stating a sum. Asquith made a last unavailing effort to get the owners to accept five shillings per shift as the amount. When he reported failure to the Cabinet on 26 March, it was Grey who suggested a solution. The Government should inform the owners that if, after a year, they suffered loss up to a certain figure, the Exchequer should indemnify them. This suggestion produced a strong difference of opinion. The Prime Minister stated that he would accept it, if *force majeure* prevailed, though it would be difficult to justify such a subvention from public funds to one of the most prosperous industries of the country. The proposal was accepted, though Burns, McKinnon Wood, Runciman and Morley were 'very adverse' to it.[61] On this basis, the miners went back to work in mid-April. Grey's coolness had apparently been justified. Early in March, as he told Bryce, he was convinced that 'the bulk of the miners have more to lose than to gain by revolution, so have the bulk of people in the country. When this is so, there ought not to be revolution.' Churchill's violent tirades and cataclysmic forecasts in Cabinet had not impressed him. After the strike was over, Grey wrote that 'the whole question of the organization and conditions of work of the mining industry should be overhauled'.[62]

While he hoped that there would be 'an orderly and gradual revolution', it would have to take place, for 'labour intends to have a larger share and has laid hold of power'.[63] He went even further in May 1911, feeling that 'the men employed in a big business have as great an interest in it as the proprietors, or shareholders'.[64] By the late summer, the strike wave seemed to be spent, though not without cost to the Government's legislative plans and to the energy of Ministers. But there had been no disorderly revolution.

The important role Grey played in domestic politics and his firm alignment with Lloyd George (described by Masterman as 'the new alliance') helps to explain why the campaign against him, roughly from the summer of 1911 to the spring of 1912, was so ineffective. His convictions, while quite genuine, enabled him to frustrate attempts to typecast him as a thorough-going 'reactionary' on all fronts. His party and press critics had no alternative candidate to offer if political attitudes were considered in the round. For example, there could be no fiercer critic of Grey's foreign policy than H. N. Brailsford but, keen supporter of the suffragettes that he was, did he want to see Harcourt advance to the inner tier of the Cabinet? Or, with his socialist convictions, did he seek the advancement of Runciman? Morley appealed to few as a replacement, and age ruled him out. Loreburn discussed the problem with C. P. Scott in December 1911: '... Grey no doubt ought to go, but who was there to take his place? Either Churchill or Haldane wd. be worse, the one irresponsible, the other with his cloudy mind and passion for intrigue. Morley was now really senile and Crewe was not at all the same man since his illness ...' In any case, Loreburn realized that Grey's resignation would mean the break-up of the Cabinet, for Churchill, Haldane and Lloyd George would go with him. He saw nothing for it 'but a change of Government. Bonar Law & Lansdowne wd. be far better ...'[65] This was not, however, a solution which appealed to all Liberals. The attack on Grey might have succeeded if Lloyd George had remained the all-purpose Radical hero, but something seemed to have gone wrong there.

The press and backbench assault on the Foreign Secretary also suffered from a diversity of enthusiasms. Some critics, notably Ponsonby and Noel Buxton, had a general concern for widening entry into the Foreign Office and increasing parliamentary influence, if not control, over foreign policy. They noted that the House of Commons had not played a significant role in the Moroccan crisis and set up a Foreign Policy Committee, under the Presidency of

Lord Courtney of Penwith, to work for their wider objectives. Grey's reticence, or secrecy, made him a frequent target, especially so after the disclosure in the French press in November 1911 of the secret clauses attached to the Anglo-French entente. Crowe rightly regarded this action as a piece of French trickery, but Grey was unperturbed, and told Lansdowne that he had decided to publish them officially. Lansdowne replied: 'We shall at any rate hear no more of the confident statements . . . that we had bound ourselves by these articles to afford one another material assistance of a definite kind in certain eventualities.'[66] The former Foreign Secretary was too optimistic. E. D. Morel returned to the fray with a best-selling pamphlet, *Morocco in Diplomacy*, which repeated the old charges and added some new ones. He and others argued that if these clauses had been inadvertently disclosed, how many others were lurking in the files of the Foreign Office? The pressure for more information built up. Lord Sanderson commented privately in a letter to Hardinge in India that the Foreign Office had not published any Blue Books for three years, except a collection of papers on Persia.[67]

The specific issues which had agitated the Cabinet were also, of course, repeated in the party at large. Noel Buxton sent a memorial to Grey stating that if, in relation to France, 'we had laid ourselves under treaty duties so incredible that we are under the obligation of a promise, Liberals of all classes, and not Liberals alone, are bound to protest against a policy of "hemming Germany in" from a share in the colonial world'.[68] Grey would have given the backbench critics the same reply as he had given Loreburn at the end of August. He did not believe that an assurance of British neutrality in the event of war between Germany and France could be conducive to peace. The same was true of any statement that would commit Britain to war.[69] All the old Boer War animosities, however, revived, and Loreburn urged Scott to remember that it was a 'Liberal League' Government. Lloyd George dismissed the charge and told Scott that Loreburn was simply 'petulant'. Grey himself consented to see Scott at the height of the crisis, but the editor derived little comfort from his interview.[70]

The attacks continued strongly, and Grey decided that the only way to meet them was to make a major speech on foreign affairs in the Commons. Rumours were in the air that the intention to send six divisions to the continent had only been frustrated by the Navy. Esher wrote in his diary: 'Fifteen members of the Cabinet against five. The Entente is decidedly imperilled. The Cabinet is so far intact. Edward Grey is to speak on Monday and Europe is awaiting his speech with some anxiety.'[71] In Berlin, there was little expectation that Grey would fall, but if the attacks on him were sufficiently strong he might have to bend his policy to meet them. It was for just this reason that there was anxiety in Paris. Sir Edward took very great care with his speech. He discussed it in advance with Asquith and Haldane. He was also careful to make contact with the new leader of the Opposition, Bonar Law, before the debate. H. A. Gwynne, of the *Morning Post*, told Law that Tyrrell was prepared to act as go-between, as he had done with Balfour. He added that Tyrrell was 'a vigorous defender of Grey but I imagine that we all are, especially as the extreme left are going for him like pickpockets'. Grey gave the Tory leader an outline of his intended speech and summed up his view as 'readiness to make a new friend whenever we can do it without losing an old one'. At the same time, Law had a conversation with the Liberal Chief Whip, who warned him that 'many of our members hold that the conversations between Sir Edward Grey & AJB are responsible for the secrecy wh. has been consistently maintained & from wh. much apprehension exists'.[72] This was indeed true. The appearance of an understanding between the two front benches on major foreign policy questions frustrated those who wanted to see a distinct 'Liberal' foreign policy.

Grey's speech in the foreign-affairs debate, which began in the Commons on 27 November, chiefly consisted of a long recital of the Moroccan crisis, though he also touched on Persia. This was largely history, and most attention was paid to his remarks on the question of secret commitments. They were very carefully phrased. He commented on the argument that if the Government kept secret little things, like the supplementary articles to the French agreement of 1904, it would, *a fortiori*, keep big things secret. 'This is absolutely untrue. There may be reasons why a Government should make secret arrangements of that kind if they are not things of first-rate importance, if they are subsidiary to matters of great importance. But that is the very reason why the British Government should not make secret engagements which commit Parliament to obligations of war. It would be foolish to do it. No British Government could embark upon a war without public opinion behind it, and such engagements as there are which really commit Parliament to anything of that kind are contained in treaties or agreements which have been laid before the House. For ourselves we have not made a single secret article of any kind since we came into office.'[73] The Prime Minister described his speech as 'a great performance', having the effect on the House which Grey alone was capable of producing.[74] It would have been surprising if the Prime Minister did not form that impression. More surprisingly, Morley glowed with praise. He knew 'no one so capable upon a critical occasion, of choosing his words with precision and felicity. . . . For judgment, temper and lucidity on a matter which required the most delicate handling, nothing could have exceeded the speech delivered last night. . . .' Morley found 'the candour of his explanation' very impressive. 'The value of character in the forefront of international controversy was never more conspicuously vindicated.'[75] Particularly in view of Morley's recent attacks in Cabinet on the military conversations, it is perhaps a little surprising that he should describe as candid a speech which contained no reference to them. They were, presumably, not matters of first-rate importance.

Whatever impression it made on his colleagues, the speech did not appease his critics. Men like Ramsay MacDonald, Arthur Ponsonby, Noel Buxton and John Dillon expressed their dissent on subsequent days of the debate. Since the Morocco crisis seemed to be subsiding, the main object of criticism was Grey's Persian policy. The complaint remained what it had been for the last few years. Russian influence and control was being consolidated in the country. The fresh cause for protest was that the attempts of the American, Morgan Shuster, to bring order to Persian finances and thus provide a realistic basis for independence, were being frustrated. The impending removal of Shuster sent the Liberal daily and periodical press into a frenzy of indignation. Again and again, from November onwards, journalists like Brailsford, Massingham, Wolf and Gardiner thundered out their protests against Grey's monstrous and feeble acquiescence in the subjection of Persia.[76] Linked with the accusation that he was an ingrained Germanophobe, this was sufficient justification for the call 'Grey must go'. As Massingham declared, 'public opinion has not authorized a government which acts in its name to follow a policy so mean and weak as this'.[77]

It would have been out of character for Grey to have bowed before this storm. He never attempted to change his style of diplomacy in response to it. He continued his long-standing reticence about what he said in public. Back in 1894, he had told his constituents in no uncertain terms on one occasion 'that he was not going to speak to them on foreign politics because it was necessary that a public speaker should know what not to say as well as what to say'.[78] He still adhered to this view. It was an essentially aristocratic conception, but not without its advantages. His reticence, however, was not merely the product of his background and disposition. It reflected a narrowing of British freedom of manœuvre in foreign affairs. When there had been a sense of superiority in relative isolation, there was more discussion in the Commons and more documents were released. The passing of that period coincided with the growth of the power of the Cabinet in many areas, not merely in foreign policy.[79] Nor was Grey greatly impressed by the claims of his critics to have an exclusive understanding of that protean entity, 'public opinion'. Remarkably, he found that 'public opinion' usually agreed with him. He was therefore able to tell Loreburn that he could not offer Germany 'a free hand' on the questions of the Baghdad railway, the Persian Gulf, or Morocco because public opinion would not sanction it.[80] It was unlikely that Grey would be removed by a newspaper agitation on behalf of the Persians. After all, even Loreburn described them as 'a corrupt and hopeless lot'.[81]

It is typical of the strong streak of obstinacy in Grey's character, that if it had not been for the strong opposition, he might have gone of his own accord. Perhaps obstinacy is not quite the word. He had a charming, but quite determined, desire to get his own way. A fatherless upbringing and three admiring sisters may have encouraged him in his normally correct belief that he could succeed in this desire. By the end of 1911 he was very tired, writing that 'though the F.O. is thought to be so interesting the weariness of its succession of worries is almost intolerable after six years of it. Do you know the definition of life as being "one damned thing after another"? It is very true of the F.O. work especially so this year . . .'[82] But in February 1912, in answer to Mrs Creighton who wrote asking whether he minded the attacks, he replied: 'Well, really I haven't had time to read my papers except *Times*, *Westminster Gazette* & *Spectator* & I have seen very little of the abuse.' He got the drift of it from extracts sent to him, 'but I have too much to do to mind'.[83] Then, at Eastertide, 1912, when the storm had subsided somewhat, he confessed in private that the Cabinet was getting tired: 'We have been in too long.'[84] A more sinister note also entered his correspondence. He wrote to Lady Lyttelton: '. . . I am full of a curious presentiment that I am very near some great change in my life: put roughly the feeling is that I shan't live out the year. . . . However, don't think I am morbid.'[85]

13

After the Storm, 1912-14

In February 1912, the King was graciously pleased to make Sir Edward Grey a Knight of the Garter. The Prime Minister intended it as a snub for the Foreign Secretary's critics and an indication that he would not be moved. There had been some Government changes. The events of the summer and the August C.I.D. meeting clearly revealed, even to Asquith, that there would have to be greater co-ordination between the services. If there had been war in the summer of 1911, the lack of an agreed plan could have been disastrous. In October 1911, Churchill became First Lord of the Admiralty, exchanging jobs with McKenna. Even if this had not been Asquith's intention in appointing him, Churchill proceeded to create a naval staff sympathetic to a 'continental' military strategy, to oust A. K. Wilson as First Sea Lord, and to co-operate with the Army. Despite Churchill's forceful initiative, a great deal of resistance remained below the surface. Lord Haldane, as he now was, had fancied the position, but amongst other reasons, the Prime Minister correctly supposed that the Admirals would not welcome a successful Secretary for War. Grey was not so sure and wrote, admittedly to Haldane, that 'till the Admirals know him, his going to the Admiralty might upset the naval men; and we can't so soon after Fisher & at the present moment have another spell of unrest in the Navy'. He had no doubt that Winston would succeed, 'but it would take a little time & I dread the interval'.[1] After the pressure put upon him, McKenna was initially disinclined to serve as Home Secretary, but Grey helped him to change his mind. 'It would be an awful pity,' he wrote, 'if you chucked office altogether.'[2] The effect of these changes was, in Haldane's view, to produce a very harmonious Cabinet.

Sir Edward fully appreciated in the opening months of 1912 that this harmony could only be maintained if a fresh attempt was made to reach agreement with Germany. Informal approaches were, in fact, already under way.[3] Ballin, the Hamburg shipowner, was in contact with Sir Ernest Cassel, suggesting that he bring Churchill on a visit to Germany. Churchill declined, but the British Government allowed Cassel to visit Berlin to explore the situation. He presented a note to the Kaiser indicating that in return for an embargo on further naval construction, Britain might encourage German colonial ambitions and welcome 'reciprocal assurances' designed to prevent either power joining coalitions which were directed against the other. This visit, on 29 January, came at a delicate juncture in German politics.[4] In October 1911, Tirpitz and the Kaiser had wanted to announce that a new Navy Bill would be brought before the Reichstag in the following spring. Some naval experts felt that fresh construction was unnecessary, while others felt that an announcement would provoke a British attack when the Kiel Canal was still unfinished. Bethmann used the latter argument to quash the proposal, whereupon the Kaiser accused him of being afraid of England. The Chancellor was not, in fact, against further expenditure in principle, but wanted to work quietly so as not to provoke Britain. For the time being, he was happy to take up suggestions that Britain would be prepared to help Germany enlarge her Colonial Empire. The Kaiser was sceptical, but the coincidence of bad election results—Grey had supposed back in September that 'the violent animosity worked up against us' was 'for the sake of the January elections'[5]—and Cassel's visit persuaded the Kaiser to follow up the initiative. He even told the Chief of his Naval Cabinet that 'refusal meant war in the spring, and in fact war on three fronts'.

These tactical disagreements in Berlin were paralleled in London. The idea of a colonial bargain was largely the work of Harcourt, the Colonial Secretary. In September he had written: 'The idea of war is monstrous and inconceivable—and if it took place it would involve the whole of Europe.' Late in December 1911 he stated privately that Anglo-German relations could be permanently improved if there were 'conversations' concerning territory which might give Germany ' "a place in the sun" without injury to our Colonial or Imperial interests'. If anything, a 'deal' should be to the definite advantage of Germany. He hoped suitable areas might be found.[6] Grey was apprehensive, writing to Churchill that 'the Germans are going to open the ball in public by something that will entail an increase of our naval expenditure'. He wanted the Germans to 'suggest what we should do to prove that agreed naval superiority on our part would not restrict their expansion'.[7] The German Government had requested that Grey himself visit Berlin, but when the Cabinet discussed the question at its meeting on 2 February, this was felt to be 'premature'. Instead, Haldane was commissioned 'to feel the way in the direction of a more definite understanding'.[8]

The Haldane Mission is still something of a puzzle. It was at once assumed in some sections of the press that Grey had been elbowed aside. This is unlikely, since Grey simply did not want to go. The obvious alternative is that the inner ring of the Cabinet decided to humour its critics by authorizing such a mission. Haldane was simply the minister who combined a knowledge of Germany and of military matters. The military correspondent, Repington, believed that the Cabinet had little expectation that the mission would succeed and, when it failed, Haldane would be able to purr the Radicals to sleep. This theory presupposes a Radical trust in Haldane which had not been conspicuous in the past. The Liberal Imperialist myth was still active, even though Lord Rosebery had just surfaced to lament the drift towards France. Yet, as he had been known to mention, Haldane had a special relationship with Germany which might, after all, make him generally acceptable, not least to the Germans. No doubt Grey watched the enterprise with mixed feelings. For their part, Nicolson and Crowe were undisguised in their hostility to the project. Predictably, the French Government began to fuss and Grey had to spend a lot of time giving reassurance.

It was in these rather confusing circumstances that Haldane departed for Berlin with Cassel and his brother John. As a diplomatic exercise it was to prove a vindication of Grey's linguistic intransigence and cultural insularity. In a series of meetings, first with Bethmann Hollweg and then with Tirpitz and the Kaiser, Haldane only succeeded in gaining an offer to reduce the tempo of shipbuilding, and this was conditional on British acceptance of a satisfactory political agreement. The activities of the unofficial advisers, Ballin and Cassel, added a further element of ambiguity. Bethmann no longer wished Ballin to be present, and Grey requested Haldane to send Cassel back. There was a certain amount of public comment in London at the role of two men who were German Jews by birth and had no official standing in either country. In further discussions, Haldane resisted Bethmann's plea for an unqualified pledge of British neutrality and the final 'sketch of a

257

conceivable formula' suggested instead that if either Power should be engaged in a 'defensive' war, the other would observe, at least, a 'benevolent neutrality'. Haldane was delighted with his enterprise and impressed by the Chancellor, 'a high-minded sincere gentleman'.[9]

The Cabinet considered Haldane's report at its meeting on 20 February. There was a long discussion and, as expected, a division of opinion. The Prime Minister and Lloyd George were adamant that there was no point in negotiating with Germany, unless Berlin kept to the old naval programme. Harcourt and Crewe, on the other hand, felt that the colonial aspects touched on by Haldane could be taken further. If a settlement looked likely, then a naval formula might be possible. Grey was distinctly uneasy, nevertheless he was prepared to discount French alarms for the moment and have fresh talks with the German Ambassador. In the company of Haldane, he asked for clarification of certain points, especially those relating to naval recruitment. The Kaiser was furious at the introduction of this point, which he interpreted as a British attempt to force Germany to abandon the new Naval Law altogether: 'I must reject out of hand such a monstrosity as being incompatible with our honour.' When in Berlin, he said, Haldane had not raised any objection. Haldane later plausibly explained that this was because he was not a specialist in naval affairs and could not anticipate the Admiralty's objections. The ambiguity on this question illustrated the dangers of this type of diplomacy. Whether his anger was genuine or contrived, the Kaiser raged at British impudence, writing to Bethmann Hollweg a letter full of such 'incredible cruelties' that it could only be interpreted as an invitation to resignation. The Chancellor duly obliged, warning against a policy which could lead Germany into an attack on France in which the victim, but not the aggressor, would receive support. If war did come, Germany might avoid disaster, 'but to cause a war ourselves so long as our honour and our vital interests are not involved, that I would regard as a sin against Germany even if we could expect victory. But that too is not the case, at least on sea.' The Kaiser retreated, agreed to respect Bethmann's office and promised changes in the Navy Law. In 1917, Bethmann wondered whether he ought at this point to have pressed his resignation, but concluded that he would have been succeeded by Tirpitz and the certainty of war.

Although the details of this conflict in Berlin were not known in

Britain, the basis of the conflict was suspected. There were those who felt that an agreement with Bethmann would strengthen his hand against Tirpitz, while others felt that there was, in the end, little significant division between them. At any rate, early in March, fresh exchanges took place, revolving around the remarks Haldane did or did not make in Berlin. Once again, deadlock seemed inevitable. Then, on the evening of 12 March, Haldane received a sudden call to the German Embassy. Metternich told him that 'if the British Government would offer a suitable political formula the proposed Fleet Law as it stood would be withdrawn'. Some law there would be, but of less magnitude. The German Ambassador thought that the reduction would extend to personnel and, even more surprisingly, that the British formula need not go beyond the disclaimer of aggressive intentions and combinations. Haldane reported this conversation to Grey, who found it 'very extraordinary'.[10] At the Cabinet two days later, Grey again commented on the 'remarkable interview'. It seemed that for the moment, Bethmann had got the better of Tirpitz. After much discussion, it was agreed to suggest the formula: 'England will make no unprovoked attack upon Germany and pursue no aggressive policy towards her. Aggression upon Germany is not the subject, and forms no part of, any treaty understanding or combination to which England is now a party, nor will she become a party to anything that has such an object.' After the Cabinet meeting, Haldane and Harcourt put pressure on Grey to allow the word 'neutrality' to appear in the formula.[11] They rightly suspected that the British proposal would not, in fact, satisfy Germany. Indeed, in the course of further exchanges, it became clear that nothing less than a declaration of 'absolute' neutrality would satisfy Berlin. Grey refused to change the formula. Crowe and Nicolson were most alarmed that members of the Cabinet should even contemplate such a concession. Germany wanted, so Crowe believed, 'an absolutely free hand in dealing with any problem of foreign policy without fear of meeting with the opposition of third parties'. Grey shared his anxiety, though suspicious of the way in which Bertie in Paris seemed to be mobilizing the French against any possibility of agreement. It had to be borne in mind, he wrote, 'that Russia and France both deal separately with Germany and that it is not reasonable that tension should be permanently greater between England and Germany than between Germany and France or Germany and Russia'.[12] If agreement had been possible on the basis of the 14 March formula, Grey would have accepted it. As things were, however, Asquith wrote on 10 April that he was becoming more and more doubtful of the wisdom of prolonging the discussions. Short of a promise of neutrality which could not be given, nothing would satisfy Germany and she made 'no firm or solid offer, even in exchange for that'.[13] Grey agreed. A delighted Kaiser pressed ahead with the supplementary Naval Law and Bethmann saw the defeat of his more subtle stratagem. Those who had been prepared to sign a 'neutrality' declaration were dispirited. Loreburn wrote that the country would never tolerate a European war against Germany 'unless Germany outraged all fair play—even if then'. He felt, however, that he was speaking to deaf ears 'and the mischief is mainly done already'.[14] Two months later he resigned, leaving to Haldane, at last, his coveted seat on the Woolsack.

Although no agreement was reached with Germany on the naval question, Grey still did not rule out the possibility of some colonial accommodation. Whether because of 'pro-German' feeling in the Cabinet, or because of a genuine shift in his own convictions, his regard for French susceptibilities was no longer as tender as it had once been. Paul Cambon noted with dismay that Grey seemed to have a childish belief in the possibility of preserving naval supremacy through agreement with Germany. When caught by the pacifist virus, it seemed that even the most intelligent of men behaved simplemindedly.[15] Indeed, the spring of 1912, when Grey had surmounted the challenge to his position, seems to mark the beginning of a new phase in his foreign policy. On a number of central issues, he seems to have been prepared to experiment. He would not retreat, under pressure, from the agreements with France and with Russia, but he was not anxious to strengthen them by formal commitments. He would not commit Britain in advance by giving a promise of unconditional neutrality to Germany, or of unconditional support to France.[16]

The sort of detachment which Grey seems to have had in mind is probably impossible. It presupposes an ability, both political and military, to join one side or the other in a potential conflict with equal facility. Britain did not possess this capacity in the years before 1914. Grey, nevertheless, strove to preserve for Britain as much freedom of choice as was possible. In one sense, therefore, the military conversations with France had created expectations and intimacies which compromised British freedom of choice. Yet, as he frequently stressed, not to allow these contacts would compromise that freedom in another direction. It would remove British capacity to act meaningfully in the event of a German invasion of France. There is little reason to challenge his basic premise that, despite the revival of nationalist sentiment in France, a German invasion of France was more to be expected than the reverse. Grey remained firm in his belief that if that happened, he and his colleagues would be confronted with a decision, not a treaty obligation. Conscious of the inexorable weight of intangible involvement, many since have questioned the distinction and accused Grey of duplicity. Perhaps all one can say is that if Grey underestimated the extent to which he was committed, and had to admit, in the end, that an element of honour was involved, he preserved as much real independence as was conceivable in the circumstances. He wrestled with a situation in which complete 'independence' from the European Balance of Power was both dangerous and anachronistic, yet it seemed clear-cut and coherent. The alternative was cloudy, fluid, imprecise but essential.

The logical reaction, of course, seemed to be to turn Britain's vague ententes into well-defined alliances. Churchill argued that the German decision to press on with the Naval Law left Britain with little option. If fresh expenditure on a large scale were to be avoided, it would be necessary to withdraw the British battle fleet from the Mediterranean and concentrate it in the North Sea. The First Lord did not altogether carry his Admirals with him in this argument. They respected Churchill's maxim that it was necessary to concentrate overpowering strength at the decisive point, but they were unhappy about completely denuding the Mediterranean of British ships. The Foreign Office, equally, was by no means enthusiastic, although initially Nicolson argued that if the Mediterranean Fleet were reduced, this would prove an ideal time for coming to terms with France. This would provide 'the cheapest, simplest and safest solution'.[17] It was precisely because of the political implications that McKenna, Morley and Harcourt, in particular, opposed Churchill's plan. Acting quite correctly, Grey brought the French request for talks on possible naval co-operation in the event of war, to the Cabinet on 16 May. The whole problem was thoroughly discussed at a series of Cabinet meetings in the summer and at a special C.I.D. meeting on 4 July. The Cabinet was in considerable confusion, but not along predictable lines. At one extremity was Churchill's argument that a naval agreement should be concluded with France and form the basis for a proper alliance. The 'radicals' reacted in horror at this notion, but equally shuddered at the alternative, which was greatly to increase naval expenditure so as to provide for the continuance of a major British force in the Mediterranean.[18] A compromise in between was inevitable and it was reached largely along lines suggested by Grey at the C.I.D. meeting on 4 July. The Foreign Secretary argued that British diplomacy in the Mediterranean would be quite ineffective if it had no power behind it. He was particularly thinking of Austria and Turkey. He was prepared to admit that Britain should give up command of the sea to France 'but if we had a one-Power standard against any other Power there, diplomacy could guard against any such combination. . . .'[19] The motley assortment responsible for carrying this conclusion rejoiced that a fleet of battle ships was still to be based on a Mediterranean port. 'Whatever the cost may be,' Esher wrote, 'it is cheaper than a conscript army and any entangling alliance.'[20] Grey was not so sanguine, telling the C.I.D. on 11 July in the presence of a Canadian delegation: 'I will sum up matters by saying that foreign policy and naval policy are now most intimately connected. The smaller our naval power, the more difficult our foreign policy. . . .'[21]

Once again, Grey had chosen the middle course and pleased few by doing so. Churchill made his discontent very plain. While acknowledging the need to safeguard 'freedom of choice', he felt that 'we have the obligations of an alliance without its advantages, and above all without precise definitions'. Arthur Balfour, too, had been urging on him the advantages of a treaty of alliance on the grounds that 'the capacities of the much tried "Entente" are now almost exhausted'. The former Conservative leader produced an elaborate formula designed to dispel the fears of those who argued that France would herself become the aggressor if she were permitted an alliance. Grey replied that the problem had been greatly exercising him, but his decision not to support Churchill was deliberately taken.[22] Yet, despite his stand against an alliance, he fully realized that he was even more constricted in his actions by what had taken place. Some clarification of Anglo-French relations was obviously necessary after the great naval debate. The Cabinet considered the subject during October and November and agreed that Grey should write to the French Ambassador in the following terms: 'We have agreed that consultation between experts is not, and ought not to be, regarded as an engagement that commits either Government to action in a contingency that has not arisen and may never arise.' This was supposed to apply in the case of the disposition of the French and British fleets. As against this, however, it was agreed that if either Government gravely feared an unprovoked attack by a third Power, both Governments should immediately discuss whether they should act together to prevent aggression and what measures they would take in common. 'If these measures involved action the plans of the general staffs would at once be taken into consideration, and the Governments would then decide what effect should be given to them.'[23] When the contingency did arise, it would be a matter of opinion which of these two paragraphs was the most important. The letters marked one further stage in the definition of the entente, although at the time they had not been a source of anything like the division of the previous November. With their customary perversity, some 'radicals' even found this exchange incriminatory. Far from limiting the entente, Loreburn wrote, the consequence of the letters was to increase British commitment to France. Poor Grey could do nothing right.

Nicolson was worried for precisely the opposite reason. He was afraid that if a collision did occur between France and Germany, Britain would waver until it was too late. The Foreign Secretary had shown great weakness in allowing himself to be drawn into a written exchange. Nor was this the only area where a lack of judgment had shown itself. He had shown a slight hardening of attitude towards Russia, something Nicolson found hard to forgive. The basic issue was again Persia. In December 1911, the Russian Ambassador, Count Benckendorff, warned St Petersburg that some sections of British opinion were in favour of a rapprochement with Germany. The Haldane Mission seemed to be a confirmation that agreement might be achieved. The consequences for Russia, in such an instance, could be serious. The Russians had taken advantage of British preoccupation with the Moroccan crisis to consolidate their position in northern Persia, having achieved the dismissal of Shuster. Sazonov was warned that any more dramatic move, such as the restoration of the former Shah, might lead to the downfall of the British Foreign Secretary. To a certain extent, therefore, Grey was able to make use of his own unpopularity at home to keep Russian activity within certain bounds. Beyond this, he was not really prepared to go, though Nicolson became so anxious that his doctor ordered him to take six weeks' rest. Grey's main debating point was that it would do the Persians little good if Britain broke with Russia.

Liberals who wanted him to do this also denounced him for acquiescing in a *de facto* division of the country. He told Scott of the *Manchester Guardian* that he did not regard British occupation as inevitable or other than undesirable. A certain section of Liberal opinion, he wrote to Spender, seemed 'to set no store by the peace we have enjoyed on our Indian frontier and seems to me to be quite reckless in attempting to make us take all Persia under our protection'.[24]

The renewed press comment on Persia was occasioned by the visit to Britain of the Russian Foreign Minister, Sazonov. He had discussions with Grey at Balmoral in late September. Sir Edward found Sazonov 'very amiable' but had doubts as to whether what he had to say would 'amount to much'.[25] The Foreign Secretary made it clear that Britain would not accept the return of the former Shah and urged the withdrawal of Russian troops from areas where their bombardment of Moslem shrines had offended opinion. He 'rubbed in' the bad effect created by the destruction of the shrine at Meshed. Although Grey was pessimistic about any considerable improvement, Russian behaviour in Persia did annoy him and he feared that the Russians were beginning to look for trouble in Afghanistan, Tibet and Central Asia. Crewe tried to reassure him.[26] Even so, the Foreign Secretary was not prepared to rupture the entente. At the same time, he was rather coy when Sazonov asked him what steps Britain would take in case of war to help Russia. He hoped that something might be done to draw the German navy away from Russia's Baltic shores. Grey said the question was a matter for experts and added: 'No British Government could go to war unless backed by public opinion. Public opinion would not support any aggressive war for a revanche or to hem Germany in. . . .'[27]

No sooner had Sazonov left the country than war broke out in the Balkans. The Russian Foreign Minister had not deigned to mention the alliance and military convention between the Balkan states which had been concluded in March 1912. Some pieces of information had filtered back to London, however, and in April Grey minuted: 'We shall have to keep out of this and what I fear is that Russia may resent our doing so; the fact that the trouble is all of her own making won't prevent her from expecting help if the trouble turns out to be more than she had bargained for.'[28] Grey wanted to restrain Russia, but it was difficult to tell who made Russian policy. Both Grey and Nicolson believed that Sazonov, having 'fomented' the alliance of the Balkan states, was now 'much concerned at the blaze he had kindled'. He was now afraid that Austria would confront him with a forward policy and his chief desire was to put out the blaze.[29] A recent study in part challenges this analysis, the author writing that: 'Even in 1912 Sazonov did not pursue an anti-Turkish policy à outrance.' While he favoured the Balkan states, he was in fact anxious to prevent the dissolution of the Ottoman Empire in 1912 and did not encourage their war plans.[30] While this may be true of Sazonov's own intentions, Grey believed that he had gravely 'underestimated the pro-Slav feeling of Russia'. Unless Russia supported the territorial demands of the Balkan states, she would lose their affections.

Grey's chief anxiety was to prevent the war spreading beyond a conflict between Greece, Bulgaria, Serbia and Montenegro on the one hand, and Turkey on the other. He did not altogether share Nicolson's belief in the inevitable penetration of Russia into the area, and both men in fact underestimated the infinite capacity of the Balkan states for creating difficulties. At the same time, he was still opposed to the complete collapse of the Ottoman Empire. By 1911, his enthusiasm for the new regime had faded. He wrote sardonically to Crewe concerning a suggestion that the best way to treat the Turks was to soothe them. He had been informed that 'they really mean to do better & are not unwilling to be influenced by us. I am willing still to give the Turks the benefit of the doubt; we cannot in fact *do* anything else. . . .'[31] Grey was angered by the Italian invasion of Tripoli in 1911—'The Italians have been very foolish in putting out their foot so far in this Tripoli business; they had a fair case for squeezing guarantees for economic interests in Tripoli . . .' but spoiled it by blundering into war to obtain them. As a result, he did not feel 'justified in making overtures to Italy for any political understanding'.[32] In November 1911, Churchill urged Grey to go even further. There was strong feeling in the Liberal Party about the way the Italians had behaved and there was a strong historical pro-Turk party among Conservatives. 'The combination of these two forces, normally in equipoise, wd afford a basis for political action of a vy decided character.' Turkey had much to offer, for 'in fixing our eyes upon the Belgian frontier and the North Sea we must not forget that we are the greatest Mahometan power in the world'. Besides, Turkey was the greatest land weapon which the Germans could use against Britain, whereas Italy would not be worth much for or against anyone for some time to come.[33]

The Foreign Secretary had substantial sympathy for this point of view. Rather to the general surprise, however, the 'great land weapon' collapsed within a month before the onslaught of the Balkan armies. In this situation, Asquith urged that 'we ought to take an initiative of our own: if we do so clearly & strongly, it may make all the difference to our future position in the Near East'.[34] Asquith, Grey and Lloyd George were afraid that Austria might invade Serbia. The military success of the Serbs had given rise to much anxiety in Vienna, and there was some pressure for the Government to take preventive measures. As usual, Grey found the Balkan situation 'very tiresome'. If time could be gained 'so that it becomes apparent that the only outstanding point of difference between the Great Powers is whether Servia is to have a port of her own on the Adriatic or guaranteed access to a neutralized free port on the Adriatic, there will be no war between the Great Powers. . . .'[35] Otherwise the situation might be serious. Grey's concern throughout was to discriminate between those matters which the Balkan states could settle among themselves, and those subjects, like Constantinople and the Adriatic, which touched on the interests of the Great Powers. To this end, he proposed an ambassadorial conference of the Great Powers which had its first session in London in December 1912. Grey's achievement in persuading Germany, France, Austria-Hungary and Italy to agree to a conference under his presidency added greatly to his personal prestige. Grey wrote to Lloyd George in December 1912 that 'the progress made is really good. Diplomatically we are past the biggest rocks & with good will we ought to be able to get past the others.' He did not believe that the Austrian military party would hold out 'against the pressure for peace of all the five Powers'.[36] His colleagues, in turn, 'warmly congratulated' him 'on the skill and success with which he is piloting the European ship through troubled waters'.[37]

The rejoicing proved somewhat premature and the voyage longer than expected. Although the Powers agreed that Albania should be autonomous, the Balkan states were not satisfied with this provision and renewed the conflict. The King of Montenegro added a fresh touch by threatening Scutari, which the Powers wished to assign to Albania. Throughout the Balkan crisis, Grey had been assiduous in bringing the problems to the attention of his colleagues, who were forced to develop an unwelcome familiarity with the geography and ethnology of the area. They agreed to British participation in a naval demonstration against Montenegro. The Russians refused to join in, and Grey lamented 'the singularly unsatisfactory declarations' made by the French Government before it finally agreed to join in this portentous expedition.[38] When Scutari fell to the Montenegrins, the Cabinet saw no reason to give in to them, and considered various coercive measures. The Concert of Europe was to be preserved at all costs.[39] In the event, the King of Montenegro gave way. No sooner had this crisis passed than Grey had to warn his colleagues that the Balkan allies might well begin fighting among themselves. This gloomy forecast proved correct. In the second Balkan War, the Bulgarians were defeated and their erstwhile allies gained disputed land and population. The Turks also took the opportunity to regain an area they had lost in the previous fighting. Once again, Grey's concern was to follow a policy of complete non-intervention and persuade the other Powers to do the same. On 10 August 1913, the victors imposed on Bulgaria the Treaty of Bucharest. 'It left Bulgaria sore, injured, and despoiled, and deprived of what she believed should belong to her,' Grey subsequently wrote.[40] While it remained, any future Balkan peace was impossible. The Ambassadors did not meet in conference again, but Grey was pleased with their deliberations.

The Balkan settlement raised Grey's international prestige, but caused complications within the Foreign Office. Nicolson never liked it when the Foreign Secretary attempted to play the 'honest broker', and was suspicious of the pretentious resurrection of the 'Concert of Europe'. Nicolson was particularly disappointed by Grey's failure to give Russia firm support when she stood by Serbia and Montenegro. For example, discussing the Scutari question, Nicolson minuted in January that the Russians had been promised diplomatic support and 'were we to abandon the Russian standpoint we should be heading straight towards a serious breach in our understanding, and this would be simply disastrous'.[41] Relations between Nicolson and Grey degenerated, and the Foreign Secretary seems to have come to depend more upon Tyrrell, his private secretary. By the spring, at least according to report, Tyrrell was becoming weary of Nicolson's policy, which seemed to be to dance to whatever tune the Russians played. He complained of the 'cynical selfishness of Russian policy in Persia, Mongolia, Pekin . . .' Russia had to be brought to her bearings and Grey showed that this could be done, without estranging her, by his firm line throughout the Balkan crisis. Tyrrell and Nicolson now openly rivalled each other for the Foreign Secretary's attention.[42] Yet there is a danger of taking the comments of the permanent officials too much at their face value. It is difficult to tell what is going on when Tyrrell writes that Grey 'ought to say no to Nicolson more often' at just the time when Nicolson felt that he was receiving a surfeit of negatives. Yet Nicolson wrote to Grey expressing his pleasure that relations were 'so frank and friendly'.[43] Perhaps more significant than these subjective judgments of 'strength' and 'weakness' is the comment of Chirol in May 1913 that the 'only member of the Govt. whose prestige stands higher than ever is Grey'.[44] The King also wrote to express his feelings of 'absolute reliance in your management of our foreign policy'. In this respect, he differed from his mother, whose judgment was that 'E. Grey has certainly proved the worst Foreign Secretary England ever had'.[45] However close Sir Edward was to Tyrrell, or however estranged from Nicolson, he was his own master.

This independence makes it all the more difficult to be sure what he really thought about policy. It looks as though he consciously cultivated good relations with Germany, and his opposite number, Kiderlen, throughout the Balkan crisis. His purpose was obviously to persuade the Germans not to give Austria-Hungary such support as might lead to war. Initially, Kiderlen, with the approval of the Kaiser, responded favourably. This time, however, Bethmann Hollweg worked with Admiral Müller to persuade the Kaiser that Germany could not afford to drop Austria, if war broke out with Serbia over the question of a Serbian outlet to the Adriatic. They felt they had won him over, and on 2 December, Bethmann pledged German support to Austria if she were attacked by Russia while defending her vital interests. In giving this pledge, he felt confident that Britain would remain neutral in such a conflict. However, on 3 December, Haldane, presumably with Grey's authority, told the German Ambassador, now Prince Lichnowsky, that Germany must not presume too much. Britain would not tolerate the crushing of France by Germany's superior military strength. The Kaiser was furious on receiving this report and summoned his chief military and naval advisers to conference. His tone changed abruptly. He now urged that Austria should gain the support of Bulgaria, Rumania and possibly Turkey. Then Germany would be free to fight France and send the Fleet against Britain. The Kaiser's excitement lasted for several weeks, during which time he raged against the nation of shopkeepers and their temerity in ranging themselves, in the final struggle between Slavs and Teutons, on the side of the Slavs and the Gauls. Tirpitz all the while maintained that the Navy was not ready and this, coupled with a renewed hope that Britain would stay neutral, helped to persuade the Kaiser that the time was not ripe. Besides, since Serbia had backed down in her demand for an Adriatic port, it was necessary to find a more popular cause for war.[46]

The estimates in Berlin concerning the chances of gaining British neutrality seem to bear little precise relationship to any attitude Grey adopted. It must be presumed that Haldane's remarks, which caused such rage in Berlin, were quite acceptable to Grey. His standard response at this juncture was to say that it would be dangerous if the German Government assumed that under no circumstances would England come to the assistance of France and Russia, if Germany and Austria went to war with them. He further admitted to the King that he judged public opinion to be 'very adverse to a war arising out of a quarrel about Servia. But if Austria attacked Servia aggressively, and Germany attacked Russia if she came to the assistance of Servia, and France were then involved, it might become necessary for England to fight. . . .'[47] He had been warned that 'bad blood' existed between Austria and Serbia 'until in course of time one of two things happens: either the Slav races in Austria break away and form a Southern Slav Kingdom together with Servia and Montenegro, or Servia is absorbed into Austria'.[48] Neither alternative particularly pleased Grey. As events were amply to justify, he was somewhat cynical about the virtues of the Christian peoples of the Balkans. The Serbs could be classified with the Persians as 'hopeless people' with whom it was the lot of the Foreign Office to deal.[49] 'A situation more full of paradoxes has rarely been seen' was his comment on the Balkans in the summer of 1913.[50]

Another reason for Grey's renewed interest in Germany lies in the appointment of Jagow as Foreign Minister. 'If we could only have ten years of a man like Jagow to deal with,' Grey wrote, 'really controlling the policy of Germany, we should be on intimate terms with her at the end of the time, and on increasingly good terms all through it.'[51] The Kaiser too was pleased with his new man, who was making 'a splendid start'. Jagow confirmed that he was of suitable stature by declaring that he would be the first to advise his sovereign to go to war if anyone should tamper with Germany's rights in the Balkans and Asia Minor. Grey had no wish to tamper with such 'rights'. Asia Minor, he told the British

Ambassador in Rome, was not Morocco. If there was going to be a partition, 'Germany must be well in it, and I should not think of trying to exclude her. . . . Security as regards the Persian Gulf and its littoral is all that we want, and it can perfectly well be reconciled with German interests.' This was an area, in contrast to the Naval problem, where he would be willingly conciliatory. If, however, 'our Fleet was not superior to the German Fleet, our very independence would depend on Germany's goodwill . . . the Prussian mentality is such that to be on really good terms with it one must be able to deal with it as an equal. . . .'[52] By making it clear that he would be both firm and conciliatory, Grey hoped to discover whether there were political forces in Germany, anxious and powerful enough to want a settlement with Britain on terms which stopped short of a British declaration of neutrality.

In December 1911, the Foreign Secretary referred to the Portuguese colonies as 'sinks of iniquity'—the phrase being decorously removed from the published documents for fear of offending Britain's oldest ally.[53] Yet he had not rushed into the revision of the Anglo-German and Anglo-Portuguese agreements of 1898 and 1899. It was Harcourt, the Colonial Secretary, who constantly prodded his colleague and explored the ground. By 1913, however, Grey approved the idea of a fresh agreement with Germany which would amend the earlier agreement in certain details. Having given his approval, Grey took little part in the detailed negotiations, much to the disgust of Crowe and Bertie, who believed that Harcourt was giving far too much away to Germany. By the end of 1913, the agreement had been initialled and seemed ready for signature. The Foreign Secretary had been in touch with Balfour, the author of the previous agreement, who agreed that it was 'an excellent thing to do anything to convince Germany that we are not animated in our relations with her either by jealousy or enmity'.[54] In the end, however, the agreement was never signed. The Germans wanted it kept a secret whereas Grey, on Crowe's advice, pressed for publicity. Nevertheless, this disagreement did not lead to bitterness and Grey liked to believe that the negotiations had contributed to the improvement of Anglo-German relations. Britain had done her part by showing a disarming willingness to discuss the partition of the colonial possessions of her oldest ally behind her back. This accommodating attitude should not, however, be mistaken for a fundamental policy shift. Grey had a sharp exchange with Harcourt in January 1914. The Colonial Secretary objected to the use of the term 'Triple Entente'—there were ententes with France and Russia, and there was an alliance between France and Russia, 'but none of these facts entail any community of action between the three'. Grey replied that he had once deprecated the term but it had become so common that he could no more stop it than he could banish split infinitives. The Powers concerned understood the real position, and the phrase gave no offence in Berlin. 'The best course', he argued, '. . . is to let things go on as they are without any new declaration of policy. The alternatives are either a policy of complete isolation in Europe, or a policy of definite alliance with one or the other group of European Powers. . . .'[55]

Grey also encouraged a further effort to reach agreement with Turkey and Germany on the Baghdad railway question. The intricate detail involved naturally meant that the negotiations were tiring and lengthy. However, in late May 1914, agreement was reached between Britain and Germany, following the conclusion of an earlier settlement with Turkey. The Baghdad railway was carefully defined and Britain undertook not to oppose its construction. Germany accepted British control over the Mesopotamian rivers. The line was to end at Basrah and, except by agreement, the German Government agreed not to establish a port or railway terminus on the Persian Gulf. It seemed an admirable agreement for both sides. It had been reached notwithstanding a certain amount of Anglo-German friction concerning the appointment of General Liman von Sanders to command the Ottoman army. Grey's initial reaction, early in December 1913, was that the appointment of a German officer put the key of the Straits in German hands.[56] On the other hand, he felt that this was not a question 'in which we can be more Russian than the Russians'.[57] Even Nicolson had to report to St Petersburg that there was 'a certain disinclination on our part to pull the chestnuts out of the fire for Russia'.[58] This disinclination was strengthened when the Germans pointed out that the position of the British Admiral charged with the reorganization of the Russian Fleet was analogous. Grey steered a careful course between Russia and Germany, and helped to reach a compromise solution.

There was, therefore, little reason to suppose in the opening months of 1914 that the international situation was markedly deteriorating and major war inevitable. The Balkans remained the most sensitive area of Europe. There, the possibility of a lasting settlement seemed far away, but the danger of complete collapse seemed far away too.

T

The approach of July 1914 has led most historians to concentrate their attention on Grey's European policy. It is true that the
Foreign Secretary did give most time to European questions, but
not to the exclusion of all else. Despite his additional responsibilities during the Balkan wars, there were a number of pressing
Far Eastern, American and Imperial questions which could not be
ignored.

The situation both in the Far East and in the Americas seemed
to be forcing Grey to draw a firmer distinction between foreign
policy to defend British 'interests', and foreign policy to defend 'the
British interest'. British economic interests in China continued to
exceed those of any other Power. In the last years of the Manchu
dynasty, Britain had been instrumental in setting up a consortium
to deal with the extensive loan business. The aim was to eliminate
what Britain regarded as wasteful competition and dangerous
international rivalry. In the eyes of those not favoured by the
operation of the consortium, there were other ways of looking at the
move. By the first year of the new presidential regime of Yuan Shih
k'ai, it was becoming apparent that, at least in respect of industrial
loans, the effect of the consortium was, strangely, to encourage
Britain's competitors. There was considerable pressure from the
City for the revision of the consortium agreement. In particular,
potential business rivals disliked the degree of dependence shown
by Grey and the Foreign Office on the advice from the Hong Kong
and Shanghai Bank. They wanted to know why Grey refused to
allow all interested financial institutions to compete on equal terms.
The answer was that the efficient operation of the consortium had
to take precedence over abstract free-trade principles and over
direct British benefits. Grey conceived the basic British interest to
be the preservation of the integrity of China and specific British
interests to be subordinate to that end. As he told the House of
Commons in May 1913, the object of policy was 'to secure first that
there should not be that very undesirable political competition
between the Powers exploiting the situation in China for their own
advantage. . . .'[59]

It was when specific and quantifiable British interests in China
came into collision with Japanese interests that the nature of the
'British interest' required careful consideration. By 1913 many
permanent officials were coming to feel that the chief importance
of the renewed Anglo-Japanese alliance was the fact that it acted
as a constraint on Japanese expansion. They suspected that Japan

had been active in giving support to the rebellion led by Sun Yat Sen in the summer of 1913. These suspicions grew as it became apparent that the Japanese were bent on expansion in the Yangtze Valley—the British sphere. Britain would prevent railway-building in this area by any other Power, even by her own ally, and Grey made this very plain in Tokyo. Several years earlier, he had himself faced the wrath of British commercial interests by agreeing to their exclusion from South Manchuria.[60] It was only cricket to expect the Japanese to respect this division of spheres, and, for the time being, Grey made his point. Yet further alarms were raised by reports of Japanese agents in Tibet and support in Japanese Pan-Asian political circles for terrorist activity in India. Crewe also drew Grey's attention to Japanese rivalry in the Indian coastal trade: 'The shipping companies are greatly exercised as you may suppose.'[61] It was obvious that there were factors both of interest and ideology which could destroy the alliance. The Foreign Secretary, however, was determined that this should not happen. From the outset, he had recognized that Japan was an expanding Power. If she did not expand in Manchuria, she would expand across the Pacific. For this reason the alliance remained in the British interest.[62]

The alternative would have been to reverse the naval strategy Churchill was following at the Admiralty. From 1912 onwards, he had been developing a policy of naval consolidation near British home waters, leaving a much reduced British Fleet in the Far East, inferior to that of Japan. The situation was galling to the Australasian Dominions, whose apprehensions of Japan were much more immediate. The First Lord believed in coming straight to the point. In the House of Commons in March 1914, he arrogantly defended his policy of concentration. 'If the British fleet were defeated in the North Sea,' he declared, 'all the dangers which it now wards off from the Australasian Dominions would be let loose.' In such a contingency, Japan could colonize with impunity. Not surprisingly, however true its basic contentions were, the speech was resented in the Dominions. Once again they were being told what they should do and what was in their best interests.

The Anglo-Japanese alliance also continued to present problems in relations between Britain and Canada. Following fresh racial trouble in British Columbia, which coincided with serious agitation in California, the Canadian Government decided to suspend all immigration for a six-month period. The Japanese Ambassador in

273

London warned Grey in the summer of 1913 that the Canadian action would stir up public opinion in Japan, 'which would lead to undesirable results detrimental to the cordial relations between Japan and Great Britain'. Fortunately, the crisis was overcome and better Canadian–Japanese relations ensued, but it was a warning that the emotions of Western Canada might upset the calculations of London.[63] Nor, in this time of constitutional transition, was there a compensating Canadian contribution towards the defence of the Empire. The Canadian Prime Minister, Borden, abandoned the idea of building a Canadian Navy and instead proposed that the British Government should build three Dreadnoughts at Canadian expense. However, because of Liberal and French Canadian opposition, which discounted the alleged German threat, Borden's Bill was rejected by the Canadian Senate in April 1913. Thus, in effect, the Canadians neither looked after their own defence nor contributed to the Imperial burden.[64] Partnership in defence and foreign policy was, in any real sense, still rudimentary, and although there were some advantages in this for the United Kingdom, the drawbacks probably outweighed them.

The question of the relationship between 'British interests' and 'the British interest' also had to be considered in dealings with the United States. It was already apparent to Churchill that 'if the power of Great Britain were shattered on the sea, the only course of the five millions of white men in the Pacific would be to seek the protection of the United States'. It was also common knowledge that much West-Coast Canadian opinion took the anti-Japanese side in the bitter Californian dispute which endangered American–Japanese relations in the summer of 1913. From the situation as it existed, it was not difficult to prophecy a future in which defence needs and racial consciousness drew some of the Dominions closer to the United States than to the mother country. British official rhetoric might gloss over such a development with talk of the 'Anglo-American heritage' but, as a number of disputes in the pre-war period showed, the reality was rather different.

In 1912, for example, a Canal Bill had been passed through Congress exempting American ships from the payment of tolls through the recently completed Panama Canal. Not unreasonably, the British regarded this as a breach of the Hay–Pauncefote treaty of 1901, which provided that the passage should be open on terms of complete equality. Bryce protested in vain, lamenting this trampling on legally established British rights. Hope of its repeal grew in the wake of the election of President Wilson in November 1912. Bryce stayed at his post in the hope of persuading the President to call for its repeal. Eventually, in the summer of 1914, Wilson did go to Congress with such a request and, after prolonged discussion, Congress agreed.[65]

A more prolonged and ill-tempered Anglo-American dispute, however, revolved around the situation in revolutionary Mexico. The enterprise of Lord Cowdray had brought for Britain an unexpectedly large economic interest in the affairs of the United States' neighbour. The basic British concern, as in China, was with the maintenance or re-establishment of law and order in the country. Unless this was maintained, trade, commerce and investment would be lost. At its simplest (though the Mexican Revolution was never simple) the question was whether the regime of General Huerta, which had accomplished the murder of the ex-President, should be recognized, in order to restore stability. Nicolson advised Grey to consult the United States, France and Germany, but the Foreign Secretary took a surprisingly firm line: 'Our interests in Mexico are so big that I think we should take our own line without making it dependent upon that of other Govts.'[66] He therefore provisionally recognized the Huerta administration, while at the same time it was becoming apparent that the American delay was being replaced by an outright refusal to do so. An anxious summer of suspicion and misunderstanding then ensued.

Bryce's successor as British Ambassador in Washington was Spring-Rice. He had been passed over for the appointment in the past. On this occasion Grey could not think of a strong enough reason to refuse him, although Spring-Rice's political friendships turned out to be with the 'wrong side'. Late in July, he wrote to Grey that it looked as if 'the most incompetent government which America has ever had' was embarking light-heartedly on a policy of securing a protectorate over Central America and the Caribbean.[67] The British, on the other hand, were being accused in Washington of indifference to the fate of good government in Mexico. They were also supposed to be dominated by financial interests. Grey found the new President's overt moralism difficult to deal with. When, for example, Ambassador Page came to report Wilson's belief that 'Governments as human institutions should be founded on a moral basis', Grey minuted gently: 'It would require about 200,000 soldiers to put Mexico on a "moral" basis.'[68] The Foreign Secretary had already had a foretaste of such attitudes

275

when the new administration withdrew from the Chinese loan consortium because it was 'undemocratic'.

Sir Edward, therefore, waited for the President to realize that the clear-cut solutions he appeared to espouse were not always applicable. He wanted Wilson to appreciate that while he was naturally defending British interests in Mexico, he was not dominated by them. There were some officials, on the other hand, who believed that he should not limit his policy to a concern for British interests. Britain should use Mexico to make a stand against the American domination of Central America. The newly appointed British Minister in Mexico, Carden, on his departure, left Grey a catalogue of American interventions. The United States Government had given repeated proof that 'far from favouring the principle of the open door in Latin America, they view with jealousy the competition of European nations for the trade of those Republics: and all their influence has been and is being directed towards obtaining such special advantages for their citizens, by reciprocity conventions and otherwise, as will ensure for them in course of time a great preponderance if not a virtual monopoly in all matters connected with finance, commerce or public works. . . .'[69] In 1913, for the first time, American exports to the British West Indies exceeded those from Britain. When Grey had been in the West Indies in 1897, his Commission had viewed the United States as the natural market for the West Indies. A subsequent Commission in 1909 noted that its predecessor in 1897 'could not foresee . . . the acquisition of tropical possessions by the United States'. It strongly advised improving the trade routes between the West Indies and Canada, otherwise American trade predominance and then outright annexation of the islands seemed inevitable.[70] If Grey had been so inclined, material existed for the defence of British interests. After all, the Central American Republics, somewhat abortively, were looking to Britain's ally, Japan, as their predestined helper.

Grey's subsequent diplomacy in the Mexican crisis made it clear, however, that the defence of British interests to the point of conflict with the United States, was not in the British interest. Occasionally, the notion of an Anglo-German partnership in Europe to resist American domination filtered through the brains of the Kaiser and other Germans. More often, however, Germans resigned themselves to Europe having to take on this task without British assistance. When they beheld the American dream, many Englishmen also saw the decline of their own interests, but if a choice had to be made between the United States and Germany, few Englishmen hesitated. In the event, during the Mexican crisis, Edward Grey successfully accomplished his modest ambitions and avoided an undesired confrontation with the United States. He may well have reflected that in time of war, if one could not have allies, it was at least necessary not to have enemies.

14

The Coming of War

If war was spoken of in the early months of 1914, most people at once thought of Ireland. There, the crisis was steadily building up in a manner which threatened to destroy the authority of the Government. The Liberals would need all the vigour and resolution they possessed to be able to deal with the question, but their morale was not very high. One reason for this was the Cabinet's continuing division on the question of votes for women. The Speaker had confounded everybody by decreeing that the women's suffrage amendment, if passed, would require the reintroduction of the Government's Reform Bill. In other words, further delay would ensue when the militant suffragettes were already causing considerable disruption. The Foreign Secretary remained firm in support of the suffrage and was the principal speaker for that cause in a debate on a private member's bill in May 1913. His chief opponent in the debate was able to muster more votes and the measure was lost. He happened to be the Prime Minister. Grey and Asquith never overcame their difference on the issue, though there was now little danger of the Cabinet falling apart because of it.

A more serious situation arose for the Government in the summer of 1913, as a result of the charges brought against the Attorney-General, Rufus Isaacs; the Postmaster-General, Herbert Samuel; the Chief Whip, the Master of Elibank, and the Chancellor of the Exchequer himself, Lloyd George. The chief charges, concerning 'injudicious' share purchases in the American Marconi Company, were directed against Lloyd George and Rufus Isaacs. Whatever his private thoughts, and despite offers of resignation, the Prime Minister stood by his erring colleagues when the select committee report on the transactions was presented to the Commons in June 1913. The Opposition was not prepared simply to accept the Ministers' regrets, but insisted that the House should itself express

278

regret. It was Grey who was put up to answer Bonar Law's speech. He declared that if the Opposition amendment was carried, the Ministers would probably resign and their political careers might be at an end. If the transactions themselves were the only matter at issue, the House might well have been justified in censuring the ministerial conduct. However, the men concerned had been suffering under reckless charges of gross corruption and, 'if justice is to be done by the House, the first thing to be emphasised is to do away, as far as lies in the power of the House, with the imputation of those charges and the effects of them'.[1] This speech, and the Government's majority, saved Lloyd George's career. Sir Edward was, of course, primarily concerned to preserve the Government rather than Lloyd George the individual. Nevertheless, the relations between the two men in 1913 were good. The Chancellor was very strongly committed to his land campaign and, in contrast to some other colleagues, Grey gave him firm support. Austen Chamberlain described Grey as being 'very Radical on the land . . .'[2] After the Marconi debate, Lloyd George wrote to thank Grey for his support. The Foreign Secretary replied: 'There was a very true sentence in your speech about mistakes being often more heavily censured than misdeeds, which is very applicable. I have often thought in public affairs that one is always being over praised or over blamed.' He concluded that despite the strain of life together, 'the personal relations of all of us have not only stood the long strain but have gained in attachment to an extent that must be very rare if not unprecedented in the history of Cabinets'.[3] The Marconi scandals did have a marginal effect on foreign policy. Grey's political private secretary, Arthur Murray, was a brother of the Master of Elibank —a fact which gave ample scope to American businessmen, politicians and officials who disliked Elibank's activities on behalf of Lord Cowdray in Latin America.[4]

Before finally settling down to the Irish dispute, the Cabinet indulged itself in what were to be the last Naval Estimates before the war. The scenario was by now quite familiar; the only interest was in the guise of the leading actors. Churchill had spent part of the summer floating the idea of a 'naval holiday'. Grey, however, had not been very enthusiastic about returning naval questions to the forefront of Anglo-German exchanges. He preferred to explore the more indirect approach. But when Churchill returned to the subject in a speech on 13 October, Grey did not reproach him: 'I think there was no choice but to say something to our own people about naval expenditure. The Continental response is very bad but that cannot be helped. . . .'⁵ The First Lord was now anxious to increase naval expenditure and pressed his case hard at a number of Cabinets in the middle of December. He misjudged the mood of his colleagues, some of whom, in any case, believed that he was on the point of disappearing back to the Opposition, where he really belonged. Churchill was forced to produce a lower figure, but his critics, McKenna, Simon, Runciman and others, stated their firm opposition to the construction of four capital ships. They would only sanction two.

Grey's position in this last naval crisis is not easy to establish. On past form, his sympathies had always been with the big-navy men, but he seems to have been less ardent in this instance. Churchill had to send him an exhortatory Christmas Day letter urging that 'unless a very serious disaster to national policy is to happen you will have to rouse yourself and exert the influence which you at the Foreign Office alone can command'.⁶ Then, on 1 January, the *Daily Chronicle* fittingly released an interview with Lloyd George in which he expressed his views on the future. The Chancellor talked of the improvement in international relations and denounced the 'organized insanity' of armaments expenditure. The chief target of the interview, Churchill, told Grey that he kept his own counsel with an effort, but 'you can imagine its effect on the Admirals!'⁷ An incident of this kind always made Grey feel obliged to express his dismay to the Prime Minister. It happened that at this juncture, the geographical distribution of Ministers was as diverse as their opinions. The argument could only begin again on 20 January. Then the Prime Minister, gathering that Lloyd George had achieved a reconciling conversation with the Foreign Secretary, urged the merits of a similar conference with Winston before he came into the matter. Grey and Lloyd George exchanged letters, deploring the German press exaggerations of the interview. Churchill remained obdurate for a little while longer. Finally, on 11 February, the Cabinet agreed both to raise the supplementary estimates and build the four capital ships. The naval crisis had followed its customary path. Nevertheless, the 'economist' Ministers remained disgruntled, and the whole episode did nothing to raise low morale. The co-incidence of these three problems—the naval disagreement, the Marconi scandal and suffragette militancy—help to explain the confusion of the Government's policy towards Ireland.

Grey thoroughly endorsed the federalist approach to the problem which inspired the third Home Rule Bill, introduced into the Commons in April 1912. The Liberals stressed the benefit to the United Kingdom as a whole, as much as to Ireland. As Grey wrote, 'In the last fifty years the amount of work demanded for particular portions of the United Kingdom, for the United Kingdom as a whole, or for the Empire has increased enormously; in all three categories the work is still increasing and will increase; one Parliament cannot do it all.' Irish Home Rule was the first step which opened the way for Federal Home Rule. As for Ireland itself, Home Rule was necessary to 'heal bitterness' and 'to effect that reconciliation without which there cannot be real union'.[8] In his speech on the second reading of the Bill in the Commons in May 1912, Grey stressed these aspects and urged that nothing but harm could come from making out that there were no differences of national opinion within the United Kingdom. 'There is an Irish national feeling and there is national feeling in other parts of the United Kingdom. You cannot help it. The thing is there. . . .' He felt confident that the last thing an Irish Executive or an Irish Parliament would do would be 'to provoke a strong minority in Ulster to resistance based upon moral wrong and unreasonable treatment'. Whatever Ulster members might say, he believed that 'the animosity which may exist between different parts of Ireland to-day is no measure whatever and no guide to what the feeling will be when the different parts of Ireland have for the first time a sense of joint responsibility'.[9] Within a few months, however, it was clear that the Ulster problem was not going to melt away in this easy fashion. Grey himself became uneasy at the Cabinet's determination to press ahead with the full Home Rule Bill, and began to contemplate alternative solutions. By the end of 1912, the Ulster Covenant had been drawn up by Carson, and the determination of Ulstermen to resist had become the main obstacle to Home Rule. By the autumn of 1913, the Bill had passed through the Commons twice and then been rejected twice in the Lords. The King brought Asquith and Bonar Law together in an attempt to resolve the deadlock. The Opposition leader gave as his terms the permanent exclusion of the four north-eastern counties, plus Tyrone and one other should they so decide, from the operation of the Bill. On 12 November, a select group of the Cabinet—Asquith, Grey, Crewe, Haldane and Lloyd George—had a meeting to discuss when to hold the next General Election. Grey strongly favoured July 1914, and the Prime Minister agreed. The development of the Ulster question was clearly vital to Liberal prospects. The Foreign Secretary suggested that Ulster should be given Home Rule within Home Rule for Ireland. Lloyd George brushed this aside. He thought the best means of avoiding armed resistance was the exclusion of Ulster for half a dozen years, with provision for its automatic inclusion thereafter.[10] The Cabinet did not want to rule out either of these alternatives, and on 25 November, Grey successfully proposed that if talks were resumed with Bonar Law, he should be told that the Liberal Party would not accept permanent or indefinite exclusion, but would discuss temporary exclusion or separate administrative treatment.[11]

At this stage, Grey was not out of line with his colleagues. Lloyd George, for example, wrote on 5 December: 'I thought your treatment of Ulster last night was simply first-rate.'[12] But as the months passed, Grey became more apprehensive. Speaking of Grey's proposal, Austen Chamberlain had written to Lansdowne that it almost filled him with despair: 'Surely if one thing is clear about Ulster it is that Ulster will not submit to Dublin, and that any proposal for Home Rule within Home Rule is only another way of saying that in the last resort Dublin must rule Belfast.'[13] By the spring of 1914, the Foreign Secretary came to see that neither his suggestion, nor Lloyd George's, would mollify the militant Ulstermen. It would require the use of force to impose Home Rule on Ulster. It was this tension that led to the so-called mutiny at the Curragh, in which British officers of Ulster domicile declared that they would refuse to obey an order compelling them to initiate action against the Ulster Volunteers.[14] The complicated pattern of events revealed how weak the political control had become. Grey urged the Secretary of State for War, Seely, not to resign, but when he did so, Asquith took over the War Office himself.[15] Sir Edward wrote to the Prime Minister 'that we cannot and ought not to use force to bring the Home Rule Bill into operation till the opinion of the country has been taken upon the situation'. Unless this was done, 'we shall be confronted with one unseen incident after another, each of which will weaken our hands and bring the situation nearer to becoming impossible'.[16] But Asquith did not want to risk an election, even though Grey's idea had royal support. Two months later, in May, the Foreign Secretary was still alarmed, not being 'at all satisfied with the opinion of the Cabinet that there should be no further statement of the circumstances under which we should or should not use armed force in Ireland'.[17] Asquith ignored the request, and the Cabinet struggled on through May and June seeking an amending Bill to the main Home Rule measure, which would satisfy Redmond, Ulster, the Opposition, the King and their own supporters. Until the implications of the European crisis finally penetrated, it seemed that there was no other political problem to consider. However, Grey's increasing alarm about the possible use of force in Ulster was, in the latter stages, a consequence of his anxiety about European developments.

The obsession with Ireland was no doubt due to the intrinsic fascination of the subject, but it also reveals the extent to which international affairs were felt to be relatively quiet. Sir Edward chose the tenth anniversary of the Anglo-French entente as the occasion for his first official visit abroad. He accompanied the King to Paris in late April. The Foreign Secretary had made it clear that 'he had not the slightest intention of going to the Races, as in the first place Racing bores him stiff, and in the second, he is anxious to see the sights of Paris'.[18] The Quai d'Orsay had other delights in store. He had been warned in advance that the French would invite him to see the benefits of closer Anglo-Russian collaboration. For several months past, the Russians had also stressed this fact. 'It is curious', Grey remarked, 'that the Russians should be suggesting more than the French have got from us.'[19] Nicolson was more sympathetic, believing that there would be 'a little disappointment at Petersburg if we do not give evidence that we are anxious that our relations with Russia should be given a more precise and definite form'. Unless this was done, Russia 'might become weary of us and throw us overboard'.[20] Grey moved carefully. Nicolson's recommendations carried little weight, for relations between the two men had deteriorated. Quite apart from foreign-policy issues, Grey had come to resent the Permanent Under-Secretary's undisguised contempt for the Government's Home Rule policy. It was believed to be only a matter of time before he was replaced by either Crowe or Tyrrell. It was the latter who accompanied him to Paris.

Sir Edward's talks in Paris covered a variety of topics, but the most important concerned the possibility of Anglo-Russian naval talks. In the absence of any formal engagement, Grey offered to inform the Russian Government of the scope of Anglo-French military and naval conversations. He thought there was a possibility that naval, but not military, conversations with St Petersburg might be initiated. On his return, Grey raised the subject in the Cabinet on 12 May. Churchill gave an optimistic report on Russian naval potential which led his colleagues to feel that 'the large contemplated increase in the Baltic fleet of Russia must necessarily ease our position vis-à-vis Germany in home waters . . .' A week later, Grey informed Count Benckendorff that staff talks could begin between Britain and Russia on the basis of the Grey–Cambon exchange. On 22 May, however, an accurate summary of the conversations appeared in the *Berliner Tageblatt*—probably the result of a French leak. Questions were asked in the press and the House of Commons. It would be an understatement to say that Grey gave little information in his reply on 11 June. He stated that 'Parliament has an unqualified right to know of any agreements or arrangements that bind the country to action or restrain its freedom. But it cannot be told of military and naval measures to meet possible contingencies.'[21]

If the approach had been pressed by the Russians themselves, Grey quite possibly would have refused authorization. His concern was to please France at the culmination of a successful royal visit. His suspicions of Russia remained very keen. The behaviour of Sazonov had given rise to critical comment in the Foreign Office. The youthful Vansittart wrote in December 1913 that 'M. Sazonow is very difficult to deal with', which Crowe capped by adding 'and his opinions almost incredibly jejune'.[22] The situation in Persia did not change and led to fresh exasperation. A telegram in mid-March led Grey to write to Crewe that 'we cannot postpone a reconsideration of the Persian question'. The Secretary for India agreed: 'Townley evidently telegraphed in a state of acute exasperation against the Russians, and it is not entirely surprising, especially when one reads his message in conjunction with Buchanan's of 15th March.'[23] Grey wrote again in the middle of May: 'I think we ought to have a joint meeting of I.O. & F.O. to discuss the situation: it looks to me as if the expected but dreaded breakdown in Persia were coming.'[24] If that did indeed happen, the British position in southern Persia might be in some jeopardy and Grey would resist Russia very firmly. The presence of the oil in the British sphere rather mollified those who held that Grey had abandoned all that was good in Persia to the Russians. Oil-fired ships needed fuel to drive them, and although Lord Cowdray could oblige with a certain amount of oil from Mexico, the real point, as Grey told the First Lord, 'is that S. Persia, near the coast, is more controllable by us than other centres of oil production in the world which are entirely out of our reach'.[25] The Foreign Secretary was aware of the growth of Russian military strength and, although he declared to Lichnowsky that he had 'no indication of any sort that it was being strengthened with any aggressive purpose', he was apprehensive.[26] It was, therefore, only partly because of a certain public outcry that Grey was happy to postpone the naval talks until August. The Anglo-Russian naval convention never existed. Certainly, Grey dissembled, for reasons that are not entirely clear, about the fact of negotiations with Russia being considered. The only 'crisis of trust' that these putative conversations created was a further blow to the ill-founded German belief that Britain would remain neutral in a European conflict.[27]

Grey's major achievement of these months, which left him 'in a mood of offensive arrogance', had not been the subject of diplomatic exchanges: he had given up smoking. 'In some thirty-three years', he wrote in February, 'there have been very few days when I haven't had a strong smoke after every meal and now for nearly five weeks I haven't had a whiff.'[28] He had been prompted to this renunciation by a developing anxiety about his sight. He had begun to have difficulty in seeing the ball accurately while playing squash. Nor could he see his favourite star in its constellation. Early in 1914, he consulted an oculist, who had advised that heavy smoking seemed to be causing the trouble, and if he stopped, his sight would be restored. By May, however, this was manifestly not happening and he went for a further specialist examination. This time the report was grave. In due course, he would lose the power of reading, though he would probably retain the ability to distinguish light from darkness. The progress of the infection would be slow, but it would probably be inexorable. He decided to wait until the end of the parliamentary session and then attend the clinic of an eminent specialist in Germany during the summer. Tyrrell might come with him and have some profitable private discussions with political figures. The shock to Grey of this news was very considerable. He had prided himself on keeping himself fit through the gruelling years of office, but now, at fifty-two, it seemed that the strain was beginning to tell. What was more, the pace of events in the Balkans might conspire to rule out the visit to Germany for a special consultation.

The assassination of Archduke Francis Ferdinand on 28 June at Sarajevo came as a shock, though, since it concerned the 'matter of

Serbia', hardly a surprise. The heir to the Habsburg throne had paid a successful private visit to England some six months previously, and, in return, King George V came unannounced to the Austro-Hungarian Embassy early on the morning after his death to express his grief. The King's distant cousin, the Austrian Ambassador, Count Mensdorff, gratefully accepted these condolences and others which flowed into the Embassy. Grey himself wrote a personal note on the loss: 'The cruel circumstances attending to it add to the tragedy. . . . Every feeling political and personal makes me sympathise with you.'[29]

These feelings among court and official circles were genuine, yet the sympathy shown towards the Dual Monarchy on this level did not correspond to policy towards her. The Dual Alliance between Austria and Germany severely limited the scope of any Anglo-Austrian rapprochement. The major topic of diplomatic interest was therefore the extent to which Vienna was being pushed by Berlin, or was itself doing the pushing. At the time of the Bosnian crisis, Grey had shown little patience with Austrian diplomacy as conducted by Aehrenthal, but by 1911 he was prepared to regard the affair as an event in the past. He told Mensdorff that he did not apprehend great difficulties between the major Powers: 'There were separate groups amongst them, but no reason remained why these groups should be hostile to each other.'[30] These fine sentiments were somewhat battered by the Balkan Wars, when Viennese opinion believed, largely correctly, that Anglo-German co-operation had been at the expense of Austrian ambitions. Grey himself held no high opinion of the final Balkan settlement, but critical Austrian opinion held that it showed the foolishness of entrusting the destinies of the Empire to the ambassadors' conference in the British Foreign Office. Nevertheless, it was consoling that over Albania, the British had not aligned themselves completely with Russia, and in the first six months of 1914 seemed to desire good relations with the monarchy. Despite naval friction in the past, there was a gesture of calculated goodwill in May with the exchange of naval visits —the British Mediterranean Fleet called at Austro-Hungarian ports and an Austro-Hungarian squadron visited Malta. Even the King let it be known that if left to himself, he would have preferred a visit to Vienna rather than Paris.[31] There was some Liberal criticism of Habsburg policy towards the 'suppressed nationalities', but advice from a British Government enmeshed in the Irish question might not have been appreciated.

286

In his note to Count Mensdorff, Grey feared the effect of the assassination on the old Emperor, whose life was so closely bound up with the peace of Europe. Few in Britain believed that the threat to peace was even more close at hand. The death of Joseph Chamberlain on 2 July provided a more acceptable topic for political commentators. On 6 July, for example, Nicolson, in a letter to the British Ambassador in Vienna, devoted the bulk of it to Albania and contented himself with the hope that the crime would have 'no serious political consequences, in any case outside of Austria-Hungary'. A strong agitation against Serbia was to be expected, but he was glad to hear that the more reasonable journals deprecated making a Government responsible for crimes committed by revolutionaries.[32] However, an interview with the German Ambassador on the same day left the Foreign Secretary more apprehensive. Speaking privately, Lichnowsky warned that the Austrians intended to take action and this might possibly mean the use of force. Grey hoped that this did not mean taking Serbian territory. It did not, Lichnowsky replied, the humiliation of Serbia was all that the Austrians desired. Germany was placed in a very difficult situation. If she held her ally back, she would be accused of neglecting her at a critical moment; if she gave support, then the consequences could be serious. He asked Grey to use his influence at St Petersburg, since German apprehensions of Russia were growing.[33] He also sought to draw Grey on the question of Britain's relations with her entente partners. The Foreign Secretary took Lichnowsky's remarks about Russia seriously. They confirmed him in his belief that 'the German government are in a peaceful mood and that they are very anxious to be on good terms with England. . . .'[34] On 9 July, Sir Edward returned to Lichnowsky's unanswered question about Britain's relations with her entente partners, and gave him a considered answer. He stressed that 'England wished to preserve an absolutely free hand so that in the event of Continental complications she might be able to act according to her judgment'. This time, he did refer to the various naval or military conversations which had taken place since 1906 but stated that they did not constitute agreements which imposed any obligations whatsoever.[35]

For the next fortnight, while it was still uncertain whether a local war would break out, Grey took steps to localize it if it should. He warned Cambon that in the event of an Austrian *démarche* against Serbia, Britain and France would have to encourage patience in St Petersburg.[36] He spoke to the Russian Ambassador on 8 July and

U

warned him of the uncertain temper in Vienna. For his part, Count Benckendorff hoped that Germany would restrain Austria. Whatever the Germans might feel, there was no ill-feeling in St Petersburg. Grey urged the Russians to do all they could to convince Germany that no coup was being prepared against her.[37] After these conversations, Grey saw the German Ambassador again, stressing that if Austrian action against Serbia was kept within certain bounds, it would be quite easy to encourage patience at St Petersburg; otherwise, Slav feeling would compel the Russian Government to send an ultimatum. He did not say what these bounds were. It still remained to be seen whether the Austrian demands would be 'reasonable', or indeed whether they would be made at all. In this uneasy period, everyone waited for the storm to break. The Austrian Ambassador did his best to urge upon British newspaper editors that Serbia should be compelled to mend her ways. In his conversations, however, he did not talk about the possibility of war. Much to the disgust of the Serbian Minister, *John Bull* appeared on 11 July with a full-scale article alleging the complicity of the Serbian Government. More embarrassingly, after a visit from a certain Baron Franckenstein on 15 July, Spender's *Westminster Gazette* declared that the Austrian Government could not be expected to remain inactive. Since the paper was sometimes known as 'Grey's own', the piece caused some consternation and the Foreign Secretary disavowed any responsibility.[38] It was clear that solid sympathy in London for the Dual Monarchy did exist if the Vienna Government chose to take any notice of it.

It has recently been argued at this juncture of events that 'even if Austria-Hungary had not been so "aggressive" in 1914, she could hardly have counted on British sympathy in a diplomatic conflict with Russia'.[39] This view perhaps underestimates the degree to which London was initially prepared to play a floating role. On 14 July, for example, the Russophil Nicolson was writing to the British Ambassador in St Petersburg: '. . . it seems to me that our relations with Russia are now approaching a point when we shall have to make up our minds as to whether we should become really intimate and permanent friends, or else to diverge into another path.'[40] He himself continued to favour the former, but was more prepared to consider an alternative than he had been previously. On 16 July, even more significantly, Grey was represented as saying that 'whereas hereto Germany has feigned alarm at the encircling policy against Germany falsely attributed to His Majesty's Government . . . she is now really frightened at the growing strength of the Russian Army, and may make another military effort additional to the recent large expenditure . . . or bring on a conflict with Russia at an early date before the increases in the Russian Army have their full effect and before the completion of the Russian strategic railways. . . .'[41] Given the unabating Russian pressure on Persia, it was by no means clear that a reasonable Austrian response would not receive a favourable hearing in London.[42] Meanwhile, Grey tried to keep British involvement to a minimum. He refused to put pressure on Belgrade, took little action to bring about Russo-Austrian talks, but also declined to agree to a joint warning to Vienna from the Triple Entente.[43]

In this curious period of waiting for the Austrian ultimatum, Foreign Office anxieties about Germany increased. Crowe was alarmed that, despite knowing the terms, German actions in Vienna seemed the reverse of conciliatory. For its part, Berlin did not believe there was a real danger of war, but hoped to persuade the British to take a decisive role and thus bring about the much desired breach between Britain and Russia. Grey was prepared to suspend judgment a little longer, being impressed by Lichnowsky's good will. It did not help that the Ambassador neither accurately transmitted an account of the British position nor reflected the mind of his own Government on Austrian matters. Mensdorff saw Grey on 23 July and outlined the Austrian demands, which would be released on the following day. The Serbian Government would be confronted by what amounted to an ultimatum. Grey was aghast, and painted a gloomy picture of the vast destruction which would ensue if war did break out.[44] Now was the time for Grey to raise the matter at the Cabinet. When his colleagues at the meeting on 24 July heard him say that the Austro-Hungarian proposals might be the prelude to a war in which at least four of the Great Powers might be involved, they blenched. Grey was urged to explore the possibility of a mediating group of states—England, Germany, France and Italy—coming between Russia and Austria-Hungary.[45] Grey himself described the Austrian proposals as 'the most formidable document ever addressed by one State to another that was independent'.[46] He confessed to the German Ambassador that his chances of restraining Russia had been much reduced by it. Indeed, the pressure was now in the other direction. He received a telegram on 24 July from Buchanan in St Petersburg in which Sazonov made it clear that he now expected Britain to proclaim her solidarity with

Russia. Poincaré and Viviani had just concluded their talks in the Russian capital. The details of these discussions have never been released, but it is clear that the French supported, if not prompted, a firm line by Russia. Crowe rightly read Sazonov's appeal as a blow to any hope of enlisting French support in holding back Russia. The chance of localizing the war, supposing it ever existed, had gone. Whatever Britain might think of the merits of the Austrian case, France and Russia had decided to make a stand. Crowe felt that the only remaining doubt was whether Germany was bent on war. She could be made to hesitate if she could be made to apprehend that the war would find England by the side of France and Russia.[47] Already on 25-6 July a number of mobilization measures had taken place, and the most dramatic step Britain could take would be to put the whole fleet on a war footing. The Foreign Secretary found these comments too crisp. He had undoubtedly been disappointed by what he interpreted as a lack of response from Berlin to his requests for restraint. Yet he was reluctant to adopt a policy of firm alignment and bold confrontation. With unflappable sang-froid, or culpable disregard of duty, Sir Edward disappeared to his fishing cottage to think on these things.

At a variety of levels, the problems confronting the Foreign Secretary were enormous. The abstract calculation of the likely effect of diplomatic moves had to be combined with an assessment of domestic opinion, in particular, the views of the Cabinet. It was not easy to bring these considerations into alignment. Grey still wanted to avoid a major war, but there came a point when it was more important to assess the conditions under which it would be fought and its likely outcome. If, at this juncture, he firmly aligned himself with Russia and France, mobilizing accordingly, such a show of united strength might have a deterrent effect. Germany would draw back and Austria with her. It might then be possible to patch up an Austrian–Serbian settlement, although, in view of the past, it might only lead to fresh trouble in the future. If such a deterrent worked, Grey could reasonably expect that colleagues and commentators who had reservations, or opposed such a course, would forget them in the aftermath of success. Looking further ahead, it might also be necessary to envisage a closer association with Germany after she had received such a diplomatic defeat. Russia might become so bumptious and powerful that some counter-weight against her would be needed. On the other hand, Grey knew that such a bold policy stood little chance of being adopted. Cabinet and public opinion, in so far as it could be discovered, seemed obsessed by the absurdity of a great international conflict on the Serbian issue. If war broke out, it was generally believed that the Serbs, the Austrians, the Russians and the Germans, probably in that order, would all be responsible. The Foreign Secretary fully realized that the fate of Serbia was no longer the only issue at stake, nevertheless, however theoretically attractive the idea, it was not emotionally feasible to stake all on deterring Germany by a close collaboration with France and Russia. Sir Edward therefore decided to continue playing as detached a role as possible before the pressure to commit Britain became inexorable. In a few days, the movement of opinion at home might be more disposed to such a course.

He came back to London on 26 July, having authorized a new proposal for an ambassadorial conference in London.[48] Grey was not very optimistic, because news had just reached him that Austria had rejected the Serbian reply and was making military preparations. On 27 July, he saw Mensdorff, who informed him that since Serbia intended to continue on her subversive way, the Austrian Government was reluctantly compelled to use force. Grey expressed his disappointment, claiming that the Serbian reply had already involved her in great humiliation. He urged the Austrians to think again: 'If they could make war on Servia and at the same time satisfy Russia, well and good; but, if not, the consequences would be incalculable.'[49] The Foreign Secretary then reported this conversation to the Cabinet. He also explained to his colleagues that the fate of his conference proposal was doubtful. France and Italy would agree, but he was sceptical about Germany. Although Nicolson and Crowe were now frankly suspicious of Germany's intentions, it was quite another matter for Grey to bring the Cabinet to a point of decision. With passion in his voice, he had told Samuel before the Cabinet began that there was some *devilry* going on in Berlin.[50] Others had different views. John Burns wrote in his diary: 'Why 4 great powers should fight over Servia no fellow can understand. . . . It must be averted by all the means in our power. Apart from the merits of the case it is my especial duty to dissociate myself and the principles I hold and the trusteeship for the working classes which I carry from such a universal crime as the contemplated war will be.'[51] After this Cabinet, Lloyd George told C. P. Scott that 'there could be no question of our taking part in any war in the first instance. He knew of no Minister who would be in favour of it.'[52] The only substantive decisions of the meeting on 27 July were to prevent the First and Second Fleets from being dispersed after their annual summer manœuvres and to agree to discuss Britain's precise obligations to Belgium at the next meeting, two days later.[53]

On the intervening day, Austria declared war on Serbia and began preparations for the bombardment of Belgrade. The Austro-Russian conversations which had finally staggered to a start came quickly to a pathetic close. In Paris, it was widely assumed that the Austrian declaration made war inevitable. Later that evening, Sazonov informed his ambassadors in Vienna, Paris, London and Rome, that in consequence, on the following day mobilization would be proclaimed in the districts of Odessa, Kiev, Moscow and Kazan. The German Government would be informed and the absence of any intention to attack Germany stressed. In the small hours of 29 July, the Tsar telegraphed the Kaiser to enlist his help in trying to avoid war. He was in danger of being overwhelmed by the pressure of events into taking drastic measures. Later that day, Moltke warned Bethmann Hollweg that Russian military measures directed against Austria would lead to Austrian general mobilization. If that happened, Germany was treaty bound to mobilize too. The Franco-Russian alliance would then be activated and the civilized states of Europe would begin to tear one another to pieces.

Would Britain be among their number? The Cabinet met on the morning of 29 July amid this mounting crisis, but it broke up without coming to a decision on the major issue. Opinions were so divided that it was impossible to elicit a promise of support for France, let alone Russia. There was a great deal of hesitation about Britain's duty and some were still of the opinion that it would be possible to consider the defence of France quite separately from an Austro-Russian war. Convictions of this sort seemed to gain strength from the reports of the British Ambassador in Paris that French opinion was against going to war because of Serbia.[54] Even in its discussion of Belgium, the Cabinet was doubtful whether a single guaranteeing state was bound to act, if the other signatories abstained or refused.[55] It agreed that if the matter should arise, it would require a decision of 'policy rather than legal obligation'. Apart from agreeing to the initiation of a 'precautionary period', the Cabinet would go no further and refused to make pledges in advance.[56] This Cabinet split was also reflected in the party at large. Ponsonby had mustered a meeting of the parliamentary Foreign Affairs Group and, on its behalf, wrote Grey a letter expressing its dismay at the trend of events. They did not want to upset the Government by premature publicity, but they did feel that 'if both France and Russia were informed that on no account would we be drawn into war even though they and other European powers were involved, it would have a moderating effect on their policy'. There was no mention of restraint by Germany. After the Cabinet meeting, Grey saw Ponsonby and agreed to pass on his message to the Prime Minister. Otherwise, he refused to make any statement about the British attitude towards intervention. He claimed that an assurance to France and Russia of the kind desired, would have the opposite to a pacific result. He insisted, once more, that Britain was 'absolutely free and working for peace'.[57]

In his interview with Ponsonby, Grey also claimed that doubt about Britain's intentions was useful to him in negotiations with both sides. While this might have been true a few days earlier, it was so no longer. The hesitation in the Cabinet on 29 July was now a decided embarrassment. It only served to revive German hopes of gaining British neutrality on the one hand, and to encourage Russian mobilization on the other. So, after the Cabinet, the Foreign Secretary warned Lichnowsky that his personal friendliness should not be interpreted to mean that Britain would stand aside if France and Germany joined in the war. In so declaring, he was going beyond what he had been authorized to say by his colleagues. But to the French Ambassador he was even more frank. He warned that British public opinion did not regard events in the Balkans as on a par with the Moroccan question. There, it had appeared that Germany was trying to pick a quarrel on a matter where Anglo-French agreement already existed. The problem of Austria and Serbia was different; 'even if the question becomes one between Austria and Russia we should not feel called upon to take a hand in it'. If France and Germany were involved, 'we were free from engagements, and we should have to decide what British interests required us to do'.[58] As the Austrians began their bombardment of Belgrade, Grey snatched a few hours' sleep and waited for the next move. It came from Bethmann Hollweg.

The German Chancellor made a clumsy bid for British neutrality by promising that if Germany defeated France, French territorial integrity would be maintained. However, he refused to make the same pledge in respect of French colonies, nor would he guarantee Belgian neutrality. Sir Edward's secretary reported to Francis

Acland that 'never before had he been seen in a white heat of passion'.[59] The proposal was rejected. It would seem that Bethmann Hollweg and the German Foreign Office, now conscious that Tirpitz was nervous about the preparedness of the German fleet, were anxious not to find themselves in conflict with Britain. The tendency of German policy, as Admiral Müller put it, was 'to keep quiet, letting Russia put herself in the wrong, but then not shying away from war'. It is a matter of opinion how genuine were the fears of Russian expansion, either in the short or long term; they may only have been a cover for German 'aggression'.[60] Whatever the verdict on the general question, this particular exercise was a total failure. Nevertheless, despite the passion which the proposal apparently engendered, Grey still refused to give much encouragement to Cambon. To the annoyance of Crowe, he resorted to last-ditch expedients, like trying to arrange that the Austrian attack should halt at Belgrade.

His reticence was again due to the delicate balance of opinion within the Cabinet. At its meeting on 31 July, it still refused to authorize any statement about British intentions should war come. Although there was some anxiety about the neutrality of Belgium, there was little suggestion that its violation would be sufficient to provide a *casus belli*. It is little wonder that Grey subsequently had a 'rather painful' interview with Cambon. The French Ambassador was told that for the moment the Cabinet and the nation did not feel that any treaties or obligations were involved. Great importance was attached to Belgian neutrality, but Grey refused to be drawn further. Moreover he added that the latest news of complete mobilization in Russia would not only precipitate a crisis but 'would make it appear that German mobilisation was being forced by Russia'.[61] In taking this view, Grey reflected the feeling of the Cabinet. Left to himself, he would probably have been more forthcoming (indeed he had hinted that morning to Lichnowsky that Britain would probably be drawn in if France and Germany became involved). Alarmed, Crowe sent the Foreign Secretary a concisely argued case for British intervention, but it began to look as though his views would be disregarded. Decisions were now being made in the heart of the Cabinet and the views of leading officials mattered little. After the meeting on 1 August, Grey had an even sterner message for Cambon. Germany was apparently now offering not to attack France if she remained neutral in a Russo-German war. If France could not take up this offer it was because she was bound by an alliance to which Britain was not a party. Britain would not send an expeditionary force to the continent. France must make her own decisions. This interview was particularly tense and emotional. Cambon tried to argue that Britain did have an obligation to help France, but Grey refused to admit it. The exchange of letters had made this quite clear. Desperately, Cambon talked about the 'obligation of British interests' compelling intervention, but Grey replied that the Cabinet could be trusted to make its own evaluation of British interests. The only concession he agreed to make was to remind his colleagues about France's undefended coasts.[62]

Asquith later recorded that at this stage he was still not quite hopeless about peace, but felt that if war came, some split in the Cabinet could not be avoided, with possibly disastrous consequences. According to the Prime Minister, 'if an out and out uncompromising policy of non-intervention at all costs is adopted' Grey would go.[63] As so often, this typically negative statement was tactically adroit. Although in an emotional state—Nicolson described him pacing up and down in his room biting his lower lip—Grey had not lost his facility for getting decisions in his own favour.[64] He did not say that he would resign unless the Cabinet agreed to intervene, but he categorically refused to be bound in the opposite direction. This gave him another day during which to assess the course of events. The situation began to look hopeless. On 2 August, a Sunday, the Cabinet assembled in the morning with the news, as a fresh cause for alarm, that Germany had just occupied Luxembourg.

Sir Edward opened the morning session by claiming that Britain had 'both moral obligations of honour and substantial obligations of policy in taking sides with France'.[65] He therefore proposed firstly, 'to announce to France & Germany that if the German ships enter the Channel we should regard that as a hostile act' and secondly, to reserve the British position on Belgian neutrality for the present. McKenna then proposed that the Channel should be formally neutralized to both Powers. Grey said that this was pointless, arguing, according to Runciman's account, 'If the Channel is closed against Germany *it is* in favour of France, & we cannot take half measures—either we must declare ourselves neutral, or in it.' If Britain were neutral, Grey declared that he would go, but would not blame the Cabinet if they disagreed with him. One way or the other, he asked for a decision. After considerable discussion, Grey was able to persuade his colleagues to allow him to warn Germany that Britain would not tolerate German naval action in the Channel or against the French coasts. This decision, Asquith recorded, was 'not only a recognition of our friendship with France, but it is also imperatively required to protect British interests'.

The Cabinet resumed its discussions on the afternoon of 2 August. This session was largely devoted to the question of Belgium. Again, Grey took a strong line, and was able, this time, to persuade his colleagues that any interference with Belgian independence would compel Britain to take action.[66] After this hectic day of argument, Grey and Haldane were dining quietly together in the evening when a dispatch came through that Germany had presented an ultimatum to Belgium. While not appealing directly for help, the Belgian Government had previously declared its intention to defend the country. The German ultimatum was therefore rejected. Weary though he was, Grey spent the rest of the evening thinking about the speech he would have to make in the Commons the following afternoon. Next morning, the Cabinet met amidst considerable uncertainty about the number of Ministers who would resign. Asquith knew that Burns and Morley, Simon and Beauchamp intended to go, but Lloyd George seemed now to be veering in favour of intervention.[67]

Just after three o'clock on Bank Holiday Monday, 3 August, Grey rose to speak to a crowded House of Commons. If he carried his audience, then the unity of the nation, so essential to success, would probably be preserved. Although he looked gaunt and austere, he did not outwardly seem nervous or uncertain. His speech was a typical Grey performance. No other member of the House could have given it at such a time. Sir Edward had few rhetorical conceits or stylistic embellishments to decorate what he had to say. Yet on major occasions the Prime Minister often put him up to speak, because he had an unrivalled impact on his audience. Even on this occasion, Asquith's sense of polish noted 'his usual ragged ends' but that did not matter.[68] The abiding impression Grey left was one of coldness and detachment, mysteriously charged with a pure emotion. Everything about him combined to produce this impression. 'His face was passionless', an observer noted, 'and sharply cut like a bird's, his voice was clear, with no warm tones in it, his language was wholly unadorned, precise, simple, accurate, austerely dignified.'[69] The first part of the speech was a rehearsal of the entente with France. He told the House of the exchange of letters in November 1912 and emphasized that the Government did not consider its freedom was restricted by them. Nevertheless, as regards friendship with France, he added, 'how far that entails an obligation let every man look into his own heart, and his own feelings, and construe the extent of the obligation for himself. I construe it myself as I feel it. . . .' It is right to stress that Grey did feel a sense of moral obligation, though it is too simple to suppose that his calculations in this crisis can be reduced in any easy fashion to the ethical code of a 'high-principled, slightly priggish Wykehamist'.[70] The sense of moral commitment was real but it was also allied to a strong calculation of interest. 'But for Belgium,' he wrote a few days after war broke out, 'we should have kept out of it . . .'[71] Happily for Grey, in respect of Belgium, treaty obligations and strategic considerations conveniently coincided. After Grey sat down, Bonar Law promised the support of the Opposition in upholding the honour and security of the country. The only sour note came from Ramsay MacDonald. He was not convinced, either that the country was in any danger, or that its honour was involved. The Foreign Secretary had failed to mention Russia and the effect her power would have in Europe at the end of the war. The House was in no mood to debate these points, and expressed its confidence in the character of the Foreign Secretary.[72] His speech had the result of convincing waverers both in the Cabinet and in the party.

On 4 August, the Cabinet heard the news of the violation of Belgian territory by German troops. Grey was authorized to send an ultimatum to Berlin requiring a satisfactory answer by midnight. Grey, Asquith and others sat around in the Cabinet room, smoking and waiting. There was no reply.

15

The War and the Liberal Government, August 1914-May 1915

Grey's conduct during the July crisis seems in retrospect to mark the highspot of his career. He had strained himself to the uttermost, trying to find a path from which all sides could emerge with honour. Yet, while his colleagues congratulated him on his patience and composure, the effort drained his confidence and strength. Asquith noted that Grey was 'much overstrained'.[1] While the Foreign Secretary might outwardly seem the most detached of men, within was a vein of wistful feeling which, if crushed, revived only slowly. For days after the outbreak of war, he was irritable and bad tempered. Nicolson's attempts to lecture him during the crisis he resented, and he did not wish to resume any intimacy. His private secretary, Tyrrell, was cracking up under the strain. Grey himself began to worry about his eyesight, with every reason. The long hours and tension of the previous month had not corresponded to the requirement of rest 'where possible'. The broodiness in his nature began to be obtrusive. No one, placed as he was, could avoid the question of personal responsibility. If he had acted differently in this or that particular, could disaster have been avoided? A nature more gregarious than his might have overcome this speculation in the company of congenial friends, but for too long, now, he had been driven in upon himself. Hardinge and Sanderson had discussed this aspect back in 1912. Grey's fault was that he was 'too detached from other people—unpopular owing to his position of splendid isolation—yet a first class Sec. of State for F. Affrs'.[2] When he was riding high, this detachment had not been a handicap politically, indeed quite the contrary. But now he had undoubtedly 'failed' and he did not disguise this fact from himself. To have brought the nation united into the war was not something on which he believed he should be congratulated, and when people ill-advisedly did so, he grumpily replied: 'I hate war, I hate war.'

It would perhaps have been better if he had resigned at once. Yet the political reasons why he should stay were compelling. To have gone, would have seemed too overt a confession of failure. His conduct of affairs during the summer had the unfortunate consequence of turning him into a symbol of national probity and purpose, and while politicians are expendable, symbols are not. Not that he ever seriously doubted the wisdom of his own diplomacy. At the time, and to the end, he maintained that 'no one could have prevented the war except the Germans, & Bethmann Hollweg when he vetoed a Conference struck the only effective instrument for peace out of my hand. The experience of the Balkan Conference ought to have assured the Germans that there was no risk of their or even Austria's losing prestige in another Conference in London and Serbia had already accepted nine-tenths of the Austrian ultimatum, so Austrian prestige was safe already.'[3] There were others, however, who soon began to take a less favourable view of his actions. The patriotic pages of F. S. Oliver's *Ordeal by Battle* recognized the difficulties he laboured under, particularly from his colleagues, but was still not satisfied. 'The criticism is', Oliver wrote early in 1915, 'that although his intentions were of the best, and his industry unflagging, he failed to realise the situation, and to adopt the only means which might have secured peace.'[4] He should have aligned himself firmly and unequivocally with Russia and France, the moment Austria sent her demands to Serbia. As well as criticism of policy in Conservative circles, there was also a certain amount of personal criticism because of Grey's known close association with Haldane. The Lord Chancellor was a marked man from the outset because of his alleged pro-German sympathies. By December 1914, the *Daily Express* found it 'disquieting' to know that Lord Haldane was 'assisting' Sir Edward Grey at the Foreign Office. In course of time, this disquiet was to take a more venomous turn.[5]

The more common criticism, however, was that Grey had gone too far in support of France. Writing privately to Haldane, Rosebery was struck by the fact that the French had approached Grey, in the first place, 'before he was warm in his seat'. He could not help suspecting that this was done 'to test his sympathies, or more probably to entangle him inextricably in an engagement of a compromising character. . . .' Haldane believed that Grey would answer that by 1905 the naval supremacy of this country over the combined

Powers of Europe was inevitably disappearing and that he had to choose with which group he would range himself. He would add that it was not safe to range Britain with Germany because German ambitions were not to be trusted. Rosebery replied that he was not so much criticizing the policy, as 'the almost indecent haste of the French to rope Edward in, and so he was committed to giving them assured assistance before he had been in office a month'. Haldane's rejoinder to this was that 'January 1906 was a really critical moment, and one in which a decision had to be taken. For the ways were parting—Delcassé's resignation & the Morocco pressure brought things to the test.'[6]

When the debate was conducted in private amongst his friends, the comments on Grey's policy were good-natured, but it was otherwise when substantially the same criticism came from Radicals and Socialists. On the extreme Left, there was little comment on Grey's policy or his ability. Those who accepted a Marxist explanation of the war were obsessed by the deep underlying forces and the inner contradictions of capitalism. To them, it was largely a matter of indifference what policy had been followed or which individual had fashioned it. War was inevitable. There were also many Radicals who felt that Grey was a victim, albeit a willing one, of an archaic system. E. D. Morel and others who founded the Union of Democratic Control wanted to see the composition of the Foreign Office changed and foreign policy made 'democratic'. Ramsay MacDonald was not convinced that these structural changes would in themselves make very much difference. 'Given Sir Edward Grey', he wrote, 'and the two or three present heads of the Foreign Office in control of our foreign policy, and I do not care whether the House of Commons ratified treaties . . . we would probably have been in this war. . . . It is public opinion and the personality of Foreign Secretaries that we must get at.'[7] But what was Grey's personality? Opinion on the Left wavered uneasily between the view that he was feeble and gullible, a mere tool of his permanent officials, and the conviction that he was devious and secretive. MacDonald, for example, again wrote to Morel lamenting the misplaced trust in Grey: 'I have never trusted him. He is well-meaning & manages to impress people with his ability, but his whole conduct of foreign affairs shows that he is both weak and short-sighted.'[8] Morel, on the other hand, found it difficult to control his personal animosity towards the Foreign Secretary. When Gilbert Murray had the temerity to publish an orthodox defence of Grey's foreign policy, the Radicals raged with fury. After attacking the critics, Murray concluded: 'The rest of us will only be grateful for ever to one who through all these years of crisis acted justly and sought no aggrandizement, who kept faith with his friends and worked for a good understanding with his enemies, who never spoke a rash word to bring the peril nearer, and never neglected a precaution to meet it when it should come.'[9] Such a statement provoked the Hon. Bertrand Russell to a scathing reply, in which he stated dogmatically: 'The interests of the British democracy do not conflict at any point with the interests of mankind.'[10] It would be wrong to pretend that these criticisms constituted a political threat to the Foreign Secretary between 1914 and 1916. His chief problems came from other directions. Nevertheless, these arguments in war time showed that the Foreign Secretary could not shake off the inheritance of his own previous actions.

The gravest handicap Grey suffered from in the war was his own attitude towards it. It was a source of weakness that in July he had not appreciated the extent to which the continental Powers were gravely circumscribed in their diplomacy by military pressures and strategic considerations. Just as, in peace, Grey had not paid undue attention to military factors, so in war he easily accepted their supremacy. He did not believe that he had any qualities which suited him for the role of amateur strategist, and it was therefore better not to pose as one. As he himself put it, 'the position of a civilian in a War Council, who feels that, from a lack of military knowledge and training, this limitation is imposed upon him, is not glorious'.[11] A nice example of Grey's attitude came in November 1914 when Crewe wrote saying that it would be necessary to decide whether or not to advance on Basrah in Mesopotamia. Grey replied: 'It seems to me to depend upon whether military experts think we are strong enough to take Basrah & hold it.' That was all. Crewe was not satisfied: '. . . the political aspect has also to be considered.' Grey then agreed to confer.[12] If not glorious, Grey's attitude was at least honest. Other members of the Cabinet felt no such inhibitions about their strategic capacities, and began to find the Foreign Secretary's reticence increasingly irksome. They wanted to do something, even if ill-considered, while their colleague seemed to be the embodiment of benevolent scepticism.

At first, it seemed that the business of the Government would go on as usual. In theory, each member of the Cabinet could express his views on the conduct of the war. The confusion, therefore, was even greater than usual. Did 'foreign policy' still exist? Was it not swallowed up in the total direction of the struggle? Where did the responsibilities of the Foreign Secretary begin and end? No one knew. At the outset, Asquith had left Haldane with the responsibility of summoning a Council of War. The Lord Chancellor picked Grey and Churchill, together with the leading soldiers, to serve on it. The Committee of Imperial Defence faded away, apart from the examination of specific problems by specialist sub-committees. The full Cabinet met frequently throughout August, September and October, but its role was uncertain. Its chief business seemed to be to receive reports from the new Secretary for War, Kitchener, and from Churchill. At the outset, Grey had approved of Kitchener's appointment because he had 'a great asset of public confidence'. Later on, he began to wonder whether a civilian, supported by an effective General Staff, might not have been a better solution. When specific decisions had to be taken quickly, it was largely a matter of luck who took them. For example, since the Prime Minister happened to be out of town, Grey, Kitchener and Churchill hastily conferred on 2 October and agreed that Churchill might go to Antwerp. As usual, Grey had felt unable to assess the military merits of such a scheme, and had merely approved it when Kitchener agreed.

This uncertainty at the top was paralleled within the Foreign Office itself. Nicolson had been asked to stay on as Permanent Under-Secretary, and reports (not without their bias) suggested that 'under his rule the office is in a state of chaos. There is no discipline and the tail waggles the dog.' The loss of his younger son drove Tyrrell to a complete breakdown and in the spring of 1915 he had to leave the Foreign Office. Before that, he and Crowe had tried to run the Office between them and had quarrelled over it. Crowe wanted to channel all matters of importance concerning the war into a special War Department. The effort involved in setting this up created animosities within the Office, while Crowe found the continuing inefficiency most taxing and, in the end, quarrelled with the Foreign Secretary over it. In December 1914, Bertie recorded: 'Crowe has completely lost his head. His Prussian blood came out and he was insubordinate and insolent to Grey, who has decided that his appointment to succeed Nicolson is impossible.'[13] He was placed in charge of a new Contraband Department instead.

Asquith tried to give some direction by summoning a meeting of the inner group of Ministers on 25 November and announcing his intention to bestow upon them the official designation of 'the War Council'. Grey was a member, together with Kitchener, Churchill, Lloyd George, Balfour (present in a personal not a party capacity), together with a couple of experts. The idea was that this group should range broadly over the conduct of the war, summoning other Ministers only if their departments were particularly involved. No 'decisive action', however, was to be taken without the assent of the full Cabinet. Grey was not a very effective member of this new Council. German behaviour in Belgium had horrified him; they seemed 'to have taken us back to the time of the Huns'.[14] Yet he was reluctant to retaliate, in kind, for the bombing of Ostend. It would 'only put us on the same plane morally as they are'. Churchill minuted brusquely: 'All right. You will have to come to it soon.'[15] This was symptomatic. It was little wonder that Asquith condescendingly described Grey's courage as 'too nervy to be put really high'. Haldane, however, described Grey as 'wonderfully well. He comes in daily on his way to the F.O. to weigh the news of the day. . . .'[16] This was not a view the Foreign Secretary himself shared. On Christmas Eve 1914 he wrote to Lady Lyttelton: 'My machinery was almost ceasing to work & I have handed over to Haldane for a few days and come away.'[17] When he got to Fallodon he slept 'at least 18 hours of the first 48 spent here' and pronounced himself much refreshed. 'I went to bed at 11 last night', he wrote to Haldane, '& woke about 11 a.m. with an uneasy sense of something unusual which soon turned to an apprehension that the Germans had landed & arrived; but full consciousness disclosed that Christmas hymns were being sung outside. . . .'[18] This break did little permanent good. The Prime Minister described him at a Cabinet in the spring of 1915 as 'most dolorous and despondent'.[19] Grey confessed to Runciman in March that he had been 'inhumanly busy & tired. I dozed in a chair this morning in intervals of work.' He had just paid a visit to Kew Gardens and felt the contrast between their peace and the fact of war. He added: 'I suppose there were people who felt the incongruity as much when Napoleon was spreading slaughter and ruin over Europe as the Prussians are doing now. But I don't recollect in Wordsworth's war poetry at the time any note except that of the stern necessity and justice of the fight. . . .' If Wordsworth had not flinched, nor would he.[20]

Asquith's War Council lasted until June 1915 when, in a different form, it emerged as the Dardanelles Committee. Grey had been present in January when the plans for a naval attack on the Dardanelles were discussed. Once again, however, he took little part in the argument. In retrospect, he accepted some blame for what happened: 'I must take the responsibility for not having urged them [the diplomatic difficulties] beforehand as a reason for not undertaking the affair at all.'[21] This remark, however, probably oversimplifies a complex position. While it is unlikely, as has been claimed, that Grey was a warm advocate and that Churchill was simply following in his wake, the Foreign Secretary had some reason to favour the expedition. It is even possible that he saw Constantinople as Russia's compensation in a future negotiated peace. These are contentious matters, however, and unfortunately largely a matter of conjecture. Different men decided to go for the Dardanelles for different reasons—whenever that decision precisely was taken.[22]

As will appear, Grey did have his own diplomatic considerations in the Near East, yet, curiously, these were mingled with his near obsession about the limitations of diplomacy in war. The situation in the Balkans provides a further illustration of this point. Some of the Cabinet looked eagerly for an impressive combination of states which would, in due course, drive a way into Central Europe. The means—a Balkan confederation—was obvious, and judicious concessions to Bulgaria could achieve this objective, or so it was believed. But long experience of the Balkans had convinced Grey that while this was a consummation devoutly to be wished, it was almost impossible to achieve. The rapacity of the Balkan States and their rulers was formidable, and a concession to one would only whet the appetite of another. In the first weeks of war, Grey had tried to prevent Ottoman Turkey from joining the Central Powers. To Churchill and Lloyd George, this was foolishness. The British Ambassador in Constantinople had led him to believe that the situation was still fluid. Churchill was scornful: 'If Mallet thinks he is dealing with a Govt. amenable to argument, persuasion & proof of good faith, he is dreaming. . . .'[23] Churchill and Lloyd George had been persuaded, largely by the Buxton brothers, that a general rearrangement of territory in the Balkans was possible. They pressed this claim strongly in the Cabinet. The Ministers had once again to brush up their Balkan geography. Several of them became annoyed, as Grey turned his increasingly blind eye to the 'offers' and hints which they claimed to be able to substantiate. Hellenophiles, in particular, were aghast at Grey's action in spurning the offer from

Venizelos to bring Greece into the war. For his part, the Foreign Secretary suspected that one of Venizelos's main purposes was to wriggle out of ceding Kavalla to Bulgaria and, quite apart from the effect of this on Bulgaria, it would alienate Russia. All roads in the Balkans seemed to lead to Petrograd and Grey regarded it as his primary duty not to act in such a way as would endanger the alliance.

From the Russian point of view, a Balkan confederation under British patronage was an example of meddling in a sphere which she traditionally regarded as her own. Indeed, there was an element of calculated interference in British policy. Grey would not, however, let it be pushed very far. He did not need Ramsay MacDonald to remind him of the existence of Russia, but for the moment, at least, Britain and Russia were fighting a common enemy. Moreover, Grey was not convinced that the internal situation in Russia made her an entirely reliable partner. There was always the possibility that having declared war on Turkey, the prize of Constantinople and hegemony over the Balkans might tempt her to transfer troops from her Western front for this purpose. Britain, France and Russia had signed an agreement on 4 September that they would not negotiate peace separately, but such agreements were not necessarily infallible. At its meeting on 2 November, the Cabinet agreed that Britain should finally abandon the formula of 'Ottoman integrity', whether in Europe or in Asia.[24] A couple of weeks later, without, it seems, consulting the Cabinet as a whole, Grey instructed the British Ambassador in Petrograd to inform Sazonov that the British Government recognized that 'the question of the Straits and of Constantinople should be settled in conformity with Russian desires'.[25] There the matter rested for the time being. The Russian military losses over the winter of 1914–15, combined with fresh apprehensions of a split in the Russian Government, kept Grey preoccupied. In the view of a recent historian, 'Grey's important concession could not have been better timed, despite its off-hand and somewhat vague nature.'[26]

Early in 1915, Grey considered that Russian military failure and the situation on the Western front crippled any major diplomatic initiative. As he wrote subsequently, there was a tendency at the time 'to make insufficient allowance for the fact that in war words count only so far as they are backed by force and victories'.[27] In regard to the Dardanelles expedition, Churchill and Lloyd George worked on the opposite principle. The Foreign Secretary believed that a success might have the effect of jolting the Bulgarians, and making them more amenable. If it really looked as though the Allies were going to win, they would be anxious to come in on their side. Lloyd George wanted to see diplomacy bring about a Balkan combination which would, in turn, provide the military assurance to guarantee the success of the expedition in the Straits. In April, Grey was angered by statements Lloyd George made to the Bulgarian Minister in London, claiming to have the authority of the Government. He told the Minister that the Chancellor's remarks could indeed be sent back to his Government, but Grey wished to see them first.[28] It is not surprising that when Lloyd George was considering alternatives to Asquith's leadership, the Foreign Secretary was not a favoured candidate. He had 'even less push and drive than the present Prime Minister'. If he had been Foreign Secretary, Lloyd George would already have paid visits to Bucharest, Sofia and Athens.

Just as the Russian and Balkan questions were closely linked, so were both connected with the problem of Italy. In the first two months of the war, when Sazonov could eagerly think in terms of destroying the Habsburg Empire, he was sympathetic to Italian hints that they might join the Entente Powers. In return for this deed Italy would expect a preponderant position in the Adriatic, including the ports of Trieste and Valona, as well as the Trentino. Grey raised no objection, but pressed the British Ambassador in Rome to see whether these suggestions were serious. Rodd saw the Italian Foreign Minister, Salandra, on 13 August. It was then made clear that while Italian neutrality was quite defensible, it might look rather bad for Italy to pass straight into the opposite camp. Instead, Salandra gave his personal assurance that Italy would never join her former allies. It was therefore clear that nothing immediate could be expected and the idea was dropped. In the black weeks of September 1914 Grey would not go any further and the Italians were understandably wary. Sazonov was only interested in immediate support in order to persuade Roumania to join in the war and help him administer the knock-out blow to Austria-Hungary. Correspondingly, from time to time, the Italians were not averse to hinting that an Anglo-Italian agreement might be a useful buffer against the westward drive of the Slav. Grey refused to be drawn into speculation upon contingencies. He also realized that as time passed, the Russian anxieties about the extent of the Italian claims grew. Nicolson shared them, writing that 'M. Sazonov is quite right. Dalmatia is Slav and anxious to unite with Croatia. Slavonia and she would utterly resent Italy attempting to incorporate her . . .' Nor was it certain that Italy would prove a worthwhile ally, even if she were persuaded to join the war.[29] Once again, it was widely held that the Dardanelles expedition would unlock all neutral hearts. The initial successes seemed to prove both in the Balkans and as regards Italy, that they would have to make offers to Britain before it was too late. On 4 March, subject to conditions, Grey was informed of the Italian intention to intervene. Grey had no doubt that this would be desirable: 'The participation on our side of Italy and the Balkan States would enormously facilitate this object; it probably would, in a comparatively short time, effect the collapse of German and Austro-Hungarian resistance.'[30]

In this six months, however, Russian resistance to Italy had steadily grown. The obvious sweetener was to formalize the November understanding about the future of Constantinople. Grey had just been informed from Petrograd that Russian public opinion would now be satisfied with no settlement which did not give Constantinople to Russia. Although Grey told the Russian Ambassador that he could not be more Russian than the Russian Government in his public utterances, he did raise the subject at a meeting of the War Council on 3 March.[31] What Russia required, he said, was an access to the sea which she could control. He was not certain that this particular subject could be safely left to the eventual peace negotiations. It was very important to avoid anything in the nature of a breach with Russia; 'it would never do for us to drift into a position of again checking Russian aspirations in the Dardanelles as we had in the past'. This preliminary discussion, which revealed differences of opinion among his colleagues, was overtaken by a formal written request from Sazonov on 4 March for unconditional post-war possession of both Constantinople and the Straits. In return Russia agreed to recognize British claims in other regions of the Ottoman Empire and elsewhere. This request was circulated to the Cabinet and discussed at its meeting on 9 March.[32] The Russian demands were accepted in principle providing Constantinople remained a free port and the Straits were kept open for the commerce of all nations. The War Council met to discuss the question on the following day. Again, Grey stressed that Germany would like a separate peace with Russia, and that Petrograd was thwarting the intervention of the Balkan neutrals and Italy. 'The urgency of the question', he concluded, 'was to remove Russian suspicions as to our attitude and to get rid of the Russian objections to the participation of other nations.' Despite some objections, Grey was authorized to accept the Russian proposal, subject to the victorious prosecution of the war. The Russians accepted the attendant British stipulations, even that the neutral sphere of Persia should come under British control, and a satisfactory solution seemed to have been reached. The day after this momentous meeting, Hankey discovered that back in February 1903 the C.I.D. had agreed that Russian possession of the Straits 'would not fundamentally alter the present strategic position in the Mediterranean'.[33]

Having gained this objective, Grey now took a firmer line with Sazonov on the question of Italian intervention. He was in some difficulty, however. The sweeping Italian claims to the Dalmatian coast had traditionally been opposed by the Foreign Office. The basis of the Italian claim was undisguisedly strategic—the coastline and ports at the end of the war would be a necessary protection against the advance of Russia. This argument struck a sympathetic chord in the War Council, where some members had been unhappy about the cession of Constantinople. Moreover, the prospect of British success at the Dardanelles, which had prompted the Italian offer, was now fading fast. No Balkan State had joined the entente side—apart from other considerations, the Russians had made it clear that they did not want Greeks or Bulgarians in Constantinople before them. Sazonov found the Italian terms quite unreasonable and for weeks haggled over them. In turn, the Italians declared that only substantial concessions would persuade them to enter a war which many of their countrymen were still firmly against. In the end, when the tide of battle turned against Russia, Sazonov became anxious for Italian assistance. The final compromise was not Grey's work. He had withdrawn to Fallodon to rest for a few weeks. It was the Prime Minister himself who produced the final settlement, and the Treaty of London, embodying his formulae, was signed on 26 April. Italy did not join the war for another month (she still had to declare war on Germany) and the results of her intervention were not immediately detectable. Meanwhile, the Russian armies were in full retreat and the Dardanelles expedition had fallen far short of expectation. In writing to his old friend Sydney Buxton, now Governor-General of South Africa, that 'it is also in my opinion certain that the war cannot last more than a few months longer. England could go on for a long time, but the Continent cannot; & particularly Germany cannot, the waste of men & money is too great', the Foreign Secretary was being unduly optimistic.[34]

No one involved in the negotiations with Italy pretended that the settlement corresponded with the principle of national self-determination. When he was trying to moderate the Italian terms, Grey noted that they would 'not only involve a sacrifice of that principle of nationality . . . but would permanently disturb relations between Italy and her new neighbours'.[35] But he did not propose to do anything about this unfortunate fact. He could not. Like an estate agent selling houses, he was arranging a complex series of transactions in which it was essential that no one should drop out. In this instance, Serbia might have been accommodated by further expansion in Macedonia at the expense of Bulgaria or Greece. Bulgaria might have been accommodated at the expense of Greece, and Greece at the expense of Turkey. Or the sequence could have been reversed. In any event, complete 'justice' was unobtainable. The Treaty of London did, however, cause some difficulties straightaway. Some of the terms leaked out and supporters of the South Slavs protested to Grey. His basic argument, in reply, was that on some occasions Great Powers had to act like Great Powers. 'The Serbs and other Slavs,' he told Seton-Watson, 'who are really going to gain more than any one else, must not deny to those who are fighting for them the means of securing victory.'[36] One might not like particular links in the chain, but it could not be broken without common disaster. Grey regretted the violations of the principle, but felt that the attacks made upon him by individuals with strong emotional links with the South Slav peoples showed a want of proportion. Whether they liked it or not, except incidentally, he had gone to war against Germany, not embarked on a Nationality Crusade. Pious aspirations to secure the rights of the smaller nationalities of Europe on an unassailable foundation certainly did not imply that they all had a right to independent statehood. In Grey's estimation, it was not a major British war aim to destroy the Habsburg Monarchy.[37]

If Grey could have succeeded in preserving Ottoman neutrality, he would equally have felt no compulsion to destroy that Empire either. Grey's hot defence of the Ambassador, Mallet, while showing commendable loyalty, also testifies to his own awareness that he had misjudged the situation.[38] The destruction of the Ottoman Empire meant, of course, far more than just the question of Constantinople. At the War Council in which the concession to Russia was made, Churchill and Kitchener both pressed for British control of Alexandretta on the Syrian coast, in order to provide a post-war base to counter France and Russia. But it was clear that the French claims in the area would be extensive. Crewe thought that Russia and France did not seem to realize that 'we may claim particular interest in the fate of the western half of Turkey in Asia, and of Palestine'. Southern Mesopotamia, with its chief town, Basrah, had been under British control since the end of 1914. This advance had been made by an expeditionary force of the Indian Army, and in February 1915, Hardinge, the Viceroy, promised that Turkish rule would not be restored in its pre-1914 form.[39] Crewe wanted the Foreign Secretary to make it clear that British desiderata were not simply confined to this area. Grey did not share that enthusiasm shown by some colleagues for snapping up a port here and a harbour there. He tried to restrain ambitions by presenting two essential questions. Would the acquisition of fresh territories make Britain stronger or weaker? Should account be taken of the strong feeling that Islam ought to have a political as well as a religious existence? In asking these questions, it was clear that Grey himself was a reluctant expansionist in the Near East. British interests might be as well served by the creation of a Moslem Arab Empire, possibly incorporating Mesopotamia.[40] Churchill felt that it had been a pity 'that we let the Russians talk of "giving" us Egypt—we have had it for years *in fact* and wanted no victorious war to give it to us *in form*'. He hoped Grey would not allow Britain to be pushed out of all interest in the Near East on the grounds that Egypt was her prize. 'That wd. be paying for Egypt twice over.'[41] The Foreign Secretary did not like carving up Asia Minor in advance. As he wrote retrospectively, 'the thing seemed rather premature: what we needed first was to concentrate on winning the war'.[42] An interdepartmental committee was appointed, under Sir Maurice de Bunsen, to examine British territorial claims in the area. When this body reported, Grey was prepared to consider the problem in greater depth.

There was one aspect of the Near East, however, on which Grey had already been button-holed by Herbert Samuel, the President of the Local Government Board. After Asquith's speech at the Guildhall on 5 November in which he declared that the Ottoman Government had rung its own death-knell, Samuel saw Grey. He pointed out that an opportunity might arise for the restoration of a Jewish state in the land of Palestine. The geographical situation, close to Egypt, would render it essential, whatever arrangement was reached for the territory, that the inhabitants should be well disposed towards the British Empire. The Jews would show that goodwill. According to Samuel's note of the interview, Grey was receptive. He even went so far as to say that 'if any proposals were put forward by France or any other Power with regard to Syria, it would be important not to acquiesce in any plan which would be inconsistent with the creation of a Jewish State in Palestine'. It is difficult to say how accurate this report is, or with what care Grey was choosing his words. Certainly when Samuel later reported to Weizmann, the Zionist leader, that 'Sir Edward Grey is interested in the project, especially from the point of view of creating a Jewish cultural centre', something very different from a sovereign state seems to have been involved.[43] In the spring of 1915, therefore, it was already clear that the settlement of the Near East would involve the solution of some formidable problems.

If the death-knell of the Ottoman Empire had already been tolled and the shape of the Habsburg Empire was in doubt, the British Empire seemed doomed to expansion. The response of the Dominions had been one of the heartening features of the war. The psychological stimulus was as important as any contribution which could be made immediately. This encouragement was achieved by glossing over some of the more painful realities. There was an Afrikaner rebellion in 1914 of some gravity. Much French-Canadian opinion was bitterly opposed to intervention. Nevertheless, these obstacles had been overcome within the countries concerned, and the Dominions were not dragooned into assisting the mother country. In each case, quite apart from sentiment, there were very good reasons for participation.[44] Yet, precisely because they were not simply trotting obediently behind Britain, the Dominions could exercise power in ways which might not altogether coincide with the views of London. They were fortunate in having a Colonial Secretary who was prepared to fight their battles for them. Having spent the previous few years trying to foist miscellaneous colonies on Germany, Harcourt was now quite anxious to strip her of those she actually held. It was discovered that Germany was not (as had been widely assumed before 1914) on a par with Britain as a colonial power. South African troops invaded German South-West Africa in January 1915 and captured the capital, Windhoek, in May. The German troops surrendered a couple of months later. German Togoland had already capitulated, and it was anticipated that victory could easily be achieved in the Cameroons and German East Africa. The latter was to prove an optimistic supposition. The Colonial Secretary, in a memorandum, 'The Spoils', in March 1915, argued that the control of these colonies would be essential for the future security of the Empire. It would mean that even if the war in Europe eventually stalemated to peace, and Germany consolidated her military gains, the British Empire would have also gained a tangible benefit. In particular, British communications with the Cape would be safeguarded. Harcourt rather fancied the fine harbour of Duala in the Cameroons, otherwise he was prepared to allow France the major part of the colony, in exchange for a general tidying up of little colonial difficulties in other parts of the globe. Grey was again anxious about this enthusiasm, writing to Harcourt: 'I contend that the occupation is *provisional* and that my language is clear . . .'[45] Sir Edward did not want to upset the French by mopping up colonies in Africa while the situation on the Western front was still so precarious. He may also have been influenced by Samuel's argument that to strip Germany of her African colonies would be to provide materials for a war of revenge in the future. This suggestion of Samuel's was not entirely disinterested, for 'if Great Britain can obtain the compensations, which public opinion will demand, in Mesopotamia and Palestine, and not in German East Africa and West Africa, there is more likelihood of a lasting peace'.[46] There was also more likelihood of a home for Jews.

It was not only in the Near East and Africa that the question of annexation presented itself. The disposal of the German colonies in the Pacific also posed formidable problems. On 1 August, Grey had seen the Japanese Ambassador and informed him that in the event of war, he did not anticipate that Britain would call on Japanese assistance, under the terms of the alliance, unless Germany attacked Hong Kong or Wei-hai-wei. On the outbreak of war, however, the Admiralty came to the conclusion that Japanese assistance in hunting down German warships in the China Sea would be invaluable. Grey was advised, both by the Minister in Peking and from Hong Kong, against this course. It would 'endanger the stability of the existing regime in China, to say nothing of the inevitable effect it would have upon our future political influence in this country and our prestige in Asia generally'. Crowe reacted strongly to this dispatch. Such a view showed a horizon limited to China. The Minister did not understand the nature of the war, in which the continued existence of Britain itself was at stake: 'What is wanted is to strike hard with all our might in all the four corners of the world.'[47] If Sir John Jordan had a Chinese horizon, Crowe had a European one. In face of Australasian and American anxiety, Grey told the Japanese that he did not wish them to intervene for the moment, using the pretext that they refused to limit the scope of their involvement. Not surprisingly, the Japanese were offended and Grey had to work hard to repair the damage he had done. Agreement was eventually reached, though the Japanese signifi-cantly refrained from mentioning any restrictions on the scope of their activity. On 23 August, Japan declared war on Germany.

In August and September, New Zealand and Australian troops occupied Samoa and German New Guinea respectively. The Dominion Ministers hoped, and pressed for assurances, that the Japanese would confine themselves to naval warfare. They became very alarmed when the Japanese occupied the German islands north of the Equator in October 1914. Opinion in London was somewhat divided. Churchill was still anxious for maximum naval co-operation with Japan—indeed, it was indispensable if the Germans were to be defeated in the Far East. Harcourt felt that he had to appease the colonial wrath. Grey stood in the middle. He wrote privately to Harcourt on 23 November: 'The Australians must hold their hand somehow till we have come to an under-standing with the Japanese. There are materials for a tragic row.'[48] Despite American anxieties, Grey was quite clear that '... Japan must have compensation after the war proportionate to her efforts' but he was again anxious to cool annexationist ardour. He insisted with regard to newly conquered territory that 'the only acceptable basis is that it should be without prejudice to final arrangements to be made in time of peace. ...'[49] Temporary arrangements, however, have a way of becoming permanent and the Australasian Dominions were to have to reconcile themselves to a Japanese presence in the Pacific north of the Equator.

One further question involving Japan had to be considered. Should she be brought formally into the wartime alliance as a full partner? For different reasons, both France and Russia favoured this idea, but the Japanese themselves were suspicious. It might complicate a Far Eastern settlement, after the war, which was bound to favour them. Japan did not sign the Declaration of London on 5 September, and Grey did not press her. Some of his colleagues had visions of extensive Japanese collaboration in Europe, but Grey knew that there was little hope of troops, and possibly grave complication if they did appear. 'It is clear', he wrote to Haldane at the end of December, 'that Japanese help would be of more use with the Russians than anywhere. If the Japanese would only send artillery it would make a great difference to the Russians.'[50]

Since the United States was not at war, Grey successfully tried to keep control over policy towards her. He was prepared to lose influence over other matters where military considerations directly impinged. He saw it as his responsibility to minimize the conflict which would inevitably arise over British blockade policy. Initially, he was helped by the fact that hopes were still entertained of a decisive battle against Germany at sea. Thereafter, when a long haul seemed more likely, the pressure grew on him to stop all German imports, including those from the United States. Almost from the outbreak of war, Grey had privately concluded that the attitude of the United States could be vital in determining its outcome. As he wrote subsequently, 'It was better therefore to carry on the war without blockade, if need be, than to incur a break with the United States about contraband, and thereby deprive the Allies of the resources necessary to carry on the war at all or with any chance of success.' The object of his diplomacy was 'to secure the maximum of blockade that could be enforced without a rupture with the United States'.[51]

The Foreign Secretary's desire to be conciliatory did not mean that he would fall in meekly with whatever the Americans proposed. In particular, he was adamant in his refusal to accept the body of rules, the so-called Declaration of London, referring to maritime warfare. These had been discussed at great length in London during 1908–9. After initial wavering, the Liberal Government had refused to give the Declaration the force of law. Now, because the Declaration was favourable to neutral trade during wartime, the Americans wished to see it enforced. Under its provisions, belligerents could still capture 'absolute' contraband (chiefly munitions and material of direct use to armed forces) and 'conditional' contraband (chiefly goods such as food and clothing), which might be used by armed forces. However, essential raw materials, including cotton, rubber and copper, were supposed to be inviolate. There was also some dispute about the right of a belligerent to capture conditional contraband bound for a neutral port, which might then reach enemy territory. Despite strong pressure on him from Wilson and Lansing, Grey would not give way.[52] In his handling of this complex matter, the Foreign Secretary was helped by the sympathetic attitude of the American Ambassador in London, Walter Hines Page, although Page's known pro-British sympathies led to considerable distrust in Washington. Late in October, the United States gave way, and Grey was 'very sensible of the friendly spirit shown by the President'. While ships might have to be detained to make sure their cargoes would be landed and consumed in a neutral territory, it was not to be assumed that the cargo was going to be captured or confiscated.[53] The subsequent British Order in Council of 29 October declared British adherence to the Declaration in general terms, but added copper, iron, aluminium, rubber, petrol and oil to the list of absolute contraband. However, the President of the Board of Trade, Runciman, helped him to block the French request that cotton should be added to the list. Page had warned Grey that 1914 had seen an exceptionally good American cotton crop. If cotton had been put on the list, the outcry in the States would have been extremely dangerous. Runciman too agreed that everything possible and effective ought to be done 'short of a quarrel with American opinion'.[54] Even so, it was obvious that friction was bound to occur when vessels were detained for inspection, but Grey did his best to see that delays were reduced to a minimum, and on occasion offered to purchase consignments of cotton if that eased the situation. For his part, Page insisted that the British were not using their sea-power to gain commercial advantage: 'They have but one thought now—to starve out the enemy.'[55] How long this uneasy equilibrium would last was another matter. As the British Ambassador, Spring-Rice, wrote, while Britain was 'undoubtedly in the right in exercising our right of search we can only exercise it at great inconvenience to neutral nations. . . .'[56]

The crisis came in late January and February 1915, although the dispute did not rise directly out of the contraband regulations. Grey was seriously alarmed by the American Ship Purchase Bill, and, in particular, by the transfer to American ownership of a German vessel, the *Dacia*, whose new owner then proposed to send her to Bremen with a cargo of cotton. On 18 January, Ambassador Page had what he described as his 'most ominous conversation' with the Foreign Secretary. Two days later, Grey made it clear that the *Dacia* would be treated as a test case and refused passage. He had little alternative, since public opinion in England was taking an increasingly anti-American turn. Naval and military pressure for an intensification of the economic blockade was also mounting.

Grey took the unusual step of writing privately to Colonel House, the President's unofficial, yet influential, adviser, to warn him that public opinion was becoming antagonized both by the attitude and by the actions of the United States. It seemed that Americans were bent on paralysing the advantage which Britain gained from her sea-power, while leaving Germany's military and scientific gains intact.[57] A direct confrontation was avoided by letting the French navy capture the ship and apply the traditionally strict rules of the French Prize Court. The situation, however, remained tense and fresh shipping crises could be expected.

The second challenge Grey had to face in the early months of 1915 presented as great a difficulty—the American attempt to mediate. Spring-Rice warned him of the strength of the German vote in America and he felt that 'this peace mission is most probably promoted by the German and Austrian Governments. . . .'[58] Grey had always been very wary of trying to counter this pro-German opinion in the United States. Some of his colleagues had wanted to see a massive expansion of British propaganda, but Grey was against this, reporting to the Prime Minister that 'we should not appear in any way to emulate what has been described as "the orgy of second-rate publicity" in which the Germans have indulged. . . .' In December 1914 he wrote again that it was 'difficult to overstate the importance of avoiding wrong methods of presenting our case. . . .'[59] He had a fine old-fashioned notion that truth would out, and that the issues of the war could be left to the uninstructed good sense of the American people.

In the last months of 1914, there had been a great deal of discussion in Washington about the possibility of American mediation. In particular, House had been having what he believed to be encouraging talks with the German Ambassador, Bernstorff. From these, he believed that it would be possible to start peace talks on the basis of evacuating and indemnifying Belgium, combined with drastic disarmament to ensure permanent peace. Grey could not refuse to consider these terms, when they were conveyed to him, without seriously compromising the Allied cause. He therefore replied through Spring-Rice that personally, he would be prepared to consider such a proposal. However, he reminded House that some of his colleagues might feel differently, and also that Britain had her allies to consider. When it became clear that, nevertheless, Washington was determined to explore the question seriously, Grey tried to dampen the enthusiasm. In a message conveyed to the

President in early January 1915, he stressed that the time had not come for peace overtures. He wanted Wilson to know that if they were in a position to do so after the war, the Allies would require the return to France of Alsace-Lorraine and the Russian acquisition of Constantinople. House ought not to forget that France and Russia would have to be consulted about European peace, and he would not dare broach the subject with them unless he was satisfied that the German disposition was genuine. Personally, he remained convinced that Germany was merely trying to embarrass Britain in the eyes of American opinion. Wilson would still not be put off, and, on his behalf, House arrived in London on 6 February. Talks began shortly afterwards.

In his report of the first conversation with Grey, House told the President that he had discussed the situation frankly and unreservedly. The Foreign Secretary had stressed to him the difficulties in which the Allies found themselves, particularly in the Balkans. Negotiations with Italy and Roumania were also not going well. As regards the terms of settlement, Grey was prepared to consider House's suggestion of neutralizing Alsace-Lorraine. He also stated that Russia might be satisfied simply with Constantinople. In turn, he pressed the United States to come into some general guarantee of world-wide peace—House claimed that he evaded answering this plea. Accompanied by Tyrrell and Page respectively, the two men met again a few days later. This time, Grey stressed that in his opinion the German approaches were quite insincere, while House disagreed. The rest of the conversation revolved around American involvement in the final settlement, but House was very coy, saying that it was an unwritten law and fixed policy of the United States not to become involved in European affairs.[60] Grey's worst fears about the mission were removed by House's assurance that he 'had no intention of pushing the question of peace, for in my opinion, it could not be brought about, in any event, before the middle of May or the first of June. I could see the necessity for the Allies to try out their new armies in the Spring. . . .'[61] This statement hardly corresponded with the President's intentions, but it did mean that when, a few weeks later, House proposed to travel on to Berlin, Grey this time raised no objection.

In his discussions in Berlin, House's great hope was that he could induce the British to consent to the freedom of the seas as one of the peace conditions, in return for which Germany would have no call to retain Belgium. The President was delighted, writing that the suggestion seemed 'very promising and may afford the opening we are looking for'.[62] House then spent some time in Paris, and from there wrote to Grey in rather different terms: 'I did not find conditions in Berlin favourable for any discussion looking towards peace, consequently I did not remain long or say much.' Nevertheless, though there were few points of contact, the visit had been of value because it had revealed interest in the concept of the 'freedom of the seas'. But, in view of his experience, he stressed that he was not going to move hastily.[63] In the meantime, he begged Grey to be as conciliatory as possible on blockade questions. The Foreign Secretary was delighted to receive this letter, for it enabled him to confirm his belief that 'the German people will not contemplate terms of peace except on the assumption that they are both the aggrieved and the victorious party'.[64] While this radical divergence remained, there was no chance of finding peace terms acceptable to both sides.

The reason for House's renewed warning about the blockade was the new British Order in Council of 11 March. This had been dictated by the need for mobility in face of the submarine menace. The idea was that instead of confiscating neutral cargoes, they would simply be prevented from ever reaching neutral or German ports. Not surprisingly, there was an outburst of protest in the United States, but after careful work by Page, who made it clear that the British were quite determined, the President reserved the legal position but took no further action beyond a formal protest. Grey recognized what he termed the 'friendly and courteous tone' of this Note. He stressed the strength of public feeling on the issue, and also his own desire to avoid interference with bona fide neutral commerce. House stayed on in London throughout May, mixing in London political society, and trying to dampen Anglo-American friction. It is difficult to believe that he was as optimistic about the chances of peace talks as has been suggested. Certainly, the Foreign Secretary, capitalizing on House's expressed disappointment in Berlin, now quietly reduced Bernstorff's peace talk in Washington, which had initiated the mission, to 'fudge'. As for the freedom of the seas, Grey firmly stated that 'if Germany means that her commerce is to go upon the sea in time of war, while she remains free to make war upon other nations at will, it is not a fair proposition'.[65] For the time being, however, Anglo-American relations were preserved by the deterioration in relations between Berlin and Washington on the submarine question, especially following the sinking of the

Lusitania on 7 May. When House finally left for home at the beginning of June, he was convinced that the United States would 'inevitably drift into war with Germany and before long'. Grey replied that 'Germany is the peril to-day, but the peril will recur every century in Europe, if Europe is left to itself. And the peril now cannot be confined to one continent—the world is too closely knit together by modern inventions and conditions.' As for the immediate future, it did seem possible that 'overconfidence may lead Germany to be reckless enough to push you into war. . . .'[66]

The House mission therefore ended in rather different circumstances from those in which it had begun. Grey had handled House skilfully, and allowed events, rather than a direct personal negative, to nullify the purpose of the exercise. He had shown himself willing to be conciliatory on the blockade question, while holding firm to the principle. He was no doubt helped by the fact that House, and therefore Wilson, realized that if they placed him in an impossible position, he would only be replaced by someone likely to take an even tougher stand. Despite his success, he did not like the work, writing to Rosebery that '. . . the F.O. is nauseous in war time—a mass of questions of contraband & kindred subjects that don't exist in time of peace and are a disagreeable brood spawned by war'.[67] Despite House's prophecy of impending American intervention, he remained sceptical and did not attempt to apply any overt pressure. He agreed strongly 'as to the folly of our endeavouring to persuade the United States to take part in the war. Should they do so it must be entirely of course as the result of their own spontaneous action.'[68] If they should go to war, he hoped that in the general aspects of the peace the United States would take the lead, 'as distinct from local and particular conditions such as the destiny of Alsace & Lorraine, which are purely European'.[69] This concern for an ill-defined pact of guarantee, or league of nations, was not a hasty expedient, devised to put him in good odour with influential segments of American opinion. It represented his own deeply felt (felt rather than thought out) reaction to the failure of his own diplomacy. Theodore Roosevelt did not like to see Grey's activities in this direction: 'The encouragement given by Grey to such movements did not in the smallest degree placate anti-English sentiment here. It did in some small degree weaken the hands of those of us who were trying to make our people see that it was ignoble and cowardly to fail in the present to do our duty against Germany and for civilization. . . .'[70] Roosevelt failed to appreciate that besides the tough-minded statesmen he had encountered in 1911, there was also a sentimental pacifist. It was another matter whether the Coalition Government would provide the right atmosphere for the cultivation of such sentiments.

When the last Liberal Government came to an end in May 1915, it was already clear that if the Allies won the war, the map of the world would show considerable changes. Despite his poor health and low spirits, it is difficult to believe that Grey blundered badly in this initial period of the war. Yet it is easy to see that his presence was not inspiring, and that moves to displace him were made. The Prime Minister claimed to have reports that Churchill was conspiring to this effect in February 1915 but he gave no encouragement. Asquith still rated Grey after Crewe at the head of the Cabinet batting order.[71] Any moves of this kind were then swallowed up in the wider manœuvres which resulted in the formation of the Coalition Government in May 1915. The Foreign Secretary was not involved in the bargaining and accepted the reshuffle with a certain foreboding.[72] The only event which shocked him was the exclusion of Haldane. Grey tried to get the decision reversed, but when Asquith made it clear that this was impossible, he offered his own resignation.[73] It is likely that the Prime Minister stressed the undesirability of leaving at such a delicate juncture in the war. He may have added that, together, they could hold the Liberal ship steady. Grey yielded, and agreed to carry on, but it is hardly likely that his feelings for Asquith remained unaltered. After they were all out of office, Grey wrote to Haldane's sister: 'Asquith is very easy going and often does not realise the situation of other people. I hear he is in his own way sore about the way he has been treated by Ll.G., but Richard's case is far more unjust & exasperating than that of any of us.'[74] Now, for better or worse, whatever his personal feelings, Grey's political survival was bound up with that of the Prime Minister himself.

16

The Final Phase,
May 1915-December 1916

There is something pathetic about the last eighteen months of Grey's political career. While he had always professed his dislike of office, he now did so with a new intensity. He felt increasingly exhausted. 'My eyes are worse', he wrote to Buxton in May 1915, 'and a third independent opinion forbids me to read or write at all for some months. I am told that if I do this and live mostly in the dark and always with dark glasses, the trouble may be stopped in a year or so and get no worse.'[1] Dark glasses he did wear, but he could not remain in office and observe the other conditions. The alternative, of course, was to resign. At the end of 1915 he wrote to Asquith that he had not pressed his resignation in May because it had been represented to him that public opinion, both at home and abroad, would have been gravely disturbed. 'Under ordinary circumstances', he added, 'I should have given up the work more than a year ago to save my eyesight. . . .' This time, he really did want to go.[2]

The decision to resign was not, however, simply because of his failing eyesight. The first six months of the Coalition Government had not been a success. The progress of the war was disappointing, and increased the strains within and between the parties. After the departure of Haldane, Grey had increasingly aligned himself with what might broadly be termed the 'civilian' party in the Cabinet —in particular with Runciman, the President of the Board of Trade, and with McKenna, the Chancellor of the Exchequer. They expressed traditional Liberal anxieties about the financing of the war and about the condition of domestic industry. The obsession of their Conservative colleagues with increasing military manpower was misplaced, if it led to a shortage of labour at home, with consequent loss of industrial production. When, under considerable pressure, Asquith supported a proposal to enroll single men, Simon declared he objected in principle and would resign. Runciman and McKenna were not opposed to conscription on this ground, but felt it would damage the economy. Grey agreed with them. He told the Prime Minister that since he did not believe that their views would prevail in the Cabinet, it would be better for him to go at this point, rather than resign separately at a later date.

Asquith claimed to receive the letter 'with profound astonishment, if indeed not disgust'. According to the King's private secretary, he was 'naturally much hurt by what seemed to him desertion by one of his oldest friends and colleagues at a time of unusual trouble if not danger'.[3] Asquith wrote to Grey saying that he would have to reconsider his own position if he were so deserted: 'I have not as yet received any definite resignation from any colleague. Yours would, of course, be universally interpreted as a German triumph.'[4] The Foreign Secretary did not immediately wilt before this moral blackmail. In the Haldane affair, he had seen the Prime Minister desert a close colleague, and the frequency of Asquith's appeals for loyalty diminished their potency. Nevertheless, he did agree to stay, though the Prime Minister had to make a concession to the rebellious trio by establishing a committee to examine the merits of the competing military and economic claims. The French were to be informed that Britain could not supply both more men and more money indefinitely. Sir Edward was therefore able to stick to his belief that 'finance may in the long run be the decisive factor in the whole war'.[5]

Grey would have done well to press his resignation at this point. Certainly, many of his friends thought so privately. His cousin Albert wrote to their mutual friend, Munro Ferguson: 'As for Edward, my cousin Hamlet, he is stale and tired, and that is a danger. He wants a long holiday in order that he may bring a fresh mind to the consideration of foreign affairs.' Munro Ferguson agreed: 'E.G. was never intended for the service of Mars.'[6] Esher wrote in his journal: 'Edward Grey's appearance shocked and distressed me. His eyes grow dimmer and he sleeps only a few hours at night. When he wakes he manages to work with a strong light and then drops off to sleep early in the morning.'[7] Less sympathetic observers wrote privately that he was 'done for', Lady Courtney suspecting that 'he has ceased to believe in himself, as some of us have long ceased to believe he was an able man'.[8] Old Hicks Beach wrote to his son that Asquith and Grey ought to resign, guessing correctly that the latter would, if allowed, but 'Asquith (and his wife) are limpets'.[9] Something of a whispering campaign also began against the Foreign Secretary. Lady Helen Primrose thought it worthwhile honouring Bonar Law with the story that Grey was quite changed: 'Ld. Haldane had taken possession of him. He seemed to be under a *hypnotic* influence & had no will of his own.'[10] Other more dangerous public persons were similarly alarmed. Lord Northcliffe believed that in mid-December 'the Foreign Secretary has been spending most, if not all, of his time during the past week at Lord Haldane's office, or house or both'. Some great pro-German conspiracy was clearly under way, especially since Northcliffe's informant told him that 'Grey was particularly lachrymose on the subject of the starving German women and children. . . .'[11] In fact, just about this time, Grey was disappointing Haldane by refusing to authorize publication of further Foreign Office documents, which the latter believed would clear his name. Nevertheless, mere association with Haldane was tantamount to treason in some quarters, and some of this malignity rubbed off on Grey.

His health did not improve. In May 1916 he again wrote to Buxton that the oculist had reported that if he could give up work for a year or more, he might keep his sight for the rest of his life, but if not, his chances were poor. The solution was for Lord Crewe to take over the Foreign Office for some ten days in every two months or six weeks. On these occasions, he fled northwards from London. He was delighted to find, on an expedition with Lord Glenconner, that he could still walk up hills, and last all day, as fit as when he was twenty-five. The loss of his eyesight interfered only with his shooting. In July 1916, he wrote from Fallodon that he was 'unwell & in almost constant pain; it is only gouty acidity . . .' but this was in itself ominous.[12] A further attempt to relieve the pressure on him was made in July. He left the House of Commons for the Lords, on condition that Crewe would still be available as an alternate at the Foreign Office: 'I should indeed be . . . in despair if that could no longer be the case.'[13] He was offered an earldom, but his cousin pointed out that much confusion was likely to result from their being two Earls Grey. Even an earldom was not sufficient to make Edward part with his family name. The King consented that he should become Viscount Grey of Fallodon and he was introduced into the Upper House by Bryce and Haldane. Yet such expedients could not go on indefinitely. It was clearly unsatisfactory that a great office of state in time of war should be held by a man suffering in such a way. Only a Prime Minister intent on his survival would have rejected further attempts to resign, on the pretext that they needed to finish together a war 'they had started'. Nevertheless, his departure was only a matter of time.

The decline in the Foreign Secretary's personal standing was paralleled to an extent by a decline in the status of the Foreign Office itself. There seems to have been a loss of morale, which a fitter Foreign Secretary might have been able to restore. The unusual step was taken, presumably with Grey's approval, of bringing Hardinge, the Viceroy of India, back to the Foreign Office in June 1916, to serve once more as Permanent Under-Secretary. But in the short run, this did little to restore confidence. Those who had been goading the Foreign Office before 1914 now renewed their attacks. The Union of Democratic Control believed that the 'old diplomacy' was discredited for ever. Nor were these views confined to dissenting outsiders. For example, Edwin Montagu, Chancellor of the Duchy of Lancaster, wrote to Eric Drummond, Grey's private secretary, in Feburary 1916 to complain that in his humble opinion 'the diplomatic service is at the root of all our ailments, past and present. And unless we take care, future.' The diplomatic service, 'with its predilection for promotion by seniority, its method of recruitment, its concomitant of divorcing the ambassadors from everything that the Home Government is thinking, its practice of refusing to speak English but of communicating amongst themselves or at home in the language of diplomatic telegrams', had robbed British diplomacy of life. A thorough overhaul was needed.[14]

Criticisms of this kind were very general; more serious were the immediate problems caused by the big increase in the volume of work connected with the blockade, especially after the Order in Council of March 1915. In the new Government, Lord Robert Cecil was appointed Under-Secretary for Foreign Affairs with special responsibility for the blockade. The official organization was at this stage very complicated, involving the Foreign Office, the Admiralty and the Board of Trade, with occasional interventions from the Treasury and the War Office. In September 1915, the War Trade Advisory Committee was formed under Lord Crewe, composed of all committees engaged in contraband work. This did not remove overlapping and friction. Therefore, in February 1916, Grey told Asquith that 'there ought to be control by some Minister in touch with the Foreign Office'. At the Cabinet on 16 February, it was decided that Cecil should undertake this work, retaining his existing office, but becoming a member of the Cabinet.[15] In effect, therefore, there was a dual command and it was Cecil's empire that seemed to be growing. Nor was this the only assault. At the end of August, Grey wrote to Runciman concerning a Board of Trade proposal that it should take over all the commercial work of Embassies and Legations, leaving to the Foreign Office such diplomatic work as could be disentangled. He was most anxious that the Foreign Office view should be considered by whoever decided, so that 'the F.O. should not be abolished without a hearing'.[16]

It is with these personal and institutional factors in mind that foreign policy in this final period should be considered. Grey's chief preoccupation, initially, was with the Balkans and the Dardanelles. Few writers have found much to praise in his conduct of these matters, and there was indeed a certain lethargy in his behaviour which infuriated his more energetic colleagues. He remained unmoved by these criticisms. Basically, his defence remained that in war, diplomacy cannot perform miracles and military considerations must be dominant. The grim fact of the matter, in his judgment, was that the initial assault on the Dardanelles was a failure and that the war was going badly for Russia. In this situation, the ardent wooing of Bulgaria which was urged upon him from many sides seemed to him doomed to disappointment. As he put it in a congenial ornithological metaphor, 'Our bird offered to Bulgaria was not only a smaller and duller bird, but it was receding more and more into the bush. The bird offered by Germany was not only a bigger and brighter bird, but seemed to be coming nearer and nearer to the hand.'[17]

At a lunch party in October 1915, a witty guest, discussing diplomacy in the Balkans, compared Grey in that context to 'sending Parsifal to a poker party'.[18] Besides doing an injustice to the Foreign Secretary's card-playing skills, this amusing remark underestimated his grasp of the Balkan situation. The intransigent selfishness of the Balkan statesmen was only too familiar to him. Confronted by a contradictory bombardment from the Balkan experts in the Cabinet, whose number was legion, he seemed to adopt a fatalistic attitude. The resignation of Carson in October 1915, because of the failure to help Serbia, was a reflection of wider and deeper discontent. The Foreign Secretary was aware of this criticism and wrote to Bonar Law in the hope that he would prevail upon Carson to moderate his remarks. He did not deny his right to a resignation statement, but hoped that he would not 'say anything that will, by encouraging the Turks, have a disastrous effect upon the position of our troops in Gallipoli'.[19] The events in the Near East were necessarily interpreted as a failure on the part of the Prime Minister to co-ordinate the operations. Something of a revolt took place in the Cabinet on 21 October. Grey wrote to Crewe that 'the present state of things cannot continue & that unless some arrangement such as the Cabinet desired is made for the conduct of the war the Cabinet will break up'. His colleagues, in Asquith's absence, had clearly wanted a small directing body, and Grey urged that the Prime Minister should 'associate 3 members with himself & include Lloyd George. . . .'[20] A promising start was subsequently made along these lines, but soon an increasing number of Ministers believed that they had an important contribution to make. Grey himself refused to accept blame for failure in the Dardanelles. In response to criticism that he had not welded together a Balkan bloc, he scrawled on the Prime Minister's copy of one such circular that the War Council had originally only agreed to the whole enterprise on the 'understanding that the Navy would do it alone, and that if the navy failed the whole thing would be treated as a demonstration & given up & that no troops would be required. It appears however from this paper signed W.S.C. that the failure for the Dardanelles is due to Lord Kitchener and myself, though neither of us have been at the Admiralty.' Grey continued to hold Churchill primarily responsible and wept few tears over his subsequent departure from the Government. Nevertheless, he did not believe that the question of responsibility was a suitable subject for wartime investigation. When the Government did give in to the pressure for an inquiry in the following summer, Hankey records Grey as having been 'very disgusted'. Subsequently, Grey wrote that 'nothing so distorted perspective, disturbed impartial judgement, and impaired the sense of strategic values as the operations on Gallipoli'. He himself was not free from those distorted and disturbed judgments.[21]

However correct Grey's comments, they form a pathetic commentary on the conduct of the war and the lack of integrated political/strategic thinking. It was little wonder that a sober estimate of the fortunes of the British Empire at the beginning of 1916 might well have prophesied defeat. Attempts to break through on the

Western front had failed. Gallipoli had ended in disaster. Bulgaria had joined the Central Powers. Serbia and Russian Poland were overrun. The Foreign Secretary had no comfort to offer in this serious situation, and was preoccupied by what he thought were the dangers of a separate peace. In order to encourage France, he supported the dispatch of British troops to Salonika. Robertson, the new C.I.G.S., circulated a memorandum stressing what influence Britain ought to be able to exercise over the policy of her allies. Grey replied in February 1916 that, while it was certainly true that if Britain withheld support, even simply financial support, the Allies could not continue, this view neglected the fact that Germany had made it clear both to France and Russia that comparatively favourable terms were available for them if they left the war. Therefore, while the Allies depended on Britain for any chance whatever of success in the war, he held that 'it is at best doubtful whether we could secure ourselves if the Allies abandon us: we are therefore dependent upon the Allies for our safety to a greater extent than they are upon us'.[22] In 1901, Arthur Acland had written to Asquith concerning Grey: '. . . I think he is a man rather to see difficulties than to help people over them.'[23] In wartime, at least, this judgment was vindicated.

It was this concern for Allied susceptibilities that led Grey to hand over 'provisionally' to the French the greater part of the Cameroons including the port of Duala. He made it clear to the French Ambassador that he expected France to recognize the magnanimity of his action. British colonial feeling would not be pleased by his decision. However, with South Africa in German South-West Africa, he did not want to give the French any grounds for thinking that Britain was bent on acquiring all the German colonies. Apparently, the Colonial Office felt that the Foreign Office had 'let them down' and, despite Bonar Law's agreement, there was criticism that 'if Grey is allowed a free hand—like in this instance— he will fritter away all our bargaining powers before the conclusion of the war. . . .'[24] Grey took the view that the war had first to be won, and a gesture to France would be a valuable means of encouraging her.

The immediate needs of war also took first place in British policy towards Japan. The presentation of the famous 'Twenty-one demands' by the Japanese to China in January 1915 had caused a considerable shock in Britain. If implemented in full, they would amount to a protectorate over China. The Cabinet discussed the question on 7 May, and Grey was instructed to warn the Japanese Government that an attempt to press the fifth part of its demands would be regarded as incompatible with the terms of the Anglo-Japanese alliance. Grey was annoyed by the fact that the demands were presented to China without previously informing London. He neither wished to antagonize Japan, nor allow her to assume that British views could be disregarded. His intervention, therefore, had a salutary effect on Sino-Japanese relations, though it was largely a matter of luck that it did so.[25] At the same time, he recognized that since the Japanese were excluded from British colonies and the United States, they had a right to claim a special position in the Far East. In conversation with the Australian Prime Minister in February 1916, Grey forcefully pointed out that Britain's professions of friendship and requests for aid hardly rang true if Japan were denied any concessions in China. Not willing to change Australian policy, Hughes took the point. Grey therefore humoured the Japanese Ambassador with assurances that 'if Japan did not pursue expansion in Europe, America, or Africa, the Powers who did expand in these Continents ought to be favourable to the expansion of Japanese influence and interest in the Far East'. There would undoubtedly be difficulties at the end of the war, but to refrain from such statements might only encourage German–Japanese peace talks. Rumours were already circulating that the Germans might allow Japan a free hand in the Pacific, China and South-East Asia in return for Japanese acknowledgment of their hegemony in Europe, Africa and the Near East.[26]

It is difficult to evaluate this policy of sweetening Britain's allies. Grey has been the victim of his policy's success. It prevented disaffection and it is therefore easy, probably too easy, to assume that no danger really existed. This balancing of short- and long-term considerations was most acute in the Near East. The War Council meeting in March had revealed a wide divergence of view about the future of the Middle East. Once again, Grey had played a restraining role and the running had been made by the Indian Government and by Kitchener. The former thought in terms of the Persian Gulf and extending treaty relations with local Arab rulers in Mesopotamia. The latter had more ambitious schemes for establishing an Arab Kingdom under British auspices, bounded in the north by the valley of the Tigris and the Euphrates, and containing the chief Moslem Holy Places. The de Bunsen Committee, which had been set up after the March meeting, reported in June 1915. Its brief had been to consider British desiderata in the event of Turkey being partitioned. While it suggested a variety of alternatives, it concluded that zones of interest were preferable to direct partition. Whether as a sphere of interest, or as annexed territory, it advocated a British area running from Acre to Ruwandiz in the north and from Aqaba to Kuwait in the south. It plumped for Haifa rather than Alexandretta as the British port, and the terminus for a possible connexion with Mesopotamia. Since France would have Alexandretta, she would have less reason to interfere in southern Syria. While Palestine would be within the British sphere on this arrangement, it was recognized that its future would have to be decided 'in special negotiations, in which both belligerents and neutrals alike are interested'.[27]

Such a scheme seems in general to have been congenial to Grey, since he thought that it would give minimum offence to France with regard to her interests in Syria. Yet his control over events was, to say the least, not complete. Sharif Husain of Mecca had been approached by Kitchener even before the outbreak of hostilities, and was encouraged to revolt against Constantinople, remove the Holy Places from Turkish control, and take the Arabs out of the war.[28] The British High Commissioner in Cairo, Sir Henry McMahon, was in negotiation with the Sharifians about the price to be paid for this assistance. McMahon seemed inclined to countenance their claims in regions which the French desired, especially in the north. The Sharif's ambitions for the independence of the Arabs, as defined in his letter to McMahon of 14 July 1915, were grandiose and were treated with considerable reserve. But in the ensuing months, the general situation changed. The Sharif began to put pressure on Cairo for clarification, alleging that Turco-German approaches had been made to various Arab societies. This, combined with nervousness about the military situation, led McMahon to become anxious. In letters to Kitchener and Grey he stressed the valuable support the Arabs could give and the need to reach a speedy settlement on the question of their boundaries. Kitchener gave him general support, but, in his reply of 20 October, Grey stressed that no impression should be given that Britain supported Arab interests in Syria in order to advance her own against France. Without further reference to London, McMahon sent a letter to the Sharif on 24 October, pleading in a subsequent letter to Grey that the matter admitted no delay. The fatal letter promised the Arabs independence within the boundaries the Sharif had demanded, subject to two major reservations. The British were to supervise a special administration in the provinces of Baghdad and Basrah, and coastal areas west of the districts of Damascus, Hama, Homs and Aleppo could not be promised without French consent. It has remained a vexed question whether McMahon intended to exclude Palestine; on the whole, it seems that he did.[29]

No doubt suspecting some such complication as this letter, Grey had been careful to suggest to Cambon three days beforehand that they should discuss the frontiers of Syria. The French were aware, though not in detail, that the British were negotiating with the Sharif. The task before Grey was to try to keep faith both with France and with the Sharif. Grey was able to state that French as well as British advisers would be acceptable in the future Arab territories. He revealed that Britain supported the idea of an Arab state—if the Arabs declared their hostility to Turkey and also agreed that it should exclude Syria. The Foreign Secretary also took steps to be certain that the text of McMahon's letter was acceptable to Arab opinion.[30] On 4 November he gave Kitchener a report from a recent visitor to Egypt that it was only necessary to promise the Arabs the four towns of Damascus, Aleppo, Homs and Hama to gain their support. 'As we are risking our Eastern Empire to help the French in a Balkan expedition against our better judgment I think the French ought to agree to this.'[31] Meanwhile, McMahon urged Husain to take active measures to marshal support for the Allies, since it was on the success of such help 'when the time for action comes, that the permanence and strength of our agreement must depend'.[32] Some of Grey's colleagues, especially Austen Chamberlain, the Secretary for India, were sceptical of the whole enterprise. In alarm the latter wrote to Grey on 29 December fearing that the Government was getting 'into a great mess with these negotiations of MacMahon's'. He wanted to know when the 'time for action' was going to be, and concluded: 'Are we then going to add the independence of "Arabia" to all the other objects which we have pledged ourselves to secure before we make peace?'[33] Unfortunately, Grey chose to see Chamberlain rather than write. A written reply might have given historians the illumination they need on the nature of this 'independence', and the extent to which Grey held himself committed to it. In June 1916, he admitted that he did not have a 'clear head' about British promises and intentions in Mesopotamia.[34] A few months later, he wrote privately on the question of recognizing an independent Arab state: 'We were, of course, prepared to do that if he [the Sharif] succeeded in establishing his independence; for all we were pledged to was that the Moslem holy places should remain in independent Moslem hands.'[35]

The negotiations with France were conducted by Sir Mark Sykes, who was aware of the letters exchanged with Mecca. He came to a provisional agreement with his French colleague, Georges-Picot, in early 1916. They then had to visit Petrograd to discuss the portions involving Russia, and the draft agreement was then sent to McMahon in Cairo. The left hand knew what the right was doing. Yet the discrepancies were not as significant as has often been supposed. Both the McMahon letter and the Sykes–Picot draft ratified the British control of southern Mesopotamia and the French control of the Lebanon/Syria coastal strip. Both provided for the independence of the Arab peoples if they played their part. But while the independence of Arab Arabia was assumed in both cases, the Sykes–Picot agreement went on to specify the areas in which British and French 'assistance' would be provided. The heart of the matter is the meaning of the term 'independence'. If the Sykes–Picot agreement went back on the British undertaking to Husain, it is hard to understand the Cambon–Grey correspondence of August 1916 in which Cambon agreed to the withdrawal of the words 'protect an independent Arab State' on the ground that it might be misunderstood to involve a sort of protectorate 'while we have simply meant to guarantee the full independence of the new State'.[36] Here again, however, there are degrees of independence and, as has been observed, 'the Sharif had not fired a shot; no one knew how far his writ ran, except that it did not extend over Ibn Saud; the Turks were still attacking the Suez Canal, threatening Aden, and holding a British force besieged in Kut'.[37] In face of this profound uncertainty, and the anxiety of the Indian Government, Grey had to insist on safeguarding British interests.

Apart from the stipulation that Britain should control Acre and Haifa outright, the Sykes–Picot agreement was simply more specific where the McMahon letter was vague. It stipulated that Palestine should have an international administration, the form of which was to be determined by the Allies and representatives of the Sharif of Mecca. There was no reference in the agreement to the interests of the Jews, and the subject had not featured in earlier Anglo-French exchanges. Nevertheless, there was one bizarre episode in which Grey was to some degree involved. The Foreign Secretary had been receiving reports from Spring-Rice and others about the pro-

German sympathies of American Jewry. It was alleged that the treatment of Jews in Russia was a major reason for this sympathy. He was also informed that Zionist sentiment in the United States was growing. Advice on the subject was taken from the Jewish, but anti-Zionist, journalist, Lucien Wolf. McMahon in Cairo also forwarded a message from the leader of the Jewish community in Alexandria that 'England could assure herself the active support of the Jews all over the neutral world if only the Jews knew that British policy accorded with their aspirations for Palestine'. Lord Robert Cecil observed at the beginning of March: 'I do not think it is easy to exaggerate the international power of the Jews.' The prospect of an 'international administration' in Palestine was undoubtedly uncongenial to some Foreign Office opinion, while its annexation had an appeal to some members of the Cabinet—though too much can be made of this fact.[38] Some were also sceptical of the real value of the Arab revolt—if it ever started.

Early in March 1916, Wolf submitted a formula for consideration by the Foreign Office. It stated that if Palestine fell into the sphere of Britain or France at the end of the war, 'the historic interest that country possesses for the Jewish community' was to be taken into account. 'The Jewish population will be secured in the enjoyment of civil and religious liberty, equal political rights with the rest of the population, reasonable facilities for immigration and colonisation, and such municipal privileges in the towns and colonies inhabited by them as may be shown to be necessary.' The Foreign Office found the formula 'unobjectionable', and Grey sent it to Paris and Petrograd, even adding the gloss that the scheme might be made even more attractive to the majority of Jews by adding the prospect that when the Jewish colonists had grown 'strong enough to cope with the Arab population, they may be allowed to take the management of the internal affairs of Palestine (with the exception of Jerusalem and the Holy Places) into their own hands'.[39] Whether or not the proposal was designed to further British interests, or whether dictated by the American situation, it came to nothing. Although the Russian Government was not unsympathetic, the French Government refused to take it up. Nevertheless, although by the summer of 1916 Grey's proposal was dead, the notion of a Jewish Commonwealth had been given diplomatic currency. Not that there is any evidence that Grey could be called a Zionist. He did not discuss the proposal with Samuel or with any Zionist leader. The *Zionist Review* was able to quote Grey in support of the Balfour

Declaration when it was made in 1917, but like many others, he had subsequent doubts: '. . . a Zionist home undoubtedly means or implies a Zionist Government over the district in which the home is planned, and if 95 per cent of the population of Palestine are Arabs, I do not see how you can establish other than an Arab Government, without prejudice to their civil rights.'[40]

When Grey left office at the end of 1916, there seemed very little to show for all this intricate and secret diplomatic activity. The agreements which have since become such a source of controversy seemed rather academic. The Sharif of Mecca did rise against the Turks in June 1916, but as the Government of India had long prophesied, it was a limited and localized rebellion. Officers in Cairo forecast that Husain's head would soon dangle from a Turkish scaffold. In a way, Grey must have been relieved that a policy of partition, for which he had little enthusiasm, should have run, literally, into the sands. This, however, is to suppose that he had a policy. The evidence seems to suggest that his role in the Near East was very shadowy. It is significant that the Anglo-French negotiations were conducted by Sykes, who was not a Foreign Office man, and who, on his own admission, worked throughout in close consultation with Kitchener's aide. Even 'Sir Edward Grey's proposal of March 1916' turns out to have been drafted in the Foreign Office by O'Beirne, with corrections and endorsement by Crewe in Grey's absence.[41] The Foreign Secretary may have 'approved', but the drive clearly came from elsewhere. It must also be remembered that where Palestine was concerned, Lord Robert Cecil had strong Zionist sympathies, and was not reluctant to indulge them. The Foreign Secretary remained nominally in control of Near Eastern policy, but how much direct control he exercised is another matter.

The already mentioned changes in the administration of blockade policy were only in part for administrative convenience. They were also the result of attacks made on the Foreign Secretary's policy. Nevertheless, the fact that these attacks were made is in itself an indication that Grey still did possess a strong, if diminishing, influence. He continued the attempt to preserve Anglo-American relations as his special domain. The first months of the Coalition Government were extremely difficult from the standpoint of these relations. President Wilson was pressing for the adequate implementation of the assurance to the United States given in the Note accompanying the March Order in Council. By the mid-summer of

1915, it seemed that his firm, but not passionate, response to the sinking of the *Lusitania* had produced a conciliatory attitude from Germany, and instead, a serious crisis with Britain was pending. By July, it had become clear that, contrary to House's prophecy, the United States was not going to fight Germany. Grey was not surprised, having been warned from various sources not to overrate the strength of American feeling. What caused him more alarm was the report that pressure was building up in America to ban the export of arms. The administration would act unwillingly in this matter, but Congressional feeling was growing and might be irresistible.[42] The most serious issue, however, was cotton.

Although the British Government had not dared to put cotton on the 'absolute' contraband list, it had nevertheless detained American and other neutral ships carrying cotton for Holland. A number of such cases were before the Prize Court when Lansing sent a firm note to Page on 14 July making it clear that the United States would insist on its rights under international law, British domestic legislation notwithstanding. Pressure on the administration from the South was growing, but equally increasing was the pressure in Britain for cotton to be added to the contraband list, and 'legality' established. Grey was trapped in the middle. Some of his colleagues were adamant that to give way on this issue would be to destroy the blockade altogether. Northcliffe mounted a formidable attack, and Grey offered to see him, writing to Balfour: 'I have never seen Northcliffe & I suppose therefore it may be said that I haven't yet quarrelled with him.' Page warned House on 21 July that 'there is a fast growing feeling here, therefore, that the American Government is pusillanimous—dallies with 'em, is affected by the German propaganda, etc, etc'.[43]

Grey shared these feelings to some extent, but he kept them under control. Following the discussions carried on by a special Cabinet committee appointed on 19 July, Grey laid two memoranda before his colleagues.[44] He rejected the maintenance of the existing system on the grounds that the friction it caused would sooner or later get out of hand. He also refused to abandon the Order in Council unless there was a change in the contraband list. But, while putting cotton on the 'absolute' list would no doubt make interference 'legal', it was hardly likely to be more palatable to opinion in the American South. An ingenious, though expensive, solution was then worked out, whereby the British contrived to make large purchases of American cotton to keep the price up and remove the discontent.[45]

Grey thought that the Germans might in fact have all the cotton they needed, but he told House that any Government that did not stop cotton from going to Germany would be condemned. As it was, he was much blamed for not stopping cotton from going to Germany in the first seven months of the war.[46] Taking advantage of the fact that on the previous day, the *Arabic* was sunk with the loss of American life, the British Government announced on 20 August that cotton was now on the 'absolute' contraband list. It was not even felt necessary to repeal the Order in Council. The elaborate steps taken by Grey to ensure that American economic interests were as little damaged as possible had largely contributed to this result. As Wilson's American biographer comments, 'The Anglo-American controversy over neutral trading rights was by no means at an end, but it would be vastly less dangerous to the good relations of the two countries in the future because cotton was no longer involved.'[47]

If cotton was no longer so contentious, there were always other problems to take its place. The standard German reply when their submarines sank merchant or passenger ships was that the British were arming merchantmen and using them offensively and illegally. Wilson knew that there was some substance in the charge and sent a warning that if the practice did not cease, all British ships calling at American ports would be required to disarm. Balfour, the First Lord of the Admiralty, vigorously protested that it was necessary for merchantmen to take the initiative if they were to have any chance against submarines. Once again, Grey's own reaction was to be conciliatory, writing to Balfour: 'I am afraid we shall have to disarm our merchant vessels & I suggest that all further arming should be stopped at once.'[48] Because of the withdrawal of German submarines from the Irish Sea, the issue was not pressed to a conclusion for the moment, but Grey's reaction was typical. His attitude led to increasing attacks on him from those, like Carson, who believed that it was 'only by using every ounce of power and advantage which our naval supremacy gives us that we can successfully bring the war to a conclusion in the shortest time. . . .'[49] Grey refused to be moved, again writing to Balfour: 'The blockade doctrine is being run very hard—in this country by people who neither know nor think—in America by people who wish to get us right with America. I cannot see how we are to deal with German exports under the American Civil War doctrine of blockade. . . .'[50] With Cecil's appointment in the following month, the formation of blockade policy was largely in other and tougher hands. General

Y

relations with the United States were, nevertheless, still very much his concern.

The failure of House's mediation mission in the early months of 1915 had not removed his itch to intervene. Throughout August and September 1915, he blew alternately hot and cold on the possibilities of a bold diplomatic initiative. Grey answered him skilfully, managing neither to offend nor encourage. Since House could not make up his own mind, this task was not too difficult. He wrote pointedly to Grey on 3 September asking directly whether the President should make peace proposals 'upon the broad basis of the elimination of militarism and navalism and a return, as nearly as possible, to the status quo?' But eleven days later he requested Grey not to take his suggestion 'too seriously'. He had 'merely' intended to inform him of the President's readiness to do whatever was best. He added: 'As far as I can see, and from all that I can hear from Germany, it is utterly hopeless to think in that direction now. . . .'[51] No doubt somewhat bewildered, Grey wrote a double-edged reply stressing that his own great objective was to eliminate militarism and navalism. Would the President be prepared to propose a League of Nations who would bind themselves to side against any Power which broke a treaty? With the use of poisonous gas and Zeppelins, 'the horror of what the state of things after the war may be, increases'. But he followed this general sentiment by expressing a longing to see 'the bullied provinces of Alsace and Lorraine returned to the freer government of France'. He stressed that 'for us and for France defeat would mean our disappearance as Powers'.[52] Greatly excited, and seemingly hardly troubling to read this second paragraph, House rushed to the President with the letter. As a result, House proposed to Grey that 'the time may soon come when this Government should intervene between the belligerents and demand that peace parleys begin upon the broad basis of the elimination of militarism and navalism'.[53] At a signal from the Foreign Secretary, he would rush across the Atlantic. Grey was amazed, and stalled by asking for information on the proposal to which he was supposed to have given his agreement. Was it the League of Nations? Before receiving House's affirmative reply, he sent a further dampening letter which was largely taken up with complaint about the American attitude to the blockade. It had little effect. Although House wrote on 7 December that his mind was 'not now moving towards peace, even upon the broad lines spoken of before' he was going to come to London himself to find out about the situation.[54]

House landed in England on 5 January. On his arrival in London he spent the next ten days in conversations with a wide range of public figures, culminating in appointments with Lloyd George, and a final session with Balfour and Grey. To them, House outlined his scheme for a settlement based on the 'freedom of the seas' and the elimination of militarism. According to House, Grey was mostly silent, and it was Balfour who tried to discover what these proposals could possibly mean. He wanted to know how Germany could be counted on to play the game fairly. House thought it all very simple, and received the support of Grey in arguing that with a League of Nations under the lead of Britain and the United States, Germany would be sure to suffer if she failed to keep her agreements. On this note, he departed for the continent, wishing that Lloyd George was Prime Minister with Grey as his Foreign Secretary, 'for I believe we could then do something'. He stressed: 'It would be a calamity if anything should happen to prevent Sir Edward's continuance in the Government until peace is made. And yet if we push them too hard upon the question of neutral trade, he is likely to go.' He made a similar point to the German Government: 'Grey is the most reasonable of English statesmen.'[55] After Berlin, House went to Paris and there convinced himself that Briand and Cambon were receptive of his plans for mediation. By the time he arrived back in London on 9 February he had convinced himself, and reported to his master, that his chances were now very good. Grey sent him a welcoming note, anticipating an early meeting. The only person to try to bring House down to earth was Page, with whom he dined that night. The Ambassador was much more aware of what political circles in London were really thinking. He wrote in his diary: 'They are laughing at the "Empty House" here.' The Colonel's scheme, he thought, was 'purely academic nonsensical stuff' and he ridiculed the contention that the French approved it. In reply, the Colonel 'flayed him'.[56]

There is little doubt that Page was nearer the truth than House. Grey did not want to offend the American gratuitously, but he did not believe the basis for a peace settlement existed. Nevertheless, he claimed to believe that the time was ripe for the President to demand a peace conference, but that his colleagues dared not, or did not, agree with him. House noted in his diary: 'Public opinion here would condemn any minister who would dare endorse such a proposal, and Grey believes they would even go so far as to smash his windows.'[57] Nevertheless, on the evening of 14 February,

Reading, Asquith, Grey, Balfour, Lloyd George and House all solemnly assembled for dinner. The conversation ranged widely, and Lloyd George formed the impression that the Americans regarded the restoration of Belgian and Serbian independence as a *sine qua non* for any settlement. They were also favourable to the surrender of Alsace-Lorraine, with compensation for Germany outside Europe, and the adjustment of the Italo-Austrian frontier. House told the Prime Minister that if the Allies proposed a settlement which the President considered unjust at a peace conference, the United States would probably withdraw. Asquith then wanted to know what Wilson would do if Germany proposed something totally unfair. 'In these circumstances,' House replied, 'I thought the President would throw the weight of the United States on the side of the Allies.' After this dinner, House fondly believed that Grey was in favour of immediate action. The Foreign Secretary drew up a memorandum of the conversation for the benefit of the French, in which he stated that if a conference failed to secure peace, 'the United States would leave the Conference as a belligerent on the side of the Allies, if Germany were unreasonable'. When Wilson received a copy of this report, he insisted that the word 'probably' be inserted after 'the United States'. When he heard of the proposal, Cambon reportedly 'laughed it to scorn' and regarded it as a device by the President to avoid English and French press criticisms during his re-election campaign. The Russian Government was given a suitably truncated account of the meeting and took no action upon it.[58]

'It is now up to you to make the next move,' wrote House on 10 March. Accordingly the Foreign Secretary invited his colleagues on the War Council to offer a verdict. Inevitably, he added: 'This decision depends, I imagine, upon the opinion of military and naval authorities on the prospects of the war.' At its meeting on 20 March, the Council decided that, since the struggle at Verdun was still taking place, it was not appropriate to think of a conference. Grey informed House that only if the French were interested would he bring the proposal to the attention of his other allies. The French were not.[59] Grey's letter was written on the same day as the sinking of an unarmed Channel passenger steamer, the *Sussex*. This action, together with the American insistence on classifying armed merchantmen into 'offensive' and 'defensive' categories, led to renewed Anglo-American hostility. There can be little doubt that Grey was rather 'fly' in his relations with House, although the

Colonel had a well-developed capacity for self-deception. As if to close the episode, Sir Edward wrote on 7 April: 'Everybody feels there must be more German failure and some Allied success before anything but an inconclusive peace could be obtained.' House had attempted to claim that if America went to war, it would only lengthen the conflict, but Grey could not agree. Having heard before that German-American relations were 'going steadily to the breaking point' he would wait and see.[60]

The chances of an improvement in Anglo-American relations were further diminished by the Easter Rising in Dublin and the arrest of Sir Roger Casement. At first, Spring-Rice reported that the attitude of the American public was on the whole satisfactory, the press agreeing that the Irish movement was 'suicidal and in the interests of Germany alone'. But after the suppression of the rebellion and the executions, the Ambassador regarded the agitation as 'growing very serious especially in view of elections'. A few days later he added: 'Delight of Germans here at executions shows that we have fulfilled their expectations and played into their hands.' The Foreign Secretary was disgusted by this misguided liberalism. He minuted: 'I wish we could get a good short interview about Ireland pointing out the number of officers & men killed compared with the number of executions. . . .'[61] He expressed his disquiet to his colleagues. Balfour, no small authority on Ireland, wrote that he was 'unwilling to believe that, if the truth about Ireland were known, there would not be a reaction in our favour'. In order to bring this about, he advocated a message in direct and simple language. Grey entirely agreed. It should stress the number of people killed by the revolutionaries and the fact that for days British troops were fighting for their lives. These facts should impress those Americans who seemed to regard the rising as 'a toy affair of misguided but comparatively harmless people, but punished with executions & outrage'.[62] Although quite unrepentant, Grey was mindful of Spring-Rice's warning, and would have been prepared to allow Casement to be sent to an asylum rather than to the gallows, but he readily accepted the decision of his colleagues that Casement should hang. He was aware of the damage this would do to Britain's reputation in the United States. It was suggested to him that he should send over a loyal Roman Catholic Irishman to the United States in order 'to silence the Irish-American part who exude poison from every pore', in the well-chosen words of a later Poet Laureate, but he rejected the idea.[63]

Despite the rebuff they had received, it never took long for the Presidential ideas on a peace settlement to revive. On 10 May, House warned that Wilson was under increasing pressure to take some action to bring the war to a close. 'The impression grows', he claimed, 'that the Allies are more determined upon the punishment of Germany than upon exacting terms that neutral opinion would consider just.' On the same day, Spring-Rice also warned that a new phase in Anglo-American relations was about to begin. Violent notes would be sent, 'and violent threats will be used. At the same time we shall be told that the President is ready to help us to make peace. If we refuse, we shall be called bloodthirsty. . . .'[64] He and others stressed that, for electoral reasons, the President wanted to appear as the great Pacificator. As predicted, House opened a fresh series of letters to Grey by stressing the purported advantages of mediation, and hinting at an Anglo-American special relationship. If America entered the war, 'it would probably lead to the complete crushing of Germany, and Russia, Italy and France would then be more concerned as to the division of the spoils than they would for any far-reaching agreement that might be brought about looking to the maintenance of peace in the future. . . .' The Colonel tried to appeal to Grey's genuine concern for the League idea, but the latter, perhaps not unmindful that he too had a concern for the spoils, simply and bluntly replied that any suggestion of peace was premature.[65] House professed grave disappointment—for two years Grey had been telling him that future international well-being depended on the United States taking a full part in world affairs. Now that the United States had indicated a willingness, Grey 'halts, stammers and questions'. He put this down to growing Allied confidence, after Verdun, in their ability to hold the German armies. House himself did not see much reason for this optimism.[66]

A further source of hard feelings was the lukewarm response to Wilson's speech on 27 May in which the President dealt with the League and with the prospects of peace. In preparing it, Wilson was of the opinion that it would be one of the most important speeches he would ever make, but the European reaction, in both belligerent camps, was sceptical.[67] Grey expressed his reactions to Page with some contempt.[68] His private secretary, Drummond, with his approval, wrote to Spring-Rice that if the United States was refusing to assume definite obligations of a military character, 'the whole value of the scheme falls to the ground and it would not,

I suppose, be worth pursuing'.[69] Eventually, Grey himself wrote a strong letter to House at the end of August commenting on the President's reported disappointment at the response to his speech. 'His statement of indifference to the causes and objects of the war, his putting the freedom of the seas in the forefront of the objects of the League of Nations without defining what was meant by it . . . and the omission of all reference to observing rules of warfare on land as well as on sea, were great obstacles to a response here.' The continued reports that American public opinion was determined to keep out of the war at all costs made people wonder 'whether even with a League of Nations the United States could be depended upon to uphold treaties and agreements by force. . . .' As for himself, he had done enough for the time being. 'It is difficult for a man who shares responsibility for the daily conduct of the war when the very existence of his country is at stake, to go as far as I have done in public about a future League of Nations, but I have not seen that what I said met with any public notice or response in the United States.' He would stand by what he had said, but would not force the pace. For good measure, he added: 'We are not favourably impressed by the action of the Senate in having passed a resolution about the Irish prisoners, though they have taken no notice of outrages in Belgium and massacres of Armenians.'[70]

The sharpness of this letter from one who thought himself, and was considered, pro-American, requires some comment. House misjudged his man when he came hawking his ill-considered formulae for peace. The sincerity of Grey's concern for a League cannot be disputed, but he wanted some assurance that American participation would be a reality. For their part, Wilson and House thought that, in the autumn of 1916, Britain was drifting into reaction and intransigence, and they must have thought Grey was going the same way. Yet the Foreign Secretary had always believed that unless there was a real change of heart in Germany, a compromise peace would solve nothing. In addition, he feared that talk of a peace settlement might lead Russia to act separately. The dismissal of Sazonov late in July 1916 came as 'a bolt from the blue', and Grey was very depressed by the news.[71] Wilson and House could not understand what the war was all about. In particular, the President's refusal to discriminate between the belligerents with regard to the origin of the war was bound to be taken personally by Grey. Impatiently, he remarked to Page that if the war did end in deadlock, and Wilson were to play a crucial part in the settlement, he had a personal longing that an independent tribunal should examine all the documents on the origins of the war so that the truth could be established.[72]

All summer long, with great loss of life, the opposing armies battled it out on the Somme to singularly little effect. Like most of his colleagues, Grey had accepted the inevitability of this strategy. He told Robertson that he was quite prepared to tell the French that they 'ought not to press us for anything about Salonica that will impede preparations for the offensive in France'.[73] In mid-August, the Russian offensive, led by General Brusilov, had unexpectedly reached the slopes of the Carpathians and captured the Bukovina. For some months Grey had been resisting suggestions that he should attempt to entice Bulgaria to revert to neutrality or change sides. He explained to Lloyd George that it would be 'most dangerous to make any move as regards Bulgaria while the entry of Roumania hangs in the balance, and I do not like the thought of approaching France about it'.[74] Fortunately, spurred on by the Russian achievement, Roumania joined the Allies on 27 August— the day before Grey wrote his letter to House and hence, perhaps, its defiant tone. On 13 September, Henry Newbolt found Grey 'absolutely himself again'. He was 'sunny, humorous, interested in everything, talkative, indiscreet and very friendly'. About the war, he was 'cheerful rather than sanguine'. We were doing well, though it would still take a great deal to defeat the German *people*. He was pleased with the Russian advance, though the situation there was not free from anxiety.[75]

By the end of September, this optimism was coming to seem misplaced. The Russian offensive was exhausted, and the Roumanians were themselves in danger. There was stalemate on the Western front. In face of these set-backs, Grey's pessimism, which was always latent, seems once more to have gained the upper hand. Spring-Rice warned him to expect another serious Anglo-American crisis in the winter. The President would be forced by Irish- and German-American opinion to make another peace move. Lloyd George then took it upon himself, without consultation, to give an interview to an American newsman in the course of which he stated that 'Peace now or at any time before the final and complete elimination of this menace is unthinkable'. Grey was furious. He complained to Lloyd George that Wilson would now be even more disposed to put pressure on Britain, and the Germans would be provided with a ready-made excuse for their submarine campaign. He concluded, significantly: 'It has always been my view that until the Allies were sure of victory the door should be kept open for Wilson's mediation. It is now closed for ever as far as we are concerned.' The Secretary for War was quite unrepentant. He repeated that it would be a disaster to stop the war at this point. He claimed that he was inoculated, and could get away with such public statements, whereas Grey could only have acted reticently and formally. Patronizingly, he concluded: 'You will find that it will work out all right. I know the American politician. He has no international conscience. He thinks of nothing but the ticket, and he has not given the least thought to the effect of his action upon European affairs.' While sorry to have added to Grey's troubles, he was callously impenitent, as he put it. The Foreign Secretary had been very firmly put in his subordinate place.[76]

This exchange, and the general military situation, prompted Asquith for the first time to test opinion among his colleagues on the possibilities of peace. Already, at the end of August, the Foreign Office had prepared a long memorandum, though it does not seem to have been considered in the Cabinet. The Prime Minister received a variety of answers.[77] Lansdowne pointed to the enormous casualties. These could no doubt be sustained if it could be shown that the sacrifice would have its reward. But could the country go on affording the price when the reward was uncertain? At the other extreme, the C.I.G.S., General Robertson, would not hear of any settlement which conserved the military might of Germany. Only 'cranks, cowards and philosophers' were likely to be convinced that Britain stood more to gain by losing the war than by winning it. Grey's memorandum, dated 27 November, as one would expect, came between the two. Typically, he believed that to talk of peace was premature if the naval and military authorities were correct in assuming that terms could eventually be dictated to Germany. So far as he could tell, he believed they were right, and so long as the Allied military position was likely to improve, then it would be better to fight on. If they did not think the situation was likely to improve, then it would be better to wind up the war on the best terms available. If, despite military optimism, the situation deteriorated, then again it would be better to wind up the war 'presumably through the medium of not unsympathetic mediation ...'[78] Thus, right to the end, despite his own reservations, he refrained from giving priority to political judgments. Privately, he regarded the financial situation as very alarming and also wrote to Balfour at the end of November: 'The submarine danger seems to me to be increasing so rapidly that unless in the next two months or so we can abate it the Germans will see their way to victory.' His impression was that the Germans 'who would have closed with a proposal for peace in terms of a draw in September or even October, are now out again for victory. Under these circumstances we must make every effort to cope with submarines & there is no time to be lost.'[79] Grey's memorandum had been intended as a contribution to the discussion. A week later he was in no position to share in it. Lloyd George, the man who was indeed to 'make every effort', had become Prime Minister and he was out of office.

17

The Life of an Elder Statesman

By a curious coincidence, Grey gave up the seal of office not only on the same day of the month, but on the same day of the week on which he had received it eleven years earlier. As he reflected to Rosebery, 'They have been years of almost continuous storm & trouble at home & abroad, ending in the greatest war the world has ever known. As I look back & reflect, I cannot but think that tremendous forces have been at work in the world & that individuals have been helpless to arrest them. We could take an honourable part but we could not control the whirlwind.'[1] He was not sorry to go. At the meeting of all Liberal Cabinet Ministers on 5 December, Asquith had foreseen 'grave evils' from the change of administration, 'because it would mean a divided nation at home, and because himself and Grey being so definitely identified with the war from the outset, the effect upon the Allies would be bad'. Grey did not agree. Lloyd George was equally identified with the policy of carrying the war on to victory.[2] His relations with Asquith were now, as Beaverbrook put it, 'of that distant but friendly kind which an ocean might have with a contiguous mountain peak'.[3] In his speech at the Reform Club Grey stated: 'There is no doubt what our course ought to be. We must support the Government in every possible way that we can.'[4]

His main feeling on leaving office was profound relief: '. . . I feel like a man who has walked 1000 miles without rest & has at last been told he may lie down.'[5] It was a particular pleasure to be free from the attacks made on him in the press, though he claimed that they had not distressed him. 'The only papers I see', he wrote to Newbolt, 'are The Times, Daily Tel: & Westminster Gazette; I have seen in these one outrageous untrue attack upon me quoted from the Daily Mail. . . . The attacks upon the diplomacy of the Allies are very ill informed & ignorant, and to hold me personally responsible for the whole of that policy is ludicrous.'[6] He wrote in stronger terms to the editor of the *Spectator* that the attacks of the *Morning Post* and the *National Review* were disgraceful. If they were really 'typical of British thought, opinion, and temperament, many of us who are devoted to the country would despair of its success in this war and of its future'.[7]

He was most anxious not to become involved in controversy over the fall of the Government and his friends in distant places had to be content with enigmatic comments to the effect that 'the real causes of the break up of the Govt. are too private to be written about. They are not to be found in any correspondence between Asquith & Ll.G. or in Ll.G.'s account of the matter. The ostensible causes in such cases are not the real causes.'[8] As regards the future, he thought one of four things would happen. 'If Lloyd George is right, there will be a great victory and he will be a national hero for all time; if not and things go wrong, his supporters may try to make out that it is his late colleagues who are to blame for everything, and may thereby extricate him at our expense. Or . . . the press may in turn assail him and his Government, and destroy them; or lastly if things go very wrong, the country, seeing that press rule and the Lloyd George Government have failed, and that the ordinary constitutional safeguards and remedies cannot operate in war, will take matters into its own hands, and make a clean sweep by mob rule.'[9] Of these alternatives, he undoubtedly preferred the first, writing to Crewe 'that the present Govt. must have the best chance the country can give it & we should leave it alone & not embarrass it'.[10] Much as he wished the war to end, it should do so 'only on terms as have been indicated by the Allies that will completely restore countries now occupied by the enemies, will repair as far as this is possible the wrongs done & will secure the peace & freedom of Europe in future'.[11] Towards the end of May 1917, he began to feel that the country was going to win and wrote that 'if so Lloyd George deserves great credit'. While there were 'certainly very many unpleasant circumstances in the way the Asquith Govt. was displaced & many of us including myself had shamefully unfair things said about us, but then so far as I was concerned I was at one time very much overpraised & I was really always miserable & out of place in public life. So as long as I am left alone in private life now I have a feeling that it is a sort of quits.'[12]

The wish to be left alone in private life could not, of course, be completely fulfilled. He could not disappear into utter oblivion in Northumberland, much as he might want to. His political friends on both sides of the Atlantic still sought him out and requested his views on current military and political developments. The March Revolution in Russia, for example, he welcomed unreservedly, rejoicing 'that Russia is changing her Govt. & striking out for freedom: but revolutions generally reach their ends through confusion & violence & I am apprehensive as to the effect upon Russia's part in the war'.[13] When President Wilson brought the United States into the war in April 1917 he wrote to Walter Hines Page: 'I can't express adequately all that I feel. Great gratitude and great hope are in my heart. I hope now that some great and abiding good will yet be brought out of all this welter of evil . . . I glow with admiration.'[14] These two great events would have more consequences 'direct & indirect than we can foresee; they are themselves consequences of the war & make me feel that the war is now beginning to have consequences more tremendous than the actual fighting. . . .'[15] In September, staying at Cloan, he gave the opinion that the war would somehow be over within twelve months. The Allies were bound to win.[16] Events in Russia might delay ultimate victory, but they could not prevent it.

The consequences of the war, to which Grey referred, were not altogether congenial to Lord Lansdowne. At the beginning of November 1917, his famous letter appeared in the *Daily Telegraph*, substantially repeating the contentions he had urged in the Cabinet a year previously. Grey's reaction to the letter was very guarded. What moved him to write in general sympathy was, he told Runciman, admiration for Lansdowne's courage, but he did not want 'to get sucked into the whirlpool again'. Runciman tried to persuade him, receiving Lansdowne's thanks for giving 'a small dose of "ginger" ' to Grey. His intervention would be 'invaluable'. They were disappointed. Grey again stressed that he had taken a peerage 'on the ground that I meant to go out altogether. To be in & out is to make the worst of both worlds.' He reiterated his belief that 'the real obstacles to peace seem to me to be the desire of the German people (it amounts to that) *not* to be masters in their own house & *not* to know anything except what their Govt. tells them; & their complete want of any sense of wrong done & of need for reparation. To make peace with them still in this frame of mind would be at best a very regrettable necessity. . . .'[17] As he explained to Gilbert Murray, 'If the German people will show the Junkers to the door & down the Tirpitzes everything else will follow.'[18]

As he refused to join the Lansdowne movement in any active sense, so he had earlier declined to serve the Government as Ambassador in Washington to replace the ineffective Spring-Rice. The question of his appointment was discussed in May 1917, and Balfour strongly supported the suggestion.[19] According to a memorandum by Stamfordham, Grey discussed the question with Asquith, who apparently pointed out the danger that he might come to see more eye to eye with President Wilson than with Lloyd George and be obliged to resign—a disaster in wartime.[20] Largely on these grounds, Grey refused, and since the notion that he was 'too pacifist' seems to have been held by other members of the War Council, he was not pressed into service. Lord Northcliffe was sent instead. Grey abhorred the social responsibility which the post would entail, but wrote to House that if he were asked at a later stage, with the confidence of the Government, to go as a special envoy to discuss the 'great object' he would seriously consider accepting.[21]

The 'great object' to which he referred was the League of Nations. For the rest of his life it was the one cause, with the Liberal Party, which would induce him to sacrifice any of his much-prized leisure. Immediately after his resignation, he warned League supporters in the country that he did not think the time was ripe for an extensive campaign of education. Even though the League idea was being attacked, he refused to enter into public controversy.[22] He stressed to Bryce in August 1917 that while he supported a League for Permanent Peace, American sensitiveness on the issue led him to feel that 'in further public action Wilson should take the lead'. Any statements by individuals or the British Government should be sure to be along the lines of the President's thinking.[23] The utopian conceptions of some advocates irritated him. There was a 'danger of injuring the movement if rigid proposals going further than the Nations are prepared to accept are pressed'. As for himself, he thought 'the League must go so far as to entail the use of force, at any rate by the Great Powers. . . .' Everything, however, depended on the attitude of the United States.[24]

The reason for his caution was still his desire not to jeopardize the war effort. As he wrote to Spender in January 1918, '. . . Isn't the German mentality a depressing thing? When one is not in office & out of London it is so uncomfortable to hate anybody & one longs more than ever for peace, but I do not see how there is to be peace with the people who still run Germany. . . .' The territorial obstacles to peace in order of importance were Belgium, Alsace-Lorraine, the German colonies, Italian and Roumanian claims in Europe, British, French and Italian claims in Asia Minor. He believed that the sensible thing for the Allies would be to accept the logic of facts and conditions. Since Russia had gone out of the war and the United States had come in, the Allies should make a joint statement of war aims and conditions for peace. If Germany was amenable on these points, they should make her an offer of economic equality after the war. It was just possible that peace might result from such an initiative but 'if the offensive fails there may be an opportunity for a just peace'.[25] While that offensive was under way, he did not dabble in League matters. In April 1918 he thought the German attack was slackening a little, but he feared that the enemy would bring up guns and make a further concentrated effort. It was to be hoped that the best German divisions were used up, 'but there must still be much ground for grave anxiety. We can do nothing but wait for the issue of the battle & hope that neither our civilians in power nor the French politicians will prevent the soldiers from doing their best in the crisis. I wish that Robertson had not been displaced.'[26]

When the crisis had been surmounted, Grey consented to the publication of his pamphlet on the League of Nations. He stressed that he wanted it to be an independent production, although 'once published it can be translated & circulated by the Ministry of Information as much as they please'.[27] In the pamphlet he stated that there were two essential conditions for the success of the League idea. It had to be adopted 'with earnestness and conviction' by the Executive Heads of State. They must adopt it only if they were serious, and not merely intent on rendering lip-service to please others. The second condition was that Governments and peoples had to recognize that the League would impose some limitation on their actions and entail inconvenient obligations. In particular, all the States had to 'forgo the right in any dispute to resort to force before other methods of settlement by conference, conciliation, or, if need be, arbitration, have been tried'. In his view, the establishment and maintenance of such a League of Nations was a more important means of securing peace than any of the actual terms that might conclude the war.[28] Following the publication of the pamphlet, he indirectly approached House to see whether his ideas met with Presidential approval and whether there was anything he could do further to help the League. House replied that the pamphlet was admirable, but the President was busy.[29]

At this stage, there were in Britain two societies devoted to furthering the League idea; the League of Nations Society and the League of Free Nations Association. Between the two bodies there were certain clashes of personality and emphasis. The latter body approached Grey to become its President, but he declined on the grounds that it was unreasonable to have two Societies. If they united, he would reconsider the invitation. Later, in August, to help overcome the difficulties in bringing about amalgamation he offered to become President. 'My failing eyesight hampers me very much', he wrote, '. . . I shall have to do without notes. All this makes me very reluctant to take a position that may or must entail such things, but I will take the risk . . .'[30] There were, he thought, 'tremendous difficulties in the way of a League of Nations, but there are also tremendous reasons why an effort should be made to overcome those difficulties'.[31] When it became apparent that the war was at last ending, the establishment of a League was what Grey meant when he wrote: 'We shall now have to show whether we are worthy of success: it is a more severe test than adversity.'[32] As the new President of the League of Nations Union, he addressed a large audience in the Central Hall, Westminster, on the subject of the League. Half-blind and reading his notes with difficulty under strong arc lights, he told his listeners what they wanted to hear. The war had taken its toll of blood and tears. Mankind would make it clear that never again would such a catastrophe overwhelm it.[33] When President Wilson came to London at the end of December 1918, Grey had the opportunity of meeting him. 'Everything you used to tell me about him', he wrote to House, 'is now evident to the world.'[34] The new order was about to be laid.

Despite the fond hope of some of his friends that just as Lloyd George had been the man to win the war, so Grey would be the man to make the peace, there was, of course, no chance of this happening. Apart from making the plea that Heligoland should be turned into a bird sanctuary, he did not attempt to intervene in the politics of peacemaking. He confined himself to making general statements in support of the League, but refused to be a member of a League of Nations Union delegation to Paris. Early in February 1919, he commented to Gilbert Murray that the League seemed to be making good progress at the conference. It seemed, indeed, 'the only question in which satisfactory progress is being made and in which the U.S.A. will be really helpful'. As for the other weighty matters, 'Diocletian, had he been alive and invited to the Peace Conference, would have been more than ever attached to his cabbages'.[35] A little later, while he was critical of some details, particularly concerning the real meaning of the armaments clause, he was delighted that 'such a great piece of work' had been done. He hoped people would support the League warmly 'without cavilling at details'. By the end of March he felt that 'the work on this side of the Atlantic is done for the present'. The danger now lay in the United States. He was fearful that the Treaty would be wrecked by the Senate.[36] Lord Robert Cecil wrote from Paris: 'I feel that a word is due to you personally and to the Union of which you are the distinguished President.' Public opinion had created the League and for that 'you and those who are working with you are in great measure responsible'.[37]

It was Grey's anxiety about the United States which led him to accept the invitation to go to Washington as Ambassador on special mission, pending the appointment of a permanent British Ambassafor. It was a curious appointment, announced in a curious way—before the formal agreement of the United States had been obtained. The reason for this procedure was undoubtedly that Grey had been very sticky about the terms on which he would accept office. Lloyd George and Curzon first mooted the idea and worked through Haldane to gain Grey's consent. Grey then drew up a memorandum on 29 July declining a full ambassadorship and stating that if he were an envoy on a special mission to deal chiefly with the League of Nations, Ireland and the Navy, he needed to know the Government's policy on these matters, to agree with it, and to feel there was a fair chance of it proving acceptable in Washington. As regards the League, he saw no reason to expect 'insuperable difficulties' between London and Washington. On Ireland, he refused to suggest a policy, except to say that 'what might have been a successful solution in 1886 and subsequent years is now out of date'. As regards the Navy, it had been accepted before the war that Britain should not build against the United States and this, after the exhaustion of war, Grey held to be *a fortiori* true. The British Naval Estimates should be based on an avowed European standard, and should be frankly defended on that basis. If the naval programme was so large that it could only be justified by admitting that it was, to some extent, based on rivalry with the United States, then the latter would certainly go one better. He strongly resisted the pressure which he feared would come from some quarters to put

z

the U.S. Navy in the place of the German Navy. If Britain's programme was 'European', then Grey believed that the United States would frame her programme mainly with reference to the Japanese Navy in the Pacific.[38]

After the Prime Minister had digested this memorandum, Grey saw him on 4 August, and as a result, felt that he would accept the post. He had found himself in agreement with Lloyd George's expressed wish that the League of Nations should become a reality and that 'as a sham it would be particularly dangerous'. Grey also felt reasonably happy with his discussions on the Navy, though he wanted to be given a figure for the next Naval Estimates. But he did not like the Government's Irish policy. To try to meet the situation in Ireland with a scheme which was over two years old, and was not even acceptable then, seemed unsatisfactory. He hoped the Government would work on the problem, he told Curzon, otherwise he would not be able to do much good in America.[39] After further discussion, Grey and the Government reached an agreement which the Foreign Secretary embodied in a formal letter.[40] Grey was not very sanguine about his mission, describing it to H. A. L. Fisher as 'a speculative adventure'.[41] But even Northcliffe sent him a letter of encouragement, though privately considering that Grey would have no more than a *succès d'estime* in Washington. Grey had never given him an impression of 'magnetic bigness'.[42] There was no message of good wishes from Asquith. Grey told Gilbert Murray: 'He never writes to me. He is not good at writing.' Murray replied that he was good at answering, always, it seemed, by return of post. 'Yes,' came the retort, 'but rather as Ld. Salisbury used to make appointments by return of post, to avoid being troubled about them. . . .'[43]

The mission was a failure almost before it began. Sending his first report to the Foreign Secretary, Grey wrote: 'I am constantly coming upon instances in which Americans are behaving badly and twisting things against us. There is an Irishman everywhere, and Irish antagonism is at the bottom of all our troubles.' He felt that he would soon be in a position to make a strong protest, 'but I gather that the only person worth talking to is the President. . . .'[44] This was true, but it was also true that the President's recent illness made him inaccessible. By early October, Grey had sized up the situation in Washington. He had accepted the appointment in the belief that, through Colonel House, he could get on well with Wilson, but 'within a week, therefore, of my arrival the reason for my coming has disappeared. For some time, with no one to take the place of the President, there will be chaos in American policy.' He could talk to individuals and departments, but it was all rather pointless. He detected a strong shrinking from Wilson's European policy, and a feeling that the President had been exploited for purposes of British policy.[45] In another letter, in mid-October, he stressed that 'a real amelioration of American feeling may result from a policy of self-government for Ireland on good lines'.[46] He also had a brush with Curzon on his Persian policy, but the Foreign Secretary took little notice, writing that '. . . he has always needlessly been alarmed about the Persian Agreement'.[47] By early November, Curzon reported to the Prime Minister that 'Grey is getting very fidgety & irritable at Washington'.[48] It was little wonder. The only matter of substance with which he was concerned was the British insistence that the British Empire should have six votes in the League for the Dominions.[49] In the middle of November he wrote testily to the Prime Minister regretting that he had ever agreed to be an ambassador and stating that he was prepared to remain till the end of the year, 'but I shall take a passage home early in January'.[50] He liked what he could see of people and places in Washington, but that, unfortunately, was not very much. 'The trees would be very interesting if I could see them,' he wrote to Buxton.[51]

On his way home, Grey brooded on his unhappy experience and wrote to Wickham Steed of *The Times*, suggesting an appointment. He had it in mind to publish a long letter which might do something, he believed, to improve Anglo-American relations. When they met, Grey 'remarked casually that Lloyd George had come very near to spoiling everything he had tried to do in the States. By charging the Americans with breach of faith and repudiation of pledges . . . he raised a storm of indignation against himself and everything English.' Although Grey still had a 'sneaking admiration' for the Prime Minister, his frequent gaffes were a drawback to the whole of Britain's foreign relations.[52] On 31 January 1920 *The Times* published a communication from Grey which it described as 'probably unique in the history of diplomacy'. Speaking as a private person, he declared that nothing seemed to him more desirable in international politics than good understanding between the United States on the one hand, and Great Britain, the Dominions and Ireland on the other. He wanted to explain to a British audience that nowhere was the impasse caused by the deadlock between the

President and the Senate more deeply regretted than in the United States itself. One possible misunderstanding should be removed at once: 'No charge of bad faith or repudiating signatures can be brought against the action of the United States.' Nor was it true to say that the United States had been motivated solely by self-interest to the disregard of higher ideals. He stressed the strength of the tradition against entangling alliances. This conservatism recognized that conditions had changed but it desired time to consider and feel its way. After discussing the constitutional position, he turned to the international situation. 'Without the United States', he wrote, 'the present League of Nations may become little better than a League of Allies for armed self-defence against a revival of Prussian militarism or against a military sequel to Bolshevism in Russia.' On the other hand, if the American people entered the League 'as a willing partner with limited obligations, it may well be that American opinion and American action inside the League will be much more fruitful than if they entered as a reluctant partner who felt that her hand had been forced'. He did not deny that some of the American reservations were material qualifications of the League as drawn up at Paris, but it was better to proceed pragmatically on the basis of what could be achieved than to hanker after what was unobtainable.[53] The letter caused a considerable stir. The American press tended to divide along party lines in its treatment of Grey's remarks. The Republican journals were generally united in a chorus of appreciation. On 6 February, the Washington Correspondent of *The Times* wrote that as the days passed 'it becomes increasingly clear that Viscount Grey's letter has had as great an effect here as the utterance of any statesman of one country ever had upon the Parliamentary and political situation in another'. The glee was all on the Republican side. Here, at last, was an eminent foreign statesman who saw that the President's discomfiture was due to facts somewhat more respectable than pique and personal prejudice. Although Grey's letter had the result of dampening the anti-British sentiment which was raging in the United States, it did not achieve the desired result of producing a majority for American adherence to the League on the basis of the Lodge reservations.

While Grey's letter reassured Republicans, the White House was furious at what it regarded as interference in a domestic American matter. It was not until May that Grey dared to write to House. 'When I heard my letter had made the President angry, it did occur to me that at the White House you might be represented as directly or indirectly responsible for any inconvenience I caused. . . .' For this he apologized. He would not retract anything he said in the letter, writing that it 'did some good here, and was accepted by fair-minded people as giving a fair account of American opinion and American difficulties. . . .'⁵⁴ While Grey fondly believed that he was helping both American parties to reach a reasonable compromise and was helping Anglo-American understanding by showing the reasonableness of some Republican objections, his successor as ambassador, Sir Auckland Geddes, thought very differently. In June he wrote to Curzon: 'The greatest blow we have had here since the war was inflicted by Lord Grey's letter. It was interpreted as a formal announcement that we were backing the Republican machine. The President has never forgiven us for what he firmly believes to have been a British government repudiation of the League of Nations Covenant. There is no doubt that the Grey letter shook Wilson's hold on the Southern Democrats badly—they moved to agree with the British Cabinet as they thought. . . .'⁵⁵ In the aftermath of this controversy, Grey resolved that the League would have to go on without the United States as best it could, and that he would never again get involved at such a high level.

When he departed for Washington, Gilbert Murray welcomed his acceptance of the mission as evidence that Grey was now back in public life. When he returned to London, his old friends were waiting for him. Lord Robert Cecil had a good talk about the political situation both at home and abroad. Cecil urged him very strongly to come back into politics. He was, after all, not yet sixty. Cecil told Runciman that he refused, but 'did not absolutely slam the door if it became necessary to do something to save the League of Nations'.⁵⁶ Cecil's great scheme was for Asquith to retire from the Liberal leadership and Grey to take his place. Gilbert Murray tried again in the summer of 1920 by trying to organize a letter from prominent people with 'Centre' political views, urging Grey to come back. Grey replied on 17 August, making the obvious reference to his poor sight, but continuing: 'Public duty is not paramount or even plain, unless a man feels very clear not only as to the policy he thinks wrong, but also as to the policy that he thinks right.' While great mistakes had been made since the war, 'I am not clear as to how the consequences of those mistakes can be avoided'.⁵⁷ Cecil wrote resignedly: 'It is as much as cld. be expected —I feel with you rather guilty in pressing him to come back—but there is really no one else. Everything he writes especially on Foreign Affairs seems to me so exactly to touch the spot. . . .'[58] What these views were can be judged from a letter to Spender at the end of July. 'The debacle in Europe', he wrote, 'is even more swift than I had feared. The two fatal mistakes have been 1. Interfering in Russian affairs at all: this put Bolshevism on its legs. 2. Allowing, still more, encouraging the Polish offensive: this made the Bolsheviks a National Party.' In his opinion, the national feeling of Russia, Germany and even France had turned against Britain and the situation was 'past redemption. We have indeed lost the peace.' Lloyd George was the cause. He had some great qualities, without being a great man. He was 'constitutionally incapable of understanding that straightforwardness is essential, "cleverness", fatal, to success in the long run'.[59]

Grey also felt strongly on the question of Ireland.[60] He spoke publicly on the subject and also wrote to the press. He had lived long enough with the Irish question to know its intractable difficulties. Yet sheer coercion appalled him. He proposed to substitute what he called 'the Coercion of Facts', though he recognized that the Irish were not good at identifying facts. They had to choose between compromise or agreement with each other, a divided Ireland or civil war.[61] By November 1920, he was in despair: 'Ireland for the present seems to me hopeless. With three or four police being murdered every day, British feeling is too indignant to discuss remedial measures. The reprisals, on the other hand, I believe pass the bounds of anything that could possibly be justified, and are making Ireland irreconcilable. . . .'[62] Again, in the end, the blame could only rest with the Prime Minister. He told Asquith that while he did not seek political talks with him, he was in fact prepared to discuss anything: 'what I do want to avoid is getting into regular political work either of Govt. or Opposition'.[63]

Liberals like Crewe and Runciman refused to allow Grey to give up the notion of a political return. A campaign to this end started again in the summer of 1921. The non-Coalition Liberals sought a leader who in some miraculous way would draw together the dispirited, ideologically divided and personally riven party. Cecil looked for the creation of a generally progressive party in which Conservatives like himself might show their disgust with the Coalition. It is ironic that they should repeatedly turn in their distress to a man who was nearly blind. One after another they courted him and wished each other good luck in their efforts.

'Our destinies as a nation', Lord Cowdray wrote, '. . . are dependent on Grey coming back & taking the reins.'[64] Certainly, Grey was still dissatisfied with the trend of events. The French seemed to him to be making impossible financial demands on Germany, though at the same time the Germans were not trying as hard to pay as they might. It seemed apposite to quote Gibbon to the effect that history was little more than the records of the crimes, the follies and the misfortunes of mankind.[65] It was rather in this mood that he consented to come down for talks, initially with Asquith, on the leadership question. He was not at all keen, writing to Lady Gladstone that, quite apart from his sight and being in the Lords, he felt that 'the possible results of my taking an active part in public affairs are being greatly overestimated by my friends'.[66]

Nevertheless, on 29 June, he had an extensive discussion with Asquith on the political future. The only really effective government could be provided by the Liberal Party, reinforced by such men as Cecil and 'moderate Labour'. The essential element for such a grouping to succeed was the 'avowed and open co-operation' of Grey himself. They then discussed a possible programme, stressing the League of Nations and urging that if the negotiations with Ireland broke down, the Irish should be left to govern themselves.[67] Following this meeting, the two men, with Cecil, Crewe, Runciman and Maclean, met again on 5 July. Asquith noted that Grey did not take 'a very active part in the discussion, but he was helpful & seemed keen. He says he has got rusty and out of touch with many departments of policy, and scouted the possibility of his becoming leader, which is, of course, what R.C. desires.'[68] But little real progress was made. Cecil did not want merely to be an auxiliary to the Liberals; and the Liberals did not want to dilute their party further in a speculative venture of this kind. Grey again refused to guarantee that he would give the time and energy needed for proper leadership. Nevertheless, the project refused to die. Runciman wrote in September 1921 concerning Grey: 'He shudders at continuous responsibility, but we must go on impressing him with what the Methodists describe as the "Call"—which he dare not shrink.'[69] Others also took the view that, 'looking round, Grey is the only man (apart from a Tory Government pure and simple) who might hope to form a responsible and reliable alternative administration. It is on these lines that we are working. . . .'[70] Grey did make a number of public speeches in the winter of 1921, but his heart was not really in the work. He put the situation very well himself in

December 1921: 'As to politics I am not the sort of person that is wanted now: Lloyd George is the modern type, suited to an age of telephones & moving pictures & modern journalism. . . . The Irish question brought me into controversial politics for a time, but I should support the agreement now made by the Govt. & shall not make new public engagements.'[71]

The break-up of the Coalition Government in October 1922 might conceivably have led to Liberal reunion, except that it was difficult for Liberals of the stamp of Asquith and Grey to forget Lloyd George's record. Sometimes, it even seemed as if Conservatives were to be preferred. Early in November, Grey was invited to address a meeting in Manchester intended to celebrate Liberal reunion. Rather to the surprise of his audience, he chose the occasion to expend his passion on the now-defunct Coalition and let the Tories off lightly.[72] Lloyd George was angry, writing to C. P. Scott: 'What is the use of talking about Liberal reunion at this Election when you have speeches like those that Grey delivered at the Free Trade Hall last night.' Grey had been given a great chance, but had used it to have a 'prolonged nag' at him. 'These men', he continued, 'are far to [*sic*] obsessed with their personal wrongs and disappointments to welcome any reunion except on the express condition that I am marooned.'[73] Rather surprisingly, Scott defended Grey: he had not 'meant to be vicious, but he is temperamentally intensely antipathetic to you & above all he is outraged by what he regards as the invasion of the prerogatives of the Foreign Office'. It had only been announced on the afternoon of the speech that the meeting would celebrate Liberal reunion. Grey now had to prepare his remarks so carefully beforehand that he probably could not change his text.[74] Lloyd George was not convinced. The result of the November 1922 General Election was a grave blow to hopes of a Liberal recovery. Labour slipped ahead of the combined Liberal total for the first time, and the Liberals were of course divided, almost equally, between Asquithians and Lloyd Georgeites. 'What a chance the Liberals did miss in not taking our advice about Grey,' Cecil optimistically wrote. 'As things have turned out I verily believe they wld. have swept the country with Grey as their alternative Prime Minister.'[75] Grey continued as Liberal Leader in the House of Lords, notwithstanding the attempts of Lloyd Georgeite Liberal peers to unseat him.[76] A year later, Baldwin, the new Conservative leader, surprisingly went to the country on the issue of Protection, and the Liberals were forced to fight again. This time they gained some forty seats, but Labour went higher still. Asquith gave MacDonald the opportunity to form the first Labour Government. Once more, Cecil modestly reflected: 'How different everything would be if Grey had . . . been acknowledged the leader of the Liberal Party, with me as one of his lieutenants.'[77] Following the defeat of friends like Murray and Runciman, Grey felt dispirited. 'Protection of course is beaten', he wrote, '& I feel quite angry with the folly of the Conservatives in throwing away their good working majority & landing the country in this mess—it will play strongest into the hands of Labour, who will urge that Ll.G. is a knave & Baldwin a fool & that both the "Capitalist" parties as they call them are discredited.'[78] He did not believe any stable government would be possible until after another election, 'for if a Conservative–Liberal Coalition was formed, I do not believe it would get the support of more than a minority of the Liberal Party, and it might mean the break-up of the Liberal Party. In that case probably some 2/3 of the Liberal voters would go to Labour, and 1/3 to the Conservatives. I still believe it very important to keep the Liberal Party as a separate entity in politics. . . .'[79]

The record of the next few years is the dismal story of this endeavour. In the election of October 1924 which gave the Conservatives their clear majority, Asquith was defeated. Shortly before the election, Grey resigned the leadership of the party in the House of Lords on the grounds that he was not able to attend regularly.[80] Asquith took a peerage and became leader of the party in the Lords while Lloyd George was the leader in the Commons. There was a great deal of talk about Liberal unity, but the twin-leadership experiment operated with hardly suppressed tension between the two men. There was constant squabbling concerning the use and control of the Lloyd George Fund. The rift came into the open in 1926 on the question of the General Strike. Asquith and Grey roundly condemned the strike and wrote messages for the Government newspaper, the *British Gazette*, to this effect. Lloyd George spoke in a different, though, it was claimed, not altogether contradictory, tone. Grey thoroughly approved of Sir John Simon's statement that the strike was illegal. He wrote to Asquith 'to say how much your action & his, by firm & consistent attitude & by constructive suggestion contributed to make the record of the Liberal party in this time of confusion both honourable & sympathetic'.[81] If it was honourable and sympathetic, it was also

359

politically sterile. In September 1926, a 'conclave of the faithful' as Asquith put it, met at Grey's house to discuss the situation. Asquith refused either to lead what he called a squalid faction fight against Lloyd George, in which the latter had all the sinews of war, or to patch up a hollow and humiliating alliance. It was the end of the road. He resigned the leadership in October and eighteen months later, he was dead. 'I saw the beginning of his Parliamentary life', Grey wrote, 'and to witness the close is the end of a long chapter of my own.'[82]

Grey felt himself called upon to continue the faction fight which Asquith had not the stomach for. He invited the old guard of the party to his house in December 1926 to form the Liberal Council, the object of which was stated to be 'to enable Liberals who desire to uphold the independence of the Party to remain within it for the furtherance of the aims of Liberalism'.[83] As President, he was supported by old friends such as Runciman, Spender, Buxton and others in this attempt to revitalize Liberalism without at the same time being excessively dependent upon the financial resources Lloyd George had under his control. But it was far from clear what programme the group had to offer, apart from the satisfying conviction that Lloyd George had corrupted the nation. In a letter to Herbert Samuel, now head of the party's organization, in November 1927, he argued that the Liberal Council was prepared to support that organization, but it would not have 'anything more to do with Ll.G.'s fund'.[84] Lloyd George flirted with novel ideas which he believed would recreate a dynamic Liberal Party, while the old guard continued to be obsessed by what it regarded as public rectitude. 'We have clean hands', Grey wrote to Crewe, appealing for money, 'but empty pockets; we want to get up a fund to finance at any rate a few candidates' elections, who will not have Ll.G.'s money.'[85] However, by the time of the 1929 General Election, relations were patched up, and Grey described Lloyd George's unemployment programme as 'absolutely right'.[86] But the great Liberal effort failed, and the party's hopes of ever again becoming an alternative government faded. Curiously enough, it seems that Grey could even have been Foreign Secretary if the Conservatives had won. In January 1929, Baldwin had written asking Grey whether, in that event, he would be prepared to serve. He declined, saying that his importance in public life was overestimated. He added: 'As long as you are at the head of a Government, it will stand for what is honourable. The iron entered into my soul, when

Ll.G.'s Govt. after the war let down and corrupted public life at home and destroyed our credit abroad.'[87] The iron never left his soul. In January 1930, speaking on behalf of the Liberal Council, he reiterated his condemnation of the party's dependence on the Lloyd George Fund, and declined to acknowledge him as party leader.[88] From this point on, until the collapse of the Labour Government in August 1931, the Liberals tottered from split to split.

Instead of resigning, MacDonald invited the Conservative and Liberal leaders to join him in a National Government. Speaking at a meeting of the National Liberal Council on 28 August, Grey strongly urged the Liberals to join the Government: 'When the Empire was in danger the only line that the Liberal Party could take was to assist it.'[89] Lloyd George was seriously ill, and there was little objection to this course. The small party was generously treated—Samuel, Crewe and Maclean being among those given office. The formation of the new Cabinet did not stop the financial crisis. The run on gold began again. A feeling of panic was created by the Invergordon 'mutiny'. On 21 September the Government abandoned the Gold Standard—the action which it had been formed to avoid. The next issue was clearly going to be whether or not to hold a General Election. Samuel, who was acting leader of the party, thought that an election might well completely undermine the Liberal position. He consulted Grey, who thought that a General Election could not be postponed. The main issue, as Grey saw it, 'ought to be between a National Govt. under Ramsay MacDonald on the one side & T.U.C. policy on the other. If the Tories insist on making Tariffs the issue, I should hope that MacDonald would refuse to remain at the head of the Govt.'[90] The General Election duly came, and although the Liberals under Samuel made plain their continued adherence to the principle of a National Government, they brought out their own manifesto. Grey took no active part in the campaign, but wrote Samuel a letter to make use of as he chose. In it, he strongly supported the National Government, though he insisted that Liberal members were needed in order to maintain its national character. He deeply regretted that Lloyd George should have advised anyone to vote for the Labour Party rather than a Conservative candidate, but 'the Conservatives, who are opposing you agree with Mr Lloyd George in thinking that Fiscal policy is in this election more important than to concentrate attention upon the danger and ruin which the opposition Labour party threatens the nation'.[91] The Liberals in fact increased their representation to 68, but approximately half of these were led by Simon, and half by Samuel—the latter refusing to recognize the former. But, as Grey commented, the Conservatives would have such an overwhelming position that to use it fairly and moderately would be a great strain on them.[92]

This strain became apparent almost immediately. The Government decided on a tariff policy, and the only way in which Liberal susceptibilities could be met was by allowing them to 'agree to differ'. Once again, Grey supported this compromise. Expressing his relief that the Government's national character had been maintained, Grey found the solution 'a novel experiment. But the British Constitution has developed by being adaptable to novel conditions. . . .'[93] Nevertheless, many younger Liberals were not happy with the decision. The Government's attempts to realize the dream of Imperial Free Trade at the Ottawa Conference in July and August 1932 would clearly bring this unease to a head. To prepare for it, Samuel saw Grey on 26 August. Grey did not like what he knew of the agreements, and felt that on balance the Liberals ought to leave the Government because of them.[94] Early in September, after careful consideration, he told Samuel he thought the decision was finely balanced. If the Liberals did come out, he hoped it would be made clear that this was simply to enable them to speak their minds on fiscal policy 'and not because you wish to see the Government displaced, or to go into general opposition to it. . . .' This remained his advice even though Walter Runciman presented the Ottawa agreements (which he helped to negotiate) in a more favourable light and declared that he would stay in the Government. It is probably true that, for different reasons, neither MacDonald nor Baldwin actually wished to see the Liberals depart. The King shared this feeling even more strongly, and empowered Runciman to deliver a personal message to Grey to say that he hoped he 'would do everything possible to help keep the National Government united as His Majesty felt that any break now would have a disastrous effect not only in this country, but in the outside world'. Runciman reported that Grey would not put pressure on Samuel to change his mind. He agreed with the acting leader on the tariff question and was sure that the existence of the Government would not be in doubt because of the Liberal withdrawal. It was Lord Grey's last contribution to the affairs of the nation.[95]

The time was near for his last public speech. On 28 April 1933, as President of the Liberal Council, he declared, perhaps significantly in view of the year: 'As long as people are what they are in this country, they will be liberal, even if they do not belong to the Liberal Party. We have been attached to individual liberty and tolerance, but the British people have shown that, while they prized liberty above everything and would not tolerate the loss of liberty, they also have the conviction that order must be preserved in order that liberty may be enjoyed.'[96]

Elder statesmen have only a minor role to play when the party which gives them their eminence is in catastrophic decline. Grey stuck to the Liberal Party doggedly, even petulantly. The final struggles with Lloyd George are all the more sad in that in earlier times, despite his different background, he had seemed capable of appreciating the Welshman's genius. Although Grey's activities for the Liberal Party and the League of Nations are not without a certain modest importance, he never strayed far, in the post-war period, from his deep-seated desire to be a private man. He wished to be free to indulge himself in those interests and activities which office had so restricted. Yet, just as his public life had, in a sense, ended in disaster, so the private anticipations of modest happiness were rewarded by surprising joy, and then yet further disaster.

His first intention, on resigning, was to leave London and his London home 'for good and all'. In Northumberland were his ducks, hills and clear burns. Once the pressure of office was removed, however, he seemed to submit to the illness which he had long resisted. For the first weeks of his new life, he was laid up with sickness and stomach pain. Yet the country brought release. 'Men', he reflected, 'will never get right till they get united by some sort of admiration and reverence for the great elemental works of God and think less of their own artifices.'[97] He had no intention of coming anywhere near London until after Easter. He left Fallodon at the end of April for a holiday in Scotland. It was the last he saw of the old house. In his absence, it was burnt, and only some furniture, books and pictures on the ground floor could be saved. It was a bitter blow and he wrote sadly: 'I kept everything in the house in the place where Dorothy put it & now I shall never see the familiar rooms again. And of course my nursery & the room where I learnt the alphabet & memories like that are swept away. It makes me feel that affections should be set on the open air & the seasons & the stars & things that are less perishable. But after all how gladly would I have had the house burnt if only Dorothy might have lived.'[98]

Sadness also came from deaths among the younger generation. He had no children to lose in the war, but profoundly sympathized with old friends who lost their sons or young friends who lost their husbands. When the Warden of All Souls, his Balliol friend, Frank Pember, lost his son (Grey's godson) he wrote: 'I know very well that there is no escape from the suffering of grief. We cannot love much without suffering much & the very pain of the suffering is an evidence of the strength of our love, so that we cannot even wish our grief to be less than it is & must be.'[99] In a later letter he wrote dolefully: '. . . I have so little left to live for that my life is more a sort of waiting for the end than living: I do live but it is in memory of past years & also in hope of what is to come after this life.'[100] He did not pretend in this confusion and distress to have a religious faith more definite than it really was. He wrote to his cousin Cyril Ryder, a Catholic priest, that he had 'a real active sense of the limitation of my own knowledge and understanding, and sincere reverence for what is beyond it and I thank you for your prayer for me'. His favourite picture of life came to him from his walks on the hills—'only when we are on very high ground can we see the direction of the paths in the country below: we may even see then, that some which appeared, when we were on low ground, to go in opposite directions really lead to the same place'.[101] Nevertheless, withal, he was satisfied: 'To have some choice in life of time & work; to be able to read for pleasure, to write what one has an impulse to write, to do work that is not uncongenial & does not entail pressure is an incredibly pleasant change from office.'[102]

Although he had been re-elected to the Board of the North Eastern Railway Company, Grey was, on his own admission, 'becoming a recluse'. He was saved from the hermitage by his friendship with Pamela Glenconner, and his later marriage to her. Pamela was one of the most strikingly beautiful women of her generation. Born a Wyndham, she was the sister of the Tory politician, George Wyndham. But by her marriage to Eddie Tennant (created Lord Glenconner in 1911), Asquith's brother-in-law, she became, perforce, a leading Liberal hostess. Inter-connexions of this kind brought down the wrath of Hilaire Belloc, who wrote scornfully in 1909: 'Alfred Lyttelton will think the power of the Peers reasonable; not his sister's husband, Masterman, who will, however, be supported by his wife's first cousin, Gladstone; while the Prime Minister will not find his brother-in-law fail him nor need he doubt Mr McKenna, since he married the daughter of the Tennant's chief friend. Oddly enough, however, while Pamela Tennant's husband will support the Government, her brother Mr George Wyndham will not find it possible to agree with them.'[103] Throughout his years in office, Edward Grey was on the fringe of this social world. Since, for a time, he lived so very near them in London, he was a frequent caller on the Glenconners. Pamela had strong and fastidious tastes. She wrote poetry herself and published a personal anthology, *The White Wallet*, which, in its day, had a certain success.[104] A favourite subject for her poetry was her country home, Wilsford, on the downs in Wiltshire. Both there, and at Queen Anne's Gate, the staff appreciated Edward's visits. He always left money in appreciation of their services, and, unlike other visitors, such as Mr Churchill, he was never late for meals.[105] To Lady Tweedsmuir, Pamela seemed 'an Olympian character, because of her aloofness from mundane things. She floated to and fro between Wilsford and the Glen, appreciating their different beauties, and so well buttressed by wealth that she never had to catch a bus or think about the price of fish.'[106]

The Glenconners were among the few people who could attract Edward Grey to their dinner table in the latter stages of the war. They too had tasted tragedy, for their eldest son had been killed in action in 1916. Henry Newbolt described one such occasion in February 1918 when, together with Grey, he was a guest. The dining-room had been turned into an air-raid bedroom so they dined in the hall: 'simplicity was attained by a menu of soup, fish potato pie, and cold rosbif'.[107] Glenconner died in 1920 and by the end of 1921, Grey was writing privately to Mrs Creighton that '. . . for some years as I supposed people knew I have had a very delightful & intimate friendship with Pamela Glenconner. It did not impair my close friendship with her husband & I was equally in the confidence of them both.' He had asked her to marry him, and although nothing was likely to happen at once, 'what would probably be best is that people should understand we are attached to each other but that nothing is likely to happen soon'.[108] However, on 4 June 1922, they were married without wedding presents, spectators or photographers.

His second marriage gave him a fresh enthusiasm for life at a time when he was likely to have fallen into despondency. The previous year he had declined the post of Chairman of the newly amalgamated London and North Eastern Railway.[109] Now Pamela encouraged him to turn to lecturing and writing on congenial topics. Simultaneously, and symbolically, the new Fallodon was being built without its previous top floor. 'I shall have no affection for the new house,' he wrote, 'but it will be a relief to have something more comfortable than the remnant of a house in which I have now lived for nearly five years. . . . And I shall enjoy having my books back from the warehouse, though I can do little in the way of reading with my crippled eyes.'[110] The lectures he gave were all on themes dear to him. He expounded such familiar topics as the pleasure of reading, making it clear that his preferences were for well-established classics. On another occasion, he regretted the development of picture papers, which were tending to divert people not only from reading, but also from thought. He quoted as an example of the ill-informed judgments such papers produced, the case of the lady who preferred the Turks to the Greeks because she judged from the pictures that Mustapha Kemal was rather a good sort of fellow. His dislike of illustrated papers was matched by his distrust of the motor car, the effect of which, under the specious guise of convenience, kept a man in a sedentary position when the real pleasure of life was to be found in exercise or rest. Industrial societies, he considered, stood in grave danger of losing the capacity for true recreation and reflection. It is not surprising that he reverted to these themes again and again in his lectures, which, when published as the *Fallodon Papers* in 1926, had to be instantly reprinted four times.

His most serious work was the writing of *Twenty-Five Years*. Again, Pamela's stimulus was invaluable. 'It becomes very clear to me', he wrote to her, 'that but for you *Twenty-Five Years* would never have been written. It is due to things and influences you brought, much rarer even than your material help, and which could have come from no one else.'[111] He also received considerable assistance from J. A. Spender. The journalist left a note of a working day with Grey in October 1924: 'We had as good a journey as getting out at Newcastle at 5 a.m. makes possible, and after it a strenuous day— work till 12, then on bicycles to Bamburgh and a long circuit back (about 28 miles altogether), then an hour before dinner, and two hours in the evening at the MS. Grey is extraordinarily tough. . . .'[112] These two volumes were the first full-length record by a Foreign Secretary of his period of office—itself perhaps an indication of a change in public attitude since he had first gone to the Foreign Office in 1892. He set out to write an account which would not simply be a *pièce justificative* for his own actions, but which would be a record of real historical value. After nearly half a century, it can be shown, of course, to have limitations. What is remarkable, however, is the extent to which the work has itself an historical importance. In his reflective conclusion, he accepted the substance of contentions which his critics had been arguing for years—indeed, accepted them with quite unwarranted ease. While he did not withdraw his criticism of German militarism, he now argued: 'The lesson of European history is so plain. It is that no enduring security can be found in competing armaments and in separate alliances; there is no security for any Power unless it be security in which its neighbours have an equal share.' Nations could learn from the past and 'the future, the life of European civilization, will depend upon whether a wider and more instructed spirit prevails now than it did before the experience of the Great War; if it does not, our present civilization will perish, as others have done before it, and the future of mankind will depend on the rise of something new, some human agency outside Europe and perhaps not of European race'. It seemed that the establishment had joined the dissenters. The book was widely translated and its sales, in its various English editions, were very high for the period. Its influence both upon the historiography of the Great War and in moulding public opinion in the inter-war period was very considerable, though impossible to estimate exactly.[113]

The publication of *Twenty-Five Years* was a debt to the past. It was his first and last 'political' work. His chief preoccupation in the last decade of his life was rather with the quality of civilization. His anxieties were not those of a refined aesthete, but of a man whose sense of oneness with nature was more than ordinary. He was not a scientific ornithologist, though he was held in high esteem by both amateurs and professionals. What impressed all who came into contact with him was his patience and skill in handling all kinds of birds, most famously, of course, the ducks in his pond at Fallodon. He had a remarkable ear for bird-songs, and though his sight became so bad that he could not find nests at all or see birds distinctly, he could judge them by their songs impeccably to the end. He captured this enjoyment in his book, *The Charm of Birds*, which went through ten editions in the decade after it was published in 1927. He was very far from any conception of Social Darwinism.

'Mankind', he wrote, 'is so separate from the wild life of Nature that the two things are not comparable at all. Man's highest concern individually and collectively is with moral problems, with right and wrong. If he imports these considerations into the study of wild birds and animals, he will distort the truth of what he sees. The wild creatures act admirably according to the inherited instinct of their kind, but they are not troubled by sense of virtue or of shame. Therefore it is that the study of their life is such a recreation to man; it opens a door through which self-consciousness escapes and leaves him free for a time from moral doubts and strivings.' He himself felt quite unselfconscious with a robin perched on his head or hand. There can be few Foreign Secretaries who have immersed themselves unconcernedly in state papers while squirrels hopped on and off the study table. This diminution of self-consciousness was not to be confused with 'dull, insensate quiescence', for interest could be quickened to the point of excitement by what was observed. Here was the paradox: 'We are keenly alive and yet remain free from all anxiety about success or failure, from shyness, embarrassment or any concern that is personal to ourselves.'[114]

He was fortunate to be able to find this release until the very end, for his last years would otherwise have been blacker than they were. Pamela died after six years of marriage, and he was left alone once more. 'It is very hard', he wrote to Mrs Creighton, 'but I lived alone for more than 16 years and I can do it again, though I am very stricken.'[115] Even little havens of memory and experience like his Hampshire cottage were denied him. It was burned in 1923 and he wrote to his old companion of many fishing expeditions, Earl Buxton, expressing his sadness. Even the mitigating factor, that since he could not fish, it was playing less and less part in his life, was itself a source of sorrow.[116] The autumn of 1928 was a time of double tragedy. Shortly before Pamela's death came news that his other brother, Charlie, had been claimed in Africa by a buffalo, just as George had previously been by a lion. 'Charlie was a very rare person & greatly beloved', he wrote. 'Like my brother George he was quite fearless & this led him as it had led George to take a fatal risk. I was the eldest of 4 brothers & I am now the last left, which makes me feel as if I must go soon.'[117] Wordsworth, as always, expressed his feelings:

> *Suffering is permanent, obscure and dark,*
> *And shares the nature of infinity.*

The public honours which came to him at the end of his life were some little consolation, but he had never cared greatly for such things. He was a Fellow of Winchester College for some years, and enjoyed his visits to his old school. Perhaps the greatest honour was his election in 1928 as Chancellor of Oxford University. The qualifications for this office had been the subject of some discussion among his friends. It was generally agreed that 'character' was required. Haldane thought that 'intellectual character' was desirable, and Grey never read a book. The little circle was aghast at this remark, which was then repeated for emphasis. Archbishop Lang then intervened to state that Grey was known to have read Wordsworth; to which Haldane replied that Wordsworth was not a book. The remark was greeted with general stupefaction and the company pressed Haldane to admit that Grey did have intellectual interests. 'Oh, yes,' came the answer, 'among birds and fishes.'[118] It is, of course, just conceivable that Haldane was attempting to make a joke. At any rate Grey was elected Chancellor and played some part in University affairs for the last five years of his life, in particular sponsoring the development of the Oxford Society. But, with his various incapacities, there was a limit to the role he could play. Occasionally, as on his seventieth birthday in 1932, he could be enticed out for a formal occasion. The birthday luncheon was organized by Sir James Barrie and attended by old friends and leading politicians. In Barrie's speech there were a number of good stories which were testimony to the affection in which he was held. Barrie reputedly discussed with his canary his intention of holding the lunch. The bird wanted to know who this 'Grey' was. Sir James replied that it was the eminent statesman, which had little impact on the bird. Suddenly, however, it perked up and exclaimed: 'You don't mean Our Grey . . . the man the grey squirrels are called after.'[119] Grey enjoyed such whimsy and replied in kind.

Away from such company, however, back at Fallodon, he was dispirited and gloomy. To add to his troubles, he began to be seriously troubled by a kidney affliction which he had suffered from for some time. Since February 1906 he had been waiting for death, and when it came, in September 1933, his ashes found their due place beside Dorothy's under the trees in the garden at Fallodon.

The tributes paid him on his death singled out his courage, integrity and character. Even the Nazi *Angriff* conceded that Lord Grey was 'neither as black as the devil nor as white as an angel but just Grey'.[120] Privately and publicly, however, doubts about his capacity could easily be found. The most notable public source was the biting comment in Lloyd George's recently published *War Memoirs*. William George had tried to restrain his brother's pen. Edward Grey was an old man, he wrote, and would soon be gone: the sharp phrases would only damage Lloyd George's own reputation. David would have none of it. Grey's reputation was not based on any achievement. He was a calamitous Foreign Secretary, both before and during the war. Nor would he desist because they had been colleagues: 'I would be bound to take that into account had he behaved in a true spirit of comradeship. Instead of that he was one of the bitterest of those who assailed me when I was chairman of the Party.' He claimed to have dealt faithfully in his book with the charlatans and skunks, and 'Grey certainly belongs in my opinion in the first category'. Members of Lloyd George's entourage anxiously sought other opinion. Lord Beaverbrook thought that if that was the way Lloyd George felt, so he ought to write. He added: 'My firm view is that in the long run he will be right. Grey's reputation will be deflated.' Hankey, too, found the character sketches admirable: 'Grey is torn rather ruthlessly from his pedestal. Much as I like the man, I have never had a high opinion of him as a statesman.'[121] Ramsay MacDonald expressed himself just as sharply about Grey: 'I believe him to have been the most incompetent Foreign Secretary—& one of the most honest men who ever held office—one who combined a most admirable intention with a tragic incapacity to drive his way to his own goal.'[122] No doubt other similar comments could be discovered, running counter to the general tributes and praise.

There is one sentence in Lloyd George's letter to his brother which helps to resolve this discrepancy of judgment, though it can never entirely be removed. He let slip that the real cause of his venom was the Liberal in-fighting of the late twenties and the controversy over the Coalition Government. Grey, like Baldwin, felt an almost physical revulsion from the methods of that administration. Undoubtedly, codes of conduct and political styles were in open confrontation. In this respect, the war marked the end of an era and, unlike his friend Haldane, Grey was unable to switch his political allegiance.[123] He had been fashioned in a political tradition whose principles and practices he had himself helped to adapt and refine. What had been the subject of academic discussion with Mandell Creighton in his Embleton Vicarage in the early eighteen-eighties had become reality. To the anxiety of his family, in the flush of youth, he had grandly accepted the extension of the suffrage and swept aside their inhibitions. Little could he foresee then that he would be Foreign Secretary when the greatest war in human history ravaged and battered the political structure. He had few illusions about its consequences: '. . . there will be changes that amount to revolution & will cause great discomfort, but will be very interesting & will I hope not be accompanied by the violence, public anxiety & private grief that are still inseparable from the war'.[124] Reflecting on Winchester in 1936, Firth found it very significant that Britain's greatest War Minister since Chatham had not been a public schoolboy at all. Much as Wykehamists reverenced Lord Grey, 'Was there just some element lacking of sheer power and drive, of the force which can shape complicated circumstances to a man's own will?' While Winchester had signally refused to capitulate to modern self-advertisement, and the criterion of success, was it not perhaps true that in the contemporary world, 'this hatred of vulgar pushfulness, may, beyond a certain point, become a form of pride and a weakness'?[125] At the time of his death, England seemed to have survived the transition from the political Liberalism of Grey's youth to the pressures of mass democracy, relatively unscathed. Yet, looking at Europe as a whole, it seemed more doubtful whether the virtues of tolerance and parliamentary government could survive into the future. In the last year of his life (and the significance of 1933 needs no reminder) he wrote to Colonel House: 'Democracy is on a new trial. When policy depended upon the political instincts of the people democracy did well, but politics are now a matter of economics and in this the instinct of people may be at fault.'[126]

All of this has little significance for the years of Grey's political prime. Although the bases of politics were shifting, the structure still seemed firm enough to allow a man of Grey's gifts and qualities to operate successfully within it. It would be folly to expect complete agreements on the merits of his foreign policy, but that for a decade at least it was *his* policy, there can be little disputing. He did not stray by accident into the Foreign Office while out fishing and remain there undisturbed—though there were diplomatists who fondly imagined that his rods were stacked in a corner of his room. He was a very perfect English gentleman but he was also a very sharp politician. 'Though I have never known a man with a more frank and straightforward manner,' Mrs Belloc Lowndes wrote,

'Grey's long training as Foreign Secretary had taught him how to evade answering a question he considered indiscreet.'[127] In the history of British foreign policy from the turn of the century there were a number of vital questions which could perhaps only be evaded and not answered. And perhaps it is not too much of a paradox to assert that only a man of Grey's stature could evade them with conviction and integrity. A Foreign Secretary with greater intellectual capacity would probably have been unable to stand the strain created by the ambiguous relations between Britain and France without wishing for sharper definition. While it may be that the international situation might have been clarified with advantage, the cost would probably have been domestic disruption and the break up of the Government. Instinctively, Grey shied away from the attempt to be rigid and precise. He preferred in his own quiet way to manœuvre for position, and in the final crisis, decide for himself the full extent of responsibility, interest and obligation. Edward Grey was the last Foreign Secretary in a great nineteenth-century tradition. Probably never again would a Prime Minister allow him such scope as did Asquith. Probably never again would the Foreign Office have such an unchallenged authority. Albeit reluctantly, he took decisions which brought the British Empire to its greatest territorial extent. His successors have only been concerned with preserving, and then dismantling, the imperial structure.

By a supreme irony, which his sense of humour would have enjoyed, his anxieties about land, cities, noise, birds and cars, which seemed the quintessence of the gentleman amateur, have reappeared under the more elaborate guise of 'Conservation' and 'the Environment' as major issues in contemporary politics. 'I feel deep in me that the civilization of the Victorian epoch ought to disappear', he wrote in 1918. 'I think I always knew this sub-consciously, but I took things as I found them and for 30 years spoke of progress as an enlargement of the Victorian industrial age—as if anything could be good that led to telephones, and cinemato-graphs and large cities and the *Daily Mail*.'[128]

Sources

CHAPTER I

1. *Journals and Correspondence of Francis Thornhill Baring, Lord Northbrook*, Vol. 1, privately printed, 1905, p. 278.
2. R. Fulford, *Samuel Whitbread*, Macmillan, London, 1967, pp. 26–30.
3. G. M. Trevelyan, *Lord Grey of the Reform Bill*, Longmans, London, 1952.
4. Unless otherwise stated, the facts about Sir George Grey are derived from M. Creighton, *Memoir of Sir George Grey, Bart.*, Newcastle, 1884. Unfortunately it would seem that Sir George's papers were destroyed in the fire at Fallodon in 1917.
5. Mrs H. Ryder to Lady Anna Grey, August 1827, Harrowby MS. CII ff. 105–6.
6. Extract from a sermon preached by the Rev. W. S. Dusautoy on the Sunday following the funeral of Sir George Grey, 12.10.28. Harrowby MS. CII f. 145.
7. Sir G. Grey to A. Rennie, 9.1.32, Harrowby MS. CII ff. 186–7.
8. D. Southgate, *The Passing of the Whigs*, Macmillan, London, 1962, p. 151.
9. Miss S. Ryder to Miss R. March-Phillipps, 22.9.48, Harrowby MS. CIV f. 52.
10. Mrs H. Ryder to Lady Anna Grey, Harrowby MS. CIII f. 395.
11. Southgate, *Passing of the Whigs*, p. 152.
12. Mrs H. Ryder to Lady Anna Grey, 16.4.48, Harrowby MS. CIV f. 35.
13. *The Poll Book for the Northern Division of Northumberland*, Newcastle, The Journal Office, 1852; N. McCord and A. E. Carrick, 'Northumberland and the General Election of 1852' in *Northern History*, Vol. 1, 1966.
14. Creighton, *Grey*, p. 83.
15. T. Burt, *Pitman and Privy Councillor: Autobiography*, Fisher Unwin, London, 1924, pp. 212–14.
16. Sir G. Grey to 3rd Earl Grey, 9.11.74; 3rd Earl Grey to Sir G. Grey, 10.11.74, Grey of Howick MS.
17. Mrs H. Ryder to Lady Anna Grey, 1839, Harrowby MS. CIII f. 362.
18. Sir G. Grey to Gen. C. Grey, 11.9.58, Royal Archives, Z 443/70.
19. Queen Victoria: Journal, 2.11.58, Royal Archives, Windsor and RA Add. C/1 54.
20. Prince Albert to Sir G. Grey, 12.9.58, Royal Archives Z 443/71.
21. Gen. Bruce to Prince Albert, 12.1.59, Royal Archives Z 444/37.
22. Gen. Bruce to Prince Albert, 23.1.59, Royal Archives Z 444/45.
23. I am greatly indebted to Lt.-Col. R. L. Clarke, Mrs Olive S. Clarke, Mr Hubert Butler and Mr Gerald Curtis for providing me with information about the Pearson family from genealogies and documents in their possession.

24. The Grey family accepted her easily after the marriage and mother and daughter-in-law were on good terms until the former's death.
25. Harriet Pearson to Louisa Thornewill. Courtesy of Mr Gerald Curtis.
26. Lady Elizabeth Waldegrave to Lady Mary Waldegrave, 14.9.66. Courtesy of the Countess Waldegrave.
27. D. Newsome, *The Parting of Friends*, Murray, London, 1966, pp. 310–12.
28. Lady Elizabeth Waldegrave to Lady Mary Waldegrave, 15.9.66.
29. Lady L. Palmer to Lady D. Palmer, 17.9.61, Waldegrave Papers.
30. A. C. Benson, *Memories and Friends*, Murray, London, 1924, pp. 30 ff.
31. Princess Alexandra to the Prince of Wales, 10.12.74, Royal Archives Z 450/142.
32. Queen Victoria: Journal, 11.12.74, Royal Archives.
33. Queen Victoria: Journal, 12.12.74, Royal Archives.
34. Knollys to the Prince of Wales, 11.12.74, Royal Archives Z 450/143.
35. The Prince of Wales to Princess Louise, 18.12.74, Royal Archives Add. A/17 652.
36. T. J. H. Bishop and R. Wilkinson, *Winchester and the Public School Elite*, Faber and Faber, London, 1967, pp. 23–4 and 104–5.
37. E. C. Mack, *Public Schools and British Opinion since 1860*, Columbia U.P., New York, 1941, Chap. 1.
38. L. Ridding, *George Ridding*, Arnold, London, 1908, p. 95.
39. H. A. L. Fisher in *The Wykehamist*, 13.10.33.
40. G. M. Trevelyan, *Grey of Fallodon*, Longmans, Green, London, 1948 impression, p. 12.
41. Mrs J. Salter, a niece of Edward Grey, to Viscount Sandon, 19.2.51, Harrowby MS., 3rd Ser., LXXII, f. 83.
42. Sir G. Grey to 3rd Earl Grey, 18.4.76, Grey of Howick MS.
43. Bishop and Wilkinson, *Winchester*, p. 131.
44. It is interesting to note that the Indian Civil Service claimed the largest group of Balliol men in Grey's year: 17 out of 71. The Law claimed 10 others, Education 10 and the Church 7. Then there were a few eccentrics who became engineers or went into business. Sir I. Elliott, *The Balliol College Register, Third Edition, 1900–50*, privately printed, Oxford, 1953, p. 7.
45. L. Creighton, *Life and Letters of Mandell Creighton*, Longmans, Green, London, 1913, i, p. 209.
46. J. A. Spender recounts the incident in his *Men and Things*, Cassell, London, 1937, p. 3.
47. J. G. Lockhart, *Cosmo Gordon Lang*, Hodder and Stoughton, London, 1949, pp. 30–1.
48. Dr E. V. Quinn, Librarian and Fellow of Balliol, kindly found me the photograph and showed me the minute book.
49. Edward Grey's autobiographical fragment cited in Trevelyan, *Grey*, pp. 19–20.
50. N. Annan, *Leslie Stephen: His thought and character in relation to his time*, MacGibbon and Kee, London, 1951, makes this claim for Grey as well as others.

CHAPTER 2
1. Miss U. Ryder to W. Ryder, 7.7.84, Harrowby MS. 507 f. 361–2.
2. Trevelyan, *Grey*, p. 23. Creighton, in a letter on 29.7.84, urged Grey to 'use every opportunity that may offer itself of making yourself a political personage, with a distinct line', and proceeded to advise him on the length of his speech. *Creighton*, i, pp. 204–5.

3. S. Childers, *The Life and Correspondence of Rt Hon. Hugh C. E. Childers, 1827–96*, Murray, London, ii, pp. 210–11.

4. Trevelyan, *Grey*, p. 27.

5. W. W. Bean, *The Parliamentary Representation of the Six Northern Counties of England, 1603–1886*, Hull, 1896, pp. 483 and 1164.

6. Creighton to Grey, 22.1.85, in *Creighton*, i, p. 305.

7. Trevelyan, *Grey*, p. 28.

8. M. Kinnear, *The British Voter*, Batsford, London, 1968, pp. 125–6.

9. Grey to D. Widdrington, 7.9.85, cited in Trevelyan, *Grey*, pp. 31–2.

10. For a stimulating brief discussion see F. M. L. Thompson, 'Land and Politics in the Nineteenth Century', *Transactions of the Royal Historical Society*, Vol. 15, 1965.

11. G. A. Grey to 3rd Earl Grey, 10.5.85, Grey of Howick MS.

12. Creighton to Grey, 18.3.85, *Creighton*, i, p. 306.

13. Grey to A. Grey, n.d. 1885, Grey of Howick MS.

14. Grey: Journal, 24.3.85, cited in Trevelyan, *Grey*, p. 28.

15. Grey to A. Grey, n.d. 1885, Grey of Howick MS.

16. Mrs S. Ryder to Col. W. Ryder, 17.7.85, Harrowby MS. 508 f. 364.

17. Grey to A. Grey, n.d. 1885, Grey of Howick MS.

18. Grey to A. Grey, n.d. 1885, Grey of Howick MS.

19. Apparently Grey's selection was made after a ballot in which the four final contenders were all asked to speak separately.

20. D. Grey to Miss Herbert, 3.11.85, cited in L. Creighton, *Dorothy Grey*, London, privately printed, 1907, pp. 22–3.

21. Grey to Lord Northbrook, 13.10.85, Rosebery MS.

22. D. Spring, *The English Landed Estate in the Nineteenth Century: its Administration*, Johns Hopkins, Baltimore, 1963, pp. 8–13.

23. Pollock on *The Land Laws*, 2nd ed., 1887, pp. 152–3, cited in H. J. Hanham, *The Nineteenth Century Constitution, 1815–1914*, Cambridge, 1969, p. 289.

24. Anon, *Sir Edward Grey, K.G.*, Newnes, London, 1915, pp. 18–19.

25. E. Pease to A. Grey, 23.6.07, Grey of Howick MS. 228/10.

26. L. Creighton, *D. Grey*, pp. 10–11.

27. L. Creighton, *D. Grey*, p. 19.

28. Miss E. Ryder to Miss S. Ryder, 13.10.85, Harrowby MS. 508 ff. 514–19.

29. Miss M. Ryder to Col. W. Ryder, 12.3.86, Harrowby MS. 509 ff. 113–14.

30. William Adam, the Liberal Whip, was sponsor for the Club and it was believed that Chamberlain made available the basement room in the Devonshire Club where the members assembled. O. Browning, *Memories of Sixty Years*, The Bodley Head, London, 1910, p. 283.

31. In 1884, when Edward joined, the Club had 200 members, of whom 36 were M.P.s. Gladstone was the President and the Vice-Presidents were Lord Richard Grosvenor, Albert Grey and Arnold Morley. Asquith, Haldane and L. Harcourt were amongst those on the Executive Committee. (*The Annual Report of the 'Eighty Club' for 1885*) Edward rose rapidly, joining the Committee in 1887 and becoming a Vice-President in 1889.

32. Grey, Journal, 28.4.85, cited in Trevelyan, *Grey*, p. 29.

33. Grey, Journal, 19.2.85, cited in Trevelyan, *Grey*, pp. 29–30.

34. For further discussion of this general question see D. A. Hamer, 'The Irish Question and Liberal Politics', *The Historical Journal*, 12,3,1969, pp. 519-20.

35. D. Grey to E. Pease, 6.2.86, L. Creighton, *D. Grey*, pp. 24–5.

36. Creighton to Grey, 3.6.85 and 1.12.85, *Creighton*, i, pp. 306–7 and 347–9. For Maine, see the biography, G. Feaver, *From Status to Contract*, Longmans, London, 1969.

37. Lord Northbrook to Mountstuart Grant Duff, 30.7.86, cited in B. Mallet, *Thomas George, Earl of Northbrook*, Longmans, London, 1908, pp. 232–3.

38. Trevelyan, *Grey*, p. 33.

39. Sir C. E. Trevelyan to Mr Woodman, 9.9.81, Trevelyan MS. 18.

40. A. E. Pease, *Elections and Recollections*, Murray, London, 1932, p. 39.

41. Bean, p. 485.

42. Grey to A. Grey, 11.7.86, Grey of Howick MS.

43. Grey to A. Pease, 2.12.86, cited in Pease, *Elections*, p. 149.

44. Grey to Pease, 6.12.86, cited in Pease, *Elections*, p. 150.

45. He declared his belief that 'From not understanding the feelings of the Irish people, we in Westminster set our hands heavily upon the most tender parts of the Irish character. I believe an Irish government will be in every way more qualified for the task.' The Home Secretary told the Queen that Sir Edward had made a maiden speech of much promise and interest, but he believed him to have made 'admissions which were very fatal to his argument if he had been seriously attacked. . . .' Royal Archives B 38/12.

46. Grey to A. Grey, 30.3.87, Grey of Howick MS.

47. See M. C. Hurst, *Joseph Chamberlain and Liberal Reunion*, Routledge, London, 1967.

48. R. Jenkins, *Asquith*, Collins, London, 1964, p. 35.

49. Grey to A. Grey, 30.3.87, Grey of Howick MS.

50. L. Creighton, *D. Grey*, pp. 31–2.

51. L. Creighton, *D. Grey*, p. 37.

52. Mrs Belloc Lowndes, *A Passing World*, Macmillan, London, 1948, pp. 174–5.

53. Though she could be nasty about him too. In 1897, after a visit from Haldane, she wrote to Mrs Herbert Paul that he had been so pleasant that she felt 'ashamed of ever having been nasty about him. He talked no gossip & was interesting and kind. . . .' D. Grey to E. Paul, 3.11.97, Paul MS.

54. Haldane to Munro Ferguson, November 1889, cited in D. Sommer, *Haldane of Cloan*, Allen and Unwin, London, 1960.

55. Grey held, 'as regarded the Home Rule movement, that it was no spurious growth founded on the surface of agrarian discontent. He held it to be a genuine movement, bound up with the life of the people.' Since that was so, Liberals had nothing to fear from supporting necessary improvements in Ireland. He and Haldane voted with the Government but Acland, Buxton, Asquith and Munro Ferguson voted with the Opposition. Hansard, CCCXXX, 20.11.88, col. 1673. For his support against Curzon for the idea of payment of members see Hansard, CCCXXXIV, 29.3.89, cols. 1195–1201.

56. In his memoirs, Morley writes of this small group as follows: 'They were a working alliance, not a school; they had idealisms, but were no Utopians. Haldane, Asquith, Grey, Acland, had the temper of men of the world and the temper of business. They had conscience, character, and took their politics to heart.' Viscount Morley, *Recollections*, Macmillan, London, 1917, i, p. 323.

57. D. A. Hamer, *John Morley, Liberal Intellectual in Politics*, Clarendon Press, Oxford, 1968, pp. 249–50.

58. Asquith to Buxton, 10.11.89, Buxton MS.

59. Hamer, *Morley, loc. cit.*

60. Harcourt to Morley, 9.1.89, Harcourt MS.
61. Jenkins, *Asquith*, pp. 48–9.
62. Grey to Haldane, 8.11.90, Haldane MS.
63. In the summer of 1890, the Unionists were concerned about their legislative programme, fearing they might have to go to the country and bring about a repeal of the Union. Harcourt considered that the Opposition had only to 'complete the rout of a defeated foe and the pursuit of a flying enemy'. L. P. Curtis, *Coercion and Conciliation in Ireland, 1880–92*, Princeton U.P., Princeton, 1963, p. 308. After the Parnell divorce case, however, 'The obstruction of Government measures in the Commons seemed to collapse overnight ... and the Government's majority on the first reading of the Land Purchase Bill soared to 138.' Curtis, p. 318. Grey and Haldane again deserted their party and voted with the Government on this issue.
64. Grey to Haldane, 8.11.90, Haldane MS.
65. E. Pease to A. Grey, 23.6.07, Grey of Howick MS.
66. Comments by A. O. J. Cockshutt, *The Unbelievers: English Agnostic Thought, 1840–90*, Collins, London, 1964, pp. 13–14.
67. Grey himself wrote of Wordsworth, 'His firm conviction [was] that it is not through knowledge that we grow—unless that knowledge be accompanied by feeling—that great, pure, exalted thoughts are due not to knowledge, but to right and elevated feeling.' *Fallodon Papers*, London, Constable, 1926, pp. 157–8.
68. In December 1891 he told Tom Ellis that he could not speak for him in North Wales because of an engagement in Durham on the following day, 'unless indeed I hired a special train, which I don't feel up to, at any rate till payment of members takes place'. Grey to T. Ellis, 15.12.91, Ellis MS. 717.
69. Speaking in the debate on the franchise in March 1891, Grey noted that there were many constituencies where working men were apathetic towards politics because they did not consider they had a real choice of candidates. 'You can only remove this apathy', he claimed, 'by manhood suffrage, payment of members, and perfect freedom of election.' Hansard, CCCLI, 3.3.91, col. 87.
70. Grey to Buxton, 13.9.91, Buxton MS.
71. Cited in Hanham, *Nineteenth Century Constitution*, pp. 217–18.
72. Speech by Grey, November 1891, cited in F. A. Channing, *Memoirs of Midland Politics*, Constable, London, 1918, pp. 123–5.
73. Grey to Buxton, 31.10.91, Buxton MS.
74. Grey to A. Grey, 18.1.92, Grey of Howick MS.
75. Sir Edward Grey, *Rural Land*, London, 1892, pp. 10–11. Published by the Eighty Club.
76. Grey to Sir G. O. Trevelyan, 10.6.92, Trevelyan MS. 23.
77. Morley to Harcourt, 28.6.92, Harcourt MS.; D. Grey to E. Paul, 7.7.92, Paul MS.
78. D. Grey to E. Paul, 7.7.92, Paul MS.

CHAPTER 3
1. Grey to Bryce, 22.8.92, Bryce MS. E15.
2. D. Grey to Bishop Creighton, 13.9.92, L. Creighton, *D. Grey*, pp. 85–6.
3. Grey to Buxton, 6.8.92, Buxton MS.
4. Grey to W. E. Gladstone, 19.8.92, W. E. Gladstone MS., Add. MS. 44515.

5. Anna, Lady Grey to 3rd Earl of Harrowby, 28.9.92, Harrowby MS., 2nd Ser. XLIV, ff. 59–61.
6. Sir Charles Mallet, *Herbert Gladstone, A Memoir*, Hutchinson, London, 1932, p. 143n.
7. R. Rhodes James, *Rosebery*, Weidenfeld and Nicolson, London, 1963, p. 244.
8. It is almost impossible to gain an accurate idea of Edward Grey's wealth. He was never less than self-sufficient, but most of his capital was locked away in the estate and he does not appear to have had a very large regular income. At his death he left £123,000, which is, of course, in contemporary values a considerable sum and in 1933 represented a great deal more.
9. D. Grey to Bishop Creighton, 13.9.92, L. Creighton, *D. Grey*, pp. 85–6.
10. D. Grey to Mrs Buxton, 12.9.92, Buxton MS.
11. Grey of Fallodon, *Twenty-Five Years*, Hodder & Stoughton, London, 1925, i, p. 2.
12. R. Munro Ferguson to his wife, 16.8.94, reporting this remark by Grey made at a dinner. I owe this reference to Mr H. C. G. Mathew.
13. Grey to A. Grey, 30.3.87, Grey of Howick MS.
14. *Journal and Letters of Viscount Esher*, Nicholson and Watson, London, 1934, i, p. 162.
15. A. Low, 'British Public Opinion and the Uganda Question, October–December 1892', *The Uganda Journal*, Sept. 1954.
16. W. E. Gladstone to Rosebery, 25.9.92, W. E. Gladstone MS., Add. MS. 44289.
17. Lord Crewe, *Lord Rosebery*, Murray, London, 1931, ii, p. 423.
18. Grey to W. E. Gladstone, 22.3.93, W. E. Gladstone MS., Add. MS. 44517.
19. Grey to Rosebery, 21.3.93, Rosebery MS. 23.
20. E. Hamilton, Diary, 31.3.93, Hamilton MS., Add. MS. 48660.
21. See L. Trainor, 'The Liberals and the Formation of Imperial Defence Policy, 1892–5', *Bulletin of the Institute of Historical Research*, November 1969.
22. Cited in Rhodes James, *Rosebery*, p. 284.
23. Grey to D. Grey, October 1892, cited in Trevelyan, *Grey*, p. 60.
24. T. B. Miller, 'The Egyptian Question and British Foreign Policy, 1892–94', *The Journal of Modern History*, March 1960.
25. E. Hamilton, Diary, 25.7.93, Hamilton MS., Add. MS. 48661.
26. E. Hamilton, Diary, 5.10.93, Hamilton MS., Add. MS. 48661.
27. Grey to H. Paul, 22.12.92, Paul MS.
28. D. Grey to Grey, 18.9.93, L. Creighton, *D. Grey*, pp. 198–9.
29. D. Grey to G. Grey, 3.11.93, L. Creighton, *D. Grey*, pp. 199–200.
30. Grey to D. Grey, 21.3.94, cited in Trevelyan, *Grey*, p. 61.
31. For quotation and comment see P. Stansky, *Ambitions and Strategies*, Clarendon Press, Oxford, 1964, pp. 102–3.
32. *The Times*, 26.7.94.
33. *The Times*, 15.10.94.
34. He did not object to the Welsh in principle. T. E. Ellis's promotion to Liberal Chief Whip in March 1894 delighted Grey: 'May the news of it give to every member of the party the same stimulus to loyalty that it has given to me.' Grey to Ellis, 7.3.94, Ellis MS.
35. I. Klein, 'Salisbury, Rosebery, and the Survival of Siam', *Journal of British Studies*, November 1968.
36. 3rd Earl Grey to Grey, 4.6.94, F.O. 800/37.
37. Grey to 3rd Earl Grey, 5.6.94, Grey of Howick MS.

38. Grey to Lord Kimberley, 4.6.94, Minute by Lord Kimberley, F.O. 800/37.
39. Grey to H. Paul, 16.1.95, Paul MS.
40. The problem of the Nile is admirably discussed by G. N. Sanderson, *England, Europe and the Upper Nile*, Edinburgh U.P., Edinburgh, 1965, and I am indebted to his account of the 'Grey Declaration' on pp. 213 ff.
41. Letter in *The Times*, 1.4.95.
42. Hansard, 4 Ser., XXXII, pp. 403–7.
43. Cited in Rhodes James, *Rosebery*, p. 374. In October 1898 Rosebery did claim responsibility, but this claim must remain doubtful.
44. Grey, *Twenty-Five Years*, i, pp. 19–20.
45. Grey to Rosebery, 30.3.95, Rosebery MS.
46. Cited, Rhodes James, *Rosebery*, p. 375.
47. E. Hamilton, Diary, 29.3.95, Hamilton MS., Add. MS. 48664.
48. A. G. Gardiner, *Life of Sir William Harcourt*, Constable, London, 1923, ii, pp. 335–7.
49. Sanderson, *The Upper Nile*, p. 216.
50. R. Robinson, J. Gallagher and A. Denny, *Africa and the Victorians*, Macmillan, London, 1961, pp. 335–6.
51. Grey to Rosebery, 30.3.95, Rosebery MS.
52. Grey to Rosebery, 24.4.95, Rosebery MS.
53. Printed in Grey, *Twenty-Five Years*, i, pp. 45 ff.
54. Grey to Buxton, 28.12.94, Buxton MS. The question of secession was on Grey's mind because he was slightly involved with the rights of self-governing colonies in trade matters. Grey felt that it was impossible to turn the clock back and prevent the colonies from negotiating separate commercial treaties, but they should be discouraged from doing so. Some limitations should be placed on the colonial power but these, he argued, were to be dictated 'not by economic doctrine, but by reasons partly of Imperial policy and partly of self interest. . . .' Cited in L. Trainor, 'The British Government and Imperial Economic Unity, 1890–1895', *The Historical Journal*, 1970, XIII, i, p. 79.
55. Grey to Rosebery, 22.6.95, Rosebery MS.
56. Grey to Rosebery, 13.3.95, Rosebery MS.
57. E. C. F. Collier, ed., *A Victorian Diarist. Extracts from the Journals of Mary, Lady Monkswell, 1873–95*, Murray, London, 1944, pp. 267–8.
58. Grey to Rosebery, 25.6.95, Rosebery MS.

CHAPTER 4

1. E. and D. Grey, *Cottage Book, Itchen Abbas, 1894–1905*, privately published, London, 1909. Entry of 22–3.6.95.
2. D. Grey to Miss E. Arnold, 13.7.95; D. Grey to Mrs F. Buxton, 26.7.95. L. Creighton, *D. Grey*, pp. 87–8.
3. Rosebery to Ripon, 13.8.95, Ripon MS., Add. MS. 43516.
4. R. A. Humphreys, *Tradition and Revolt in Latin America and other essays*, Weidenfeld and Nicolson, London, 1969, pp. 196–9.
5. Cited in Humphreys, *Tradition and Revolt*, p. 203.
6. J. A. S. Grenville, *Lord Salisbury and Foreign Policy, the close of the nineteenth century*, Athlone Press, London, 1964, pp. 60–69; Humphreys, *Tradition and Revolt*, p. 205.
7. Cited in Grenville, *Lord Salisbury*, p. 65.
8. Gardiner, *Harcourt*, ii, pp. 396–7.

9. Grey to Buxton, 31.12.95, Buxton MS.
10. Grey to Munro Ferguson, 7.1.96, Rosebery MS.
11. Grey to Buxton, 11.1.96, Buxton MS.
12. Grey to Buxton, 11 & 17.1.96, Buxton MS.
13. Grey to Munro Ferguson, 7.1.96, Rosebery MS.
14. D. Grey to G. Grey, 3.11.93, L. Creighton, *D. Grey*, pp. 199–200.
15. T. O. Ranger, 'African Reactions in East and Central Africa', in L. H. Gann and P. Duignan, *Colonialism in Africa, 1870–1960*, Cambridge U.P., Cambridge, 1969, i, pp. 306–7.
16. *Some Account of George Grey and His Work in Africa*, privately printed, London, 1914, p. 118.
17. J. Butler, *The Liberal Party and the Jameson Raid*, The Clarendon Press, Oxford, 1968.
18. Grey to Buxton, 31.12.95, Buxton MS.
19. Grenville, *Lord Salisbury*, pp. 50–3 and 74–5.
20. Grey to Buxton, 31.12.95, Buxton MS.
21. Rhodes James, *Rosebery*, pp. 395–6.
22. Grey to Buxton, 24.7.96, Buxton MS.; Grey to Ellis, 16.8.96, Ellis MS.
23. Grey to Rosebery, 6.9.96, Rosebery MS.
24. Grey to Rosebery, 13.10.96, Rosebery MS.
25. Grey to Rosebery, 6.9.96, Rosebery MS.
26. E. C. F. Collier, *A Victorian Diarist, Later extracts from the journals of Mary, Lady Monkswell, 1895–1909*, Murray, London, 1946, p. 20. Entry of 24.11.96.
27. Grey to Munro Ferguson, 16.12.96, cited in Trevelyan, *Grey*, p. 71.
28. Morley to Harcourt, 14.12.96, Harcourt MS.
29. Harcourt to Morley, 15.12.96, Harcourt MS.
30. Grey to Rosebery, 14.12.96, Rosebery MS.
31. Sir Henry Lucy, *The Diary of a Journalist*, Murray, London, 1922, ii, p. 180.
32. D. Grey to Miss E. Robins, 16.3.97, L. Creighton, *D. Grey*, p. 96.
33. J. L. Garvin, *Life of Joseph Chamberlain*, Macmillan, London, 1951, iv, pp. 234–43.
34. D. Judd, *Balfour and the British Empire*, Macmillan, London, 1968, pp. 280–1.
35. Grey to Buxton, 27.10.97, Buxton MS.
36. Grey to Buxton, 21.1.98, Buxton MS.
37. Grey to Ellis, 28.3.97, Ellis MS.
38. *The Times*, 1.1.96 and 27.11.96.
39. Grey to Munro Ferguson, January 1897, cited in Trevelyan, *Grey*, pp. 62–3.
40. For further details see P. M. Holt, *The Mahdist State in the Sudan, 1881–1898*, The Clarendon Press, Oxford, 1958, Chap. 12, The Overthrow of the Mahdist State.
41. Grey to Rosebery, 14.11.97, Rosebery MS. Harcourt wrote to Morley in January 1898: 'There is much danger of our coming to issue with France on our pretensions to the whole of the Nile basin . . . which will bring up again the blessed history of the Anglo-Belgian Convention of unhappy memory & the speech which E. Grey was instructed to make thereupon.' Harcourt to Morley, 6.1.98, Harcourt MS.
42. Grey to Munro Ferguson, May 1897, cited in Trevelyan, *Grey*, p. 65.
43. *The Times*, 21.10.97. Grey thought Roberts to blame for the forward policy and if this was correct he would always look upon him as 'one of the greatest dangers to the Empire'. Grey to Munro Ferguson, 3.9.97, Rosebery MS.

44. D. Dilks, *Curzon in India*, Hart Davis, London, 1969, i, pp. 58–62.
45. Salisbury to Currie, 19.10.97, cited in Grenville, *Lord Salisbury*, p. 94.
46. P. M. Holt, *A Modern History of the Sudan*, Weidenfeld and Nicolson, London, 1963, pp. 106–7.
47. Grey to K. Lyttelton, 20.6.98, Lyttelton MS.
48. Harcourt to L. Harcourt, 12.9.98, Harcourt MS.
49. Grey to Ellis, 27.9.98, Ellis MS.
50. *The Times*, 28.10.98. Dorothy, however, described Edward as going 'gloomily' off to make this speech. 'We are getting very sick of the "unfriendly act". If we go to war with France I think he ought at least to volunteer to fight. It would only be a proper punishment. . . . Civilization and humanity could have been so much better established by Marchand than by the English. It has all been a sad waste of effort on our part. . . .' D. Grey to H. Paul, 27.10.98, Paul MS.
51. Harcourt to Morley, 10.10.98, Harcourt MS.
52. Gardiner, *Harcourt*, ii, pp. 470–1.
53. *The Times*, 15.12.98.
54. Sir G. O. Trevelyan to G. M. Trevelyan, 15.2.15, Runciman MS.
55. Grey to Buxton, 24.12.98, Buxton MS.
56. Gardiner, *Harcourt*, ii, p. 591.
57. Harcourt to Grey, 16.12.98, Harcourt MS.
58. Harcourt to Buxton, 15.12.98, Harcourt MS.
59. Harcourt to Fowler, 15.12.98, Harcourt MS.
60. Grey to Harcourt, 19.12.98, Harcourt MS.
61. Grey to Haldane, 16.12.98, Haldane MS.
62. Grey to Buxton, 24.12.98, Buxton MS.
63. Stansky, *Ambitions*, p. 277.
64. Grey to Buxton, 24.12.98, Buxton MS.
65. Grey to Munro Ferguson, 16.12.98, Rosebery MS.
66. Grey of Fallodon, *Fly-Fishing*, Dent, London, 1934 edition, pp. 31–2.
67. D. Grey to K. Lyttelton, 31.5.99, Lyttelton MS.
68. Grey to H. Paul, 4.9.99, Paul MS.
69. *Cottage Book*, 9.7.99; Grey to H. Paul, 4.9.99, Paul MS.

CHAPTER 5
1. Haldane to Rosebery, 10.1.99, Rosebery MS.
2. Rhodes James, *Rosebery*, p. 408.
3. Jenkins, *Asquith*, pp. 121–2.
4. Grey to Milner, 9.4.97, Milner MS. 4.
5. H. W. McCready, 'Sir Alfred Milner, the Liberal Party and the Boer War', *The Canadian Journal of History*, March 1967. Asquith, Haldane and Milner had taken holidays together, but not Grey.
6. Milner to Asquith, 18.11.97, quoted in C. Headlam, ed., *The Milner Papers*, Cassell, London, 1931, pp. 177–80.
7. British policy in South Africa and Milner's role in particular has now been thoroughly studied by a number of South African, or former South African, historians. What follows is heavily dependent on their works, though they place an undue stress on the 'Imperial factor'. See J. Butler, 'Sir Alfred Milner on British policy in South Africa in 1897' in *Boston University Papers in African History*, i, Boston U.P., Boston, 1964; J. S. Marais, *The Fall of Kruger's*

Republic, Clarendon Press, Oxford, 1961; G. H. Le May, *British Supremacy in South Africa, 1899–1907*, Clarendon Press, Oxford, 1965. See also J. E. Wrench, *Alfred, Lord Milner, the Man of no Illusions, 1854–1925*, Eyre and Spottiswoode, London, 1958.

8. Grey to Milner, 13.7.99, Milner MS. 16.
9. Milner to Grey, 7.8.99, Milner MS. 8.
10. Grey to Rosebery, 5.9.99, Rosebery MS.
11. Grey to Buxton, 12.9.99, Buxton MS.
12. Grey to Rosebery, 19.9.99, Rosebery MS.
13. Grey to Rosebery, 30.9.99, Rosebery MS.
14. Grey to Milner, 4.10.99, Milner MS. 17.
15. Grey to K. Lyttelton, 17.10.99, Lyttelton MS.
16. Grey to N. Lyttelton, 23.10.99, Lyttelton MS.
17. D. Grey to K. Lyttelton, 14.10.99, Lyttelton MS.; D. Grey to A. Kay-Shuttleworth, 29.9.99. Courtesy of Mrs Janet Young.
18. D. Grey to Bishop Creighton, 19.10.99, L. Creighton, *D. Grey*, pp. 209–10.
19. D. Grey to H. Paul, 21.11.99, Paul MS.
20. Campbell-Bannerman to Gladstone, 19.9.99, cited in J. A. Spender, *The Life of Sir Henry Campbell-Bannerman*, Hodder and Stoughton, London, 1924, i, pp. 242–3.
21. Butler, *Liberal Party and Jameson Raid*, pp. 231–3; Morley, Harcourt, Bryce and Reid all voted with Stanhope against the Government. Morley felt that the Imperialists had suffered a serious setback, writing to Harcourt: '. . . The Haldane–Grey gang worked as hard as ever they could all the time to draw our men with them. They only voted *15* after all, against our 92!! They are much mortified. . . . I thought Grey hardly concealed his chagrin, in talking to you on the bench after the division.' J. Morley to W. Harcourt, 23.10.99, Harcourt MS. Morley and Grey had clashed earlier in the year when the former brought in a critical motion on the Sudan while Grey with a dozen other Liberals voted in the Government lobby. Stansky, *Ambitions*, p. 293. After this brush, Morley wrote to Harcourt: 'Grey went out of his way, like the good fellow he is, to talk on the old terms. But I fancy I wore the look of a grim beast. . . .' Morley to Harcourt, 8.2.99, Harcourt MS.
22. Jenkins, *Asquith*, pp. 125–6.
23. Grey to Rosebery, 20.10.99, Rosebery MS.
24. Grey to Rosebery, 22.10.99, Rosebery MS.
25. Haldane to Rosebery, 23.10.99, Rosebery MS.
26. *The Times*, 26.10.99.
27. Grey to Haldane, 10.11.99, Haldane MS. Haldane, meanwhile, was assuring Milner that four-fifths of 'our people' supported his policy. Haldane to Milner, 11.10.99, Headlam, *Milner Papers*, pp. 559–60.
28. Campbell-Bannerman to Buxton, 31.10.99, Spender, *Campbell-Bannerman*, i, pp. 253–4. Speech at Birmingham, p. 257.
29. Gardiner, *Harcourt*, ii, p. 513. Asquith's adherence to the other side greatly alarmed Morley and Harcourt. Morley wrote: '. . . undoubtedly, with Asquith, Fowler, and Grey in a cave, they will have the preponderance in speaking power over C.B. unless you join him in some way. . . .' Morley to Harcourt, 28.11.99, Harcourt MS.
30. *The Times*, 6, 28 & 30.11.99.
31. Grey to Buxton, 1.12.99, Buxton MS.

32. Grey to Buxton, 1.12.99, Buxton MS. Nevertheless, he had written to Milner in November to say that while he did not retract his criticisms of policy, he was not quite clear that in the circumstances war could not have been avoided. Grey to Milner, 1.11.99, Milner MS. 17.
33. Grey to Haldane, 4.12.99, Haldane MS.
34. Grey to Buxton, 1.12.99, Buxton MS.
35. Grey to Buxton, 12.1.00, Buxton MS.
36. Grey to Rosebery, 9.1.00, Rosebery MS.
37. Reported in R. Spence Watson, *The National Liberal Federation, 1877 to 1906*, Fisher Unwin, London, 1907, pp. 246–7. G. B. Pyrah's statement that Grey and not Campbell-Bannerman was elected Chairman of the National Liberal Council in March 1900 does not seem to bear the implication he places upon it. G. B. Pyrah, *Imperial Policy and South Africa, 1902–10*, Clarendon Press, Oxford, 1955, p. 52.
38. Grey to Rosebery, 1.4.00, Rosebery MS.
39. Harcourt described Lawson's move as 'very mischievous' since 'it gave to the Grey–Perks party exactly the handle they desired. . . .' Harcourt to Morley, 27.7.00, Harcourt MS.
40. Grey to Rosebery, 26.7.00, Rosebery MS. Jenkins, *Asquith*, p. 129, is wrong in supposing that Asquith voted with the Government. He abstained.
41. Haldane to Rosebery, 25.7.00, Rosebery MS.
42. Grey to Rosebery, 30.7.00, Rosebery MS.
43. Kinnear, *British Voter*, p. 26.
44. Garvin, *Chamberlain*, iii, p. 603.
45. Grey to Munro Ferguson, 18.10.00, cited in Trevelyan, *Grey*, p. 79.
46. D. Crane, *Sir Robert Perks*, p. 201; Perks to Rosebery, 20.2.00 and 10.4.00, Rosebery MS.
47. Harcourt to Spencer, 18.8.00, Spencer MS.
48. Perks to Rosebery, 7 & 19.10.00, Rosebery MS. The Imperial Liberal Council had aroused the wrath of the pro-Boers by endorsing the unimpeachable patriotism of some 56 candidates and declaring that after the election those unworthy to guide the Empire would be purged. This plan misfired.
49. Haldane to Buxton, 19.10.00, Buxton MS.
50. Spender, *Campbell-Bannerman*, Campbell-Bannerman to Ripon, 29.10.00, p. 298; Campbell-Bannerman to Buxton, 21.11.00, pp. 307–8.
51. Haldane to Rosebery, 17.11.00, Rosebery MS.
52. Grey to Campbell-Bannerman, 17.11.00; Campbell-Bannerman to Grey, 19.11.00; Grey to Campbell-Bannerman, 22.11.00: Campbell-Bannerman MS., Add. MS. 41218.
53. Rhodes James, *Rosebery*, pp. 419–21; Grey to Rosebery, 20.11.00, Rosebery MS.
54. Haldane to Milner, 3.3.01, Milner Papers, 31.
55. D. W. Kruger, 'The British Imperial Factor in South Africa' in Gann and Duignan, ed., *Colonialism in Africa*, p. 347.
56. Gardiner, *Harcourt*, ii, pp. 526–7.
57. Spender, *Campbell-Bannerman*, i, p. 336.
58. Grey to Milner, 24.5.01, Milner MS. 39.
59. Grey to Haldane, 28. 5. 01, Haldane MS.
60. Haldane to Milner, 6.6.01, Milner MS. 31.
61. Asquith to Campbell-Bannerman, 15.6.01, Jenkins, *Asquith*, p. 135.

62. Asquith to Perks, 19.6.01. Courtesy of Sir Malcolm Perks. Jenkins, *Asquith*, p. 136.
63. Acland to Asquith, 20.1.99, Asquith MS.
64. Sir Henry Newbolt, *My world as in My Time*, Faber and Faber, London, 1932, pp. 273–4. Notes of conversation with Grey on 27.6.01.
65. Grey to L. Creighton, 7.7.01, Creighton MS.
66. Grey to Asquith, 12.7.01, Asquith MS.
67. Rhodes James, *Rosebery*, p. 425.
68. *The Times*, 18.7.01.
69. Rhodes James, *Rosebery*, p. 426.
70. Rhodes James, *Rosebery*, p. 424.
71. Acland to Asquith, 15.7.01 and 17.7.01, Asquith MS.
72. Grey to Rosebery, 20.7.01, Rosebery MS.
73. Cited, Rhodes James, *Rosebery*, p. 427.
74. Asquith to Rosebery, 22.7.01, Rosebery MS.
75. Grey to D. Grey, 16.8.01, cited in Trevelyan, *Grey*, pp. 79–80.
76. D. Grey to F. Buxton, 24.10.01, L. Creighton, *D. Grey*, p. 226.
77. Grey to Rosebery, 2.10.01, Rosebery MS.
78. *The Times*, 18.12.01.
79. Grey to Rosebery, 17.12.01; Haldane to Rosebery, 16.12.01, Rosebery MS.
80. Grey to Buxton, 18.12.01, Buxton MS.
81. Grey to Spender, 21.12.01, Spender MS., Add. MS. 46389.
82. Grey to H. Gladstone, 24.12.01; H. Gladstone to Grey, 28.12.01, H. Gladstone MS., Add. MS. 45992.
83. Grey to Campbell-Bannerman, 2.1.02, Campbell-Bannerman MS., Add. MS. 41218.
84. Campbell-Bannerman to Harcourt, 2.1.02, cited in Gardiner, *Harcourt*, ii, p. 538.
85. Campbell-Bannerman to H. Gladstone, 18.12.01, Spender, *Campbell-Bannerman*, ii, p. 14.
86. Campbell-Bannerman to Grey, 4.1.02, Campbell-Bannerman MS., Add. MS. 41218.
87. Haldane to Rosebery, 3.1.02, Rosebery MS.
88. Grey to D. Grey, 28.1.02, cited in Trevelyan, *Grey*, p. 80.
89. Rhodes James, *Rosebery*, pp. 437–8.
90. Grey to Rosebery, 22.2.02, Rosebery MS.
91. Perks to Rosebery, 7.8.01, Rosebery MS.
92. Jenkins, *Asquith*, p. 144.
93. H. Fowler to Perks, 28.12.01. Courtesy of Sir Malcolm Perks.
94. Grey to Milner, 16.3.02, Milner MS. 40.

CHAPTER 6
1. L. Creighton, *D. Grey*, p. 226.
2. Grey to K. Lyttelton, 12.4.03, Lyttelton MS.
3. I am grateful to Mr E. C. Marsden for making available his unpublished history of the North Eastern Railway Company. The minutes of the board are kept in the British Railways Archives at York.
4. H. Parris, *Government and the railways in nineteenth-century Britain*, Routledge, London, 1965, pp. 226–7; H. A. Clegg, A. Fox and A. F. Thompson, *A*

History of British Trade Unions since 1889, Clarendon Press, Oxford, 1964, pp. 236–7.

5. Cited, Trevelyan, *Grey*, p. 86.
6. Grey to K. Lyttelton, 12.4.03, Lyttelton MS.
7. Grey to Buxton, 25.12.04, Buxton MS.
8. L. Creighton, *D. Grey*, p. 136.
9. Grey to K. Lyttelton, 22.3.05, Lyttelton MS.
10. Newbolt, *My World*, pp. 273–4. Notes of a conversation with Grey, 27.6.01.
11. Grey to Rosebery, 11.8.02, Rosebery MS.
12. L. Creighton, *D. Grey*, p. 227.
13. Grey to Albert, Earl Grey, 27.9.03, Grey of Howick MS. 239/4.
14. B. Webb, *Our Partnership*, Longmans, London, 1948, pp. 226–7 and 250.
15. Grey to S. Webb, 7.10.02, Passfield MS.
16. H. G. Wells, *Experiment in Autobiography*, Gollancz and The Cresset Press, London, 1934, ii, pp. 768–9.
17. B. Russell, *Portraits from Memory and other Essays*, Allen and Unwin, London, 1956, p. 77.
18. Grey to K. Lyttelton, 12.4.03, Lyttelton MS.
19. L. S. Amery, *My Political Life*, Hutchinson, London, 1953, i, p. 224.
20. W. A. S. Hewins, *The Apologia of an Imperialist*, Constable, London, 1929, i, p. 69.
21. He certainly never committed himself to any public statement of doubts about Free Trade.
22. Grey to Rosebery, 11.6.03, Rosebery MS.
23. Grey to Rosebery, 13.7.03, Rosebery MS.
24. Haldane to Asquith, 5.10.03, Asquith MS.
25. Grey to Asquith, 7.10.03, Asquith MS. Jenkins, *Asquith*, p. 158, is wrong in stating that Grey's account conflicted 'at no point' with Haldane's. According to Haldane, the two men stated that they would not serve under C-B 'either as P.M. or as leader in the H. of C.'. Grey, however, merely reported his determination not to take office 'with C.B. as Prime Minister in any Govt. in which C-B was leader in the House of Commons'.
26. Grey to Asquith, 10.10.03, Asquith MS.
27. L. Creighton, *D. Grey*, p. 236.
28. The *Monthly Review*, October 1903.
29. Grey to Albert, Earl Grey, 27.9.03, Grey of Howick MS. 239/4.
30. Grey to H. Gladstone, 18.9.03, Gladstone MS., Add. MS. 45992. For a general account of Liberal political activity see M. Craton and H. W. McCready, *The Great Liberal Revival 1903–1906*, The Hansard Society, London, 1966.
31. D. Lloyd George, *War Memoirs*, Odhams, London, 1938, i, Chap. 3. Lloyd George omitted this last section from the published version. It can be found in the Lloyd George MS. G/211.
32. Grey to H. Gladstone, 31.12.03, Gladstone MS., Add. MS. 45992.
33. *North Wales Observer*, 8.1.04.
34. Perks to Rosebery, 26.12.03, Rosebery MS.
35. Wells, *Experiment*, i, pp. 768–9.
36. Grey to Gladstone, 18.9.03, Gladstone MS., Add. MS. 45992. For the situation in Barnard Castle see F. Bealey and H. Pelling, *Labour and Politics, 1900–06*, Macmillan, London, 1958, pp. 152–4. They also remark (p. 147) that 'even Liberal Leaguers such as Grey and Haldane were very favourable to a greater

representation of Labour in Parliament'. It is difficult to see the force of the 'even' in view of Grey's early espousal of this cause.

37. Sir Edward Grey, *Questions of Today*, Liberal League Pamphlets, No. 36, London, 1903.
38. Burt, *Autobiography*, p. 260.
39. Grey to Spencer, 22.12.01, Spencer MS.
40. Grey to Gladstone, 11.10.01, Gladstone MS., Add. MS. 45992.
41. Sir Edward Grey, *The Irish Question*, Liberal League Pamphlets, No. 39a, London, 1903.
42. Grey to W. Allard, Allard MS., L. Add. 140.
43. Cited in Trevelyan, *Grey*, p. 87.
44. Grey to Albert, Earl Grey, 1.4.05, Grey of Howick MS.
45. Grey to Albert, Earl Grey, 4.8.05, Grey of Howick MS.
46. L. Creighton, *D. Grey*, p. 247.
47. R. B. Haldane, *Autobiography*, Hodder and Stoughton, London, 1929, p. 158.
48. Cited, Trevelyan, *Grey*, p. 96.
49. Ripon to Spencer, 24.9.03, Spencer MS.
50. Grey to Asquith, 2.10.05, Asquith MS.
51. M. Asquith, *Autobiography*, Eyre and Spottiswoode, London, 1962, pp. 236–7.
52. Grey to Asquith, 24.11.05, Asquith MS.
53. Morley to Campbell-Bannerman, 25.11.05, Campbell-Bannerman MS., Add. MS. 41223.
54. Morley wrote to Campbell-Bannerman to say that he did not believe Asquith and Grey were in collusion with Rosebery. There had not been a 'whisper of discontent' when he had discussed the subject with Grey. Morley to Campbell-Bannerman, 27.11.05, Campbell-Bannerman MS., Add. MS. 41223.
55. Grey to Rosebery, 27.11.05, Rosebery MS.
56. Grey to Rosebery, 2.12.05, Rosebery MS.; Trevelyan, *Grey*, pp. 94–5.
57. Trevelyan, *Grey of the Reform Bill*, pp. 110–12.
58. Grey to Asquith, 25.11.05, Asquith MS.
59. Grey to Asquith, 2.12.05, Asquith MS.
60. Grey to Rosebery, 3.12.05, Rosebery MS.
61. Grey to Asquith, 4.12.05, Asquith MS.
62. Grey to Campbell-Bannerman, 4.12.05, Campbell-Bannerman MS., Add. MS. 41218.
63. Grey to Asquith, 5.12.05, Asquith MS.
64. M. Asquith, *Autobiography*, p. 239.
65. Cited, Trevelyan, *Grey*, p. 100.
66. M. Asquith, *Autobiography*, pp. 240–1.
67. Grey to Campbell-Bannerman, 7.12.05, Campbell-Bannerman MS., Add. MS. 41218.
68. Haldane, *Autobiography*, pp. 168 ff. A somewhat different interpretation of this sequence of events can be found in J. F. Harris and C. Hazlehurst, 'Campbell-Bannerman as Prime Minister', *History*, October 1970.
69. Grey to Rosebery, 8.12.05, Rosebery MS.

CHAPTER 7
1. Almeric Fitzroy, *Memoirs*, Hutchinson, London, 1925, ii, pp. 219–20.
2. Grey to M. Asquith, 11.12.05, in M. Asquith, *Autobiography*, p. 243.
3. H. S. Wilkinson, *Thirty-Five Years*, Constable, London, 1933, pp. 273–4.

4. S. R. Williamson, *The Politics of Grand Strategy, Britain and France Prepare for War, 1904–1914*, Harvard U.P., Cambridge, Mass., 1969, p. 63.
5. Asquith to Spencer, 11.2.03, Spencer MS.
6. For a recent survey see H. W. Koch, 'The Anglo-German Alliance Negotiations: Missed Opportunity or Myth?', *History*, October 1969.
7. I. H. Nish, *The Anglo-Japanese Alliance*, The Athlone Press, London, 1966, p. 224.
8. Grenville, *Salisbury*, pp. 281–3; Grey to Haldane, 4.12.99, Haldane MS.
9. Cited in R. H. Heindel, *The American Impact on Great Britain, 1898–1914*, Pennsylvania U.P., Philadelphia, 1940, p. 70. Grey was also among the politicians who contributed statements advocating Anglo-American 'reunion' to the June 1898 number of W. T. Stead's *Review of Reviews*: C. S. Campbell, *Anglo-American Understanding, 1898–1903*, Johns Hopkins, Baltimore, 1957, p. 44.
10. D. C. Watt, *Personalities and Policies*, Longmans, London, 1965, p. 23.
11. Grey to A. Carnegie, 22.10.01, Carnegie MS. 16256–9. I owe this reference to Mr H. C. G. Mathew.
12. Grey to Newbolt, 10.9.03, Newbolt MS.
13. Grey to H. Gladstone, 2.7.02, Gladstone MS., Add. MS. 45992.
14. Grey to Newbolt, 5.1.03, Newbolt MS.
15. Cited in Trevelyan, *Grey*, p. 83.
16. There are some examples in A. J. P. Taylor, *The Troublemakers*, Hamish Hamilton, London, 1957, pp. 110–11.
17. Cited in Trevelyan, *Grey*, p. 84.
18. E.g., Morley to Spencer, 2.10.05, Ripon to Spencer, 28.9.05, Asquith to Spencer, 8.10.05, Spencer MS.
19. Spencer to Asquith, 5.10.05, Spencer MS.
20. Grey to Asquith, 2.10.05, Asquith MS.
21. Grey to W. Allard, 24.5.04, Allard MS., L. Add. 140.
22. G. W. Monger, *The End of Isolation*, Nelson, London, 1963, p. 286, notes the Liberal suspicion but adds that 'even' Grey shared it. If Monger is correct in arguing that Grey was bent on downgrading Anglo-Japanese relations for the sake of agreement with Russia one would have expected him to join in the sharper criticisms of some of his colleagues. On the other hand, the fact that his reservations are quite mild, casts doubt on the notion that the new treaty was irrelevant or even an obstacle to his supposed new policy. It is not in fact true that 'intimate contact between London and Tokyo ceased with the change of government'.
23. Grey to Spender, 19.10.05, Spender MS., Add. MS. 46389.
24. *The Times*, 21.10.05.
25. Bryce to Spencer, 21.8.05, Spencer MS.
26. Campbell-Bannerman to Spencer, 29.8.05, Spencer MS.
27. Campbell-Bannerman to Spencer, 13.9.05, Spencer MS.
28. H. Paul, 'Liberals and Foreign Policy', *Nineteenth Century and After*, November 1905.
29. J. A. Spender to J. St Loe Strachey, 21.10.05, cited in A. Strachey, *St Loe Strachey: His Life and His Paper*, Gollancz, London, 1930, pp. 237–8.
30. Grey to H. Samuel, 10.8.02, Samuel MS. A/155.
31. Grey to Newbolt, 10.9.03, Newbolt MS.
32. Grey, *Questions of Today*, 1903.

33. Grey to Spencer, 17.12.01, Spencer MS.
34. Grey to Allard, 24.5.04, Allard MS., L. Add. 140.
35. Amery, *My Life*, i, p. 200.
36. Campbell-Bannerman to Spencer, 4.3.03, Spencer MS.; Grey, *Questions of Today*, 1903.
37. J. P. Mackintosh, 'The Role of the Committee of Imperial Defence before 1914', *The English Historical Review*, July 1962.
38. Grey to Buxton, 27.10.97, Buxton MS.
39. Cited, Monger, *End of Isolation*, p. 264. On the reform of the Foreign Office see Z. S. Steiner, *The Foreign Office and Foreign Policy, 1898–1914*, Cambridge U.P., Cambridge, 1969, especially pp. 70 ff.
40. Monger, *End of Isolation*, p. 265.
41. R. S. Churchill, *Winston S. Churchill*, Companion ii, Part i, Heinemann, London, 1969, p. 417.
42. Grey to Albert, Earl Grey, 22.12.05, Grey of Howick MS.
43. L. Creighton, *D. Grey*, p. 184.
44. Grey to Campbell-Bannerman, 19.1.06, Campbell-Bannerman MS., Add. MS. 52514.

CHAPTER 8
1. Cited in Taylor, *The Troublemakers*, p. 111.
2. N. Rich, *Friedrich von Holstein*, Cambridge U.P., Cambridge, 1965, ii, p. 745.
3. Monger, *End of Isolation*, p. 244.
4. C. Andrew, *T. Delcassé and the Entente Cordiale*, Macmillan, London, 1968, p. 281.
5. See Williamson, *Politics of Grand Strategy*, p. 72.
6. Grey to Campbell-Bannerman, 9.1.06, Campbell-Bannerman MS., Add. MS. 41218.
7. *British Documents on the Origins of the War, 1898–1914* (henceforth B.D.), iii, pp. 180–5; Grey to Campbell-Bannerman, 10.1.06, Campbell-Bannerman MS., Add. MS. 41218.
8. Haldane, *Autobiography*, p. 190.
9. Grey to Bertie, 15.1.06, printed in Grey, *Twenty-Five Years*, i, p. 76.
10. Haldane to Grey, 17.1.06, F.O. 800/102.
11. B.D., ii, No. 216.
12. Grey to Campbell-Bannerman, 19.1.06, Campbell-Bannerman MS., Add. MS. 52514.
13. Campbell-Bannerman to Grey, 21.1.06; Grey to Campbell-Bannerman, 22.1.06, Campbell-Bannerman MS., Add. MS. 52514.
14. Ripon to Grey, 23.1.06, F.O. 800/99.
15. L. Wolf, *Life of the First Marquess of Ripon*, ii, Murray, London, 1921, pp. 292–3. In quoting from this letter in his book, Dr Monger omits this final expression of confidence in Grey.
16. Cited in Williamson, *Politics of Grand Strategy*, pp. 80–1.
17. D.D.F., 2 ser., IX, pt. 1, no. 106.
18. In a post-war conversation with G. P. Gooch, Grey claimed: 'We should doubtless have had criticism but not, I should say, opposition.' G. P. Gooch, *Under Six Reigns*, Longmans, London, 1958, pp. 227–30.
19. Monger, *End of Isolation*, p. 255.
20. Monger, *End of Isolation*, p. 256.

21. Earl Loreburn, *How the War Came*, Methuen, London, 1919, pp. 76 ff. A note by Fitzmaurice on Campbell-Bannerman to Fitzmaurice, 14.1.06, Campbell-Bannerman MS., Add. MS. 41214, makes it clear, as Monger, p. 254n, acknowledges, but on p. 308n questions, that he was kept informed of these conversations. Fitzmaurice to Pentland, n.d. 1919, Campbell-Bannerman MS., Add. MS. 41252, states: 'If nobody else told Loreburn of the conversations of that month with Cambon, I did.' He was specifically commenting on the above passage in Loreburn's book. Since, as he says, he never saw eye to eye with Grey, particularly about Russia, the comment is very significant and casts doubt on the reality of Loreburn's ignorance. Monger, *End of Isolation*, p. 254, does not mention the letter.

22. Haldane, *Autobiography*, p. 191; Harris, *Spender*, p. 149.

23. B.D., iii, pp. 180–5.

24. For a recent account see S. L. Mayer, 'Anglo-German Rivalry at the Algeciras Conference' in P. Gifford and W. R. Louis, *Britain and Germany in Africa*, Yale U.P., New Haven, 1967.

25. B.D., iii, No. 299.

26. Memorandum by Mallet, 26.2.06; Grey to Tweedmouth, 28.2.06, F.O. 800/87.

27. Grey to Campbell-Bannerman, 10.3.06, Campbell-Bannerman MS., Add. MS. 41218.

28. Grey to Haldane, 2.2.06 and 4.2.06, Haldane MS. Entries in the Ellingham C.E. School Log Book kindly copied for me by Mr J. W. Manners, the present headmaster.

29. Grey to L. Creighton, 24.6.05, Creighton MS.

30. Grey to L. Creighton, 5.2.06, Creighton MS.; Grey to Haldane, 4.2.06, Haldane MS.

31. Collier, *A Victorian Diarist, Later Extracts*, p. 162.

32. E. Pease to Albert, Earl Grey, 23.6.07; Albert, Earl Grey, to E. Pease, 5.6.07; Albert, Earl Grey, to L. Creighton, 17.6.07, Grey of Howick MS.

33. Grey to L. Creighton, 6.10.06, Creighton MS.

34. Grey to Campbell-Bannerman, 4.2.06, Campbell-Bannerman MS., Add. MS. 41207.

35. Grey to H. Paul, 10.2.06, Paul MS.

36. Grey to E. Paul, 20.2.06, Paul MS.

37. Grey to L. Creighton, 22.2.06, Creighton MS.

38. Grey to K. Lyttelton, 15.4.06, Lyttelton MS.

39. B.D., iii, No. 418.

40. Monger, *End of Isolation*, p. 301.

41. Grey to Haldane, 3.9.06, Haldane MS.

42. W. S. Blunt, *My Diaries*, Secker, London, 1920, ii, pp. 160–1.

43. B.D., iii, No. 435.

44. Cited, Trevelyan, *Grey*, pp. 114–16.

45. B.D., iii, Appendix A; Grey to Ripon, 27.7.06, Ripon MS., Add. MS. 43640.

46. Williamson, *Politics of Grand Strategy*, pp. 101–2.

47. Minute by Hardinge, 29.7.07, F.O. 371/261, cited in Monger, *End of Isolation*, p. 317.

48. Grey to Haldane, 4.9.07 and 4.10.07, Haldane MS.

49. Grey to Campbell-Bannerman, 4.9.07, Campbell-Bannerman MS., Add. MS. 52514.

50. Grey to Campbell-Bannerman, 11.1.07, Campbell-Bannerman MS., Add. MS. 52514.

51. Morley to Minto, 29.8.06, Morley MS., i, also cited in Monger, *End of Isolation*, p. 283.

52. Grey to Campbell-Bannerman, 6.4.06, Campbell-Bannerman MS., Add. MS. 52514.

53. Campbell-Bannerman to Grey, 24.7.06, F.O. 800/100.

54. Grey to Nicolson, 3.10.06, F.O. 800/72.

55. 'Military considerations involved with regard to an entente cordiale between Great Britain and Russia', Memorandum by W. R. Robertson, 22.3.06, F.O. 800/102. See also B. J. Williams, 'The Strategic Background to the Anglo-Russian Entente of August 1907', *The Historical Journal*, 1966.

56. B. C. Busch, *Britain and the Persian Gulf, 1894-1914*, U. of California Press, Berkeley, 1967, pp. 357-69. F. Kazemzadeh, *Russia and Britain in Persia, 1864-1914*, Yale U.P., New Haven, 1968, pp. 475 ff.

57. Grey to Campbell-Bannerman, 31.8.07, Campbell-Bannerman MS., Add. MS. 52514.

58. Lord Ronaldshay, *Life of Lord Curzon*, ii, Benn, London, 1928, p.38.

59. Grey, *Twenty-Five Years*, i, p. 160.

60. Kazemzadeh, *Russia and Britain*, p. 504.

61. Cited in Kazemzadeh, *Russia and Britain*, p. 492.

62. S. Gwynn, ed., *The Letters and Friendships of Sir Cecil Spring-Rice*, ii, Constable, London, 1929, p. 98.

63. Gwynn, *Spring-Rice*, ii, p. 105.

64. Kazemzadeh, *Russia and Britain*, p. 502. See also P. Avery, *Modern Iran*, Benn, London, 1965, pp. 133-5.

65. Grey to Campbell-Bannerman, 16.4.06, Campbell-Bannerman MS., Add. MS. 52514.

66. Campbell-Bannerman to Grey, 1.5.06, F.O. 800/100. The First Sea Lord also wrote: 'May I congratulate you on the Sultan as some of your colleagues who privately I heard speak gave me the "shivers".' Sir J. Fisher to Grey, 15.5.06, F.O. 800/87.

67. Grey to Lascelles, 1.5.06, printed in *Twenty-Five Years*, i, p. 130.

68. R. L. Tignor, *Modernization and British Colonial Rule in Egypt, 1882-1914*, Princeton U.P., Princeton, 1966, pp. 278-9.

69. P. J. Vatikiotis, *The Modern History of Egypt*, Weidenfeld and Nicolson, London, 1969, pp. 194-5.

70. Afaf Lufti al-Sayyid, *Egypt and Cromer*, Murray, London, 1968, pp. 174-5.

71. Hardinge to Bryce, 8.8.07, Bryce MS.

72. Cited, Trevelyan, *Grey*, p. 197. He wrote to Lady Lyttelton, 'The going of Cromer is very pathetic. . . . My first little job was to be called his private secretary for a month in 1884 while he was in London for the Egyptian Conference. Lord Northbrook got that for me. . . . I have lived a whole lifetime since 1884 & am alone.' Grey to K. Lyttelton, 14.4.07, Lyttelton MS.

73. Loreburn to Grey, 10.10.07; Grey to Gorst, 12.10.07, F.O. 800/99. It has recently been noted that Grey gauged the volume of nationalist feeling in Egypt more accurately than his officials, one of whom had minuted following the death of Mustapha Kamel: 'It appears probable that the Nationalist party will collapse.' Grey thought that the demonstration of feeling at his

funeral was an indication of nationalist strength. Hyam, *Elgin and Churchill*, p. 537n.

74. Grey to Selborne, 22.12.05, F.O. 800/111.
75. Elgin to Grey, 17.12.05 and 23.12.05, F.O. 800/91.
76. Grey to Elgin, 24.12.05, F.O. 800/91.
77. Elgin to Grey, 17.2.06, F.O. 800/91.
78. Hyam, *Elgin and Churchill*, pp. 256–7.
79. Grey to Albert, Earl Grey, 15.3.06, Grey of Howick MS.
80. Elgin to Grey, 22.2.08, F.O. 800/91.
81. Elgin to Grey, 7.3.08, F.O. 800/91.
82. Grey to Durand, 13.12.05, F.O. 800/81.
83. See P. Neary, 'Grey, Bryce and the settlement of Canadian–American Differences, 1905–11', in *Canadian Historical Review*, December 1968.
84. Grey to Roosevelt, 2.12.06, cited in Trevelyan, *Grey*, pp. 142–3.
85. E. E. Morison, *The Letters of Theodore Roosevelt*, Harvard U.P., Cambridge, Mass., 1952, v, pp. 152 and 528–9.
86. Grey to St Loe Strachey, 9.10.07, Strachey MS.
87. Grey to Bryce, 30.3.08, Bryce MS.
88. Grey to Campbell-Bannerman, 21.11.06, Campbell-Bannerman MS., Add. MS. 41207.
89. Grey to St Loe Strachey, 2.1.07, Strachey MS.
90. Bryce to Grey, 26.2.07, F.O. 800/81.
91. Grey to Bryce, 7.6.07, Bryce MS.
92. Grey to Bryce, 19.9.07, Bryce MS.
93. Bryce to Grey, 6.3.08, F.O. 800/81.
94. Grey to Bryce, 30.3.08, Bryce MS.
95. Hardinge to Bryce, 22.5.08, Bryce MS.

CHAPTER 9

1. Monger, *End of Isolation*, p. 313. For a discussion of naval and military attitudes towards the United States at this time see K. Bourne, *Britain and the Balance of Power in North America, 1815–1908*, Longmans, London, 1967, pp. 394 ff. When the question of Canadian frontiers was brought before the C.I.D. in 1908 Grey stated that he had no wish to discuss the question of what action Britain should take in the event of war with the United States.
2. Asquith to Campbell-Bannerman, 30.12.06, Campbell-Bannerman MS., Add. MS. 41210.
3. B.D., viii, p. 192.
4. B.D., viii, pp. 198–9.
5. Cited in E. L. Woodward, *Great Britain and the German Navy*, Cass, London, 1964, p. 129.
6. Morison ed., *Roosevelt Letters*, v, pp. 600–1.
7. Hansard, 4th Ser., CLXXIX, 1316, 1.8.07.
8. Grey to E. Fry, 22.6.07, F.O. 800/69.
9. Crowe to Tyrrell, 6.8.07, F.O. 800/69.
10. Woodward, *Britain and the German Navy*, pp. 135–9.
11. The private and personal letter from Emperor William II to Lord Tweedmouth of February 1908 and his reply, together with a commentary by Lord Tweedmouth's then private secretary Sir Vincent Baddeley, MS. Eng. Hist. c. 264, Bodleian Library, Oxford.

12. Hardinge to Knollys, 23.2.08, Royal Archives W 53/9.
13. M. V. Brett, *Journals and Letters of Reginald, Viscount Esher*, Nicholson and Watson, London, 1934, ii, p. 162, 9.5.06.
14. S. E. Koss, *Lord Haldane, Scapegoat for Liberalism*, Columbia U.P., New York & London, 1969, pp. 44 ff.
15. *Esher Journals*, ii, p. 186.
16. Sinclair to Campbell-Bannerman, 8.1.07, Campbell-Bannerman MS., Add. MS. 41230.
17. Haldane to Campbell-Bannerman, 9.1.07, Campbell-Bannerman MS., Add. MS. 41218.
18. Grey to Mrs Haldane, 1.3.07, Haldane MS.
19. Fitzroy, *Memoirs*, pp. 329–30.
20. Cited, Williamson, *Politics of Grand Strategy*, pp. 102–3 and 107.
21. Mackintosh, 'Role of the C.I.D.', p. 497.
22. C.I.D., 96, 28.2.07, Asquith MS. 132.
23. Grey to Bryce, 7.6.07, Bryce MS.
24. L. Masterman, *C. F. G. Masterman*, London, Nicholson and Watson, 1939, pp. 111–12.
25. Cited in J. H. Grainger, *Character and Style in English Politics*, Cambridge U.P., 1969, pp. 157–8.
26. Grey to Bryce, 29.11.07, Bryce MS.
27. Grey to Bryce, 30.3.08, Bryce MS.
28. Grey to Newbolt, 27.11.06, Newbolt MS.
29. Grey to L. Creighton, 17.4.06, Creighton MS.
30. Grey to L. Creighton, 14.8.06, Creighton MS.
31. Grey to K. Lyttelton, 18.9.06, Lyttelton MS.
32. Grey to L. Creighton, 13.10.06, Creighton MS.
33. Grey to L. Creighton, 30.12.06, Creighton MS.
34. Grey to L. Creighton, 20.10.07, Creighton MS.; Grey to E. Paul, 13.10.06, Paul MS.; Grey to K. Lyttelton, 14.4.07, Lyttelton MS.
35. Grey to E. Paul, 20.1.07, Paul MS.
36. Grey to L. Creighton, 2.2.07, Creighton MS.
37. Grey to Newbolt, 8.5.07, Newbolt MS.
38. Grey to E. Paul, 27.12.07, Paul MS.
39. Newbolt's journal, entry for 27.1.08. M. Newbolt, ed., *The Later Life and Letters of Sir Henry Newbolt*, Faber and Faber, London, 1942, p. 139.
40. Grey to Newbolt, 20.8.06, Newbolt MS.
41. Newbolt's journal, 4.3.08, in Newbolt, *Later Life and Letters*, pp. 142–3.
42. Grey to Campbell-Bannerman, 7.4.08, Campbell-Bannerman MS., Add. MS. 41218.

CHAPTER 10
1. Sir Charles Petrie, *The Life and Letters of Rt Hon. Sir Austen Chamberlain*, Cassell, London, 1939, i, p. 213.
2. Churchill, *Churchill*, Companion ii, Part ii, pp. 705, 708 and 721–2.
3. A. G. Gardiner, *Prophets, Priests and Kings*, Dent, London, 1914, pp. 78–9.
4. Grey to Bryce, 30.3.08, Bryce MS.
5. Memorandum by Hardinge, 12.6.08, B.D., v, No. 195.
6. E. E. Ramsaur, *The Young Turks, Prelude to the Revolution of 1908*, Khayats, Beirut, 1965, p. 147.

7. 'How little either of us foresaw, when you were appointed, the reception you would actually get!' wrote Grey to the newly appointed British Ambassador, Sir Gerard Lowther, on 31 July. B.D., v, p. 263.

8. British policy can be followed in more detail in the article by M. B. Cooper, 'British Policy in the Balkans, 1908–9', *The Historical Journal*, vii, 1964–5, to which I am indebted in the following section.

9. D. C. M. Platt, *Finance, Trade and Politics in British Foreign Policy, 1815–1914*, Clarendon Press, Oxford, 1968, pp. 192–3 and 217–18.

10. M. S. Anderson, *The Eastern Question, 1774–1923*, Macmillan, London, 1966.

11. Grey to Asquith, 5.10.08; Asquith to Grey, 6.10.08, F.O. 800/100.

12. Cabinet letter, 12.10.08, Asquith MS.

13. Hardinge to Bryce, 23.10.08, Bryce MS.

14. Esher, *Journals*, ii, p. 327.

15. Grey to K. Lyttelton, 4.2.08, Lyttelton MS.

16. Hardinge to Grey, B.D., vi, No. 116.

17. Grey to Crewe, 17.6.08 and 23.6.08, Crewe MS. c/17.

18. B.D., vi, No. 100.

19. Asquith to Grey, 7.9.08, F.O. 800/100.

20. Grey to Loreburn, 5.1.09, F.O. 800/99. Grey was being somewhat optimistic in ignoring a Franco-German dispute over Casablanca in the late autumn 1908. He had to face French pressure for Anglo-French naval co-operation. In this delicate situation, the Foreign Secretary was disinclined to take up Churchill's generous offer to have consultations when on a visit to Paris in January 1909. Churchill to Grey, 24.12.08; Grey to Churchill, 26.12.08, F.O. 800/89. Agreement was reached later in 1909 between France and Germany. See, E. W. Edwards, 'The Franco-German Agreement on Morocco, 1909', *The English Historical Review*, July 1963.

21. Grey to K. Lyttelton, 8.11.08, Lyttelton MS.

22. Grey to Cartwright, 16.12.08, F.O. 800/40.

23. Grey to Bryce, 25.12.08, Bryce MS.

24. Hardinge to Bryce, 4.12.08, Bryce MS.

25. Grey to Asquith, 31.12.08, F.O. 800/100.

26. Grey to Cartwright, 8.1.09, F.O. 800/41.

27. Grey to Cartwright, 31.12.08, F.O. 800/40.

28. Hardinge to Bryce, 15.1.09, Bryce MS.

29. Grey to Lowther, 8.2.09, F.O. 800/79.

30. Hardinge to Bryce, 26.2.09, Bryce MS.

31. A. K. S. Lambton, 'Persian Political Societies, 1906–11' in *St Antony's Papers, No. 16, Middle Eastern Affairs No. 3*, Chatto and Windus, London, 1963, pp. 86–7.

32. Morley to Grey, 22.3.09 and 30.3.09, F.O. 800/98. S. A. Wolpert, *Morley and India, 1906–10*, University of California Press, 1967, p. 217.

33. P. Avery, *Modern Iran*, Benn, London, 1965, p. 138.

34. Cited in Lambton, 'Persian Political Societies', p. 87.

35. Grey to K. Lyttelton, 14.8.08, Lyttelton MS.

36. Grey to Asquith, 23.12.08, Asquith MS.; McKenna to Grey, 30.12.08, cited in S. McKenna, *Reginald McKenna*, Eyre and Spottiswoode, London, 1948, pp. 71–2.

37. Churchill, *Churchill*, Companion ii, Part ii, p. 850.

38. Churchill, *Churchill*, Companion ii, Part ii, p. 818.

39. Hardinge to Bryce, 15.1.09, Bryce MS.
40. Grey to Asquith, 5.2.09, Asquith MS.
41. Cabinet letter, 15.2.09, Asquith MS.
42. Cited in Trevelyan, *Grey*, pp. 214–15.
43. E. Marsh to W. Tyrrell, 12.2.09; Churchill to Grey, 16.2.09, F.O. 800/89.
44. Cited in Jenkins, *Asquith*, p. 216.
45. Hardinge to Knollys, 26.2.09, Royal Archives W55/8.
46. This particular example was published in *Review of Reviews*, December 1909 and is cited in Z. Steiner, 'Grey, Hardinge and the Foreign Office, 1906–10', *The Historical Journal*, 3, 1967, pp. 426–7. Grey to Asquith, 13.1.09, F.O. 800/100.
47. Grey to St Loe Strachey, 29.12.09, Strachey MS.
48. Masterman, *Masterman*, p. 128.
49. Fisher to the King, 12.3.09, Royal Archives W59/70.
50. Fisher minuted that the original word had been 'resignation' and that Grey had declared his willingness to go with him. *Fear God and Dread Nought. The Correspondence of Lord Fisher of Kilverstone*, ii, *The Years of Power, 1904–14*, Cape, London, 1956, pp. 227–8 and 230–1.
51. Asquith to Grey, 19.3.09, cited Trevelyan, *Grey*, p. 213.
52. A. M. Gollin, *The Observer and J. L. Garvin, 1908–14*, O.U.P., London, 1960, pp. 77–82.
53. For an analysis see G. J. Marcus, 'The Naval Crisis of 1909 and the Croydon By-Election', *Journal of the Royal United Services Institute*, November 1958.
54. H. Gladstone to the King, 29.3.09, Royal Archives R 38/107.
55. Hardinge to the King, 31.3.09, Royal Archives W 55/15.
56. Grey to Asquith, 9.4.09, Asquith MS.
57. Grey to Asquith, 12.9.09, Asquith MS.
58. For discussion see Williamson, *Politics of Grand Strategy*, pp. 108 ff.
59. Fisher to Esher, 31.1.08, cited in *Fear God and Dread Nought*, ii, pp. 160–1.
60. Hardinge to Bryce, 26.2.09, Bryce MS.
61. Grey to Hardinge, 6.8.09, cited in Steiner, 'Grey, Hardinge', p. 423n.
62. B.D., vi, Minute in No. 187.
63. Grey to Master of Elibank, 1.2.09, F.O. 800/90.
64. B.D., vi, Enclosure in No. 204.
65. W. S. Churchill, *The World Crisis, 1911–18*, Odhams, London, 1938, i, pp. 25–6.
66. Tyrrell to Bertie, 22.10.09, Bertie MS.
67. Grey to Bryce, 12.12.09, Bryce MS.
68. Cited, Trevelyan, *Grey*, p. 170.
69. Masterman, *Masterman*, p. 146.
70. Grey to K. Lyttelton, 24.10.09, Lyttelton MS.
71. Grey to K. Lyttelton, 18.4.09, Lyttelton MS.
72. *Annual Register for 1909*, p. 192.
73. Grey to Bryce, 12.12.09, Bryce MS.
74. Grey to K. Lyttelton, 8.11.08 and 4.12.08, Lyttelton MS.
75. Grey to L. Creighton, 10.1.09, Creighton MS.
76. Grey to K. Lyttelton, 4.12.08, Lyttelton MS.
77. Grey to Newbolt, 27.4.09, Newbolt MS.
78. H. Lucy, *The Diary of a Journalist: Later Entries*, Murray, London, 1922, p. 202.
79. Grey to Buxton, 11.9.91, Buxton MS.

80. Grey to K. Lyttelton, 9.4.09, Lyttelton MS.
81. Esher, *Journals*, ii, p. 346.
82. Grey to L. Creighton, 28.1.10, Creighton MS.

CHAPTER II

1. Grey to L. Creighton, 28.1.10, Creighton MS.
2. McNair Wilson, *Doctor's Progress*, Eyre and Spottiswoode, London, 1938, p. 101.
3. Churchill to Grey, 23.1.10, F.O. 800/89.
4. There was also to be no change in the practice or privilege with regard to money bills. C. C. Weston, 'The Liberal Leadership and the Lords' Veto, 1907–10', *The Historical Journal*, XI, 3, 1968.
5. Hardinge to Knollys, 27.1.10, Royal Archives W 55/89 and 90.
6. Grey to Runciman, 29.1.10 and 3.2.10, Runciman MS.
7. Grey to Crewe, 2.2.10, Crewe MS.
8. Grey to Asquith, 7.2.10, Asquith MS.
9. Hardinge to Knollys, 12.2.10, Royal Archives W 55/103.
10. Grey to Crewe, 15.3.10, Crewe MS.
11. Cabinet letter, 16.3.10, Asquith MS.
12. Grey to Asquith, 25.3.10, Asquith MS.; cited, Jenkins, *Asquith*, p. 229.
13. Runciman to McKenna, 27.3.10, McKenna MS.
14. McKenna to Runciman, 28.3.10, Runciman MS.
15. Cited in R. Jenkins, *Mr Balfour's Poodle*, Heinemann, London, 1954, pp. 90–1.
16. Cited in Jenkins, *Asquith*, p. 88.
17. Grey to K. Lyttelton, 19.4.10, Lyttelton MS.
18. Sir P. Magnus, *King Edward the Seventh*, Murray, London, 1964, pp. 409–10.
19. Hardinge to Knollys, 3.5.10, Royal Archives W 55/110.
20. Hardinge to Knollys, 9.5.10, Royal Archives W 55/109.
21. Grey to Crewe, 3.6.10, Crewe MS.
22. Churchill to Lloyd George, 6.10.10; Churchill, *Churchill*, Companion ii, Part ii, pp. 1024–5.
23. Grey to Asquith, 26.10.10, Asquith MS.
24. Asquith to Crewe, 27.10.10, Asquith MS.
25. Personal information from Miss M. Gregson, M.B.E., Berwick-upon-Tweed.
26. Cited, Trevelyan, *Grey*, p. 173.
27. Grey to K. Lyttelton, 4.12.10 and 26.12.10, Lyttelton MS.
28. C. H. Hoare to Alice, Lady Hylton, 23.12.10, Newbolt MS.
29. Grey to Newbolt, 16.12.10, Newbolt MS. Part of the letter is cited, Trevelyan, *Grey*, p. 174.
30. B.D., vi, No. 336.
31. Hardinge to Bryce, 1.4.10, Bryce MS.
32. B.D., vi, No. 337.
33. B.D., vi, No. 344.
34. B.D., vi, No. 387.
35. B.D., vi, No. 392.
36. Churchill to Grey, 20.5.10, F.O. 800/97.
37. Cabinet Letters, 20.7.10 and 29.7.10, Asquith MS.
38. B.D., vi, No. 407.
39. B.D., vi, No. 425.

40. H. Nicolson, *King George V, His Life and Reign*, Constable, London, 1952, pp. 177-8.
41. Churchill to Grey, 6.10.10, F.O. 800/97.
42. Haldane to Grey, 26.12.10, F.O. 800/102.
43. Grey to Lord Althorp, 21.5.10 and 27.5.10, F.O. 800/99.
44. Avery, *Modern Iran*, p. 141; Kazemzadeh, *Russia and Britain in Persia*, pp. 549 ff.
45. G. M. Trevelyan to W. Runciman, 24.10.10, Runciman MS.; E. G. Browne, *The Persian Revolution of 1905-1909*, Cambridge, 1910; Blunt, *Diaries*, ii, p. 250.
46. Cited, Kazemzadeh, *Russia and Britain in Persia*, p. 565.
47. Grey to Lowther, 3.3.10; Lowther to Grey, 21.9.10, F.O. 800/79.
48. Grey to Asquith, 22.12.10, F.O. 800/100.
49. Hardinge to Gorst, 13.5.10, Hardinge MS., cited Steiner, *Foreign Office and Foreign Policy*, p. 238.
50. Morison, *Roosevelt Letters*, 7, pp. 402-3.
51. See 'Theodore Roosevelt and the British Empire', in M. Beloff, *The Great Powers*, Allen and Unwin, London, 1958.
52. Grey to T. Roosevelt Jr, 9.4.33, Roosevelt Jr MS.
53. Morison, *Roosevelt Letters*, 7, pp. 402-3.
54. Grey to Crewe, 3.6.10; Crewe to Grey, 5.6.10, F.O. 800/91.
55. Blunt, *Diaries*, ii, pp. 325-8.
56. Morel's own *History of the Congo Reform Movement* has recently been edited and published by W. R. Louis and J. Stengers, The Clarendon Press, Oxford, 1968.
57. Morel to Grey, 2.2.09, cited in S. J. S. Cookey, *Britain and the Congo Question, 1885-1913*, Longmans, London, 1968, p. 238.
58. Morel to Hodgkin, 11.8.09, cited in Cookey, *Britain and the Congo*, p. 249.
59. *The Times*, 5.10.09; Morel to Gilmour, 5.10.09, cited in C. A. Cline, 'E. D. Morel and the Crusade against the Foreign Office', *Journal of Modern History*, June, 1967.
60. Grey to Churchill, 5.11.09, F.O. 800/89.
61. Morel to Holt, 21.9.10, cited in Cookey, *Britain and the Congo*, p. 271.

CHAPTER 12

1. A. J. Mayer, 'Domestic Causes of the First World War' in L. Krieger and F. Stern, ed., *The Responsibility of Power*, Macmillan, London, 1968, pp. 291-2.
2. H. Gollwitzer, *Europe in the Age of Imperialism, 1880-1914*, Thames and Hudson, London, 1969, p. 179.
3. Grey to K. Lyttelton, 19.4.10 and 8.4.12, Lyttelton MS.
4. Gooch, *Under Six Reigns*, pp. 109-10; M. Asquith, *Autobiography*, 1962, p. 276.
5. Cabinet letter, 9.3.11, Asquith MS.
6. Large extracts from the speech are cited in Woodward, *Great Britain and the German Navy*, pp. 299-303.
7. Asquith to Knollys, 6.2.11, Royal Archives GV K 540/1; Harcourt to Gladstone, 3.4.11, Harcourt MS.
8. Cabinet letter, 17.5.11, Asquith MS.
9. Grey to Bryce, 11.8.10, Bryce MS.
10. For a discussion see E. Ions, *James Bryce and American Democracy*, Macmillan, London, 1968, pp. 230 ff.
11. J. B. Brebner, *North Atlantic Triangle: the interplay of Canada, the United States and Britain*, New Haven, 1945, p. 245.
12. Grey to Albert, Earl Grey, 27.1.11, Grey of Howick MS.

13. Grey to Bryce, cited Ions, *Bryce*, p. 235.
14. A. J. Ward, *Ireland and Anglo-American Relations, 1899–1921*, Weidenfeld and Nicolson, London, 1969, pp. 66–7.
15. Cabinet letters, 16.2.11 and 30.3.11, Asquith MS.
16. See the discussion in I. H. Nish, 'Australia and the Anglo-Japanese Alliance, 1901–11', *Australian Journal of Politics and History*, November 1963.
17. Grey to Albert, Earl Grey, 27.1.11, Grey of Howick MS.
18. The speech is in B.D., vi, pp. 781–90.
19. J. E. Kendle, *The Colonial and Imperial Conferences, 1887–1911*, Longmans for the Royal Commonwealth Society, London, 1967, pp. 195–6.
20. Grey to Albert, Earl Grey, 29.5.07, Grey of Howick MS.
21. Grey to Lady Helen Munro Ferguson, 19.4.08, cited in Trevelyan, *Grey*, p. 153.
22. B.D., vi, No. 192.
23. Cited, Williamson, *Politics of Grand Strategy*, p. 137.
24. B.D., vi, No. 460.
25. Grey, *Twenty-Five Years*, i, p. 94. The first paragraph should properly read: '. . . I have marked it for you, Morley, & Haldane, and I would suggest that, as soon as Haldane returns it, you and Morley should have a talk with him.' F.O. 800/100.
26. Williamson, *Politics of Grand Strategy*, p. 140.
27. Williamson, *Politics of Grand Strategy*, p. 170. No doubt Grey's previous experience as a railway director was of some assistance, but Williamson errs in stating that Grey continued to serve as a director while at the Foreign Office.
28. Williamson, *Politics of Grand Strategy*, p. 140.
29. B.D., vii, No. 339.
30. B.D., vii, No. 352; B.D., vii, No. 354.
31. I owe these remarks to Dr Zara Steiner.
32. See Steiner, *Foreign Office and Foreign Policy*, pp. 124–5.
33. Cabinet letters, 4, 11 and 19.7.11, Asquith MS.
34. B.D., vii, No. 339.
35. Cabinet letter, 22.7.11, Asquith MS.
36. For a discussion see R. A. Cosgrove, 'A Note on Lloyd George's Speech at the Mansion House, 21 July 1911', *The Historical Journal*, xii, 4 (1969). See also O. J. Hale, *Publicity and Diplomacy*, Appleton-Century, New York, 1940, pp. 384 ff.
37. B.D., vii, No. 383.
38. See J. S. Mortimer, 'Commercial Interests and German Diplomacy in the Agadir Crisis', *The Historical Journal*, x (1967).
39. Grey, *Twenty-Five Years*, i, p. 241.
40. Williamson, *Politics of Grand Strategy*, p. 140.
41. Grey to K. Lyttelton, 5.8.11, Lyttelton MS.
42. Grey, *Twenty-Five Years*, i, p. 238.
43. Churchill, *Churchill*, ii, p. 357.
44. C. E. Callwell, *Field-Marshal Sir Henry Wilson: His Life and Diaries*, Cassell, London, 1927, i, pp. 98–9.
45. 114th Meeting of the C.I.D. Minutes, Asquith MS.
46. Runciman to Harcourt, 24.8.11, Runciman MS.
47. Harcourt to Runciman, 26.8.11, Runciman MS.
48. Lloyd George to Churchill, 27.8.11, Lloyd George MS. C/3/15/6.

49. Grey to Churchill, 30.8.11, Lloyd George MS. C/3/15/7.
50. Asquith to Grey, 3.9.11, F.O. 800/100.
51. Grey to Lloyd George, 5.9.11, Lloyd George MS. C/4/14/5.
52. Asquith to Grey, 5.9.11; Grey to Asquith, 8.9.11, Grey, *Twenty-Five Years*, i, p. 95.
53. Asquith to Grey, 9.9.11, F.O. 800/100.
54. Cabinet letter, 1.11.11, Asquith MS.
55. Cabinet letter, 15.11.11, Asquith MS.; Fitzroy, *Memoirs*, ii, p. 468.
56. C. P. Scott, Diary, 16.3.11, Scott MS., Add. MS. 50901.
57. Churchill to Elibank, 18.12.11; Churchill to Grey, 20.12.11; Churchill to Asquith, 21.12.11, Churchill, *Churchill*, Companion ii, Part iii, pp. 1473–5.
58. Harcourt to Grey, 22.12.11, F.O. 800/91.
59. Grey to L. Creighton, 31.1.12 and 4.2.12, Creighton MS.
60. Sir Edward Grey, *Sir David Dale. Inaugural Address delivered for the Dale Memorial Trust*, Murray, London, 1911, pp. 93–4.
61. Jenkins, *Asquith*, pp. 263–4.
62. Grey to Bryce, 11.3.12 and 30.3.12, Bryce MS.
63. Grey to K. Lyttelton, 8.4.12, Lyttelton MS.
64. Lord Riddell, *More Pages from my Diary, 1908–14*, Country Life, London, 1934, p. 58.
65. C. P. Scott, Diary, 1.12.11, Scott MS., Add. MS., 1.12.11. For a fuller account of Radical views on foreign policy see H. Weinroth, 'The British Radicals and the Balance of Power, 1902–1914', *The Historical Journal*, XIII, 4, 1970.
66. Lansdowne to Grey, 22.11.11, F.O. 800/108.
67. Sanderson to Hardinge, 26.1.12, cited in Steiner, *Foreign Office*, p. 126.
68. M. Anderson, *Noel Buxton: A Life*, Allen and Unwin, London, 1952, pp. 50–1.
69. Loreburn to Grey, 27.7.11, F.O. 800/99.
70. J. L. Hammond, *C. P. Scott of the Manchester Guardian*, London, 1934, pp. 154–62.
71. Esher, *Journals*, iii, p. 74.
72. H. A. Gwynne to Bonar Law, 20.11.11, 24/6/63; Memorandum by Bonar Law of conversation with Elibank, 22.11.11, 24/3/70; Grey to Bonar Law, 25.11.11, 24/4/80, Bonar Law MS.
73. Parl. Deb., 5 Ser., xxii, cols. 57–8.
74. Cited in Jenkins, *Asquith*, pp. 272–3. Asquith was writing to Crewe.
75. Fitzroy, *Memoirs*, ii, p. 471.
76. For Wolf, see M. Beloff, *Lucien Wolf and the Anglo-Russian Entente, 1907–14*, Jewish Historical Society, London, 1951.
77. Cited, with many other similar examples, in J. A. Murray, 'Foreign Policy Debated: Sir Edward Grey and his Critics, 1911–12' in L. P. Wallace and W. C. Askew, *Power, Public Opinion and Diplomacy*, Durham, North Carolina, 1959. Murray is, however, wide of the mark in places, especially in saying that the Cabinet Foreign Affairs Committee was set up in October 1911. The committee functioned before the Agadir crisis and seems to have ceased some time during it.
78. Speech reported in *The Times*, 11.10.94.
79. These aspects are discussed in F. Gosses, *The Management of British Foreign Policy before the First World War*, Sijthoff, Leiden, 1948, *passim*.
80. Grey to Loreburn, 30.8.11, F.O. 800/99.
81. C. P. Scott, Diary, 1.12.11, Scott MS., Add. MS. 50901.

82. Grey to Runciman, 2.10.11, Runciman MS.
83. Grey to L. Creighton, 4.2.12, Creighton MS.
84. Recorded by W. R. Inge in his diary, 2.4.12. W. R. Inge, *Diary of a Dean*, Hutchinson, London, 1950, p. 15.
85. Grey to K. Lyttelton, 19.1.12, Lyttelton MS.

CHAPTER 13

1. Grey to Haldane, 5.10.11, Haldane MS.
2. Grey to McKenna, 11.10.11, McKenna MS.
3. L. Cecil, *Albert Ballin: Business and Politics in Imperial Germany, 1888–1918*, Princeton U.P., Princeton, 1967, pp. 180 ff.
4. What follows is based on F. Fischer, *Kreig der Illusionen*, Droste, Düsseldorf, 1969, pp. 169 ff; J. C. G. Röhl, 'Von Müller and the Approach of War, 1911–14', *The Historical Journal*, December 1969; Koss, *Lord Haldane*; F. Stern, 'Bethmann Hollweg and the War: The Limits of Responsibility' in L. Krieger and F. Stern, *The Responsibility of Power*, Macmillan, London, 1968. These works supplement and, in part, supersede older accounts of the Haldane Mission.
5. Grey to Asquith, 13.9.11, Asquith MS.
6. Harcourt to H. Gladstone, 12.9.11; Harcourt to Sir John Anderson, 23.12.11, Harcourt MS.
7. Grey to Churchill, 31.1.12, Lloyd George MS. C/13/15/15.
8. Cabinet letter, 3.2.12, Asquith MS.
9. B.D., vi, No. 506. After the outbreak of war, Haldane wrote that he did not 'even now, in the least realise that the German Government treacherously and consciously deceived me in 1912. I do not believe they thought of doing anything of the sort. . . .' Haldane to Gosse, 9.9.17, Gosse MS.
10. B.D., vi, Nos. 533 and 535.
11. Notes by Harcourt, 14.3.12, Harcourt MS.
12. Minutes by Crowe and Grey, on B.D., vi, No. 564.
13. B.D., vi, No. 571.
14. Loreburn to Runciman, 2.4.12, Runciman MS.
15. P. Cambon to X. Charles, 10.2.12; H. Cambon ed., *Paul Cambon: correspondance*, iii, Grasset, Paris, 1940–6.
16. B. Dexter, 'Lord Grey and the Problem of Alliance', *Foreign Affairs*, January 1952.
17. H. Nicolson, *Lord Carnock*, Constable, London, 1930, pp. 371–3.
18. Williamson, *Politics of Grand Strategy*, pp. 264 ff.
19. 117th Meeting of the C.I.D., 4.7.12, Minutes, Asquith MS.
20. Esher, *Journals*, iii, p. 101.
21. 118th Meeting of the C.I.D., 11.7.12, Minutes, Asquith MS.
22. R. Churchill, *Churchill*, ii, p. 596; Balfour to Grey, 12.6.12; Grey to Balfour, 16.6.12, Balfour MS., Add. MS. 49731.
23. Grey to Cambon, 22.11.12, cited in Grey, *Twenty-Five Years*, i, pp. 97–8.
24. Grey to Spender, 24.9.12; Scott to Grey, 20.9.12; Grey to Scott, 21.9.12, F.O. 800/111.
25. Grey to Crewe, 24.9.12, Crewe MS.
26. Crewe to Grey, 16.12.12, Crewe MS.
27. B.D., ix (1), No. 805. Kazemzadeh, *Russia and Britain*, p. 674, citing Sazonov's report to the Tsar, quotes Grey as saying, 'England would make every attempt

to deal the most severe blow to German naval might.' The version in the British Documents seems preferable.

28. B.D., ix (2), p. 1008.
29. B.D., ix (1), No. 813.
30. E. C. Thaden, *Russia and the Balkan Alliance of 1912*, Pennsylvania U.P., 1965, pp. 131–2.
31. Grey to Crewe, 17.2.11, Crewe MS.
32. Grey to Rodd, 14.11.11, F.O. 800/64. A recent study of Grey's Italian policy in general in this period concludes that he 'did not have the details of policy towards her at his fingertips. He lacked the time to make an intellectual appraisal of the ideal means and ends of his Italian policy'. Bosworth, 'Britain and Italy's Acquisition of the Dodecanese, 1912–15', *The Historical Journal*, XIII, 4, 1970.
33. Churchill to Grey, 4.11.11, Churchill, Companion ii, Part iii, pp. 1369–70.
34. Asquith to Grey, 4.11.12, Asquith MS.
35. Grey to Rodd, 26.11.12, F.O. 800/64.
36. Grey to Lloyd George, 21.12.12, Lloyd George MS. C/4/14/8.
37. Cabinet letter, 9.1.13.
38. Cabinet letter, 3.4.13.
39. Cabinet letter, 30.4.13.
40. The details can be followed in E. C. Helmreich, *The Diplomacy of the Balkan Wars, 1912–13*, London, 1938. Grey, *Twenty-Five Years*, i, p. 263.
41. B.D., ix (2), No. 431.
42. Steiner, *Foreign Office and Foreign Policy*, pp. 149–50.
43. Nicolson to Grey, 21.10.13, F.O. 800/94.
44. Chirol to Hardinge, 29.5.13, Hardinge MS. 93.
45. G. Battiscombe, *Queen Alexandra*, Constable, London, 1969, p. 278.
46. Fischer, *Krieg*, pp. 236 ff; Röhl, 'Von Müller'.
47. Grey to the King, 9.12.12, F.O. 800/103.
48. Paget to Grey, 30.11.12, F.O. 800/76.
49. Masterman, *Masterman*, pp. 245–7.
50. Cabinet letter, 3.7.13, Asquith MS.
51. Grey to Rodd, 13.1.13, F.O. 800/64.
52. Röhl, 'Von Müller', p. 665.
53. Grey to Goschen, 29.12.11, F.O. 800/62.
54. Balfour to Grey, 16.12.13, Balfour MS., Add. MS. 49731.
55. Harcourt to Grey, 8.1.14; Grey to Harcourt, 10.1.14, F.O. 800/91.
56. B.D., x (1), No. 387.
57. B.D., x (1), No. 388.
58. B.D., x (1), No. 393.
59. P. Lowe, *Great Britain and Japan, 1911–13*, Macmillan, London, 1969, Chap. 4.
60. E. W. Edwards, 'Great Britain and the Manchurian Railways Question, 1909–10', *The English Historical Review*, 1966.
61. Crewe to Grey, 11.12.13, Crewe MS.
62. Lowe, *Great Britain and Japan*, pp. 175–6.
63. Lowe, *Great Britain and Japan*, Chap. 8, *passim*.
64. See D. C. Gordon, *The Dominion Partnership in Imperial Defence, 1870–1914*, Johns Hopkins, Baltimore, 1965, for a thorough examination of the whole subject.
65. Ions, *Bryce*, pp. 237–41.

66. P. Calvert, *The Mexican Revolution, 1910–1914: The Diplomacy of Anglo-American Conflict*, Cambridge, 1968, pp. 162–3.
67. Spring-Rice to Grey, 21.7.13, F.O. 800/83.
68. Cited in Calvert, *Mexican Revolution*, p. 238.
69. Carden to Grey, 12.9.13, cited in Calvert, *Mexican Revolution*, pp. 220 ff.
70. Heindel, *American Impact*, p. 165.

CHAPTER 14
1. F. Donaldson, *The Marconi Scandal*, Hart-Davis, London, 1962, p. 230.
2. A. Chamberlain, *Politics from the Inside*, Cassell, London, 1936, p. 533.
3. Grey to Lloyd George, 20.6.13, Lloyd George MS. C/4/14/9.
4. Calvert, *Mexican Revolution*, p. 176.
5. Grey to Churchill, 21.10.13, F.O. 800/87.
6. Churchill to Grey, 25.12.13, F.O. 800/87.
7. Churchill to Grey, 8.1.14, F.O. 800/88.
8. H. Spender, *Home Rule*, Hodder and Stoughton, London, 1912. Preface by Sir Edward Grey.
9. *Home Rule from the Treasury Bench*, Fisher Unwin, London, 1912, pp. 187–9.
10. Memorandum by Lloyd George, 12.11.13, Lloyd George MS. C/14/1/10.
11. Jenkins, *Asquith*, p. 328.
12. Lloyd George to Grey, 5.12.13, F.O. 800/101.
13. Chamberlain, *Politics from the Inside*, p. 567.
14. See Sir J. Fergusson, *The Curragh Incident*, Faber and Faber, London, 1964.
15. Grey to Seely, n.d. May 1914, Mottistone MS.
16. Grey to Asquith, 23.3.14, F.O. 800/100.
17. Grey to Asquith, 20.5.14, F.O. 800/100.
18. F. Ponsonby to F. Bertie, 8.4.14, Royal Archives GV M 627/23.
19. B.D., x (2), No. 539.
20. B.D., x (2), No. 540.
21. Grey, *Twenty-Five Years*, i, pp. 289–92.
22. B.D., x (1), No. 412.
23. Grey to Crewe, 22.3.14; Crewe to Grey, 24.3.14, Crewe MS.
24. Grey to Crewe, 11.5.14, Crewe MS.
25. Grey to Churchill, 28.5.14, F.O. 800/88.
26. B.D., x (2), No. 521.
27. E. Zechlin, 'Deutschland zwischen Kabinetts-und Wirtschaftskrieg', *Historiche Zeitschrift*, 199, 1964; L. C. F. Turner, *Origins of the First World War*, Arnold, London, 1970, pp. 72–3.
28. Grey to L. Creighton, 8.2.14, Creighton MS.
29. Grey to Mensdorff, 29.6.14, F.O. 800/41.
30. Grey to Cartwright, 3.2.11, F.O. 800/41.
31. For a detailed discussion see F. R. Bridge, 'The British Declaration of War on Austria-Hungary in 1914', *Slavonic and East European Review*, July 1969.
32. B.D., xi, No. 33.
33. B.D., xi, No. 32.
34. Memorandum by Bertie, 27.6.14, F.O. 800/161. I owe this reference to Dr M. Dockrill.
35. Prince Lichnowsky, *Heading for the Abyss*, Constable, London, 1928, p. 372.
36. B.D., xi, No. 38.
37. B.D., xi, No. 39.

38. B.D., xi, Nos. 47 and 58.
39. Bridge, 'British Declaration of War', p. 405.
40. B.D., x (2), p. 821.
41. Memorandum by Bertie, 16.7.14, F.O. 800/161, cited in Steiner, *Foreign Office*, p. 137n.
42. B.D., xi, No. 72.
43. For a stimulating discussion, see H. Butterfield, 'Sir Edward Grey in July 1914', *Historical Studies*, 5, 1965.
44. B.D., xi, No. 86.   45. Cabinet letter, 25.7.14, Asquith MS.
46. B.D., xi, No. 91.   47. B.D., xi, No. 101.
48. B.D., xi, No. 139.   49. B.D., xi, No. 188.
50. J. Bowle, *Viscount Samuel*, Gollancz, London, 1957, p. 118.
51. J. Burns, Diary, 27.7.14, Burns MS., Add. MS. 46336. When Burns did subsequently resign, Grey wrote expressing his regret and wishing to see friendly personal relations maintained. Grey to Burns, 5.8.14, Burns MS., Add. M.S. 46303.
52. Hammond, *Scott*, pp. 177–8.   53. Cabinet letter, 28.7.14, Asquith MS.
54. Ed. Lady Algernon Gordon Lennox, *The Diary of Lord Bertie of Thame, 1914–18*, Hodder and Stoughton, London, 1931, i, pp. 1–4.
55. For discussion of the Belgian question see J. Helmreich, 'Belgian Concern over Neutrality and British Intentions, 1906–14', *Journal of Modern History*, December, 1964; M. E. Thomas, 'Anglo-Belgian Military Relations and the Congo Question, 1911–13', *Journal of Modern History*, June 1953; Williamson, *Politics of Grand Strategy*, pp. 215–18. Cookey, *Britain and the Congo Question*, pp. 312–13, concludes that British recognition of the Belgian Congo in 1913 was granted on the merits of the case.
56. Cabinet letter, 30.7.14.
57. Ponsonby to Grey, 29.7.14; notes by Ponsonby of his interview with Grey, 29.7.14, Ponsonby MS.; A. Murray to M. Bonham Carter, 29.7.14, A. Murray MS. 8805. Dr G. C. L. Hazlehurst's book, *Politicians at War*, Cape, London, 1971, came too late to be noted in the text of this, and the ensuing, chapter. It contains much useful information on opinions in the Cabinet. It is, however, difficult to believe his contention, pp. 86–7, that Asquith accepted Ponsonby's estimate of neutralist strength in the Liberal Party.
58. B.D., xi, Nos. 283 and 286.
59. War Diary, 1914, written by Eleanor Acland, Acland MS. I am indebted to Dr G. C. L. Hazlehurst for making this available to me.
60. B.D., xi, No. 293; Röhl, 'Von Müller'; L. C. F. Turner, 'The Russian Mobilization in 1914', *The Journal of Contemporary History*, i, 1968.
61. B.D., xi, No. 367.   62. B.D., xi, Nos. 426 and 447.
63. Jenkins, *Asquith*, p. 366. Grey's attitude to the sending of an expeditionary force 'at the moment' is discussed in Hazlehurst, *Politicians at War*, pp. 88–90.
64. Nicolson, *Carnock*, p. 419.
65. Lord Morley, *Memorandum on Resignation*, Macmillan, London, 1928, p. 11.
66. Cabinet letter, 2.8.14, Asquith MS.; notes on the Cabinet meeting, 2.8.14, Runciman MS.
67. Despite the fact that Runciman is regularly listed as having attended a luncheon at Earl Beauchamp's house on that Sunday, along with other waverers, he denied this in a letter to Samuel in 1943: 'I can safely tell you that I was absent from the historic luncheon with Beauchamp and the others.

My attitude was clear and I did not feel it necessary to join him ... I acted with Grey throughout.' Runciman to Samuel, 14.1.43, Samuel MS. A/45.

68. Jenkins, *Asquith*, p. 368.
69. J. Johnson, *Westminster Voices*, Hodder and Stoughton, London, 1928, pp. 94 ff.
70. J. Joll, *1914: The Unspoken Assumptions*, L.S.E./Weidenfeld and Nicolson, London, 1968, p. 12.
71. Grey to L. Creighton, 9.8.14, Creighton MS.
72. The speeches are conveniently collected by P. Stansky, ed., *The Left and War: The British Labour Party and World War I*, O.U.P., London, 1969, pp. 41 ff.

CHAPTER 15

1. Jenkins, *Asquith*, p. 369.
2. Sanderson to Hardinge, 26.1.12; Hardinge to Sanderson, 12.2.12, Hardinge MS. 92. Mr K. Wilson kindly drew my attention to this remark.
3. Grey to Newbolt, 5.4.18, Newbolt MS.
4. F. S. Oliver, *Ordeal by Battle*, Macmillan, London, 1915, p. 35.
5. Koss, *Haldane*, p. 162.
6. Rosebery to Haldane, 11.8.16 and 16.8.16, Haldane MS. 5913; Haldane to Rosebery, 14.8.16 and 17.8.16, Rosebery MS. 24.
7. MacDonald to Morel, 24.8.14, Morel MS.
8. MacDonald to Morel, 24.9.14, Morel MS.
9. G. Murray, *The Foreign Policy of Sir Edward Grey, 1906–15*, Oxford, 1915, p. 127. Murray told Bryce, 'The fact is that I was so disturbed at the statements about our policy & about Grey which were freely made in Democratic Control meetings—statements which really amounted to a campaign of slander—that I read up the whole story as best I could to clear my own mind.' G. Murray to Bryce, 23.9.15, Bryce MS.
10. B. Russell, *Justice in War-Time*, London, 1916, p. 211.
11. Grey, *Twenty-Five Years*, ii, p. 70.
12. Crewe to Grey; Grey to Crewe; Crewe to Grey, 16.11.14, Crewe MS.
13. Memorandum by Bertie, 19.12.14, F.O. 800/163, cited by Steiner, *Foreign Office*, p. 164.
14. Grey to K. Lyttelton, 4.9.14, Lyttelton MS.
15. Churchill to Grey, 25.9.14, F.O. 800/88.
16. Jenkins, *Asquith*, p. 377; Haldane to Buxton, 12.12.14, Buxton MS.
17. Grey to K. Lyttelton, 24.12.14, Lyttelton MS.
18. Grey to Haldane, 25.12.14, Haldane MS.
19. Jenkins, *Asquith*, p. 382.
20. Grey to Runciman, 14.3.15, Runciman MS.
21. Grey, *Twenty-Five Years*, ii, p. 77.
22. I am grateful to Dr M. Ekstein for sending me a chapter on Grey's policy on Constantinople which he is contributing to a forthcoming symposium on Grey's foreign policy, and for discussing his views with me. See also C. Jay Smith, 'Great Britain and the 1914–15 Straits Agreement with Russia', *The American Historical Review*, CXXX, 4, 1963.
23. Churchill to Grey, 6.9.14, F.O. 800/88.
24. Cabinet letter, 3.11.14, Asquith MS.
25. See W. A. Renzi, 'Great Britain, Russia, and the Straits, 1914–1915', *The Journal of Modern History*, March 1970, p. 8. In Ekstein's view, it was a concern to buy Russia out of Persia, rather than fear of Russian expansion in Europe,

which led Grey to offer compensation in Turkey. It is difficult to see why both motives should not have been present.

26. C. Jay Smith, *The Russian Struggle for Power, 1914–17*, Philosophical Library, New York, 1956, p. 88.
27. Grey, *Twenty-Five Years*, ii, pp. 159–60.
28. I deal with the complexities of the Balkan situation in an article 'British Diplomacy and Bulgaria, 1914–15' to appear in the *Slavonic and East European Review*. See also *Bulgaria, 1914–15*, a confidential document drawn up for the use of the Cabinet, July 1915, p. 8, Asquith MS.
29. For further details see C. J. Lowe, 'Britain and Italian Intervention, 1914–1915' in *The Historical Journal*, 3, 1969.
30. Cited, Lowe, 'Britain and Italian Intervention', p. 541.
31. War Council, 3.3.15, notes by Hankey, Cab/42/2.
32. Cabinet letter, 9.3.15, Asquith MS.
33. Renzi, 'Great Britain, Russia, and the Straits'.
34. Grey to Buxton, 21.3.15, Buxton MS.
35. Grey to Rodd, 1.4.15, cited in Lowe, 'Britain and Italian Intervention', p. 546.
36. Grey to Seton-Watson, 3.5.15, F.O. 800/112.
37. For further discussion see H. Hanak, *Great Britain and Austria-Hungary during the First World War*, O.U.P., London, 1962, pp. 84–6; H. Hanak, 'The Government, the Foreign Office and Austria-Hungary, 1914–1918', *The Slavonic and East European Review*, January 1969.
38. As a result of attacks on Mallet in *The Times*, Grey refused that newspaper access to the Foreign Office.
39. Crewe to Grey, 22.3.15, F.O. 800/98; V. H. Rothwell, 'Mesopotamia in British War Aims, 1914–1918', *The Historical Journal*, 2, 1970.
40. See J. Nevakivi, *Britain, France and the Arab Middle East, 1914–20*, Athlone Press, London, 1969, pp. 15–17.
41. Churchill to Grey, 2.3.15, F.O. 800/88.
42. Grey, *Twenty-Five Years*, ii, p. 230.
43. L. Stein, *The Balfour Declaration*, Vallentine Mitchell, London, 1961, pp. 103–4.
44. Beloff, *Imperial Sunset*, i, p. 178.
45. Memorandum by Harcourt, 'The Spoils', 25.3.15, Asquith MS. For discussion see W. R. Louis, *Great Britain and Germany's Lost Colonies, 1914–1919*, Clarendon Press, Oxford, 1969, pp. 58 ff. Grey to Harcourt, n.d., Harcourt MS., C.O. Box 10.
46. Memorandum by Samuel, 'Palestine', 11.3.15, Asquith MS.
47. Lowe, *Great Britain and Japan*, pp. 183–4 and Chap. 6 *passim*.
48. Grey to Harcourt, 23.11.14, F.O. 800/91.
49. Minute to Grey, c. 17.12.14, cited in Louis, *Great Britain and Germany's Lost Colonies*, p. 40.
50. Grey to Haldane, 24.12.14, Haldane MS. 5910.
51. Grey, *Twenty-Five Years*, ii, p. 103.
52. For discussion of the Admiralty and the Declaration of London see Williamson, *Politics of Grand Strategy*, pp. 240–3.
53. F.R.U.S., *The Lansing Papers, 1914–20*, i, p. 257. See also A. S. Link, *Wilson: the Struggle for Neutrality, 1914–15*, Princeton U.P., Princeton, 1960, Chap. 4.
54. Runciman to Grey, 27.10.14, F.O. 800/89.
55. *Lansing Papers*, i, p. 259.
56. Spring-Rice to Grey, 8.1.15, F.O. 800/85.

57. Grey to Spring-Rice (for the attention of House), 22.1.15, House MS.
58. Spring-Rice to Grey, 23.1.15, F.O. 800/85.
59. H. Montgomery to M. Bonham-Carter, 23.11.14; Grey to Asquith, 5.12.14, Asquith MS.
60. C. Seymour, *The Intimate Papers of Colonel House*, Benn, London, 1926, i, pp. 367 ff.
61. House, Diary, 11.2.15, cited in Link, *Wilson: Struggle*, p. 219.
62. Wilson to House, 1.4.15, cited in Link, *Wilson: Struggle*, p. 227.
63. House to Grey, 12.4.15, House MS. Link does not cite this letter in which House shows a degree of frankness to Grey which his President could hardly have relished had he known.
64. Grey to House, 16.4.15, House MS.
65. Grey to House, 24.4.15, House MS.
66. House to Grey, 1.6.15; Grey to House, 2.6.15, House MS.
67. Grey to Rosebery, 7.2.15, Rosebery MS.
68. Grey to Sanderson, 22.5.15, F.O. 800/111.
69. Grey to House, 6.6.15, House MS.
70. Roosevelt to Bryce, 30.6.18, in Morison, *Roosevelt Letters*, viii, pp. 1341–3.
71. Jenkins, *Asquith*, p. 381.
72. Runciman to McKenna, 19.5.15, McKenna MS.; 'E.G. knows nothing more. Neither he nor R.B.H. have seen or heard from the P.M.'
73. Grey to Asquith, 26.5.15, F.O. 800/100.
74. Grey to E. Haldane, 18.9.17, Haldane MS. 6027.

CHAPTER 16
1. Trevelyan, *Grey*, p. 327.
2. Grey to Asquith, 29.12.15, Asquith MS.
3. Memorandum by Lord Stamfordham, December 1915, Royal Archives GV K 869/3.
4. Asquith to Grey, 29.12.15, cited in Trevelyan, *Grey*, p. 327.
5. Grey to Asquith, 23.11.15, F.O. 800/100.
6. Munro Ferguson, as Lord Novar, was now Governor-General of Australia. Albert, Earl Grey, to Novar, 1.12.15; Novar to Albert, Earl Grey, 24.1.16, National Library of Australia, Canberra MS., 696/7533–6 and 696/7544 (Novar MS.).
7. Esher, *The Captains and Kings Depart*, p. 298. December 1915.
8. K. Courtney, *Extracts from a Diary during the War*, privately published, 1927, p. 67. November 1915.
9. Lady Victoria Hicks Beach, *Life of Sir Michael Hicks Beach*, Macmillan, London, 1932, ii, p. 351. December 1915.
10. Lady Helen Primrose to Bonar Law, 17.12.15, Bonar Law MS. 52/1/41.
11. R. Pound and G. Harmsworth, *Northcliffe*, Cassell, London, 1959, p. 491.
12. Grey to Newbolt, 20.7.16, Newbolt MS.
13. Grey to Crewe, 11.8.16, Crewe MS.
14. Montagu to Drummond, 26.2.16, in S. D. Waley, *Edwin Montagu*, Asia Publishing, London, 1964, p. 92.
15. Grey to Asquith, 15.2.16, F.O. 800/100; Cabinet letter, 16.2.16, Asquith MS.
16. Grey to Runciman, 31.8.16, Runciman MS.; Drummond to Runciman, 4.9.16, F.O. 800/89.
17. Grey, *Twenty-Five Years*, ii, p. 198.

18. Lady Cynthia Asquith, *Diaries, 1915–18*, Hutchinson, London, 1968, pp. 87–8.
19. Grey to Bonar Law, 20.10.15, Bonar Law MS. 51/4/23.
20. Grey to Crewe, 22.10.15, Crewe MS.
21. Marginal note by Grey on memorandum by Churchill dated 6.10.15. Asquith MS.; S. Roskill, *Hankey, Man of Secrets*, Collins, London, 1970, i, p. 293; R. Rhodes James, *Gallipoli*, Batsford, London, 1970, p. 350.
22. Cab. 22/8.
23. Acland to Asquith, 17.7.01, Asquith MS. 10.
24. Louis, *Germany's Lost Colonies*, pp. 61–2.
25. Lowe, *Great Britain and Japan*, Chapter 7.
26. Louis, *Germany's Lost Colonies*, pp. 48–9.
27. *Report of the Committee on Asiatic Turkey*, June 1915.
28. J. Nevakivi, 'Lord Kitchener and the Partition of the Ottoman Empire, 1915–16', in K. Bourne and D. C. Watt, ed., *Studies in International History presented to W. N. Medlicott*, Longmans, London, 1967.
29. I. Friedman, 'The McMahon–Hussein Correspondence and the question of Palestine' in *Journal of Contemporary History*, 5, 2, 1970.
30. E. Kedourie, *England and the Middle East*, Bowes and Bowes, Cambridge, 1956, pp. 36–40.
31. Grey to Kitchener, 4.11.15, F.O. 800/102.
32. McMahon to Hussein, 17.12.15, cited in Friedman, p. 94.
33. Chamberlain to Grey, 29.12.15, F.O. 800/98.
34. Cited in Rothwell, 'Mesopotamia in British War Aims', p. 275.
35. Grey to Rodd, 21.9.16, cited in Friedman, pp. 84–5.
36. Cambon to Grey, 25.8.16, B.D., iv, pp. 248–9. See the discussion in Nevakivi, *Britain, France and the Arab Middle East*, pp. 36–44.
37. E. Monroe, *Britain's Moment in the Middle East, 1914–1956*, Chatto and Windus, London, 1963, p. 35.
38. M. Vereté, whose article 'The Balfour Declaration and its Makers', *Middle Eastern Studies*, January 1970, cites the comment from Alexandria and the remark by Cecil, does appear to make too much of this. For example, he cites Kitchener as among the few members of the Cabinet he names who wanted to secure Palestine for Britain. But at the March 1915 War Council meeting, Kitchener remarked: 'Palestine would be of no value to us whatever.' War Council minutes, 10.3.15, Cab. 22/1/2.
39. Stein, *Balfour Declaration*, pp. 222–4.
40. Stein, *Balfour Declaration*, cited on p. 114.
41. I owe this information to Vereté, 'The Balfour Declaration', f. 7.
42. Spring-Rice to Grey, 10.6.15 and 13.6.15, F.O. 800/85.
43. Grey to Balfour, 30.7.15, Balfour MS., Add. MS. 49731; Page to House, 21.7.15, in B. J. Hendrick, *Life and Letters of Walter H. Page*, Heinemann, London, 1924, ii, pp. 24–5.
44. Besides Grey, the members were Crewe, Lansdowne, McKenna, Kitchener and Runciman. Cabinet letter, 19.7.15, Asquith MS.
45. Link, *Wilson*, ii, pp. 602–15.
46. Grey to House, 10.8.15, House MS.
47. Link, *Wilson*, iii, pp. 615–16.
48. Memo, n.d., by Grey, Balfour MS., Add. MS. 49731.
49. Cited, with other similar criticisms, in E. R. May, *The World War and American Isolation, 1914–17*, Harvard U.P., Cambridge, 1959, pp. 315–19.

50. Grey to Balfour, 21.1.16, Balfour MS., Add. MS. 49731.
51. House to Grey, 3.9.15; House to Grey, 14.9.15, House MS. Link, *Wilson*, iv, makes no mention of this second letter which helps to explain Grey's surprise at subsequent developments.
52. Grey to House, 22.9.15, House MS. Seymour, *House Papers*, ii, pp. 88–9, only quotes the first part of this letter.
53. House to Grey, 17.10.15, House MS.
54. House to Grey, 11.11.15 and 7.12.15, House MS.
55. House to Wilson, 16.1.16 and 28.1.16, in Seymour, *House Papers*, ii, pp. 133 and 141.
56. Link, *Wilson*, iv, p. 129.
57. House, Diary, 11.2.16, cited in May, *World War*, p. 373.
58. For a more detailed account see Link, *Wilson*, iv, pp. 130–7.
59. House to Grey, 10.3.16, House MS.; Link, *Wilson*, iv, pp. 140–1. Link, however, errs in describing E. S. Montagu, whose comments he quotes, as representing the views of the Foreign Office. Montagu was Financial Secretary to the Treasury and shortly to become Minister of Munitions.
60. Grey to House, 7.4.16; House to Grey, 7.4.16, House MS.
61. Spring-Rice to Grey, 28.4.16, 15.5.16, 19.5.16. Grey's minute is on the second of these messages. F.O. 800/86.
62. Balfour to Grey, 29.5.16; Grey to Asquith, 30.5.16, Asquith MS. 30.
63. Cabinet letter, 5.7.16; John Masefield, cited in Ward, *Ireland and Anglo-American Relations*, pp. 96–7.
64. House to Grey, 10.5.16, House MS. Spring-Rice to Grey, 19.5.16, F.O. 800/86.
65. House to Grey, 11.5.16; Grey to House, 12.5.16, House MS.
66. House, Diary, 13.5.16, cited in Link, *Wilson*, v, p. 20; House to Grey, 8.6.16, House MS.
67. Link, *Wilson*, v, pp. 23 ff.
68. Hendrick, *Page*, ii, pp. 160–3. Record of conversation between Grey and Page, 27.7.16.
69. Drummond to Spring-Rice, 25.7.16, F.O. 800/86.
70. Grey to House, 28.8.16, House MS.
71. Grey to Crewe, 22.7.16, Crewe MS. While some opinion was very fearful of the situation in Russia, the Ambassador, Buchanan, wrote to Hardinge: 'I do not myself believe that there is any danger of such a peace being concluded between Russia and Germany, but I do very much fear that when peace negotiations begin, influences may be brought to bear to make things easier for Germany than we should wish.' 17.10.16. Copy in Lloyd George MS. E/3/23/1.
72. Grey to Spring-Rice, 29.7.16, F.O. 800/86.
73. Grey to Robertson, 12.6.16, F.O. 800/102.
74. Grey to Lloyd George, 4.8.16, F.O. 800/102.
75. Newbolt, Diary, 13.9.16, in Newbolt, *Later Life*, pp. 227–9.
76. Grey to Lloyd George, 29.9.16; Lloyd George to Grey, 2.10.16, Lloyd George MS. E/2/13/5–6. Grey's letter in full, and most of the reply, are printed in Lloyd George, *War Memoirs*, i, pp. 511–12.
77. See H. I. Nelson, *Land and Power*, Routledge and Kegan Paul, London, 1963, pp. 8–14.
78. Trevelyan, *Grey*, pp. 322–4.

79. Link, *Wilson*, v, pp. 180–2. Grey to Balfour, n.d. (Nov. 1916), Balfour MS., Add. MS. 49731.

CHAPTER 17

1. Grey to Rosebery, 10.12.16, Rosebery MS.
2. Memorandum on the resignation of the Asquith Government, 5.12.16, Samuel MS. For a general assessment of the new Government's position see S. Kernek, 'The British Government's Reactions to President Wilson's "Peace" Note of December 1916', *The Historical Journal*, XIII, 4, 1970.
3. Lord Beaverbrook, *Politicians and the War, 1914–1916*, Thornton Butterworth, London, 1928, p. 225.
4. *The Change of Government*, Liberal Publications, London, 1917, pp. 9–12.
5. Grey to L. Creighton, 8.12.16, Creighton MS.
6. Grey to Newbolt, 31.12.16, Newbolt MS.
7. Grey to Strachey, 9.10.16, Strachey MS.
8. Grey to Buxton, 2.2.17, Buxton MS.
9. Grey to Pember, 4.1.17, Pember MS.
10. Grey to Crewe, 2.2.17, Crewe MS.
11. Grey to A. Chamberlain, 23.1.17, Chamberlain MS.
12. Grey to Buxton, 29.5.17, Buxton MS.
13. Grey to L. Creighton, 25.3.17, Creighton MS.
14. Hendrick, *Page*, ii, p. 234.
15. Grey to H. Runciman, 9.4.17, Runciman MS.
16. Haldane to Gosse, 12.9.17, Gosse MS.
17. Grey to Runciman, 5/9/15.12.17; Lansdowne to Runciman, 9.12.17, Runciman MS.
18. Grey to G. Murray, 8.10.17, G. Murray MS.
19. W. B. Fowler, *British–American Relations, 1917–18, The Role of Sir William Wiseman*, Princeton U.P., Princeton, 1969, p. 31.
20. Memorandum by Lord Stamfordham, 18.5.17, Royal Archives GV K 1185/2.
21. Grey to House, 15.11.17, House MS.
22. Grey to G. Murray, 23.12.16, G. Murray MS.; Grey to L. Creighton, 5.12.17, Creighton MS.
23. Grey to Bryce, 1.1.18, Bryce MS. Uncat. E 15.
24. Grey to Strachey, 30.10.17, Strachey MS.
25. Grey to Spender, 27.1.18 and 14.2.18, Spender MS.
26. Grey to Asquith, 3.4.18, Asquith MS.
27. Grey to Spender, 12.6.18, Spender MS.
28. Viscount Grey of Fallodon, *The League of Nations*, London, 1918.
29. A. Murray to W. Wiseman, 5.7.18; W. Wiseman to A. Murray, 9.7.18 (transmitting messages between Grey and House), House MS.
30. Grey to G. Murray, 15.8.18, G. Murray MS.
31. Grey to W. H. Page, 1.7.18, Page MS.
32. Grey to L. Creighton, 14.10.18, Creighton MS.
33. See the eye-witness account in V. Markham, *Return Passage*, O.U.P., London, 1953, p. 165.
34. Grey to House, 29.12.18, House MS.
35. Grey to G. Murray, 17.1.19 and 7.2.19, G. Murray MS.
36. Grey to G. Murray, 19.2.19 and 21.3.19, G. Murray MS.
37. Cecil to Grey, 24.3.19, Lloyd George MS. F/6/6/19.

38. Curzon to Lloyd George, 23.7.19, Lloyd George MS. F/12/1/28: Curzon to Lloyd George, F/12/1/30, including a memorandum by Grey, 29.7.19.
39. Memorandum by Grey, 5.8.19; Grey to Curzon, 5.8.19, Lloyd George MS. F/12/1/35.
40. *Documents on British Foreign Policy*, First Series, v, pp. 997–1000.
41. Grey to Fisher, 25.8.19, Fisher MS.
42. Pound and Harmsworth, *Northcliffe*, pp. 749–52.
43. Memorandum by G. Murray of conversation with Grey, 13.9.19, Murray MS.
44. Grey to Curzon, 29.9.19, Lloyd George MS. F/60/3/6.
45. Grey to Lloyd George, 5.10.19, Lloyd George MS. F/60/3/7.
46. Grey to Lloyd George, 17.10.19, Lloyd George MS. F/60/3/9.
47. Grey to Curzon, 17.10.19; Curzon to Lloyd George, n.d., Lloyd George MS. F/12/2/4.
48. Curzon to Lloyd George, 2.11.19, Lloyd George MS. F/12/2/6.
49. His mission can be followed in B.D.F.P., First Series, v, Chap. 2.
50. Grey to Lloyd George, 11.11.19, Lloyd George MS. F/66/3/18.
51. Grey to Buxton, 2.11.19, Buxton MS.
52. Grey to Steed, 29.12.19; Steed to Northcliffe, 16.1.20, Steed MS.
53. *The Times*, 31.1.20. For reaction to the letter, see the issues for the following week.
54. Grey to House, 18.5.20, House MS.
55. Geddes to Curzon, 29.6.20, Lloyd George MS. F/60/4/4.
56. Cecil to Runciman, 2.1.20 and 24.1.20, Runciman MS.
57. Grey to G. Murray, 17.8.20, G. Murray MS.
58. Cecil to G. Murray, 23.8.20, G. Murray MS.
59. Grey to Spender, 30.7.20, Spender MS.
60. Asquith and Grey, *Ireland*, Liberal Publications, London, 1920.
61. Grey to G. Murray, 21.9.20, G. Murray MS.
62. Grey to House, 5.11.20, House MS.
63. Grey to Asquith, 20.10.20, Asquith MS.
64. Cowdray to A. Murray, 28.4.21, A. Murray MS. 8808.
65. Grey to L. Creighton, 14.3.21, Creighton MS.
66. Grey to Lady Gladstone, 7.6.21, Bodleian Library, Oxford, MS. Eng. Lett. d. 122.
67. Jenkins, *Asquith*, p. 555.
68. Memorandum by Asquith on his talks, 5.7.21, Asquith MS.
69. Runciman to A. Murray, 22.9.21, A. Murray MS. 8808.
70. A. Murray to R. Isaacs, 7.10.21, A. Murray MS. 8808.
71. Grey to H. Paul, 9.12.21, Paul MS.
72. T. Wilson, *The Downfall of the Liberal Party, 1914–1935*, Collins (Fontana), London, 1968, pp. 249–50.
73. Lloyd George to Scott, 8.11.22, Lloyd George MS. G/17/11/1.
74. Scott to Lloyd George, 15.11.22, Lloyd George MS. G/17/11/2.
75. Cecil to G. Murray, 2.11.22, G. Murray MS.
76. For example, Lord St Davids to Lloyd George, 31.2.23, Lloyd George MS. G/17/6/2.
77. Cecil to G. Murray, 21.11.23, G. Murray MS.
78. Grey to A. Murray, 8.12.23, A. Murray MS. 8808.
79. Grey to Cecil, 14.4.24, Cecil MS., Add. MS. 51073.

80. Grey to Gladstone, 26.8.24, Gladstone MS.
81. Grey to Asquith, 6.6.26, Asquith MS.
82. Grey to Crewe, 2.2.28, Crewe MS.
83. Trevelyan, *Grey*, pp. 357–9; Wilson, *Liberal Downfall*, pp. 365–7.
84. Grey to Samuel, 2.11.27, Samuel MS.
85. Grey to Crewe, 10.6.28, Crewe MS.
86. Wilson, *Liberal Downfall*, p. 373.
87. Grey to Baldwin, 5.1.29, in T. Jones, *Whitehall Diary*, O.U.P., London, 1969, ii, pp. 165–166.
88. Wilson, *Liberal Downfall*, p. 382.
89. Notes by A. J. Sylvester of the speeches at the National Liberal Council, 28.8.31, Lloyd George MS. G/20/2/43.
90. Grey to Samuel, 29.9.31 and 30.9.31, Samuel MS.
91. Grey to Samuel, 22.10.31, Samuel MS.
92. Grey to Samuel, 28.10.31, Samuel MS.
93. Grey to Samuel, 27.1.32, Samuel MS.
94. Memorandum by Samuel of conversation with Grey, 26.8.32, Samuel MS.
95. Grey to Samuel, 4.9.32 and 12.9.32, Samuel MS.; Memoranda by Sir Clive Wigram, 15.9.32 and 18.9.32, Royal Archives GV K 2357/3 and 5.
96. Cited, Trevelyan, *Grey*, p. 359.
97. Grey to Lyttelton, 5.2.17, Lyttelton MS.
98. Grey to E. Paul, 21.5.17, Paul MS.
99. Grey to Pember, 6.10.17, Pember MS.
100. Grey to Pember, 13.12.17, Pember MS.
101. Grey to C. Ryder, 5.5.17, Harrowby MS.
102. Grey to Pember, 14.1.18, Pember MS.
103. R. Speaight, *The Life of Hilaire Belloc*, Hollis and Carter, London, 1957, p. 303.
104. P. Glenconner, *The White Wallet*, Fisher Unwin, London, 1912.
105. Mrs E. Bourner to the author, 6.6.69.
106. Susan, Lady Tweedsmuir, *The Edwardian Lady*, Duckworth, London, 1966, pp. 87–8.
107. Newbolt, *Later Life*, pp. 246–7.
108. Grey to L. Creighton, 8.11.21, Creighton MS.
109. Grey to Butterworth, 21.8.21, Courtesy of Mr E. C. Marsden.
110. Grey to E. Paul, 9.12.21, Paul MS.
111. Mrs Belloc Lowndes, *A Passing World*, Macmillan, London, 1948, p. 186.
112. Harris, *Spender*, p. 57.
113. Grey, *Twenty-Five Years*, ii, Chap. 31; Mrs Frances Trueman of A. P. Watt & Son kindly informs me that the first two-volume edition sold over 12,000 copies and the various three-volume editions together sold over 35,000 copies. The book earned Lord Grey nearly £7,000.
114. Lord Grey of Fallodon, *The Charm of Birds*, Hodder and Stoughton, London, 1937 edition, pp. 293–4. See also Seton Gordon, *Edward Grey of Fallodon and his birds*, Country Life, London, 1937. I am indebted to Mr Gordon for sending me his impressions of Grey as a naturalist and for allowing me to see some letters, moving in their brevity, written by Grey in the last years of his life concerning the behaviour of his birds. Sir Hugh Elliott kindly drew my attention to the obituary of Grey in *Ibis, The Journal of the British Ornithologists' Union*, iv, 1934, and the steps which led to the creation of the

Edward Grey Institute of Field Ornithology in the University of Oxford. *Second and Fourth Reports of the British Trust for Ornithology*, Spring 1936 and Summer 1938. Dr D. A. Bannerman, O.B.E., M.B.E., also kindly gave me an assessment of Grey in which he stressed his uncanny and extraordinary influence over all the wild-life on his estate.

115. Grey to L. Creighton, 23.11.28, Creighton MS.
116. Grey to Buxton, 2.2.23, Buxton MS. After Edward's death, Lord Buxton published privately a tribute, *Edward Grey, Bird Lover and Fisherman*, 1933. 'He was born a fisherman; and as a fisherman, especially as a dry-fly fisherman, he was supreme . . .' pp. 7–8.
117. Grey to Pember, 7.10.28, Pember MS.
118. Newbolt, *Later Life*, pp. 356–7.
119. *The Times*, 5.5.32.
120. Reported in *The Times*, 8.9.33.
121. W. George to Megan Lloyd George, 14.5.33, George, *My Brother and I*, p. 238; David Lloyd George to William George, 28.5.33, Lloyd George MS. G/211; Beaverbrook to Miss Stevenson, n.d., G/211; Hankey to Lloyd George, 4.4.33, G/212.
122. MacDonald to G. Murray, 14.5.25, G. Murray MS.
123. After his remarriage, Grey does not seem to have seen very much of Haldane. However, when his old friend died in 1928 he paid him a handsome tribute, both privately and publicly. Grey to Miss Haldane, 20.8.28, Haldane MS.; Lord Grey of Fallodon *et al.*, *Viscount Haldane of Cloan, O.M.: The Man & His Work*, O.U.P., London, 1928.
124. Grey to Pember, 14.1.18, Pember MS.
125. J. d'E. Firth, *Winchester*, Blackie, London, 1936, pp. 86–7.
126. Grey to House, n.d. (December 1931), House MS.
127. Belloc Lowndes, *Passing World*, p. 176.
128. Grey to K. Lyttelton, 16.1.18, Lyttelton MS.

Bibliography

A. UNPUBLISHED PAPERS

Acland MS. The Diary of Mrs Eleanor Acland. In the keeping of Dr G. C. L. Hazlehurst, The Queen's College, Oxford.

Allard MS. The papers of William Allard in the University of Birmingham Library.

Asquith MS. The papers of the 1st Earl of Oxford and Asquith, Bodleian Library, Oxford.

Balfour MS. The papers of the 1st Earl of Balfour, The British Museum.

Bertie MS. The papers of Lord Bertie of Thame, Public Record Office.

Bonar Law MS. The papers of Andrew Bonar Law, The Beaverbrook Library, London.

Bryce MS. The papers of Viscount Bryce of Dechmont, Bodleian Library, Oxford.

Burns MS. The papers of John Burns, The British Museum.

Buxton MS. The papers of the 1st Earl Buxton at Newtimber Place, Hassocks, Sussex.

Campbell-Bannerman MS. The papers of Sir Henry Campbell-Bannerman, The British Museum.

Carnegie MS. The papers of Andrew Carnegie, The Library of Congress, Washington, D.C.

Cecil of Chelwood MS. The papers of Viscount Cecil of Chelwood, The British Museum.

Chamberlain MS. The papers of Sir Austen Chamberlain, The University of Birmingham Library.

Creighton MS. The papers of Mrs Louise Creighton, Bodleian Library, Oxford.

Crewe MS. The papers of the 1st Marquess of Crewe, The University Library, Cambridge.

Ellis MS. The papers of T. E. Ellis, The National Library of Wales, Aberystwyth.

Fisher MS. The papers of H. A. L. Fisher, The Bodleian Library, Oxford.

Gladstone MS. The papers of W. E. Gladstone, The British Museum. The papers of Herbert, Viscount Gladstone, The British Museum.

Gosse MS. The papers of Edmund Gosse, The Brotherton Library, The University of Leeds.

Grey of Fallodon MS. The public papers of Viscount Grey of Fallodon, F.O. 800/35–112, Public Record Office.

412

Grey of Howick MS. The papers of the 3rd Earl Grey; The Papers of the 4th Earl Grey: Dept. of Palaeography and Diplomatic, University of Durham.

Haldane MS. The papers of Viscount Haldane of Cloan, The National Library of Scotland, Edinburgh.

Hamilton MS. The papers of Sir Edward Hamilton, The British Museum.

Harcourt MS. The papers of Sir William Harcourt; The papers of Lewis, Viscount Harcourt at Stanton Harcourt, Oxfordshire.

Hardinge MS. The papers of Lord Hardinge of Penshurst, The University Library, Cambridge.

Harrowby MS. Ryder Family Papers at Sandon Hall, Stafford.

House MS. The papers of Colonel E. M. House, Yale University Library.

Lloyd George MS. The papers of the 1st Earl Lloyd George of Dwyfor, The Beaverbrook Library, London.

Lyttelton MS. The papers of Lady Katharine Lyttelton, Westfield College, The University of London.

McKenna MS. The papers of Reginald McKenna, Churchill College, Cambridge.

Milner MS. The papers of Alfred, Viscount Milner, The Bodleian Library, Oxford.

Morel MS. The papers of E. D. Morel, The British Library of Economics and Political Science.

Mottistone MS. The papers of the 1st Lord Mottistone, in the keeping of Dr G. C. L. Hazlehurst, The Queen's College, Oxford.

Munro Ferguson MS. The papers of Ronald Munro Ferguson, 1st Lord Novar, The National Register of Archives (Scotland), Edinburgh.

A. Murray MS. The papers of the Murrays of Elibank, The National Library of Scotland, Edinburgh.

G. Murray MS. The papers of Gilbert Murray, The Bodleian Library, Oxford.

Newbolt MS. The papers of Sir Henry Newbolt. In private hands.

Novar MS. The papers of 1st Lord Novar as Governor-General of Australia, National Library of Australia, Canberra.

Page MS. The papers of Walter Hines Page, The Houghton Library, Harvard University.

Passfield MS. The papers of Sidney Webb, 1st Lord Passfield, The British Library of Economics and Political Science.

Paul MS. The papers of Herbert and Eleanor Paul. In the possession of Beatrix, Lady Aldenham. To be deposited in Hertfordshire County Record Office.

Perks MS. The papers of Sir Robert Perks. In private hands.

Pember MS. Letters to F. W. Pember, in the author's keeping.

Ripon MS. The papers of the 1st Marquess of Ripon, The British Museum.

Roosevelt Jr. MS. The papers of Theodore Roosevelt Jr., The Library of Congress, Washington, D.C.

Rosebery MS. The papers of the 5th Earl of Rosebery, National Library of Scotland, Edinburgh.

Royal Archives. The papers and journals of Queen Victoria, King Edward VII and King George V, The Royal Archives, Windsor Castle.

Runciman MS. The papers of Walter, Viscount Runciman of Doxford, The University of Newcastle-upon-Tyne.

Samuel MS. The papers of the 1st Viscount Samuel, The House of Lords Record Office.

Scott MS. The papers of C. P. Scott, The British Museum.
Spencer MS. The papers of the 5th Earl Spencer. In private hands at Althorp, Northampton.
Spender MS. The papers of J. A. Spender, The British Museum.
Steed, MS. The papers of Wickham Steed, *The Times* Archives, Printing House Square, London.
Strachey MS. The papers of J. St Loe Strachey, The Beaverbrook Library, London.
Trevelyan MS. Trevelyan Family Papers, The University of Newcastle-upon-Tyne.
Waldegrave MS. Palmer and Waldegrave Family Papers, Chewton Mendip, Somerset.

B. PUBLISHED PAPERS

British Documents on the Origins of the War, 1898–1914. Eleven volumes, London, 1926–38. Edited by G. P. Gooch and H. W. V. Temperley.
Documents on British Foreign Policy, 1919–1939, First Series, Volume Five.
Hansard, *Parliamentary Debates.*
The Times.
Foreign Relations of the United States, The Lansing Papers, 1914–20.

C. BOOKS

AL-SAYYID, A. L., *Egypt and Cromer,* London, 1968.
AMERY, L. S., *My Political Life,* London, 1953.
ANDERSON, M., *Noel Buxton: A Life,* London, 1952.
ANDERSON, M. S., *The Eastern Question,* London, 1966.
ANDREW, C., *Théophile Delcassé and the Entente Cordiale,* London, 1968.
ANNAN, N. G., *Leslie Stephen,* London, 1951.
ASQUITH, LADY C., *Diaries, 1915–18,* London, 1968.
ASQUITH, H. H., and GREY, *Ireland,* London, 1920.
ASQUITH, M., ed. Bonham Carter, M., *Autobiography,* London, 1962.
AVERY, P., *Modern Iran,* London, 1965.
BATTISCOMBE, G., *Queen Alexandra,* London, 1969.
BEACH, LADY VICTORIA HICKS, *Life of Sir Michael Hicks Beach,* London, 1932.
BEALEY, F., and PELLING, H., *Labour and Politics, 1900–06,* London, 1958.
BEAN, W. W., *The Parliamentary Representation of the Six Northern Counties of England, 1603–1886,* Hull, 1896.
BEAVERBROOK, LORD, *Politicians and the War, 1914–1916,* London, 1928.
BELOFF, M., *Lucien Wolf and the Anglo-Russian Entente, 1907–14,* London, 1951.
— *The Great Powers,* London, 1958.
— *The Imperial Sunset,* London, 1969.
BENSON, A. C., *Memories and Friends,* London, 1924.
BISHOP, T. J. H., and WILKINSON, R., *Winchester and the Public School Elite,* London, 1967.
BLUNT, W. S., *My Diaries,* London, 1919.
BOURNE, K., *Britain and the Balance of Power in North America, 1815–1908,* London, 1967.
BOURNE, K., and WATTS, D. C., *Studies in International History,* London, 1967.

BOWLE, J., *Viscount Samuel*, London, 1957.

BREBNER, J. B., *North Atlantic Triangle: The Interplay of Canada, the United States and Britain*, Toronto and New Haven, 1945.

BROWNE, E. G., *The Persian Revolution of 1905–09*, Cambridge, 1910.

BROWNING, O., *Memories of Sixty Years*, London, 1910.

BURT, T., *Autobiography*, London, 1924.

BUSCH, B., *Britain and the Persian Gulf, 1894–1914*, Berkeley, 1967.

BUTLER, J., *The Liberal Party and the Jameson Raid*, Oxford, 1968.

BUXTON, LORD, *Edward Grey, Bird Lover and Fisherman*, 1933.

CALLWELL, C. E., *Field Marshal Sir Henry Wilson, His Life and Diaries*, London, 1927.

CALVERT, P., *The Mexican Revolution, 1910–1914: The Diplomacy of Anglo-American Conflict*, Cambridge, 1968.

CAMBON, H., *Paul Cambon; Correspondance*, Paris, 1940–6.

CAMPBELL, C. S., *Anglo-American Understanding, 1898–1903*, Baltimore, 1957.

CECIL, L., *Albert Ballin: Business and Politics in Imperial Germany, 1888–1918*, Princeton, 1967.

CHAMBERLAIN, A., *Politics from the Inside*, London, 1936.

CHANNING, F. A., *Memories of Midland Politics, 1885–1910*, London, 1918.

CHILDERS, S., *The Life and Correspondence of the Rt. Hon. H. C. E. Childers*, London, 1901.

CHURCHILL, R. S., *Winston S. Churchill*, London, 1967–9.

CHURCHILL, W. S., *The World Crisis, 1911–1918*, London, 1938.

CLEGG, H. A., FOX, A., and THOMPSON, A. F., *A History of British Trade Unions since 1889*, Oxford, 1964.

COCKSHUTT, A. O. J., *The Unbelievers: English Agnostic Thought, 1840–90*, London, 1964.

COLLIER, E. C. F., ed., *A Victorian Diarist. Extracts from the Journals of Mary, Lady Monkswell, 1873–95*, London, 1944.

— *A Victorian Diarist. Later extracts . . .* , London, 1946.

COOKEY, S. J. S., *Britain and the Congo Question, 1885–1913*, London, 1968.

COURTNEY, K., *Extracts from a Diary during the War*, London, 1927.

CRANE, D., *The Life Story of Sir Robert W. Perks*, London, 1909.

CRATON, M., and MCCREADY, H. W., *The Great Liberal Revival, 1903–1906*, London, 1966.

CREIGHTON, L., *Dorothy Grey*, London, 1907.

— *The Life and Letters of Mandell Creighton*, London, 1913.

CREIGHTON, M., *Memoir of Sir George Grey, Bart.*, Newcastle, 1884.

CREWE, MARQUESS OF, *Lord Rosebery*, London, 1931.

DILKS, D., *Curzon in India*, London, 1969.

DONALDSON, F., *The Marconi Scandal*, London, 1962.

ELLIOTT, SIR I., *The Balliol College Register, Third Edition*, Oxford, 1953.

ESHER, VISCOUNT, *Journals and Letters*, London, 1934.

FEAVER, G., *From Status to Contract*, London, 1969.

FERGUSSON, SIR J., *The Curragh Incident*, London, 1964.

FIRTH, J. D'E., *Winchester*, London, 1936.

FISCHER, F., *Krieg der Illusionen*, Düsseldorf, 1969.

FITZROY, SIR A., *Memoirs*, London, 1925.

FOWLER, W. B., *British-American Relations, 1917–18, The Role of Sir William Wiseman*, Princeton, 1969.

FULFORD, R., *Samuel Whitbread*, London, 1967.

GANN, L. H., and DUIGNAN, P., *Colonialism in Africa, 1870–1960*, Cambridge, 1969.
GARDINER, A. G., *Prophets, Priests and Kings*, London, 1914.
— *Life of Sir William Harcourt*, London, 1923.
GARVIN, J. L., *Life of Joseph Chamberlain*, London, 1951.
GEORGE, D. LLOYD, *War Memoirs*, London, 1938.
GEORGE, W., *My Brother and I*, London, 1958.
GIFFORD, P., and LOUIS, W. R., *Britain and Germany in Africa*, New Haven, 1967.
GLENCONNER, LADY, *The White Wallet*, London, 1912.
GOLLIN, A. M., *The Observer and J. L. Garvin*, London, 1960.
GOLLWITZER, H., *Europe in the Age of Imperialism, 1880–1914*, London, 1969.
GOOCH, G. P., *Under Six Reigns*, London, 1958.
GORDON, D. C., *The Dominion Partnership in Imperial Defence, 1870–1914*, Baltimore, 1965.
GORDON, H. S., *Edward Grey of Fallodon and His Birds*, London, 1937.
GOSSES, F., *The Management of British Foreign Policy before the First World War*, Leiden, 1948.
GRAINGER, J. H., *Character and Style in English Politics*, Cambridge, 1969.
GREY, EDWARD, VISCOUNT, *Rural Land*, London, 1892.
— *Fly Fishing*, London, 1899.
— *Cottage Book. Itchen Abbas, 1894–1905*, London, 1909.
— *Sir David Dale Inaugural Lecture*, London, 1911.
— *Twenty-Five Years*, London, 1925.
— *Fallodon Papers*, London, 1926.
— *The Charm of Birds*, London, 1927.
— *Haldane of Cloan*, London, 1928.
Some account of George Grey and his work in Africa, London, 1914.
GWYNN, S., ed., *The Letters and friendships of Sir Cecil Spring Rice*, London, 1929.
HALDANE, RICHARD, VISCOUNT, *An Autobiography*, London, 1929.
HALE, O. J., *Publicity and Diplomacy*, New York, 1940.
HAMER, D. A., *John Morley, Liberal Intellectual in Politics*, Oxford, 1968.
HAMMOND, J. L., *C. P. Scott of the Manchester Guardian*, London, 1934.
— *Gladstone and the Irish Nation*, London, 1938.
HANAK, H., *Great Britain and Austria-Hungary during the First World War*, London, 1962.
HANHAM, H. J., *The Nineteenth Century Constitution*, Cambridge, 1969.
HARRIS, W., *J. A. Spender*, London, 1946.
HAZLEHURST, C., *Politicians at War, July 1914 to May 1915*, London, 1971.
HEADLAM, C., ed., *The Milner Papers*, London, 1931.
HEINDEL, R. H., *The American Impact on Great Britain, 1898–1914*, Philadelphia, 1940.
HELMREICH, E. C., *The Diplomacy of the Balkan War, 1912–13*, London, 1938.
HENDRICK, B. J., *The Life and Letters of Walter H. Page*, London, 1924.
HEWINS, W. A. S., *The Apologia of an Imperialist*, London, 1929.
HOLT, P. M., *The Mahdist State in the Sudan, 1881–1898*, Oxford, 1958.
— *A Modern History of the Sudan*, London, 1963.
HUMPHREYS, R. A., *Tradition and Revolt in Latin America*, London, 1969.
HURST, M. C., *Joseph Chamberlain and Liberal Reunion*, London, 1967.
HYAM, R., *Elgin and Churchill at the Colonial Office, 1905–08*, London, 1969.
INGE, W. R., *Diary of a Dean*, London, 1950.
IONS, E. S. A., *James Bryce and American Democracy*, London, 1968.
JENKINS, R., *Mr Balfour's Poodle*, London, 1954.

JENKINS, R., *Asquith*, London, 1967.

JOHNSON, J., *Westminster Voices*, London, 1928.

JOLL, J., *Unspoken Assumptions*, London, 1968.

JONES, T., *Whitehall Diary*, London, 1969.

JUDD, D., *Balfour and the British Empire*, London, 1968.

KAZEMZADEH, F., *Russia and Britain in Persia, 1864–1914*, New Haven, 1968.

KEDOURIE, E., *England and the Middle East*, Cambridge, 1956.

KENDLE, J. E., *The Colonial and Imperial Conferences, 1887–1911*, London, 1967.

KINNEAR, M., *The British Voter*, London, 1969.

KOSS, S., *Lord Haldane, Scapegoat for Liberalism*, New York, 1969.

KRIEGER, L., and STERN, F., *The Responsibility of Power*, London, 1968.

LE MAY, G. H., *British Supremacy in South Africa, 1899–1907*, Oxford, 1965.

LENNOX, LADY ALGERNON GORDON, *The Diary of Lord Bertie of Thame, 1914–18*, London, 1931.

LICHNOWSKY, PRINCE KARL MAX VON, *Heading for the Abyss*, London, 1928.

LINK, A. S., *Wilson*, Vols. 3, 4 and 5, Princeton, 1960–65.

LOCKHART, J. G., *Cosmo Gordon Lang*, London, 1949.

LOREBURN, EARL, *How the War Came*, London, 1919.

LOUIS, W. R., and STENGERS, J., *E. D. Morel's History of the Congo Reform Movement*, Oxford, 1968.

LOUIS, W. R., *Great Britain and Germany's Lost Colonies, 1914–19*, Oxford, 1969.

LOWE, P., *Great Britain and Japan, 1911–13*, London, 1969.

LOWNDES, MRS BELLOC, *A Passing World*, London, 1948.

LUCY, SIR HENRY, *The Diary of a Journalist*, London, 1922.

— *The Diary of a Journalist, Later Entries*, London, 1922.

MACK, E. C., *Public Schools and British Opinion since 1860*, New York, 1941.

MCKENNA, S., *Reginald McKenna*, London, 1948.

MAGNUS, SIR P., *King Edward the Seventh*, London, 1964.

MALLET, B., *Thomas George, Earl of Northbrook*, London, 1908.

MALLET, SIR C., *Herbert Gladstone*, London, 1932.

MARAIS, J. S., *The Fall of Kruger's Republic*, Oxford, 1961.

MARDER, A. J., ed., *Fear God and Dread Nought: the Correspondence of Admiral of the Fleet Lord Fisher of Kilverstone*, London, 1952–9.

— *From the Dreadnought to Scapa Flow: The Road to War*, London, 1961.

MARKHAM, V., *Return Passage*, London, 1953.

MASTERMAN, L., *C. F. G. Masterman*, London, 1939.

MAY, E. R., *The World War and American Isolation, 1914–17*, Cambridge, Mass., 1959.

MONGER, G. W., *The End of Isolation: British Foreign Policy, 1900–07*, London, 1963.

MONROE, E., *Britain's Moment in the Middle East, 1914–1956*, London, 1963.

MORISON, E. E., ed., *The Letters of Theodore Roosevelt*, Cambridge, Mass., 1952–4.

MORLEY, JOHN, VISCOUNT, *Recollections*, London, 1917.

— *Memorandum on Resignation*, London, 1928.

MURRAY, G., *The Foreign Policy of Sir Edward Grey, 1906–1915*, Oxford, 1915.

NELSON, H. I., *Land and Power*, London, 1963.

NEVAKIVI, J., *Britain, France and the Arab Middle East, 1914–20*, London, 1969.

NEWBOLT, SIR H., *My World in my Time*, London, 1932.

NEWBOLT, M., ed., *The Later Life and Letters of Sir Henry Newbolt*, London, 1942.

NEWSOME, D. H., *The Parting of Friends*, London, 1966.

NICOLSON, SIR H., *Lord Carnock: A Study in the old diplomacy*, London, 1930.

— *King George the Fifth*, London, 1952.

NISH, I. H., *The Anglo-Japanese Alliance: The Diplomacy of two Island Empires*, London, 1966.

OLIVER, F. S., *Ordeal by Battle*, London, 1915.

PARRIS, H., *Government and the Railways in Nineteenth Century Britain*, London, 1965.

PEASE, SIR A. E., *Elections and Recollections*, London, 1932.

PETRIE, SIR C., *The Life and Letters of Rt. Hon. Sir Austen Chamberlain*, London, 1939.

PLATT, D. C. M., *Finance, Trade, and Politics in British Foreign Policy, 1815–1914*, Oxford, 1968.

Poll Book for the Northern Division of Northumberland, Newcastle, 1852.

POUND, R., and HARMSWORTH, G., *Northcliffe*, London, 1959.

PYRAH, G. B., *Imperial Policy and South Africa, 1902–10*, Oxford, 1955.

RAMSAUR, E. E., *The Young Turks, Prelude to the Revolution of 1908*, Beirut, 1965.

RHODES JAMES, R., *Rosebery*, London, 1963.

— *Gallipoli*, London, 1965.

RICH, N., *Friedrich von Holstein*, Cambridge, 1965.

RIDDELL, LORD, *More Pages from my Diary, 1908–14*, London, 1934.

RIDDING, L., *George Ridding*, London, 1908.

ROBINSON, R., GALLAGHER, J., with DENNY, A., *Africa and the Victorians*, London, 1961.

RONALDSHAY, EARL OF, *The Life of Lord Curzon*, London, 1928.

ROSKILL, S., *Hankey, Man of Secrets*, London, 1970.

RUSSELL, BERTRAND, EARL, *Justice in War Time*, London, 1916.

— *Portraits from Memory*, London, 1956.

St Antony's Papers, No. 16, Middle Eastern Affairs No. 3, London, 1963.

SANDERSON, G. N., *England, Europe & the Upper Nile, 1882–1899*, Edinburgh, 1965.

SEYMOUR, C., *The Intimate Papers of Colonel House*, London, 1926.

Sir Edward Grey, K.G., London, 1915.

SMITH, C. JAY, *The Russian Struggle for Power, 1914–17*, New York, 1956.

SOMMER, D., *Haldane of Cloan*, London, 1960.

SOUTHGATE, D., *The Passing of the Whigs*, London, 1962.

SPEAIGHT, R., *The Life of Hilaire Belloc*, London, 1957.

SPENDER, H., *Home Rule*, London, 1912.

SPENDER, J. A., *The Life of Sir Henry Campbell-Bannerman*, London, 1924.

— *Men and Things*, London, 1937.

SPRING, D., *The English Landed Estate in the Nineteenth Century: Its Administration*, Baltimore, 1963.

STANSKY, P., *Ambitions and Strategies*, Oxford, 1964.

— ed., *The Left and War: The British Labour Party and World War I*, London, 1969.

STEIN, L., *The Balfour Declaration*, London, 1961.

STEINER, Z. S., *The Foreign Office and Foreign Policy, 1898–1914*, Cambridge, 1969.

STRACHEY, A., *St Loe Strachey: His Life and His Paper*, London, 1930.

TAYLOR, A. J. P., *The Troublemakers*, London, 1957.

THADEN, E. C., *Russia and the Balkan Alliance of 1912*, Pennsylvania, 1965.

TIGNOR, R. L., *Modernization and British Colonial Rule in Egypt, 1882–1914*, Princeton, 1966.

TREVELYAN, G. M., *Grey of Fallodon*, London, 1948.

— *Grey of the Reform Bill*, London, 1952.

TURNER, L. C. F., *Origins of the First World War*, London, 1970.

TWEEDSMUIR, SUSAN, LADY, *The Edwardian Lady*, London, 1966.

VATIKIOTIS, P. J., *The Modern History of Egypt*, London, 1969.

WALEY, S. D., *Edwin Montagu*, London, 1964.

Bibliography

WALLACE, L. P., and ASKEW, W. C., *Power, Public Opinion and Diplomacy*, Durham, N.C., 1959.

WARD, A. J., *Ireland and Anglo-American Relations, 1899–1921*, London, 1969.

WATSON, R. SPENCE, *The National Liberal Federation, 1877 to 1906*, London, 1907.

WATT, D. C., *Personalities and Policies*, London, 1965.

WEBB, B., *Our Partnership*, London, 1948.

WELLS, H. G., *Experiment in Autobiography*, London, 1934.

WILKINSON, H. S., *Thirty-Five Years, 1874–1909*, London, 1933.

WILLIAMSON, S. R., *The Politics of Grand Strategy, Britain and France Prepare for War, 1904–1914*, Cambridge, Mass., 1969.

WILSON, MCN., *Doctor's Progress*, London, 1938.

WILSON, T., *The Downfall of the Liberal Party, 1914–1935*, London, 1968.

WOLF, L., *Life of the First Marques of Ripon*, London, 1921.

WOLPERT, S. A., *Morley and India, 1906–10*, Berkeley, 1967.

WOODWARD, SIR E. L., *Great Britain and the German Navy*, London, 1964.

WRENCH, SIR J. E., *Alfred, Lord Milner, the man of no illusions*, London, 1958.

D. ARTICLES AND REPORTS

Annual Register for 1909.
Annual Report of the Eighty Club, 1885.

BOSWORTH, R., 'Britain and Italy's Acquisition of the Dodecanese, 1912–15', *The Historical Journal*, XIII, 4, 1970.

BRIDGE, F. R., 'The British Declaration of War on Austria-Hungary in 1914', *The Slavonic and East European Review*, July 1969.

BUTTERFIELD, SIR H., 'Sir Edward Grey in July 1914', *Historical Studies*, 5, 1965.

CLINE, C. A., 'E. D. Morel and the Crusade against the Foreign Office', *Journal of Modern History*, June 1967.

COOPER, M. B., 'British Policy in the Balkans, 1908–9', *The Historical Journal*, VII, 1964–5.

COSGROVE, R. A., 'A Note on Lloyd George's Speech at the Mansion House, 21 July 1911', *The Historical Journal*, XII, 4, 1969.

DEXTER, B., 'Lord Grey and the Problem of Alliance', *Foreign Affairs*, January 1952.

EDWARDS, E. W., 'The Franco-German Agreement on Morocco, 1909', *The English Historical Review*, July 1963.

— 'Great Britain and the Manchurian Railways Question, 1909–10', *The English Historical Review*, 1966.

FRIEDMAN, I., 'The McMahon–Hussein Correspondence and the question of Palestine', *Journal of Contemporary History*, 5.2.1970.

GREY, EDWARD, VISCOUNT, 'Mr Chamberlain's Tariff Policy', *The Monthly Review*, October 1903.

— *The Irish Question*, Liberal League Pamphlets, 1903.

— *Questions of Today*, Liberal League Pamphlets, 1903.

HAMER, D. A., 'The Irish Question and Liberal Politics', *The Historical Journal*, 12.3.1969.

HANAK, H., 'The Government, the Foreign Office and Austria-Hungary, 1914–1918', *Slavonic and East European Review*, January 1969.

HARRIS, J. F., and HAZLEHURST, C., 'Campbell-Bannerman as Prime Minister', *History*, October 1970.

HELMREICH, J., 'Belgian Concern over Neutrality and British Intentions, 1906–14', *Journal of Modern History*, December 1964.

Home Rule from the Front Bench, London, 1912.

KERNEK, S., 'The British Government's Reactions to President Wilson's "Peace" Note in December 1916', *The Historical Journal*, XIII, 4, 1970.

KLEIN, I., 'Salisbury, Rosebery and the Survival of Siam', *Journal of British Studies*, November 1968.

KOCH, H. W., 'The Anglo-German Alliance Negotiations: Missed Opportunity or Myth?', *History*, October 1969.

LOW, A., 'British Public Opinion and the Uganda Question, October–December 1892', *The Uganda Journal*, September 1954.

LOWE, C. J., 'Britain and Italian Intervention, 1914–15', *The Historical Journal*, 3, 1969.

MCCORD, N., and CARRICK, A. E., 'The Northumberland Election of 1852', *Northern History*, 1, 1966.

MCCREADY, H. W., 'Sir Alfred Milner, the Liberal Party and the Boer War', *The Canadian Journal of History*, March 1967.

MACKINTOSH, J. P., 'The Role of the Committee of Imperial Defence before 1914', *The English Historical Review*, July 1962.

MARCUS, G. J., 'The Naval Crisis of 1909 and the Croydon By-election', *Journal of the Royal United Services Institution*, November 1958.

MILLER, T. B., 'The Egyptian Question and British Foreign Policy, 1892–94', *The Journal of Modern History*, March 1960.

MORTIMER, J. S., 'Commercial Interests and German Diplomacy in the Agadir Crisis', *The Historical Journal*, 4, 1967.

NEARY, P., 'Grey, Bryce and the Settlement of Canadian-American Differences', *The Canadian Historical Review*, December 1968.

NISH, I. H., 'Australia and the Anglo-Japanese Alliance, 1901–11', *The Australian Journal of Politics and History*, November 1963.

PAUL, H., 'Liberals and Foreign Policy', *Nineteenth Century and After*, November 1905.

RENZI, W. A., 'Great Britain, Russia and the Straits, 1914–15', *Journal of Modern History*, March 1970.

RÖHL, J. C. G., 'Von Müller and the Approach of War, 1911–14', *The Historical Journal*, December 1969.

ROTHWELL, V. H., 'Mesopotamia in British War Aims', *The Historical Journal*, 2, 1970.

SMITH, C. JAY, 'Great Britain and the 1914–15 Straits Agreement with Russia', *The American Historical Review*, CXXX, 4, 1963.

STEINER, Z. S., 'Grey, Hardinge and the Foreign Office, 1906–10', *The Historical Journal*, 3, 1967.

THOMAS, M. E., 'Anglo-Belgian Military Relations and the Congo Question', *Journal of Modern History*, June 1953.

THOMPSON, F. M. L., 'Land and Politics in the Nineteenth Century', *Transactions of the Royal Historical Society*, 15, 1965.

TRAINOR, L., 'The Liberals and the Formation of Imperial Defence Policy, 1892–95', *Bulletin of the Institute of Historical Research*, November 1969.

— 'The British Government and Imperial Economic Unity', *The Historical Journal*, 1, 1970.

VERETÉ, M., 'The Balfour Declaration and its Makers', *Middle Eastern Studies*, January 1970.

WEINROTH, H., 'The British Radicals and the Balance of Power, 1902–1914', *The Historical Journal*, XIII, 4, 1970.

WESTON, C. C., 'The Liberal Leadership and the Lords' Veto, 1907–10', *The Historical Journal*, 3, 1968.

WILLIAMS, B. J., 'The Strategic Background to the Anglo-Russian Entente of August 1907', *The Historical Journal*, 1966.

ZECHLIN, E., 'Deutschland zwischen Kabinetts-und Wirtschaftskrieg', *Historische Zeitschrift*, 199, 1964.

Index